# Lecture Notes in Computer Science 3810

Commenced Publication in 1973
Founding and Former Series Editors:
Gerhard Goos, Juris Hartmanis, and Jan van Leeuwen

Yvo G. Desmedt   Huaxiong Wang
Yi Mu   Yongqing Li (Eds.)

# Cryptology and Network Security

4th International Conference, CANS 2005
Xiamen, China, December 14-16, 2005
Proceedings

 Springer

Volume Editors

Yvo G. Desmedt
University College London, Department of Computer Science
Gower Street, London WC1E 6BT, UK
E-mail: y.desmedt@cs.ucl.ac.uk

Huaxiong Wang
Macquarie University, Department of Computing
NSW 2109, Australia
E-mail: hwang@ics.mq.edu.au

Yi Mu
University of Wollongong, School of Information Technology and Computer Science
Wollongong, NSW 2522, Australia
E-mail: ymu@uow.edu.au

Yongqing Li
Fujian Normal University, School of Mathematics and Computer Science
Fujian, Fuzhou 350007, China
E-mail: yqli@fjnu.edu.cn

Library of Congress Control Number: 2005936808

CR Subject Classification (1998): E.3, D.4.6, F.2.1, C.2, J.1, K.4.4, K.6.5

ISSN        0302-9743
ISBN-10     3-540-30849-0 Springer Berlin Heidelberg New York
ISBN-13     978-3-540-30849-2 Springer Berlin Heidelberg New York

Springer is a part of Springer Science+Business Media

springeronline.com

© Springer-Verlag Berlin Heidelberg 2005
Printed in Germany

Typesetting: Camera-ready by author, data conversion by Scientific Publishing Services, Chennai, India
Printed on acid-free paper      SPIN: 11599371      06/3142      5 4 3 2 1 0

# Preface

The 4th International Conference on Cryptology and Network Security (CANS 2005) was held in Xiamen, Fujian Province, China, December 14–16, 2005. The conference was sponsored by the Fujian Normal University and Fujian Digital Certificate Authority Co. Ltd and was organized in cooperation with the International Association for Cryptologic Research (IACR).

The first International Workshop on Cryptology and Network Security was in Taipei, Taiwan, 2001. The second one was in San Francisco, California, USA, September 26–28, 2002, and the third in Miami, Florida, USA, September 24–26, 2003. CANS 2005 was the first CANS with proceedings published in the *Lecture Notes in Computer Science* series by Springer.

The Program Committee received 118 submissions, and accepted 28 papers from which 1 withdrew and thus 27 papers were included in the proceedings. The reviewing process took eight weeks, each paper was carefully evaluated by at least three members from the Program Committee. We appreciate the hard work of the members of the Program Committee and external referees who gave many hours of their valuable time. Thanks to Carl Ellison, Goce Jakimoski, Bart Preneel, Yongge Wang, Christopher Wolf and Shouhuai Xu, who acted as the shepherds of 6 papers included in the proceedings.

In addition to the contributed papers, there were two invited talks: Wenbo Mao spoke on "Research Issues in Network Security" — a practical viewpoint; and Matt Franklin on "Research Issues in Network Security" — a foundations viewpoint.

The best paper award was given to Hongbo Yu, Gaoli Wang, Guoyan Zhang and Xiaoyun Wang for their joint paper: The Second-Preimage Attack on MD4.

We would like to thank all the people involved in organizing this conference. In particular we would like to thank the Chair of the Organizing Committee, Xu Li, and people from the School of Mathematics and Computer Science, Fujian Normal University, for their time and efforts, as well as Vijayakrishnan Pasupathinathan and Qingsong Ye for their excellent work on maintaining the submission/reviewing software.

December 2005

Yvo Desmedt
Huaxiong Wang
Yi Mu
Yongqing Li

# 4ᵀᴴ International Conference on Cryptology and Network Security (CANS 2005)

**Sponsored by**
Fujian Normal University
Fujian Digital Certificate Authority Co. Ltd.

**In Cooperation with**
The International Association for Cryptologic Research (IACR)

## General Chairs

| | |
|---|---|
| Yongqing Li | Fujian Normal University, China |
| Yi Mu | University of Wollongong, Australia |

## Program Chairs

| | |
|---|---|
| Yvo G. Desmedt | University College London, UK & Florida State Univ., USA |
| Huaxiong Wang | Macquarie University, Australia |

## Program Committee

| | |
|---|---|
| Farooq Anjum | Telcordia, USA |
| Amos Beimel | Ben Gurion University, Israel |
| John Black | University of Colorado, USA |
| Carlo Blundo | University of Salerno, Italy |
| Jung Hee Cheon | Seoul Natl. Univ., South Korea |
| Cunsheng Ding | Hong Kong Univ. Sci. Tech., China |
| Carl Ellison | Microsoft, USA |
| Helena Handschuh | Gemplus, France |
| Thomas Johansson | University of Lund, Sweden |
| Antoine Joux | Université de Versailles, France |
| Kaoru Kurosawa | Ibaraki University, Japan |
| Xuejia Lai | Shanghai Jiao Tong University, China |
| Tanja Lange | Technical University of Denmark, Denmark |
| Pil Joong Lee | Pohang University, South Korea |
| Arjen Lenstra | Lucent, USA & Tech. Univ. Eindhoven, The Netherland |
| Radia Perlman | Sun Microsystems, USA |
| Josef Pieprzyk | Macquarie University, Australia |
| David Pointcheval | École Normale Supérieure, France |
| Bart Preneel | Katholieke Universiteit Leuven, Belgium |

## Organizing Committee

## External Referees

# Table of Contents

## Signcryption

## E-mail Security

## Cryptosystems

# Privacy and Tracing

# Information Hiding

# Firewalls, Denial of Service and DNS Security

# Trust Management

# The Second-Preimage Attack on MD4

Hongbo Yu, Gaoli Wang, Guoyan Zhang, and Xiaoyun Wang*

School of Mathematics and System Sciences,
Shandong University, Jinan 250100, China
yhb@mail.sdu.edu.cn, xywang@sdu.edu.cn

**Abstract.** In Eurocrypt'05, Wang et al. presented new techniques to find collisions of Hash function MD4. The techniques are not only efficient to search for collisions, but also applicable to explore the second-preimage of MD4. About the second-preimage attack, they showed that a random message was a weak message with probability $2^{-122}$ and it only needed a one-time MD4 computation to find the second-preimage corresponding to the weak message. A weak message means that there exits a more efficient attack than the brute force attack to find its second-preimage. In this paper, we find another new collision differential path which can be used to find the second-preimage for more weak messages. For any random message, it is a weak message with probability $2^{-56}$, and it can be converted into a weak message by message modification techniques with about $2^{27}$ MD4 computations. Furthermore, the original message is close to the resulting message (weak message), i.e, the Hamming weight of the difference for two messages is about 44.

**Keywords:** Hash function, collision differential path, second-preimage, weak message.

## 1 Introduction

In 1990[1], Rivest introduced the hash function MD4 which is the first dedicated hash function. After MD4, many hash functions such as MD5[2], HAVAL[3], RIPEMD [4], SHA-0[5], SHA-1[6], SHA-256[7] were designed subsequently.

For a hash function $h$ with inputs $x$, $x'$ and outputs $y$, $y'$, three potential security properties should be satisfied:

1. **Preimage resistance:** for any pre-specified output $y$, it is computationally infeasible to find an input $x$ such that $h(x) = y$.
2. **Second-preimage resistance:** for any input $x$, it is computationally infeasible to find another input $x'$ such that $h(x) = h(x')$
3. **Collision resistance:** it is computationally infeasible to find any two distinct inputs $x$, $x'$ with the same output, i.e., $h(x) = h(x')$.

* Supported by the National Natural Science Foundation of China(NSFC Grant No.90304009) and 973 Project( No.2004CB318000).

Y.G. Desmedt et al. (Eds.): CANS 2005, LNCS 3810, pp. 1–12, 2005.

The original design purpose of MD4 is that there is no better collision attack than the birthday attack which should take about $2^{64}$ MD4 computations to find a collision, and no better attack than brute force attack which should take $2^{128}$ MD4 computations to find a preimage corresponding to a pre-specified hash-value or the second preimage corresponding to a given message. The existing attack reveals that MD4 fails to reach the designer's goals both on collision resistance and second-preimage resistance. In 1996, Dobbertin presented a successful attack on MD4 which find a collision with probability $2^{-22}$[8]. In 1998, H.Doberrtin[9] showed that the first two (out of the total three) rounds of MD4 are not one-way. This means it is possible to find the preimage and the second-preimage for the first two rounds of MD4. Wang et al. [11] described a new kind of collision attack on the hash function MD4 and RIPEMD which is also applied to break MD5[10], HAVAL-128[14], SHA-0[12] and SHA-1[13]. Simultaneously, the collision attack on MD4 [11] can be used to explore the second-preimage attack on MD4, and the main results are as follows:

1. A random message is a weak message with probability $2^{-122}$. For a weak message, it only needs a one-time MD4 computation to find a second-preimage of the resulting hash value.
2. Any message $M$ can be modified with the basic message modification techniques. The resulting message $M'$ is a weak message with probability $2^{-23}$. $M$ and $M'$ are close and the Hamming weight of the difference for two messages is 50 on average.
3. Under the advanced message modification, any message $M$ can be modified into $M'$ which is a weak message with probability $2^{-2}$ to $2^{-6}$. However, the Hamming weight of their difference increases quickly up to 110.

In this paper, we give a further research on the second-preimage attack on MD4. Our results are as follows:

1. We find a new differential path which is efficient to find more weak messages. Utilizing this path, any message $M$ is a weak message with probability $2^{-56}$. For a weak message, it only needs a one-time MD4 computation to find a second-preimage.
2. For any message, we apply message modification techniques to convert it into a weak message with $2^{27}$ MD4 computations, the Hamming weight for their difference is about 44.

The paper is organized as follows: In section 2, we describe MD4 details. In section 3, we give some basic properties of nonlinear round functions for MD4 and some notations. Our main results are introduced in section 4. We summarize the paper in section 5.

## 2   Description of MD4

The message digest algorithm MD4 takes a message of length less than $2^{64}$ bits and produces a 128-bit hash value. The input message is padded and then processed in 512-bit blocks by Damgard/Merkle iterative structure. Each iteration invokes a compression function which takes a 128-bit chaining value and a 512-bit message block and outputs another 128-bit chaining value. The initial chaining value (called IV) is a set of fixed constants, and the final chaining value is the hash value of the message.

MD4 has three rounds, and every round employs a round function. The three round functions are defined as follows:

$$F(X, Y, Z) = (X \wedge Y) \vee (\neg X \wedge Z)$$
$$G(X, Y, Z) = (X \wedge Y) \vee (X \wedge Z) \vee (Y \wedge Z)$$
$$H(X, Y, Z) = X \oplus Y \oplus Z$$

Here $X, Y, Z$ are 32-bit words. The operations of three functions are all bitwise. $\neg X$ is the bitwise complement of $X$, $\wedge$, $\oplus$ and $\vee$ are respectively the bitwise AND, XOR and OR.

Each round of the compression function repeats 16 similar step operations, and in each step, one of the four chaining variables $a$, $b$, $c$, $d$ is updated. "$\ll s$" is the circularly left-shift by s bit positions and "$\gg s$" is the circularly right-shift by s bit positions.

$$\phi_0(a, b, c, d, m_k, s) = ((a + F(b, c, d) + m_k) \bmod 2^{32}) \ll s$$
$$\phi_1(a, b, c, d, m_k, s) = ((a + G(b, c, d) + m_k + 0x5a827999) \bmod 2^{32}) \ll s$$
$$\phi_2(a, b, c, d, m_k, s) = ((a + H(b, c, d) + m_k + 0x6ed9eba1) \bmod 2^{32}) \ll s$$

The initial value for MD4 is defined as:

$$(a, b, c, d) = (0x67452301, \ 0xefcdab89, \ 0x98badcfe, \ 0x10325476)$$

**MD4 Compression Function.** For one 512-bit block $M$ of the padded message $\overline{M}$, $M = (m_0, m_1, ..., m_{15})$, the compressing process is as follows:

1. Let $(aa, bb, cc, dd)$ be input of compressing process for $M$. If $M$ is the first message block to be hashed, $(aa, bb, cc, dd)$ is selected as the initial value. Otherwise it is the output for compressing the previous message block. $a$, $b$, $c$, $d$ are the chaining variables which are initialized by the initial values.
2. Perform the following 48 steps (three rounds):
   For j=0, 1, 2
      For i=0, 1, 2, 3

$$a = \phi_j(a, b, c, d, w_{j,4i}, s_{j,4i})$$
$$d = \phi_j(d, a, b, c, w_{j,4i+1}, s_{j,4i+1})$$
$$c = \phi_j(c, d, a, b, w_{j,4i+2}, s_{j,4i+2})$$
$$b = \phi_j(b, c, d, a, w_{j,4i+3}, s_{j,4i+3})$$

$s_{j,4i+k}$ ($k = 0, 1, 2, 3$) are step-dependent constants. $w_{j,4i+k}$ is a message word. The details of the message order and shift positions can be referred to Table 3.

3. Add $a$, $b$, $c$ and $d$ respectively to the chaining variables in the input value.

$$aa = (a + aa) \bmod 2^{32}$$
$$bb = (b + bb) \bmod 2^{32}$$
$$cc = (c + cc) \bmod 2^{32}$$
$$dd = (d + dd) \bmod 2^{32}$$

If $M$ is the last message block, $H(\overline{M}) = aa||bb||cc||dd$ is the hash value for the message $\overline{M}$. Otherwise repeat the above compression function with the next 512-bit message block and $(aa, bb, cc, dd)$ as inputs.

# 3 Preliminaries

## 3.1 Some Basic Conclusions of the Three Nonlinear Functions

The collision differential path and its sufficient conditions are closely related to the following properties of the three round functions.

**Proposition 1.** For the nonlinear function $f(x, y, z) = (x \wedge y) \vee (\neg x \wedge z)$ in the first round, the following properties hold:

1. $f(x, y, z) = f(\neg x, y, z)$ if and only if $y = z$.
   $f(x, y, z) = x$ and $f(\neg x, y, z) = \neg x$ if and only if $y = 1$ and $z = 0$.
   $f(x, y, z) = \neg x$ and $f(\neg x, y, z) = x$ if and only if $y = 0$ and $z = 1$.

2. $f(x, y, z) = f(x, \neg y, z)$ if and only if $x = 0$.
   $f(x, y, z) = y$ and $f(x, \neg y, z) = \neg y$ if and only if $x = 1$.

3. $f(x, y, z) = f(x, y, \neg z)$ if and only if $x = 1$.
   $f(x, y, z) = z$ and $f(x, y, \neg z) = \neg z$ if and only if $x = 0$.

**Proposition 2.** For the nonlinear function $g(x, y, z) = (x \wedge y) \vee (x \wedge z) \vee (y \wedge z)$, the following properties hold:

1. $g(x, y, z) = g(\neg x, y, z)$ if and only if $y = z$.
   $g(x, y, z) = x$ and $g(\neg x, y, z) = \neg x$ if and only if $y = \neg z$.

2. $g(x, y, z) = g(x, \neg y, z)$ if and only if $x = z$.
   $g(x, y, z) = y$ and $g(x, \neg y, z) = \neg y$ if and only if $x = \neg z$.

3. $g(x, y, z) = g(x, y, \neg z)$ if and only if $x = y$.
   $g(x, y, z) = z$ and $g(x, y, \neg z) = \neg z$ if and only if $x = \neg y$.

**Proposition 3.** For the nonlinear function $h(x, y, z) = x \oplus y \oplus z$ , the following properties hold:

1. $h(x, y, z) = \neg h(\neg x, y, z) = \neg h(x, \neg y, z) = \neg h(x, \neg y, z)$

2. $h(x, y, z) = h(\neg x, \neg y, z) = h(x, \neg y, \neg z) = h(\neg x, y, \neg z)$

Here, $x$, $y$, $z \in \{0, 1\}$ and $\neg$ is the bit complement operation.

### 3.2   Basic Notations

1. $M = (m_0, m_1, ..., m_{15})$ and $M' = (m'_0, m'_1, ..., m'_{15})$ represent two 512-bit messages.
2. $a_i$, $d_i$, $c_i$, $b_i$ respectively denote the outputs of the $(4i - 3)$-th, $(4i - 2)$-th, $(4i - 1)$-th and $4i$-th steps for compressing $M$, where $1 \le i \le 16$.
3. $a'_i$, $b'_i$, $c'_i$, $d'_i$ respectively denote the outputs of the $(4i - 3)$-th, $(4i - 2)$-th, $(4i - 1)$-th and $4i$-th steps for compressing $M'$.
4. $\Delta m_i = m'_i - m_i$ denotes the difference of two words $m_i$ and $m'_i$. It is noted that $\Delta m_i$ is an modular difference and not a XOR difference.
5. $a_{i,j}$, $b_{i,j}$, $c_{i,j}$, $d_{i,j}$ represent respectively the $j$-th bit of $a_i$, $b_i$, $c_i$, $d_i$, where the least significant bit is the 1-st bit, and the most significant bit is 32-nd bit.
6. $x_i[j]$, $x_i[-j]$ ($x$ can be $a$, $b$, $c$, $d$) are the resulting values by only changing the $j - th$ bit of the word $x_i$. $x_i[j]$ is obtained by changing the $j$-th bit of $x_i$ from 0 to 1. $x_i[-j]$ is obtained by changing the $j$-th bit of $x_i$ from 1 to 0.
7. $x_i[\pm j_1, \pm j_2, ..., \pm j_l]$ is the value by changing $j_1$-th, $j_2$-th, ..., $j_l$-th bits of $x_i$. The " $+$ " sign means that the bit is changed from 0 to 1, and the " $-$ " sign means that the bit is changed from 1 to 0.

## 4   The Second-Preimage Attack on MD4

In this section, we describe a second-preimage attack to find more weak messages and the corresponding second-preimages. The collision differential path in [11] is efficient to find collisions of MD4, but it isn't efficient to find weak messages and second-preimages because the path has too many conditions. Our purpose is to find another collision differential path with fewer conditions which is easily used to find weak messages and second-preimages.

### 4.1   Constructing the Specific Collision Differential Path

In order to find such a path, we select $\Delta M = M' - M$ as:

$$M = (m_0, m_1, \ldots, m_{15})$$
$$\Delta M = (0, 0, 0, 0, e2^i, 0, \ldots, 0), where \ e = \pm 1 \ and \ 0 \le i \le 31$$

We find a collision differential path when $e = 1$ and $i = 22$ with 62 variable conditions which are showed in Table 3.

The following description shows how to construct such a path. The main idea of constructing a valid collision differential path is to cancel out the propagations of message difference $\Delta m_4 = 2^{22}$ which occurs in step 5, 18 and 35 respectively.

1. In step 5, the message difference can cause the chaining variable difference $a_2[26]$.
2. In step 18, the message difference can be cancelled out by previous chaining variable difference or cause new difference $d_5[28]$.
3. In step 35, we select a chaining variable difference $\Delta c_8 = -2^{22}$ to cancel out the difference $\Delta m_4 = 2^{22}$, so we set $c_8' = c_8[-23]$.

In order to guarantee $M$ and $M'$ consist of a collision in step 35, the differences $\Delta b_8$, $\Delta a_9$, $\Delta d_9$ must remain zero. According to Proposition 3, the difference $\Delta c_8$ results in the nonzero differences $\Delta a_9$ and $\Delta d_9$. In order to cancel out these two differences, we set $d_8' = d_8[23]$. From $a_2[26]$, we get two simple lines reaching $d_8[23]$ and $c_8[23]$. They are expressed as follows:

$$a_2[26] \rightarrow a_3[-29, 30] \rightarrow a_4[32] \rightarrow a_5[3] \rightarrow d_5[8] \rightarrow d_6[13] \rightarrow d_7[18] \rightarrow d_8[23]$$

$$a_2[26] \rightarrow a_3[-29] \rightarrow c_3[-8] \rightarrow c_4[-19] \rightarrow c_5[-28] \rightarrow c_6[5, -6] \rightarrow c_7[-14] \rightarrow c_8[-23]$$

In addition, the difference $a_2[26]$ produces $a_3[29]$, we expand $a_3[29]$ to $a_3[-29, 30]$ by bit carry so that the bit difference $a_3[-29]$ can produce $c_3[-8]$. Similarly, the difference $c_5[-28]$ produces $c_6[-5]$, and we expand $c_6[-5]$ to $c_6[5, -6]$ by bit carry so that $c_6[-6]$ can offset $a_6[6]$.

Finally, the message difference $\Delta m_4 = 2^{22}$ in step 18 produces $d_5[28]$ which can be cancelled out by bit difference of $c_5[-28]$. The whole route can be expressed in table 3 where the first column defines the operating step. The second is the chaining variable in each step for $M$. The third denotes the message word of $M'$. The fourth is shift rotation. The fifth is the message word difference. The sixth is the chaining variable difference. The seventh is the chaining variable for $M'$ and the last column is the sufficient condition that guarantee the differential path to hold.

## 4.2   Deriving Conditions on Chaining Variable

From the differential path in Table 3, we derive a set of sufficient conditions on chaining variables from the Boolean function properties and the bit carry. For example,

The condition $b_{1,26} = c_{1,26}$ guarantees that the difference $a_2[26]$ results in no bit change in $d_2$.

The conditions $d_{2,26} = 0$ and $c_{2,26} = 1$ guarantee that $a_2[26]$ causes no bit change in $c_2$ and $b_2$ respectively.

The conditions $a_{3,29} = 1$ and $a_{3,30} = 0$ guarantee that the difference in $a_3$ has 1-bit carry.

Similarly, we can derive all the other conditions that are showed in the 8-th column of Table 3. They are also listed in Table 4.

What deserves particularly to mention is that constructing the path and deriving the conditions go on simultaneously. On one hand, we derive the sufficient conditions according to the differential path. On the other hand, we can adjust the path to avoid the contradictory conditions.

### 4.3   How to Verify Whether a Message Is a Weak Message

From the conditions in Table 4, we know that if $M$ satisfies all the 62 conditions, $M' = M + \Delta M$ is the second-preimage of $h(M)$. In fact, for every $\Delta m_4 = \pm 2^i$, $0 \leq i \leq 31$, we can find a differential path similar to Table 3 and derive the corresponding 62 conditions which guarantee the path to hold. So any message $M$ is a weak message with probability about $2^{-62} \times 2^5 \times 2 = 2^{-56}$. The probability can be further improved as long as we can find better differential path with less conditions.

### 4.4   Modifying Any Message into a Weak Message

Given message $M_0$, we use the **basic message modification**, **advanced message modification** and **bit searching** techniques to modify $M_0$ into a weak message $M$.

**Basic message modification.** The basic message modification technique is a kind of simple message modification used to ensure all the conditions in the first round to hold. A condition for chaining variable from compressing $M_0$ which isn't consistent with the condition in Table 4 is called a wrong condition. Usually correcting a wrong condition in the first round needs about single bit message modification.

For example, we can correct the condition $a_{2,26} = 1$ to $a_{2,26} = 0$ by changing the 23-rd bit of $m_4$, i.e,

$$m_4 \leftarrow m_4 \oplus 0x400000.$$

This can be easily seen from the following equation:

$$a_2 = (a_1 + f(b_1, c_1, d_1) + m_4) \lll 3.$$

Using a similar technique, we can correct all the wrong conditions by modifying their corresponding message words in the first 16 steps. If more than one condition need to be corrected in a step, we can correct them from the lower bit to the higher bit in order to avoid influencing the corrected conditions. For example, in step 9, we first correct the condition $b_{2,29} = c_{2,29}$, then $b_{2,30} = c_{2,30}$.

For any random message $M_0$, if we only fulfil the basic message modification, the modified message $M$ is a weak message with probability $2^{-38}$, and the Hamming weight between $M_0$ and $M$ is about 12 because there are total 24 conditions in first 16 steps.

**Advanced message modification.** We can correct part of conditions in round 2 by the advanced message modification which includes various technique details.

1. The correction of $a_{5,3}$, $a_{5,8}$, $a_{5,19}$ and $a_{5,28}$ in Table 4.
   From
   $$a_5 = (a_4 + G(b_4, c_4, d_4) + m_0 + 0x5a827999) \lll 3$$
   we know that these conditions can be corrected by modifying $m_0$, $m_1$, $m_2$, $m_3$, $m_4$ which consists of a partial collision from 1-5 steps which ensures

that all the conditions in round 1 unchanged. But one condition correction depends on at least 5 bits of these messages that will increase about 3 Hamming weights for the difference. In order to keep the low Hamming weights, we correct them by only modifying the message words $m_{14}$ and $m_{15}$ mainly. For example, if $a'_{5,3} \neq 0$, we correct it as follows:

$$b_4 = b_4 \oplus 0x80000000$$
$$m_{15} = b_4 \ggg 19 - b_3 - F(c_4, d_4, a_4)$$
$$a_5 = (a_4 + G(b_4, c_4, d_4) + m_0 + 0x5a827999) \lll 3$$

Due to $c_{4,32} \neq d_{4,32}$, from the proposition 2, we know that the change of $b_{4,32}$ will cause the change of $a_{5,3}$. Similarly, it's easy to correct the other three conditions of $a_5$. The computation of the Hamming weights is included in the next part.

2. The correction of $d_{5,3}$, $d_{5,8}$, $d_{5,28}$, $c_{5,3}$, $c_{5,8}$, $b_{5,6}$ and $b_{5,8}$.

   These conditions can be corrected by the similar method. We take $c_{5,3}$ for example. If $c_{5,3} \neq d_{5,3}$, we correct it by changing $c_{4,26}$ and keep the conditions in $c_4$, $b_4$, $a_5$, $d_5$ hold. The modification details are given in Table 1. The conditions $b_{4,26} = d_{4,26}$ and $a_{5,26} = b_{4,26}$ are set in advance to ensure nochange of $a_5$ and $d_5$. Indeed, there are many kinds of methods to correct a condition and this kind of advanced message modification is very flexible.

*Remark 1.* The condition $c_{5,28}$ can't be corrected by the method above since the condition $c_{4,19}$, $b_{4,19}$ and $a_{5,19}$ are all fixed in table 4.

**Searching Conditions and Estimating Hamming Weight.** There are still 27 conditions undetermined in table 4 after the correction of basic message modification and advanced message modification. We can search them exhaustively by choosing $m_{14}$ and $m_{15}$ randomly. For any couple of $m_{14}$ and $m_{15}$, we first modify them to ensure the conditions(except $c_{5,28}$) from step 15 to step 20 hold and then check whether all the remaining 27 conditions hold. If all the conditions hold, the resulting message is a weak message. There are 15 conditions from step 15 to step 20 of Table 4 which can be corrected and they depend on about 20 bits of $m_{14}$ and $m_{15}$. Therefore, there leave about a message space of $2^{40}$ which is large enough to search the remaining 27 conditions.

According to our analysis, we can estimate the Hamming weight for the difference of the original message $M_0$ and the resulting message $M$ by counting the

**Table 1.** The modification for correcting $c_{5,3}$

| | | | | |
|---|---|---|---|---|
| 15 | $m_{14}$ | 11 | $c'_4 = c_4 \oplus 2^{25}, d_4, a_4, b_3$ | $m_{14} \leftarrow c'_4 \ggg 11 - c_3 - F(d_4, a_4, b_3)$ |
| 16 | $m_{15}$ | 19 | $b_4, c'_4, d_4, a_4$ | $m_{15} \leftarrow b_4 \ggg 19 - b_3 - F(c'_4, d_4, a_4)$ |
| 17 | $m_0$ | 3 | $a_5, b_4, c'_4, d_4$ | $b_{4,26} = d_{4,26}$ |
| 18 | $m_4$ | 5 | $d_5, a_5, b_4, c'_4$ | $a_{5,26} = b_{4,26}$ |
| 19 | $m_8$ | 9 | $c'_5, d_5, a_5, b_4$ | |

**Table 2.** A weak message and its second-preimage. $H$ is the common Hash value for the message $M$ and $M'$ with little-endian and no message padding.

| $M_0$ | ffffffff | ffffffff | ffffffff | ffffffff | ffffffff | ffffffff | ffffffff | ffffffff |
|---|---|---|---|---|---|---|---|---|
| | ffffffff | ffffffff | ffffffff | ffffffff | ffffffff | ffffffff | ffffffff | ffffffff |
| $M$ | ffffffff | ffffffff | ffffffff | ffffffff | ffbfffff | fffbffff | ffffbfff | ffff9ff |
| | ffffffff | ffdfffff | fffbffff | ffffefff | ffffffff | f73ff7ff | adac30f9 | 2e2b983e |
| $M'$ | ffffffff | ffffffff | ffffffff | ffffffff | ffffffff | fffbffff | ffffbfff | ffff9ff |
| | ffffffff | ffdfffff | fffbffff | ffffefff | ffffffff | f73ff7ff | adac30f9 | 2e2b983e |
| $H$ | 36c6ff7 | b4f8abf9 | bcaaff6e | faa6e73d | | | | |

numbers of the conditions in table 4. The average Hamming weight of first 13 difference words is 9 , that of the 14-th word is 3, that of the 15-th and 16-th words is 32, so the total Hamming weight is about 44.

In order to easily observe the Hamming weight for a message and its corresponding weak message, we choose a special message $M_0$ with 512 one-bit, a weak message $M$ for $M_0$ and the second-preimage $M'$ for $M$ are given in Table 2. The Hamming weight for $M_0$ and $M$ is 43 which is one bit less than the average Hamming weight.

## 5    Conclusion

In this paper, we prove that any message is a weak message with probability about $2^{-56}$, and for a weak message, it only needs a one-time MD4 computation to find its second-preimage. For any message $M_0$, especially for meaningful message, it can be modified into a weak message $M$ which is very close to $M_0$ by the message modification techniques. In fact, we can utilize a more precise message modification such that the weak message $M$ is not only meaningful, but also is close to $M_0$. Our result about weak message is very useful for the key recovery of the MACs based-MD4. Due to the space limitations we will elaborate it in the other paper.

## References

1. R. L. Rivest, The MD4 Message Digest Algorithm, Advances in Cryptology, Crypto'90, Springer-Verlag, 1991, 303-311.
2. R. L. Rivest, The MD5 message-digest algorithm, Request for Comments (RFC 1320), Internet Activities Board, Internet Privacy Task Force, 1992.
3. Y. L. Zheng, J. Pieprzyk, J. Seberry, HAVAL–A One-way Hashing Algorithm with Variable Length of Output, Advances in Cryptology, AUSCRYPT'92 Proceedings, Springer-Verlag.
4. RIPE, Integrity Primitives for Secure Information Systems. Final Report of RACE Integrity Primitives Evaluation (RIPE-RACE 1040), LNCS 1007, Springer-Verlag, 1995.
5. FIPS 180, Secure Hash standard, NiST, May 1993.

6. FIPS 180-1, Secure hash standard, NIST, US Department of Commerce, Washington D. C., Springer-Verlag, 1996.
7. FIPS 180-2, Secure Hash Standard, http://csrc.nist.gov/publications/, 2002.
8. H. Dobbertin, Cryptanalysis of MD4, Fast Software Encryption, LNCS 1039, D. Gollmann, Ed., Springer-Verlag, 1996.
9. H. Dobbertin, The First Two Rounds of MD4 are Not One-Way, Fast Software Encryption, 1998.
10. X. Y. Wang, H. B. Yu, How to Break MD5 and Other Hash Functions. In Eurocrypt'05, May 2005.
11. X. Y. Wang, X. J. Lai, D. G. Feng, H. Chen, X. Y. Yu, Cryptanalysis for Hash Functions MD4 and RIPEMD. In Eurocrypt'05, May 2005.
12. X. Y. Wang, H. B. Yu, Y. L. Yin, Efficient Collision Search Attacks on SHA-0. To be appear in Crypto'05, August 2005.
13. X. Y. Wang, Y. L. Yin, H. B. Yu, Finding Collisions in the Full SHA-1. To be appear in Crypto'05, August 2005.
14. X. Y. Wang, D. G. Feng, X. Y. Yu, An Attack on Hash Function HAVAL-128, Science in China Series E, 2005.

# Appendix

**Table 3.** The collision differential path on MD4 for finding more weak messages and corresponding second-preimages

| Step | Output for $M$ | $m_i$ | $s_i$ | $\Delta m_i$ | Output difference | Output for $M'$ | Sufficient conditions |
|------|------|------|------|------|------|------|------|
| 1 | $a_1$ | $m_0$ | 3 | | | | |
| 2 | $d_1$ | $m_1$ | 7 | | | | |
| 3 | $c_1$ | $m_2$ | 11 | | | | |
| 4 | $b_1$ | $m_3$ | 19 | | | | |
| 5 | $a_2$ | $m_4$ | 3 | $2^{22}$ | $2^{25}$ | $a_2[26]$ | $a_{2,26}=0$ |
| 6 | $d_2$ | $m_5$ | 7 | | | $d_2$ | $b_{1,26}=c_{1,26}$ |
| 7 | $c_2$ | $m_6$ | 11 | | | $c_2$ | $d_{2,26}=0$ |
| 8 | $b_2$ | $m_7$ | 19 | | | $b_2$ | $c_{2,26}=1$ |
| 9 | $a_3$ | $m_8$ | 3 | | $2^{28}$ | $a_3[-29,30]$ | $a_{3,29}=1,\ a_{3,30}=0$ |
| 10 | $d_3$ | $m_9$ | 7 | | | $d_3$ | $b_{2,29}=c_{2,29},\ b_{2,30}=c_{2,30}$ |
| 11 | $c_3$ | $m_{10}$ | 11 | | $-2^7$ | $c_3[-8]$ | $c_{3,8}=1,\ d_{3,29}=1,\ d_{3,30}=0$ |
| 12 | $b_3$ | $m_{11}$ | 19 | | | $b_3$ | $c_{3,29}=1,\ c_{3,30}=1,\ d_{3,8}=a_{3,8}$ |
| 13 | $a_4$ | $m_{12}$ | 3 | | $2^{31}$ | $a_4[32]$ | $a_{4,32}=0,\ b_{3,8}=0$ |
| 14 | $d_4$ | $m_{13}$ | 7 | | | $d_4$ | $b_{3,32}=c_{3,32},\ a_{4,8}=1$ |
| 15 | $c_4$ | $m_{14}$ | 11 | | $-2^{18}$ | $c_4[-19]$ | $c_{4,19}=1,\ d_{4,32}=0$ |
| 16 | $b_4$ | $m_{15}$ | 19 | | | $b_4$ | $d_{4,19}=a_{4,19},\ c_{4,32}=1$ |
| 17 | $a_5$ | $m_0$ | 3 | | $2^2$ | $a_5[3]$ | $a_{5,3}=0,\ b_{4,19}=d_{4,19}$ |
| 18 | $d_5$ | $m_4$ | 5 | $2^{22}$ | $2^7+2^{27}$ | $d_5[8,28]$ | $d_{5,8}=0,\ d_{5,28}=0,$ $a_{5,19}=b_{4,19},\ b_{4,3}=c_{4,3}+1$ |
| 19 | $c_5$ | $m_8$ | 9 | | $-2^{27}$ | $c_5[-28]$ | $c_{5,28}=1,\ a_{5,8}=b_{4,8},$ $d_{5,3}=b_{4,3},\ a_{5,28}=b_{4,28}$ |
| 20 | $b_5$ | $m_{12}$ | 13 | | | $b_5$ | $c_{5,3}=d_{5,3},\ c_{5,8}=a_{5,8}$ |
| 21 | $a_6$ | $m_1$ | 3 | | $2^5$ | $a_6[6]$ | $a_{6,6}=0,\ b_{5,8}=c_{5,8}$ |
| 22 | $d_6$ | $m_5$ | 5 | | $2^{12}$ | $d_6[13]$ | $d_{6,13}=0,\ b_{5,6}=c_{5,6},$ $a_{6,28}=b_{5,28}+1$ |
| 23 | $c_6$ | $m_9$ | 9 | | $-2^4$ | $c_6[5,-6]$ | $c_{6,5}=0,\ c_{6,6}=1,\ d_{6,6}=b_{5,6},$ $a_{6,13}=b_{5,13}$ |
| 24 | $b_6$ | $m_{13}$ | 13 | | | $b_6$ | $d_{6,5}=a_{6,5},\ c_{6,13}=a_{6,13}$ |
| 25 | $a_7$ | $m_2$ | 3 | | | $a_7$ | $b_{6,6}=d_{6,6}+1,\ b_{6,5}=d_{6,5},$ $b_{6,13}=c_{6,13}$ |
| 26 | $d_7$ | $m_6$ | 5 | | $2^{17}$ | $d_7[18]$ | $a_{7,5}=b_{6,5},\ a_{7,6}=b_{6,6},\ d_{7,18}=0$ |
| 27 | $c_7$ | $m_{10}$ | 9 | | $-2^{13}$ | $c_7[-14]$ | $c_{7,14}=1,\ a_{7,18}=b_{6,18}$ |
| 28 | $b_7$ | $m_{14}$ | 13 | | | $b_7$ | $d_{7,14}=a_{7,14},\ c_{7,18}=a_{7,18}$ |
| 29 | $a_8$ | $m_3$ | 3 | | | $a_8$ | $b_{7,14}=d_{7,14},\ b_{7,18}=c_{7,18}$ |
| 30 | $d_8$ | $m_7$ | 5 | | $2^{22}$ | $d_8[23]$ | $d_{8,23}=0,\ a_{8,14}=b_{7,14}$ |
| 31 | $c_8$ | $m_{11}$ | 9 | | $-2^{22}$ | $c_8[-23]$ | $c_{8,23}=1,\ a_{8,23}=b_{7,23}$ |
| 32 | $b_8$ | $m_{15}$ | 13 | | | $b_8$ | |
| 33 | $a_9$ | $m_0$ | 3 | | | $a_9$ | |
| 34 | $d_9$ | $m_8$ | 9 | | | $d_9$ | $a_{9,23}=b_{8,23}$ |
| 35 | $c_9$ | $m_4$ | 11 | $2^{22}$ | | $c_9$ | |
| 36 | $b_9$ | $m_{12}$ | 15 | | | $b_9$ | |

**Table 4.** A set of sufficient conditions for the MD4 differential path

| step | output variable | condition |
|------|-----------------|-----------|
| 1 | $a_1$ | |
| 2 | $d_1$ | |
| 3 | $c_1$ | |
| 4 | $b_1$ | $b_{1,26} = c_{1,26}$ |
| 5 | $a_2$ | $a_{2,26} = 0$ |
| 6 | $d_2$ | $d_{2,26} = 0$ |
| 7 | $c_2$ | $c_{2,26} = 1$ |
| 8 | $b_2$ | $b_{2,29} = c_{2,29}$, $b_{2,30} = c_{2,30}$ |
| 9 | $a_3$ | $a_{3,29} = 1$, $a_{3,30} = 0$ |
| 10 | $d_3$ | $d_{3,8} = a_{3,8}$, $d_{3,29} = 1$, $d_{3,30} = 0$ |
| 11 | $c_3$ | $c_{3,8} = 1$, $c_{3,29} = 1$, $c_{3,30} = 1$ |
| 12 | $b_3$ | $b_{3,8} = 0$, $b_{3,32} = c_{3,32}$ |
| 13 | $a_4$ | $a_{4,8} = 1$, $a_{4,32} = 0$ |
| 14 | $d_4$ | $d_{4,19} = a_{4,19}$, $d_{4,32} = 0$ |
| 15 | $c_4$ | $c_{4,19} = 1$, $c_{4,32} = 1$ |
| 16 | $b_4$ | $b_{4,3} = c_{4,3} + 1$, $b_{4,19} = d_{4,19}$ |
| 17 | $a_5$ | $a_{5,3} = 0$, $a_{5,8} = b_{4,8}$, $a_{5,19} = b_{4,19}$, $a_{5,28} = b_{4,28}$ |
| 18 | $d_5$ | $d_{5,3} = b_{4,3}$, $d_{5,8} = 0$, $d_{5,28} = 0$ |
| 19 | $c_5$ | $c_{5,3} = d_{5,3}$, $c_{5,8} = a_{5,8}$, $c_{5,28} = 1$ |
| 20 | $b_5$ | $b_{5,6} = c_{5,6}$, $b_{5,8} = c_{5,8}$, |
| 21 | $a_6$ | $a_{6,6} = 0$, $a_{6,13} = b_{5,13}$, $a_{6,28} = b_{5,28} + 1$ |
| 22 | $d_6$ | $d_{6,5} = a_{6,5}$, $d_{6,6} = b_{5,6}$, $d_{6,13} = 0$ |
| 23 | $c_6$ | $c_{6,5} = 0$, $c_{6,6} = 1$, $c_{6,13} = a_{6,13}$ |
| 24 | $b_6$ | $b_{6,5} = d_{6,5}$, $b_{6,6} = d_{6,6} + 1$, $b_{6,13} = c_{6,13}$ |
| 25 | $a_7$ | $a_{7,5} = b_{6,5}$, $a_{7,6} = b_{6,6}$, $a_{7,18} = b_{6,18}$ |
| 26 | $d_7$ | $d_{7,14} = a_{7,14}$, $d_{7,18} = 0$ |
| 27 | $c_7$ | $c_{7,14} = 1$, $c_{7,18} = a_{7,18}$ |
| 28 | $b_7$ | $b_{7,14} = d_{7,14}$, $b_{7,18} = c_{7,18}$ |
| 29 | $a_8$ | $a_{8,14} = b_{7,14}$, $a_{8,23} = b_{7,23}$ |
| 30 | $d_8$ | $d_{8,23} = 0$ |
| 31 | $c_8$ | $c_{8,23} = 1$ |
| 32 | $a_9$ | $a_{9,23} = b_{8,23}$ |

# On the Security of Certificateless Signature Schemes from Asiacrypt 2003*

Xinyi Huang[1], Willy Susilo[2], Yi Mu[2], and Futai Zhang[1,**]

[1] College of Mathematics and Computer Science,
Nanjing Normal University, P.R. China
xinyinjnu@126.com, zhangfutai@njnu.edu.cn
[2] Centre for Information Security Research,
School of Information Technology and Computer Science,
University of Wollongong, Australia
{wsusilo, ymu}@uow.edu.au

**Abstract.** In traditional digital signature schemes, certificates signed by a trusted party are required to ensure the authenticity of the public key. In Asiacrypt 2003, the concept of certificateless signature scheme was introduced. In the new paradigm, the necessity of certificates has been successfully removed. The security model for certificateless cryptography was also introduced in the same paper. However, as we shall show in this paper, the proposed certificateless signature is insecure in their defined model. We provide an attack that *can successfully forge* a certificateless signature in their model. We also fix this problem by proposing a new scheme.

**Keywords:** Certificateless Signature, Certificateless Cryptography, Attack Model, Bilinear Pairing.

## 1 Introduction

In traditional digital signature schemes, the binding between a user and his public key needs to be ensured. A typical way to provide this assurance is by providing certificates that are signed by a trusted third party. In [13], Shamir introduced a new notion called identity-based cryptography (and hence, identity-based signature scheme) where the user's public key is indeed his identity (such as an email, IP address, etc.). This way, the need of certification can be avoided. However, this approach creates a new inherent problem namely the key escrow of a user's private key, since the trusted third party called the Private Key Generator (PKG) must be completely trusted, since he has the knowledge of the user's secret key.

* This work is supported by ARC Discovery Grant DP0557493.
** Partially supported by Ministry of Education of Jiangsu Province Project 03KJA520066 and Open Project of Key Laboratory on Computer Network and Information Security of Ministry of Education of China.

Y.G. Desmedt et al. (Eds.): CANS 2005, LNCS 3810, pp. 13–25, 2005.

To fill the gap between traditional cryptography and identity-based cryptography, Al-Riyami and Paterson proposed a new paradigm called *certificateless cryptography* in [1]. In contrast to traditional cryptography, certificateless cryptography does not require the use of any certificates to ensure the authenticity of public keys. Certificateless cryptography relies on the existence of a trusted third party who has the master-key. In this sense, it is similar to identity-based cryptography. Nevertheless, certificateless cryptography does not suffer from the key escrow property that seems to be inherent in identity-based cryptography. We note that the concept of certificateless cryptography has been around [7, 9, 10, 12], but the first formalization was provided in [1].

Intuitively, the characteristic of certificateless cryptography is as follows. The trusted third party, called the $KGC$, does not have access to the users' private keys. The $KGC$ only supplies a user with a *partial private key* $D_i$, which the $KGC$ computes from an identifier $\mathsf{ID}_i$. As in the identity-based cryptography, the partial private key needs to be delivered securely to the user. Then, the user combines his partial private key $D_i$ with some secret information to generate his actual private key $S_i$. This way, the user's private key is *not* available to the $KGC$. The user also combines his secret information with the $KGC$'s public parameters to generate his public key $P_i$. The user's public key $P_i$ needs to be made available to the other participants by transmitting it along with messages, in the case of message signing. Hence, it is no longer an identity-based cryptography, since the public key needs to be provided (but in contrast to the traditional cryptography, the public key does not require any certificate).

Due to the lack of public key authentication, it is important to assume that an adversary can replace the user's public key by a false key of its choice [1]. In order to provide a secure certificateless signature scheme, this type of attacks must not be able to produce signatures that verify with the false public key [1]. An assumption that must be made is that the $KGC$ does not mount a public key replacement attack since he is armed with a partial private key. Hence, we must assume that the $KGC$, who posses the master-key and hence all partial private keys, is trusted not to replace user's public keys. This way, the level of trust is similar to the trust in a CA in a traditional PKI. We will review the adversarial model defined in [1] in the next section.

Following, the work of [1], there are several certificateless public key encryption proposed (eg. [3, 5, 4, 15]). In [14], a generic construction of certificateless signature from any identity-based signature scheme and a secure public key signature scheme in the sense of [8] was proposed.

*Our Contribution*
In this paper, we show that the proposed certificateless signature scheme in [1] *does not* satisfy the security requirement of certificateless cryptography, in terms of the defined adversarial model in [1]. To be more precise, we show that an attacker who does *not* posses the master-key but can only do a public key replacement attack, can always successfully forge a signature. We also provide a new scheme that resists against this type of attacks and hence, it satisfies the requirements of certificateless signature schemes as defined in [1].

*Organization of the Paper*

In the next section, we will review some preliminaries required throughout the paper. In Section 3, we review the proposed certificateless signature scheme in [1]. The security of this scheme was not provided in [1], and therefore, firstly we show that the unforgeability of the scheme in Section 4. Unfortunately, as we will also show in Section 4, the scheme fails to resist against the adversarial model type I as defined in [1]. We will show how to fix this problem in Section 5. Finally, Section 6 concludes the paper.

# 2 Preliminaries

In this section, we will review some fundamental backgrounds required in this paper, namely bilinear pairing and the certificateless cryptography definition.

## 2.1 Bilinear Pairing

Let $\mathbb{G}_1$ denote an additive group of prime order $q$ and $\mathbb{G}_2$ be a multiplicative group of the same order. Let $P$ denote a generator in $\mathbb{G}_1$. Let $\hat{e} : \mathbb{G}_1 \times \mathbb{G}_1 \to \mathbb{G}_2$ be a bilinear mapping with the following properties:

- The map $\hat{e}$ is bilinear: $\hat{e}(aP, bQ) = \hat{e}(P, Q)^{ab}$ for all $P, Q \in \mathbb{G}_1, a, b \in \mathbb{Z}_q$.
- The map $\hat{e}$ is non-degenerate: $\hat{e}(P, P) \neq 1_{\mathbb{G}_2}$.
- The map $\hat{e}$ is efficiently computable.

A Bilinear pairing instance generator is defined as a probabilistic polynomial time algorithm $\mathcal{IG}$ that takes as input a security parameter $\ell$ and returns a uniformly random tuple $param = (q, \mathbb{G}_1, \mathbb{G}_2, \hat{e}, P)$ of bilinear parameters, including a prime number $q$ of size $\ell$, a cyclic additive group $\mathbb{G}_1$ of order $q$, a multiplicative group $\mathbb{G}_2$ of order $q$, a bilinear map $\hat{e} : \mathbb{G}_1 \times \mathbb{G}_1 \to \mathbb{G}_2$ and a generator $P$ of $\mathbb{G}_1$. For a group $\mathbb{G}$ of prime order, we denote the set $\mathbb{G}^* = \mathbb{G} \setminus \{\mathcal{O}\}$ where $\mathcal{O}$ is the identity element of the group.

**Definition 1. Computational Diffie-Hellman (CDH) problem in $\mathbb{G}_1$.** *Given $(P, aP, bP)$, for some $a, b \in \mathbb{Z}_q^*$, compute $abP$.*

The success probability of any probabilistic polynomial-time algorithm $\mathcal{A}$ in solving CDH problem in $\mathbb{G}_1$ is defined to be

$$\mathrm{Succ}_{\mathcal{A}, \mathbb{G}_1}^{CDH} = Pr[\mathcal{A}(P, aP, bP) = abP : a, b \in \mathbb{Z}_q^*]$$

The CDH assumption states that for every probabilistic polynomial-time algorithm $\mathcal{A}$, $\mathrm{Succ}_{\mathcal{A}, \mathbb{G}_1}^{CDH}$ is negligible.

## 2.2 Certificateless Signature Schemes

A certificateless signature scheme is defined by seven algorithms: Setup, Partial-Private-Key-Extract, Set-Secret-Value, Set-Private-Key, Set-Public-Key, Sign and Verify. The description of each algorithm is as follows.

- Setup: The master key and parameter generation algorithm is a probabilistic algorithm that accepts as input a security parameter $1^k$ and returns a master-key and a parameter list params.
- Partial-Private-Key-Extract: The partial private key issuance algorithm is a deterministic algorithm that accepts as input a user identity $ID_i$, a parameter list param and a master-key to produce the user's partial private key $D_i$.
- Set-Secret-Value: The set secret value setup algorithm is a probabilistic algorithm that accepts as input a parameter list param and a user identity $ID_i$ to produce the user's secret value $x_i$.
- Set-Private-Key: The secret value setup algorithm is a probabilistic algorithm that accepts as input a parameter list param, the user's partial private key $D_i$ and the user's secret value $x_i$ to produce a private signing key $S_i$.
- Set-Public-Key: The public key generation algorithm is a deterministic algorithm that takes as input a parameter list param, a user identity $ID_i$ and the user's secret value $x_i$ to produce a public key $P_i$.
- Sign: The signing algorithm is a probabilistic algorithm that accepts a message $M \in \mathcal{M}$, $\mathcal{M}$ is the message space, a user's identity $ID_i$, a parameter list param and the user's signing key $S_i$ to produce a signature $\sigma$.
- Verify: The verification algorithm is a deterministic algorithm that accepts a message $M$, a signature $\sigma$, a parameter list param, the public key $P_i$ and the user's identity $ID_i$ to output true if the signature is correct, or $\perp$ otherwise.

### 2.3 Adversarial Model of Certificateless Signature Schemes

As defined in [1], there are two types of adversary with different capabilities:

**Type I Adversary:** This type of adversary $\mathcal{A}_I$ does not have access to the master-key, but $\mathcal{A}_I$ has the ability to *replace* the public key of any entity with a value of his choice, because there is no certificate involved in certificateless signature schemes.

**Type II Adversary:** This type of adversary $\mathcal{A}_{II}$ has access to the master-key but cannot perform public keys replacement.

Nevertheless, no formal security model was presented in neither [1] nor [2]. In this section, firstly we provide a formal definition of existential unforgeability of a certificateless signature (CLS) scheme under both two types of chosen message attack. They are defined using the following game between an adversary $\mathcal{A} \in \{\mathcal{A}_I, \mathcal{A}_{II}\}$ and a challenger $\mathcal{C}$.

*Type I Adversary*

- Setup: $\mathcal{C}$ runs the algorithm to obtain the system parameter lists params, $\mathcal{C}$ then sends params to the adversary $\mathcal{A}_I$.
- Partial-Private-Key Queries: $\mathcal{A}_I$ can request the Partial-Private-Key of the user whose identity is ID. In respond, $\mathcal{C}$ outputs the Partial-Private-Key $D_{ID}$.
- Public-Key-Replacement: For any user whose identity is ID, $\mathcal{A}_I$ can choose a new Secret-Value $x$ and compute the new public key $(X, Y)$. $\mathcal{A}_I$ then set $(X, Y)$ as the new public key of this user and submit $(x, X, Y, ID)$ to $\mathcal{C}$. $\mathcal{C}$ will record these replacements which will be used later.

- Sign Queries: $\mathcal{A}_I$ can request user's (whose identity is ID) signature on a message $M$. In respond, $\mathcal{C}$ outputs a signature $\sigma$ for a message $M$ which is a valid signature under the public key $\mathcal{A}_I$ has replaced earlier.
- Output: Finally, $\mathcal{A}_I$ outputs a target message/signature pair $(M^*, \sigma^*)$ of the user whose identity is ID$^*$. This message/signature pair must satisfy the following requirements:
  1. This signature is valid under the public key $(X^*, Y^*)$ chosen by $\mathcal{A}_I$.
  2. $\mathcal{A}_I$ does not request the Partial-Private-Key of this user whose identity is ID$^*$.
  3. $M^*$ has never been queried during the Sign Queries.

The success probability of an Type I adversary to win the game is defined by

$$Succ_{\mathcal{A}_I}^{EF-CLS-CMA}$$

**Definition 2.** *A certificateless signature scheme is existential unforgeable against Type I chosen-message attacks iff the probability of success of any polynomially bounded Type I adversary in the above game is negligible. In other words,*

$$Succ_{\mathcal{A}_I}^{EF-CLS-CMA}(k) \le \epsilon$$

*k is the system's security parameter.*

*Type II Adversary*

- Setup: $\mathcal{C}$ runs the algorithm to obtain the system parameter lists params and also the system's master-key:$s$, $\mathcal{C}$ then sends params and $s$ to the adversary $\mathcal{A}_{II}$.
- Sign Queries: $\mathcal{A}_{II}$ can request user's(whose identity is $ID$) signature on a message $M$. In respond, $\mathcal{C}$ outputs a signature $\sigma$ for a message $M$.
- Output: Finally, $\mathcal{A}_{II}$ outputs a target message/signature pair $(M^*, \sigma^*)$ of the user whose identity is $ID$. This message/signature pair must satisfy the following requirements:
  1. This signature is a valid one, i.e. it passes the verification algorithm.
  2. $M^*$ has never been queried during the Sign Queries.

The success probability of an Type II adversary to win the game is defined by

$$Succ_{\mathcal{A}_{II}}^{EF-CLS-CMA}$$

**Definition 3.** *A certificateless signature scheme is existential unforgeable against Type II chosen-message attacks iff the probability of success of any polynomially bounded Type II adversary in the above game is negligible. In other words,*

$$Succ_{\mathcal{A}_{II}}^{EF-CLS-CMA}(k) \le \epsilon$$

*k is the system's security parameter.*

**Definition 4.** *[1] A certificateless signature scheme is existential unforgeable against chosen-message attacks iff it is secure against both types of adversaries.*

# 3   Review of Al-Riyami-Paterson's Certificateless Signature Scheme from Asiacrypt 2003

In this section, we review the certificateless signature scheme from [1]. The certificateless signature scheme is defined as follows.

- Setup: This algorithm runs as follows.
  1. Run $\mathcal{IG}$ on input $k$ to generate $(\mathbb{G}_1, \mathbb{G}_2, \hat{e})$ where $\mathbb{G}_1$ and $\mathbb{G}_2$ are groups of some prime order $q$ ( $q \geq 2^k$ ) and $\hat{e} : \mathbb{G}_1 \times \mathbb{G}_1 \to \mathbb{G}_2$ is a bilinear pairing.
  2. Select a random generator $P \in \mathbb{G}_1$.
  3. Select a master-key $s$ randomly from $\mathbb{Z}_q^*$ and set $P_0 = sP$.
  4. Select cryptographic hash functions $H_1 : \{0,1\}^* \to \mathbb{G}_1^*$ and $H_2 : \mathbb{G}_2 \to \{0,1\}^n$, where $n$ denote the bit-length of plaintexts [1].

  The system parameters param $= (\mathbb{G}_1, \mathbb{G}_2, \hat{e}, n, P, P_0, H_1, H_2)$. The master-key is $s \in \mathbb{Z}_q^*$. The message space is $\mathcal{M} = \{0,1\}^n$.
- Partial-Private-Key-Extract: This algorithm accepts an identity $\mathsf{ID}_i \in \{0,1\}^*$ and constructs the partial private key for the user as follows.
  1. Compute $\mathsf{Q}_i = H_1(\mathsf{ID}_i)$.
  2. Output the partial private key $D_i = s\mathsf{Q}_i$.
- Set-Secret-Value: This algorithm takes as input param and the user's identity $\mathsf{ID}_i$, and selects a random $x_i \in \mathbb{Z}_q^*$ and outputs $x_i$ as the user's secret value.
- Set-Private-Key: This algorithm accepts param, a user's partial private key $D_i$ and the user's secret value $x_i \in \mathbb{Z}_q^*$ to transform the partial private key $D_i$ to a full private key $S_i$ by computing $S_i = x_i D_i = x_i s \mathsf{Q}_i$ and output $S_i$.
- Set-Public-Key: This algorithm accepts param and a user's secret value $x_i \in \mathbb{Z}_q^*$ to produce the user's public key $P_i = (X_i, Y_i)$, where $X_i = x_i P$ and $Y_i = x_i P_0 = x_i sP$.
- Sign: To sign a message $M \in \mathcal{M}$ using the private key $S_i$, perform the following steps.
  1. Select a random $r \in \mathbb{Z}_q^*$.
  2. Compute $R = \hat{e}(rP, P)$.
  3. Set $v = H_2(M, R)$.
  4. Compute $U = vS_i + rP$.
  5. Output $(U, v)$ as the signature on $M$.
- Verify: To verify a signature $(U, v)$ on a message $M \in \mathcal{M}$ for an identity $\mathsf{ID}_i$ and public key $(X_i, Y_i)$, perform the following steps.
  1. Verify whether $\hat{e}(X_i, P_0) \stackrel{?}{=} \hat{e}(Y_i, P)$ holds with equality. If not, then output $\perp$ and abort.
  2. Compute $R = \hat{e}(U, P)\hat{e}(\mathsf{Q}_i, -Y_i)^v$.
  3. Verify whether $v \stackrel{?}{=} H_2(M, R)$ holds with equality. If it does, output true. Otherwise, output $\perp$.

# 4   Security Analysis of Al-Riyami-Paterson's Certificateless Signature Schemes

A formal security proof for the provided certificateless public key encryption scheme in [1] has already provided in [1]. Unfortunately, the security proof for their certificateless signature scheme is not provided in the same paper. As we shall show in this section, the scheme in [1] does not resist against type I adversary, defined in the same paper. We will show how to fix this problem in section 5.

## 4.1   An Attack on Al-Riyami-Paterson's Scheme Using Type I Adversary

As defined in [1], a certificateless signature scheme is existentially unforgeable iff it resists against type I and type II adversaries. Recall that type I adversary does not possess the knowledge of the master-key, $s$, but the adversary can perform public key replacement, i.e. replacing the public key with its choice. We will show that the scheme in [1] does not resist against type I adversary since the adversary can successfully forge a user's signature on a message of its choice. The attack is as follows.

Without losing generality, we only define the Sign and Verify algorithms in this section. The rest of the algorithms are the same as the original scheme defined in [1]. Recall that the Sign algorithm will be performed by an attacker who can replace the user's public key. The attack is successful, iff the signature verification with respect to the replaced public key is correct.

**Sign:** To sign an arbitrary message $M \in \mathcal{M}$, the adversary performs the following.

1. Select a random $U \in \mathbb{G}_1$.
2. Compute $R = \hat{e}(U, P)\hat{e}(Q_i, -P_0)$, where $Q_i = H_1(\mathsf{ID}_i)$ and $\mathsf{ID}_i$ denotes a valid user's identity.
3. Compute $v = H_2(M, R)$.
4. Let $x_i = v^{-1} \pmod{q}$.
5. Compute $X_i = x_i P$ and $Y_i = x_i P_0$.
6. Replace the user's public key with $(X_i, Y_i)$.
7. Publish $(U, v)$ as the user's signature on a message $M$.

The attack is said to be *successful*, iff the verification of the signature on a message returns `true`. This is justified as follows.

Verify: To verify a signature $(U, v)$ on a message $M$, using the public key $(X_i, Y_i)$ for an identity $\mathsf{ID}_i$, anyone can perform the verification algorithm as defined in [1]. As we shall see below, the verification will return `true`.

1. Verify whether $\hat{e}(X_i, P_0) \stackrel{?}{=} \hat{e}(Y_i, P)$ holds. This verification will pass because

$$\hat{e}(X_i, P_0) = \hat{e}(x_i P, sP)$$
$$= \hat{e}(x_i sP, P)$$
$$= \hat{e}(Y_i, P)$$

2. Compute $R' = \hat{e}(U, P)\hat{e}(Q_i, -Y_i)^v$.

3. Verify whether $v \stackrel{?}{=} H_2(M, R')$ holds. This verification will pass because

$$R' = \hat{e}(U, P)\hat{e}(Q_i, -Y_i)^v$$
$$= \hat{e}(U, P)\hat{e}(Q_i, -v \cdot x_i \cdot P_0)$$
$$= \hat{e}(U, P)\hat{e}(Q_i, -v \cdot v^{-1} \cdot P_0)$$
$$= \hat{e}(U, P)\hat{e}(Q_i, -P_0)$$
$$= R$$

Since $R' = R$ holds, then $v \stackrel{?}{=} H_2(M, R)$ will hold with equality.   □

**Theorem 1.** *The Al-Riyami-Paterson's certificateless signature scheme is universally forgeable against type I adversary.*

*Remarks:* We note that this attack is a strong attack that belongs to the *no-message attack* classes, where *no* signing oracle is required, in the adversarial model type I. The authors of [1] revised their Asiacrypt 2003 paper in [2], but the signature scheme in their revised version is the same as the Asiacrypt version in [1].

## 4.2 Security of Al-Riyami-Paterson's Certificateless Signature Scheme Against Type II Adversary

Fortunately, as we shall show in this section, the proposed scheme is secure against type II adversary. This is shown in the following theorem.

**Theorem 2.** *The certificateless signature scheme proposed in [1] is unforgeable against the type II adversary in the random oracle [6] model under the CDH assumption in $\mathbb{G}_1$.*

*Proof (sketch).* Let $\mathcal{A}$ be our type II adversary. Recall that $\mathcal{A}$ has access to the master-key, $s$, but cannot perform any public key replacement. Having the access to $s$, $\mathcal{A}$ can forge any message-signature pair for any user. We will show how to build algorithm $\mathcal{B}$ that will solve the CDH problem using $\mathcal{A}$'s capability as follows.

We model the hash function $H_2$ as a random oracle and hence, we will need to keep a list of the oracle queries that have been made. The purpose of algorithm $\mathcal{B}$ is to compute $abP$ given $aP, bP$, for some unknown $a, b \in \mathbb{Z}_q^*$. Firstly, $\mathcal{B}$ sets the user's public key $X_i = aP$ and the user's public identity $Q_i = bP$. Then, $\mathcal{B}$ selects the system parameter param $= (\mathbb{G}_1, \mathbb{G}_2, \hat{e}, n, P, P_0, H_1, H_2)$. Finally, the master-key is $s \in \mathbb{Z}_q^*$ is selected. The public key $Y_i$ can be computed afterwards from $Y_i = sX_i$.

When the simulation is started, $\mathcal{A}$ is provided with param and the master-key, $s$. The interaction with the hash oracle, $H_2$, is recorded in the list of oracle queries. Eventually, applying the forking technqie [11], a set of two forged signatures on the same message $M$ will be obtained. When this happens, $\mathcal{B}$ obtains

$$R = \hat{e}(U, P)\hat{e}(Q_i, -Y_i)^v$$

and
$$R = \hat{e}(U', P)\hat{e}(Q_i, -Y_i)^{v'}$$

for both signatures $(U, v), (U', v')$ on the same message $M$. Therefore, $\mathcal{B}$ obtains the following equations

$$\hat{e}(U, P)\hat{e}(Q_i, -Y_i)^v = e(U', P)\hat{e}(Q_i, -Y_i)^{v'}$$
$$\hat{e}(U - U', P) = \hat{e}(Q_i, -Y_i)^{v'-v}$$
$$\hat{e}(U - U', P) = \hat{e}((v - v')Q_i, x_i s P)$$
$$\hat{e}(U - U', P) = \hat{e}((v - v')x_i s Q_i, P)$$

From this equation, $\mathcal{B}$ has the following

$$U - U' = (v - v')x_i s Q_i$$
$$(v - v')^{-1}s^{-1}(U - U') = x_i Q_i$$

Since $x_i Q_i$ can be computed from

$$x_i Q_i = (v - v')^{-1}s^{-1}(U - U')$$

and $\mathcal{B}$ has the knowledge of $(v, v', s, U, U')$, then $x_i Q_i$ is computable by $\mathcal{B}$. Note that $x_i Q_i = x_i b P = ab P$ in our setting above, and hence, $\mathcal{B}$ has successfully obtains the solution of CDH. We obtain the contradiction and hence, complete the proof. $\qquad\square$

## 5   A Secure Certificateless Signature Scheme

In this section, we provide a modification to the certificateless signature scheme proposed in [1]. Unlike the scheme in [1], our scheme is secure against type I and II adversaries. Firstly, we provide an intuition why the proposed scheme in [1] fails against type I adversary.

In the scheme in [1], the receiver of the message verifies the validity of user's public key by testing whether the equation

$$\hat{e}(X_i, P_0) \stackrel{?}{=} \hat{e}(Y_i, P)$$

holds with equality. However, this is *not sufficient* to deter against type I adversary. This equality only ensures that $Y_i = sX_i$ holds. The test should also cover a mechanism to make sure that the secret value $x_i$, chosen by the user, has been used correctly to obtain $S_i = x_i D_i$, for $X_i = x_i P$ and $Y_i = x_i P_0$. This important aspect is neglected in the design of the certificateless signature scheme in [1]. There is no way to check whether $x_i$ in $X_i$ and $Y_i$ is identical to that of $x_i$ in $S_i$. In this section, we show how to fix this problem.

## 5.1   A Secure Scheme

Without losing generality, we only describe the Sign and Verify algorithms as the other algorithms are the same as the one defined in [1].

Sign: To sign a message $M \in \mathcal{M}$ using the private key $S_i$, perform the following steps.

1. Select a random $r \in \mathbb{Z}_q^*$.
2. Compute $R = \hat{e}(rP, P)$.
3. Compute $v = H_2(M, R, \hat{e}(S_i, P))$.
4. Compute $U = vS_i + rP$.
5. Output the signature on a message $M$ as $(U, v)$.

Verify: To verify a signature $(U, v)$ on a message $M \in \mathcal{M}$ for a public key $(X_i, Y_i)$, perform the following steps.

1. Test whether
$$\hat{e}(X_i, P_0) \stackrel{?}{=} \hat{e}(Y_i, P)$$
   holds with equality. If not, then output $\perp$ and abort.
2. Compute $R = \hat{e}(U, P)\hat{e}(Q_i, -Y_i)^v$.
3. Test whether
$$v \stackrel{?}{=} H_2(M, R, \hat{e}(Q_i, Y_i))$$
   holds with equality. If that so, then output `true`. Otherwise, output $\perp$.

*Remarks:* Intuitively, the scheme is secure against the attack model presented earlier. This is due to the following arguments. In the signature scheme, the value $v$ is the output of the hash on input $(M, R, e(S_i, P))$ which is determined by the message $M$, a random choice $R$ and $S_i = x_i s Q_i$. In this scheme, the attacker $\mathcal{A}_I$ cannot use $v$ to change the public key of the signer because $S_i$ is determined by the signer's public key. The formal proof is presented as follows.

**Theorem 3.** *Our scheme is unforgeable against type I adversary in the random oracle model under the CDH assumption in $\mathbb{G}_1$.*

*Proof (sketch).* Let $\mathcal{B}$ be a CDH attacker. Suppose that $\mathcal{B}$ is given an instance $(q, P, aP, bP)$. Let $\mathcal{A}$ be a forger that breaks the proposed signature scheme under chosen message attack. We show how $\mathcal{B}$ can use $\mathcal{A}$ to solve the CDH problem, i.e. to compute $abP$.

First, $\mathcal{B}$ sets $P_0 = aP$ where $P_0$ denotes the $KGC$'s public key and gives $(q, P, P_0)$ to $\mathcal{A}$. $\mathcal{B}$ then simulates the random oracle $H_1$ as follows. Let $q_{H_1}$ be the maximum number of queries to the random oracle $H_1$. $\mathcal{B}$ picks $j \in [1, q_{H_1}]$ uniformly at random. Then, whenever $\mathcal{A}$ issues a query denoted $\mathsf{ID}_i$ to $H_1$ where $1 \le i \le q_{H_1}$, $\mathcal{B}$ does the following: If $i \ne j$, pick $l_i \in \mathbb{Z}_q^*$, compute $l_i P$ and return $H(\mathsf{ID}_i) = l_i P$ as answer. Else (if $i = j$) return $H(\mathsf{ID}_j) = bP$ as answer.

From now on, we let $\mathsf{ID}_j = \mathsf{ID}^*$ where $\mathsf{ID}_j$ is the $j$-th query to the random oracle $H_1$ and $j$ is chosen at the beginning of the above simulation of $H_1$.

Now, let $q_{ex}$ be the maximum number of partial private key extraction queries. Whenever $\mathcal{A}$ issues such a query each of which is denoted $\mathsf{ID}_i$, where $1 \le i \le q_{ex}$,

$\mathcal{B}$ does the following: If $\mathsf{ID}_i \neq \mathsf{ID}^*$, find $l_i \in \mathbb{Z}_q^*$ that used to compute $H(\mathsf{ID}_i) = l_i P$ or pick $l_i \in \mathbb{Z}_q^*$ at random (this is the case when $\mathsf{ID}_i$ has not been asked to $H_1$), compute $l_i a P$ and return $D_i = l_i P_0$ as answer. Else (if $i = j$) abort and stop the simulation.

From the above simulation of partial private key extraction and the random oracle $H_1$, it can be easily seen that the distribution of the simulated private keys are identical to those in the real attack except for the partial private key associated with $\mathsf{ID}^*$ as $D_j = l_j P_0 = l_j a P = a l_j P = a H(\mathsf{ID}_j)$.

The random oracle $H_2$ can naturally be simulated. Namely, whenever $\mathcal{A}$ issues a query $(M_i, R_i, \hat{e}(S_i, P))$ to $H_2$, $\mathcal{B}$ does the following: Pick $v_i \in \mathbb{Z}_q^*$ at random and return it as answer.

Note that at any time during the simulation, $\mathcal{A}$ can generate a private/public key pair and replace the user's public key with its own. We assume that $\mathcal{B}$ *keeps track* of all such private/public key pairs.

Equipped with those private keys and the partial private keys for any $\mathsf{ID}_i \neq \mathsf{ID}^*$, $\mathcal{A}$ is able to create signatures on any message. Hence, assume that $\mathcal{A}$ issues a query $(M_i, (X_i, Y_i))$, where $M_i$ denotes a message and $(X_i, Y_i)$ denotes a public key chosen by $\mathcal{A}$, to the signing oracle whose secret key is associated with $\mathsf{ID}^*$. Upon receiving this, $\mathcal{B}$ creates a signature as follows:

1. Pick $U_i \in \mathbb{G}_1$ and $v_i \in \mathbb{Z}_q^*$ at random.
2. Compute $R_i = \hat{e}(U_i, P)\hat{e}(H_1(\mathsf{ID}^*), -Y_i)^{v_i}$. (Note that $H_1(\mathsf{ID}^*) = bP$).
3. Set $v_i = H_2(M_i, R_i, \hat{e}(H_1(\mathsf{ID}^*), Y_i))$.
4. Return $(U_i, v_i)$ as a signature on $M_i$.

Notice that the above simulated signature is identically distributed as the one in the real attack.

The next step of the simulation is to apply the 'forking' technique formalized in [11]: Let $(M, (U, v), \mathsf{ID}^*, (X, Y))$ be a forgery that output by $\mathcal{A}$ at the end of the attack. Note here that if $\mathcal{A}$ does not output $\mathsf{ID}^*$ as a part of the forgery, $\mathcal{B}$ just aborts the simulation. (The probability that $\mathcal{B}$ does not abort the simulation is $O(1/q_{H_1})$). $\mathcal{B}$ then replays $\mathcal{A}$ with the same random tape but different choice of the hash function $H_2$ to get another forgery $(M, (U', v'), \mathsf{ID}^*, (X, Y))$. From these two forgeries, $\mathcal{B}$ obtains

$$R = \hat{e}(U, P)\hat{e}(H_1(\mathsf{ID}^*), -Y)^v$$

and

$$R = \hat{e}(U', P)\hat{e}(H_1(\mathsf{ID}^*), -Y)^{v'}.$$

Since $(U, v)$ and $(U', v')$ are valid signatures on $M$, $\mathcal{B}$ consequently obtains the following:

$$\hat{e}(U, P)\hat{e}(H_1(\mathsf{ID}^*), -Y)^v = e(U', P)\hat{e}(H_1(\mathsf{ID}^*), -Y)^{v'}$$
$$\hat{e}(U, P)\hat{e}(bP, -xaP)^v = e(U', P)\hat{e}(bP, -xaP)^{v'}$$
$$\hat{e}(U - U', P) = \hat{e}(bP, -xaP)^{v'-v}$$
$$\hat{e}(U - U', P) = \hat{e}((v - v')xP, abP)$$
$$\hat{e}(U - U', P) = \hat{e}((v - v')xabP, P)$$

From this equation, $\mathcal{B}$ has the following

$$U - U' = (v - v')xabP$$
$$(v - v')^{-1}(U - U') = xabP$$

Recall that $\mathcal{B}$ is assumed to keep track of private/public key pairs of $\mathcal{A}$. Hence, the Diffie-Hellman key $abP$ can be obtained by computing $(v - v')^{-1}x^{-1}(U - U') = abP$. Therefore, we complete the proof. $\square$

It is easy to see that our scheme is unforgeable against type II adversary under the same assumption. The proof is very similar to the proof of theorem 2 and hence, it is omitted.

## 6  Conclusion

In this paper, we reviewed the security of the certificateless signature scheme proposed in [1]. The authors of [1] did not provide a security proof for this scheme. We showed that the scheme does not resist against type I adversary as defined in the adversarial model in [1]. However, we also show that the scheme is unforgeable against type II adversary. We modified the scheme in [1] and proposed a new scheme that resists against both types of adversaries.

## Acknowledgement

The authors would like to express their gratitude thanks to Dr. Joonsang Baek for his fruitful discussion and suggestion on the security proof for our paper. We would also like to thank the anonymous referees of International Conference on Cryptology and Network Security (CANS05) for the suggestions to improve this paper.

## References

1. S. S. Al-Riyami and K. G. Paterson. Certificateless Public Key Cryptography. *Advances in Cryptography - Asiacrypt 2003, Lecture Notes in Computer Science 2894*, pages 452–473, Springer-Verlag, Berlin, 2003.
2. S. S. Al-Riyami and K. G. Paterson. Certificateless Public Key Cryptography. Cryptology ePrint Archive. Available online: Http:// eprint.iacr.org/2003/126.
3. S. S. Al-Riyami and K. G. Paterson. CBE from CLPKE: A Generic Construction and Efficient Schemes. *Public Key Cryptography, PKC 2005, Lecture Notes in Computer Science 3386*, pages 398–415, Springer-Verlag, Berlin, 2005.
4. J. Baek, R. Safavi-Naini and W. Susilo. Certificateless Public Key Encryption without Pairing. *8th Information Security Conference, ISC 2005, Lecture Notes in Computer Science*, Springer-Verlag, Berlin, 2005.
5. Z. Cheng and R. Comley. Efficient Certificateless Public Key Encryption. Cryptology ePrint Archive. Available online: http://eprint.iacr.org/2005/012.

6. M. Bellare and P. Rogaway. Random Oracles are Practical: A Paradigm for Designing Efficient Protocols. *ACM CCCS '93*, pp. 62–73, 1993.

7. M. Girault. Self Certified Public Keys. *Advanced in Cryptology - Eurocrypt 1991, Lecture Notes in Computer Science 547*, pp. 490–497, Springer-Verlag, 1992.

8. S. Goldwasser, S. Micali, and R. Rivest. A Secure Digital Signature Scheme. *SIAM Journal on Computing 17*, pages 281 – 308, 1988.

9. E. Okamoto. Key distribution systems based on identification information. *Advances in Cryptology - Crypto 1987, Lecture Notes in Computer Science 293*, pp. 194 – 202, Springer-Verlag, Berlin, 1987.

10. H. Petersen and P. Horster. Self-Certified Keys – Concepts and Applications. *International Conference on Communications and Multimedia Security*, Chapman and Hall, 1997.

11. D. Pointcheval and J. Stern. Security Proofs for Signature Schemes. *Advanced in Cryptology - Eurocrypt 1996, Lecture Notes in Computer Science 1070*, pages 387 – 398, Springer-Verlag, Berlin, 1996.

12. S. Saeednia. Identity-Based and Self-Certified Key-Exchange Protocols. *Information Security and Privacy, ACISP 1997, Lecture Notes in Computer Science 1270*, pp. 303–313, Springer-Verlag, 1997.

13. A. Shamir. Identity-based cryptosystems and signature schemes. *Advances in Cryptology - Crypto '84, Lecture Notes in Computer Science 196*, pages 47–53, Springer-Verlag, Berlin, 1985.

14. D. H. Yum and P. J. Lee. Generic Construction of Certificateless Signature. *Information Security and Privacy, ACISP 2004, Lecture Notes in Computer Science 3108*, pages 200 – 211, Springer-Verlag, Berlin, 2004.

15. D. H. Yum and P. J. Lee. Generic Construction of Certificateless Encryption. *ICCSA 2004, Lecture Notes in Computer Science 3043*, pp. 802–811, Springer-Verlag, Berlin, 2004.

# On the Security of a Group Signcryption Scheme from Distributed Signcryption Scheme

Haiyong Bao, Zhenfu Cao, and Haifeng Qian

Department of Computer Science and Engineering,
Shanghai Jiao Tong University,
1954 Huashan Road, Shanghai 200030, PRC
{bhy, zfcao, ares}@sjtu.edu.cn
http://tdt.sjtu.edu.cn

**Abstract.** Signcryption denotes a cryptographic method, which can process encryption and digital signature simultaneously. So, adopting such schemes, computational cost of encryption and signature compared to traditional signature-then-encryption can be reduced to a great extent. Based on the existing distributed signcryption schemes, Kwak and Moon proposed a new distributed signcryption scheme with sender ID confidentiality and extended it to a group signcryption. Their scheme is more efficient in both communication and computation aspects. Unfortunately we will demonstrate that their scheme is insecure by identifying some security flaws. Exploring these flaws, an attacker without any secret can mount universal forging attacks. That is, anyone (not necessary the group member) can forge valid group signatures on arbitrary messages of his/her choice.

## 1 Introduction

In [1], Y. Zheng proposed an asymmetric cryptographic method called signcryption, which can simultaneously provide message confidentiality and unforgeability with a little computational and communicational overhead. After that, several signcryption schemes [2], [3], [4] have been put forward. Then, Mu et al. proposed the distributed signcryption scheme [5]. In such scheme, any party can *"signcrypt"* a message and distribute it to a designed group, and any member in the receiving group can *"unsigncrypt"* the message. However, in most practical circumstances, in order to protect the user's privacy, persons who signcrypt the messages should be anonymous, i.e. requiring sender ID confidentiality. The basic scheme [5] cannot fulfill such properties. In order to make up these flaws, Kwak and Moon generalized the original scheme [5] and presented a new distributed signcryption scheme and extended to group signcryption [6]. They also presented a security analysis of their scheme and claimed that their scheme satisfied all the security requirements of distributed signcryption with sender ID confidentiality and group signcryption. However, this is not the fact.

In this paper, some serious security flaws of Kwak et al.'s scheme are successfully identified. By using our attack methods, anyone (not necessary the group

Y.G. Desmedt et al. (Eds.): CANS 2005, LNCS 3810, pp. 26–34, 2005.

member) can forge valid group signatures on any messages such that the forged messages cannot be opened by the group manager.

The rest of this paper is organized as follows. Section 2 first illustrates some preliminaries of Kwak et al.'s scheme. Section 3 presents the existing distributed signcryption and its extension, which is the basic scheme of Kwak et al.'s scheme. We then review and analyze Kwak et al.'s scheme in section 4 and 5, respectively. Finally, some conclusions and remarks are given in section 6.

## 2    Preliminaries

This section briefly introduces some basic concepts of Kwak et al.'s scheme. We put our emphasis on how to initialize of a group. In Kwak et al.'s scheme, some members of one group can send signcrypted messages to a designated group. Then, any valid member in the designated group can unsigncrypt the message using his/her private key.

**Initialization of a group**
Assume p denotes a large prime number, $Z_p^*$ a multiplicative group of order q for $q|p-1$ and $g \in Z_p^*$ a primitive element. $Hash(\cdot)$ denotes a strong one-way function, $Hash_k(\cdot)$ a keyed one-way hash function with key $k$, and $E_k(D_k)$ a symmetric encryption (decryption).

In order to construct a group including $n$ members, the manager selects a set of integers, $\varepsilon_i \in_R Z_q$, for $i = 1, 2, \cdots, n$, and computes the coefficients $\alpha_0, \cdots, \alpha_n \in Z_q$ of the following polynomial:

$$f(x) = \prod_{i=1}^{n} (x - \varepsilon_i) = \sum_{i=0}^{n} \alpha_i x^i. \tag{1}$$

Define $g \in Z_p^*$ and $g_i = g^{\alpha_i} \mod p$, for $i = 0, 1, \cdots, n$, which procedures

$$F(\varepsilon_l) = \prod_{i=0}^{n} g_i^{\varepsilon_l^i} = 1 \mod p, \tag{2}$$

where $\varepsilon_l$ is an element of the set $\{\varepsilon_i\}$.

This is because $F(\varepsilon_l) = g^{f(\varepsilon_l)}$ and $f(\varepsilon_l) = 0$ in $Z_q$.

In [6], the authors specify incorrectly as $F(\varepsilon_l) = \sum_{i=0}^{n} g_i^{\varepsilon_l^i} = 1 \mod p$. We correct their errors in our description.

For the given $\{\alpha_0, \alpha_1, \cdots, \alpha_n\}$, a new set is defined as $\{\alpha_0', \alpha_1', \cdots, \alpha_n'\}$, where $\alpha_0' = \alpha_0$, $\alpha_n' = \alpha_n$, $\alpha_1' = \cdots = \alpha_{n-1}' = \sum_{i=1}^{n-1} \alpha_i$. Define $\beta_i = g^{\alpha_i}$ and $A_l = \sum_{i=1, j=1, i \neq j}^{n-1} \alpha_j \varepsilon_l^i$, then equation (2) can be rewritten as

$$F'(\varepsilon_l) = g^{-A_l} \prod_{i=0}^{n} \beta_i^{\varepsilon_l^i} = g^{-A_l} g^{\sum_{i=0}^{n} \alpha_i' \varepsilon_l^i} = 1 \mod p. \tag{3}$$

The group manager picks a random number $\gamma \in_R Z_q$, then computes its inverse $\gamma^{-1}$ and $\rho_l = -\gamma A_l \bmod q$ for member $l$. The group public key is defined as a $n+2$ tuple, $\{\beta_0, \cdots, \beta_{n+1}\} = \{\beta_0, \cdots, \beta_n, g^{\gamma^{-1}}\}$. The manager keeps $\gamma$ and all $\{\alpha_i\}$ secret and gives $\varepsilon_l$ and $\rho_l$ to a group member $l$ who then uses $\varepsilon_l$ and $\rho_l$ as his/her *group private key pair*.

## 3   Existing Distributed Signcryption

This section reviews the existing distributed signcryption [5], which is the original scheme that Kwak et al. aimed to improve.

Assume Alice is the sender who signcrypts a message $m$ and sends the message to a designated group. Bob is a member of the designated group and he unsigncrypts the message. $(x_a, y_a = g^{x_a})$ is the private key and public key of Alice.

**The signcryption.** Alice does the following and sends to Bob the signcrypted message $(c_1, c_2, r, s)$.

Choose $z \in_R Z_q$ and compute $k = g^z \bmod p$
Split $k$ into $k_1$ and $k_2$
Compute $r = hash_{k_2}(m)$
Compute $s = z(kr + x_a)^{-1} \bmod q$
Compute $w = hash(m)$
The encrypted message is as follows:

$$c_1 = \{a_0, \cdots, a_n, a_{n+1}\} = \{g^{kr}\beta_0^w, \beta_1^w, \cdots, \beta_{n+1}^w\}$$

$$c_2 = E_{k_1}(m)$$

**The unsigncryption.** Bob who is one of the designated group members and has group private key pair $(\varepsilon_b, \rho_b)$ can unsigncrypt the signcrypted message by discovering the secret session key $k$ as follows:

$$k = (y_a a_0 (\prod_{i=1}^{n} a_i^{\varepsilon_b^i}) a_{n+1}^{\rho_b})^s = (y_a g^{rk} \prod_{i=0}^{n} g^{w\alpha_i^{\varepsilon_b^i}})^s = (y_a g^{rk} g^{wf(\varepsilon_b)})^s = g^z \bmod p.$$

Then Bob splits $k$ into $k_1$ and $k_2$ as agreed earlier and verifies $m? = D_{k_1}(c_2)$.

Kwak et al. also extended the above scheme to a group signcryption, which is relatively irrelevant to our discussion. So we omit these procedures. But, by the way, we should point out here that in their signcrypt procedures Alice needs to compute $s_j = w(\varepsilon_a^j - ru_j) \bmod q$ not $s_j = z(\varepsilon_a^j - ru_j) \bmod q$, for $j = 1, \cdots, n$. Because otherwise the verification accomplished by Bob cannot process successfully.

## 4   Review of Kwak et al.'s Scheme

In this section, we review Kwak et al.'s distributed singcryption scheme with sender ID confidentiality and their extended distributed group signcryption scheme.

## 4.1 Distributed Signcryption with Sender ID Confidentiality

**The Signcryption.** Alice does the following and sends to Bob who belong to a designated group the message $(c_1, c_2)$. Where $Cert_a$ is Alice's certificate including her public key, and $x||y$ denotes the concatenation of x and y.

Choose $z \in_R Z_q$ and compute $k = g^z \bmod p$

Split $k$ into $k_1$ and $k_2$

Compute $r = hash_{k_2}(m)$

Compute $s = z(r + x_a)^{-1} \bmod q$

Compute $w = hash(m)$

The encrypted message is as follows:

$$c_1 = \{a_0, \cdots, a_n, a_{n+1}\} = \{k\beta_0^w, \beta_1^w, \cdots, \beta_{n+1}^w\}$$

$$c_2 = E_{k_1}(m||r||s||Cert_a)$$

**The unsigncryption.** Bob or anyone of the designated group can unsigncrypt the signcrypted message using his $(\varepsilon_b, \rho_b)$ based on discovering the secret session key k as follows:

$$k = a_0 \left(\prod_{i=1}^{n} a_i^{\varepsilon_b^i}\right) a_{n+1}^{\rho_b} = g^z \prod_{i=0}^{n} g^{w\alpha_i \varepsilon_b^i} = g^z g^{wf(\varepsilon_b)} = g^z \bmod p$$

Split $k$ into $k_1$ and $k_2$

Decrypt $D_{k_1}(c_2) = m||r||s||Cert_a$

Verify

$$r? = hash_{k_2}(m)$$

$$g^z? = (y_a g^r)^s.$$

## 4.2 Extension to Group Singcryption

There are five procedures involved in group signcryption: setup, join, signcryption, unsigncryption, and tracing or open, enabling a member of one group to signcrypt a message on behalf of the group and send it to another member in another group with anonymity.

**Setup.** To derive the information related to a group, the group manager computes the following values:

- p, q, and g are the same as the above and $h \in Z_p^*$ is newly generated.
- Group manager's RSA signature key denotes $d_A$, verification key $e_A$, and $n_A$ a large RSA modulus with two random prime factors of approximately equal length. It satisfies $e_A d_A \equiv 1 \bmod \varphi(n_A)$, where $\varphi(n_A)$ is Euler phi function.

The manager keeps $d_A$ as his secret signature key and opens $(p, q, g, h, n_A, e_A)$ as the system parameters.

**Join.** Each entity who wants to join the group generates his own group private key $\varepsilon_l$ and computes $\tau_l (= h^{\varepsilon_l} \bmod p)$ as *group membership key*. Then he transfers

$\tau_l$ to the group manager through secure channel and proves to the manager that he knows the discrete logarithm of $\tau$ to the base $h$. $\varepsilon_l$ should be kept secret by the entity.

Each group manager generates $v_l(= \tau_l^{d_A} \bmod n_A)$ as membership certificate. In order to setup a group, the manager computes the coefficients of the following polynomial:

$$f(x) = \prod_{i=1}^{n} (x - \tau_i) = \sum_{i=0}^{n} \alpha_i x^i. \tag{4}$$

Define $A_l = \sum_{i=1, j=1, i \neq j}^{n-1} \alpha_j \tau_l^i$, then Equation (4) has the following property:

$$F'(\tau_l) = g^{-A_l} \prod_{i=0}^{n} \beta_i^{\tau_l^i} = g^{-A_l} g^{\sum_{i=0}^{n} \alpha_i' \tau_l^i} = g^{f(\tau_l)} = 1 \bmod p. \tag{5}$$

**Signcryption.** After the above group construction, consider two designated groups, $G_A$ and $G_B$, and assume that Alice belongs to $G_A$ and Bob is one of recipients belonging to $G_B$. In order to signcrypt the message $m$, Alice needs to do the following using his $\varepsilon_a, \tau_a$ and $v_a$:

Choose $z$ and $t \in_R Z_q$ and compute $k = g^z \bmod p$
Split $k$ into $k_1$ and $k_2$
Compute $r = hash_{k_2}(m)$
Compute $s = z(r + \varepsilon_a t)^{-1} \bmod q$
Compute $w = hash(m)$
Compute $\lambda_a = (t^{e_A} \tau_a \bmod n_A) \bmod q$, $\delta_a = g^{\varepsilon_a t}$ and $\theta_a = t \cdot v_a \bmod n_A$
The encrypted message is as follows:

$$c_1 = \{a_0, \cdots, a_{n+2}\} = \{k\beta_0^{w\tau_a}, \beta_1^{w\tau_a}, \cdots, \beta_{n+1}^{w\tau_a}, g^{\lambda_a}\}$$

$$c_2 = E_{k_1}(ID_{G_A} || m || r || s || \delta_a || \theta_a)$$

Where, $ID_{G_A}$ is the identity of group $G_A$. The rest notations are the same as those in the previous section.

**Unsigncryption.** Bob or any member of $G_B$ can unsigncrypt the signcrypted message using his $(\tau_b, \rho_b)$ based on discovering the secret session key $k$ as follows:

$$k = a_0 (\prod_{i=1}^{n} a_i^{\tau_b^i}) a_{n+1}^{\rho_b} = g^z \prod_{i=0}^{n} g^{w\alpha_i \tau_b^i} = g^z g^{wf(\tau_b)} = g^z \bmod p$$

Split $k$ into $k_1$ and $k_2$
Decrypt $D_{k_1}(c_2) = ID_{G_A} || m || r || s || \delta_a || \theta_a$
Compute $\lambda_a' = (\theta_a^{e_A} \bmod n_A) \bmod q$
Verify

$$r? = hash_{k_2}(m)$$
$$g^z? = (\delta_a \cdot g^r)^s$$
$$a_{n+2}? = g^{\lambda_a'}.$$

**Tracing or Open.** In case of disputes, Bob forwards $c_1$ and $w$ $(= hash(m))$ to group $G'_A s$ manager after decrypting $c_2$ and knowing group $G'_A s$ identity. Then, only the manager can find the group member, Alice, who issued this signcryption by testing $\{a_i? = (\beta_i^w)^{\tau_l}\}_{i=1}^{n+1}$ for all his group members' $\tau_l$ in $G_A$.

## 5   Security of Kwak et al.'s Scheme

Kwak et al. claimed that their scheme satisfied all the security requirements of distributed signcryption with sender ID confidentiality and group singcryption. However, this is not the fact.

### 5.1   Distributed Signcryption with Sender ID No Confidentiality

The authors contain $r, s$ and $Cert_a$ in $c_2$ encryption, where $Cert_a$ is sender Alice's certificate including her public key. So any group member having valid group private key pair $(\varepsilon_i, \rho_i)$ after unsigncryption can use symmetric key $k_1$ to obtain the sender's identity. In other words, their improved scheme cannot guarantee the requirement of sender ID confidentiality. The author pointed out that the sender's ID is included in the encrypted message $c_2$, so the adversary cannot discover any information without decrypting the ciphertext. However, this is of no practical value.

Because in various security protocols such as e-cashes, e-votings, e-biddings and so on, the anonymity of the candidates should be kept confidentiality to everyone except the group manager.

Even though it can be accepted to some extent, we will still point out that their scheme has no improvements comparing with the original distributed encryption scheme.

In the original scheme, the verifier cannot unsigncrypt the signcrypted messages without the singer's public key $y_a$ as follows:

$$k? = (y_a a_0 (\prod_{i=1}^{n} a_i^{\varepsilon_b^i}) a_{n+1}^{\rho_b})^s.$$

In their improved scheme, the verifier also needs the signer's public key $y_a$ to check the validity of unsigncryption as follows:

$$k? = (y_a g^r)^s.$$

Thus, the sender's ID is of no anonymity or the newly proposed scheme is of no advantages comparing with the original scheme.

### 5.2   Security Analysis of Kwak et al.'s Group Signcryption

**Forging Signatures.** The authors pointed out that due to discrete logarithm problems, the signer's private key $\varepsilon_a$ cannot be revealed to anyone, so only valid group members are able to signcrypt the message on behalf of the group.

However, we notice that this does not imply that an attacker cannot adopt other ways to generate valid signatures. We will present a method to forge a valid group signature on any given message under the assumption that we do not know any valid membership certificate $(\varepsilon_i, \tau_i, v_i)$.

Assume an attacker Malice wants to signcrypt the message to Bob who is one of recipients belonging to $G_B$.

The concrete forging attacks are as follows:

**Forged Signcryption**

Choose $t, t_1$ and $z \in_R Z_q$ and compute $k = g^z \bmod p$

Split $k$ into $k_1$ and $k_2$

Compute $r = hash_{k_2}(m)$

Compute $s = z(r + t_1)^{-1} \bmod q$

Compute $w = hash(m)$

Choose $u \in_R Z_{n_A}^*$, compute $\theta_a = u \bmod n_A$

Compute $\lambda_a = (\theta_a^{e_A} \bmod n_A) \bmod q = (u^{e_A} \bmod n_A) \bmod q$, $\delta_a = g^{t_1}$

Select $t_2 \in_R Z_q^*$

The encrypted message is as follows:

$$c_1 = \{a_0, \cdots, a_{n+2}\} = \{k\beta_0^{wt_2}, \beta_1^{wt_2}, \cdots, \beta_{n+1}^{wt_2}, g^{\lambda_a}\}$$

$$c_2 = E_{k_1}(ID_G||m||r||s||\delta_a||\theta_a)$$

Where, $ID_G$ is an arbitrary string.

**Unsigncryption**

Bob or any member of $G_B$ can unsigncrypt the signcrypted message using his $(\tau_b, \rho_b)$ as follows:

$$k = a_0 \left(\prod_{i=1}^{n} a_i^{\tau_b^i}\right) a_{n+1}^{\rho_b} = g^z \prod_{i=0}^{n} g^{wt_2\alpha_i\tau_b^i} = g^z g^{wt_2 f(\tau_b)} = g^z \bmod p$$

Split $k$ into $k_1$ and $k_2$

Decrypt $D_{k_1}(c_2) = ID_G||m||r||s||\delta_a||\theta_a$

Compute $\lambda_a' = (\theta_a^{e_A} \bmod n_A) \bmod q = (u^{e_A} \bmod n_A) \bmod q$

Verify

$$r = hash_{k_2}(m)$$

$$g^z = (\delta_a \cdot g^r)^s$$

$$a_{n+2} = g^{\lambda_a'}.$$

According to the above discussion, the attacker Malice successfully forges signcrypted messages. The security weakness comes from the fact that the verification equation does not check the validity of the membership certificate $(\varepsilon_a, \tau_a, v_a)$.

**No Traceability.** In the above forking signatures, the attacker uses a random number $t_2$ to generate the signature. Thus no one can identify the actual signer by testing $\{a_i = (\beta_i^w)^{\tau_l}\}_{i=1}^{n+1}$ for all group members even if in all groups $G's$, because $a_i = (\beta_i^w)^{t_2}$, for $i = 1, \cdots, n+1$, where $t_2 \in_R Z_q^*$. Furthermore, due to the above design faults, other security properties of group signature [7], [8], [9], [10] such as exculpability, coalition-resistance cannot be satisfied.

Besides, in Kwak et al.'s group signcryption scheme, when initially constructing a group, the group manager should compute and create group private key pair $\{(\varepsilon_i, \rho_i)\}_{i=1}^n$ for all the members first. Then the largest number of group members in such scheme is at most $n$. Thus such scheme cannot allow group members to join or to leave the group dynamically.

## 6   Conclusions

In this paper, we present the security analysis of Kwak et al.'s improved distributed signcryption scheme with sender ID confidentiality and group signcryption scheme. By successfully identifying several attacks, we demonstrate that their scheme is insecure. More specifically, our results show that their distributed signcryption cannot keep the sender's ID confidentiality, so it is of no advantages over the original scheme. Besides, the group signcryption scheme they proposed is forgeable, untraceable, no coalition-resistant and so on. Thus, how to design a secure and more efficient group signcryption scheme in which group members can join and leave the group dynamically based on the existing distributed signcryption scheme is still a hot problem.

## Acknowledgments

The authors would like to thank anonymous referees and reviewers for their suggestions to improve this paper. Besides, this article is supported by the National Natural Science Fund for Distinguished Young Scholars under Grant No. 60225007, the National Research Fund for the Doctoral Program of Higher Education of China under Grant No. 20020248024 and the Science and Technology Research Project of Shanghai under Grant Nos. 04JC14055 and 046407067.

## References

1. Zheng, Y.: Digital signcryption or how to achieve cost(signature & encryption) ≪ cost(signature) + cost(encryption). In: *Advanced in Cryptology– CRYPTO '97 Proceedings*, LNCS, Vol. 1294. Springer-Verlag (1997) 165–179
2. Bao, F., Deng, R. H.: A signcryption scheme with signature directly verifiable by public key. In: *Public Key Cryptography – PKC '98*, LNCS, Vol. 1431. Springer-Verlag (1998) 55–59
3. Kwak, D., Ha, J., Lee, H., Kim, H., Moon, S.: A WTLS handshake protocol with user anonymity and forward secrecy. In: *CDMA International Conference– CIC '2002*, LNCS, Vol. 2524. Springer-Verlag (2002) 219–230

4. Lee, K., Moon, S.: AKA protocol for mobile communications. In: *Australasian Conference Informations Security and Privacy – ACISP '2000*, LNCS, Vol. 1841. Springer-Verlag (2000) 400–411
5. Mu, Y., Varadharajan, V.: Distributed signcryption. In: *Advanced in Cryptology – INDOCRYPT '2000 Proceedings*, LNCS, Vol. 1977. Springer-Verlag (2000) 155–164
6. Kwak, D., Moon, S.: Efficient Distributed Signcryption Scheme as Group Signcryption. In: *Applied Cryptography and Network Security (ACNS'03)*, LNCS, Vol. 2846. Springer-Verlag (2003) 403-417
7. Ateniese, G., Camenisch, J., Joye, M., Tsudik, G.: A practical and provably secure coalition-resistant group signature scheme. In: *Advanced in Cryptology– CRYPTO '2000*, LNCS, Vol. 1880. Springer-Verlag (2000) 255–270
8. Bresson, E., Stern, J.: Efficient revocation in group signatures. In: *Public Key Cryptography – PKC '2001*, LNCS, Vol. 1992. Springer-Verlag (2001) 190–206
9. Camenisch, J., Stadler, M.: Efficient group signature schemes for large groups. In: *Advances in Cryptography – CRYPTO '97*, LNCS, Vol. 1294. Springer-Verlag (1997) 410–424
10. Lyuu, Y., Wu, M.: Convertible Group Undeniable Signatures. In: *International Conference on Information Security and Cryptology – ICISC '2002*, LNCS, Vol. 2587. Springer-Verlag (2002) 48–61

# Cryptanalysis of Two Group Key Management Protocols for Secure Multicast

Wen Tao Zhu

State Key Laboratory of Information Security,
Graduate University of Chinese Academy of Sciences,
P.O. Box 4588, Beijing 100049, P.R. China
wtzhu@gucas.ac.cn

**Abstract.** Many emerging network applications are based upon group communication models and are implemented as either one-to-many or many-to-many multicast. As a result, providing multicast confidentiality is a critical networking issue and multicast security has become an active research area. To secure the sessions, a common group key is maintained to encrypt the traffic, and the key is updated whenever a new member joins the group or an existing member leaves. In this paper we analyze the security of a centralized key distribution protocol for one-to-many multicast and a decentralized key agreement protocol for many-to-many multicast. We show that they both fail to provide forward and backward security. The first protocol is revealed to be vulnerable to a single adversary due to an algorithmic issue. The second protocol, however, is subject to sophisticated collusion. Remedial approaches are proposed for both key management schemes to effectively resist relevant attacks.

## 1   Introduction

In the Internet, multicast has been used successfully to provide an efficient, best-effort delivery service to large user groups that are dynamic in nature. As a result, multicast confidentiality has become a critical networking issue, since the original Internet protocols paid little attention to security concerns [1]. Specifically, the Internet Group Management Protocol (IGMP) has been designed to provide an open group model and it does not provide an access control mechanism; anyone can join the group and thus obtain a copy of every multicast packet by simply sending membership reports to its neighboring router. It would be very easy to launch a theft of service when the multicast data is transmitted in plaintext.

The standard approach to control access to group communication is to use symmetric cryptography (for minimal computation) with a common shared group key, known as the session encryption key (SEK), to securely distribute data to all intended members. In this paper, we define secure multicast as a private session with such symmetric key encryption of group-oriented data content. Whenever there is a membership change, the SEK needs to be updated to assure backward security that a joining user cannot access previous group communication, and forward security that a leaving user cannot access data multicast after its departure unless

Y.G. Desmedt et al. (Eds.): CANS 2005, LNCS 3810, pp. 35–48, 2005.

it is added back. Ensuring only the valid members of the group hold the SEK at any instant is the secure multicast key management problem [2].

Secure multicast in the Internet has many applications such as subscription CD/TV broadcasting, stock quote updates, remote education, and distributed interactive simulation. Some of them have a single sender distributing secret data to a large number of subscribers while the others have multiple (usually all) registered users communicating privately with each other. In the first case, to protect SSM (Source-Specific Multicast) [3] confidentiality, a centralized key server known as the Group Controller (GC) is preferred to manage the SEK [1, 4–12]. In the second case, to support many-to-many secure multicast among dynamic peers, distributed group key agreement is desirable [13–17]. In this paper, the terms SSM and one-to-may multicast are used interchangeably, so do ASM (Any-Source Multicast) and many-to-many multicast.

The balance of this paper is organized as follows. Section 2 presents an overview of the centralized group key distribution approaches for SSM. One of these schemes, called the Secure Filter [7], is presented and analyzed in Section 3. We show that it has a security breach that may fail to assure forward and backward security, and propose a remedy to invalidate potential attacks. Section 4 presents DISEC [13], an efficient distributed framework for scalable secure many-to-many communication, as a case study of distributed group key agreement protocols for ASM. Section 5 performs security analysis on DISEC. We show that it also fails to provide forward and backward security, and propose two remedial approaches. Our conclusions are in Section 6.

Throughout this paper, we denote the group size of the secure multicast session by $N$. We use the notation $K\{m\}$ to denote the encryption of plaintext message $m$ with key $K$, and the notation A→B: $K\{m\}$ to denote the secure delivery of message $m$ from A to B. For instance, the Group Controller rekeys at time $t_1$ and sends the group key to member $M_i$, encrypted with a pair-wise key $K_i$, and this is denoted as GC→$M_i$: $K_i\{SEK(t_1)\}$. This $K_i$, usually pre-assigned, is secretly shared between $M_i$ and the GC only, and thus we call it the user private key or the individual key of $M_i$. As $K_i$ is used to protect another cryptographic key (herein the group key $SEK(t_1)$), it is called a Key Encryption Key (KEK). In most cases, a KEK is only used to encrypt one key per message, which conforms to the key-oriented strategy [8]. We now address the centralized group key distribution schemes for securing one-to-many group communication.

## 2   Centralized Group Key Distribution Approaches for SSM

As most of the commercial applications that benefit from multicast communication have a single sender and multiple recipients, it is the model of interest in this section. To secure SSM traffic, a trusted authority, the GC, is introduced to be responsible for the group key distribution. The main requirement is confidentiality: only valid users should be able to decrypt the group communication even if the data is broadcast to the entire network.

Since the group is distributed over the untrustworthy network, whenever the SEK is invalidated, there needs to be another set of keys (the KEKs) to securely transmit the updated SEK to the valid group members. Quite a few approaches have been proposed in the literature. We now abstract away the implementation details from the GKMP [4] and outline the simplified protocol as follows.

In the GKMP, when a new member $M_j$ with its pair-wise key $K_j$ joins at time $t_1$, the GC changes the group key from a former $SEK(t_0)$ to a fresh $SEK(t_1)$. It multicasts $SEK(t_0)\{SEK(t_1)\}$, which can be decrypted by every member except $M_j$. The GC then unicasts $K_j\{SEK(t_1)\}$ to $M_j$. Hence the join admission requires two encryptions, one for multicast and one for unicast. When a member $M_d$ is deleted, say at $t_2$ that follows $t_1$, $SEK(t_1)$ known to $M_d$ is compromised and cannot be used to protect $SEK(t_2)$. The GC then contacts every residual member individually to distribute $SEK(t_2)$. Hence to delete a member from an $N$-user group, $(N\text{-}1)$ encrypted unicasts are required. As we comply with the key-oriented rekeying [8], the encryption overhead is always proportional to that of communication, and we mainly consider the latter henceforth.

While member addition can be handled easily in the GKMP, deletion poses challenges when $N$ increases. We also note that in the case of member addition, if we let $SEK(t_1) = f(SEK(t_0))$ where $f()$ is a public one-way function and thus it is computationally infeasible for $M_j$ to derive $SEK(t_1)$ from $SEK(t_0)$, the GC then needs only to broadcast a plaintext announcing the admission of $M_j$. On receiving the announcement, each member except $M_j$ can rekey the SEK by applying $f()$, therefore only one encryption $(GC{\rightarrow}M_j: K_j\{SEK(t_1)\})$ is required. Hence in the remainder of this section we focus on member deletion.

In [5], an impressive method of group key distribution based upon the mathematics of the Chinese Remainder Theorem was presented. In the scheme the GC constructs a rekey message called the Secure Lock from individual KEKs held by each valid group member, and then broadcasts it to the group to securely convey the SEK. We comment that the Secure Lock is essentially a combination of all the $K_i\{SEK\}$'s for each valid member $M_i$. Therefore, it is considered to be a particular variation of the GKMP. Under a member deletion, it also incurs $\mathcal{O}(N)$ communication overhead counted in the length of the bits transmitted.

In [6], another mathematical approach was proposed. It differs observably from GKMP-style rekeying as it does not encrypt the SEK with the KEKs of the valid group members. Instead, the GC composes the rekey message as

$$\alpha = SEK + \prod_{i=1}^{N-1} (2^B + f(K_i, \mu)) \tag{1}$$

where the SEK, the KEKs, and the output of a public one-way function $f()$ are of the same length of $B$ bits. Function $f()$ takes $\mu$ as one of its arguments, which is a $B$-bit seed generated randomly and broadcast in plaintext on each rekeying. Note that $f(K_N, \mu)$ is excluded in (1), as herein without loss of generality $M_N$ is the member to be deleted. As $SEK < 2^B$, on receiving broadcast messages $\alpha$ and $\mu$, each residual member $M_i$ can extract the new group key according to

$$SEK \equiv \alpha \pmod{(2^B + f(K_i, \mu))}, \text{ for all } i \in [1, N-1] \tag{2}$$

We make the observation that $\mu$ is randomly selected on each rekeying, thus $f(K_i, \mu)$ varies on each rekeying. This sheds light on the security analysis of the Secure Filter approach [7], which we will address in Section 3.

The above key distribution schemes [4, 5, 6, 7] are generally known as flat approaches as they all involve $\mathcal{O}(N)$ rekeying communication overhead under a member deletion. Therefore, they all face a serious scalability problem. This paper focuses on security issues, and flat schemes are also taken into consideration.

In [8] and [9] a scalable group key distribution scheme known as the logical key hierarchy (LKH) was independently proposed and has led to a family of variations [1, 10, 11, 12]. LKH constructs a key tree in which each member is represented by a unique leaf node and is associated with its individual key. The inner nodes are associated with auxiliary intermediate KEKs while the root node is with the group key. The set of keys associated with the nodes along the path from a leaf node to the root are assigned to the member at that leaf node, which include the user private key, the intermediate KEKs, and the SEK. Tree-based schemes reduce rekeying communication cost from $\mathcal{O}(N)$ to $\mathcal{O}(\log N)$, and they are generally studied in [2]. As later we will return to a tree-based approach in Section 4, we now analyze a flat key distribution scheme, the Secure Filter [7].

## 3    Cryptanalysis of the Secure Filter Scheme

In [7] the Secure Filter was proposed as the main building block of a solution to the secure multicast key distribution problem. Similar to (1) its rekey message is a special function $sf(x)$, with the group key to be distributed ($SEK$) and each of the valid user private keys ($K_i$) sent via a hash function $h()$ as its inputs:

$$sf(x) = SEK + \prod_{i=1}^{N-1}(x - h(K_i)) \qquad (3)$$

Note that $K_N$ is again excluded in constructing (3) as herein $M_N$ is taken as the member to be deleted. Although the authors of [7] also adopt $sf(x)$ to rekey the group when a new member joins, we prefer the GKMP-style rekeying described in Section 2 as it only occurs $\mathcal{O}(1)$ communication cost.

Officially, a Secure Filter is defined as a polynomial in the indeterminate $x$ over Galois field $\mathbf{GF}(p)$, where $p$ is a public large prime. The function is actually broadcast by transmitting ($N$-1) coefficients after a polynomial expansion:

$$sf(x) = x^{N-1} + a_{N-2}x^{N-2} + a_{N-3}x^{N-3} + \cdots + a_1 x + a_0 \qquad (4)$$

It is easy to see that on receiving the ($N$-1) coefficients $\{a_{N-2}, a_{N-3}, \cdots, a_1, a_0\}$ from the GC, each valid group member $M_i$ can acquire the $SEK$ with

$$SEK \equiv sf(h(K_i)) \pmod{p}, \text{ for all } i \in [1, N-1] \qquad (5)$$

We note that the $SEK$ should also belong to $\mathbf{Z}_p$ with respect to (5). Hence such SEKs generated by the GC may not be as evenly distributed as expected. However, this is not the real security weakness, which we present now.

Suppose a malicious user, $M_m$, is already a member at time $t_1$ and thus knows $SEK(t_1)$. As the coefficients $\{a_{N-2}, a_{N-3}, \cdots, a_1, a_0\}$ are broadcast, $M_m$ can easily compose another function by subtracting $SEK(t_1)$ from $sf_1(x)$:

$$sf_1(x) - SEK(t_1) = \prod_{i=1}^{N-1} (x - h(K_i)), \; m \in [1, N-1] \tag{6}$$

As factorization of polynomials over $\mathbf{GF}(p)$ may be achieved at only a computational cost of $\mathcal{O}(\log p)$ [18], it is possible for $M_m$ to obtain an $h(K_n)$ of another member $M_n$ who remains in the group when $M_m$ departs at time $t_2$. Although GC rekeys at $t_2$ in order to evict $M_m$ by broadcasting

$$sf_2(x) = SEK(t_2) + \prod_{\substack{i=1 \\ i \neq m}}^{N-1} (x - h(K_i)) \tag{7}$$

$M_m$ still can acquire $SEK(t_2)$ with (5) as it has got $h(K_n)$. Thus the scheme fails to provide forward security against $M_m$. On the other hand, if $M_n$ is already a group member at a time $t_0$ ($t_0 < t_1$) when GC rekeys to delete someone else, $M_m$ (who joins the group between $t_0$ and $t_1$) can acquire $SEK(t_0)$ by buffering the polynomial coefficients of $sf_0(x)$ before joining the group and playing the same trick described above after its joining. Hence the scheme also fails to provide backward security against $M_m$. The scenario is depicted in Fig. 1.

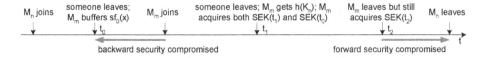

**Fig. 1.** Both forward and backward security of the Secure Filter are compromised as a single adversary $M_m$ factors polynomial (6) to obtain $h(K_n)$ and acquires the group keys distributed before its admission and after the eviction. We note that on member joining, if $sf(x)$ is used instead of the GKMP-style rekeying (described in Section 2), backward security may become compromised as early as $M_n$ joins the group.

We borrow the idea from [6] to fix the vulnerability. We propose the remedy by replacing $h(K_i)$ in (3) and (5) with $f(K_i, \mu)$ in (1), where $\mu$ is changed and broadcast on each rekeying, thus altering $f(K_i, \mu)$ under every member eviction. It is obvious that the one-way function $f()$ with a volatile argument $\mu$ effectively stalls the attacks of malicious members. The improved scheme assures both forward and backward security.

## 4    Distributed Group Key Agreement Protocols for ASM

Although it presents a single point of failure, using a centralized GC (as in section 2 and 3) is natural for one-to-many secure multicast. However, in the presence of multiple senders (especially, all members being senders), it is desirable that the key management be operational as long as the group exists. Therefore, ASM prefers decentralized key management. Moreover, in environments such as peer-to-peer and ad hoc networks, centralized resources are usually not readily available, and thus secure groups naturally turn to distributed key agreement in which the SEK is generated in a contributory and collaborative fashion.

Based upon group-extensions to the Diffie-Hellman protocol, quite a few distributed key agreement approaches have been proposed [14, 15, 16, 17]. This paper, however, chooses a somewhat different approach [13] as a case study, which avoids expensive public-key operations of Diffie-Hellman based protocols. We show that it also fails to provide forward and backward security against adversarial members, but in a manner quite different from the Secure Filter.

In [13], DISEC, the DIstributed framework for Scalable sEcure many-to-many Communication, was proposed to delegate key management tasks evenly to all group members. It is essentially a decentralization of an LKH [8, 9] variation, the One-way Function Tree (OFT) [10]. DISEC employs a virtual key tree which is approximately balanced (thus its height scales as $\mathcal{O}(\log N)$) but strictly binary (thus each interior node has exactly two children). Fig. 2 illustrates such an OFT for DISEC with respect to a secure multicast group of nine members (A to I).

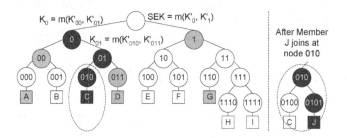

**Fig. 2.** A One-way Function Tree for a group (A to I) of $N = 9$. Each node $n$ in the tree is associated with a node key $K_n$ and its blinded counterpart $K'_n$ computed by applying a public one-way function. As the node key of an interior node (also the root) is computed by mixing the blinded node keys of both its children, member C can step by step (in a bottom-up manner) compute the SEK with only its own secret key $K_{010}$ and the blinded keys $\{K'_{011}, K'_{00}, K'_1\}$ received from its key association $\{D, A, G\}$.

Each leaf node in the tree is associated with a member, who respectively generates a unique secret key as its contribution towards the root key (i.e. the SEK). For every node $n$, there is a node key $K_n$ and its blinded version $K'_n$ computed by applying a public one-way function. The node key of an interior node (also the root) is computed by applying a mixing function $m()$ (typically the bitwise XOR) to its two children's blinded keys. Each member knows all and only the unblinded keys of the nodes in its path to the root and the blinded keys of the siblings of those nodes. For example, in Fig. 2, C knows the unblinded keys of the solid nodes $\{010, 01, 0\}$ plus the root key, the blinded keys of the shadowed nodes $\{011, 00, 1\}$, and none of the other keys either blinded or unblinded.

Each member has a binary ID $X = b_h b_{h-1} \cdots b_1$ and is responsible for generating its secret node key. To compute the group key, it needs exactly $h = |X|$ blinded keys from other members. For the $i$th bit in $X$ ($i = 1, 2, \cdots, h$) there is a member that supplies the corresponding blinded key, as specified in Alg. 1. The set of the $h$ members that supplies the $h$ blinded keys to the member with ID $X$ is defined as its key association. For example, H in Fig. 2 has the key association I, G, F, and D, who provides H with $K'_{1111}$, $K'_{110}$, $K'_{10}$, and $K'_0$ respectively.

---

**Algorithm 1. Finding the $i$th member of a key association**

```
Find_Key_Association(X = bₕbₕ₋₁···b₁, i)
{
    Xᵢ = bₕbₕ₋₁···bᵢ₊₁b̄ᵢbᵢ₋₁···b₂b₁;
    AS = bₕbₕ₋₁···bᵢ₊₁b̄ᵢ;
    if (leaf_node(Xᵢ) == true) return (Xᵢ, K'ₐₛ);
    if (internal_node(Xᵢ) == true) {
        do {
            Xᵢ = bit_concatenate(Xᵢ, 0)
        } until (leaf_node(Xᵢ) == true);
    } else { //Xᵢ does not exist
        do {
            Xᵢ = right_shift(Xᵢ, 1);
        } until (leaf_node(Xᵢ) == true);
    }
    return (Xᵢ, K'ₐₛ);
}
```

---

The key computation process for C in Fig. 2 is as follows. First, it generates $K_{010}$, sends $K'_{010}$ to D, and receives $K'_{011}$ in return. Both C and D can then compute $K_{01}$ by apply the mixing function $m()$. Next, C sends $K'_{01}$ to A and receives $K'_{00}$ accordingly. After the key exchange both C and A can compute $K_0$. Then C and G exchange $K'_0$ and $K'_1$ with each other, and compute the group key according to $SEK = m(K'_0, K'_1)$. Similarly, in a bottom-up manner, each member can compute the unblinded keys of the internal nodes in its path to the root plus the SEK with its own secret key and approximately $\log_2 N$ blinded keys received from its key association. We now outline the join and leave operations of DISEC.

*A. Join protocol*

A new member joins the group by splitting the leaf node with the shortest ID to keep the tree reasonably balanced. In Fig. 2 for example, to include a new member J, C splits node 010, assigning new ID 0100 to itself and 0101 to J. C also generates a new key $K_{0100}$ and sends $K'_{0100}$ to J. J generates its node key $K_{0101}$ and sends $K'_{0101}$ to C. Both C and J now know the new $K_{010}$. All the keys of the internal nodes in the path from J to the root change due to the join, and thus the SEK is updated. According to Alg. 1, J knows that D, A, and G are the rest ones in its key association. Note that these members and a few others also need the blinded keys that J holds. To elaborate, J exchanges $K'_{010}$ with D for $K'_{011}$. After computing $K_{01}$, J exchanges $K'_{01}$ for $K'_{00}$ with A. In DISEC, A is also required to locally multicast $K_{00}\{K'_{01}\}$ which can only be decrypted by A and B. J then computes $K_0$, exchanges $K'_0$ with G for $K'_1$, and computes the new SEK. G is also required to multicast $K_1\{K'_0\}$, which can only be decrypted by E, F, G, H, and I. After the above deliveries, all members will have all and only the keys they are entitled to know, and be able to compute the new SEK.

The join protocol is generalized in Alg. 2, which takes the new member X and the node ID of the joining point Y as arguments. In all, a member joining incurs about $2\log_2 N$ unicast messages between itself and its key association, and $\log_2 N$ multicast messages by its key association. Some of the multicasts can be suppressed, as shown in the above example.

---

**Algorithm 2. Adding a member into the group**

```
Join(X, Y = b_h b_{h-1} ··· b_1) //Y has the shortest ID
{
    Y = b_h b_{h-1} ··· b_1 0; X = b_h b_{h-1} ··· b_1 1; //node splitting
    K_X = generate_new_key(); //so does Y (omitted here)
    for (i=1; i<=h+1; i++) {
        (M, K'_AS) = Find_Key_Association(X, i);
        K_OG = K'_right_shift(X, i-1); //the outgoing key
        exchange_key(X, K_OG, M, K'_AS);
        multicast(M, K_AS{K_OG});
        K_right_shift(X, i) = m(K_OG, K'_AS);
    } //2 unicasts plus 1 multicast in one round
}
```

---

We note that in Fig. 2, none of the blinded keys known to C is changed when J is added, and thus on receiving $K'_{0101}$ only, C can compute all the new values of $K_{010}$, $K_{01}$, $K_0$, and $SEK$. J may freely choose another joining point other than node 010 as in Fig. 2 the leaf nodes associated with members A to G are all assigned 3-bit IDs, which is the shortest length.

### B. Leave protocol

When a member X leaves, its neighbor (defined as the $1st$ member in its key association) Y changes its secret key and sponsors the rekeying. If Y is the sibling of X, it simply takes over their parent's position by right shifting Y by one bit. Otherwise X's neighbor Y is a leaf node of the subtree rooted at X's sibling S, and the subtree is then moved closer to the root by one level. To do so, all the nodes in the subtree change their IDs: for every $Z = b_h b_{h-1} \cdots b_{i+1} b_i b_{i-1} \cdots b_2 b_1$, Z's new ID would be $b_h b_{h-1} \cdots b_{i+1} b_{i-1} \cdots b_2 b_1$, where $i = |Z| - |X| + 1$. For example, in Fig. 2, if E leaves, F assumes node 10 and sponsors the rekeying; if G leaves, H gets ID 110 and sponsors the rekeying while I gets ID 111.

In both cases, X's neighbor Y sends the updated blinded keys to members of its key association, who are responsible for propagating them by encrypted multicasts similar to the join case. The leave protocol is generalized in Alg. 3. In Fig. 2, for example, C leaves the group, and its neighbor is its sibling J. J notices the departure and changes its ID from 0101 to 010. The sponsor generates its new secret key $K_{010}$ and sends $K'_{010}$ to D so that they can both compute $K_{01}$. J then sends $K'_{01}$ to A, who then notifies B by multicasting $K_{00}\{K'_{01}\}$. Finally, J sends $K'_0$ to G, who then multicasts $K_1\{K'_0\}$ to inform E, F, H, and I. J does not need any keys in return from its key association $\{D, A, G\}$ as it already holds $K'_{011}$, $K'_{00}$, and $K'_1$. The deleted member C also holds those blinded keys, but it cannot compute the updated SEK due to not knowing the updated $K'_{010}$.

---

**Algorithm 3. Deleting a member from the group**

```
Leave(X) //X's neighbor will be the sponsor
{
    Y = Find_Key_Association(X, 1); //the neighbor
    for each Z in {Y} ∪ {descendants(sibling(X))}
        Z = delete_ith_bit(Z, |Z|-|X|+1);
    K_Y = generate_new_key();
    compute_path_node_keys(Y);
    for (i=1; i<=|Y|; i++) {
        (M, K'_AS) = Find_Key_Association(Y, i);
        K_OG = K'_right_shift(Y, i-1); //the outgoing key
        send_key_from_to(K_OG, Y, M);
        multicast(M, K_AS{K_OG});
    } //1 unicast plus 1 multicast in one round
}
```

---

We note that a departure incurs about $\log_2 N$ unicasts by the leaving member's neighbor, and $\log_2 N$ multicasts by the neighbor's key association (some may be suppressed). This is unusual, as a basic observation on group key management protocols is that deleting a member tends to involve no less overhead than adding one, which has been exemplified with GKMP in Section 2. We will further comment on our observation in the next two sections.

# 5   Cryptanalysis of the DISEC Framework

In ASM environments, as there is no centralized authority, usually all group members are equally trusted. However, it is possible for collusion to take place in DISEC and it may even be impractical to detect them. We now illustrate its vulnerability with Fig. 3, in which two colluding scenarios are depicted.

*Scenario* 1: Suppose G leaves the group at time $t_1$, its neighbor F assumes their parent's position 101, generates $K_{101}(t_1)$, and sponsors the rekeying. Note that the blinded keys $K'_{100}$, $K'_{11}$, $K'_0$ do not change on G's departure. Then, at time $t_2$ a new member L chooses to join at the point of node 100 since E has the shortest ID. The blinded key $K'_{101}(t_2)$ assigned to L is actually identical to $K'_{101}(t_1)$. Although $K_{10}$ is updated at time $t_2$, G and L can collude to recover $K_{10}(t_1)$ when G offers $K'_{100}(t_1)$ and L offers $K'_{101}(t_1)$. As G knows $K'_{11}(t_1)$ (which is identical to $K'_{11}(t_2)$ known by L) and $K'_0(t_1)$ (which is identical to $K'_0(t_2)$ known by L), G can recover $SEK(t_1)$ and thus forward security is comprised. L can also recover $SEK(t_1)$ and thus backward security is comprised, too.

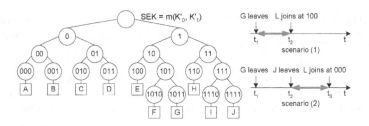

**Fig. 3.** Two scenarios to illustrate the vulnerability of DISEC. In the first case, G knows $K'_{100}(t_1)$ and L holds $K'_{101}(t_2)$, therefore they can collude to acquire $K_{10}(t_1)$ and recover $SEK(t_1)$. In the second case, G knows $K'_0(t_1)$ and L holds $K'_1(t_3)$ and they can collude to acquire $SEK(t_2)$. In both cases, DISEC fails to provide forward security against the evictee G and backward security against the new member L.

*Scenario* 2: Suppose G leaves the group at time $t_1$. Due to a departure of J at time $t_2$, $K'_{11}(t_1)$ known to G is updated to $K'_{11}(t_2)$. However, similar to scenario 1, $K'_0(t_1)$ is identical to $K'_0(t_2)$. Then at time $t_3$ a new member L chooses to join at node 000 since A has the shortest ID. L is notified $K'_1(t_3)$, which is identical to $K'_1(t_2)$. Therefore, G and L can collude to recover $SEK(t_2)$, which is used between the deletion of J and the addition of L. Note that we do not assume J in collusion with L as it does not yield much difference from scenario 1.

In both scenarios, DISEC fails to provide forward security against G and backward security against L. We note that in scenario 1 and in Fig. 1, forward security is comprised immediately after the evictee departs. However, in scenario 2, forward security is not compromised until another member J leaves, in which it makes little sense for J to collude with G (as $SEK(t_1)$ is delegated to J).

As observed in Section 4, DISEC takes less trouble to remove a member than to admit one, which leads to the fact that some of the unchanged blinded node keys used in subsequent group key agreement may be exploited by a departed member to collude with a joining member to recover the SEK that they should not acquire. We now propose two remedial approaches to fix the security breach.

The first remedy is a straightforward one. We update all the blinded keys $\{K'_S\}$ known to an evictee by having relevant members regenerate their leaf node keys. For each sibling S of the nodes in the path from the leaving member to the root, if S is a leaf node, we nominate the associated member to be the sponsor, otherwise we specify the member who is associated with the shallowest leaf node in the subtree rooted at S as the sponsor. We then have the sponsor generate a new secret key and have its key association propagate the new values of the blinded counterparts of the affected node keys. Similar to Alg. 3, updating $K'_S$ incurs about $\log_2 N$ unicasts by the sponsor, and $\log_2 N$ multicasts by its key association. As $\{S\}$ is approximately of size $\log_2 N$, updating $\{K'_S\}$ to securely delete a member incurs $\mathcal{O}(\log_2^2 N)$ messages for both unicast and multicast.

For example in Fig. 3 when G leaves, F takes over their parent's position 101 and refreshes $K_{101}$, E sponsors the rekeying for $K'_{100}$, H sponsors the rekeying for $K'_{11}$, and one of the members A to D sponsors the rekeying for $K'_0$. As node 1011 is deleted and all the keys known to G (either blinded or unblinded) are invalidated, the remedy effectively stalls the evictee's attack to collude with any new member to gain access to any SEK that they are not entitled to know.

Although this approach achieves forward and backward security, we show that it is not optimized. For simplicity we employ a well balanced key tree as depicted in Fig. 4, and we focus on the number of unicast messages involved.

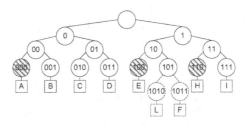

**Fig. 4.** L leaves and the residual members form a group of size $N = 8$. The number of unicasts needed to delete L securely can be reduced from $h(h+1)$ to $h(h+3)/2$, where $h = \log_2 N$ is the tree height. Similar communication reduction holds for multicast.

Suppose in Fig. 4 L departs and F assumes their parent's position 101, and thus the key tree is of height $h = 3$. To invalidate all the keys known to L, four members, F, E, H, and A, sponsor each of the following rekeying rounds respectively: (1) F → E: $K'_{101}$, F → I: $K'_{10}$, F → B: $K'_1$; (2) E → F: $K'_{100}$, E → H: $K'_{10}$, E → A: $K'_1$; (3) H → I: $K'_{110}$, H → E: $K'_{11}$, H → C: $K'_1$; (4) A → B: $K'_{000}$, A → C: $K'_{00}$, A → E: $K'_0$. In all, 12 unicast messages are delivered. We note that the $K'_{10}$ in round 1 is updated by the one in round 2, and the $K'_1$ in round 2 is also updated by the one in round 3. This yields unnecessary communication cost. We now propose the second and optimized remedial approach.

To securely delete member $L = b_h b_{h-1} \cdots b_1 b_0$, its neighbor F assumes position $b_h b_{h-1} \cdots b_2 b_1$ and refreshes its node key. Instead of serving as a sponsor, F only plays the role of a passive collaborator. This is different from the behavior specified in Alg. 3 as well as in the first remedy. The optimized rekeying consists of $h$ rounds. In the $i$th round, for node $S = b_h b_{h-1} \cdots \overline{b_i}$, if $S$ is a leaf node, we nominate the associated member to be the sponsor, otherwise we specify the member with the smallest ID in the subtree rooted at $S$ as the sponsor. The sponsor updates $K'_S$ by refreshing its secret node key, but it only sends relevant updated blinded keys to the first $i$ members in its key association (instead of the whole). The $i$th round ends with a key exchange between the sponsor and its $i$th key association member, and this is the only key exchange in one round.

We describe out optimized remedial leave protocol in Alg. 4 as a revision of Alg. 3. As the $i$th round incurs $(i + 1)$ unicasts, the rekeying in all involves $h(h+3)/2$ unicasts. In Fig. 4, $N = 8$ and $h = 3$, thus only 9 unicasts are delivered: (1) E → F: $K'_{100}$, F → E: $K'_{101}$; (2) H → I: $K'_{110}$, H → E: $K'_{11}$, E → H: $K'_{10}$; (3) A → B: $K'_{000}$, A → C: $K'_{00}$, A → E: $K'_0$, E → A: $K'_1$. In Fig. 4, leaf secret keys associated with the hatched nodes are regenerated by the $h = 3$ sponsors.

**Algorithm 4. Securely deleting a member from the group**

```
Leave(X = bₕbₕ₋₁···b₁b₀)
{
    Y = bₕbₕ₋₁···b₁; //X's sibling assumes parent node
    K_Y = generate_new_key();
    for (i=1; i<=h; i++) {
        S = bₕbₕ₋₁···b̄ᵢ; //K'_S needs updating
        for (j=0, SP=S; !leaf_node(SP); j++) {
            SP = bit_concatenate(S, j);
        }
        K_SP = generate_new_key(); //SP is the sponsor
        for (j=1; j<=i; j++) {
            (M, K'_AS) = Find_Key_Association(SP, j);
            K_OG = K'_right_shift(SP, j-1); //the outgoing key
            send_key_from_to(K_OG, SP, M);
            multicast(M, K_AS{K_OG});
        }
        send_key_from_to(K'_AS, M, SP);
        multicast(SP, K'_OG{K'_AS});
    } //(i+1) unicasts(multicasts) in the ith round
}
```

## 6   Conclusion and Discussion

In this paper, we have shown the importance of assuring forward and backward security in group key management. Firstly, we have studied a few centralized key distribution approaches. We have revealed and fixed the vulnerability of a polynomial based scheme, the Secure Filter [7]. The vulnerability is caused by an algebraic issue in the algorithm, and may be exploited by a single adversary.

Centralized key distribution approaches can be roughly classified as non-tree-based and tree-based, and this paper focuses on the former case. For a review of the latter case, we refer the readers to [2], in which the key distribution models are systematically studied with basic concepts from information theory.

Secondly, we have addressed distributed group key agreement protocols with DISEC [13] as a case study, which is essentially a decentralization of one of the aforementioned tree-based approaches, the OFT [10]. We note that a letter [19] has demonstrated the vulnerability of OFT, which sheds light on our cryptanalysis of the DISEC scheme. However, the letter just showed a specific example by assuming that there is no key update between the evictee is deleted and the colluding member is added, and that the two colluding members are in different subtrees of the root node. We have found that neither of the two assumptions is a necessary condition to comprise the security of OFT, and two more general colluding attacks have been depicted in Fig. 3 in the context of DISEC.

We have noted that DISEC takes unusually less trouble to remove a member than to admit one, which leads to the vulnerability that an evictee can exploit the unchanged blinded keys to collude with a joining member to recover the SEK that they should not acquire. Furthermore, we have proposed two remedial approaches to fix the security breach. The first proposal incurs approximately $\log_2^2 N$ unicasts (multicasts) to securely delete a member, while the second remedy involves nearly half of that. Although a communication overhead of order $\mathcal{O}(\log_2^2 N)$ may not seem highly scalable for a centralized solution like OFT [10], it would be fairly acceptable for a decentralized solution in which the overhead is distributed over at least $\mathcal{O}(\log_2 N)$ devoted members (called sponsors in this work, as well as their key association groups), as proposed in our Alg. 4.

Finally, we comment on our observation that deleting a member tends to involve no less overhead than adding one. We state that it is only a constructive reference and by no means a qualification for a key management protocol to be secure. For better explanation, we define a factor $r$ as the first-order approximation of the ratio of the communication cost of evicting a member to that of admitting one. We then study a few approaches and tabulate their $r$ factors in table 1. For LKH and its variations, parameter $d$ denotes the degree of the key tree. For DISEC and its remedial approaches, we focus on the unicast messages counted with reference to $h = \log_2 N$ (the height of the key tree).

**Table 1.** Summarization of a Few Key Management Protocols and Their $r$ Factors

| Scheme | $C_{join}$ | $C_{leave}$ | $r = C_{leave}/C_{join}$ | Security |
|---|---|---|---|---|
| LKH [8,9] | $2\log_d N$ | $d\log_d N - 1$ | $d/2$ | |
| IHC [11] | $1 + \log_d N$ | $(d-1)\log_d N$ | $d-1$ | |
| SD-LKH [11] | $1 + \log_d N$ | $(d-1)\log_d N$ | $d-1$ | |
| GKMP [4] | $2$ | $N-1$ | $N/2$ | |
| Secure Filter [7] | $2$ | $N-1$ | $N/2$ | Vulnerable |
| Complete Key Graph [8] | $2^{N+1} - 2$ | $1$ | $1/2^N$ | |
| Complementary Variable [9] | $N+3$ | $1$ | $1/N$ | Vulnerable |
| DISEC[13] | $2h$ | $h$ | $1/2$ | Vulnerable |
| DISEC with remedy 1 | $2h$ | $h(h+1)$ | $h/2$ | |
| DISEC with remedy 2 | $2h$ | $h(h+3)/2$ | $h/4$ | |

For a considerable $N$, the Secure Filter [7] has an $r$ greater than 1 but the algorithm is vulnerable due to an algebraic issue. Hence our constructive reference is not a sufficient condition. On the other hand, three approaches, Complete Key Graph [8], Complementary Variable [9], and DISEC [13], have an $r$ factor less than 1. However, Complete Key Graph is supposed to be secure, though it has the poorest scalability of all. Therefore, it is not a necessary condition, either. Nevertheless, we still expect out reference to shed light on future research works.

## Acknowledgement

The author is grateful to Dr. Chuan-Kun Wu for his valuable comments. This work was supported by the National Natural Science Foundation of China under Grant No. 60503046 and Grant No. 60403006.

# References

1. R. Canetti, J. Garay, G. Itkis, D. Micciancio, M. Naor, B. Pinkas, "Multicast security: A taxonomy and some efficient constructions". Proceedings of IEEE IN-FOCOM'99, vol. 2, pp. 708-716, March 1999.
2. R. Poovendran, J. S. Baras, "An information-theoretic approach for design and analysis of rooted-tree-based multicast key management schemes". IEEE Transactions on Information Theory, vol. 47, pp. 2824-2834, November 2001.
3. S. Bhattacharyya, "An Overview of Source-Specific Multicast (SSM)", RFC3569, July 2003.
4. H. Harney, C. Muckenhirn, "Group key management protocol (GKMP) specification". RFC2093, July 1997.
5. G.-H. Chiou, W.-T. Chen, "Secure broadcasting using the secure lock". IEEE Transactions on Software Engineering, vol. 15, pp. 929-934, August 1989.
6. W. Trappe, J. Song, R. Poovendran, K.J.R. Liu, "Key distribution for secure multimedia multicasts via data embedding". Proceedings of IEEE ICASSP'01, vol. 3, pp. 1449-1452, May 2001.
7. K.-P. Wu, S.-J. Ruan, F. Lai, C.-K. Tseng, "On key distribution in secure multicasting". Proceedings of the 25th Annual IEEE Conference on Local Computer Networks, pp. 208-212, November, 2000.
8. C. K. Wong, M. Gouda, S. S. Lam, "Secure group communications using key graphs". IEEE/ACM Transactions on Networking, vol. 8, pp. 16-30, February 2000.
9. D. M. Wallner, E. J. Harder, and R. C. Agee, "Key management for multicast: Issues and architectures". RFC 2627, June 1999.
10. D Balenson, D. McGrew, A. Sherman, "Key management for large dynamic groups: One-way function trees and amortized initialization". IRTF Internet Draft, available at http://www.securemulticast.org/smug-drafts.htm, September 2000.
11. W. T. Zhu, "Optimizing the tree structure in secure multicast key management". IEEE Communications Letters, vol. 9, pp. 477-479, May 2005.
12. H. Lu, "A novel high-order tree for secure multicast key management". IEEE Transactions on Computers, vol. 54, pp. 214-224, February 2005.
13. L. R. Dondeti, S. Mukherjee, A. Samal, "DISEC: A distributed framework for scalable secure many-to-many communication". Proceedings of 5th IEEE Symposium on Computers and Communications, pp. 693-698, July 2000.
14. G. Ateniese, M. Steiner, G. Tsudik, "New multiparty authentication services and key agreement protocols". IEEE Journal on Selected Areas in Communications, vol. 18, pp. 628-639, April 2000.
15. M. Steiner, G. Tsudik, M. Waidner, "Key agreement in dynamic peer groups". IEEE Transactions on Parallel and Distributed Systems, vol. 11, pp. 769-780, August 2000.
16. Y. Kim, A. Perrig, G. Tsudik, "Simple and fault-tolerant key agreement for dynamic collaborative groups". Procedings of the 7th ACM Conference on Computer and Communications Security, pp. 235-244, November 2000.
17. Y. Amir, Y. Kim, C. Nita-Rotaru, J. L. Schultz, J. Stanton, G. Tsudik, "Secure group communication using robust contributory key agreement". IEEE Transactions on Parallel and Distributed Systems, vol. 15, pp. 468-480, May 2004.
18. E. Bach, V. Shoup, "Factoring polynomials using fewer random bits". Journal of Symbolic Computation, vol. 9, pp. 229-239, March 1990.
19. G. Horng, "Cryptanalysis of a key management scheme for secure multicast communications". IEICE Transactions on Communications, vol. E85-B, pp. 1050-1051, May 2002.

# Security Analysis of Password-Authenticated Key Agreement Protocols*

Kyung-Ah Shim[1] and Seung-Hyun Seo[2]

[1] Department of Mathematics
[2] Department of Computer Science and Engineering,
Ewha Womans University, Seoul, Korea
kashim@ewha.ac.kr, seosh@ewhain.net

**Abstract.** Recently, there have been proposed a number of password-authenticated key agreement protocols for two-party setting or three-party setting. In this paper, we show that recently proposed three password-authenticated key agreement protocols in [11, 12, 10] are insecure against several active attacks including a stolen-verifier attack, an off-line password guessing attack and impersonation attacks.

## 1 Introduction

Two entities, who only share a password, and who are communicating over an insecure network, want to authenticate each other and agree on a session key to be used for protecting their subsequent communication. This is called the *password-authenticated key exchange* problem. The first password-authenticated key exchange (PAKE) protocol, known as Encrypted Key Exchange (EKE), was suggested by Bellovin and Merritt [1]. By using a combination of symmetric and public-key cryptography, EKE resists dictionary attacks by giving a passive attacker insufficient information to verify a guessed password. Since it was invented, many password-authenticated key agreement protocols that promised increased security have been developed [2-4, 8, 9, 14-16].

In 1995, Steiner, Tsudik, and Waidner [15] extended two-party EKE protocol to three-party one (STW-3P-EKE), in which all clients share a password with a trusted server $S$ only and in which $S$ mediates between two communication parties to allow their mutual authentication. The three-party EKE protocol is particularly well-suited for large communication environments because it is inconvenient in key management that every two communication parties mutually share a secret. Unfortunately, Ding and Horster [7] showed that the STW-3P-EKE is not resistant to undetectable on-line password guessing attacks. Lin, Sun and Hwang [13] also pointed out that the STW-3P-EKE is not only vulnerable to undetectable on-line password guessing attacks but also vulnerable to off-line password guessing attacks. They proposed a new three-party EKE, in which the server holds a long-term and publicly known public key to prevent both off-line

---

* This work was supported by the Korea Research Foundation Grant funded by the Korean Government(MOEHRD).(KRF-2005-217-C00002).

Y.G. Desmedt et al. (Eds.): CANS 2005, LNCS 3810, pp. 49–58, 2005.

and undetectable on-line password guessing attack. However, in their protocol, communication parties have to obtain and verify the public key of the server, a task which puts a high burden on the user. Later, there have been proposed several key agreement protocols for three-parties, in which two clients establish a common session key through a authentication server. Most of those protocols require to use server's public key to prevent password guessing attacks. However, the protocols may not be practical for some environments since clients need to verify and keep the server's public key. Recently, Lee *et al* [12] proposed a new efficient verifier-based key agreement protocol for three parties, which does not require server's public key. They argued that the protocol was secure against impersonation attacks and server compromise. In this paper, we show that the protocol is still insecure against a stolen-verifier attack and impersonation attacks. Also, Lee *et al* [11] proposed a two-party password-authenticated key agreement protocol PAKA and its verifier-based version PAKA-X. In the PAKA-X protocol, the client uses a plaintext of the password, while the server stores a verifier for the password. So the protocol does not allow an adversary who compromises the server to impersonate a client without actually running a dictionary attack on the password file. We will show that the PAKA-X protocol is insecure against a stolen-verifier attack and an off-line password-guessing attack.

At ICICS'02, Byun *et al* [5] proposed two password-authenticated key exchange protocol between clients with different passwords, so-called Client-to-Client Password-Authenticated Key Exchange (C2C-PAKE) protocol. One is for a cross-realm setting where two clients are in two different realms and hence there exist two servers involved, the other is for a single-server setting where two clients are in the same realm. The protocol being circulated for consideration at the 27th SC27/WG2. Subsequently, Chen [6] and Kim *et al* [10] showed that their protocol was insecure against a dictionary attack by a malicious server in a different realm and Denning-Sacco attacks mounted by insiders, respectively. And Kim *et al* [10] also proposed a modified protocol to resist these attacks. In this paper, we point out that the modified protocol is also insecure against impersonation attacks.

The rest of the paper is organized as follows. The next section presents the attacks on the PAKA-X protocol. In section 3, we point out the Lee *et al*'s PAKE for three-party is insecure against a stolen-verifier attack. In section 4, we show that the modified C2C-PAKE protocol is insecure against partition attacks and impersonation attacks. Concluding remarks are given in section 5.

## 2   Cryptanalysis of the PAKA-X Protocol

Lee *et al* [11] proposed a password-based authenticated key agreement protocol, PAKA and its verifier-based version, PAKA-X. In this section, we show that the PAKA-X protocol is insecure against a stolen-verifier attack and an off-line password guessing attack. First, we review the PAKA-X protocol.

## 2.1   The PAKA-X Protocol

Let $g$ be a generator of $\mathbb{Z}_p^*$, where $p$ is a large prime and $h$ a collision-resistant one-way hash function. Henceforth, we will omit the operation 'mod $p$' for simplicity. We assume that there is an initialization in which the client, Alice chooses a memorable password, $\pi$, computes a verifier $\nu = g^{h(Id_A, Id_B, \pi)}$ and then sends $\nu$ to the server, Bob, over a secure channel. Bob stores $(Id_A, \nu)$, where $Id_A$ indicates an identifier of Alice. To enhance the efficiency of the protocol, $\nu = g^{h(Id_A, Id_B, \pi)}$ and $h(Id_A, Id_B, \pi)^{-1}$ can be precomputed by Alice before the protocol runs. The PAKA-X protocol is as follows;

1. Alice computes $X_A = g^a \oplus \nu$ by choosing $a \in_R \mathbb{Z}_p^*$ and then sends $\{Id_A, X_A\}$ to Bob.
2. After receiving the message, Bob retrieves $\nu$ from a password file, computes $X_B = \nu^b \oplus \nu$ by choosing $b \in_R \mathbb{Z}_p^*$ and then sends $X_B$ to Alice. While waiting for a message from Alice, Bob computes $K_B = (X_A \oplus \nu)^b = g^{ab}$ and $V_A' = h(Id_A, X_B, K_B)$ and $V_B = h(Id_B, X_A, K_B)$, in sequence.
3. After receiving the message from Bob, Alice computes

$$K_A = (X_B \oplus \nu)^{ah(Id_A, id_B, \pi)^{-1}} = g^{ab}$$

   and $V_A = h(Id_A, X_B, K_A)$ and then sends $V_A$ to Bob. While waiting for a message from Bob, Alice computes $V_B' = h(Id_B, X_A, K_A)$.
4. On the receipt the message $V_A$, Bob checks whether $V_A = V_A'$ holds or not. If it holds, Bob is convinced that $K_A$ is validated, and then sends $V_B$ to Alice.
5. On the receipt the message $V_B$, Alice checks whether $V_B = V_B'$ holds or not. If it holds, Alice is convinced that $K_B$ is validated.
6. Finally, Alice and Bob compute the common session key $K = h(K_A) = h(K_B) = h(g^{ab})$.

## 2.2   Attacks on the PAKA-X Protocol

Lee *et al* [11] argue that the PAKA-X is secure against sever compromise, i.e., an attacker who steals password file from the server cannot use that information directly to impersonate the client. Now, we show that the PAKA-X protocol is still vulnerable to server compromise, i.e., a stolen-verifier attack. If the host's password file is captured and then an adversary learns the value of the verifier $\nu$, it should still not allow the adversary to impersonate the user without an expensive dictionary search. Then we say that the protocol is secure against stolen-verifier attack or server compromise attack.

**• Stolen-Verifier Attack on the PAKA-X Protocol**
Suppose that an adversary $E$ has captured $A$'s verifier $\nu$ and wishes to impersonate $A$ to $B$. $E(A)$ represents $E$ impersonating $A$.

1. First, the adversary $E$ chooses $a \in_R \mathbb{Z}_p^*$ and computes $X_A = \nu^a \oplus \nu$ from $\nu$. Then $E$ starts a protocol run sending $\{Id_A, X_A\}$ to $B$ impersonating $A$.

2. After receiving the message, $B$ retrieves $A$'s verifier $\nu$ from a password file. He chooses a random $b$, computes $X_B = \nu^b \oplus \nu$ and sends it to $E(A)$. Then $B$ computes $K_B = (X_A \oplus \nu)^b = (\nu^a \oplus \nu \oplus \nu)^b = \nu^{ab}$, and $V_B = h(Id_B, X_A, K_B)$. While waiting for a message from $E(A)$, $B$ computes $V_A' = h(Id_A, X_B, K_B)$.
3. On the receipt the message, $E(A)$ can obtain $K_A$ (which is the same as $K_B$) by computing $(X_B \oplus \nu)^a = (\nu^b \oplus \nu \oplus \nu)^a = \nu^{ab} = K_A$ from $X_B$, $\nu$ and $a$. And then $E(A)$ computes $V_A = h(Id_A, X_B, K_A)$ and sends it to $B$.
4. After receiving the message $V_A$, $B$ checks whether $V_A = V_A'$ holds or not. The equation holds since $K_A = K_B$. Then $B$ is convinced that $K_A$ is validated and sends $V_B = h(Id_B, X_A, K_B)$ to $A$. Next, $B$ computes the session key $K = h(K_B) = h(\nu^{ab})$.
5. After receiving the message $V_B$, $E(A)$ computes $V_B' = h(Id_B, X_A, K_A)$ and checks $V_B = V_B'$ holds or not. Finally, $E$ succeeds to impersonate $A$ to $B$ as well as the knowledge of the session key $K = h(K_A) = h(\nu^{ab})$.

By using the verifier, an adversary can compute the first transmitted message $X_A$ to confine the shared secret to a predictable value from the message computed by the legitimate user $B$. In other words, by fabricating the message from the compromised verifier, the adversary can impersonate $A$ and compute the shared secret, $K_A = K_B = \nu^{ab}$ established between $E(A)$ and $B$ without the knowledge of the password $\pi$ and an expensive dictionary search. Therefore, the PAKA-X is insecure against the stolen-verifier attack unlike their claim in [11].

We also show that the PAKA-X protocol is insecure against an off-line password guessing attack. The attack on the PAKA-X is mounted as follows;

### • Off-line Password Guessing Attack on the PAKA-X Protocol
When $A$ starts a protocol run by sending a message $\{Id_A, X_A = g^a \oplus \nu\}$ to $B$, an attacker $E(B)$ intercepts it and sends $X_B = 0$ to $A$ impersonating $B$. On the receipt the message, $A$ computes

$$K_A = (X_B \oplus \nu)^{ah(A,B,\pi)^{-1}} = \nu^{ah(A,B,\pi)^{-1}} = g^a, \quad V_A = h(Id_A, X_B, K_A)$$

and then sends $V_A$ to $E(B)$. After receiving the message, $E$ stores it and stops the protocol run.

$$
\begin{aligned}
(1.1) \quad &A \longrightarrow E(B): \quad Id_A, \quad X_A = g^a \oplus \nu \\
(1.2) \quad &E(B) \longrightarrow A : \quad\quad\quad X_B = 0 \\
(1.3) \quad &A \longrightarrow E(B): V_A = h(Id_A, X_B, K_A) \\
(1.4) \quad &E(B) \longrightarrow A : \quad\quad\quad stop.
\end{aligned}
$$

Finally, $E$ executes an off-line password guessing attack and then finds the password $\pi$ iterating upon all possible choices of $\pi$;

1. Pick a candidate $\pi'$.
2. Compute $\nu' = g^{h(Id_A, Id_B, \pi')}$ and $K_A' = X_A \oplus \nu' = (g^a \oplus \nu) \oplus \nu'$ from the recorded message $X_A$.
3. Compare $V_A$ with $h(Id_A, X_B, K_A')$.

Since $V_A = h(Id_A, X_B, K_A) = h(Id_A, X_B, g^a)$, a match in the last step indicates correct guess of the password. Therefore, an attacker succeeds to guess the valid password $\pi$.

# 3  Cryptanalysis of the LKY Protocol

## 3.1  The LKY Protocol

We review the Lee $et$ $al$'s verifier-based key agreement protocol (called the LKY protocol)[12] for three parties without server's public key. We assume that each client uses a memorable password, while the server stores corresponding verifiers instead of plaintext-equivalent passwords to resist to server compromise. Let $p$ be a large prime and $g$ a generator of $\mathbb{Z}_p^*$. Let $h(\cdot)$ be a collision-resistant one-way hash function. Assume that two clients, $A$ and $B$, want to agree a common session key though a authentication server, called $AS$. For registering for $AS$, $A$ and $B$, respectively, choose passwords $\pi_A$ and $\pi_B$, compute verifiers $v_A = g^{t_A}$, $t_A = h(A, S, \pi_A)$ and $v_B = g^{t_B}$, $t_B = h(B, S, \pi_B)$, and then send $v_A$ and $v_B$ to $AS$ over a secure channel. $AS$ stores $v_A$ and $v_B$ in a password file. The protocol runs as follows;

1. $A$ computes $X_A = g^a$ by choosing a random $a \in \mathbb{Z}_p^*$ and sends $\{A, X_A\}$ to $B$.
2. After receiving the message from $A$, $B$ choose a random $b \in \mathbb{Z}_p^*$, computes $X_B = g^b$ and sends $\{A, X_A, B, X_B\}$ to $AS$. $B$ also sends $X_B$ to $A$.
3. After receiving the message from $B$, $AS$ retrieves $v_A$ and $v_B$ from a password file. Then $AS$ chooses $c, d \in \mathbb{Z}_p^*$ computes $X_{SA} = (v_A)^c \oplus v_A$ and $X_{SB} = (v_B)^d \oplus v_B$ and sends $X_{SA}$ and $X_{SB}$ to $A$ and $B$, respectively. While waiting for messages from $A$ and $B$, $AS$ computes $K_{SA} = (X_A)^c = g^{ac}$ and $K_{SB} = (X_B)^d = g^{bd}$.
4. After receiving the messages from $AS$ and $B$, $A$ computes $K_{AS} = (X_{SA} \oplus v_A)^{t_A^{-1}a} = g^{ac}$, $V_{AS} = h(A, B, S, X_A, X_B, X_{SA}, K_{AS})$ and sends $V_{AS}$ to $AS$. Similarly, after receiving the message from $AS$, $B$ computes $K_{BS} = (X_{SB} \oplus v_B)^{t_B^{-1}b} = g^{bd}$, $V_{BS} = h(B, A, S, X_B, X_A, X_{SB}, K_{BS})$ and sends $V_{BS}$ to $AS$.
5. After receiving the messages from $A$ and $B$, $AS$ checks whether $V_{AS} = h(A, B, S, X_A, X_B, X_{SA}, K_{SA})$ and $V_{BS} = h(B, A, S, X_B, X_A, X_{SB}, K_{SB})$ hold or not. If they hold, $AS$ is convinced that $A$ and $B$ are validated. Then $AS$ computes $V_{SA} = h(S, A, B, X_A, X_B, K_{SA})$, $V_{SB} = h(S, B, A, X_B, X_A, K_{SB})$ and sends $V_{SA}$ and $V_{SB}$ to $A$ and $B$, respectively.
6. After receiving the message from $AS$, $A$ checks whether $V_{SA} = h(S, A, B, X_A, X_B, K_{AS})$ holds or not. If it holds, $A$ is convinced that both $B$ and $AS$ are validated. Similarly, $B$ checks whether $V_{SB} = h(S, B, A, X_B, X_A, K_{BS})$ holds or not. If it holds, $B$ is convinced that both $A$ and $AS$ are validated. Finally, $A$ and $B$ compute $K_{AB} = (X_B)^a = g^{ab}$ and $K_{BA} = (X_A)^b = g^{ab}$, respectively, and then compute a common session key $K = h(A, B, S, g^{ab})$.

## 3.2   Stolen-Verifier Attack on the LKY Protocol

Now, we point out that the LKY protocol is insecure against a stolen-verifier attack.

• **Stolen-Verifier Attack on the LKY Protocol**

Suppose that an adversary $E$ has captured the verifiers $v_A$ and $v_B$ of $A$ and $B$, respectively, and wishes to impersonate both $A$ and $B$ to $AS$, simultaneously.

1. First, the adversary $E$ sets $X_A = v_A$ and $X_B = v_B$ and then starts a protocol run by sending $\{A, X_A, B, X_B\}$ to $AS$ impersonating $B$.
2. After receiving the message from $B$, $AS$ retrieves $v_A$ and $v_B$ from a password table. Then $AS$ chooses $c, d \in \mathbb{Z}_p^*$, computes $X_{SA} = (v_A)^c \oplus v_A$ and $X_{SB} = (v_B)^d \oplus v_B$ and sends $X_{SA}$ and $X_{SB}$ to $A$ and $B$, respectively. While waiting for messages from $A$ and $B$, $AS$ computes $K_{SA} = (X_A)^c = v_A^c$ and $K_{SB} = (X_B)^d = v_B^d$.
3. After receiving the messages from $AS$, from known value $v_A$, $E$ computes $K_{AS} = X_{SA} \oplus v_A = v_A^c$, $V_{AS} = h(A, B, S, X_A, X_B, X_{SA}, K_{AS})$ and sends $V_{AS}$ to $AS$ impersonating $A$. Similarly, $E$ computes $K_{BS} = X_{SB} \oplus v_B = v_B^d$, $V_{BS} = h(B, A, S, X_B, X_A, X_{SB}, K_{BS})$ and sends $V_{BS}$ to $AS$ impersonating $B$.
4. After receiving the messages from $A$ and $B$, $AS$ checks whether $V_{AS} = h(A, B, S, X_A, X_B, X_{SA}, K_{SA})$ and $V_{BS} = h(B, A, S, X_B, X_A, X_{SB}, K_{SB})$ hold or not. The equations hold since $K_{AS} = K_{SA} = v_A^c$ and $K_{BS} = K_{SB} = v_B^d$ as intended by the adversary. Thus, $AS$ is convinced that $A$ and $B$ are validated. Then, $AS$ computes $V_{SA} = h(S, A, B, X_A, X_B, K_{SA})$, $V_{SB} = h(S, B, A, X_B, X_A, K_{SB})$ and sends $V_{SA}$ and $V_{SB}$ to $A$ and $B$, respectively.
5. After receiving the message from $AS$, $E$ checks whether $V_{SA} = h(S, A, B, X_A, X_B, K_{AS})$ and $V_{SB} = h(S, B, A, X_B, X_A, K_{BS})$ hold or not. Finally, $E$ succeeds to impersonate both $A$ and $B$ to $AS$, simultaneously.

In above attack, by fabricating the messages and impersonating both $A$ and $B$, the adversary can compute the shared secrets, $K_{AS}$ and $K_{BS}$ established between $A$ and $AS$ and $B$ and $AS$, respectively, without the knowledge of genuine passwords $\pi_A$ and $\pi_B$, equivalently, $t_A$ and $t_B$.

## 4   Cryptanalysis of the Modified C2C-PAKE Protocol

### 4.1   The Modified C2C-PAKE Protocol

We first review the modified C2C-PAKE protocol [10] in a cross-realm setting. The following notation is used throughout this section.

- $A$, $B$                    Two clients in two different realms.
- $ID_A$, $ID_B$              Identities of $A$ and $B$, respectively.
- $KDC_A, KDC_B$     Key Distribution Centers which store passwords of $A$ and $B$, resp.

- $K$             A symmetric key shared between $KDC_A$ and $KDC_B$.
- $E_K(\cdot)$           A symmetric encryption under the symmetric key $K$.
- $E_{pwa}(\cdot)/D_{pwa}(\cdot)$    A symmetric encryption/decryption under the password $pwa$.

The modified C2C-PAKE protocol runs as follows;

## [Protocol Initialization]

1. Let $p$ and $q$ be sufficiently large primes such that $q|p-1$, and let $\mathbb{G} =<g>$ be a subgroup of $\mathbb{F}_p^*$ with order $q$. Let $g$ be a generator of $\mathbb{G}$. Let $H_i$ $(i = 1, 2)$ be cryptographic hash functions. The public system parameters are $< p, q, g, H_1, H_2 >$. The system parameters are shared by all protocol participants.
2. $A$ chooses a password $pwa$, then transfers it to $KDC_A$ through a secure channel. $B$ also transfers $pwb$ to $KDC_B$, similarly. $KDC_A$ and $KDC_B$ store $(ID_A,\ pwa)$ and $(ID_B,\ pwb)$, respectively, in their database.

## [Ticket Issuing Stage]

1. First, $A$ chooses a random $x \in \mathbb{Z}_p^*$ and sends $\{E_{pwa}(g^x),\ ID_B\}$ to $KDC_A$.
2. On the receipt of the message from $A$, $KDC_A$ obtains $g^x$ by decrypting $E_{pwa}(g^x)$ under $A$'s password $pwa$. Next, $KDC_A$ selects a random $r \in \mathbb{Z}_p^*$ and issues $Ticket_B = E_K(g^{xr}, g^r, ID_A, ID_B, L)$, where $K$ is a symmetric key shared between $KDC_A$ and $KDC_B$ and $L$ is a lifetime of $Ticket_B$. Then $KDC_A$ sends $\{Ticket_B,\ ID_A,\ ID_B,\ L\}$ to $A$.

## [Mutual Authentication and Key Exchange Stage]

1. Upon receiving $Ticket_B$ from $KDC_A$, $A$ forwards $Ticket_B$ to $B$ with $ID_A$.
2. $B$ chooses a random $y \in \mathbb{Z}_p^*$ and computes $E_{pwb}(g^y)$. Then $B$ sends $\{E_{pwb}(g^y),\ ID_A,\ ID_B,\ Ticket_B\}$ to $KDC_B$.
3. After receiving the message from $B$, $KDC_B$ obtains $g^{xr}$ and $g^r$ by decrypting $Ticket_B$ with $K$, selects a random $r' \in \mathbb{Z}_p^*$ and computes $(g^{xr})^{r'}$ and $(g^r)^{r'}$. Next, $KDC_B$ sends $\{g^{xrr'},\ g^{rr'}\}$ to $B$.
4. When $B$ receives the message, $B$ computes $cs = H_1(g^{xyrr'})$ from $g^{xrr'}$ and $y$, chooses a random $a \in \mathbb{Z}_p^*$ and computes $E_{cs}(g^a)$ and $g^{rr'y}$. Finally, $B$ sends $\{E_{cs}(g^a),\ g^{rr'y}\}$ to $A$.
5. On the receipt of the message, $A$ computes $cs = H_1(g^{xyrr'})$ from $g^{yrr'}$ and $x$ and then obtains $g^a$ by decrypting $E_{cs}(g^a)$ under $cs$. Next, $A$ chooses a random $b \in \mathbb{Z}_p^*$ and computes the session key $sk = H_2(g^{ab})$ and $E_{cs}(g^b)$. Then $A$ sends $\{E_{sk}(g^a),\ E_{cs}(g^b)\}$ to $B$ for the session key confirmation.
6. By decrypting $E_{cs}(g^b)$ with $cs$, $B$ gets $g^b$ and computes $sk = H_2(g^{ab})$. Then $B$ verifies $g^a$ by decrypting $E_{sk}(g^a)$ with $sk$ and sends $E_{sk}(g^b)$ to $A$.
7. After receiving the message, $A$ verifies $g^b$ by decrypting $E_{sk}(g^b)$ with $sk$. Finally, $A$ (resp., $B$) authenticates $B$ (resp., $A$)and share the session key.

Kim *et al* [10] argued that the modified C2C-PAKE protocol is secure against all kinds of attacks considered in [5] including the Denning-Sacco attack and Chen's dictionary attacks [6]. However, we will show that the modified C2C-PAKE protocol is totally broken by an active adversary without the knowledge of any secret information such as past session keys and the shared symmetric key.

### 4.2   Attacks on the Modified C2C-PAKE Protocol

Now, we show that the modified protocol is insecure against partition attacks and two types of impersonation attacks.

**• Partition Attacks**
Both Byun *et al*'s original protocol [5] and the modified C2C-PAKE protocol [10] use $g$ as a generator of $\mathbb{G}$, where $\mathbb{G}$ is a subgroup of $\mathbb{F}_p^*$ of order $q$. However, it is known that the protocols with such a generator are insecure against partition attacks [9]. Thus, the C2C-PAKE and the modified C2C-PAKE protocols are also insecure the attacks. However, the attacks can be easily prevented if $g$ is taken as a primitive element of $\mathbb{F}_p^*$, i.e., a generator of $\mathbb{F}_p^*$.

**• Impersonation Attack I on the Modified C2C-PAKE Protocol**
Suppose that an adversary $E$ wants to impersonate $A$ to $B$ on the protocol.

**[Ticket Issuing Stage]**

1. An adversary $E(A)$ chooses a random $k \in \mathbb{Z}_p^*$ and sends $\{k, ID_A, ID_B\}$ to $KDC_A$ impersonating $A$.
2. On the receipt of the message from $E(A)$, $KDC_A$ thinks that the stage is initiated by $A$. Then $KDC_A$ obtains $D_{pwa}(k)$ by decrypting $k$ under $pwa$, selects a random $r \in \mathbb{Z}_p^*$ and generates $Ticket_B = E_K(D_{pwa}(k)^r, g^r, ID_A, L)$. Next, $KDC_A$ sends $\{Ticket_B, ID_A, ID_B\}$ to $E(A)$.

**[Mutual Authentication and Key Exchange Stage]**

1. After receiving $Ticket_B$ from $KDC_A$, $E(A)$ sends $\{Ticket_B, ID_A\}$ to $B$ impersonating $A$.
2. Then $B$ computes $E_{pwb}(g^y)$ and sends $\{E_{pwb}(g^y), ID_A, ID_B, Ticket_B\}$ to $KDC_B$.
3. $E$ intercepts the message from $B$, chooses random $k', k'' \in \mathbb{Z}_p^*$ and computes $g^{k'}$ and $g^{k'k''}$. Then $E(KDC_B)$ sends $\{g^{k'}, g^{k'k''}\}$ to $B$ impersonating $KDC_B$.
4. After receiving $\{g^{k'}, g^{k'k''}\}$ from $E(KDC_B)$, $B$ thinks that it is sent from $KDC_B$. $B$ computes $cs = H_1(g^{k'y})$ from $g^{k'}$ and computes $E_{cs}(g^a)$ and $g^{k'k''y}$. Then, $B$ sends $\{E_{cs}(g^a), g^{k'k''y}\}$ to $E(A)$.
5. On the receipt of the message, $E(A)$ can obtain $g^{k'y}$ from $g^{k'k''y}$ by computing $(g^{k'k''y})^{k''-1}$. Next, $E$ computes $cs = H_1(g^{k'y})$ and then recover $g^a$ from $E_{cs}(g^a)$. Next, $E(A)$ chooses a random $b \in \mathbb{Z}_p^*$ and computes a session key $sk = H_2(g^{ab})$ and $E_{cs}(g^b)$. Then $E(A)$ sends $\{E_{sk}(g^a), E_{cs}(g^b)\}$ to $B$.
6. After receiving $E_{sk}(g^a)$ and $E_{cs}(g^b)$, $B$ first obtains $g^b$ by decrypting $E_{cs}(g^b)$ and computes $sk = H_2(g^{ab})$ and then verifies $g^a$ from $E_{sk}(g^a)$. $B$ computes $E_{sk}(g^b)$ and sends it to $E(A)$.
7. Finally, $E$ succeeds to impersonate both $A$ and $KDC_B$ to $B$ as well as the knowledge of the session key $sk = H_2(g^{ab})$.

**• Impersonation Attack II on the Modified C2C-PAKE Protocol**
Another impersonation attack can be mounted on the protocol without performing the **Ticket Issuing Stage**.

1. First, without issuing $Ticket_B$, $E(A)$ chooses a random $k \in \mathbb{Z}_p^*$ and sends $\{k, ID_A\}$ to $B$ impersonating $A$.
2. After receiving the message, $B$ believes that $k$ is a $Ticket_B$ issued by $KDC_A$. Because there is no way to confirm that it is issued by $KDC_A$. Then $B$ computes $E_{pwd}(g^y)$ and sends $\{E_{pwb}(g^y), ID_A, ID_B, k\}$ to $KDC_B$.
3. Intercepting the message sent from $B$, $E$ chooses $k', k'' \in \mathbb{Z}_p^*$, computes $g^{k'}$ and $g^{k'k''}$ and sends them to $B$ impersonating $KDC_B$.
4. The remainder of this attack is the same as the impersonation attack I. Finally, $E$ succeeds to impersonate $A$ to $B$ as well as the knowledge of the session key without issuing $Ticket_B$.

The weaknesses of the protocol against the impersonation attacks are due to the fact that; i) in the **Ticket Issuing Stage**, anyone can obtain a valid ticket of $A$ from $KDC_A$, because there is no device to verify whether the sender is $A$, i.e., there is no way to verify the received message is a valid encryption under $A$'s password $pwa$. ii) Similarly, in the **Mutual Authentication and Key Exchange Stage**, $B$ cannot assure that, in the step 3 in the modified C2C-PAKE protocol, the received message is sent from $KDC_B$, because, unlike the original C2C-PAKE protocol, $KDC_B$ does not use $B$'s password or any secret information between $KDC_B$ and $B$ to generate the messages $g^{xrr'}$ and $g^{rr'}$ for $B$, and so it is impossible to verify the message is generated by a genuine $KDC_B$. Thus, in the modified C2C-PAKE protocol, $KDC_A$ and $KDC_B$ do not perform the key distribution centers' role as required.

## 5    Conclusion

We have shown that the PAKA-X and LKY protocol are insecure against the stolen-verifier attacks. We have shown that the modified C2C-PAKE protocol is insecure against the partition attack and impersonation attacks. These results imply that the protocol is insecure against active adversaries without the knowledge of any secret information such as past session keys and the shared symmetric key.

## References

1. S. M. Bellovin and M. Merritt, Encrypted key exchange: Password-based protocols secure against dictionary attacks, Proc. of the 1992 IEEE Computer Society Conference on Research in security and Privacy, pp. 72-84, 1992.
2. S. M. Bellovin and M. Merritt, Augmented encrypted key exchange: Password-based protocols secure against dictionary attacks and password file compromise, Technical report, AT&T Bell Laboratories, 1994.

3. M. Bellare, D. Pointcheval and P. Rogaway, Authenticated Key Exchange Secure Against Dictionary Attacks, Advances in Cryptography-Eurocrypt'00, LNCS 1807, Springer-Verlag, pp. 139-155, 2000.
4. V. Boyko, P. MacKenzie, and S. Patel, Provably Secure Password-Authenticated Key Exchange Using Diffie-Hellman, Advances in Cryptography-Eurocrypt'00, LNCS 1807, Springer-Verlag, pp. 156-171, 2000.
5. J. Byun, I. Jeong, D. Lee and C. Park, Password-authenticated key exchange between clients with different passwords, ICICS'02, LNCS 2513, Springer-Verlag, pp. 134-146, 2004.
6. L. Chen, A weakness of the password-authenticated key exchange between clients with different passwords scheme, The documnet was being circulated for consideration at the 27th SC27/WG2 meeting in Paris, France, 2003-10-20/24(2003).
7. Y. Ding and P. Horster, Undetectable on-line password guessing attacks, ACM Operating Systems Review, vol. 29(4), 1995, pp. 77-86.
8. D. Jablon, Extended password methods immune to dictionary attack, Proc. of the WETICE'97 Enterprise Security Workshop, Cambridge, MA, June 1997.
9. D. Jablon, Strong password-only authenticated key exchange, Computer Communication Review, 26(5), pp. 5-26, 1996.
10. J. Kim, S. Kim, J. Kwak and D. Won, Cryptanalysis and improvment of password-authenticated key exchange between clients with different passwords, ICcsa'04, LNCS 3043, Springer-Verlag, pp. 895-902, 2002.
11. S-W Lee, W-H Kim, H-S Kim, and K-Y Yoo, Efficient password-based authenticated key agreement protocol, ICCSA'04, LNCS 3046, Springer-Verlag, pp. 617-626, 2004.
12. S-W Lee, H-S Kim and K-Y Yoo, Efficient verifier-based key agreement protocol for three parties without server's public key, Applied Mathematics and Computation, in Press.
13. C.-L. Lin, H.-M. Sun and T. Hwang, Three-party encrypted key exchange: attacks and a solution, ACM Operating Systems Review, vol. 34(4), 2000, pp. 12-20.
14. P. MacKenzie and R. Swaminathan, Secure Network Authentication with Password Identification, 1999 Submission to IEEE P1363a.
15. M. Steiner, G. Tsudik and M. Waidner, Refinement and extension of encrypted key exchange, ACM Operating System review, 29(3), July, 1995.
16. T. Wu, The secure remote password protocol, Internet Society Symposium on Network and Distribute System Security, pp. 97-111, 1998.

# An Immune-Based Model for Computer Virus Detection

Tao Li[1], Xiaojie Liu[1], and Hongbin Li[2]

[1] Department of Computer Science,
Sichuan University, Chengdu 610065, China
litao@scu.edu.cn
[2] Department of Electrical and Computer Engineering,
Stevens Institute of Technology,Hoboken, NJ07030, USA
hli@stevens.edu

**Abstract.** Inspired by biological immune systems, a new immune-based model for computer virus detection is proposed in this paper. Quantitative description of the model is given. A dynamic evolution model for self/nonself description is presented, which reduces the size of self set. Furthermore, an evolutive gene library is introduced to improve the generating efficiency of mature detectors, reducing the system time spending, false-negative and false-positive rates. Experiments show that this model has better time efficiency and detecting ability than the classical model ARTIS.

## 1 Introduction

As the fast development of Internet, the generating and spreading speed of new computer viruses is getting higher and higher. Then, computer viruses and worms are becoming an increasing problem in the world [1,2]. Therefore, it is necessary to detect and eliminate computer viruses, especially the unknown viruses, in real-time. However, it is very difficult for traditional preventing methods [3-5] to solve this problem effectively. In recent years, researchers have taken some researches on the computer network topologies and the spreading mechanism of computer viruses [6-8], then presented some methods to restrain virus spreading [9-11]. These methods can reduce the speed of virus spreading, however, they can not prevent virus spreading [11]. Especially, the problem for unknown virus detection is still not solved.

The problems found in computer security systems are quite similar to the ones encountered in Biological Immune Systems (BIS). BIS has successfully solved the problem of unknown virus detection [12]. Therefore, Artificial Immune System (AIS) [13-15] is considered as a new way to defeat fast-proliferating computer viruses. In 1994, Forrest presented a method of computer virus detection based on the negative selection algorithm[16], which is the first time to use immune mechanism for virus detecting and has greatly promoted the research of computer virus immune system (CVIS). The most important works should be the general

Y.G. Desmedt et al. (Eds.): CANS 2005, LNCS 3810, pp. 59–71, 2005.

framework ARTIS for AIS and the computer virus immune model proposed, respectively, by Hofmeyr [17,18] and Kephart [19,20]. In ARTIS, the concepts and mechanisms of BIS, including self, nonself, self tolerance, immune cell (detectors), memory cell (memory detectors), and costimulation were well simulated. Many CVISs are mainly derived from ARTIS. For example, the computer virus detection system proposed by Okamoto and Ishida [21], the agent based computer virus immune architecture proposed by Harmer [22], and the HMM [23] based computer immune model proposed by Jensen [24]. Different from ARTIS, the computer virus immune model [19,20] proposed by IBM laboratory uses only partial immune mechanisms, however, some other techniques such as automatic extraction of computer virus signatures [19], virus trap [20], etc. have also been adopted.

There are three major defects in the present CVISs: The first is that the self set is very large in size. For example, during the experiments of LISYS [25], a famous application of CVIS based on ARTIS, Hofmeyr and his colleagues collected over 2.3 million self elements in 50 days. The cost for mature detector training is exponentially related to the size of self set [22], making it impossible to directly collect self data from the network for the self tolerance of immature detectors. LISYS has to aim at the detection of 7 kinds of network intrusions, where the services provided by the network, as well as the normal network activities, were simplified in order to decrease the size of self set. After laborious and complicated classification, Hofmeyr finally selected over 3900 elements as self for the tolerance process of the detectors, reducing the training cost for the tolerance of detectors. However, the computation cost is still high.

The second deficiency is that the definitions of self and nonself in the system are described in a static way with almost no changes. However, it is very difficult to use a fixed definition for self and nonself in most practical applications. Furthermore, the roles of self and nonself may exchange at times, e.g., the legal network behaviors today may be dangerous tomorrow, and vice versa. Therefore, it is necessary to update the definitions of self and nonself from time to time. The static description model for self/nonself lacks the adaptability, and thus cannot cater for the network monitoring in the real network environment.

The third, the absence of rigorous quantitative descriptions in most presented CVIS models results in the randomicity of CVIS implementation. Therefore, it is not convenient to put these models into practical applications.

The above three problems have become the major obstacles to CVIS applications. Inspired by biological immune systems, a new immune-based model for computer virus detection is proposed in this paper. Quantitative description of the model is given. A dynamic evolution model for self/nonself description is presented, which reduces the size of self set. Furthermore, an evolutive gene library is introduced to improve the generating efficiency of mature detectors, reducing the system time spending, false-negative and false-positive rates. Experiments show that this model has better time efficiency and detecting ability than the classic model ARTIS.

## 2   Proposed Theoretical Models

Given problem domain $\Omega$, where $\Omega = \{0,1\}^l$, $l$ is a natural number. Antigens[1] $(Ag, Ag \subset \Omega)$ are defined as binary strings composed of program characteristics, and is divided into two set: *Self* and *Nonself*, such that $Self \cup Nonself = Ag$, $Self \cap Nonself = \Phi$, where *Self* is the normal program characteristic set, and *Nonself* is the program characteristic set infected by virus, respectively. The task of a virus detection system is to classify an input pattern $x \in Ag$ as either *Self* or *Nonself*. This detection methodology can generate two types of errors: false-positive error and false-negative error. A false-positive error occurs when a member of *Self* set is incorrectly classified as malicious. Conversely, a false-negative error is the classification of a member of *Nonself* set as benign. Given detector set $B = \{< a, age, count > | a \in \{0,1\}^l \wedge age, count \in Z^+ \wedge age \leq max\_age\}$, where $a$ is antibody, $l$ is the length of antibody $a$, $age$ is the detector age, $count$ is the detector affinity, and $max\_age$ is the upper limit of the detector age. $B$ is divided into immature, mature and memory detectors. Immature detectors are newly generated ones given by $I = \{x | x \in B \wedge x.age < \lambda \wedge x.count = 0\}$, where $\lambda$ is tolerance period. Mature detectors are the ones that are tolerant to *Self* but not activated by antigens, and given by $T = \{x | x \in B \wedge \lambda \leq x.age < max\_age \wedge x.count < \varepsilon \wedge \forall y \in Self \ (f_{match}(x.a, y) = 0)\}$, where the lifecycle of mature detector is from $\lambda$ to $max\_age$, $\varepsilon$ is the activation threshold, $f_{match}$ is the matching function based on the affinity between the detector and an antigen: if the affinity is greater than a specified threshold, then 1 is returned, otherwise, 0 is returned. Memory detectors evolve from mature ones that accumulate enough affinity in their lifecycle, and given by $M = \{x | x \in B \wedge x.age = max\_age \wedge \forall y \in Self \ (f_{match}(x.a, y) = 0)\}$. Given antibody gene library $G = \{0,1\}^{[l/4]}$, where $l$ is the antibody length of detectors.

Fig. 1 illustrates the framework of our proposed model. Antigens $(Ag)$ are binary strings, having the program characteristics in a computer system. This model serves to classify an input set $(Ag)$ into self $(Ag_{Self})$ and nonself $(Ag_{Nonself})$ by mature and memory detectors.

The new immature detectors, which are generated from antibody gene library through some evolutionary strategies (e.g., gene edit, genetic operator, etc.), have to experience a self tolerance period: the detector will be eliminated if it matches any self antigens (negative selection). The immature detectors that survived in self tolerance period will evolve into mature ones, there the mature detectors have a fixed lifecycle: the detectors will be eliminated if they do not accumulate enough affinity in their lifecycle; they will be activated if they get enough affinity, i.e., viruses are found. However, the activated detectors will be eliminated if they do not receive co-stimulation, i.e., false positive error, there the detected antigens are self elements. Meanwhile, the acti-

---

[1] The classification method of antigens used in this paper is the one in the academic immunology, which means antigens are classified into self antigen and nonself antigen, called self and nonself for short.

vated detectors will evolve into memory ones with the help of co-stimulation, there the detected antigens are sure nonself elements. The memory detectors have an infinite lifecycle, and will be activated as soon as they match an antigen.

When a detector (e.g., a memory detector, or a mature one) detects a virus, it will also clone itself and create a lot of similar detectors to protect the system against similar virus infection. In each step, our proposed model will delete the mutated self antigens from *Self* set in time through the dynamic description of self. The tolerance of immature detectors to mutated self antigens is thus prevented. Therefore, the false-negative error rate is reduced. Furthermore, the false-positive error rate is also reduced by adding new self antigens into *Self*. As the self set is dynamically defined, the immune tolerance in our model is also called dynamic tolerance.

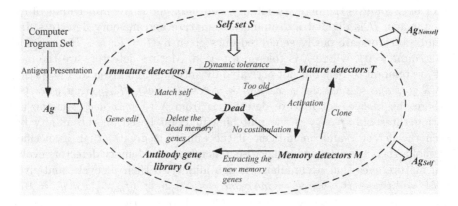

**Fig. 1.** The framework of our proposed model

In the following sections, the self set, antibody gene library, immature detector set, mature detector set, memory detector set, and antigen set, are, respectively, described in a quantitative way of set algebra.

### 2.1   The Evolution of Self

$$S(t) = \begin{cases} S_{first}, & t = 0 \\ f_{s\_lim}((S(t-1) \cup S_{del}(t)) \cup S_{new}(t)), & t > 0 \end{cases} \quad (1)$$

where $S(t), S(t-1) \subset Self$ are, respectively, indicate the self-set at time $t$ and $t$-1. $S_{first}$ is the initial self set. $f_{s\_lim}$ is a function used to limit the number of self set: if the number of self set is larger than a given value $max\_s\_size$, the least resent used self antigen is selected and discarded, and this procedure continues until the size of self set is equal to $max\_s\_size$. $S_{del}(t)$ are the mutated self antigens discarded at time $t$, which includes three parts: 1) the unloaded software; 2) the elements recognized by new memory detectors; 3) the elements infected by viruses. $S_{new}(t)$ are the new self antigens (e.g., loading new software) added into self set at time $t$.

## 2.2   The Evolution of Antibody Gene Library

$$G(t) = \begin{cases} G_{first}, & t = 0 \\ (G(t) - G_{dead}(t)) \cup G_{new}(t), & t > 0 \end{cases} \tag{2}$$

where $G(t), G(t-1) \subset G$ are, respectively, the antibody gene library at time $t$ and $t$-1. $G_{first}$ is the initial gene-library, $G_{dead}(t) = \bigcup_{x \in M_{dead}(t)} \{f_{g\_ext}(x)\}$ are the genes eliminated at time $t$, where $M_{dead}(t)$ are the dead memory detectors which cause false-positive error. $G_{new}(t) = \bigcup_{x \in T_{cloned}(t)} \{f_{g\_ext}(x)\}$ are some excellent genes added into the gene-library at time $t$, where $T_{cloned}(t)$ are the activated mature detectors[2] at time $t$, $f_{g\_ext}(x)(x \in B)$ is a function used to extract genes from a given detector $x$. The antibody gene-library is used to generate immature detectors more efficiently, since the new immature detectors, which are generated from antibody gene library through some evolutionary strategies (e.g., gene edit, genetic operator, etc.), have a higher probability to go through the self-tolerance than those generated randomly.

## 2.3   The Evolution of Immature Detectors

$$I(t) = \begin{cases} \Phi, & t = 0 \\ (f_{age\_crt}(I(t-1)) - (I_{untolerance}(t) \cup I_{matured}(t))) \cup I_{new}(t), & t > 0 \end{cases} \tag{3}$$

$$I_{untolerance}(t) = \{x | x \in f_{age\_crt}(I(t-1)) \wedge \exists y \in S(t-1)(f_{match}(x.a, y) = 1)\} \tag{4}$$

$$I_{matured}(t) = \{x | x \in f_{age\_crt}(I(t-1) - I_{untolerance}(t)) \wedge x.age > \lambda\} \tag{5}$$

Equation (3) simulates the lymphocytes growth in the marrow, where the immature detectors have to pass through the negative selection (see Eq.(4)), and undergo $\lambda(\geq 1)$ tolerance period steps of tolerance to evolve into mature ones. $I(t), I(t-1) \subset I$ are, respectively, the immature detector set at time $t$ and $t$-1. $f_{age\_crt}(I(t-1))$ is to increase the age of each detector in $I(t$-1) by 1. $I_{untolerance}(t)$ are the immature detectors which do not tolerate the self antigens. $I_{matured}(t)$ are the new mature detectors. $I_{new}(t)$ are the newly generated immature detectors. The generation of $I_{new}(t)$ is based on the antibody gene library $G$, where the key step is to generate the antibodies of detectors. The newly generated antibodies of immature detectors are usually composed of two parts: some antibodies are generated randomly, the others are derived from $G$, while the deriving methods include gene edit, genetic algorithm, etc.

---

[2] The viruses detected by mature and memory detectors are, respectively, new viruses and known ones.

## 2.4   The Evolution of Mature Detectors

$$T(t) = \begin{cases} \Phi, & t = 0 \\ (T_{prod}(t) - (T_{dead}(t) \cup T_{cloned}(t))) \cup I_{matured}(t) \cup T_{permutation}(t), & t > 0 \end{cases} \tag{6}$$

$$T_{prod}(t) = f_{age\_crt}(f_{count\_crt}(T(t-1), Ag(t-1))) \tag{7}$$

$$T_{dead}(t) = \{x | x \in T_{prod}(t) \wedge x.age = max\_age \wedge x.count < \varepsilon\} \tag{8}$$

$$T_{cloned}(t) = \{x | x \in (T_{prod}(t) - T_{dead}(t)) \wedge x.count \geq \varepsilon\} \tag{9}$$

$$T_{permutated}(t) = f_{clone\_mutation}(T_{cloned}(t) \cup M_{cloned}(t)) \tag{10}$$

where $T(t), T(t-1) \subset T$ are, respectively, the mature detector set at time $t$ and $t$-1. $T_{prod}(t)$ refers to the detectors evolving into the next generation detectors, there the age and affinity of the detectors are increased. $T_{dead}(t)$ is the set of mature detectors that have not accumulate enough affinity ($\varepsilon > 0$) in their lifecycle or are activated with no co-stimulation at time $t$. $T_{cloned}(t)$ is the set of mature detectors activated by antigens. $T_{matured}(t)$ is the set of newly matured detectors. $T_{permutated}(t)$ is the set of clone detectors generated by the cloning of activated detectors. $f_{count\_crt}(X, Y)(X \subset B, Y \subset Nonself)$ is used to accumulate the affinity of each detector in $X$, where the affinity of detector $x \in X$ is increased by $|\{y | y \in Y \wedge f_{match}(x.a, y) = 1\}|$. $f_{clone\_mutation}(A)(A \subset B)$ is a clone and mutation function, where each element $x \in A$ will clone $\lceil \theta * x.count \rceil$ ($\theta > 0$) new detectors, and, the new clone detectors will undergo a process of mutation, there the mutation operation is to reedit the gene of the detector. $M_{cloned}(t)$ refers to equation (13). The evolution of mature detectors simulates the primary response in BIS, whereas the clone selection mechanism and the gene edit give the proposed model the learning ability.

## 2.5   The Evolution of Memory Detectors

$$M(t) = \begin{cases} M_{first}, & t = 0 \\ (M(t-1) - M_{dead}(t)) \cup f_{age\_set}(T_{cloned}(t)), & t > 0 \end{cases} \tag{11}$$

$$M_{dead}(t) = \{x | x \in M(t-1) \wedge \exists y \in S(t-1) \ f_{match}(x.a, y) = 1\} \tag{12}$$

$$M_{cloned}(t) = \{x | x \in M(t-1) \wedge \exists y \in Ag(t-1) \ f_{match}(x.a, y) = 1\} - M_{dead}(t) \tag{13}$$

where $M(t), M(t-1) \subset M$ are, respectively, the memory detector set at time $t$ and $t$-1. $M_{first}$ is the initial memory detector set. $M_{dead}(t)$ are the memory detectors which recognize self antigens (false-positive error) and need to be eliminated. $f_{age\_set}$ is used to set the age of new memory detectors ($T_{cloned}(t)$) to $max\_age$. $M_{cloned}(t)$ are the activated memory detectors at time $t$.

Similar to BIS, our model has two types of immune response for antigens: the primary response and secondary response, which are, respectively, performed by mature detectors and memory ones. The primary response performed by mature detectors requires a relatively long period of time for learning: firstly, some time is needed to generate suitable immature detectors; secondly, these detectors have to undergo $\lambda$ steps of tolerance period for evolving into mature detectors; thirdly, they will not be activated until they accumulate adequate affinity. Therefore, the primary response has a lower efficiency. During this learning process, those detectors, which play no effective function in classifying antigens, will be killed. However, those superior detectors that have a good effective function in classifying antigens will be reserved and evolve into memory ones. Therefore, similar antigens will be detected quickly when they intrude the system again. The secondary response, issued by memory detectors, is prompt, robust, and needs no learning process, i.e. a memory detector will be activated immediately once it matches with an antigen.

## 2.6 Antigen Detection

$$Ag(t) = \begin{cases} Ag_{first}, & t = 0 \\ (Ag(t-1) - Ag_{checked}(t)) \cup Ag_{new}, & t > 0 \end{cases} \tag{14}$$

$$Ag_{Nonself}(t) = \{x | x \in Ag_{checked}(t) \wedge \exists y \in (T_{cloned}(t) \cup M_{cloned}(t)) \\ (f_{match}(y.a, x) = 1)\} \tag{15}$$

$$Ag_{Self}(t) = \{x | x \in Ag_{checked}(t) \wedge \forall y \in (M(t) \cup T(t))(f_{match}(y.a, x) = 0)\} \tag{16}$$

Where $Ag(t), Ag(t-1) \subset Ag$ are, respectively, the antigen set at time $t$ and $t$-1. $Ag_{new}$ are the new antigens collected at time $t$. $Ag_{first}$ is the initial antigen set. $Ag_{checked}(t)$ are the antigens detected by mature or memory detectors at time $t$, where $Ag_{Nonself}(t)$ and $Ag_{Self}(t)$ are, respectively, detected as self and nonself antigens.

# 3  Performance Analysis

Suppose the program number in a computer system is $N_p$, the average proportion of nonself antigens in the system is $\rho_N(0 < \rho_N < 1)$, the size of self set is $|S|$, the size of mature detector set is $|T|$, the size of memory detector set is $|M|$, the active threshold is $\varepsilon$ , the probability of a detector matching an antigen is $P_m$, and $P(A)$ is the probability of event $A$.

**Theorem 1.** *Given $P_n$ the probability that a detector matching a self antigen which is not listed in the self definition, such that $P_n = (1 - P_m)^{|S|} \bullet [1 - (1 - P_m)^{\lceil N_p \bullet (1-\rho_N)\rceil - |S|}]$ .*

*Proof.* Suppose $A$ is the event that a detector does not match any self antigen, $B$ is the event that a detector matches at least one self antigen which is not listed in the self definition. From (3), (4), and (5), we have $P_n = P(AB)$. As events $A$ and $B$ are independent each other, so $P(AB) = P(A)P(B)$. Suppose $X$ is the number of a detector matching an antigen in event $A$, from [30] we have $X \sim b(n, p)$, where $n = |S|, p = P_m$. Therefore, $P(A) = P(X = 0) = (P_m)^0(1 - P_m)^{|S|} = (1 - P_m)^{|S|}$. Furthermore, suppose $Y$ is the number of a detector matching an antigen in event $B$, $Y \sim b(n,p)$, where $n = N_p(1 - \rho_n) - |S|, \rho = P_m$. Then, $P(B) = 1 - P(Y = 0) = 1 - (1 - P_m)^{\lceil N_p \bullet (1-\rho_N) \rceil - |S|}$ , so $P_n = (1 - P_m)^{|S|} \bullet [1 - (1 - P_m)^{\lceil N_p \bullet (1-\rho_N) \rceil - |S|}]$. □

**Theorem 2.** *Given a randomly selected nonself antigen $x$, the probability of which is correctly recognized is $P_r = 1 \quad (1 - P_m)^{[|M|+|T|(1/\varepsilon)](1-P_n)} \approx 1 - e^{-P_m[|M|+|T|(1/\varepsilon)](1-P_n)}$.*

*Proof.* Suppose $A$ is the event that $x$ matches the detectors, including memory detectors and mature ones. From (15), we have $P_r = P(A)$. Let $X$ be the number of a detector matching an antigen in event $A$, from [30] we have $X \sim b(n,p)$, where $n$ is number of the really used detectors for detecting the nonself antigens. Suppose the stimulate level of mature detectors is between 0 and $\varepsilon - 1$ [12], then the number of really used mature detectors is $|T|/\varepsilon$. As the detectors which recognize self antigens are not considered, so the total number of the really used detectors for detecting the nonself antigens is $n = (|M| + |T|/\varepsilon)(1 - P_n)$, where $P_n$ is shown in Theorem 1, and $p = P_m$. Therefore, $P_r = P(A) = 1 - P(X = 0) = 1 - (1 - P_m)^{[|M|+|T|(1/\varepsilon)](1-P_n)}$. According to Poisson theorem [30], $P_r \approx 1 - e^{-P_m(|M|+|T|(1/\varepsilon))(1-P_n)}$ , when $P_m$ is very small and $(|M| + |T|/\varepsilon)(1 - P_n)$ is very big. □

**Theorem 3.** *Given a randomly selected nonself antigen $x$, the probability of which is classified as a self antigen by mistake $P_{neg} = (1 - P_m)^{(|M|+|T|)(1-P_n)} \approx e^{-P_m(|M|+|T|)(1-P_n)}$ . Given a randomly selected self antigen $y$, the probability of which is classified as a nonself antigen by mistake $P_{pos} = 1 - (1 - P_m)^{(|M|+|T|(1/\varepsilon))P_n} \approx 1 - e^{-P_m(|M|+|T|(1/\varepsilon))P_n}$.*

*Proof.* Suppose $A$ is the event that $x$ does match any memory and mature detectors, $B$ is event that $y$ matches the memory detectors or mature ones. From (15) and (16), $P_{neg} = P(A), P_{pos} = P(B)$. Let $X$ be the number of a detector matching a nonself antigen in event $A$, from [30] we have $X \sim b(n,p)$, where $n = (|M| + |T|)(1 - P_n)$ is number of detectors which recognize nonself antigens, and $p = P_m$. Then, $P_{neg} = P(A) = P(X = 0) = (1 - P_m)^{(|M|+|T|)(1-P_n)}$ . According to Poisson Theorem [30], $P_{neg} \approx e^{-P_m(|M|+|T|)(1-P_n)}$, when $P_m$ is very small and $(|M| + |T|)(1 - P_n)$ is very big. Furthermore, suppose $Y$ is the number of a detector matching a self antigen in event $B$, where $Y \sim b(n,p), n = (|M|+|T|/\varepsilon)P_n$ is the number of detectors which recognize self antigens, $p = P_m$. From the same way of $P_{neg}$, we have $P_{pos} = 1 - (1 - P_m)^{(|M|+|T|(1/\varepsilon))P_n} \approx 1 - e^{-P_m(|M|+|T|(1/\varepsilon))P_n}$. □

**Theorem 4.** *The number of self set is less than a constant, and the description of self is macroscopically complete.*

*Proof.* From equation (1), we have that the number of self set is always less than a constant $max\_s\_size$. Although a few of self elements are collected by the dynamic model for self description (i.e., section 2.1) in each step, however, $\bigcup_{t=0}^{\infty} S(t)$ will cover the whole self space as time goes on. In other words, we have that the description of self is macroscopically complete. □

## 4    Simulations and Experimental Results

A fixed length binary string ($l$=128) is used as the pattern characteristics of software. IBM lab shows that the characteristic code with 128bit long is enough [19], furthermore, the 128bit long characteristic code is become an industry standard [22]. The length of antibody is also 128bit. The self set is defined as 200 important system files. The experiment aims at the detection of 100 computer viruses, and the antigen set is formed by 200 self files and 200 files infected by experimental viruses. In the experiments, the parameter $\lambda$ and $max\_age$ are, respectively, set to 5 and 15. And the matching function is defined by

$$f_{match}(x, y) = \begin{cases} 1, f_{h\_dis}(x, y)/min(l_x, l_y) \geq \beta \\ 0, otherwise \end{cases} \tag{17}$$

where $\beta > 0$ is threshold, $f_{h\_dis}(x, y)$ is the Hamming distance [15] and given by

$$f_{h\_dis}(x, y) = \sum_{i=1}^{l} \delta_i \tag{18}$$

where $\delta_i = \begin{cases} 1, & y_i = x_i \\ 0, & otherwise \end{cases}, 1 \leq i \leq l.$

Fig.2 and Fig.3 show how parameter $\beta$ affects the performance of the model, where $|M| = 50, |S| = 100$. The results show that the smaller the $\beta$, the stronger the recognition ability of the model, and the lower the false-negative rate, however, the higher the false-positive rate. The results fit to Theorem 2 and 3.

The false-negative rate is mainly caused by the size of initial memory detector-set (please refer to Fig.4). Although the $\beta$ increasing will result in the increasing of false-negative rate, however, it will not exceed 50%. According to Fig.2 and Fig.3, we set $\beta$=0.8.

Fig.4 and Fig.5 show how parameter $|M|$ affects the performance of the model, where $\beta = 0.8, |S| = 100$. The false-negative rate of the model is nearly 100% when $|M|$ equals 0, and the recognition ability of the model is weak. However, with the increasing of the size of memory detector-set, the recognition ability is

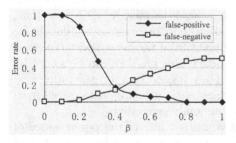

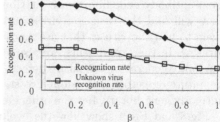

**Fig. 2.** The effect of matching threshold $\beta$ to the error rate

**Fig. 3.** The effect of matching threshold $\beta$ to the recognition ability

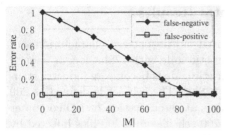
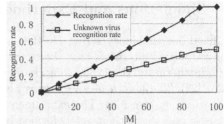

**Fig. 4.** The effect of the memory detector size to the error rate

**Fig. 5.** The effect of the memory detector size to the recognition ability

improved rapidly. When $|M|$ equals to 90, the model can recognize almost all 200 computer viruses (100 original viruses, 100 are their variations). The model can detect almost all the variation viruses and new viruses (10% of all viruses). This indicates that this model has a strong ability of self-learning. It also indicates that the detection ability will be improved while increasing the size of memory detector-set.

To test the performance of our model, the corresponding comparison experiments were undertaken, with ARTIS [17, 18], proposed by Hofmeyr and Forrest et al, selected as the opponent. ARTIS is a typical model in traditional CVIS, which has significant impact on the design of CVIS.

Fig.6 shows the situation that the number of the needed immature detectors for generating a fixed number (here is 20) of the mature detectors, where $\beta = 0.8, |M| = 50$. The result shows that our proposed model has a higher efficiency than ARTIS. The number of candidate immature detectors is exponentially related to the size of self-set in ARTIS, however, it is linear in our model. This indicates that the time needed in self tolerance is much reduced when the candidate immature detectors are generated through the antibody gene-library.

Fig.7 shows how the size of memory detector-set affects the performance for both ARTIS and our model, where $\beta = 0.8, |S| = 100$. The result shows that our model is better than ARTIS. Since the antibody genes are extracted from memory detectors, thus, the larger the memory detector-set, the more excellent genes, therefore, better candidate immature detectors can be generated from antibody gene library. In the experiments, we found that the mature detectors generated from antibody gene library are distributed around the memory detectors, thus, they will find the variation viruses or similar ones, however, it is difficult for them to find the viruses that are much different from the known ones (i.e., new viruses). In the experiments, we also found that this problem can be solved by randomly generating immature detectors. Thus, a good idea for generating new immature detectors is to adopt two strategies: some detectors are derived from antibody gene library, but the others are randomly generated.

Fig.8 and Fig.9 show how the evolutive self-set affects the performance of ARTIS and our proposed model, where some viruses are put into self-set, and $\beta = 0.8, |M| = 50$. In the experiments we found that: 1) the size of self-set will little affect the false-positive rate; 2) the size of memory detector set will affect

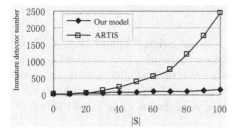

**Fig. 6.** The comparison experiment for the mature detector generating efficiency of ARTIS and our model

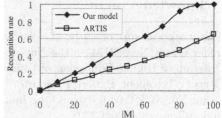

**Fig. 7.** The comparison experiment for the recognition ability of ARTIS and our model

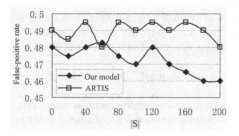

**Fig. 8.** The comparison experiment for the false positive rate of ARTIS and our model under different size of self set

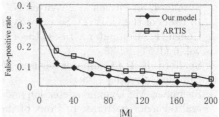

**Fig. 9.** The comparison experiment for the false positive rate of ARTIS and our model under different size of memory detector set

the false-positive rate, the reason is that the description of self is not completed; 3) the evolutive self-set can effectively reduce the false-positive rate, the reason is that the nonself elements in self-set will be eliminated by the evolutive self model through the feedback ability of memory detectors and the costimulation from a outside system. The experimental results show that our proposed model has a lower false-positive rate than ARTIS.

## 5   Conclusion

The previous models or methods, such as ARTIS, lack the ability of self-adaptation, have a higher false-positive and false-negative rate, therefore, have limited applications. In this paper, a quantitatively depiction for dynamic evolutions of *self-set, antibody gene-library, immature detector-set, mature detector-set* and *memory detector-set* are presented. Then, an immune-based dynamic model for computer virus is thus built. This model can efficiently reduce both the false-positive rate and false-negative rate, and enhance the ability of self-adaptation and diversity.

## Acknowledgement

This work was supported by the National Natural Science Foundation of China under Grant No.60373110, the National Research Foundation for the Doctoral Program of Higher Education of China under Grant No.20030610003, the New Century Excellent Expert Program of Ministry of Education of China under Grant No. NCET-04-0870, and the Innovation Foundation of Sichuan University under Grant No.2004CF10.

## References

1. F-Secure Corporation's Data Security Summary for 2004. F-Secure Corporation. Available: http://www.f-secure.com/2004/. April 2005
2. Staniford, S., Paxson, V., Weaver, N.: How to own the internet in your spare time. In Proc. of the USENIX Security Symposium, San Francisco Marriott (2002)
3. Cohen, F.: Computer viruses: theory and experiments. Computers and Security, vol. 6 (1987) 22-35
4. Spafford, E. H.: Computer Viruses—A Form of Artificial Life? Technical Report, Purdue University (1994)
5. Swimmer, M.: Dynamic detection and classification of computer viruses using general behavior patterns. In Proc. of the Fifth International Virus Bulletin Conference, Boston (1995)
6. Albert, R., Jeong, H., Barabasi, A. L.: Diameter of the world wide web. Nature, vol. 401 (1999) 130-131
7. Lloyd, A. L., May, R. M.: How viruses spread among computers and people. Science, vol. 292 (2002) 1316-1317
8. Newman, M. E. J., Forrest, S., Balthrop, J.: Email networks and the spread of computer viruses. Phys. Rev. E, vol. 66(035101) (2002)
9. Albert, R., Jeong, H., Barabasi, A. L.: Attack and error tolerance of complex networks. Nature, vol. 406 (2002) 378-382
10. Callaway, D. S., Newman, M. E. J., Strogatz, S. H., Watts, D. J.: Network robustness and fragility: percolation on random graphs. Phys. Rev. Lett., vol. 85 (2002) 5468-5471
11. Balthrop, J., Forrest, S., Newman, M. E. J., Williamson, M. M.: Technological networks and the spread of computer viruses. Science, vol. 304 (2004) 527-529
12. Perelson, A. S., Weisbuch, G.: Immunology for physicists. Review of Modern Physics, vol. 69(4) (1997) 1219-1263
13. De Castro, L. N, Timmis, J. I.: Artificial immune systems as a novel soft computing paradigm. Soft Computing journal, vol. 7(8) (2003) 526-544
14. Li, T.: An Introduction to Computer Network Security. Publishing House of Electronics Industry, Beijing (2004)
15. Li, T.: Computer Immunology. Publishing House of Electronics Industry, Beijing (2004)
16. Forrest, S., Perelson, A. S.: Self-nonself discrimination in a computer. in Proc. of IEEE Symposium on Security and Privacy, Oakland (1994) 202-213
17. Hofmeyr, S.: An Immunological Model of Distributed Detection and its Application to Computer Security. Ph.D. dissertation, Univ. New Mexico (1999)
18. Hofmeyr, S., Forrest, S.: Architecture for an artificial immune system. Evolutionary Computation, vol. 8(4) (2000) 443-473

19. Kephart, J. O., Arnold, W. C.: Automatic extraction of computer virus signatures. In Proc. of the Fourth International Virus Bulletin Conference, St. Helier, Jersey, UK (1994)

20. Kephart, J. O., Sorkin, G. B., Swimmer, M., White, S. R.: Blueprint for a computer immune system. In Proc. of the 1997 International Virus Bulletin Conference, San Francisco, California (1997)

21. Okamoto, T., Ishida, Y.: A distributed approach against computer viruses inspired by the immune system. IEICE Trans. on Communication, E83-B(5) (2000) 908-915

22. Harmer, P. K., Williams, P. D., Gunsch, G. H., Lamont, G. B.: An artificial immune system architecture for computer security applications. IEEE Transactions on Evolutionary Computation, vol. 6(3) (2002) 252-280

23. Rabiner, L.: A tutorial on Hidden Markov Models and selected applications in speech recognition. In Proc. of the IEEE, 77(2) (1989) 257-286

24. Jensen, R. S.: Immune system for virus detection and elimination. Master's Thesis, Technical University of Denmark, DTU (2002)

25. LISYS. Available: http://www.cs.unm.edu/ forrest/software/lisys/, April 2005

26. Li, T.: An immunity based network security risk estimation. Science in China Ser. F Information Sciences, vol. 48(5) (2005) 798-816

27. Li, T.: An immune based dynamic intrusion detection model. Chinese Science Bulletin, vol. 50(17) (2005)

28. Li, T.: A new model of immune-based network surveillance and dynamic computer forensics. Lecture Notices in Computer Science, vol. 3611 (2005) 799-808

29. Xu, C., Li, T.: A weather forecast system based on artificial immune system. Lecture Notices in Computer Science, vol. 3611 (2005) 795-798

30. Shen, J., Xie, S.: Probability and Statistics. Higher Education Press, Beijing (1989)

# A New Model for Dynamic Intrusion Detection

Tao Li[1], Xiaojie Liu[1], and Hongbin Li[2]

[1] Department of Computer Science,
Sichuan University, Chengdu 610065, China
litao@scu.edu.cn
[2] Department of Electrical and Computer Engineering,
Stevens Institute of Technology,Hoboken, NJ07030, USA
hli@stevens.edu

**Abstract.** Building on the concepts and the formal definitions of self, nonself, antigen, and detector introduced in the research of network intrusion detection, the dynamic evolution models and the corresponding recursive equations of self, antigen, immune-tolerance, lifecycle of mature detectors, and immune memory are presented. Following that, an immune-based model, referred to as AIBM, for dynamic intrusion detection is developed. Simulation results show that the proposed model has several desirable features including self-learning, self-adaption and diversity, thus providing a effective solution for network intrusion detection.

## 1 Introduction

The problems found in a computer security system [1] are quite similar to those encountered in a Biological Immune System (BIS) [2]. Both systems have to keep stability in a changing environment. Due to numerous desirable characteristics, such as diversity, self-tolerance, immune-memory, distributed and parallel management, self-organization, self-learning, self-adaptation, and robustness, BIS has attracted many researchers' attentions in recent years [3-5]. With the concepts of immunology introduced into many research fields, exciting results have been obtained, especially in the research of network intrusion detection system (NIDS) [2-22].

The negative selection algorithm [8], proposed by Forrest et al. in 1994, has greatly promoted the research of computer immune system (CIS). Hofmeyr and Forrest proposed a general framework for CIS, called ARTIS [9-11], where the concepts and mechanisms of BIS, including self, nonself, self tolerance, immune cell (detectors), memory cell (memory detectors), and costimulation were well simulated. The CISs are mainly derived from ARTIS [2]. For example, Dasgupta and Harmer built an agent-based CIS framework [12-13] upon ARTIS to monitor the network activities.

However, there are two major defects in the present CISs: One is that the self set is very large in size. As the cost for mature detector training is exponentially related to the size of self set [14], the efficiency of the traditional CIS models is very low.

Y.G. Desmedt et al. (Eds.): CANS 2005, LNCS 3810, pp. 72–84, 2005.

The other deficiency is that the definitions of self (normal network behaviors) and nonself (abnormal network behaviors) allow little change after they have been defined in many immune-based models or methods for NIDS [3-14]. In fact, it is very difficult to use fixed definition for self and nonself in most practical applications, since the roles of self and nonself may exchange at times (e.g., the legal network behaviors today may be dangerous tomorrow). Therefore, it is necessary to update the definitions of self and nonself from time to time. The dynamic clonal selection algorithm (DynamiCS) [15] attempted to solve this problem. In DynamiCS, the self elements used in the self tolerance for immature detectors are the survived antigens (those antigens are taken as self elements since they passed the detection) in each detection step, reducing the training cost of the immature detectors. However, as the whole self set in the system is roughly replaced by the survived antigens in each step, too much useful self information is lost, resulting in a high error rate, then, having limited applications.

In addition, the absence of rigorous quantitative descriptions in most presented CIS models results in the randomicity of CIS implementation; therefore, it is not convenient to put these models into practical applications. In this paper, we first present the dynamic evolution models and the corresponding recursive equations of self, antigen, immune-tolerance, lifecycle of mature detectors, and immune memory. Then, we develop a new immune-based model, which is called AIBM, for dynamic intrusion detection. Similar to DynamiCS, AIBM uses a very small dynamic self set during the self tolerance for immature detectors, resulting in a high efficiency in generating new mature detectors. However, different from DynamiCS, the definition of self and nonself in AIBM is dynamic. As time goes on, AIBM can add new self elements into, or eliminate the mutated ones from the self set, resulting in the dynamic evolution of self set, mature and memory detectors, having a lower error rate than traditional CIS models. Our experimental results show that AIBM is an effective solution for network intrusion detection.

The rest of the paper is organized as follows. In Section 2, we establish an immune-based mathematical model for dynamic intrusion detection. In Section 3, simulations and experimental results are provided. Finally, Sections 4 contains our summary and conclusions.

## 2   Proposed Theoretical Models

Antigens ($Ag, Ag \subset D, D = \{0,1\}^l$ ) in our approach are fixed-length binary strings extracted from the Internet Protocol (IP) packets transferred in the network. An antigen consists of the source and destination IP addresses, port number, protocol type, IP flags, IP overall packet length, TCP/UDP/ICMP fields, etc., having the characteristics of network activity. And the process of extracting the features of an IP packet to form an antigen is also called the antigen presentation. The structure of an antibody is the same as that of an antigen. Nonself patterns (*Nonself*) represent IP packets from a computer network attack, while self patterns (*Self*) are normal sanctioned network service transactions and nonmalicious background clutter, such that $Self \cup Nonself = Ag$

and $Self \cap Nonself = \Phi$ . Given the waiting detection antigen set $sAg \subset Ag$, where $|sAg| = \eta * |Ag|, 0 < \eta < 1$(detective coefficient, see section 2.2 "Dynamic Evolution Model of Antigen". Let $B$ denote the set of intrusion detectors given by $B = \{< d, age, count > | d \in D \wedge age \in N \wedge count \in N\}$ , where $d$ is the antibody (antibody gene), $age$ is the age of antibody $d$, $count$ (affinity) is the number of antigens matched by antibody $d$, and $N$ is the set of natural numbers. $B$ contains two subsets: mature detector ($T_b$) and memory detector ($M_b$), such that $B = M_b \cup T_b$, $M_b \cap T_b = \Phi$. A mature detector is a detector that is tolerant to self but not activated by antigens. A memory detector evolves from a mature detector matched enough antigens in its lifecycle. Therefore, $T_b = \{x | x \in B, \forall y \in Self(< x.d, y > \notin Match \wedge x.count < \beta)\}$, and $M_b = \{x | x \in B, \forall y \in Self(< x.d, y > \notin Match \wedge x.count \geq \beta)\}$, where $\beta(> 0)$ represents the activation threshold, $Match = \{< x, y > | x, y \in D \wedge f_{r\_con}(x, y) = 1\}$, and $f_{r\_con}(x, y)$ is a *r-contiguous bits* matching function given by $f_{r\_con}(x, y) = \begin{cases} 1 & \exists i, j, j-i \geq r, 0 < i < j \leq l, x_i = y_i, x_{i+1} = y_{i+1}, ..., x_j = y_j \\ 0 & otherwise \end{cases}$ . Let $I_b$ denote the set of immature detectors given by $I_b = \{< d, age > | d \in D, age \in N\}$ , which is used to generating mature detectors.

Basically, the mature detectors try to learn to find new intrusions, corresponding to the primary response in BIS. During this learning process, those detectors that play no effective function in classifying network activities, will be killed. However, those superior detectors that have good effective function in detecting network attacks will be reserved and evolve into memory ones. Therefore, similar attacks will be detected quickly by the memory detectors when they intrude the system again, corresponding to the secondary response in BIS.

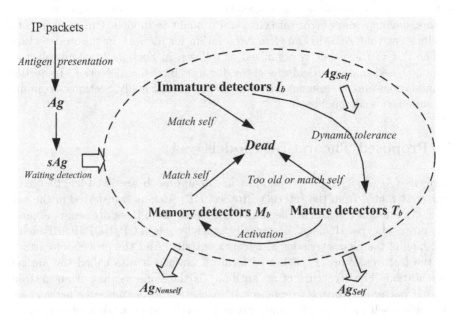

**Fig. 1.** The framework of our proposed model.

Fig. 1 illustrates the framework of *AIBM*, where the new immature detectors have to experience a self tolerance period: the detectors will be eliminated if it matches any self antigens (negative selection). The immature detectors that survived in self tolerance period will evolve into mature ones, there the mature detectors have a fixed lifecycle: the detectors will be eliminated if they do not match enough antigens or match self elements in their lifecycle; they will be activated if they get enough antigens. However, the activated detectors will be eliminated if they do not receive costimulation, i.e. false positive error, there the detected antigens are self elements. Meanwhile, the activated detectors will evolve into memory ones with the help of costimulation, there the detected antigens are sure nonself elements. The memory detectors have an infinite lifecycle, and will be activated as soon as they match an antigen.

*AIBM* serves to classify an input set $(Ag)$ into self $(Ag_{Self})$ and nonself $(Ag_{Nonself})$ by $B$ within $\delta$ steps. In each step, a fixed amount of antigens are selected from $Ag$ to form $sAg$ for detection. The antigens classified into $Ag_{Self}$ are used as self elements for the self tolerance of immature detectors. Since the $Ag_{Self}$ is dynamic, so does the self tolerance, thus, two detectors may exist in the system simultaneously: one is tolerant of a certain self element, but the other is not. This problem is solved by costimulation.

As time goes on, the model can add new self elements into, or eliminate the mutated ones from the self set, resulting in the dynamic evolution of self set, mature and memory detectors.

In the following sections (Sections 2.1~2.5), the self set *Self*, antigen set *Ag*, immature detector set $I_b$, mature detector set $T_b$, and memory detector set $M_b$ in Fig. 1 are, respectively, described in a quantitative way of set algebra.

## 2.1   Dynamic Evolution Model of Self

In a real-network environment, due to the existence of security bugs (e.g., back door), some network activities, which were regarded as normal behaviors before, are forbidden after the bugs are fixed. Meanwhile, the network administrator may open additional ports to provide more services (e.g., port 80 is opened to provide WWW services now), and, as a result, some network activities, which were forbidden before, are permitted now. Therefore, a dynamic model for the normal network activities $(Self)$ is needed to depict the variation of *Self*.

$$Self(t) = \begin{cases} \{x_1, x_2, ..., x_n\} & t = 0 \\ Self(t-1) - Self_{variation}(t) \cup Self_{new}(t) & t \geq 1 \end{cases} \quad (1)$$

where

$$Self_{variation}(t) = \{x | x \in Self(t-1), \exists y \in B(t-1) \\ (f_{check}(y, x) = 2 \wedge f_{costimulation}(x) = 0)\} \quad (2)$$

$$Self_{new}(t) = \{ y | \ y \text{ is the new self element collected at time } t\} \quad (3)$$

$$f_{check}(y, x) = \begin{cases} 2 & f_{r\_con}(y, x) = 1 \wedge x \in Self(t-1) \\ 1 & f_{r\_con}(y, x) = 1 \wedge x \notin Self(t-1) \\ 0 & otherwise \end{cases} \quad (4)$$

$$f_{costimulation}(x) = \begin{cases} 1 & x \text{ is a self antigen confirmed by an external signal.} \\ 0 & otherwise \end{cases}$$

(5)

$$B(t) = M_b(t) \cup T_b(t), t \geq 0 \tag{6}$$

Equation (1) depicts the dynamic evolution of self, where $x_i \in D(i > 1, i \in N)$ is the initial self element defined by the security administrator, $Self_{new}$ is the set of newly defined self elements at time $t$, and $Self_{variation}$ is the set of mutated self elements representing current abnormal behaviors. $f_{check}(y, x)(y \in B, x \in Ag)$ is used to classify antigens as either self or nonself: if $x$ is matched and does not belong to $Self(t-1)$, then $x$ is sure a nonself antigen, and 1 is returned; if $x$ is matched and belongs to $Self(t-1)$, then $x$ may be a nonself antigen (needs co-stimulation), and 2 is returned; however, if $x$ is not matched, then $x$ is sure a self antigen, and 0 is returned. $f_{costimulation}(x)(x \in Ag)$ simulates the co-stimulation in a biological immune system and indicates whether $x$ is a self antigen by an external signal. The external signal is usually a response from the network-security administrator.

There are two crucial points in this model. 1) *Self immune surveillance*: The model will delete the mutated self antigens ($Self_{variation}$) in time through self immune surveillance. The tolerance of immature detectors to mutated self antigens ($Self_{variation}$) is thus prevented. Therefore, the false-negative error, where an abnormal network activity is detected as a normal network activity, is reduced. 2) *The dynamic growth of Self*: The model can extend the depiction scope of self through adding new self antigens ($Self_{new}$) into *Self*. Therefore, the false-positive error, where a normal network activity is detected as an abnormal network activity, is prevented.

## 2.2 Dynamic Evolution Model of Antigen

$$Ag(t) = \begin{cases} Self(0) & t = 0 \\ Ag(t-1) - Ag_{Nonself}(t) & t > 0, t \bmod \delta \neq 0 \\ Ag_{new}(t) & t > 0, t \bmod \delta = 0 \end{cases}$$

(7)

where

$$sAg(t) \subset Ag(t), |sAg(t)| = \eta * |Ag(t)|, t \geq 0 \tag{8}$$

$$Ag_{Nonself}(t) = \{x | x \in sAg(t-1), \exists y \in B(t-1) \\ ((f_{check}(y, x) = 2 \wedge f_{costimulation}(x) = 0) \\ \vee f_{check}(y, x) = 1)\}$$

(9)

$$Ag_{Self}(t) = \begin{cases} Ag(t) & t = 0, t \bmod \delta \neq 0 \\ Ag(t-1) & t > 0, t \bmod \delta = 0 \end{cases} \tag{10}$$

where $sAg$ is selected from $Ag$ randomly in the proportion of $\eta$(detective coefficient, $0 < \eta \leq 1$). $Ag_{Nonself}$ is the set of nonself antigens detected by detectors at time $t$, where $Ag(0) = Self(0)$ indicates that at this time the model is try to do the job of self tolerance for the newly generated immature detectors and produce new mature detectors (see Section 2.3 "Dynamic Immune Tolerance"). $\delta$ is called antigen update period, indicating that $Ag$ is replaced by the new antigen set $(Ag_{new})$ every $\delta$ steps. In each antigen update period, the detected nonself antigens are deleted from $Ag$, then, the remaining antigens in $Ag$ are classified into self elements $(Ag_{Self})$.

## 2.3   Dynamic Immune Tolerance

$$
I_b(t) = \begin{cases} \{x_1, x_2, ..., x_\xi\} & t = 0 \\ I_{tolerance}(t) - I_{maturation}(t) \cup I_{new}(t) & t \geq 1 \end{cases} \tag{11}
$$

where

$$
\begin{aligned}
I_{tolerance}(t) = \{y | y.d = x.d, y.age = x.age + 1, \\
x \in (I_b(t-1) - \{x | x \in I_b(t-1), \\
\exists y \in Ag_{Self}(t-1) f_{r\_con}(x, y) = 1\})\}
\end{aligned} \tag{12}
$$

$$
I_{maturatiion}(t) = \{x | x \in I_{tolerance}(t), x.age > \alpha\} \tag{13}
$$

$$
I_{new}(t) = \{y_1, y_2, ..., y_\xi\} \tag{14}
$$

Equation (11) simulates the lympholcytes growth in the marrow, where $x_i =< d, 0 > (d \in D, 1 \leq i \leq \xi)$ is the initial immature detector generated randomly. $I_{tolerance}$ is the set of surviving immature detectors in $I_b(t-1)$ after one step of tolerance process. Immature detectors need undergo $\alpha(\geq 1$, tolerance period) steps of tolerance processes and then evolve into mature detectors. $I_{maturation}$ is the set of immature detectors which have undergone $\alpha$ steps of tolerance processes at time $t$. $I_{new}$ is the set of new immature detectors generated randomly at time $t$.

Since the number of $Ag_{Self}$ is small, therefore, the model will generate mature detectors efficiently. Meanwhile, the randomicity of $I_{new}$ makes the new mature detectors having more diversity. Furthermore, as $Ag_{Self}$ is changed time after time, thus the corresponding immune tolerance is dynamic: if a self antigen does not occur in a period of time, the newly generated mature detectors may not tolerant to it any more. Thus, two different detectors may exist in the system: one is tolerant to a certain antigen, but the other is not. Competition between these detectors is arbitrated by the external system (co-stimulation, see Equation (5)). However, if a self antigen occurs frequently, the newly generated detectors will always tolerate to it.

Dynamic immune tolerance simulates the situation of the real network environment very well: The network activities, which often occurs, have a higher possibility to be the legal ones, however, the activity, which suddenly occurs, has a higher possibility to be an intrusion.

## 2.4   Mature-Detector Lifecycle

$$
T_b(t) = \begin{cases} \phi & t = 0 \\ T_b'(t) \cup T_{new}(t) - T_{memory}(t) - T_{dead}(t) & t \geq 1 \end{cases} \tag{15}
$$

where

$$T_b'(t) = T_b''(t) - P(t) \cup T_{clone}(t) \tag{16}$$

$$T_b''(t) = \{y|y.d = x.d, y.age = x.age + 1, \\ y.count = x.count, x \in T_b(t-1)\} \tag{17}$$

$$P(t) = \{x|x \in T_b''(t), \exists y \in sAg(t-1)(f_{check}(x,y) = 1 \\ \vee(f_{check}(x,y) = 2 \wedge f_{costimulation}(y) = 0))\} \tag{18}$$

$$T_{clone}(t) = \{y|y.d = x.d, y.age = x.age, \\ y.count = x.count + 1, x \in P(t)\} \tag{19}$$

$$T_{new}(t) = \{y|y.d = x.d, y.age = 0, y.count = 0, x \in I_{maturation}(t)\} \tag{20}$$

$$T_{memory}(t) = \{x|x \in T_b'(t), x.count \geq \beta\} \tag{21}$$

$$T_{dead}(t) = \{x|x \in T_b'(t) \wedge (x.age > \lambda \wedge x.count < \beta)\} \\ \cup\{x|x \in T_b''(t) \wedge \exists y \in Ag(t-1) \\ f_{check}(x,y) = 2 \wedge f_{costimulation}(y) = 1\} \tag{22}$$

Equation (15) depicts the lifecycle of the mature detectors. All mature detectors have a fixed lifecycle ($\lambda$). If a mature detector matches enough antigens($\geq \beta$) in its lifecycle, it will evolve to a memory one ($T_{memory}$). However, the detectors will be killed and replaced by newly generated mature detectors ($T_{new}$) if they do not match enough antigens in their lifecycle. $T_{dead}$ is the set of detectors that haven't match enough antigens ($\leq \beta$) in lifecycle $\lambda$ or classified self antigens as nonself (i.e., false-positive error) at time $t$. $T_b'$ simulates that the mature detectors undergo one step of evolution. $T_b''$ indicates that the mature detectors are getting older. $P$ depicts the set of mature detectors whose antibodies match nonself antigens. $T_{clone}$ depicts the clone process of mature detectors, which is simplified by just adding matching count by 1.

In the mature-detector lifecycle, the inefficient detectors on classifying antigens are killed through the process of clone selection. However, the efficient detectors on classifying antigens will evolve to memory detectors. Therefore, similar antigens representing abnormal network behaviors can be detected quickly when they intrude the system again.

## 2.5   Dynamic Model of Immune Memory

$$M_b(t) = \begin{cases} \phi & t = 0 \\ M_b(t-1) - M_{dead}(t) \cup T_{memory}(t) & t \geq 1 \end{cases} \tag{23}$$

where

$$M_{dead}(t) = \{x|x \in M_b(t-1), \exists y \in Ag(t-1) \\ (f_{check}(x,y,t) = 2 \wedge f_{costimulation}(y) = 1)\} \tag{24}$$

Equation (23) depicts the dynamic evolution of $M_b$, where $T_{memory}$ is the set of newly generated memory detectors. A memory detector will be deleted if it matches a known self antigen ($M_{dead}$, i.e., false-positive error).

The dynamic model of immune memory, as well as the 4 dynamic models (Section 2.1~2.4) discussed above, reduce both the false positive error rate and false negative error rate in contrast to the traditional NIDS techniques, and have enhanced the ability of self-adaptation for the system.

## 3   Simulations and Experimental Results

The experiment was carried out in the Laboratory of Computer Network and Information Security at Sichuan University. A total of 40 computers in a network were under surveillance. An antigen was defined as a fixed length binary string ($l$=256) composed of the source/destination IP address, port number, protocol type, IP flags, IP overall packet length, TCP/UDP/ICMP fields, and etc. The task aimed to detect network attacks. The r-contiguous bits matching rule was used to compute the affinity between antigens and antibodies ($r$=8) [8]. The size of initial self set $n$ is randomly set to 40, and the number of newly generated immature detectors $\xi$ =10 [20]. 100 IP packets were captured from network each time, and, they were transformed into antigen format to be processed by the detection system. The detective coefficient $\eta$ was randomly set to 0.8. The network was attacked by 20 kinds of attacks, such as Syn Flood, Land, Smurf, Teardrop, ..., etc. The proportion between self and nonself packets was 9:1, i.e. there was one nonself packet among 10 packets. The experimental results were evaluated by TP rate (the true positive rate, the nonself detection probability) and FP rate (the false positive rate, the probability of the self antigens being detected by mistake).

Fig.2 illustrates the effect of the activation threshold $\beta$, where $\alpha = 50, \lambda = 40, \delta = 50$. If $\beta$ is small, TP rises rapidly, and so does FP. However, both TP and FP decrease while $\beta$ increases. This is because $\beta$ determines the amount of

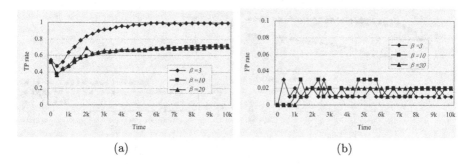

(a)                                        (b)

**Fig. 2.** The effect of activation threshold $\beta$, (a) TP rate. (b) FP rate.

memory detectors. In the antigen space, since only 80% antigens (the detective coefficient $\eta$ =0.8) are selected for detection in each step, mature detectors will evolve into memory ones after detecting a few of antigens if $\beta$ is very small. This makes the system to generate lots of memory detectors whose antibodies distribute widely in the antigen space. Therefore, a high TP is obtained. However, a high FP is also obtained since the memory detectors have not been trained enough.

However, if $\beta$ is too large, the mature detectors is very hard to be activated. Possibly, there are no memory detectors in the system. Since the lifecycle $\lambda$ of mature detectors may be smaller than the tolerance period of immature detectors ($\alpha$), the worst thing may happen: no mature or memory detector can be used to protect the network system against intrusions.

As $\alpha$ increases, the immature detectors may have a larger population than the mature detectors, resulting in a decrease of the memory detectors' population, and finally resulting in the falling down of TP and FP. Fig. 3 illustrates that $\alpha$ changes in inverse proportion to TP and FP, where $\beta = 5, \lambda = 40, \delta = 50$.

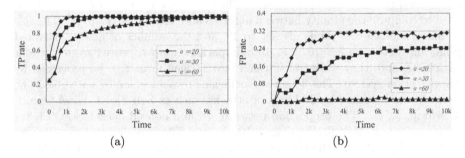

**Fig. 3.** The effect of tolerance period $\alpha$, (a) TP rate. (b) FP rate.

Fig. 4 shows the effect of lifecycle ($\lambda$) of mature detectors, where $\alpha = 50, \beta = 5, \delta = 50$. In this case, the TP and FP change in direct proportion to $\lambda$.

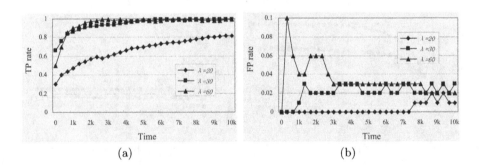

**Fig. 4.** The effect of lifecycle $\lambda$, (a) TP rate. (b) FP rate.

Fig.5 shows that TP and FP change in inverse proportion to $\delta$, where $\alpha = 50, \lambda = 40, \beta = 5$. If $\delta$ is greater than $\alpha$, FP will increase sharply. In this case, immature detectors become mature ones without enough self-tolerance.

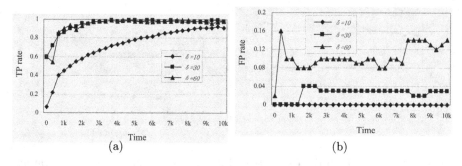

**Fig. 5.** The effect of updating cycle $\delta$, (a) TP rate. (b) FP rate.

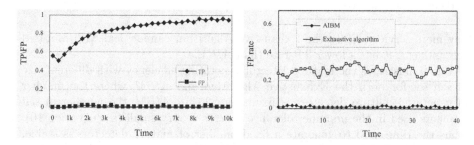

**Fig. 6.** The satisfied TP and FP, where $\delta = \alpha = 50, \beta = 5, \lambda = 40$

**Fig. 7.** FP rates for both the Exhaustive Algorithm and *AIBM*, where 40 of each 100 packets are self antigens, and half of them are newly defined

Fig. 6 is a satisfied result obtained in the experiments.

In contrast to the previous works on immune-based models or methods for NIDS [3-14,20-22], whose definitions of self and nonself allow little change after they have been defined. However, our proposed method has a dynamic evolution model for the definitions of self and nonself, and thus, offers more self-adaptability. To test the effectiveness of our proposed model, the corresponding comparison experiments were performed, with Exhaustive algorithm, proposed by Forrest et al [20], selected as the opponent. The Exhaustive algorithm is a typical one among the algorithms used in the traditional CIS, which has a strong impact on the design of CIS. Fig. 7 illustrates the FP rates for both the Exhaustive Algorithm and *AIBM*, where 40 of each 100 packets are self antigens, and half of them are newly defined (e.g., another 20 ports are now opened to provide more services). Since the Exhaustive Algorithm cannot alter the self elements during the training of the immature detectors, the detectors generated by the algorithm will not be tolerant of the newly defined self antigens, which is the reason why it has a higher FP rate than *AIBM*. Fig. 8 illustrates the TP rates for both the Exhaustive Algorithm and *AIBM*, where 80 of each 100 packets are nonself antigens, and half of them were self antigens before, but are nonself behaviors now. That is, 40 ports in the system are now closed and do not provide

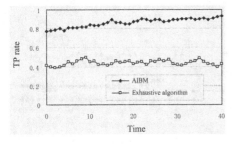
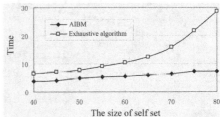

**Fig. 8.** TP rates for both the Exhaustive Algorithm and *AIBM*, where 80 of each 100 packets are nonself antigens, and half of them are new defined

**Fig. 9.** The mature detector generating efficiency for both the Exhaustive Algorithm and *AIBM*

any more services. Since the Exhaustive Algorithm cannot deal with mutated self antigens, it has a lower TP rate than *AIBM*.

Fig. 9 illustrates the mature detector generating efficiency with different size of self set for both the Exhaustive Algorithm and *AIBM*, where the number of generated mature detectors is fixed, e.g., 20. In *AIBM*, the number of self elements used in the immune tolerance process is very small (see equation 10). Thus the time used to generate a fixed number of mature detectors is stable. However, the Exhaustive Algorithm uses all self elements to train the immature detectors. Therefore, it takes much more time than *AIBM* to generate mature detectors when the size of self set increases.

## 4   Conclusion

In NIDS, it is difficult to describe self exactly. Most existing models or methods for the depiction of self are based on static description, which provides little support for dynamic evaluation, lacks the ability of self-adaptation, has high error rate, and, therefore, have limited applications. In this paper, a quantitatively depiction for dynamic evolutions of *self, antigen, immune-tolerance, lifecycle of mature detectors*, and *immune-memory* have been presented. Furthermore, an immune-based dynamic model called *AIBM* for network intrusion detection has been developed. This model can efficiently reduce both the false-positive error rate and false-negative error rate, and enhance the ability of self-adaptation and diversity for the NIDS.

*AIBM* is a general model, and can be used in other fields. For example, if the self set is considered as the normal status of file systems, or specified patterns, etc., this model can be used for virus detection, pattern recognition, and others.

## Acknowledgement

This work was supported by the National Natural Science Foundation of China under Grant No.60373110, the National Research Foundation for the Doctoral

Program of Higher Education of China under Grant No.20030610003, the New Century Excellent Expert Program of Ministry of Education of China under Grant No. NCET-04-0870, and the Innovation Foundation of Sichuan University under Grant No.2004CF10.

# References

1. Li, T.: An Introduction to Computer Network Security. Publishing House of Electronics Industry, Beijing (2004)
2. Li, T.: Computer Immunology. Publishing House of Electronics Industry, Beijing (2004)
3. De Castro, L. N., Timmis, J. I.: Artificial immune systems as a novel soft computing paradigm. Soft Computing journal, vol. 7(8) (2003) 526-544
4. Spears, W. M., De Jong, K. A.: An overview of evolutionary computation. in Proc. of the European Conf. on Machine Learning, Springer Verlag, vol. 667 (1993) 442-459
5. De Castro, L. N., Timmis, J. I.: Artificial Immune Systems: A New Computational Intelligence Approach. Springer-Verlag (2002)
6. Bradley, D. W., Tyrrell, A. M.: A hardware immune system for benchmark state machine error detection. in Proc. of the Conf. on Evolutionary Computation, Honolulu (2002) 813-818
7. Tyrrell, A. M.: Computer know thy self: a biological way to look at fault-tolerance. in Second Euromicro/IEEE Workshop on Dependable Computing Systems, Milan, Italy (1999) 129-135
8. Forrest, S., Perelson, A. S.: Self-nonself discrimination in a computer. in Proc. of IEEE Symposium on Security and Privacy, Oakland (1994) 202-213
9. Forrest, S., Hofmeyr, S., Somayaji, A.: Computer immunology. Communications of the ACM, vol. 40(10) (1997) 88-96
10. Hofmeyr, S., Forrest, S.: Immunity by design: an artificial immune system. in Proc. of the Genetic Evolutionary Computation Conf., San Francisco, CA (1999) 1289-1296
11. Hofmeyr, S., Forrest, S.: Architecture for an artificial immune system. Evolutionary Computation, vol. 8(4) (2000) 443-473
12. Dasgupta, D.: Immunity-based intrusion detection system: a general framework. in Proc. of the 22nd National Information Systems Security Conf., Crystal City (1999) 147-160
13. Harmer, P. K., Williams, P. D., Gunsch, G. H., and Lamont, G. B.: An artificial immune system architecture for computer security applications. IEEE Trans. on Evolutionary Computation, vol. 6(3) (2002) 252-280
14. D'haeseleer, P., Forrest, S.: An immunological approach to change detection: algorithm, analysis and implication. in Proc. of IEEE Symposium on Research in Security and Privacy, Oakland (1996) 110-119
15. Kim, J., Bentley, P. J.: Towards an artificial immune system for network intrusion detection: an investigation of dynamic clonal selection. in Proc. of the Conf. on Evolutionary Computation, Honolulu (2002) 1015-1020
16. Perelson, A. S., Weisbuch, G.: Immunology for physicists. Review of Modern Physics, vol. 69(4) (1997) 1219-1263
17. Li, T.: An immunity based network security risk estimation. Science in China Ser. F Information Sciences, vol. 48(5) (2005) 798-816

18. Li, T.: An immune based dynamic intrusion detection model. Chinese Science Bulletin, vol. 50(17) (2005)

19. Li, T.: A new model of immune-based network surveillance and dynamic computer forensics. Lecture Notices in Computer Science, vol. 3611 (2005) 799-808

20. Timmis, J., Bentley, P. J.: Negative selection: how to generate detectors. in Proc. of the 1st International Conf. on Artificial Immune Systems, University of Kent at Canterbury (2002) 89-98

21. Haeseleer, P. D., Forrest, S., et al.: An immunological approach to change detection. in Proc. of IEEE Symposium on Research in Security and Privacy, Oakland, CA (1996)

22. Somayaji, A., Hofmeyr, S., Forrest, S.: Principles of a computer immune system. in Proc. of the New Security Paradigms Workshop, Langdale, United Kingdom (1997) 75-82

# Self Debugging Mode for Patch-Independent Nullification of Unknown Remote Process Infection

Ruo Ando and Yoshiyasu Takefuji

Keio University, Graduate School of Media and Governance,
Endo 5322, Fujisawa, 2528520 Japan
{Ruo, Takefuji}@sfc.keio.ac.jp
http://www.neuro.sfc.keio.ac.jp

**Abstract.** The rapid increase of software vulnerabilities shows us the limitation of patch-dependent countermeasures for malicious code. We propose a patch-independent protection technique of remote infection which enables each process to identify itself with "being infected" and nullify itself spontaneously. Our system is operating system independent and therefore does not need software rebuilding. Previously, no method for stopping malicious process without recompiling source code or rebuilding software has been proposed. In proposal system, target process is running under self debugging mode which is activated by enhancing debug() exception handler and utilizing MSR debug register. In this paper we show the effectiveness of proposal method by protecting the remote process infection without patching security holes. Implemention of device driver call back function and BranchIP recorder provides the real-time prevention of unregistered worm attack through Internet. In experiment, function test of stack buffer overflow of Win32.SQLExp.Worm is presented. Also CPU utilization corresponding to the number of calling function and some database operations is showed.

**Keywords:** self-debugging mode, real-time nullification, debug register, improved debug exception handler, branchIP recorder.

## 1 Introduction

The rapid increase of software vulnerabilities and its exploitation imposes a great burden on network administrators and client users. Recent cyber attacks, worms and virsuses become more sophisticated. Some obfuscation and avoidance techniques which evade network traffic inspection such is called polymorphic and metamorphic coding. These techniques is now applied in malicious code writing.Win32.Evol and Simile virus is valid example which shows us the limitation of naive signature based inspection of network traffic. The rapid spread of Win32.SQLExp.Worm infection also shows the limitation of patch-based couvermeasures for new attack. Previously, instead of signature matching, the adaptive prevention technique has been proposed. Some technique inspect the target file

Y.G. Desmedt et al. (Eds.): CANS 2005, LNCS 3810, pp. 85–95, 2005.

by executing it both on run-time environment and on virtual machine emulation. Another run-time protection is mainly represented by compiler solutions and operating system based method. Openwall Linux kernel patch project is to improve the protection against buffer overflows. OpenBSD also provides the new feature of stack protection technology against buffer overflows which is embedded in the system compiler. Stack-smash protection compilers are used against buffer overflows including the GCC extensions, libsafe, propolice, stackguard, libmib, and MS .net compiler. However, their disadvantage lies in that kernels and software components must be rebuilt.

In this paper we propose the method for the real-time infected process nullfication using improved debug exception handler. This could be described as automated debugging based on improved loader, driver-supplied callback function and debug exception handler. On this system attribute of self-debugging is added to the target process, which makes it possible to control by itself when attacked and infected without the file scanner or IDS.

Figure1 illustrates the concept of automated debug using improved debug exception handler. In conventional debug method, the system needs to launch debugging process and API. The target process can be executed in the memory of debugging process. In proposal method, process does not need their debugging process and API because exception handler is improved so that the debug specified for malicious code is automated in running each process.

In this paper, the proposal system is constructed on 80x86 processor. The 80x86 processor has 20 different exception handlers. Table 1 shows the exception handlers mainly concerned with debugging issues. In this paper we present improved exception handler. Particularly, we enhance debug() function with sig-

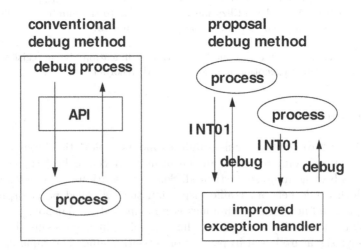

**Fig. 1.** Automated debugging. By improving exception handler INT01H, the self-debugging attribute is added to the target process. In proposal method, process under inspection does not need debugging process and its memory, which provides sense of infection and self-defense.

**Table 1.** Comparison of proposal system with previous method

| No | Exception | Exception Handler | Signal |
|----|-----------|-------------------|--------|
| 1 | Debug | debug() | SIGTRAP |
| 2 | NMI | nmi() | None |
| 3 | Breakpoint | int3() | SIGTRAP |
| 4 | Overflow | overflow() | SIGSEGV |
| 5 | BoundsCheck | bound() | SIGSEGV |
| 12 | StackException | stack_segment() | SIGBUS |
| 14 | Page Fault | page_fault() | SIGSEGV |

nal SIGTRAP. Debug facilty is called when we set the T flag of eflags or when the address of an instruction fall the range of an active debug register. The concept of proposal method is automated debugging by the implementation of some additional process within the debug() function. To achieve the concept of proposal method, IDT (interrupt descriptor table) must be initialized and over-written for dealing with the bugs hooked by INT01 insertion. In other words, to enable exception, the kernel should initialize the IDT properly. The correspondence between interrupt or exception vector and the address of each recognized interrupt or exception handler is stored to IDT.

## 2   Self Debugging Mode

In this section we discuss the self debugging mode added to the target process. Figure2 illustrated the activation of self debugging attribute to the target process. The proposal method is divided into steps. First, we insert the INT01H

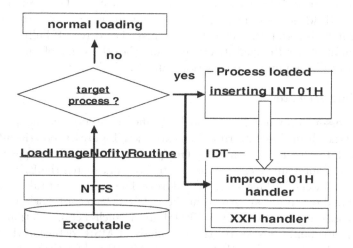

**Fig. 2.** Changing the self debug mode of the target process. When the executable file is loaded, INT01H debug point is inserted and improved exception handler is registerd to IDT. These steps begin the automated debug mode applying loader processing module such as LoadImageNoiftyRoutine and bin_fmt.

debug instruction into the process like binary translation technique. Second, the enhanced exception handler which is specified for the INT01H software bug hooking is registered to IDT. These steps are executed when the executable is loaded. In detail, we apply LoadImageNotifyRoutine in Win32 or loader processing module such as bin_fmt in linux in order to insert INT01H break point and register the improved exception handler. Regardless of the kind of opearting system, exception handler is speficied for bugs that causes exploitation. Now that we completed this manipulation, the new attribute described as self-debugging is added to the target process loaded. This mode makes it possible for the process to be nullified by itself if it is infected by unregistered malicious code. The detailed facilities of proposal system are discussed in the following.

## 2.1   Driver-Supplied Callback Function

To implement the proposal concept, we selected driver-based callback function, which is notified whenever an image is loaded for execution. Driver-based callback function is utilized for the identification of loading the target process. Highest-level system profiling drivers can call PsSetImageNotifyRoutine to set up their load-image notify routines. This could be declared as follows, particularly in Win32.

*void LoadImageNotifyRoutine (*
*PUNICODE_STRING FullImageName,*
*HANDLE ProcessId,*
*PIMAGE_INFO ImageInfo );*

Once the driver's callback has been registered, the operating system calls the callback function whenever an executable image is mapped into virtual memory. When the LoadImageNotifyRoutine is called, the input FullImageName points to a buffered Unicode identifying the executable image file. The argument of list showing handle identities of process has been mapped when we call this function. But this handle is zero if the newly loading image is a driver. If FullImageName, which is input of LoadImageNotifyRoutine matches the name of target process, we go on to call the improved exception handler.

## 2.2   Debug Register

IA-32 processors provides MSR(model specific registers) for the purpose of recording taken brunches, interrupts and exception. Figure 3 shows the allocation in debugCtlMSR register of Intel P6 family processors. In this paper we focus on last branch interrupt / exceptions flag to save and search the EIP(32 bit instructional pointer). EIP means return address. The most recent taken branches, interrupts and exception are stored in the last branch record stack MSRs. The branch records inform us of branch-FROM and branch-TO instruction address. Concerning F6 family processor, the five kinds of MSR, debugCtlMSR, LastBranchToIP, LastBranchFromIP, LastExceptionToIP and LastExecutionFromIP and available. It is possible to set break points on branches, interrupts and exception and execute single step debugging through these registers. These registers

```
┌─────────────────────────────────────────┐
│          Reserved [7-31]                 │
└─────────────────────────────────────────┘
┌─────────────────────────────────────────┐
│      TR : Trace messages enable [6]      │
└─────────────────────────────────────────┘
┌─────────────────────────────────────────┐
│        performance monitoring            │
│        break point pins [2-5]            │
└─────────────────────────────────────────┘
┌─────────────────────────────────────────┐
│      single step-on baranches [1]        │
└─────────────────────────────────────────┘
┌─────────────────────────────────────────┐
│       last branch / interrupt /          │
│           exceptions [0]                 │
└─────────────────────────────────────────┘
```

**Fig. 3.** Allocation in debugCtlMSR register. When the LBR is set, the proceesor records the source and target address at the time the branch instruction or interrupt is taken before the debug exception being generated.

can be used to collect last branch records, to set breakpoints on branches, inter-rrupts, exceptions and to single step from on branch to the next.

## 3    Experiments

### 3.1    Win32.SQLExp.Worm

Recent security incident for the mission critial servers connected to networks has been occurred at very high rates. In mission critical operation, server should be running all the time under many accesses. Once the vulnerability and its exploitation is found, this can be availeble for attackers all over the world. Particularly, the SQL slammer worms, emerged in 2003, caused more then 90 of vulnerable servers all over the world to be infected within a few hours. This worm attack exploits the vulnerability within the vulnerable SQL server. The vulnerable SQL server when it is infected it will send 376 bytes packets via UDP port 1434 to the original attack launcher and other random destinations to prop-agate the worms. According to the mailing list of snort (open-source instruction detection system), the signature of SQL slammer is as follows at 09:45:52 Sat Jan 25 2003.

*0x00b0 89e5 5168 2e64 6c6c 6865 6c33 3268 6b65*
*..Qh.dllhel32hke*
*0x00c0 726e 5168 6f75 6e74 6869 636b 4368 4765*
*rnQhounthickChGe*
*0x00d0 7454 66b9 6c6c 5168 3332 2e64 6877 7332*
*tTf.llQh32.dhws2*

*0x00e0 5f66 b965 7451 6873 6f63 6b66 b974 6f51*
*_f.etQhsockf.toQ*
*0x00f0 6873 656e 64be 1810 ae42 8d45 d450 ff16*
*hsend....B.E.P..*

After a while(half a day), the signature is changed as follows:

*81 f1 03 01 04 9b xor ecx, 9B040103h*
*81 f1 01 01 01 01 xor ecx, 1010101h*
*51 push ecx*
*9B040103 xor 1010101 = 9A050002 = port 1434 -¿AF_INET*

However,this signature describes very specific features of implementation, sending packets to port 1434. Actually, when we implemented and tested the same kind of exploitation by VC++, the binary code is different from the signature above.

This worm exploits the buffer overflow vulnerabilities of MSDE SQL server 2000 unpatched with PORT TCP1433 and UDP1434. In this case, the systematic prevention of buffer overflow should be the first priority. against exploitation of SQL slammer.

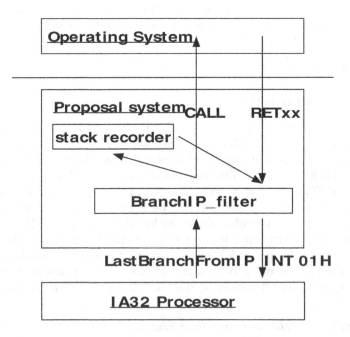

**Fig. 4.** BranchIP recorder. When the automated debug mode is enabled and the mode of the target process is changed to self debug, the system executes inspection function whenever the Branch instruction is called. BranchIP recoder hook the CALL/RET instrcution and store the saved EIP to stack recorder to check whether the bufferoverflow attack is occurred. The saved EIP is obtained from LastBranchFromIP.

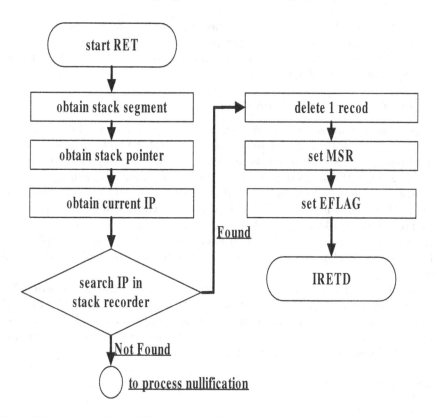

**Fig. 5.** Flow chart of BranchIP recorder. The self debug mode process checks whether EIP changes after executing local function by using stack recorder. In nested calling function, some saved EIPs are stored to the stack recorder. The proposal method checks the overwriting return address by searching EIP in stack recorder. When the saved EIP is found, this module is terminated in normal mode.

We implemented the Branch IP recorder for inspecting the overwriting EIP after executing function occuring buffer overflow. Figure 4 illustrates the structure of Branch IP recorder. With the memory called stack recorder, we check the transition of EIP while executing function occurring buffer overflow. In experiment, we prototype this system on IA-32 processor because IA-32 family enhanced facilities for debugging are available about inspecting code execution and processor performance. The LastBranchToIP and LastBranchFromIP MSRs are 32-bit registers for recording the instruction pointers for the last branch, interrupt, or exception that the processor took prior to a debug exception being generated. In our system, the inspecting the transition of EIP is possible by monitoring LastBrachFromIP. Branch IP recorder has a FIFO memory for EIP as follows. The inspection flow of saved EIP using Branch IP recorder is shown in Figure5.Although this recording facility has FIFO structure, we can detect the overwriting EIP that is not done in FIFO flow. because proposal system check all stored EIPs when the branch insturction is executed. Experimental result of table 2-5 shows that our system is effective regrdless of the kinds of buffer overflow signature as long as the target process is running on self debug mode. We succeeded to stop SQL slammer infection on Windows 2000 SP0, without patching security hole of MSDE.

## 3.2  Performance Measurements

The performance measurements were collected on a Windows 2000 host computer system using Pentium III 1000 MHz with 1024 RAM. Concerning experimental result 5.2, We measured the utilization of MS SQL server 2000.

Table 2 lists CPU utilization corresponding to the number of calling function. We vary the number of executing local function from 100 to 10000. From 100 to 100, utilization is not changed rapidply, comparetively stable about less than 10%. From 1000 to 10000, it was showed that utilzation is not increased linearly. It is showed that the proposal system is effective in the point that utilization is less than 25 % when the function is executed 10000 times without the linear increase.

Table 3 lists CPU utilization of SQL server processing SELECT queries. We vary the number of READ queries from 5 to 30. CPU utilization is 9.14, 17.5 and 47.85, almost doubled corresponding to the number of queries. The performance of proposal system is not reasonable compared with the lower column of unprotected case. Although the utilization differences are caused partly by the

**Table 2.** CPU utilization corresponding to number of times of calling local funcation(%)

| times of calling function | CPU utilization |
|---|---|
| 100 | 8.75 |
| 200 | 9.12 |
| 500 | 9.6 |
| 700 | 9.93 |
| 1000 | 10.33 |
| 5000 | 14.25 |
| 7000 | 17.31 |
| 10000 | 24.89 |

**Table 3.** CPU utilization (%) according to the number of SELECT queries

| the number of queries | 30 | 10 | 5 |
|---|---|---|---|
| proposal system enabled | 1.48 | 1.21 | 0.97 |
| proposal system disabled | 1.28 | 1.08 | 0.89 |

**Table 4.** CPU utilization (%) according to the length of SELECT query

| data length(byte) | 500 | 200 | 50 |
|---|---|---|---|
| proposal system enabled | 1.89 | 1.61 | 1.39 |
| proposal system disabled | 1.71 | 1.37 | 1.18 |

**Table 5.** Comparison of proposal system with previous method

| - | rebuild | prevention | utilization |
|---|---|---|---|
| StackGuard | O | O | mid |
| Bounds Checking | O | O | high |
| OpenWall | X | O | low |
| proposal system | X | O | high |

implementation of INSERT command, the complementary system is considered below.

Table 4 lists CPU utilization of SQL server processing SELECT queries. We vary the length of READ queries from 50byte to 500byte. The increase of CPU utilization is insignificant in changing the data length while the proposal system is sensitive to the number of query operation as shown in table. This result is caused by the fact that the proposal system inspects the transition of instructional pointer stored in 32bit register (LastBranchFromIP) while in the conventional scanning methods the length of signature changes according to the various kinds of payload of malicious code. In other words, proposal system only requires inspection the value of constant 32bit length, which makes it possible to keep utilization reasonably low.

## 4   Conclusion

In this paper, we introduce the automated debug technique, utilizing the facility of debug and instruction trace in processor level for real-time malicious process nullification. The conventional anti-virus softwares are all based on stored signatures. Consequently these schemes have the limitation against the unknown exploit occuring buffer overflow and the unregistered attack such as metamorphic and polymorphic viruses and worms Instead of modifying the sophisticated operating system for reducing vulnerabilities, we work out the new attributes for target process called self-debugging. When the process is translated into memory, this mode is activated by enhanced debug() exception handler. For the implementation of proposal system, driver supplied callback function is utilized for the event-driven insertion of self debug facility. The each process which is INT0H break point embeddedi is running on self debugging mode where software bugs is controlled by improved debug() exception handler. In proposal system, we can prevent of the exploitation of every kind of software bugs for which we can write the controlling of exception of INT01H handler. Without rebuilding applications and kernel, the system loading automated debugging technology can contorl infected process to identify its infection and nullify by itself. In experiment, CPU utilization of detecting buffer overflow, CPU time corresponding the number of calling function and some operation of SQL database server was measured and evaluated. Function test of stack buffer overflow of Win32.SQLExp.Worm is also presented.

Table 5 shows the comparison of proposal method and another adaptive protection techniques. The disadvantage of stack guard and bounds checking lies in that kernels and software components must be rebuilt. Concerning OpenWall, the kernel must be rebuild while the application with overflow vulnerability need not recompiling. The proposal system takes advantage in the point that it does not need rebuilding both kernel and application. Our method has also flexibility for all kind of vulnerabilities such stack overflow, heap overflow, race condition and so on as long as we can describe the property of software bugs in debug() exception handler. The proposal system is experimented in MS SQL vulnerability in 2003 and some database operations. The proposal scheme using a new concept of sense of self is based on the automated debugging mode where the execution of malicious code is nullified by autonomous control of target process. The proposed scheme does not need the software-rebuilding, while the existing schemes need the software-rebuilding. Finally, the concept of self debug mode is operating system independent.

## Acknowledgement

We are indebted to K.Shoji, T.Kawade and T.Nozaki, by courtesy of Sciencepark Cooporation. Some idea in this paper grew out of the ongoing collaboration with their team.

## References

1. Crispin Cowan, Perry Wagle, Calton Pu, Steve Beattie, and Jonathan Walpole: Buffer Overflows - Attacks and Defenses for the Vulnerability of the Decade, DARPA Information Survivability Conference and Expo, 2000.
2. Roesch, M:Snort - lightweight intrusion detection for networks. Proceedings of Thirteenth Systems Administration Conference (LISA '99), pp. 229-238,1999.
3. Symantec Corporation: Bloodhound Technology. http://securityresponse.symantec.com/
4. Gene H. Kim and Eugene H. Spafford:Tripwire A File System Integrity Checker, ACM Conference on Computer and Communications Security , pp. 18-29,1994.
5. Kosoresow, Andrew P. and Steven A. Hofmeyr, "Intrusion Detection Via System Call Traces", IEEE Software,pp 35-40,1997.
6. Zeshan Ghory:Openwall Improving security with the openwall patch ,securityfocus,2002.
7. Linux Openwall project. http://www.openwall.com/
8. David Larochelle and David Evans,Statically Detecting Likely Buffer Overflow Vulnerabilities,2001 USENIX Security Symposium, Washington, D.C., August 13-17, 2001.
9. C.Cowan, C.Pu, D.Maier, J.Walpole, P.Bakke, S.Beattie, A.Grier, P.Wagle, Q.Zhang, and H.Hinton:StackGuard Automatic adaptive detection and prevention of buffer-overflow attacks, In Proc. 7th USENIX Security Conference, pp 63–78,1998.
10. Baratloo, A., N. Singh and T. Tsai, Libsafe: Protecting critical elements of stacks, http://www.research.avayalabs.com/project/libsafe/.

11. J. Bergeron, M. Debbabi, J. Desharnais, M. M. Erhioui, Y. Lavoie and N. Tawbi, "Static Detection of Malicious Code in Executable Programs". Proc. of the International Symposium on Requirements Engineering for Information Security, 2001.
12. Richard W M Jones,Paul H J Kelly: Backwards-compatible bounds checking for array and pointers in C programs, AADEBUG97,1997.
13. Intel Corporation: IA-32 IntelR Architecture Software Developer's Manual, Volume 2A: Insruction Set Reference A-M,2004.
14. Intel Corporation: IA-32 IntelR Architecture Software Developer's Manual, Volume 2B: Insruction Set Reference N-Z,2004.
15. Intel Corporation: IA-32 IntelR Architecture Software Developer's Manual, Volume 3: System Programming Guide,2004.

# A New Unsupervised Anomaly Detection Framework for Detecting Network Attacks in Real-Time

Wei Lu and Issa Traore

Department of Electrical and Computer Engineering, University of Victoria,
PO Box 3055 STN CSC, Victoria, B.C., Canada
{wlu, itraore}@ece.uvic.ca

**Abstract.** In this paper, we propose a new unsupervised anomaly detection framework for detecting network intrusions online. The framework consists of new anomalousness metrics named IP Weight and an outlier detection algorithm based on Gaussian mixture model (GMM). IP Weights convert the features of IP packets into a four-dimensional numerical feature space, in which the outlier detection takes place. Intrusion decisions are made based on the outcome of outlier detections. Two sets of experiments are conducted to evaluate our framework. In the first experiment, we conduct an offline evaluation based on the 1998 DARPA intrusion detection dataset, which detects 16 types of attacks out of a total of 19 network attack types. In the second experiment, an online evaluation is performed in a live networking environment. The evaluation result not only confirms the detection effectiveness with DARPA dataset, but also shows a strong runtime efficiency, with response times falling within seconds.

## 1   Introduction

Intrusion detection has been extensively studied since the seminal report written by Anderson [1]. Traditionally, intrusion detection techniques are classified into two categories: misuse detection and anomaly detection. Misuse detection is based on the assumption that most attacks leave a set of signatures in the stream of network packets or in audit trails, and thus attacks are detectable if these signatures can be identified by analyzing the audit trails or network traffic behaviors. However, misuse detection approaches are strictly limited to the latest known attacks. How to detect new attacks or variants of known attacks is one of the biggest challenges faced by misuse detection.

To address the weakness of misuse detection, the concept of anomaly detection was formalized in the seminal report of Denning [4]. Denning assumed that security violations could be detected by inspecting abnormal system usage patterns from the audit data. As a result, most anomaly detection techniques attempt to establish normal activity profiles by computing various metrics, and an intrusion is detected when the actual system behavior deviates from the normal profiles. According to Axelsson, "the early anomaly detection systems were

Y.G. Desmedt et al. (Eds.): CANS 2005, LNCS 3810, pp. 96–109, 2005.

self-learning, that is, they automatically formed an opinion of what the subject's normal behavior was" [2]. Self-learning techniques combine the early statistical model based anomaly detection approaches [10][12][17], and the AI based approaches [8] or the biological models based approaches [9], and thus they are still applied for current anomaly detection schemes. According to whether they are based on supervised or unsupervised learning techniques, anomaly detection schemes can be classified into two categories: unsupervised anomaly detection and supervised anomaly detection [14].

Supervised anomaly detection establishes the normal profiles of systems or networks through training based on labeled datasets. In contrast, unsupervised anomaly detection attempts to detect intrusions without using any prior knowledge of attacks or normal instances. The main drawback of supervised anomaly detection is the need of labeling the training data, which makes the process error-prone, costly and time consuming. Unsupervised anomaly detection addresses these issues by allowing training based on unlabelled datasets and thus facilitating online learning and improving detection accuracy.

Clustering algorithm is one of the most widely used unsupervised learning techniques. Some examples of using clustering algorithms for intrusion detection were suggested in literature [5], [6] and [14]. Although clustering techniques have showed their capability for intrusion detection, labeling clusters is still a difficult problem faced by this kind of approach. In order to label the clusters, the approach usually makes two assumptions: (1) data instances always belong to two categories: normal clusters and intrusive clusters; (2) the number of normal data instances largely outnumbers the number of intrusions. However, these assumptions are not always the case in practice. The number of clusters is not supposed to be determined in advance. When data instances include only normal behavioral data, the assumptions will lead a high false alert rate. In order to obtain an efficient and effective detection, we propose in this paper a new unsupervised anomaly detection framework based on outlier detection techniques. The proposed detection scheme consists of a feature extraction technique based on new anomalousness metrics, named IP Weight and an outlier detection algorithm based on Gaussian mixture model (GMM).

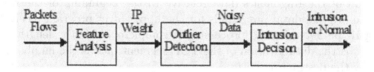

**Fig. 1.** General architecture

Fig. 1 illustrates the general architecture of our framework, which consists of three components, namely feature analysis, outlier detection and intrusion decision. During feature analysis, IP Weights are generated from standard IP packet flows. This allows extracting salient and useful domain knowledge and reducing significantly the dimensionality of the feature space. Then, noisy data of IP Weights are detected in outlier detection phase. Intrusion decision is made based on the outcome of outlier detections.

We discuss each of these phases in the rest of the paper. Specifically, Section 2 outlines empirical observations based on network traffic, and derives the IP Weight metrics based on these observations. Section 3 presents the outlier detection algorithm and the corresponding intrusion decision strategy. Section 4 presents the experimental evaluation of our approach and discusses the obtained results. Section 5 makes some concluding remarks and discusses future work.

## 2 Feature Analysis

Feature analysis consists of feature selection and extraction. In this paper we primarily focus on the detection of network attacks, and thus the main data source for our approach consists of network packets. Through empirical observations to network traffic behaviors, we derive a collection of empirical utility functions. We name these utility functions IP Weight metrics. IP Weight metrics measure the degree of anomalousness of IP packet flows. In the remainder of this section, we define the feature space, summarize these empirical observations, which are the basis of our feature selection process, and then derive the IP Weight metrics.

### 2.1   Feature Selection

**Feature Space.** Based on the standard characteristics of IP packets on networks, we define a set of features to describe a single IP packet. Let us denote by $P$ the set of IP packets. A packet $p \in P$ can be represented as a 13-dimensional feature vector $< t, dip, dp, sip, sp, ihl, pktl, ident, fragoff, pro, thl, seq, ack >$; $t$ is the time stamp corresponding to the appearing time of the packet in a certain time window; $dip$ is the destination IP address and it usually corresponds to the address of a host we want to protect; $dp$ stands for the destination port; $sip$ stands for the source IP address; $sp$ means source port; $ihl$ refers to the length of IP header for the IP packet; $pktl$ is the packet length including header and data; $ident$ is an integer that identifies the current data in a packet, which can be used to piece together data fragments; $fragoff$ is the offset of the IP packet indicating the position of the fragment's data relative to the beginning of the fragment data in the original data; $pro$ stands for the upper-layer program receiving the incoming IP packets after IP processing is complete; $thl$ is the length of TCP header; $seq$ is the data location of the TCP segment; $ack$ is the number of data received by the destination host.

We define a packet flow as group of packets flowing to a specified destination during a specified observation period. Let us denoted by $F$ the set of all packet flows. A packet flow $f \in F$ is defined as a 6-dimensional vector $f = < g, t, \delta_t, dip, nop, nodp_{max} >$; where $g \in \wp(P)$ is the set of packets observed and $\wp(P)$ denotes the power set of $P$; $t$ is the starting time of the observation; $\delta_t$ is the observation time window; $dip$ refers to the destination IP address that we want to protect; $nop$ stands for the total number of packets in the flow; $nodp_{max}$ means the maximum number of packets over all destination ports in the packet flow.

**Empirical Observations.** The goal for the feature selection is not to provide a full description about anomalous activities; instead, we are interested in identifying a limited number of facts that can allow achieving an effective and efficient detection. Specifically, the work is based on the following four intuitive observations:

1. Network traffic involving a high frequency of packets flowing to the same destination address within a very short time period, or network traffic involving a high frequency of packets flowing to the same destination address with same destination port during a very short time period, is likely anomalous.
2. During the normal network usage, for those network traffic flowing to the same destination over a given time period, the likelihood of their corresponding destination ports to be randomly distributed is low. The same observation applies for their corresponding source IP addresses and source ports.
3. Network traffic containing one or several packets that violate basic structural rules of packets is likely anomalous.
4. For a normal host, its incoming traffic and (matching) outgoing traffic are most likely similar.

Observation 3 simply derives from the TCP/IP protocol specification. To confirm other three observations, we conducted a pilot study, in which network data are collected over three weeks: two weeks for normal network usage and one week for anomalous network usage including some known attacks. The destination server was deployed behind the firewall. We ensured that the traffic over two weeks' normal usage was normal by auditing the after-event logs of the firewall. During the anomalous network usage over one week, the server operated as a honey pot. Several utilities including known vulnerabilities were purposely installed on the server and exposed to the public.

Fig. 2-a to Fig. 7-b illustrate the analysis made from the collected data. In these figures, we denote the IP address of the server by *dip* and the size of the

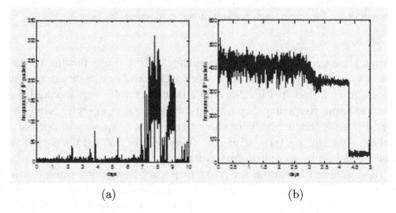

(a)                                    (b)

**Fig. 2.** (a) Frequency of normal packets flowing to same *dip* over $\delta_t$. (b) Frequency of anomalous packets flowing to same *dip* over $\delta_t$.

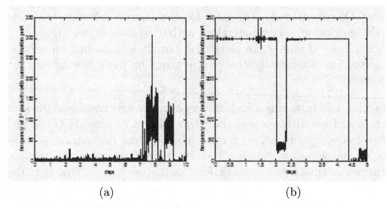

(a)                                    (b)

**Fig. 3.** (a) Maximum frequency of normal packets flowing to same *dip* with same *dp* over $\delta_t$. (b) Maximum frequency of anomalous packets flowing to same *dip* with same *dp* over $\delta_t$.

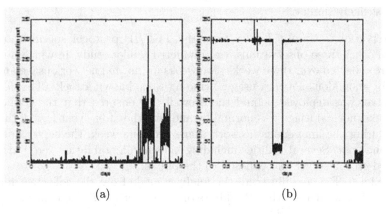

(a)                                    (b)

**Fig. 4.** (a) Randomness of *dp* for normal packets flowing to same *dip* over $\delta_t$. (b) Randomness of *dp* for anomalous packets flowing to same *dip* over $\delta_t$.

observation time window by $\delta_t$. The frequency of IP packets flowing to the same *dip* during $\delta_t$ in two weeks normal network usage and one week anomalous network usage are plotted in Fig. 2-a and 2-b respectively. Fig. 3-a and Fig. 3-b plot the maximum frequency of packets flowing to same *dip* with same destination port during $\delta_t$, respectively. In these figures, the frequency of normal packet flows follow a regular pattern, while the frequency of anomalous packet flows is persistently high. These confirm observation 1.

The randomness of destination ports in packet flows with same destination port during $\delta_t$ over two weeks' normal network usage and one week's anomalous network usage are plotted in Fig. 4-a and Fig. 4-b, respectively. Similarly, Fig. 5-a and Fig. 5-b plot the randomness of source ports in corresponding packet flows. Fig. 6-a and Fig. 6-b plot the randomness of source IP addresses. In these

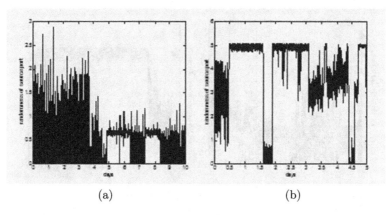

(a)                                        (b)

**Fig. 5.** (a) Randomness of *sp* for normal packets flowing to same *dip* over $\delta_t$. (b) Randomness of *sp* for anomalous packets flowing to same *dip* over $\delta_t$.

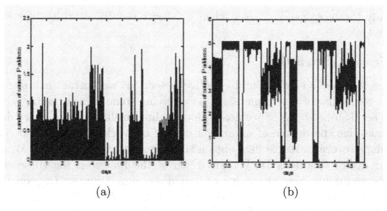

(a)                                        (b)

**Fig. 6.** (a) Randomness of *sip* for normal packets flowing to same *dip* over $\delta_t$. (b) Randomness of *sip* for anomalous packets flowing to same *dip* over $\delta_t$.

graphs, the randomness of destination ports, source IP addresses and source ports of anomalous packet flows is more often higher than those of normal packet flows, which supports observation 2.

For the server we protect, Fig. 7-a and Fig. 7-b plot the load ratio of its corresponding incoming traffic to outgoing traffic over two weeks normal network usage and one week anomalous network usage. Both the incoming traffic and outgoing traffic correspond to the same destination IP address. The load ratio for the specified destination IP address of anomalous traffic is much higher than those of normal traffic, which confirms the observation 4.

Exceptions for these observations may occur in some special cases. For instance, a normal web sever working on high traffic load will violate the first observation. However, this kind of violations has a slight impact on the final intrusion decisions according to later experimental evaluations. This is because the outlier detection technique eliminates empirical observation errors. We con-

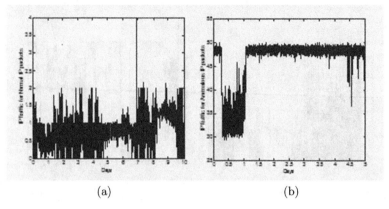

**Fig. 7.** (a) Load ratio for normal packets with same *dip* over $\delta_t$. (b) Load ratio for anomalous packets with same *dip* over $\delta_t$.

sider only the most generic cases when we derive empirical utility functions of network traffic.

## 2.2   Feature Extraction

In order to achieve efficient and effective detection, we extract a limited feature set consisting of four dimensions by applying some transformations on the feature set denoted by $F$. Specifically, four ordinal utility functions are defined to characterize the degree of anomalousness of network activities, and each of them maps several features in $F$ into a single numerical feature [16]. We name the four utility functions IP Weight. Each of the functions measures empirically the anomalousness along one of four dimensions, namely frequency, randomness, structure and load. We denote by $ipw_{freq}:F \rightarrow R$, $ipw_{ran}:F \rightarrow R$, $ipw_{str}:F \rightarrow R$, and $ipw_{load}:F \rightarrow R$ respectively the frequency, randomness, structure and load component of IP Weight, where $R$ is the set of real numbers. An empirical assumption behind IP Weight metrics is that *the greater the value of IP Weight, the more anomalous a packet flow $f \in F$ is*. All four components of IP weight metrics must satisfy this empirical assumption, and as a result, the underlying logic to derive the corresponding four utility functions is that *the greater the value of utility functions, the more anomalous a packet flow $f \in F$ is*.

**Frequency-Based Feature Extraction.** Given a packet flow $f \in F$ with same *dip* during $\delta_t$, we denote by $x_1$ and $x_2$ the appearing frequency of IP packets during $\delta_t$ and the maximum appearing frequency of IP packets over all destination ports during $\delta_t$, respectively. Thus, we have:

$$x_1 = \frac{nop}{\delta_t} \text{ and } x_2 = \frac{nodp_{\max}}{\delta_t}$$

Empirical observations show that the greater the value of $x_1$ and $x_2$, the more likely the corresponding network packet flow is anomalous. Both $x_1$ and $x_2$ contribute to some extent the anomalousness of network traffic. As a result, we define $ipw_{freq}$ by adopting a polynomial representation, which is expressed as follows:

$$ipw_{freq}(f) = (x_1 f_1(x_1, x_2) + x_2 f_2(x_1, x_2))g(x_1, x_2).\qquad(1)$$

Where $f_1: R \times R \to [0,1]$ and $f_2: R \times R \to [0,1]$ are two numerical functions that represent the contributions of $x_1$ and $x_2$ respectively; $g : R \times R \to R$ is a numerical function adjusting the value of $ipw_{freq}$, which is selected as $x_2/x_1$. Given $x_1$ and $x_2$, the constraints $x_2 \le x_1$ and $f_1(x_1, x_2) + f_2(x_1, x_2) = 1$ are always satisfied, and thus by selecting $f_2$ as $x_2/x_1$, we can derive the expression of $f_1$. By substituting $f_1$, $f_2$ and $g$ in equation (1), we can express the empirical utility function $ipw_{freq}$ as follows:

$$ipw_{freq}(f) = \left(x_1 - x_2 + x_1^{-1}x_2^2\right)\frac{x_2}{x_1}.\qquad(2)$$

**Randomness-Based Feature Extraction.** The entropy is selected to measure the randomness of variables according to information theory. Given a packet flow $f \in F$ with same $dip$ during $\delta_t$, the randomness of their corresponding source IP addresses, ports, and destination ports is denoted by $H_{sip}$, $H_{sp}$ and $H_{dp}$, respectively; $p(sip)$ refers to the appearing probability associated with source IP addresses $sip$, which is computed by taking the ratio of number of packets with specified source IP address $sip$ by the total number of packets observed in the flow $f$. Using the same approach, we can compute the $p(sp)$ and $p(dp)$, which refer to the probabilities associated with source port $sp$ and destination port $dp$, respectively.

Since each of these features has the same contribution to the anomalousness of network traffic, we combine them into a single feature by selecting their maximum value in order to satisfy the empirical assumption of IP weight metrics. Consequently, the utility function $ipw_{ran}$ is defined as follows:

$$ipw_{ran}(f) = \max(H_{sip}(f), H_{sp}(f), H_{dp}(f))\qquad(3)$$

**Load-Based Feature Extraction.** For a normal target host $dip$, the magnitudes of its incoming and (matching) outgoing traffic are most likely similar. However, when denial of service (DoS) attacks are used to compromise this host, its outgoing traffic is usually low compared to its incoming traffic. Empirical observations made earlier confirm this.

Given a packet flow $f \in F$, we extract two new features $traffic_{in}$ and $traffic_{out}$ to represent the appearing frequency of packets flowing to $dip$ over $\delta_t$ and the appearing frequency of packets outgoing from $dip$ over $\delta_t$. The ratio between $traffic_{in}$ and $traffic_{out}$ describes the load balance of the host we want to protect. Thus the utility function $ipw_{load}$ is defined as follows:

$$ipw_{load}(f) = \frac{traffic_{in}}{traffic_{out}}\qquad(4)$$

**Load-Based Feature Extraction.** Normal IP packets must satisfy some basic structural rules. In most cases, TCP/IP implementation will help to check the structures of packets. However, in some cases, the structure violation is difficult to be found by TCP/IP stack implementation. According to our domain knowledge on the structure of IP packets, we define a limited number of rules, which are usually satisfied by any pair of packets belonging to the same TCP/UDP connection. Fig. 8 describes the rule base for these rules. Given a packet flow $f \in F$ with same $dip$ during $\delta_t$ and a pair of packets $p_1, p_2 \in g$ observed during $\delta_t$, the utility function $ipw_{str}$ is defined as follows:

$$ipw_{str}(f) = \frac{1}{nop(nop - 1)} \sum_{p \in g} \sum_{\substack{q \in g, \\ p \neq q}} \varepsilon_{pq} e^{-|ident(p) - ident(q)|} \qquad (5)$$

rule 1 - if $ident_1 = ident_2$, then $fragoff_1 \neq fragoff_2$
rule 2 - if $ident_1 > ident_2 + 1$ then $seq_1 \geq seq_2$ and $ack_1 \geq ack_2$
rule 3 - if $ident_2 > ident_1 + 1$ then $seq_2 \geq seq_1$ and $ack_2 \geq ack_1$
rule 4 - if $ident_1 = ident_2 + 1$ then $seq_1 = seq_2 + pktl_2 - ihl_2 - thl_2$ and $ack_1 \geq ack_2$
rule 5 - if $ident_2 = ident_1 + 1$ then $seq_2 = seq_1 + pktl_1 - ihl_1 - thl_1$ and $ack_2 \geq ack_1$

**Fig. 8.** Rule-base for packets in the same connection

Where $|ident(p)-ident(q)|$ stands for the absolute value of the difference between identification fields of packets $p$ and $q$; Coefficient $nop(nop\text{-}1)$ is a normalizing factor, and $nop$ stands for the total number of packets in the flow $f$. $\varepsilon_{pq}$ is a positive integer, which takes the following values: $\varepsilon_{pq}=1$ if packets $p$ and $q$ belong to the same TCP/UDP connection and violate the rule base simultaneously; $\varepsilon_{pq}=0$ otherwise.

$|ident(p)\text{-}ident(q)|$ is used to measure the uncertainty of two packets belonging to the same connection. It is difficult to establish that two packets belong to the same connection with full certainty although the notion of connection-similarity has defined a precondition that IP packets belonging to the same TCP/UDP connection must have *the same source IP addresses and ports, the same destination IP addresses and ports, and the same protocol types.* The standard specification and empirical observation show that given two packets $p$ and $q$ which satisfy the connection-similarity precondition, the smaller the difference value $|ident(p)\text{-}ident(q)|$, the higher the probability of two packets $p$ and $q$ belonging to the same connection.

## 3    Outlier Detection and Intrusion Decision

We use Gaussian mixture model (GMM) to detect the outlier from a given dataset. In pattern recognition, it was established that Gaussian mixture distribution could approximate any distribution up to arbitrary accuracy, as long as a sufficient number of components are used [15], and thus the unknown probability density function can be expressed as a weighted finite sum of Gaussian with different parameters and mixing proportions [18]. Given a random variable $x$, its probability density function $p(x)$ can be represented as a weighted sum of components:

$$p(x) = \sum_{i=1}^{k} a_i f_i(x; u_i, v_i)$$

Where $k$ is the number of mixture components; $a_i$ $(1 \leq i \leq k)$ stand for the mixing proportions, whose sum is always equal to 1. $f_i(x; u_i, v_i)$ refers to the component density function, in which $u_i$ stands for the mean of variable $x$ and $v_i$ is the variance of $x$,. The density function can be a multivariate Gaussian or a univariate Gaussian.

**Table 1.** Proposed outlier detection algorithm

---
**Function:** GMM_Outlier_Detection (dataset and k) **returns** outlier data set
**Inputs:** *dataset* $X \sim \{x_n | n = 1, 2, ..., N\}$, *and the estimated number of components k*
**Output:** Outlier Data Set
**Initialization:**
Outlier Data Set = $\phi$; $j \leftarrow 0$;
Initial parameters $\{\alpha_i^j, \mu_i^j, \nu_i^j\}$, $1 \leq i \leq k$, are randomly generated;
Calculate the initial log-likelihood $L_j$;
**Repeat:**
For $1 \leq i \leq k, 1 \leq n \leq N$
**If** ( $\alpha_i^j \geq outlier_{thres}$) **then** compute posterior probability $p_j(i|x_n)$;
**Else** $p_j(i|x_n) = 0$;
$j \leftarrow j + 1$;
Re-estimate $\{\alpha_i^j, \mu_i^j, \nu_i^j\}$ by using $p_{j-1}(i|x_n)$, $1 \leq i \leq k, 1 \leq n \leq N$;
Calculate the current log-likelihood $L_j$;
**Until:** $|L_j - L_{j-1}| < th_1$ or $j > th_2$
For $1 \leq i \leq k, 1 \leq n \leq N$
**If** ($p_{j-1}(i|x_n) = 0$), assign $x_n$ to Outlier Data Set
**Return** Outlier Data Set;

---

Expectation-Maximization (EM) algorithm has been suggested as an effective algorithm to estimate the parameters of GMM [3]. In the E-step, the posterior probability $p(i|x_n)$ is calculated for each data $X \sim \{x_n | n=1,2,...,N\}$ and each mixture component $i(1 \leq i \leq k)$. In M-step, the set of parameters $\{a_i, u_i, v_i\}$ are re-estimated based on posterior probabilities $p(i|x_n)$, which maximize the likelihood function. The EM algorithm starts with some initial random parameters and then repeatedly applies the E-step and M-step to generate better parameter estimates until the algorithm converges to a local maximum.

Our outlier detection algorithm is based on the posterior probability generated by EM algorithm. The posterior probability describes the likelihood that the data pattern approximates to a specified Gaussian component. The greater the posterior probability for a data pattern belonging to a specified Gaussian component, the higher the approximation is. As a result, data are assigned to the corresponding Gaussian components according to their posterior probabilities. However, in some cases there are some data patterns whose posterior probability of belonging to any component of GMM is very low or close to zero. These data are naturally seen as the outliers or noisy data. We illustrate the detailed outlier detection algorithm in Table 1.

Thresholds $th_1$ and $th_2$ correspond to the termination conditions associated with the outlier detection algorithm: $th_1$ measures of the absolute precision required by the algorithm and $th_2$ is the maximum number of iterations of our algorithm. Threshold $outlier_{thres}$ refers to the minimum mixing proportion. Once the mixing proportion corresponding to one specified Gaussian component is below $outlier_{thres}$, the posterior probability of the data pattern belonging to this Gaussian component will be set to 0.

The intrusion decision strategy is based on the outcome of outlier detection: *if no outlier data are detected, the network packet flows is normal; otherwise, the packet flows represented by this outlier is reported as the intrusion.* This strategy is reasonable based on the empirical assumption that *the greater the value of IP Weight metrics, the more anomalous the network packet flows.*

## 4    Evaluation

### 4.1    Offline Evaluation

The 1998 DARPA intrusion detection dataset is the first standard corpus used for evaluating intrusion detection approaches offline [11]. Over 300 attacks are simulated in nine weeks. Training data are generated in the first seven weeks and testing data are derived in the rest two weeks. The attacks consisting of a total of 33 different attack types are divided into four different attack categories, namely DoS, R2L, U2S and Probing. In this paper, the proposed IP Weight metrics characterize the anomalousness of packet flows and hence we are interested in those multiple-connection based network intrusions, in which attacks are involved into multiple network connections and IP Weight metrics can be calculated from these multiple connections (i.e. packet flows). During the experiment, we extracted these attacks from the DARPA dataset and established a new multiple-connection based network intrusion dataset, which contains a combination of DoS, R2L, and Probing attacks. Specifically, we select 17 days' data from the total 45 days' (nine weeks) dataset. The corresponding attack types include *synflood, smurf, pod, teardrop, portsweep, ipsweep, land, back, saint, udpstorm, guest, nmap, satan, imap, dict, apache2, processtable, mscan* and *mailbomb.*

One data record for the 1998 DARPA intrusion detection dataset mainly includes nine fields, namely index, traffic start date, traffic start time, duration, service type, source port, destination port, source IP address and destination IP address. Based on these data, we calculate three components of IP Weight metrics, namely $ipw_{freq}$, $ipw_{ran}$ and $ipw_{str}$. The fourth component $ipw_{load}$ cannot be derived in the offline evaluation since the DARPA dataset didn't provide the exact incoming or outgoing traffic information for the protected target host. As a result, the specified network traffic in DARPA dataset are represented by total 3600 instances along with three dimensions, namely $ipw_{freq}$, $ipw_{ran}$ and $ipw_{str}$. 3493 instances represent the normal network traffic and 107 instances represent the intrusive traffic, which include 19 types of multiple-connection based network intrusions.

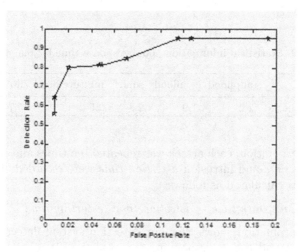

**Fig. 9.** ROC curves for our detection system

Two performance metrics are used to evaluate the detection effectiveness, namely detection rate (DR) and false positive rate (FPR). DR is the ratio of the number of attack instances detected to the total number of attack instances and FPR is the ratio of the number of normal instances detected as alerts to the total number of normal instances. We calculate the DR and FPR by varying the threshold $outlier_{thres}$ and then plot the receiving operator characteristic (ROC) curve in Fig. 9. The best detection result is obtained at a threshold of $10^{-8}$, which corresponds to <DR = 80.37%, FPR = 2.03%> and 16 types of multiple-connection based attacks out of a total of 19 attack types are detected at this point. Attacks *processtable*, *dictionary*, and *guest* (variant of *dictionary*) are missed by our detection system.

## 4.2   Online Evaluation

Online evaluation in a real networking environment is conducted to assess the efficiency and effectiveness of our detection system. The implementation of our system includes two modules, namely grader and detector. In the grader, IP packets are collected and then IP Weights are calculated according to the corresponding metrics. The IP Weights are then stored on a database. Synchronously, the detector reads IP Weights from database, detects the outlier data for IP Weights and then makes intrusion decisions.

The hardware topology of the live networking environment includes two LANs: LAN1 and LAN2. The internal attack traffic is generated from LAN1;

LAN2 is the victim network. Our detection system is deployed on a specified sever in LAN2. During the evaluation, we executed six types of network attacks from LAN 1, four of which, categorized as distributed denial of service (DDoS) attacks, include *synflood, smurf, udpflood* and a mixture of *synflood* and *udpflood.* The other two attacks fall into the category of probing attacks, namely *xscan* [19] and *fluxay* [7].

**Table 2.** Statistical information about response time for real attacks

| Attack | udpflood | synflood | smurf | mixture flood | fluxay | xscan |
|---|---|---|---|---|---|---|
| Avg. res. time (s) | 2.2 | 1.9 | 2.8 | 2.5 | 5.7 | 7.6 |

During the evaluation, each attack was repeated ten times and corresponding attack *starting time* and intrusion *detection time* were recorded. The intrusion *response time* is calculated as follows:

$$response\ time = detection\ time - starting\ time$$

The online evaluation shows that our detection system detected all the six types of attacks and the corresponding response time is on the second level. Table 2 illustrates the average response time for each attack over 10 times.

## 5    Conclusions

In this paper, we propose a real-time online intrusion detection framework, in which network packet flows are first characterized and quantified by using some anomalousness metrics named IP Weight and then an online outlier detection algorithm is used to detect the outlier (noisy) data of IP Weight metrics. Intrusion decisions are made according to the outcome of outlier detections. The offline evaluation with the 1998 DARPA intrusion detection dataset and the online evaluation in a live networking environment show the efficiency and effectiveness of our detection system.

The future works include improving the detection rate and decreasing false alarm rate for our system. The best result in the offline evaluation yields a 80.37% detection rate with a 2.03% false alarm rate. Although it was suggested that the DARPA dataset itself has some flaws [13], the offline experimental results still provide a strong criteria for the performance of our detection framework. In order to address the above issues, two substantial works are necessary in the future. One is the characterization of the 'normal' network packet flows by deriving new metrics under the constraint of effectiveness and efficiency. The other is related to the detection techniques discriminating anomalous behaviors from normal profiles and the decision strategies verifying intrusive or normal.

# References

1. Anderson, J.P.: Computer Security Threat Monitoring and Surveillance. Technical Report, James P. Anderson Co., Fort Washington, Pennsylvania (1980)
2. Axelsson, S.: The Base-Rate Fallacy and the Difficulty of Intrusion Detection. ACM Transactions on Information and System Security (TISSEC), Vol. 3. (2000) 186-201
3. Dempster, A. P., Laird, N. M. and Rubin, D. B.: Maximum Likelihood from Incomplete Data via the EM Algorithm (with discussion). Journal of the Royal Statistical Society B, Vol. 39. (1977) 1-38
4. Denning, D. E.: An Intrusion Detection Model. IEEE Transactions on Software Engineering, No. 2. (1987) 222-232
5. Eskin, E.: Anomaly Detection over Noisy Data using Learned Probability Distributions. Proceedings of 17th International Conference on Machine Learning. (2000) 255-262
6. Eskin, E., Arnold, A., Prerau, M., Portnoy, L. and Stolfo, S.: A Geometric Framework for Unsupervised Anomaly Detection: Detecting Intrusions in Unlabeled Data. On Application of Data Mining in Computer Security, Kluwer Academic Publisher (2002)
7. Fluxay, http://www.netxeyes.com
8. Frank, J.: Artificial Intelligence and Intrusion Detection: Current and Future Directions. Proceedings of the 17th National Computer Security Conference, (1994) 11-21
9. Forrest, S., Hofmeyr, S.A. and Longstaff, T.A.: A Sense of Self for Unix Processes. Proceedings of 1996 IEEE Symposium on Security and Privacy. (1996) 120-128
10. Hochberg, J., Jackson, K., Stallings, C., McClary, J. F., DuBois, D. and Ford, J.: NADIR: An Automated System for Detecting Network Intrusion and Misuse. Computers & Security, 12 (3). (1993) 235-248
11. Kendall, K.: A Database of Computer Attacks for the Evaluation of Intrusion Detection Systems. Master's Thesis, Massachusetts Institute of Technology (1998)
12. Lunt, T., Jagannathan, R., Lee, R., Listgarten, S., Edwards, D., Neumann, P., Javitz, H. and Valdes, A.: IDES: The Enhanced Prototype, A Real-time Intrusion Detection System. Technical Report, SRI Project 4185-010, Computer Science Laboratory, CA. (1988)
13. McHugh, J.: The 1998 Lincoln Lab IDS Evaluation - A Critique. Proceedings of Recent Advances in Intrusion Detection, No. 1907 in LNCS. (2000) 145-161
14. Portnoy, L., Eskin, E. and Stolfo, S.: Intrusion Detection with Unlabeled Data using Clustering. Proceedings of ACM CSS Workshop on Data Mining Applied to Security (2001)
15. Ripley, B.D.: Pattern Recognition and Neural Networks. Cambridge, U.K., Cambridge University Press (1996)
16. Roberts, F. S.: Measurement Theory. Addison-Wesley Publishing Company (1979)
17. Smaha, S. E.: Haystack: An Intrusion Detection System. Proceedings of the IEEE Fourth Aerospace Computer Security Applications Conference. (1988) 37-44
18. Titterington, D., Smith, A. and Makov, U.: Statistical Analysis of Finite Mixture Distributions. John Wiley & Sons, New York (1985)
19. X-scan, http://www.xfocus.org

# ID-Based Aggregate Signatures from Bilinear Pairings

Jing Xu[1,2], Zhenfeng Zhang[1,3], and Dengguo Feng[1,3]

[1] State Key Laboratory of Information Security, P.R. China
[2] Graduate School of Chinese Academy of Sciences,
Beijing 100039, P.R. China
[3] Institute of Software, Chinese Academy of Sciences,
Beijing 100080, P.R. China
{xujing, zfzhang, feng}@is.iscas.ac.cn

**Abstract.** Aggregate signature scheme was recently proposed by Boneh, Gentry, Lynn and Shacham, which presented a method for combining $n$ signatures from $n$ different signers on $n$ different messages into one signature. In this paper, we propose an identity-based aggregate signature scheme based on the bilinear pairings. This enhances the efficiency of communication and signature verification process. We show that the security of our scheme is tightly related to the computational Diffie-Hellman assumption in the random oracle model.

**Keywords:** ID-based signatures, aggregate signatures, bilinear pairings.

## 1 Introduction

Authentication constitutes one of the core problems in cryptography. Much modern research focuses on constructing authentication schemes that are: (1) as secure as possible, i.e., provably secure under the most general assumptions; and (2) as efficient as possible, i.e., communication- and computation-efficient. For cryptographic schemes to be adopted in practice, efficiency is crucial. Moreover, communication and storage efficiency—namely, the size of the authentication data, for example the size of a signature—lays an even greater role than computation: while computational power of modern computers has experienced rapid growth over the last several decades, the growth in bandwidth of communication networks seems to have more constraints.

Recently, Boneh et al. [1] introduced and realized aggregate signatures. An aggregate signature scheme is a signature scheme which, in addition to the usual setup, signing, and verification algorithms, admits an efficient algorithm for aggregating $n$ signatures under $n$ different public keys into one signature. Namely, suppose each one of $n$ users has a public-private key pair $(PK_i, SK_i)$ ; each wishes to attest to a message $m_i$. Each user first signs her message $m_i$, obtaining a signature $\sigma_i$; the $n$ signatures can then be combined by an unrelated party into an aggregate $\sigma$. An aggregate signature scheme also includes an extra verification algorithm that verifies such an aggregate signature. An aggregate

Y.G. Desmedt et al. (Eds.): CANS 2005, LNCS 3810, pp. 110–119, 2005.

signature provides non-repudiation simultaneously on message $m_1$ for User 1, message $m_2$ for User 2, and so forth. Crucially, such repudiation holds for each user regardless of whether other users are malicious.

In 1984, Shamir proposed a new model for public key cryptography, called identity (ID)- based encryption and signature schemes, to simplify key management procedures of certificate-based public key infrastructures (PKIs) [2]. Since then, several ID-based encryption and signature schemes have been proposed based on integer factorization problem [3][4].

The bilinear pairings, namely the Weil pairing and the Tate pairing of algebraic curves, are important tools for research on algebraic geometry. They have been found various applications in cryptography recently [5][6][7][8][9]. More precisely, they can be used to construct ID-based cryptographic schemes [10].

In spite of several advantages of ID-based signature schemes based on pairings, they suffer some restriction on applications due to efficiency problem: Their signature verifications are ten times or one hundred times slower than that of DSS or RSA [11]. This problem may be critical in some applications such as electronic commerce or banking service in which one server has to verify many signatures simultaneously. In order to enhance the efficiency of verification process and make efficient communication, we consider ID-based aggregate signatures.

Cheon et al.[12] proposed the first ID-based aggregate signature scheme. Their security proofs were obtained through Pointcheval and Stern's forking lemma [13][14]. However, this reduction is inefficient: to break the computational problem with a probability comparable to the success probability of the signature forger, the reduction algorithm needs to execute a full run of the forging algorithm $q_H$ times, where $q_H$ denotes the number of hash function queries made by the forger.

In the area of provable security, the last couple of years saw the rise of a new trend consisting of providing tight security reductions for asymmetric cryptosystems : the security of a cryptographic protocol is said to be tightly related to a hard computational problem if an attacker against the scheme implies an efficient algorithm solving the problem with roughly the same advantage.

In this paper, we begin by giving a formal definition of ID-based aggregate signatures and its security model. We then propose an efficient ID-based aggregate signature scheme whose security can be proved tightly related to computational Diffie-Hellman (CDH) problem in the random oracle model. Unlike [12], we do not rely on the forking lemma in our security reduction,hence the advantage relation can be shown to be linear, which is almost the best possible. Moreover, as pointed out in [12], our scheme seems to be the only known ID-based aggregate signature which has tight security reduction.

The rest of the paper is organized as follows. In Section 2 we give formal definitions of presumed hard computational problems from which our reductions are made and then recall an ID-based signature scheme SOK-IBS [15]. In Section 3, we present an ID-based aggregate signature scheme and formally analyze its security and efficiency. And we end with concluding remarks in Section 4.

## 2    Preliminary

### 2.1    The Bilinear Pairing

Let $G$ be a cyclic additive group generated by $P$, whose order is a prime $q$, and $L$ be a cyclic multiplicative group of the same order. Let $\hat{e} : G \times G \to L$ be a pairing which satisfies the following conditions:

1. Bilinearity: For any $P, Q, R \in G$, we have $\hat{e}(P + Q, R) = \hat{e}(P, R)\hat{e}(Q, R)$ and $\hat{e}(P, Q + R) = \hat{e}(P, Q)\hat{e}(P, R)$. In particular, for any $a, b \in \mathbf{Z}_q$,

$$\hat{e}(aP, bP) = \hat{e}(P, P)^{ab} = \hat{e}(P, abP) = \hat{e}(abP, P).$$

2. Non-degeneracy: There exists $P, Q \in G$, such that $\hat{e}(P, Q) \neq 1$.
3. Computability: There is an efficient algorithm to compute $\hat{e}(P, Q)$ for all $P, Q \in G$.

The typical way of obtaining such pairings is by deriving them from the Weil-pairing or the Tate-pairing on an elliptic curve over a finite field.

### 2.2    Gap Diffie-Hellman (GDH) Groups

Let $G$ be a cyclic group of prime order $q$ and $P$ be a generator of $G$.

1. The decisional Diffie-Hellman (DDH) problem is to decide whether $c = ab$ in $Z/qZ$ for given $P, aP, bP, cP \in G$. If so, $(P, aP, bP, cP)$ is called a valid Diffie-Hellman (DH) tuple.
2. The computational Diffie-Hellman (CDH) problem is to compute $abP$ for given $P, aP, bP \in G$.

**Definition 1.** The advantage of an algorithm $\mathcal{F}$ in solving the computational Diffie-Hellman problem on group $G$ is

$$AdvCDH_{\mathcal{F}} = Pr[\mathcal{F}(P, aP, bP) = abP : \forall a, b \in Z_q]$$

The probability is taken over the choice of $a, b$ and $\mathcal{F}$'s coin tosses. An algorithm $\mathcal{F}$ is said $(t, \varepsilon)$-breaks the computational Diffie-Hellman problem on $G$ if $\mathcal{F}$ runs in time at most $t$, and $AdvCDH_{\mathcal{F}}$ is at least $\varepsilon$.

Now we present a definition for a gap Diffie-Hellman (GDH) group.

**Definition 2.** A group $G$ is a $(t, \varepsilon)$-gap Diffie-Hellman (GDH) group if the decisional Diffie-Hellman problem in $G$ can be efficiently computable and there exists no algorithm $(t, \varepsilon)$-breaks computational Diffie-Hellman on $G$.

If we have an admissible bilinear pairing $\hat{e}$ in $G$, we can solve the DDH problem in $G$ efficiently as follows:

$(P, aP, bP, cP)$ is a valid DH tuple $\Leftrightarrow \hat{e}(aP, bP) = \hat{e}(P, cP)$

Hence an elliptic curve becomes an instance of a GDH group if the Weil (or the Tate) pairing is efficiently computable and the CDH is sufficiently hard on the curve.

### 2.3   Brief Review of Sakai et al.' Scheme

It comprises four algorithms: $(\mathcal{G}, \mathcal{K}, \mathcal{S}, \mathcal{V})$.

- $\mathcal{G}$: Assume $k$ is a security parameter, $G$ is a GDH group of prime order $q > 2^k$ generated by $P$, and $\hat{e} : G \times G \to L$ is a bilinear map. Pick a random master key $s \in Z_q^*$ and set $P_{pub} = sP$. Choose two hash functions $H_1, H_2 : \{0,1\}^* \to G$.
- $\mathcal{K}$: Given a user's identity ID, compute $Q_{ID} = H_1(ID) \in G$ and the associated private key $d_{ID} = sQ_{ID} \in G$.
- $\mathcal{S}$: In order to sign a message $m$,
   1.Randomly pick $r \in Z_q^*$ and compute $U = rP \in G$ and then put $\tilde{H} = H_2(ID, m, U) \in G$.
   2. Compute $V = d_{ID} + r\tilde{H} \in G$.
   The signature on $m$ is the pair $\sigma = \langle U, V \rangle \in G \times G$.
- $\mathcal{V}$: To verify a signature $\sigma = \langle U, V \rangle \in G \times G$ on a message $m$ for an identity ID, the verifier first takes $Q_{ID} = H_1(ID) \in G$ and $\tilde{H} = H_2(ID, m, U) \in G$. He then accepts the signature if $\hat{e}(P, V) = \hat{e}(P_{pub}, Q_{ID})\hat{e}(U, \tilde{H})$ and rejects it otherwise.

## 3   ID-Based Aggregate Signatures

We define ID-based aggregate signatures and propose an ID-based aggregate signature scheme based on SOK-IBS. Also we define security models and provide proofs of tight security reductions for the signature scheme.

Consider a set R of users. Each user $ID_i \in R$ has a signing key pair $(ID_i, d_i)$. We wish to aggregate the signatures of some subset $R' \subseteq R$. Each user $ID_i \in R'(i = 1, 2, \cdots, n)$ produces a signature $(U_i, V_i)$ on a message $m_i$ of her choice. These signatures are then combined into an aggregate signature $(U_1, U_2, \cdots, U_n, V)$ by an aggregating party. Moreover, the aggregation can be performed incrementally. The aggregating party, who can be different from and untrusted by the users in $R'$, has access to the users' ID, to the messages, and to the signatures on them, but not to any private keys. This aggregation has the property that a verifier given an aggregate signature along with ID of the parties involved and their respective messages is convinced that each user signed her respective message.

### 3.1   The Proposed ID-Based Aggregate Signature Schemes

The scheme comprises six algorithms: $\mathcal{G}, \mathcal{K}, \mathcal{S}, \mathcal{V}, \mathcal{AG}, \mathcal{AV}$.

- $\mathcal{G}, \mathcal{K}, \mathcal{S}, \mathcal{V}$: These algorithms are the same as in the Sakai et al.' scheme presented above .
- $\mathcal{AG}$: Denote by $(ID, m, U, V)$ a signature $(U, V)$ for a message $m$ generated by a signer with an identity ID. Given $n$ signatures $(ID_1, m_1, U_1, V_1), (ID_2, m_2, U_2, V_2), \cdots, (ID_n, m_n, U_n, V_n)$ compute $V = \sum_{i=1}^{n} V_i$ and output an aggregate signature $\sigma = (U_1, U_2, \cdots, U_n, V)$ .

– $\mathcal{AV}$: The verifier is given an aggregate signature $\sigma$ as above, the original messages $m_i \in \{0,1\}^*$ and $ID_i$ for all users. To verify the aggregate signature $\sigma$, compute $Q_i = H_1(ID_i)$ and $\tilde{H}_i = H_2(ID_i, m_i, U_i)$ for $i = 1, 2, \cdots, n$. The aggregate signature $\sigma$ is accepted if and only if

$$\hat{e}(P, V) = \prod_{i=1}^{n} \hat{e}(P_{pub}, Q_i)\hat{e}(U_i, \tilde{H}_i)$$

Unlike the aggregate signature scheme in [1], the signed messages are not required be distinct. In the ID-based aggregate signature scheme, a potential attack on aggregate signatures of the same message discussed by [1] can be avoided.

### 3.2   ID-Based Aggregate Signature Security

We formalize the ID-based aggregate signature security model. In this aggregate model, the adversary $\mathcal{F}$ is given a single ID. His goal is the existential forgery of an aggregate signature. We allow an aggregate forger to choose all IDs except the challenge ID. The aggregate forger is also given access to a signing oracle with respect to the challenge ID. His advantage $\mathbf{Adv}_{\mathcal{AGG},\mathcal{F}}$, is defined to be his probability of success in the following game.

- (**Setup:**) The aggregate forger $\mathcal{F}$ is provided with $ID_1$, which is an identity generated at random.
- (**Extraction Queries:**) Given an identity $ID_i(i \neq 1)$, the challenger returns the private key $d_i$ corresponding to $ID_i$.
- (**Signature Queries:**) Proceeding adaptively, $\mathcal{F}$ requests signatures with respect to identity $ID_1$ on messages of his choice.
- (**Response:**) Finally, $\mathcal{F}$ outputs $n - 1$ additional identities $ID_2, ID_3, \cdots, ID_n$. Here $n$ is at most $N$, a game parameter. The forger $\mathcal{F}$ shall also output messages $m_1, m_2, \cdots, m_n$ and an aggregate signature $\sigma$ with respect to these $n$ identities, on the corresponding messages.

The forger $\mathcal{F}$ wins if the aggregate signature $\sigma$ is valid on messages $m_1, m_2, \cdots, m_n$ under $ID_1, ID_2, \cdots, ID_n$, and $\mathcal{F}$ did not request a signatue on $m_1$ under $ID_1$. The probability is over the coin tosses of the key-generation algorithm and of $\mathcal{F}$.

**Definition 3.** An aggregate forger $\mathcal{F}$ is said $(t, q_{H_1}, q_{H_2}, q_E, q_S, N, \varepsilon)$ -breaks an $N$ -user aggregate signature scheme in the aggregate model if: $\mathcal{F}$ runs in time at most $t$; $\mathcal{F}$ makes at most $q_{H_i}$ queries to the hash function $H_i(i = 1, 2)$, at most $q_E$ queries to the key extraction oracle and at most $q_S$ queries to the signing oracle; $\mathbf{Adv}_{\mathcal{AGG},\mathcal{F}}$ is at least $\varepsilon$; and the forged aggregate signature is by at most $N$ users. An ID-based aggregate signature scheme is $(t, q_{H_1}, q_{H_2}, q_E, q_S, N, \varepsilon)$ - secure against existential forgery in the aggregate model if no forger $(t, q_{H_1}, q_{H_2}, q_E, q_S, N, \varepsilon)$ -breaks it.

**Theorem 1.** Given a security parameter $k$, let $G$ be a $(t', \varepsilon')$ -GDH group of prime order $q > 2^k$, $P$ be a generator of $G$, and $\hat{e} : G \times G \to L$ be a bilinear map. Then the ID-based aggregate signature scheme on $G$ is $(t, q_{H_1}, q_{H_2}, q_E,$ $q_S, N, \varepsilon)$-secure against existential forgery in the aggregate model for any $t$ and $\varepsilon$ satisfying

$$\varepsilon \geq e(q_E + N)(1 - q_S(q_S + q_{H_2})/2^k)^{-1}\varepsilon'$$
$$t \leq t' - C_G(q_{H_1} + q_{H_2} + q_E + 5q_S + 3N + 2),$$

where $e$ is the base of natural logarithms, and $C_G$ is the time of computing a scalar multiplication and inversion on $G$.

**Proof.** Suppose $\mathcal{F}$ is a forger algorithm that $(t, q_{H_1}, q_{H_2}, q_E, q_S, N, \varepsilon)$ -breaks the signature scheme. We show how to construct a $t'$ -time algorithm $\mathcal{C}$ that solves CDH in $G$ with probability at least $\varepsilon'$. This will contradict the fact that $G$ is a $(t', \varepsilon')$ -GDH group.

Algorithm $\mathcal{C}$ is given $X = xP \in G$ and $Y = yP \in G$. Its goal is to output $xY = xyP \in G$. Algorithm $\mathcal{C}$ simulates the challenger and interacts with forger $\mathcal{F}$ as follows.

***Setup:*** Algorithm $\mathcal{C}$ initializes $\mathcal{F}$ with $P_{pub} = X$ as a system's overall public key and provides $\mathcal{F}$ with a randomly generated identity $ID_1$.

***Queries on oracle $H_1$:*** At any time algorithm $\mathcal{F}$ can query the random oracle $H_1$. To respond to these queries, $\mathcal{C}$ maintains a list $L_1$ of tuples $\langle ID_i, w_i, b_i, c_i \rangle$ as explained below. The list is initially empty. When an identity ID is submitted to the $H_1$ oracle, algorithm $\mathcal{C}$ responds as follows:

1. If the query ID already appears on the $L_1$ in some tuple $\langle ID, w, b, c \rangle$ then algorithm $\mathcal{C}$ responds with $H_1(ID) = w \in G$.
2. Otherwise, $\mathcal{C}$ generates a random coin $c \in \{0, 1\}$ such that $Pr[c = 0] = \frac{1}{q_E + N}$.
3. Algorithm $\mathcal{C}$ picks a random $b \in Z_q$. If $c = 0$ holds, $\mathcal{C}$ computes $w = bY \in G$. If $c = 1$ holds, $\mathcal{C}$ computes $w = bP \in G$.
4. Algorithm $\mathcal{C}$ adds the tuple $\langle ID, w, b, c \rangle$ to the list $L_1$ and responds to $\mathcal{F}$ with $H_1(ID) = w$.

***Queries on oracle $H_2$:*** To respond to queries to $H_2$ oracle, $\mathcal{C}$ maintains a list $L_2$ of tuple $\langle ID_i, m_i, U_i, v_i \rangle$ as explained below. When a tuple $\langle ID, m, U \rangle$ is submitted to the $H_2$ oracle, algorithm $\mathcal{C}$ responds as follows:

1. If the query tuple already appears on the $L_2$ in some tuple $\langle ID, m, U, v \rangle$ then algorithm $\mathcal{C}$ responds with $H_2(ID, m, U) = vP \in G$.
2. Otherwise, algorithm $\mathcal{C}$ picks $v \in Z_q^*$ at random, stores the tuple $\langle ID, m, U, v \rangle$ in the list $L_2$ and returns $vP$ as a hash value to $\mathcal{F}$ .

***Key Extraction Queries:*** When $\mathcal{F}$ requests the private key associated to an identity ID, $\mathcal{C}$ recovers the corresponding $\langle ID, w, b, c \rangle$ from $L_1$. If $c = 0$, then $\mathcal{C}$ output *"failure"* and halts. Otherwise, it means that $H_1(ID)$ was previously defined to be $bP$ and $bP_{pub} = bX \in G$ is then returned to $\mathcal{F}$ as a private key associated to ID.

**Signature Queries**: Algorithm $\mathcal{F}$ requests a signature on some message $m$ under $ID_1$. Algorithm $\mathcal{C}$ responds to this query as follows: algorithm $\mathcal{C}$ first recovers the previously defined value $Q_{ID} = H_1(ID_1) \in G$ from the list $L_1$. It then chooses $r_1, r_2 \in Z_q^*$ at random, sets $V = r_1 P_{pub} = r_1 X \in G$, $U = r_2 P_{pub} = r_2 X \in G$ and defines the hash value $H_2(ID_1, m, U)$ as $r_2^{-1}(r_1 P - Q_{ID}) \in G$ ( $\mathcal{C}$ output "*failure*" and halts if $H_2$ turns out to be already defined for the input $(ID_1, m, U)$ ). The pair $(U, V)$ is a valid signature on message $m$ under $ID_1$. Algorithm $\mathcal{C}$ gives $(U, V)$ to algorithm $\mathcal{F}$.

**Output**: Finally, $\mathcal{F}$ halts. It either concedes failure, in which case so does $\mathcal{C}$, or it returns a value $n$ ($n \leq N$), $n - 1$ identities $ID_2, ID_3, \cdots, ID_n$, $n$ messages $m_1, m_2, \cdots, m_n$, and a forged aggregate signature $(U_1, U_2, \cdots, U_n, V)$. Forger $\mathcal{F}$ must not have requested a signature on $m_1$. Algorithm $\mathcal{C}$ recovers the corresponding $n$ tuples $\langle ID_i, w_i, b_i, c_i \rangle$ on the list $L_1$.

Algorithm $\mathcal{C}$ now proceeds only if $c_1 = 0$ and $c_i = 1$ for $2 \leq i \leq n$. Otherwise, $\mathcal{C}$ declares failure and halts. Since $c_1 = 0$, it follows that $Q_1 = b_1 Y$. And for $i > 1$, since $c_i = 1$, it follows that $Q_i = b_i P$. The aggregate signature $(U_1, U_2, \cdots, U_n, V)$ must satisfy the aggregate verification equation

$$\hat{e}(P, V) = \prod_{i=1}^{n} \hat{e}(P_{pub}, Q_i)\hat{e}(U_i, \tilde{H}_i)$$

Next, algorithm $\mathcal{C}$ recovers the $n$ corresponding tuples $\langle ID_i, m_i, U_i, v_i \rangle$ on the list $L_2$. Let $V_i = b_i P_{pub} + v_i U_i$ for $i > 1$. Then we have

$$\hat{e}(P, V_i) = \hat{e}(P, b_i P_{pub})\hat{e}(P, v_i U_i) = \hat{e}(P_{pub}, Q_i)\hat{e}(U_i, v_i P) = \hat{e}(P_{pub}, Q_i)\hat{e}(U_i, \tilde{H}_i)$$

Thus $(U_i, V_i)$ is a valid signature on $m_i$ under $ID_i$. Now $\mathcal{C}$ constructs $V_1$ as $V_1 = V - \sum_{i=2}^{n} V_i$. Then we can deduce

$$\hat{e}(P, V_1) = \hat{e}(P, V - \sum_{i=2}^{n} V_i) = \prod_{i=1}^{n} \hat{e}(P_{pub}, Q_i)\hat{e}(U_i, \tilde{H}_i) \prod_{i=2}^{n} \hat{e}(P_{pub}, Q_i)^{-1}\hat{e}(U_i, \tilde{H}_i)^{-1}$$
$$= \hat{e}(P_{pub}, Q_1)\hat{e}(U_1, \tilde{H}_1)$$

Here $\tilde{H}_1 = v_1 P$. Then $\mathcal{C}$ calculates and outputs the required $xY$ as $xY = b_1^{-1}(V_1 - v_1 U_1)$.

This completes the description of algorithm $\mathcal{C}$. To complete the proof, we shall show that $\mathcal{C}$ solves the given instance of CDH problem in $G$ with probability at least $\varepsilon'$. First, we analyze the four events needed for $\mathcal{C}$ to succeed:

- $\Sigma_1$: $\mathcal{C}$ does not abort as a result of any of $\mathcal{F}$'s key extraction queries.
- $\Sigma_2$: $\mathcal{C}$ does not abort as a result of any of $\mathcal{F}$'s signature queries.
- $\Sigma_3$: $\mathcal{F}$ generates a valid and nontrivial aggregate signature forgery $(U_1, U_2, \cdots, U_n, V)$.
- $\Sigma_4$: Event $\Sigma_3$ occurs, and, in addition, $c_1 = 0$, and $c_i = 1$ for $2 \leq i \leq n$, where for each $i$, $c_i$ is the $c$-component of the tuple containing $ID_i$ on the list $L_1$.

Algorithm $\mathcal{C}$ succeeds if all of these events happen. The probability $Pr[\Sigma_1 \wedge \Sigma_2 \wedge \Sigma_3 \wedge \Sigma_4]$ can be decomposed as

$$Pr[\Sigma_1 \wedge \Sigma_2 \wedge \Sigma_3 \wedge \Sigma_4] = Pr[\Sigma_1]Pr[\Sigma_2|\Sigma_1]Pr[\Sigma_3|\Sigma_1 \wedge \Sigma_2]Pr[\Sigma_4|\Sigma_1 \wedge \Sigma_2 \wedge \Sigma_3] \tag{1}$$

**Claim 1.** The probability that algorithm $\mathcal{C}$ does not abort as a result of $\mathcal{F}$'s key extraction queries is at least $(1 - 1/(q_E + N))^{q_E}$. Hence we have $Pr[\Sigma_1] \geq (1 - 1/(q_E + N))^{q_E}$.

**Proof.** As $Pr[c = 0] = 1/(q_E + N)$, for a key extraction query, the probability that $\mathcal{C}$ does not abort is $1 - 1/(q_E + N)$. Since $\mathcal{F}$ makes at most $q_E$ queries to the key extraction oracle, the probability that algorithm $\mathcal{C}$ does not abort as a result of $\mathcal{F}$'s key extraction queries is at least $(1 - 1/(q_E + N))^{q_E}$. □

**Claim 2.** The probability that algorithm $\mathcal{C}$ does not abort as a result of $\mathcal{F}$'s signature queries is at least $1 - q_S(q_{H_2} + q_S)2^{-k}$. Thus there hold $Pr[\Sigma_2|\Sigma_1] \geq 1 - q_S(q_{H_2} + q_S)2^{-k}$.

**Proof.** As the list $L_2$ never contains more than $q_{H_2} + q_S$ entries, the probability of $\mathcal{C}$ to fail in handling a signing query because of a conflict on $H_2$ is at most $q_S(q_{H_2} + q_S)2^{-k}$. And events $\Sigma_1$ and $\Sigma_2$ are independent, so $Pr[\Sigma_2|\Sigma_1] \geq 1 - q_S(q_{H_2} + q_S)2^{-k}$. □

**Claim 3.** If algorithm $\mathcal{C}$ does not abort as a result of $\mathcal{F}$'s signature queries and key extraction queries then algorithm $\mathcal{F}$'s view is identical to its view in the real attack. Hence, $Pr[\Sigma_3|\Sigma_1 \wedge \Sigma_2] \geq \varepsilon$.

**Claim 4.** The probability that algorithm $\mathcal{C}$ does not abort after $\mathcal{F}$ outputting a valid and nontrivial forgery is at least $(1 - 1/(q_E + N))^{N-1} \cdot 1/(q_E + N)$. Hence

$$Pr[\Sigma_4|\Sigma_1 \wedge \Sigma_2 \wedge \Sigma_3] \geq (1 - 1/(q_E + N))^{N-1} \cdot 1/(q_E + N)$$

**Proof.** Events $\Sigma_1$, $\Sigma_2$ and $\Sigma_3$ have occurred, and $\mathcal{F}$ has generated some valid and nontrivial forgery $(ID_1, \cdots, ID_n, m_1, \cdots, m_n, U_1, \cdots, U_n, V)$. For each $i$, $1 \leq i \leq n$, let $\langle ID_i, m_i, U_i, v_i \rangle$ be the tuple corresponding to $ID_i$ on the $L_1$-list. Algorithm $\mathcal{C}$ will abort unless $\mathcal{F}$ generates a forgery such that $c_1 = 0$ and, for $i > 1$, $c_i = 1$.

In the forged aggregation, $c_1 = 0$ occurs with probability $1/(q_E + N)$. And the probability that $c_i = 1$ for all $i, 2 \leq i \leq n$, is at least $(1 - 1/(q_E + N))^{n-1} \geq (1 - 1/(q_E + N))^{N-1}$.

Therefore $Pr[\Sigma_4|\Sigma_1 \wedge \Sigma_2 \wedge \Sigma_3] \geq (1 - 1/(q_E + N))^{N-1} \cdot 1/(q_E + N)$. □

According to the equation (1), algorithm $\mathcal{C}$ produces the correct answer with probability at least

$$\left(1 - \frac{q_S(q_{H_2} + q_S)}{2^k}\right) \cdot (1 - 1/(q_E + N))^{q_E+N-1} \cdot \frac{1}{q_E + N} \cdot \varepsilon$$

$$\geq \left(1 - \frac{q_S(q_{H_2} + q_S)}{2^k}\right) \frac{\varepsilon}{e(q_E + N)}$$

$$\geq \varepsilon'$$

as required.

Algorithm $\mathcal{C}$'s running time is the same as $\mathcal{F}$'s running time plus the time to respond to $(q_{H_1} + q_{H_2} + q_S)$ hash queries, $q_E$ key extraction queries and $q_S$ signature queries, and the time to transform $\mathcal{F}$'s final forgery into the CDH solution. Hence, the total running time is at most $t + C_G(q_{H_1} + q_{H_2} + q_E + 5q_S + 3N + 2) \leq t'$ as required. This completes the proof of Theorem.     □

### 3.3   Efficiency

Our identity based aggregate signature scheme enhances efficiency of verification. Given $n$ signatures $(U_1, V_1), \cdots, (U_n, V_n)$ for messages $m_1, m_2, \cdots, m_n$ issued by $ID_1, ID_2, \cdots, ID_n$ respectively. The $n$ signatures are accepted if and only if

$$\hat{e}(P, \sum_{i=1}^{n} V_i) = \hat{e}(P_{pub}, \sum_{i=1}^{n} Q_i) \prod_{i=1}^{n} \hat{e}(U_i, \tilde{H}_i)$$

Since elliptic curve additions and hash operations are far more efficient than pairing operations, the aggregate verification of our scheme is more efficient than individual verification of signatures.

When we verify signatures, we need only $\sum_{i=1}^{n} V_i$ rather than individual $V_i$, so we can compress almost a half of signature size. Note that all $U_i$s can not be aggregated into one element, because each of them is used as an input of the hash function.

## 4   Conclusion

In this paper we proposed an identity-based aggregate signature scheme from bilinear pairings. Our scheme is secure against existential forgery under adaptively chosen messages attacks, and the security is tightly related to Computational Diffie-Hellman (CDH) problem in the Random Oracle model. Furthermore, we showed that optimal security reductions are also achievable for ID-based aggregate signatures.

Boneh's aggregate signature scheme [1] is a method for combining $n$ signatures from $n$ different signers on $n$ different messages into one signature whose length is independent of $n$. It is an open problem to find an ID-based aggregate signature scheme whose signature length is a constant.

# Acknowledgements

This work is supported by the National Grand Fundamental Research Program of China under Grant No. G1999035802, the National Natural Science Foundation of China under Grant No. 60373039, and the Youth Foundation of the National Natural Science of China under Grant No. 60025205. The authors would like to thanks the anonymous referees for their helpful comments.

# References

1. D. Boneh, C. Gentry, B. Lynn, and H. Shacham. Aggregate and verifiably encrypted signatures from bilinear maps. Advances in Cryptology-Eurocrypt 2003, LNCS 2656, 416-432, Springer-Verlag, 2003.
2. A. Shamir. Identity-based cryptosystems and signature schemes. Advances in Cryptology-Crypto 1984, LNCS 196, 47-53, Springer-Verlag, 1984.
3. U. Maurer and Y. Yacobi. Non-interactive public-key cryptography. Advances in Cryptology- Eurocrypto 1991, LNCS 547, 458-460, Springer-Verlag, 1992.
4. S. Tsuji and T. Itoh. An ID-based Cryptosystem based on the Discrete Logarithm Problem. IEEE Journal of Selected Areas in Communications, Vol.7, 467-473, 1989.
5. D. Boneh and M. Franklin. Identity-based encryption from the Weil pairing. Advances in Cryptology-Crypto 2001, LNCS 2139, 213-229, Springer-Verlag, 2001.
6. D. Boneh, B. Lynn, and H. Shacham. Short signatures from the Weil pairing. Advances in Cryptology-Asiacrypt 2001, LNCS 2248, 514-532, Springer-Verlag, 2001.
7. A. Joux. The Weil and Tate Pairings as Building Blocks for Public Key Cryptosystems. ANTS 2002, LNCS 2369, 20-32, Springer-Verlag, 2002.
8. M.S. Kim and K. Kim. A new identification scheme based on the bilinear Diffie-Hellman problem. Proc. of ACISP(The 7th Australasian Conference on Information Security and Privacy) 2002, LNCS 2384, 464-481, Springer-Verlag, 2002.
9. D.Boneh and X.Boyen. Short Signatures without Random Oracles. Advances in Cryptology-Eurocrypt 2004,LNCS 3027,56-73,Springer-Verlag, 2004.
10. Xun Yi. An Identity-Based Signature Scheme from the Weil Pairing. IEEE Communications Letters, 7(2), 76-78, 2003.
11. P. Barreto, H. Kim, B. Lynn and M. Scott. Efficient Algorithms for Pairing-Based Cryptosystems. Advances in Cryptology - Crypto 2002, LNCS 2442, 354-368, Springer-Verlag, 2002.
12. J.H.Cheon, Y.Kim, and H.J.Yoon. A New ID-Based Signature with Batch Verification. Available from http://eprint.iacr.org/2004/131.
13. R.Cramer, and V.Shoup. Signature Schemes Based on the Strong RSA Assumption. ACM Transactions on Information and System Security,3(3),161-185,2000.
14. R.Gennaro, S.Halevi and T.Rabin. Secure Hash-and-Sign Signatures without the Random Oracle. Advances in Cryptology-Eurocrypt 1999, LNCS 1592,123-139, Springer-Verlag, 1999.
15. R. Sakai, K. Ohgishi, and M. Kasahara. Cryptosystems based on pairing. 2000 Symposium on Cryptography and Information Security, Okinawa, Japan, 26-28, 2000.
16. B.Libert, and J.J.Quisquater. The Exact Security of an Identity Based Signature and Its Applications. Available from http://eprint.iacr.org/2004/102.

# Efficient Identity-Based Signatures and Blind Signatures⋆

Zhenjie Huang[1,2,3], Kefei Chen[1], and Yumin Wang[3]

[1] Department of Computer Science and Engineering,
Shanghai Jiaotong University, Shanghai 200030, P.R. China
zhj_huang@hotmail.com, chen-kf@cs.sjtu.edu.cn
[2] Department of Mathematics and Information Science,
Zhangzhou Normal University, Fujian, 363000, P.R. China
[3] State Key Laboratory of Integrated Service Networks,
Xidian University, Xi'an, Shaanxi, 710071, P.R. China
ymwang@xidian.edu.cn

**Abstract.** In this paper, we first propose an efficient provably secure identity-based signature (IBS) scheme based on bilinear pairings, then propose an efficient identity-based blind signature (IBBS) scheme based on our IBS scheme. Assuming the intractability of the Computational Diffie-Hellman Problem, our IBS scheme is unforgeable under adaptive chosen-message and ID attack. Efficiency analyses show that our schemes can offer advantages in runtime over the schemes available. Furthermore, we show that, contrary to the authors claimed, Zhang and Kim's scheme in ACISP 2003 is one-more forgeable, if the ROS-problem is solvable.

**Keywords:** Identity-based, Signature, Blind signature, Bilinear pairings, Gap Diffie-Hellman group.

## 1 Introduction

The key generation procedure in the usual sense of public-key cryptography renders all public keys random. Consequently, it is necessary to associate a public key with the identity information of its owner. Such an association can be realized by a public-key authentication framework: a tree-like hierarchical public-key certification infrastructure (e.g., X.509 certification framework). In a certificate-based public key system, before using the public key of a user, the participants must verify the certificate of the user at first. As a consequence, this system requires a large storage and computing time to store and verify each user's public key and the corresponding certificate. In 1984 Shamir [16] introduced the concept of identity-based (simply ID-based) public key cryptosystem to simplify key management procedures in certificate-based public key setting. Since then, many ID-based encryption and signature schemes have been proposed.

---

⋆ This work is supported by the National Natural Science Foundation of China under Grant No.60273049.

Y.G. Desmedt et al. (Eds.): CANS 2005, LNCS 3810, pp. 120–133, 2005.

ID-based cryptosystems have a property that a user's public key can be easily calculated from his identity by a publicly available function, while his private key can be calculated for him by a trusted authority, called Key Generation Center (KGC). They enable any pair of users to communicate securely without exchanging public key certificates, without keeping a public key directory, and without using online service of a third party, as long as a trusted key generation center issues a private key to each user when he first joins the network, so they can be a good alternative for certificate-based public key infrastructure, especially when efficient key management and moderate security are required.

Early, the bilinear pairings, namely Weil pairing and Tate pairing of algebraic curves, were used in cryptography for the Menezes-Okamoto-Vanstone (MOV) attack [11] (using Weil pairing) and Frey-Rück (FR) attack [7] (using Tate pairing) to reduce the discrete logarithm problem on some elliptic curves or hyperelliptic curves to the discrete logarithm problem in a finite field. Recently, the bilinear pairings have been found positive applications in cryptography to construct new ID-based cryptographic primitives. In 2000, Joux [10] used the Weil pairing to construct a tripartite one round Diffie-Hellman key agreement protocol. After Joux's breakthrough, many ID-based cryptographic schemes have been proposed using the bilinear pairings [5]. In Crypto 2001, Boneh and Franklin [2] presented an ID-based encryption scheme based on bilinear pairings which to be the first fully functioning, efficient and provably secure ID-based encryption scheme. In Asiacrypt 2001, Boneh, Lynn and Shacham [3] proposed a basic signature scheme using pairings which has the shortest length among signature schemes in classical cryptography.

There are five ID-based signature (IBS) schemes based on bilinear pairings have been proposed. Sakai, Ohgishi and Kashara proposed a first IBS Scheme using Weil pairing in 2000.Then, in 2002, Paterson proposed a new IBS scheme using bilinear pairing. But, these two schemes without any formal proof of security. In 2003, there are three provably secure IBS scheme have been proposed. Yi proposed a provably secure IBS scheme using Weil pairing in [18], Cha and Cheon [4] proposed a provably secure IBS scheme from Gap Diffie-Hellman group in PKC2003, and Hess proposed a efficient scheme [9] in SAC 2002.

Blind signature, first introduced by Chaum [6] at Crypto'82, is a variant of digital signatures, which allows the user to get a signature without giving the signer any information about the actual message or the resulting signature. Formally, blindness means that the signer's view and the resulting signature are statistically independent, where the signer's view is the set of all values that can be gotten by the signer during the execution of the signature issuing protocol. This blindness property plays a central role in applications such as electronic voting and electronic cash systems. Up to now, two ID-based blind signature (IBBS) schemes based on bilinear pairings have been proposed. The first scheme was proposed by Zhang and Kim [19] in Asiacrypt 2002. Later, in ACISP 2003, Zhang and Kim [20] proposed a new ID-based blind signature scheme based on bilinear pairings. They claim that the security against generic parallel attack to their new scheme doesn't depend on the difficulty of ROS-problem.

In this paper, we first propose an efficient provably secure ID-based signature scheme based on bilinear pairings, then propose an efficient ID-based blind signature scheme based on our IBS scheme. We discuss the security and efficiency of our schemes. We prove that our IBS scheme is unforgeable in the random oracle model and show that our schemes can offer advantages in runtime, communication and memory requirements over the schemes available. Furthermore, we show that, contrary to the authors claimed, Zhang and Kim's scheme in [20] is one-more forgeable under the generic parallel attack if the ROS-problem is solvable, namely the security against generic parallel attack to this scheme also depends on the difficulty of ROS-problem.

The rest of the paper is organized as follows: Section 2 gives some notions. In Section 3, we first give definitions for ID-based signature, and then propose a provably secure ID-based signature scheme with a proof of security. ID-based blind signature is discussed in Section 4. We give some definitions and propose an efficient ID-based blind signature scheme there. We conclude in Section 5.

## 2    Bilinear Pairings and Gap Diffie-Hellman Groups

Let $G_1$ be a cyclic additive group generated by $P$ with order prime $q$, and $G_2$ be a cyclic multiplicative group with the same order $q$. A bilinear pairing is a map $e : G_1 \times G1 \to G_2$ with the following properties:

**Bilinear:** For all $P_1, P_2, Q_1, Q_2 \in G_1$,

$$e(P_1 + P_2, Q_1) = e(P_1, Q_1)e(P_2, Q_1),$$
$$e(P_1, Q_1 + Q_2) = e(P_1, Q_1)e(P_1, Q_2).$$

These two equations above imply that $e(aP, bQ) = e(P, Q)^{ab}$, for all $a, b$ .

**Non-degenerate:** There exists $P, Q \in G_1$ such that $e(P, Q) \neq 1$;

**Computable:** There is an efficient algorithm to compute $e(P, Q)$ for all $P, Q \in G_1$.

Modified Weil pairing [17] and Tate pairings [1, 8] are examples of bilinear maps.

Following are three important mathematical problems.

**Discrete Logarithm Problem (DLP):** Given $P, Q \in G_1$, find an integer $a$ such that $Q = aP$, whenever such an integer exists.

**Decisional Diffie-Hellman Problem (DDHP):** For $a, b, c$, given $P, aP, bP, cP \in G_1$, decide whether $c = ab \bmod q$.

**Computational Diffie-Hellman Problem (CDHP):** For $a, b$, given $P, aP, bP \in G_1$, compute $abP$.

We call $G$ a **Gap Diffie-Hellman (GDH) group** if DDHP can be solved in polynomial time but no probabilistic algorithm can solve CDHP with non-negligible advantage within polynomial time in $G$.

In the following, we use the notation $a \in_R A$ to mean that $a$ is randomly chosen from $A$.

# 3   ID-Based Signatures

## 3.1   Definitions

**Definition 1.** *(ID-Based Signature, IBS) An ID-based signature scheme consists of four algorithms, **Setup**, **Extract**, **Sign** and **Verify**, where*

***Setup** is a probabilistic polynomial-time algorithm for the key generation center KGC, which takes a security parameter $1^n$, and returns system parameters SP and master key.*

***Extract** is a probabilistic polynomial-time algorithm for the KGC, which takes input security parameter $1^n$, system parameters SP, master key and signer's identity ID, returns the signer's private key $S_{ID}$.*

***Sign** is a probabilistic polynomial-time signature issuing algorithm, which takes input security parameter $1^n$, system parameters SP, message m, signer S's identity ID and his private key $S_{ID}$, outputs a signature $\sigma_{m,ID}$ on message m.*

***Verify** is a polynomial-time algorithm that takes input security parameter $1^n$, system parameters SP, signer's identity ID, message m and signature $\sigma_{m,ID}$, outputs either "Accept" or "Reject", simply 1 or 0.*

The same as the normal signature, a secure ID-based signature scheme should have two properties: completeness and unforgeability.

**Definition 2.** *(IBS-Completeness) If the signer S runs the signature issuing algorithm and outputs signature $\sigma_{m,ID}$, then for any constant c, and for sufficiently large n,*

$$\Pr[\mathbf{Verify}(1^n, SP, m, ID, \sigma_{m,ID}) = 1] > 1 - n^{-c}.$$

**Definition 3.** *(**Game A**) Let $\mathcal{A}$ be a probabilistic polynomial-time algorithm and let $\mathcal{C}$ be a challenger.*

1. *$\mathcal{C}$ runs **Setup** and sends the system parameters SP to $\mathcal{A}$.*
2. *$\mathcal{A}$ can issue the following queries as he wants:*
   (a) ***Hash function query.** $\mathcal{C}$ computes the value of the hash function for the requested input and sends the value to $\mathcal{A}$.*
   (b) ***Extract query.** Given an identity ID, $\mathcal{C}$ runs **Extract** and sends the private key corresponding to ID to $\mathcal{A}$.*
   (c) ***Sign query.** Given an identity ID and a message m, returns a signature $\sigma_{m,ID}$ to $\mathcal{A}$.*
3. *$\mathcal{A}$ outputs a signature $(ID, m, \sigma_{m,ID})$, where ID and $(ID, m)$ never query to **Extract** and **Sign**, respectively.*

*$\mathcal{A}$ wins the Game A iff $(ID, m, \sigma_{m,ID})$ is a valid signatures.*

**Definition 4.** *(IBS-Unforgeability) An ID-based signature scheme is unforgeable if any probabilistic polynomial-time algorithm $\mathcal{A}$ wins Game A with a advantage $\epsilon \leq n^{-c}$ for any constant c and sufficiently large n.*

### 3.2  Provably Secure ID-Based Signature Scheme

1. **Setup.** Choose a GDH group $G_1$, which is a cyclic additive group generated by $P$ with prime order $q$. Choose a cyclic multiplicative group $G_2$ with the same order $q$ and a bilinear pairing $e : G_1 \times G_1 \rightarrow G_2$. Pick a random $s \in_R \mathbb{Z}_q^* = \mathbb{Z}_q \setminus \{0\}$, set $P_{pub} = sP$. Choose cryptographic hash functions $H_1 : \{0,1\}^* \times G_2 \rightarrow \mathbb{Z}_q^*$ and $H_2 : \{0,1\}^* \rightarrow G_1$. Publish the system parameter $SP = (G_1, G_2, e, q, P, P_{pub}, H_1, H_2)$, and keep the master key $s$ privately.

2. **Extract.** Given an identity ID, compute $P_{ID} = H_2(ID)$ and return the corresponding private key $S_{ID} = sP_{ID}$.

3. **Sign.** The signer randomly chooses $r \in_R \mathbb{Z}_q^*$, computes

$$R = e(P_{ID}, P_{pub})^r,$$
$$h = H_1(m, R),$$
$$V = (rh + 1)S_{ID},$$

and publishes the signature $\sigma_{m,ID} = (R, V)$ on message $m$.

(For notational purposes, in the proof of the security, signatures will be denoted by $(m, ID, R, h, V)$.)

4. **Verify.** To verify a signature $\sigma_{m,ID} = (R, V)$ on message $m$ for an identity ID, the verifier checks whether

$$e(V, P) = R^{H_1(m,R)} e(P_{ID}, P_{pub}).$$

### 3.3  Security

The completeness can easily be proved by straightforward calculating. In the following, we prove the unforgeability in the **Random Oracle Model**. The proof is done in two steps. We firstly reduce ID attacks to *given* ID attacks and then treat given ID attacks.

For the first case, we have below Lemma 1, since the **Setup** and **Extract** of our scheme is the same as that of the Cha-Cheon scheme [4].

**Lemma 1.** *If there is an algorithm $\mathcal{A}_0$ for an adaptively chosen message and ID attack to our scheme with running time $t_0$ and advantage $\epsilon_0$, then there is an algorithm $\mathcal{A}_1$ for an adaptively chosen message and given ID attack which has running time $t_1 \leq t_0$ and advantage $\epsilon_1 \geq \epsilon_0(1 - \frac{1}{q})/q_{H_2}$, where $q_{H_2}$ is the maximum number of queries to $H_2$ asked by $\mathcal{A}_0$. In addition, the numbers of queries to hash function $H_2$, Extract, and Sign asked by $\mathcal{A}_1$ are the same as those of $\mathcal{A}_0$.*

**Lemma 2.** *Let $\mathcal{A}$ be a probabilistic polynomial time algorithm and let $q_{H_1}$ and $q_S$ be the maximum number of queries to the random oracle $H_1$ and Sign oracle asked by $\mathcal{A}$, respectively. If $\mathcal{A}$ can produce a valid signature $(m, ID, R, h, V)$ with probability $\epsilon \geq 10(q_S + 1)(q_S + q_{H_1})/q$, then there is another algorithm $\mathcal{B}$ can produce two valid signatures $(m, ID, R, h, V)$ and $(m, ID, R, h', V')$ such that $h \neq h'$ in expected time $t' \leq 120686 q_{H_1} t / \epsilon$.*

*Proof.* We only have to prove that the signature can be simulated with an indistinguishable distribution probability without the knowledge of the signer's private key. Once this is done, the result directly follows from Theorem 3 (The Forking Lemma) in [13].

We first gave a simulator $\mathcal{S}$: In order to sign the message $m$, $\mathcal{S}$ chooses $r \in_R \mathbb{Z}_q$, $h \in_R \mathbb{Z}_q^*$, then computes $V = rP_{pub}$ and $R = e(V, P)^{h^{-1}} e(P_{ID}, P_{pub})^{-h^{-1}}$. If $R = 1$, $\mathcal{S}$ restarts the simulation. Otherwise, it returns the triple $(R, h, V)$.

Now we consider the following distributions:

$$\xi = \left\{ (R, h, V) \;\middle|\; \begin{array}{l} r \in_R \mathbb{Z}_q^* \\ h \in_R \mathbb{Z}_q^* \\ R = e(P_{ID}, P_{pub})^r \\ V = (rh+1)S_{ID} \end{array} \right\}$$

and

$$\zeta = \left\{ (R, h, V) \;\middle|\; \begin{array}{l} r \in_R \mathbb{Z}_q \\ h \in_R \mathbb{Z}_q^* \\ V = rP_{pub} \\ R = e(V, P)^{h^{-1}} e(P_{ID}, P_{pub})^{-h^{-1}} \neq 1 \end{array} \right\}$$

Let $(T, a, U)$ be a valid signature, namely $T \in G_2 \setminus \{1\}, a \in \mathbb{Z}_q^*, U \in G_1$ such that $e(U, P)e(P_{ID}, P_{pub})^a = T \neq 1$, we have following probabilities of this signature appearing in above distributions:

$$\Pr_{\xi}[(R, h, V) = (T, a, U)] = \Pr_{r \neq 0, h}\left[ \begin{array}{l} e(P_{ID}, P_{pub})^r = T \\ a = h \\ (rh+1)S_{ID} = U \end{array} \right] = \frac{1}{(q-1)^2}$$

$$\Pr_{\zeta}[(R, h, V) = (T, a, U)] = \Pr_{T \neq 1, h}\left[ \begin{array}{l} e(V, P)^{h^{-1}} e(P_{ID}, P_{pub})^{-h^{-1}} = T \\ a = h \\ rP_{pub} = U \end{array} \right] = \frac{1}{(q-1)^2}$$

It shows that two distributions above are the same, thus the signature can be simulated by simulator $\mathcal{S}$ with an indistinguishable distribution probability without the knowledge of the signer's private key.

**Theorem 1.** *If there is an algorithm $\mathcal{A}$ for an adaptively chosen message and ID attack to our scheme with running time $t$ and advantage $\epsilon \geq 10(q_S+1)(q_{H_1} + q_S)q_{H_2}/(q-1)$, then CDHP can be solved within expected time $t' \leq 120686 q_{H_1} t/\epsilon$ with probability $1 - 1/(q-1)$, where $q_{H_1}$, $q_{H_2}$ and $q_S$ be the maximum number of queries to the random oracle $H_1$, $H_2$ and **Sign** oracle asked by $\mathcal{A}$, respectively.*

*Proof.* Under the assumption of the theorem, from Lemma 1, there is an algorithm $\mathcal{A}_1$ can forge a valid signature $(m, ID, R, h, V)$ with running time $t_1 \leq t$ and advantage $\epsilon_1 \geq \epsilon(1 - \frac{1}{q})/q_{H_2} \geq 10(q_S + 1)(q_S + q_{H_1})/q$ under adaptively chosen message and given ID attack. Then from Lemma 2, there is algorithm $\mathcal{B}$ can produce two valid signatures $(m, ID, R, h, V)$ and $(m, ID, R, h', V')$ such that $h \neq h'$ in expected time $t' \leq 120686 q_{H_1} t/\epsilon$.

Armed with these two valid signatures $(m, ID, R, h, V)$ and $(m, ID, R, h', V')$, we can solve CDHP with probability $1 - 1/(q - 1)$ as follows.

We run the simulator $\mathcal{S}$ in Lemma 2 with $P_{ID} = xP, P_{pub} = yP, x, y \in_R \mathbb{Z}_q^*$. As signatures $(m, ID, R, h, V)$ and $(m, ID, R, h', V')$ are validly, we have

$$e(V, P) = R^h e(P_{ID}, P_{pub}) = R^h e(xyP, P),$$
$$e(V', P) = R^{h'} e(P_{ID}, P_{pub}) = R^{h'} e(xyP, P),$$

then have

$$h^{-1}(V - xyP) = h'^{-1}(V' - xyP),$$

so

$$xyP = (h^{-1}V - h'^{-1}V')/(h'^{-1} - h^{-1}),$$

when $h' \neq h$.

Since both $h$ and $h'$ are randomly chose from $\mathbb{Z}_q^*$, the probability of $h' = h$ is $1/(q - 1)$. So, we can compute $xyP$ from $(P, xP, yP)$, i.e. solve CDHP, with probability $1 - 1/(q - 1)$.

### 3.4   Efficiency

We compare our schemes to the five available ID-based signature schemes based on bilinear pairings. In the following we denote by E an exponentiation in $G_2$, by M a scalar multiplication in $G_1$, by A a addition in $G_1$, by SM a simultaneous scalar multiplication of the form $aP + bQ$ in $G_1$, and by P a computation of the pairing. The **Setup** and **Extract** stages are virtually identical for all six schemes. We do not take hash evaluations into account, since all schemes are require two hash evaluations. Five out of these six schemes (excepting the Scheme in [4]) can be optimized by precomputing some pairings, such as $e(P_{ID}, P_{pub})$ in our scheme, and using in later when it needed. So we will eliminate these pairing computation. The computation overheads of all six schemes (optimized by precomputing) are summarized in Table 1.

The pairing computation is the operation which by far takes the most running time, the simultaneous scalar multiplication and the scalar multiplication are the second and third time-consuming, respectively. The Table 1 shows that

**Table 1.** Comparison of Six IBS Schemes

| Schemes | Sign | Verify | Security |
|---------|------|--------|----------|
| Our Scheme | 1M+1E | 1P+1E | Provable |
| Scheme in [9] | 1M+1E | 1P+1E | Provable |
| Scheme in [4] | 2M | 2P+1M+1A | Provable |
| Scheme in [18] | 1SM+1M | 2P+1M+1A | Provable |
| Scheme in [12] | 1SM+1M | 1P+2E | |
| Scheme in [14] | 2M | 2P | |

our schemes only require 1P+1M and are far more efficient than other schemes except [9].

We conclude that our schemes can offer advantage in runtime over other schemes except [9].

## 4   ID-Based Blind Signatures

### 4.1   Definitions

**Definition 5.** *(ID-Based Blind Signature, IBBS) An ID-based blind signature scheme, which involves three parties, the key generation center KGC, the signer S and the user U, consists of four algorithms, **Setup**, **Extract**, **Sign** and **Verify**, where*

*   **Setup** *is a probabilistic polynomial-time algorithm for the key generation center KGC, which takes a security parameter $1^n$, and returns system parameters SP and master key.*

*   **Extract** *is a probabilistic polynomial-time algorithm for the KGC, which takes input security parameter $1^n$, system parameters SP, master key and signer's identity ID, returns the signer's private key $S_{ID}$.*

*   **Sign** *is an interactive probabilistic polynomial-time signature issuing protocol between the signer S and the user U, in which they input security parameter $1^n$, system parameters SP, the signer S's identity ID in common, the signer S inputs his private key $S_{ID}$ and the user U inputs message m privately, respectively. They engage in the signature issuing protocol and stop in polynomial-time. When they stop, the user outputs either "False" or a signature $\sigma_{m,ID}$ on message m.*

*   **Verify** *is a polynomial-time algorithm that takes input security parameter $1^n$, system parameters SP, signer's identity ID, message m and signature $\sigma_{m,ID}$, outputs either "Accept" or "Reject", simply 1 or 0.*

A secure ID-based blind signature scheme should have the property of blindness.

**Definition 6.** *(Blindness) Let $S'$ be a probabilistic polynomial-time algorithm, $U_0$ and $U_1$ be two honest users. $U_0$ and $U_1$ engage in the signature issuing protocol with $S'$ on messages $m_b$ and $m_{1-b}$, and output signatures $\sigma_b$ and $\sigma_{1-b}$, respectively, where b is randomly chosen from $\{0,1\}$. Sends $(m_0, m_1, \sigma_b, \sigma_{1-b})$ to $S'$ and then $S'$ outputs $b' \in \{0,1\}$. For all such $S'$, $U_0$ and $U_1$, for any constant c, and for sufficiently large n,*

$$| \Pr[b = b'] - 1/2| < n^{-c}.$$

### 4.2   Our ID-Based Blind Signature Scheme

The **Setup**, **Extract** and **Verify** are the same as that of ID-based signature scheme above. The **Sign** is as follows. The user may chooses $P_1 \in G_1$ and computes $e(P_1, P)$ beforehand outside of the signing protocol.

**Sign.**

a. The signer randomly chooses $r \in_R \mathbb{Z}_q^*$, computes

$$R' = e(P_{ID}, P_{pub})^r,$$

and sends $R'$ to the user as the commitment.

b. The user randomly chooses $t_1, t_2 \in_R \mathbb{Z}_q^*$ as blinding factors, and computes

$$R = R'^{t_1} e(P_1, P)^{t_2},$$
$$h = H_1(m, R),$$
$$h' = ht_1,$$

then sends $h'$ to the signer as the challenge.

c. The signer computes

$$V' = (rh' + 1)S_{ID},$$

then sends $V'$ to the user as the response.

d. The user checks whether

$$e(V', P) = R'^{h'} e(P_{ID}, P_{pub}).$$

If the user accepts, he computes

$$V = V' + ht_2 P_1,$$

and publishes the signature $\sigma_{m,ID} = (R, V)$ on message $m$. Otherwise, outputs "False".

The protocol is shown in Fig. 1.

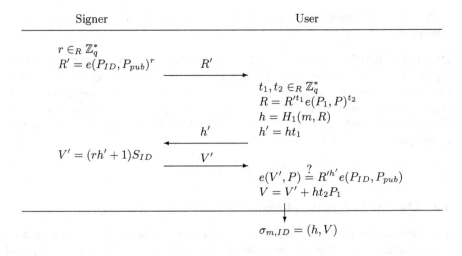

**Fig. 1.** ID-Based Blind Signature Scheme

### 4.3   Security and Efficiency

The completeness can easily be proved by straightforward calculating.

**Blindness.** For $i = 0, 1$, let $(R'_i, h'_i, V'_i, r_i)$ be data appearing in the view of the signer during the execution of the signature issuing protocol with the user on message $m_i$, and let $(m_i, R_i, h_i, V_i)$ be the corresponding message-signature pair. It is sufficient to show that there exists factors $(t_1, t_2)$ that maps $(R'_i, h'_i, V'_i, r_i)$ to $(m_j, R_j, h_j, V_j)$ for each $i, j \in \{0, 1\}$. To this end, we define $t_1 = h'_i h_j^{-1}$, and $t_2$ satisfying $V_j = V'_i + h_j t_2 P_1$. Since

$$e(V'_i, P) = R'^{h'_i}_i e(P_{ID}, P_{pub}),$$
$$e(V_j, P) = R^{h_j}_j e(P_{ID}, P_{pub}),$$

we have

$$R'^{h'_i}_i = e(V'_i, P)e(P_{ID}, P_{pub})^{-1},$$
$$R_j = e(V_j, P)^{h_j^{-1}} e(P_{ID}, P_{pub})^{-h_j^{-1}}.$$

Then we see that

$$
\begin{aligned}
R'^{t_1}_i e(P_1, P)^{t_2} &= R'^{h'_i h_j^{-1}}_i e(P_1, P)^{t_2} \\
&= e(V'_i, P)^{h_j^{-1}} e(P_{ID}, P_{pub})^{-h_j^{-1}} e(P_1, P)^{t_2} \\
&= e(V'_i + h_j t_2 P_1, P)^{h_j^{-1}} e(P_{ID}, P_{pub})^{-h_j^{-1}} \\
&= e(V_j, P)^{h_j^{-1}} e(P_{ID}, P_{pub})^{-h_j^{-1}} \\
&= R_j
\end{aligned}
$$

Thus, $(R'_i, h'_i, V'_i, r_i)$ and $(m_j, R_j, h_j, V_j)$ have exactly the same relation defined by the signature issuing protocol. Such $(t_1, t_2)$ always exist regardless of the values of $(R'_i, h'_i, V'_i, r_i)$ and $(m_j, R_j, h_j, V_j)$. Therefore, even an infinitely powerful $S'$ outputs a correct value $b'$ with probability exactly $1/2$, so the scheme is unconditional blind.

**Unforgeability.** Our blind scheme is based on the provably secure signature scheme above. The **Setup** and **Extract** stages and the signing and verification equations of our blind scheme are the same as those of the provably secure signature scheme above. If an adversary can forge a valid signature of our blind scheme, he can forge a valid signature of the scheme above too. The scheme above was proven to be unforgeable under the hardness assumption of CDHP, so we believe that our scheme is unforgeable too.

The most powerful attack on blind signature is one-more forgery introduced by Pointcheval and Stern [13]. Unfortunately, up to now, there is no ID-based blind signature scheme based on bilinear pairings can be proved secure in this model, neither our scheme nor Zhang and Kim's schemes. Finding a provably secure ID-based blind signature scheme or finding a formal proof for some available scheme remains an open problem.

In [20], the authors claim that the security against generic parallel attack to their scheme doesn't depend on the difficulty of ROS-problem. Unfortunately, in fact, the scheme in [20] is also forgeable under the generic parallel attack if the ROS-problem is solvable, namely the security against generic parallel attack to this scheme also depends on the difficulty of ROS-problem.

First we describe the ROS-problem.

**ROS-Problem [15]:** Given an oracle random function $F : \mathbb{Z}_q^l \to \mathbb{Z}_q$, find coefficients $a_{k,i} \in \mathbb{Z}_q$ and a solvable system of $l+1$ distinct equations of Eqs. (1) in the unknowns $c_1, c_2, \cdots, c_l$ over $\mathbb{Z}_q$.

$$a_{k,1}c_1 + \cdots + a_{k,l}c_l = F(a_{k,1}, \cdots, a_{k,l}) \tag{1}$$

for $k = 1, 2, \cdots, t$.

Next we describe how an adversary $\mathcal{A}$ uses the generic parallel attack to forge $l+1$ valid ID-based blind signatures of the scheme in [20], assuming the ROS-problem is solvable. Let $q_{H_1}$ be the maximum number of queries of $H_1$ from adversary.

1. The signer sends commitments $R_1 = r_1 P_{ID}, R_2 = r_2 P_{ID}, \cdots, R_l = r_l P_{ID}$.
2. $\mathcal{A}$ randomly chooses $a_{k,1}, \cdots, a_{k,l} \in_R \mathbb{Z}_q$ and messages $m_1, m_2, \cdots, m_t$. He computes $U_k = \sum_{i=1}^{l} a_{k,i} R_i$ and $H_1(m_k, U_k)$ for $k = 1, 2, \cdots, t$. Here $t < q_{H_1}$.
3. $\mathcal{A}$ solves $l+1$ of $t$ Eqs. (2) in the unknowns $c_1, c_2, \cdots, c_l$ over $\mathbb{Z}_q$.

$$H_1(m_k, U_k) = \sum_{j=1}^{l} a_{k,j} c_j \tag{2}$$

for $k = 1, 2, \cdots, t$.

4. $\mathcal{A}$ sends the solutions $c_1, c_2, \cdots, c_l$ as challenge to the signer.
5. The signer sends back $V_i = (r_i + c_i) S_{ID}$ for $i = 1, 2, \cdots, l$.
6. For each solved Eq. (2), $\mathcal{A}$ gets a valid signature $(m_k, V_k', U_k')$ by setting

$$U_k' = U_k = \sum_{i=1}^{l} a_{k,i} R_i$$

$$V_k' = \sum_{i=1}^{l} a_{k,i} V_i$$

7. $\mathcal{A}$ outputs $l+1$ signatures $(m_k, V_k', U_k')$ for $k = 1, 2, \cdots, l+1$. It is easy to see that the forged signatures are valid. According to Eq. (2), we have

$$e(U_k' + H_1(m_k, U_K')P_{ID}, P_{pub}) = e(\sum_{i=1}^{l} a_{k,i} R_i + (\sum_{i=1}^{l} a_{k,i} c_i)P_{ID}, P_{pub})$$

$$= e((\sum_{i=1}^{l} a_{k,i} r_i)P_{ID} + (\sum_{i=1}^{l} a_{k,i} c_i)P_{ID}, P_{pub})$$

$$= e(\sum_{i=1}^{l} a_{k,i}(r_i + c_i)P_{ID}, P_{pub})$$

$$= e(\sum_{i=1}^{l} a_{k,i}(r_i + c_i)S_{ID}, P)$$

$$= e(\sum_{i=1}^{l} a_{k,i}V_i, P)$$

$$= e(V_k', P)$$

for $k = 1, 2, \cdots, l + 1$.

**Efficiency.** We compare our scheme to the two available ID-based blind signature schemes based on bilinear pairings. We also do not take hash evaluation and the pairing computation which can be precomputed into account.

In Zhang and Kim's schemes [19, 20], before issuing a signature, the user does not check whether the response that the signer sent is valid or not, namely the user issues a signature regardless whether the signer performs the signature issuing protocol right or not. This will damage the completeness. To avoid a dishonest signer cheating a user, like our schemes, checking the response before issuing a signature is necessary in these two schemes too. Thus, we take it into account in the following discussion.

The computation overheads of all three schemes (optimized by precomputing) are summarized in Table 2. (The number in bracket is the computation overhead for checking response).

**Table 2.** Comparison of Three IBBS Schemes

| Schemes | Sign | Verify |
|---------|------|--------|
| Our Scheme | 2M+3E+1A+(1P+1E) | 1P+1E |
| Scheme in [19] | 1P+2SM+2M+2A+(1P+1E) | 1P+1E |
| Scheme in [20] | 1SM+3M+(2P+1M+1A) | 2P+1M+1A |

The Table 2 shows that our scheme only require 2P+2M and is far more efficient than the schemes of [19] and [20], while the scheme in [19] requires 3P+2SM+2M and the scheme in [20] requires 4P+1SM+5M. The **Sign** stage of our scheme taking less than half the runtime of [19] and [20], and the **Verify** stage of our scheme and [19] taking less than half the runtime of [20]. The scheme in [20] is hence the slowest. We conclude that our scheme can offer advantage in runtime over the schemes [19, 20].

## 5   Conclusion

ID-based cryptosystem has a property that a user's public key can be easily calculated from his identity by a publicly available function, and can be hence a good alternative for certificate-based public key infrastructure. Blind signature has the anonymity and plays a central role in applications such as electronic voting and electronic cash systems. In this paper, we first propose a efficient provably secure identity-based signature scheme based on bilinear pairings, then propose an efficient identity-based blind signature scheme based on our IBS scheme. Furthermore, we show that the scheme in [20] is also forgeable under the generic parallel attack if the ROS-problem is solvable.

Up to now, there is no ID-based blind signature scheme can be proved secure, neither our scheme nor Zhang and Kim's schemes. Finding a provably secure ID-based blind signature scheme or finding a formal proof for some available scheme remains an open problem.

# References

1. P. Barreto, H. Kim, B. Lynn and M. Scott, Efficient algorithms for pairingbased cryptosystems, In: *Advances in Cryptology-Crypto 2002*, Lecture Notes in Computer Science, Vol.2442, Springer-Verlag, 2002, pp.354- 368.
2. D. Boneh, M. Franklin, Identity-based encryption from the Weil pairing, In: *Advances in Cryptology - Crypto 2001*, Lecture Notes in Computer Science, Vol.2139, Springer-Verlag, 2001, pp.213-229.
3. D. Boneh, B. Lynn, H. Shacham, Short signatures from the Weil pairing, In: *Advances in Cryptol-ogy-Asiacrypt 2001*, Lecture Notes in Computer Science, Vol.2248, Springer-Verlag, 2001, pp.514-532.
4. J. Cha, J.Cheon, An identity-based signature from gap Diffie-Hellman groups, In: *Public Key Cryp-tography - PKC 2003*, Lecture Notes in Computer Science, Vol. 2567, Springer- Verlag, 2003, pp.18-30.
5. R. Dutta, R. Barua, P. Sarkar, Pairing-based cryptography: a survey, *IACR preprint sever*, submission 2004/064, 2004.
6. D. Chaum, Blind signatures for untraceable payments, In: *Advances in Cryptology-Crypto 82*, 1983, Plenum, NY, pp.199-203.
7. G. Frey, H. Rück, A remark concerning m-divisibility and the discrete logarithm in the divisor class group of curves, *Mathematics of Computation*, 1994, 62: 865-874.
8. S. Galbraith, K. Harrison and D. Soldera, Implementing the Tate pairing, In: *Algorithm Number Theory Symposium- ANTS 2002*, Lecture Notes in Computer Science, Vol.2369, Springer-Verlag, 2002, pp.324-337.
9. F. Hess, Efficient identity based signature schemes based on pairings, In: *Selected Areas in Cryptography - SAC 2002*, Lecture Notes in Computer Science, Vol.2595, Springer-Verlag, 2002, pp.310-324.
10. A. Joux, The Weil and Tate Pairings as Building Blocks for Public Key Cryptosystems, In: *Algorithm Number Theory Symposium- ANTS 2002*, Lecture Notes in Computer Science, Vol.2369, Springer-Verlag, 2002, pp.20-32.
11. A. Menezes, T. Okamoto, and S. Vanstone, Reducing elliptic curve logarithms to logarithms in a finite field, *IEEE Transaction on Information Theory*, 1993, 39:1639-1646.
12. K. Paterson, ID-based signatures from pairings on elliptic curves, *Electronics Letters*, 2002, 38(18):1025-1026.
13. D. Pointcheval, J. Stern, Security arguments for digital signatures and blind signatures, *J. of Cryptology*, 2000, 13: 361-396.

14. R. Sakai, K. Ohgishi and M. Kasahara, Cryptosystems based on pairing, In: *2000 Symposium on Cryptography and Information Security (SCIS2000)*, Okinawa, Japan, 2000, pp.26-28.
15. C. Schnorr, Security of blind discrete log signatures against interactive attacks, In: *Information and Communications Security - ICICS 2001*, Lecture Notes in Computer Science, Vol.2229, Springer-Verlag, 2001, pp. 1-12.
16. A. Shamir, Identity-base cryptosystems and signature schemes, In: *Advances in Cryptology - Crypto'84*, Lecture Notes in Computer Science, Vol. 196, Springer-Verlag, 1985, pp. 47-53.
17. K. Shim, Efficient ID-based authenticated key agreement protocol based on Weil pairing, *Electronics Letters*, 2003, 39(8): 653-654.
18. X. Yi, Efficient ID-based key agreement from Weil pairing, *Electronics Letters*, 2003, 39(2): 206-208.
19. F. Zhang, K. Kim, ID-based blind signature and ring signature from pairings, In: *Advances in Cryptology - Asiacrpt2002*, Lecture Notes in Computer Science, Vol.2501, Springer-Verlag, 2002, pp.533-547.
20. F. Zhang, K. Kim, Efficient ID-based blind signature and proxy signature from bilinear pairings, In: *Proc. of ACISP2003 (The 8th Australasian Conference on Information Security and Privacy)*, Lecture Notes in Computer Science, Vol. 2727, Springer-Verlag, 2003, pp.312-3323.

# How to Authenticate Real Time Streams Using Improved Online/Offline Signatures

Chong-zhi Gao[1] and Zheng-an Yao[2]

[1] Information, Machinery and Electronics College,
Guangzhou University,
GuangZhou 510000, China
[2] College of Mathematic and Computational Science,
Sun Yat-Sen University,
GuangZhou 510275, China

**Abstract.** Providing authentication protocols for real time streams is a challenging task. This is because the authentication rate is very important for real time streams, whereas it is usually a bottleneck. Using improved online/offline signatures and hash chain techniques as tools, our proposed protocol greatly reduces the online computational and communicational cost and thus is more applicable to authenticate real time streams.

**Keywords:** Stream Authentication, Real Time Streams, Online/Offline Signatures.

## 1 Introduction

A digital stream is a (potentially infinite) sequence of bits that a sender transmits to a receiver. With the growth of the Internet and the popularization of electronic commerce, there are more and more applications that need data transmissions such as live video/radio broadcastings and real time stock quote systems. In the data transmission, people are usually concerned with the following issues:

1) *Privacy:* the sender keeps information secret from those who are unauthorized to see it.
2) *Integrity:* the receiver can ensure that information has not been altered by any unauthorized parties.
3) *Authenticity:* the receiver can corroborate that the received information is sent by a certain party.
4) *Non-repudiation:* the receiver can prove to a third party that the information is sent by a certain party.

Over the years, researchers have proposed various techniques to achieve these objects. For example, public encryption schemes[21, 3, 13] were proposed to ensure the privacy of data and signature schemes[2, 21, 20] were proposed to ensure the authenticity.

Y.G. Desmedt et al. (Eds.): CANS 2005, LNCS 3810, pp. 134–146, 2005.

## 1.1   Authentication for Real Time Streams

In this paper, our goal is to provide authenticity as well as integrity and non-repudiation for real time streams. A real time stream is quite different from a non-real time stream since the sender cannot be expected to obtain the entire stream before or on sending the stream. Thus, the sender can only buffer few packets while transmitting these streams. In addition, the authentication rate must be higher than the stream generation rate while this is not required for non-real time streams.

## 1.2   Related Work

A trivial authentication method is to sign each packet[7]. The sender first splits the stream into packets and signs each packet one by one. The receiver then verifies these signatures after he/she receives the packets and their corresponding signatures. However, this method has its disadvantage since every packet requires a sign/verify computation and thus the computational cost is quite heavy. In addition, adding a signature to each packet will greatly increase the communication overhead.

In 1997, Gennaro and Rohatgi [7] proposed two paradigms for stream authentications. In the paradigm for streams that can be known in advance by the sender, they use hash chain techniques and signature techniques to authenticate streams. In this paradigm, although a signature is amortized over several packets, the computational cost is still high since a signature operation is very inefficient. In the paradigm for streams that can not be known in advance, they employ one time signatures introduced in [12, 14]. This paradigm results in a large communication overhead since the signature size and the key size of one-time signatures are very large.

In 1998, Wong and Lam [23] proposed a tree chaining technique to authenticate streams. Their construction is robust to any number of losses in streams. However, the communication overhead per packet is quite large (even larger than the size of a digital signature) and thus is not practical.

Miner and Staddon [15] proposed a graph-based authentication protocol in 2001. In their transmission model, each packet is assumed to be lost independently with the same probability and the protocol is designed based on this probability.

There are other authentication protocols for streams such as Perrig et al.'s EMSS and TESLA scheme[18], Wu et al.'s object-based scheme[24] and Pannetract and Molva's EC scheme[17]. Some of them, e.g., the TESLA scheme in [18] and the objected based scheme in [24], do not offer non-repudiation.

## 1.3   Contribution

In previous works, using ordinary signature schemes such as RSA[21], DSA[16], FFS[6, 5] or eFFS[23] will result in heavy computational cost[7, 15, 24, 17] or a large communication overhead[23]. However, the so-called online/offline signatures[4, 22] can avoid this shortcoming by dividing the authentication procedure into two phases. The first phase is offline phase: this phase's work can be carried out any time before the stream to be transmitted is generated. The second phase is online phase: this phase starts once the stream begins to be generated. Dividing authentication into two phases can avoid the computational and communicational bottlenecks that usually occur at the time of transmitting streams.

In this paper, using our improved online/offline signature schemes and the hash chain techniques[7, 19, 10] as building blocks, we construct an efficient authentication protocol for real time streams. Compared to previous protocols, our new construction has the following advantages:

1. By using our improved online/offline technique, we have greatly reduced the computational and communicational cost of authenticating streams.
2. By using the hash chain techniques, we amortize a single signing/verification operation over many packets.
3. Our protocol can tolerate 1 bursty loss of packet in a block. In addition, the ability of tolerating packet loss can be strengthened by using more complex hash chain constructions[18, 10].

### 1.4  Organization

The rest of this paper is organized as follows. In section 2, we give preliminaries. Section 3 reviews online/offline signatures and proposes a new scheme to improve the performance. Using the improved online/offline signature as a crucial building block, section 4 proposes an efficient authentication protocol for real time streams. Section 5 concludes this paper.

## 2  Preliminaries

### 2.1  Notations

The most of the following notations are borrowed from [8]. We denote by $\mathbb{N}$ the set of natural numbers. If $k \in \mathbb{N}$, we denote by $1^k$ the concatenation of $k$ ones and by $\{0, 1\}^k$ the set of bitstrings of bitlength $k$. By $\{0, 1\}^*$, we denote the set of bitstrings of arbitrary bitlength.

If $S$ is a finite set, then the notation $x \xleftarrow{R} S$ denotes that $x$ is selected randomly from the set $S$. If $\mathcal{A}$ is a algorithm, by $\mathcal{A}(\cdot)$ we denote that $\mathcal{A}$ receives only one input. If $\mathcal{A}$ receives two inputs we write $\mathcal{A}(\cdot, \cdot)$ and so on. If $\mathcal{A}(\cdot)$ is a probabilistic algorithm, $y \leftarrow \mathcal{A}^{\mathcal{O}_1, \mathcal{O}_2, \cdots}(x_1, x_2, \ldots)$ means that on input $x_1, x_2, \ldots$ and with access to oracles $\mathcal{O}_1, \mathcal{O}_2, \ldots$, $\mathcal{A}$'s output is $y$. If $p(\cdot, \cdot, \ldots)$ is a predicate, the notation $Pr[p(x, y, \ldots) : x \xleftarrow{R} S; y \xleftarrow{R} T; \ldots]$ denotes the probability that $p(x, y, \ldots)$ will be true after the ordered execution of the algorithms $x \xleftarrow{R} S, y \xleftarrow{R} T, \ldots$. "PPT" is an abbreviation for "probabilistic polynomial-time" and "$\|$" represents the concatenation operation.

# 3   Online/Offline Signatures and Our Improvement

The main building blocks of our authentication protocol are our improved on-line/offline signature scheme (which was first introduced in[4]) and the hash chain techniques. In this section, we first review the definition and the state of art of online/offline signatures. Then, In order to improve the performance, we propose an improved online/offline signature scheme as well as a security proof.

An online/offline signature scheme is a signature scheme used in a particular scenario where the signer must response quickly once the message to be signed is presented. This notion was first introduced by Even, Goldreich and Micali in 1990[4]. The idea of online/offline signatures is to split the signing procedure into two phases. The first phase is offline: in this phase, the signer does some preparatory work before the message to be signed is presented. The second phase is online: once the message to be signed is known, the signer utilizes the result of the pre-computation and use a very short time to accomplish the signing procedure.

Even et al. utilized one-time signature schemes to construct online/offline signatures. Their method can convert any signature schemes into online/offline signature schemes. Due to the use of one-time signatures, the resulting length of signatures is very long. Therefore, the method is not practical.

In 2001, Shamir and Tauman[22] proposed a new online/offline signature scheme which is based on trapdoor hash functions[11]. A trapdoor hash function is a special type of hash function which is associated with a public (hashing) key $pk$ and a secret key. It has two inputs and is written as $H_{pk}(\cdot;\cdot)$. Given $pk$ and an input pair $(m, r)$, everyone can compute the value of $H_{pk}(m; r)$. But only the person who holds the secret key can find collisions of the hash function. Shamir and Tauman's improved scheme highly enhanced the efficiency of signing, especially the efficiency in the online phase.

We call the schemes proposed by Even et al.[4] $\mathcal{OT}$-$\mathcal{OS}$ scheme (online/offline signatures based on one-time signatures) and the schemes proposed by Shamir et al.[22] $\mathcal{HSS}$-$\mathcal{OS}$ scheme (online/offline signatures using the hash-sign-switch paradigm). Both $\mathcal{OT}$-$\mathcal{OS}$ and $\mathcal{HSS}$-$\mathcal{OS}$ utilize a standard signature and another type of complex computation ($\mathcal{OT}$-$\mathcal{OS}$ should compute one-time signatures and $\mathcal{HSS}$-$\mathcal{OS}$ should evaluate trapdoor hash functions). This increases the complexity of online/offline signatures. Although $\mathcal{HSS}$-$\mathcal{OS}$'s efficiency in the online phase is very high, the computational cost of the offline phase and verification procedure is heavy. Furthermore, $\mathcal{HSS}$-$\mathcal{OS}$ requires the signer hold two private keys: one is for standard signatures, the other is for trapdoor hash functions. Exposure of any of the keys could lead to a total break of the scheme.

In the following, we give a formal syntax of online/offline signatures.

## 3.1   The Syntax of Online/Offline Signatures

An online/offline signature scheme ($\mathcal{OS}$) is a triple of algorithms ($\mathcal{G}$, Sign, Ver).

- $(pk, sk) \leftarrow \mathcal{G}(1^k)$ is a PPT algorithm which on input a security parameter $k \in \mathbb{N}$, outputs a public/private key pair $(pk, sk)$.

- $\sigma \leftarrow \mathsf{Sign}(sk, M)$ is a PPT algorithm which on input a private key $sk$ and a message $M$, outputs a signature $\sigma$. The signing algorithm consists of two sub-algorithms:
  - $St \leftarrow \mathsf{Sign\_off}(sk)$ is a PPT algorithm which on input the private key $sk$, outputs a state information $St$.
  - $\sigma \leftarrow \mathsf{Sign\_on}(St, M)$ is a PPT algorithm which on input a state $St$ and a message $M$, outputs a signature $\sigma$.

  The signing algorithm $\mathsf{Sign}$ first runs $\mathsf{Sign\_off}(sk)$ to get $St$, then transfers $St$ and the message $M$ to $\mathsf{Sign\_on}(\cdot, \cdot)$, finally it returns the signature $\sigma$ which is the output of $\mathsf{Sign\_on}(St, M)$ .
- $0/1 \leftarrow \mathsf{Ver}(pk, M, \sigma)$ is a PPT algorithm which on input the public key $pk$, a message $M$ and a signature $\sigma$, outputs 0 or 1 for reject or accept respectively.

**Completeness:** It is required that if $\mathsf{Sign}(sk, M) = \sigma$ then $\mathsf{Ver}(pk, M, \sigma) = 1$ for all $(pk, sk)$ generated by $\mathcal{G}(1^k)$.

## 3.2   Security Notion

On defining the security notion of an online/offline signature scheme, we view an $\mathcal{OS}$ scheme as a standard signature scheme and use the security notion called existential unforgeability under chosen message attacks [9] in the random oracle model [1].

**Existential Unforgeability:** Existential unforgeability for $\mathcal{OS}$ under chosen message attacks in the random oracle model is defined in the following game. This game is carried out between a simulator $\mathcal{S}$ and an adversary $\mathcal{A}$. The adversary $\mathcal{A}$ is allowed to make queries to a sign-oracle $\mathsf{Sign}(sk, \cdot)$ and a hash oracle $h(\cdot)$. The attacking game is as follows:

1. The simulator runs $\mathcal{G}$ on input $1^k$ to get $(pk, sk)$. $pk$ is sent to $\mathcal{A}$.
2. On input $(1^k, pk)$, $\mathcal{A}$ is allowed to query the sign-oracle $\mathsf{Sign}(sk, \cdot)$ and the hash oracle $h(\cdot)$ polynomial times.
3. $\mathcal{A}$ outputs a pair $(M, \sigma)$.

The adversary wins the game if the message $M$ has never been queried to the oracle $\mathsf{Sign}(sk, \cdot)$ and $\mathsf{Ver}(pk, M, \sigma) = 1$ holds. Let $\mathrm{Adv}_{\mathcal{A}, \mathcal{OS}}$ be the *advantage* of the adversary $\mathcal{A}$ in breaking the signature scheme, i.e.

$$\mathrm{Adv}_{\mathcal{A}, \mathcal{OS}} = \Pr[\mathsf{Ver}(pk, M, \sigma) = 1 : (pk, sk) \leftarrow \mathcal{G}(1^k); (M, \sigma) \leftarrow \mathcal{A}^{h(\cdot), \mathsf{Sign}^{h(\cdot)}(sk, \cdot)}]$$

where $\mathcal{A}$ has never requested $M$ to the signing oracle and the probability is taken over the internal coin tosses of the algorithm $\mathcal{G}$ and $\mathcal{A}$.

**Definition 1.** *An adversary $\mathcal{A}$ $(t, q_s, q_h, \epsilon)$-breaks an online/offline signature scheme $\mathcal{OS}$ if $\mathcal{A}$ runs in time at most $t$, makes at most $q_s$ queries to the signing oracle and at most $q_h$ queries to the hash oracle, and $\mathrm{Adv}_{\mathcal{A}, \mathcal{OS}}$ is at least $\epsilon$.*

*A signature scheme $\mathcal{OS}$ is existentially unforgeable under chosen message attacks if for every PPT adversary $\mathcal{A}$, $\mathrm{Adv}_{\mathcal{A}, \mathcal{OS}}$ is negligible.*

### 3.3 Our New Construction of Online/Offline Signatures

To improve Shamir and Tauman's online/offline signature scheme $\mathcal{HSS}$-$\mathcal{OS}$, we propose a new construction and prove its security. Compared to the scheme $\mathcal{HSS}$-$\mathcal{OS}$, there is an almost 50% reduction in signature size and overall computational cost.

The new online/offline signature scheme $\mathcal{TH}$-$\mathcal{OS}$ is based on a trapdoor hash family $\mathcal{TH} = (\mathcal{G}, \mathcal{H}, \mathcal{F})$ (A formal definition of a trapdoor hash family including a security definition is given in Appendix A). A standard collision free hash function $h : \{0,1\}^* \to \{0,1\}^{\alpha(k)}$ (where $\alpha()$ is a polynomial function of the security parameter $k$) is also needed, which will be treated as a random oracle in the proof of security.

The scheme $\mathcal{TH}$-$\mathcal{OS} = (\mathcal{G}', \mathsf{Sign}, \mathsf{Ver})$ is constructed as follows:

- $\mathcal{G}'(1^k)$. The key generation algorithm is set to be $\mathcal{G}$, i.e., $\mathcal{G}' = \mathcal{G}$. It takes as input a security parameter $k$, outputs a key pair $(pk, sk)$. Let $\mathcal{M}_{pk}, \mathcal{R}_{pk}$ and $\mathcal{Q}_{pk}$ be $\mathcal{TH}$'s message space, tag space and range set resp. It is required that $\{0,1\}^{\alpha(k)} \subset \mathcal{M}_{pk}$ holds.
- $\mathsf{Sign\_off}(sk)$. Given a secret key $sk$ , proceeds as follows:
  1. Select at random $(m, r) \in_R \mathcal{M}_{pk} \times \mathcal{R}_{pk}$, and compute $\theta = H_{pk}(m; r)$.
  2. Let $St = (sk, \theta, m, r)$.

  *Remark 1.* Assigning $(sk, \theta, m, r)$ instead of $(sk, m, r)$ to $St$ is to avoid recomputing the value $\theta = H_{pk}(m; r)$ in the online phase.

- $\mathsf{Sign\_on}(St, M)$. Given $St = (sk, \theta, m, r)$ and a message $M \in \{0,1\}^*$, computes the signature as follows:
  1. Compute $m' = h(M\|\theta)$.
  2. Run the collision-finding algorithm $\mathcal{F}$ of $\mathcal{TH}$ with the input $(1^k, sk, m, r, m')$ to obtain $r'$ such that $H_{pk}(m'; r') = H_{pk}(m; r)$.
  3. Output the signature as $\sigma = (\theta, r')$.
- $\mathsf{Ver}(pk, M, \sigma)$. Given a public key $pk$, a message $M$, and a signature $\sigma = (\theta, r')$, checks that $H_{pk}(h(M\|\theta); r') \stackrel{?}{=} \theta$. Output 1 if this check succeeds and output 0 otherwise.

**Completeness:** it is straightforward.

### 3.4 Security and Efficiency

**Theorem 1.** *Let $\mathcal{TH}$ be a uniform trapdoor hash family with a super-logarithmic min-entropy $\beta(\cdot)$. Let $\mathcal{TH}$-$\mathcal{OS}$ be the associated online/offline signature scheme as constructed in Section 3.3. Then $\mathcal{TH}$-$\mathcal{OS}$ is existentially unforgeable under chosen message attacks in the random oracle model if $\mathcal{TH}$ is collision resistant.*

The proof of the above is based on relatively standard ideas, but is complicated by details of the simulations and models. Due to the page limitation, we present it in the full paper.

**Efficiency.** In the new scheme $\mathcal{TH}\text{-}\mathcal{OS}$, the offline phase involves only one evaluation of an trapdoor hash function. The online phase involves one operation of finding a collision and one evaluation of a standard hash function. Using the trapdoor hash family proposed by [22], the operation of finding a collision requires about 0.1 modular multiplication of two 1024 bit numbers. Our scheme's verification algorithm involves one evaluation of an trapdoor hash function and one evaluation of a standard hash function. We compare the efficiency of the Hash-Sign-Switch paradigm ($\mathcal{HSS}\text{-}\mathcal{OS}$) [22] and our new scheme in Table 1.

**Table 1.** The cost of two online/offline signature schemes. Abbreviations used are: "eva-TH" for an evaluation of a trapdoor hash function; "eva-SH" for an evaluation of a standard hash function; "sign-SS" and "ver-SS" for the signing and verification algorithm of a standard signature scheme respectively. Note that the evaluation of a standard hash function is very efficient, therefore we use an asterisk to remark it.

| Schemes | Sign_off | Sign_on | Ver | Signature size |
|---|---|---|---|---|
| $\mathcal{HSS}\text{-}\mathcal{OS}$ (The Hash-Sign- Switch Paradigm) | 1 eva-TH 1 sign-SS | 1 finding collision | 1 eva-TH 1 ver-SS | 1 standard sig; 1 point in $\mathcal{Q} \times \mathcal{R}$ |
| The New Scheme $\mathcal{TH}\text{-}\mathcal{OS}$ | 1 eva-TH | 1 eva-SH * 1 finding collision | 1 eva-SH * 1 eva-TH | 1 point in $\mathcal{Q} \times \mathcal{R}$ |

We can see that operations of the standard signature are eliminated in the new scheme, at the cost of additional single hash evaluation in the online phase. Thus, the new scheme need only one private key instead of two private keys in the $\mathcal{HSS}\text{-}\mathcal{OS}$ scheme and there is an almost 50% reduction in the signature size and the overall computational cost.

## 4   Authenticating Real Time Streams

### 4.1   The New Protocol

Using improved online/offline signatures and the hash chain techniques as building blocks, we can construct an efficient protocol to authenticate real time streams. The basic idea is to split the authentication procedure into two phases just like in online/offline signature schemes. In the first phase(offline phase) , the sender does some preparatory work before the streams to be send are known. In the second phase(online phase), on obtaining the streams, the sender attaches authentication information on streams and send these data to the receiver. The following is the details of this protocol.

Suppose the sender is capable of buffering $n$ packets. Suppose $\mathcal{TH} = (\mathcal{G}, \mathcal{H}, \mathcal{F})$ is a trapdoor hash family and $h : \{0,1\}^* \to \{0,1\}^{\alpha(k)}$ is a standard collision free hash function. Let $pk$ be the sender's public key and $sk$ be the corresponding private key. Consider $n$ packets that constitute a block.

**Offline phase:**

1. The sender randomly selects $s$ pairs:

$$(\widetilde{m_1}, \widetilde{r_1}); (\widetilde{m_2}, \widetilde{r_2}); \ldots ; (\widetilde{m_s}, \widetilde{r_s}) \qquad ( \ (\widetilde{m_j}, \widetilde{r_j}) \in \mathcal{M} \times \mathcal{R} \ , 1 \le j \le s)$$

and computes $\theta_j = H_{pk}(\widetilde{m}_j; \widetilde{r}_j)$ $(1 \le j \le s)$.
2. The sender stores $\widetilde{m}_j, \widetilde{r}_j, \theta_j$ $(j = 1, 2, \ldots)$ and sends $\theta_j$ $(j = 1, 2, \ldots)$ to the receiver.

*Remark 2.* The number $s$ depends on the number of blocks that the sender want to send.

*Remark 3.* The offline phase can be carried out any time before the streams to be send are known. Thus, we can greatly reduce the computational cost and communication overhead while sending the streams. This is the most important contribution of our scheme.

**Online phase:**

Suppose the $j$-th block's packets are $m_1, m_2, \ldots, m_n$. For the $j$-th block, the sender

1. Computes

$$D_n = h(m_n \| 00 \ldots 0)$$
$$D_{n-1} = h(m_{n-1} \| D_n \| 00 \ldots 0)$$
$$D_i = h(m_i \| D_{i+1} \| D_{i+2}) \quad (1 \le i \le n - 2)$$

2. uses the private key $sk$ and $(\widetilde{m}_j, \widetilde{r}_j)$ to compute $r_j$ (see section 3.3 for details) such that

$$H_{pk}(h(D_1 \| \theta_j); r_j) = H_{pk}(\widetilde{m}_j; \widetilde{r}_j).$$

3. sends $< (r_j, D_1); (m_1, D_2, D_3); (m_2, D_3, D_4); \ldots ; (m_{n-2}, D_{n-1}, D_n); (m_{n-1}, D_n); m_n >$ to the receiver where $(r_j, D_1)$ is the header and $(m_i, D_{i+1}, D_{i+2})$ is the $i$-th packet.

*Remark 4.* If we use the trapdoor hash family in Appendix A, then the second step of this phase (computing $r_j$) has a complexity of approximate 0.1 modular multiplication. This is very efficient compared to a standard signature evaluation.

*Remark 5.* The reader can see that every $D_i$ is repeated twice. Doing it in this fashion is to avoid packet loss. We will explain this issue later.

**Verification of streams:**

On receiving the $j$-th block $< (r_j, D_1); (m_1, D_2, D_3); (m_2, D_3, D_4); \ldots ; (m_{n-2}, D_{n-1}, D_n); (m_{n-1}, D_n); m_n >$, the receiver carries out the following steps.

– On receiving $(r_j, D_1)$, check that

$$H_{pk}(h(D_1 \| \theta_j); r_j) \stackrel{?}{=} \theta_j$$

– On receiving the $i$-th packet $(m_i, D_{i+1}, D_{i+2})$ $(1 \leq i \leq n - 2)$, check that

$$h(m_i \| D_{i+1} \| D_{i+2}) \overset{?}{=} D_i$$

– On receiving $(m_{n-1}, D_n)$ , check that

$$h(m_{n-1} \| D_n \| 00 \ldots 0) \overset{?}{=} D_{n-1}$$

– On receiving $m_n$ , check that

$$h(m_n \| 00 \ldots 0) \overset{?}{=} D_n$$

## 4.2   Performance Analysis

We analyze the performance of our protocol from four aspects:

– **buffering of sender.** The maximum number of packets that need to be stored by the sender in order to compute the authentication information is $n$. Depending on the buffering capability of the sender and the situation of the networks, $n$'s value can be flexible.
– **Computational cost.** This is one of the most important measurements of the performance. We place our emphasis on the online phase since the bottleneck of authenticating real time streams always occurs in transmitting the streams (the computation of offline phase can be carried out any time before the stream transportation). For a block ($n$ packets), the sender needs to do $n$ evaluations of a standard hash function plus 0.1 modular multiplication of two 1024 bit numbers (this is the computational cost of finding collisions of a trapdoor hash function) if we use the trapdoor hash family in Appendix A. For the receiver, $n$ evaluations of a standard hash function and one evaluation of a trapdoor hash function are needed.

**Table 2.** the performance of several authentication protocols. Abbreviations used are: "eva-TH" for an evaluation of a trapdoor hash function; "eva-SH" for an evaluation of a standard hash function; "sign-SS" and "ver-SS" for the signing and verification algorithm of a standard signature scheme respectively. Note that the evaluation of a standard hash function is very efficient, therefore we use an asterisk to remark it. We also note that 1 sign-SS $\gg$ 0.1 modular multiplication.

| Protocols | Online computational cost of the sender | Online communicational cost | Computational cost of the receiver |
|---|---|---|---|
| Wong98[23] Star chaining | 1 sign-SS $n + 1$ eva-SH * | $n$ standard sig; $n(n - 1)$ hash lengths | 1 ver-SS $n + 1$ eva-SH * |
| Wong98[23] Tree chaining | 1 sign-SS $2n - 1$ eva-SH * | $n$ standard sig; $n\log_2 n$ hash lengths | 1 ver-SS $2n - 1$ eva-SH * |
| Pannetract03[17] EC scheme | 1 sign-SS $n$ eva-SH * 2 coding operations | $\approx 2n$ hash lengths (while $p = 1/4$) | 1 ver-SS $n$ eva-SH * |
| Our protocol | 0.1 multiplication $n$ eva-SH * | $\approx 2n - 1$ hash lengths | 1 ver-SS $n$ eva-SH * |

- **Communication overhead.** For the same reason of analyzing the computational cost, we place our emphasis on the online phase. For a block ($n$ packets), the communication overhead (i.e., the additional authentication information embedded in the stream) is $2n - 1$ hash lengths.
- **Tolerance of bursty loss.** Our protocol can tolerate 1 bursty loss of packet, i.e., the rest of packets can also be authenticated even if one packet is lost. In addition, the ability of tolerating packet loss can be strengthened by using more complex hash chain constructions[18, 10].

We compare the performance of several authentication protocols in Table 2 where our protocol uses the trapdoor hash family of Appendix A.

## 5   Conclusion

In this paper, we consider the authentication of digital streams over an insecure network. Using our improved online/offline signature schemes and the hash chain techniques as building blocks, we construct an efficient authentication protocol for digital streams. Compared to previous protocols, our protocol greatly reduces the online computational and communicational cost and thus is more applicable to authenticate real time streams.

## References

1. Mihir Bellare and Phillip Rogaway. Random oracles are practical: A paradigm for designing efficient protocols. In Proceedings of the 1st ACM Conference on Computer and Communications Security, pages 62–73, Fairfax, Virginia, November 1993. ACM Press.
2. W. Diffie and M. E. Hellman. Multiuser cryptographic techniques. In Proc. AFIPS 1976 National Computer Conference, pages 109–112, Montvale, N.J., 1976. AFIPS.
3. Taher ElGamal. A public key cryptosystem and a signature scheme based on discrete logarithms. IEEE Trans. Inform. Theory, 31:469–472, 1985.
4. Shimon Even, Oded Goldreich, and Silvio Micali. On-line/off-line digital signatures. In Proc. CRYPTO 89, volume 435 of Lecture Notes in Computer Science, pages 263–277. Springer-Verlag, 1990.
5. Uriel Feige, Amos Fiat, and Adi Shamir. Zero knowledge proofs of identity. In Proc. 19th ACM Symp. on Theory of Computing, pages 210–217, May 1987.
6. A. Fiat and A. Shamir. How to prove yourself: practical solutions to identification and signature problems. In Proc. CRYPTO 86, volume 263 of Lecture Notes in Computer Science, pages 186–194. Springer, 1987.
7. R. Gennaro and P. Rohatgi. How to sign digital streams. Lecture Notes in Computer Science, 1294:180–197, 1997.
8. Shafi Goldwasser, Silvio Micali, and Ron L. Rivest. A digital signature scheme secure against adaptive chosen-message attacks. SIAM Journal on Computing, 17(2):281–308, April 1988.
9. Shafi Goldwasser, Silvio Micali, and Ronald L. Rivest. A digital signature scheme secure against adaptive chosen-message attacks. SIAM Journal on Computing, 17(2):281–308, April 1988. Special issue on cryptography.

10. P. Golle and N. Modadugu. Authenticating streamed data in the presence of random packet loss. In Proceedings of the Symposium on Network and Distributed Systems Security (NDSS 2001), pages 13–22, San Diego, CA, February 2001. Internet Society.

11. Hugo Krawczyk and Tal Rabin. Chameleon signatures. In Proceedings of the Symposium on Network and Distributed Systems Security (NDSS '00), pages 143–154, San Diego, CA, February 2000. Internet Society.

12. L. Lamport. Constructing digital signatures from a one-way function. Technical Report CSL-98, SRI International, October 1979.

13. R. J. McEliece. A public-key cryptosystem based on algebraic coding theory. DSN Progress Report, pages 42–44, 1987.

14. Ralph C. Merkle. A digital signature based on a conventional encryption function. In Proc. CRYPTO 87, volume 293 of Lecture Notes in Computer Science, pages 369–378. Springer-Verlag, 1988.

15. Sara Miner and Jessica Staddon. Graph-based authentication of digital streams. In Proceedings of the IEEE Symposium on Research in Security and Privacy, pages 232–246, Oakland, CA, May 2001. IEEE Computer Society, Technical Committee on Security and Privacy, IEEE Computer Society Press.

16. National Bureau of Standards. Digital signature standard. Technical Report FIPS Publication 186, National Bureau of Standards, 1994.

17. Alain Pannetrat and Refik Molva. Efficient multicast packet authentication. In NDSS, 2003.

18. Adrian Perrig, Ran Canetti, Doug Tygar, and Dawn Song. Efficient authentication and signature of multicast streams over lossy channels. In Proceedings of the IEEE Symposium on Research in Security and Privacy, Oakland, CA, May 2000. IEEE Computer Society Press.

19. Adrian Perrig, Ran Canetti, J. D. Tygar, and Dawn Xiaodong Song. Efficient authentication and signing of multicast streams over lossy channels. In IEEE Symposium on Security and Privacy, pages 56–73, 2000.

20. M. O. Rabin. Digitalized signatures. In Foundations of Secure Computation, pages 155–168. Academic Press, 1978.

21. Ronald L. Rivest, Adi Shamir, and Leonard M. Adleman. A method for obtaining digital signatures and public-key cryptosystems. Communications of the ACM, 21(2):120–126, 1978.

22. Adi Shamir and Yael Tauman. Improved online/offline signature schemes. In Advances in Cryptology – CRYPTO '2001, volume 2139 of Lecture Notes in Computer Science, pages 355–367. International Association for Cryptologic Research, Springer-Verlag, Berlin Germany, 2001.

23. Chung Kei Wong and Simon S. Lam. Digital signatures for flows and multicasts. In IEEE ICNP '98, 1998.

24. Yongdong Wu, Di Ma, and Changsheng Xu. Efficient object-based stream authentication. In INDOCRYPT, pages 354–367, 2002.

# A    Trapdoor Hash Families

**Definition 2 (Trapdoor hash families).** *A trapdoor hash family is a triple* $(\mathcal{G}, \mathcal{H}, \mathcal{F})$ *such that:*

– $\mathcal{G}$: *key generation algorithm, a PPT algorithm, which, on input* $1^k$ *produces a pair* $(pk, sk)$ *where* $pk$ *is called the public hash key, and* $sk$ *is the corresponding private key.*

- $\mathcal{H}$ is a family of randomized hash functions. Every hash function in $\mathcal{H}$ is associated with a public hash key $pk$, takes input of a message from the message space $\mathcal{M}_{pk}$ and a random element from the tag space $\mathcal{R}_{pk}$, and outputs a value in the range $\mathcal{Q}_{pk}$. This hash function is written as $H_{pk}(\cdot;\cdot)$ and has the following properties:
  1. Efficiency: Given a public hash key $pk$ and a pair $(m,r) \in \mathcal{M}_{pk} \times \mathcal{R}_{pk}$, $H_{pk}(m;r)$ is computable in polynomial time.
  2. Collision resistance: Without private key, any PPT algorithm can not find $(m,r)$ and $(m',r')$ such that $m' \neq m$ and $H_{pk}(m';r') = H_{pk}(m;r)$. A formal description is given in Definition 4.
- $\mathcal{F}$: collision-finding algorithm, a PPT algorithm satisfies:

$$\Pr[H_{pk}(m';r') = H_{pk}(m;r) : (pk,sk) \xleftarrow{\mathrm{R}} \mathcal{G}(1^k); (m,r) \xleftarrow{\mathrm{R}} \mathcal{M}_{pk} \times \mathcal{R}_{pk};$$

$$m'(\neq m) \xleftarrow{\mathrm{R}} \mathcal{M}_{pk}; r' \xleftarrow{\mathrm{R}} \mathcal{F}(1^k, sk, m, r, m')] = 1.$$

Every member in a trapdoor hash family is called a **trapdoor hash function**.

**Definition 3 (Uniform).** A trapdoor hash family $(\mathcal{G}, \mathcal{H}, \mathcal{F})$ is **uniform** if and only if whenever the input $(m,r)$ is uniformly distributed in $\mathcal{M}_{pk} \times \mathcal{R}_{pk}$, the output of the collision-finding algorithm $\mathcal{F}$ is uniformly distributed in $\mathcal{R}_{pk}$.

**Definition 4 (Collision resistance).** Let $\mathcal{TH} = (\mathcal{G}, \mathcal{H}, \mathcal{F})$ be a trapdoor hash family. The **advantage** of an adversary $\mathcal{I}$ in breaking $\mathcal{TH}$'s collision resistance is:

$$\mathrm{Adv}_{\mathcal{I},\mathcal{TH}} = \Pr[m' \neq m \text{ and } H_{pk}(m';r') = H_{pk}(m;r) : (pk,sk) \xleftarrow{\mathrm{R}} \mathcal{G}(1^k);$$

$$(m,r,m',r') \xleftarrow{\mathrm{R}} \mathcal{I}(1^k, pk)]$$

where the probability is taken over the internal coin tosses of the algorithm $\mathcal{G}$ and $\mathcal{I}$.

An adversary $\mathcal{I}$ $(t,\epsilon)$-breaks $\mathcal{TH}$'s collision resistance if with running time of at most $t$, $\mathcal{I}$'s advantage $\mathrm{Adv}_{\mathcal{I},\mathcal{TH}}$ is at least $\epsilon$.

A trapdoor hash family $\mathcal{TH}$ is **collision resistent** if for every PPT adversary $\mathcal{I}$, $\mathrm{Adv}_{\mathcal{I},\mathcal{TH}}$ is negligible.

## An instantiation of trapdoor hash families[22]:

- **Setup:** Select at random two safe primes $p, q \in \{0,1\}^{L/2}$ (i.e., primes such that $p' \overset{\text{def}}{=} \frac{p-1}{2}$ and $q' \overset{\text{def}}{=} \frac{q-1}{2}$ are primes) and compute $N = pq$. Choose at random an element $g \in \mathbb{Z}_N^*$ of order $\lambda(N)$ ($\lambda(N) \overset{\text{def}}{=} \mathrm{lcm}(p-1,q-1) = 2p'q'$). The public key is $(N,g)$ and the private trapdoor key is $(p,q)$.
- **The Hash Family:** For $pk = (N,g)$, $H_{pk} : \mathbb{Z}_N \times \mathbb{Z}_{\lambda(N)} \longrightarrow \mathbb{Z}_N^*$ is defined to be $H_{pk}(m;r) \overset{\text{def}}{=} g^{m\|r} \pmod{N}$ ($m\|r$ denotes the concatenation of $m$ and $r$).

– **Finding trapdoor collisions:** Given $pk = (N, g)$, $sk = (p, q)$, a pair $(m_1, r_1) \in \mathbb{Z}_N \times \mathbb{Z}_{\lambda(N)}$ and an additional message $m_2 \in \mathbb{Z}_N$. We can find $r_2$ such that $g^{m_1 \| r_1} = g^{m_2 \| r_2} \pmod{N}$ as follows:

$$r_2 = 2^k(m_1 - m_2) + r_1 \pmod{\lambda(N)}.$$

Note that the computational cost of above operation is about one tenth of a single modular multiplication of two 1024 bit numbers.

We refer the reader to[4, 22] for the details of constructions of secure and efficient uniform trapdoor hash families.

# New Authentication Scheme Based on a One-Way Hash Function and Diffie-Hellman Key Exchange

Eun-Jun Yoon and Kee-Young Yoo

Department of Computer Engineering, Kyungpook National University,
Daegu 702-701, South Korea
ejyoon@infosec.knu.ac.kr, yook@knu.ac.kr

**Abstract.** In 2004, Wu-Chieu proposed improvements to their original authentication scheme in order to strengthen it to withstand impersonation attacks. In 2005, Lee-Lin-Chang proposed improvements on Wu-Chieu's original scheme so that not only could it withstand a forgery attack, but it required less computational costs and it was suitable for mobile communication. The current paper, however, demonstrates that Wu-Chieu's improved scheme is vulnerable to an off-line password guessing attack and an impersonation attack by the use of a stolen smart card. Also, we demonstrates that Lee-Lin-Chang's scheme is vulnerable to a forgery attack. Furthermore, we present a new authentication scheme based on a one-way hash function and Diffie-Hellman key exchange in order to isolate such problems and to provide mutual authentication between the user and the remote system.

**Keywords:** Authentication, Password, Guessing attack, Smart card.

## 1   Introduction

User authentication is an important part of security, along with confidentiality and integrity, for systems that allow remote access over untrustworthy networks, like the Internet. As such, a remote password authentication scheme authenticates the legitimacy of users over an insecure channel, where the password is often regarded as a secret shared between the remote system and the user. With knowledge of the password, the user can use it to create and send a valid login message to a remote system in order to gain access. Meanwhile, the remote system also uses the shared password to check the validity of the login message and to authenticate the user. ISO 10202 standards have been established for the security of financial transaction systems that use integrated circuit cards (IC cards or smart cards). The smart card originates from the IC memory card which has been in the industry for about 10 years [1][2]. The main characteristics of a smart card are its small size and low-power consumption. In general, a smart card contains a microprocessor which can quickly manipulate logical and mathematical operations, RAM, which is used as a data or instruction buffer,

Y.G. Desmedt et al. (Eds.): CANS 2005, LNCS 3810, pp. 147–160, 2005.

and ROM which stores the user's secret key and the necessary public parameters and algorithmic descriptions of the executing programs. The merits of a smart card regarding password authentication are its simplicity and its efficiency in terms of the log-in and authentication processes.

In 1981, Lamport [3] proposed a remote password authentication scheme using a password table to achieve user authentication. In 2000, Hwang and Li [4] pointed out that Lamport's scheme suffers from the risk of a modified password table. Also, there is the cost of protecting and maintaining the password table. Therefore, they proposed a new user authentication scheme using smart cards to eliminate risks and costs. Hwang and Li's scheme can withstand replay attacks and it can also authenticate users without maintaining a password table. Later, Sun [5] proposed an efficient smart card-based user authentication scheme to improve the efficiency of Hwang and Li's scheme. In 2003, Wu-Chieu [6] proposed an improvement on Sun's scheme to make the protocol a user-friendly remote authentication scheme, through which the user can choose and change their password based on a secure channel. They claimed that their scheme provided effective authentication and also eliminated the drawback of Sun's scheme that required lengthy passwords.

In 2004, Wu-Chieu, [7], however, pointed out that their original scheme is vulnerable to an impersonation attack. They proposed an improvement to their original scheme in order to protect the scheme from an impersonation attack. At the same time, Yang-Wang [8] also pointed out Wu-Chieu's original scheme [6] is susceptible to a forgery attack. Thereafter, in 2005, Lee-Lin-Chang [9] proposed improvements to Wu-Chieu's original scheme so that not only could it withstand a forgery attack, but it required less computational costs and it was suitable for mobile communication. Lee-Lin-Chang claimed that their scheme provided effective authentication and it also eliminated the drawbacks of Wu-Chieu's original scheme.

The current paper, however, demonstrate that Wu-Chieu's improved remote authentication scheme [7] is vulnerable to an off-line password guessing attack [10], where an attacker can easily guess a legal users's password and can impersonate an legal users by using a stolen smart card. Also, we demonstrate that Lee-Lin-Chang's scheme is vulnerable to a forgery attack, where an attacker can easily masquerade as another legal users in order to access the resources of a remote system. Furthermore, we present an improved authentication scheme based on a one-way hash function and Diffie-Hellman key exchange to the schemes, in order to isolate such problems. As a result, the proposed scheme is more secure than Wu-Chieu's improved scheme and Lee-Lin-Chang's scheme. Also, it provides mutual authentication between the user and remote system and it has the same advantages as the other schemes. In addition, the proposed scheme does not require time synchronization or delay-time limitations between the user and remote system, unlike the other schemes. A timestamp-based authentication scheme is suitable for tightly synchronized system clocks, such as local area networks (LAN). For a large network where clock synchronization is difficult to work, such as wide area networks (WAN), mobile communication networks, and satellite communication networks, a nonce-based authentication scheme is advised. Therefore, the proposed scheme can securely perform a key agreement for secure communication and is applicable to various environment.

The remainder of this paper is organized as follows: Section 2 briefly reviews Wu-Chieu's improved scheme and Lee-Lin-Chang's scheme. Section 3 demonstrates the security weaknesses of Wu-Chieu's improved scheme and Lee-Lin-Chang's scheme. The proposed authentication scheme is presented in Section 4, while Sections 5 and 6 discuss the security and efficiency of the proposed protocol. The conclusion is given in Section 7.

## 2   Related Works

This section briefly reviews Wu-Chieu's improved authentication scheme [7] and Lee-Lin-Chang's authentication scheme [9].

### 2.1   Review of Wu-Chieu's Improved Scheme

Wu-Chieu's improved scheme [7] consists of three phases: Registration, login, and authentication phase. Figure 1 shows Wu-Chieu's improved authentication scheme. The scheme works as follows:

**Registration Phase:** The user $U_i$ submits his identifier $ID_i$ and chosen password $PW_i$ to the remote system. These private data must be sent in person or over a secure channel. Upon receiving the registration request, the system computes $A_i = h(ID_i, x)$ and $B_i = g^{A_i \cdot h(PW_i)}(\bmod p)$, where $x$ is a secret key maintained by the system, $h(\cdot)$ is a collision resistant one-way hash function, $p$ is a large prime number, and $g$ is a public, primitive element in $GF(p)$. Then, the system personalizes the smart card with the secure information: $\{ID_i, B_i, h(\cdot), p, g\}$.

**Login Phase:** If the user $U_i$ wants to login, the user attaches the smart card to the card reader and keys in their identifier $ID_i$ and password $PW_i^*$, then the smart card performs the following operations:

(1) Compute the following two integers:
$C_1 = h(T \oplus B_i)$ and $D_i^* = g^{h(PW_i^*)}(\bmod p)$, where $T$ is the current date and time of the input device and $\oplus$ is the bit-wise XOR operation.
(2) Send a message $m = \{ID_i, C_1, D_i^*, T\}$ to the remote system.

**Authentication Phase:** Upon receiving message $m$ at time $T'$, the remote system authenticates the user based on the following steps:

(1) Verify the format of $ID_i$. If the format is incorrect, the system rejects the login request.
(2) Verify the validity of the time interval between $T$ and $T'$. If $(T' - T) \geq \Delta T$, where $\Delta T$ denotes the expected valid time interval for a transmission delay, the remote system rejects the login request.

(3) Compute $A_i = h(ID_i, x)$, $B_i^* = (D_i^*)^{A_i} \pmod{p}$ and $C_1^* = h(T \oplus B_i^*)$, and compare $C_1$ and $C_1^*$. If they are equal, this indicates that the password $PW_i^*$ is equal to $PW_i$, then the system accepts the login request; otherwise the login request is rejected.

Shared Information: $h(\cdot)$, $p$, $g$.
Information held by User $U_i$: $ID_i$, $PW_i$, Smart card($B_i$).
Information held by Remote System: $x$.

**User $U_i$**                                                    **Remote System**

**Registration Phase:**
Select $ID_i, PW_i$                        $\xrightarrow{\quad ID_i, PW_i \quad}$                        $A_i = h(ID_i, x)$
$$B_i = g^{A_i \cdot h(PW_i)} \pmod{p}$$
Store $ID_i, B_i, h(\cdot), p, g$ in Smart Card
$\xleftarrow{\quad \text{Smart Card} \quad}$

**Login and Authentication Phase:**
Input $ID_i, PW_i^*$
Generate $T$
$C_1 = h(T \oplus B_i)$
$D_i^* = g^{h(PW_i^*)} \pmod{p}$      $\xrightarrow{\quad ID_i, C_1, D_i^*, T \quad}$      Verify $ID_i$ and $T$
$$A_i = h(ID_i, x)$$
$$B_i^* = (D_i^*)^{A_i} \pmod{p}$$
$$C_1^* = h(T \oplus B_i^*)$$
Verify $C_1 \overset{?}{=} C_1^*$

**Fig. 1.** Wu-Chieu's Improved Authentication Scheme

## 2.2 Review of Lee-Lin-Chang's Scheme

Like Wu-Chieu's improved scheme, Lee-Lin-Chang's scheme [9] also consists of three phases: Registration, login, and authentication phase. Figure 2 shows Lee-Lin-Chang's authentication scheme. The scheme works as follows:

**Registration Phase:** The user $U_i$ submits their identifier $ID_i$ and chosen password $PW_i$ to the remote system. These private data must be sent in person or over a secure channel. Upon receiving the registration request, the remote system performs the following steps:

(1) Compute $A_i = h(ID_i, x)$, where $x$ is a secret key maintained by the system and $h(\cdot)$ is a collision resistant one-way hash function with an output size of 512 bits, e.g. SHA-512.
(2) Compute $B_i = h(A_i || h(PW_i))$.
(3) The remote system then personalizes the smart card with the secure information: $\{ID_i, A_i, B_i, h(\cdot)\}$.

Shared Information: $h(\cdot)$.
Information held by User $U_i$: $ID_i$, $PW_i$, Smart card($A_i,B_i$).
Information held by Remote System: $x$.

| **User $U_i$** | | **Remote System** |
|---|---|---|

**Registration Phase:**

Select $ID_i,PW_i$

$\xrightarrow{\quad ID_i, PW_i \quad}$

$A_i = h(ID_i,x)$
$B_i = h(A_i||h(PW_i))$
Store $ID_i, A_i, B_i, h(\cdot)$ in Smart Card

$\xleftarrow{\quad \text{Smart Card} \quad}$

**Login and Authentication Phase:**

Input $ID_i,PW_i^*$
Generate $T$
$B_i^* = h(A_i||h(PW_i^*))$
$C_1 = h(T \oplus B_i)$
$C_2 = B_i^* \oplus A_i$

$\xrightarrow{\quad ID_i, C_1, C_2, T \quad}$

Verify $ID_i$ and $T$
$A_i = h(ID_i||x)$
$B_i^* = C_2 \oplus A_i$
$C_1^* = h(T \oplus B_i^*)$
Verify $C_1 \overset{?}{=} C_1^*$

**Fig. 2.** Lee-Lin-Chang's Authentication Scheme

**Login Phase:** If the user $U_i$ wants to login, the user attaches the smart card to the card reader and keys in their identifier $ID_i$ and password $PW_i^*$, then the smart card performs the following operations:

(1) Compute the following three integers:
$B_i^* = h(A_i||h(PW_i^*))$, $C_1 = h(T \oplus B_i)$ and $C_2 = B_i^* \oplus A_i$, where $T$ is the current date and time of the input device.
(2) Send a message $m = \{ID_i, C_1, C_2, T\}$ to the remote system.

**Authentication Phase:** Upon receiving message $m$ at time $T'$, the remote system authenticates the user based on the following steps:

(1) Verify the format of $ID_i$. If the format is incorrect, the system rejects the login request.
(2) Verify the validity of the time interval between $T$ and $T'$. If $(T' - T) \geq \Delta T$, where $\Delta T$ denotes the expected valid time interval for a transmission delay, the remote system rejects the login request.
(3) Compute $A_i = h(ID_i||x)$ and obtain $B_i^*$ by computing $B_i^* = C_2 \oplus A_i$.
(4) Compute $C_1^* = h(T \oplus B_i^*)$, and compare $C_1$ and $C_1^*$. If they are equal, this indicates that the password $PW_i^*$ is equal to $PW_i$, then the system will accept the login request; otherwise the login request is rejected.

# 3   Cryptanalysis

This section demonstrates that Wu-Chieu's improved authentication scheme and Lee-Lin-Chang's authentication scheme are vulnerable to some attacks.

## 3.1   Two Attacks on Wu-Chieu's Improved Scheme

This subsection demonstrates that Wu-Chieu's improved remote authentication scheme is vulnerable to an off-line password guessing attack and an impersonation attack by using a stolen smart card.

**An Off-Line Password Guessing Attack:** Suppose that an attacker has eavesdropped a valid message $m = \{ID_i, C_1, D_i^*, T\}$ from an open network. It is easy to obtain the information since it is are exposed over an open network. Then, the off-line password guessing attack proceeds as follows:

(1) In order to obtain the password $PW_i$ of user $U_i$, the attacker $E$ makes a guess at the secret password $PW_i'$.
(2) $E$ computes $g^{h(PW_i')}(\mathrm{mod}\,p)$ and checks if $D_i^* = g^{h(PW_i')}(\mathrm{mod}\,p)$. If the computed value is the same as $D_i^*$, then $E$ guesses the legitimate user $U_i$'s password $PW_i$. Otherwise, $E$ repeatedly performs it until $D_i^* = g^{h(PW_i')}(\mathrm{mod}\,p)$.

If a user loses his smart card and it is found out by an attacker or an attacker stoles a user's smart card, then the attacker can easily impersonate the legitimate user $U_i$ by using the guessed password $PW_i'$ in the login phase. Furthermore, if some users employ the same password for multiple accounts, those will be compromised as well. As a result, Wu-Chieu's improved scheme is vulnerable to an off-line password guessing attack.

**An Impersonation Attack Using Stolen Smart Card:** The purpose of guessing a password is usually for further impersonation attacks. In the above described password guessing attack, in order to launch an impersonation attack on Wu-Chieu's improved scheme, an attacker still needs the smart card of the user. If the attacker $E$, however, has the smart card, $E$ can perform an impersonation attack without having to guess the password. This can be done as follows:

(1) $E$ attaches $U_i$'s smart card to the card reader and keys in $U_i$'s identifier $ID_i$ and arbitrary selects value $PW_a$ as $U_i$'s password, then the smart card will compute the following two integers: $C_1 = h(T_a \oplus B_i)$ and $D_a^* = g^{h(PW_a)}(\mathrm{mod}\ p)$, where $T_a$ is the current date and time of the input device, and then, a message $m = \{ID_i, C_1, D_a^*, T_a\}$ is sent to the remote system.
(2) Without knowing $PW_i$, $E$ can launch an impersonation attack by simply replaying $D_i^*$ instead of $D_a^*$, which can be obtained by eavesdropping, in a forged message $m = \{ID_i, C_1, D_a^*, T_a\}$. It is easy to check whether the remote system will accept this forged message $m = \{ID_i, C_1, D_i^*, T_a\}$, as $C_1 = C_1^* = h(T_a \oplus B_i^*)$ in the authentication phase.

## 3.2    Forgery Attack on Lee-Lin-Chang's Scheme

This subsection demonstrates that Lee-Lin-Chang's scheme is vulnerable to a forgery attack, where an attacker can easily masquerade as a legal user in order to access the resources of a remote system. In the login phase, the attacker can perform a forgery attack as follows:

(1) Has eavesdropped a valid message $m = \{ID_i, C_1, C_2, T\}$ from an open network.
(2) Compute $C_{2a}$ as follows:

$$C_{2a} = T \oplus C_2 \oplus T_a$$
$$= T \oplus B_i^* \oplus A_i \oplus T_a,$$

where $T_a$ is the attacker's current date and time.
(3) Send a forged message $m_a = (ID_i, C_1, C_{2a}, T_a)$ to the remote system.

When the remote system receives the message $m_a$, the remote system will go into the authentication phase and perform the following checks:

(1) The remote system will check the format of the $ID_i$. Of course, it is correct.
(2) Then, the remote system will check whether the time is valid. Because $(T' - T_a) \geq \Delta T$, where $T'$ is the received timestamp of message $m_a$, the remote system will accept this check.
(3) Then, the remote system will compute $A_i = h(ID_i||x)$ and obtain $B_a^*$ by computing the following:

$$B_a^* = C_{2a} \oplus A_i$$
$$= T \oplus B_i^* \oplus A_i \oplus T_a \oplus A_i$$
$$= T \oplus B_i^* \oplus T_a.$$

(4) Finally, the remote system will compute $C_1^*$ as follows:

$$C_1^* = h(T_a \oplus B_a^*)$$
$$= h(T_a \oplus T \oplus B_i^* \oplus T_a)$$
$$= h(T \oplus B_i^*),$$

and compare $C_1^*$ and $C_1$. It is easy to check whether the remote system will accept this forged message $m_a$, as $C_1 = C_1^* = h(T \oplus B_i^*)$. Finally, the remote system accepts the attacker's login request, making Lee-Lin-Chang's scheme insecure.

## 4    Proposed Scheme

This section proposes improvements to Wu-Chieu's improved scheme and Lee-Lin-Chang's scheme so that they can withstand the above mentioned attacks. In addition, the proposed scheme provides mutual authentication between the user and a remote system and does not require time synchronization or a delay-time limitations between the user and the remote system. In order to prevent the problems of clock synchronization or a delay-time limitations, the proposed scheme adopts a nonce-based protocol [11] instead of a timestamp-based protocol. The security of the proposed scheme is based on a one-way hash function and a discrete logarithm problem [12], and consists of registration, login, and session key agreement phases. Figure 3 shows the proposed authentication scheme. For simplicity, we omit $(\bmod p)$ from expressions.

**Registration Phase:** Like Wu-Chieu's improved scheme and Lee-Lin-Chang's scheme, let $x$ be a secret key maintained by the remote system. The user $U_i$ submits his identifier $ID_i$ and chosen password $PW_i$ to the system. These private data must be sent in person or over a secure channel. Upon receiving the registration request, the remote system performs the following steps:

(1) Compute $A_i = h(ID_i, x)$, where $h(\cdot)$ is a collision resistant one-way hash function with an output size of 512 bits, e.g. SHA-512.
(2) Compute $B_i = A_i \oplus PW_i$, where $\oplus$ is a bit-wise XOR operation.
(3) The remote system then personalizes the smart card with secure information: $\{ID_i, B_i, h(\cdot), p, g\}$.

**Login Phase:** If the user $U_i$ wants to login, the user attaches the smart card to the card reader and keys in the identifier $ID_i$ and password $PW_i^*$, then the smart card performs the following operations:

(1) Extracts $A_i = h(ID_i, x)$ from the smart card by computing $B_i \oplus PW_i^*$.
(2) Chooses a fresh random value $c \in Z_p^*$, and computes $C_1 = g^c$.
(3) Sends a message $m = \{ID_i, C_1\}$ to the remote system.

**Session Key Agreement Phase:** Upon receiving the authentication request message $m = \{ID_i, C_1\}$, the remote system and smart card execute the following steps for mutual authentication and session key agreement between the user $U_i$ and the remote system.

(1) The system verifies the format of $ID_i$. If the format is incorrect, the system rejects the login request. Otherwise, the system computes $A_i^* = h(ID_i, x)$. Then, the system chooses a fresh random value $s \in Z_p^*$, and computes $sk = (C_1)^s = g^{cs}$, $C_2 = g^s$ and $C_3 = h(ID_i, A_i^*, sk, g^c)$. The system sends back the message $\{C_2, C_3\}$.
(2) Upon receiving the message $\{C_2, C_3\}$, the smart card computes $sk^* = (C_2)^c = g^{sc}$ and $C_3^* = h(ID_i, A_i, sk^*, g^c)$. Then, the smart card compares $C_3$ and $C_3^*$. If they are equal, the user $U_i$ believes that the responding part is the real system, otherwise the user $U_i$ interrupts the connection. Finally, the smart card computes $C_4 = h(ID_i, A_i, sk^*, g^s)$ and sends this authentication token to the system for mutual authentication and session key agreement.

(3) Upon receiving the message $\{C_4\}$, the system computes $C_4^*$ $= h(ID_i, A_i^*, sk, g^s)$ and compares $C_4$ and $C_4^*$. If they are equal, the system can ensure that the user $U_i$ is legal.

After mutual authentication and session key agreement between the user and the remote system, $sk$ and $sk^*$ are used as a session key, respectively.

Shared Information: $h(\cdot)$, $p$, $g$.
Information held by User: $ID_i$, $PW_i$, Smart card($B_i$).
Information held by Remote System: $x$.

|                          **User $U_i$**                          |                          | **Remote System**                          |
| --- | --- | --- |

**Registration Phase:**

Select $ID_i, PW_i$      $\xrightarrow{\quad ID_i, PW_i \quad}$      $A_i = h(ID_i, x)$

$B_i = A_i \oplus PW_i$

Store $ID_i, B_i, h(\cdot), p, g$ in Smart Card

$\xleftarrow{\quad \text{Smart Card} \quad}$

**Login and Session Key Agreement Phase:**

Input $ID_i, PW_i^*$

$A_i = B_i \oplus PW_i^*$

Choose $c \in Z_p^*$

$C_1 = g^c (\mathrm{mod}\, p)$      $\xrightarrow{\quad \{ID_i, C_1\} \quad}$      Verify $ID_i$

$A_i^* = h(ID_i, x)$

Choose $s \in Z_p^*$

$sk = (C_1)^s = g^{cs}(\mathrm{mod}\, p)$

$C_2 = g^s(\mathrm{mod}\, p)$

$sk^* = (C_2)^c = g^{sc}(\mathrm{mod}\, p)$    $\xleftarrow{\quad \{C_2, C_3\} \quad}$    $C_3 = h(ID_i, A_i^*, sk, g^c)$

$C_3^* = h(ID_i, A_i, sk^*, g^c)$

Verify $C_3 \stackrel{?}{=} C_3^*$

$C_4 = h(ID_i, A_i, sk^*, g^s)$      $\xrightarrow{\quad \{C_4\} \quad}$      $C_4^* = h(ID_i, A_i^*, sk, g^s)$

Verify $C_4 \stackrel{?}{=} C_4^*$

Session Key: $sk = sk^* = g^{cs}(\mathrm{mod}\, p)$

**Fig. 3.** Proposed Authentication Scheme

# 5 Security Analysis

This section provides the proof of correctness of the proposed scheme. First, the security terms [12] needed for the analysis of the proposed scheme are defined . They are as follows:

**Definition 1.** *A weak secret key (user's password $PW_i$) is the value of low entropy $W(k)$, which can be guessed in polynomial time.*

**Definition 2.** *A strong secret key (system's secret key $x$) is the value of high entropy $S(k)$, which cannot be guessed in polynomial time.*

**Definition 3.** *The discrete logarithm problem (DLP) is as follows: given a prime p, a generator g of $Z_p^*$, and an element $\beta \in Z_p^*$, find the integer $\alpha$, $0 \le \alpha \le p - 2$, such that $g^\alpha \equiv \beta(\bmod p)$.*

**Definition 4.** *The Diffie-Hellman problem (DHP) is the following: given a prime p, a generator g of $Z_p^*$, and an element $y^c(\bmod p)$ and $g^s(\bmod p)$, find $g^{cs}(\bmod p)$.*

**Definition 5.** *A secure one-way hash function $y = h(x)$ is where given x to compute y is easy and given y to compute x is hard.*

Here, six security properties: passive attack, active attack, guessing attack, known-key attack, mutual authentication and perfect forward secrecy, would be considered for the proposed scheme [12][13]. Under the above definitions, the following theorems are used to analyze the six security properties in the proposed scheme.

**Theorem 1.** *The proposed scheme can resist a passive attack.*

*Proof.* If an attacker, called $E$, who eavesdrops on a successful proposed scheme run can make a guess at the session key by using only information obtainable over a network and a guessed value of the remote system's secret key $x$, $E$ could break a Diffie-Hellman key exchange [14]. The reason will be clear. Such a problem can be reduced to the computing of a keying material $g^{cs}$ from the value $C_1$ and $C_2$ in the scheme. Thus, we claim that it is as difficult as to break the Diffie-Hellman problem. Without the ability to compute the keying material $g^{cs}$, the messages $C_3$ and $C_4$ do not leak any information to the passive attacker. Since the user $U_i$ and the system do not leak any information either, the proposed scheme can resist a passive attack.

**Theorem 2.** *The proposed scheme can resist an active attack.*

*Proof.* Active attacks can take many different forms, depending on what information is available to the attacker. An attacker who knows the remote system's secret key $x$ can easily pretend to be $U_i$ and communicate with the system. Similarly, an attacker with $x$ can masquerade as the system when $U_i$ tries to contact him. A man-in-the middle attack, which requires an attacker to fool both sides of a legitimate conversation, cannot be carried out by an attacker who does not know the system's secret key $x$. For example, suppose that attacker $E$ wants to fool the system into thinking he is talking to $U_i$. First, $E$ can compute $C_1' = g^e$, where $e$ is a fresh random value, and send it to the system. Then, the system will compute $sk = (C_1')^s = g^{es}$, $C_2 = g^s$ and $C_3 = h(ID_i, A_i^*, sk, C_1')$, and send $C_2$ and $C_3$ to $E$. When $E$ receives $C_2$ and $C_3$ from the remote system, $E$ has to make $C_4' = h(ID_i, A_i', sk', C_2)$ and send it to the system. Since the problem is combined with the Diffie-Hellman problem and a secure one-way hash function, in order to compute valid $C_4'$, $E$ cannot guess $sk'$ or $A_i'$ from $C_3$. Thus, the proposed scheme can withstand the man-in-the-middle attack.

**Theorem 3.** *The proposed scheme can resist guessing attacks.*

*Proof.* Assume a user loses his smart card and it is found by an attacker or an attacker steals a user's smart card. The attacker, however, cannot impersonate a legitimate user $U_i$ by using the smart card because no one can reveal the $PW_i$ from value $B_i$ in the smart card without knowing the system's secret key $x$.

**Theorem 4.** *The proposed scheme can resist the known-key attack.*

*Proof.* Known-key security means that each run of a key agreement protocol between two entities $U_i$ and a remote system should produce unique secret keys; such keys are called session keys. If the session key $sk$ is revealed to a passive attacker $E$, $E$ does not learn any new information from combining $sk$ with publicly-visible information. This is true because the messages $C_3$ or $C_4$ do not leak any information to the attacker. We have already established that $E$ cannot make meaningful guesses at the session key $sk$ from the guessed passwords, and there does not appear to be an easy way for $E$ to carry out an off-line password guessing attack. It means that the attacker, having already obtained some past session keys, cannot compromise current or future session keys. Thus, it can resist the known-key attack.

**Theorem 5.** *The proposed scheme provides the mutual authentication.*

*Proof.* Mutual authentication means that both the user and remote system are authenticated to each other within the same protocol, while explicit key authentication is the property obtained when both implicit key authentication and key confirmation hold. As such, the proposed scheme uses the Diffie-Hellman key exchange algorithm in order to provide mutual authentication. Then, the key is explicitly authenticated by a mutual confirmation session key, $g^{cs}$.

**Theorem 6.** *The proposed scheme provides perfect forward secrecy.*

*Proof.* Perfect forward secrecy means that if a long-term private key (e.g. user password $PW_i$ or system's private key $x$) is compromised, this does not compromise any earlier session keys. In the proposed scheme, since the Diffie-Hellman

**Table 1.** A comparison of security properties

| Security properties | Wu-Chieu's Scheme | Lee-Lin-Chang's Scheme | Proposed Scheme |
|---|---|---|---|
| Passive attack | Secure | Secure | Secure |
| Active attack | Secure | Insecure | Secure |
| Guessing attack | Insecure | Secure | Secure |
| Stolen smart card attack | Insecure | Secure | Secure |
| Mutual authentication | N/A | N/A | Provide |
| Session key distribution | N/A | N/A | Provide |
| Perfect forward secrecy | N/A | N/A | Provide |

key exchange algorithm is used to generate a session key $g^{cs}$, perfect forward secrecy is ensured because an attacker with a compromised system's secret key $x$ is only able to obtain the $g^c$ and $g^s$ from an earlier session. In addition, it is also computationally infeasible to obtain the session key $g^{cs}$ from $g^c$ and $g^s$, as it is a discrete logarithm problem and a Diffie-Hellman problem.

The security properties of Wu-Chieu's improved scheme, Lee-Lin-Chang's scheme and the proposed scheme are summarized in Table 1.

## 6    Performance Analysis

Comparisons between Wu-Chieu's improved scheme, Lee-Lin-Chang's scheme and our proposed scheme are shown in Table 2. Wu-Chieu's improved scheme requires a total of three exponent operations, six hashing operations and two exclusive-or operations. Lee-Lin-Chang's scheme requires a total of eight hashing operations and four exclusive-or operations. The proposed protocol, however, requires a total of four exponent operations, six hashing operations and two exclusive-or operations. Four exponent operations are needed in order to provide mutual authentication and perfect forward secrecy.

**Table 2.** A comparison of computation costs

| Computational type | Wu-Chieu's Scheme | | Lee-Lin-Chang's Scheme | | Proposed Scheme | |
|---|---|---|---|---|---|---|
| | User | System | User | System | User | System |
| Modular exponential | 1 | 2 | 0 | 0 | 2 | 2 |
| Hash operation | 2 | 4 | 3 | 5 | 2 | 4 |
| XOR operation | 1 | 1 | 2 | 2 | 1 | 1 |
| Timestamp | Required | | Required | | Not Required | |

When considering hashing and exclusive-or operations, in Wu-Chieu's improved scheme, two hashing and one exclusive-or operations are needed for the user and four hashing and one exclusive-or operations are required for the system. In Lee-Lin-Chang's scheme, three hashing and two exclusive-or operations are required for the user and five hashing and two exclusive-or operation are required for the system. In the proposed scheme, however, two hashing and one exclusive-or operations are needed for the user and four hashing and one exclusive-or operations are required in the system. When considering hashing and exclusive-or operations, we can see that the proposed scheme and Wu-Chieu's improved scheme have the same computational costs. The proposed scheme, however, provides mutual authentication. Obviously, the proposed protocol is more efficient than Wu-Chieu's improved scheme and Lee-Lin-Chang's scheme.

# 7   Conclusion

The current paper demonstrated that Wu-Chieu's improved remote authentication scheme is vulnerable to an off-line password guessing attack and an impersonation attack by using stolen smart card. Also, we demonstrated that Lee-Lin-Chang's scheme is vulnerable to a forgery attack, where an attacker can easily masquerade as another legal user in order to access the resources of a remote system. Thus, improvements to Wu-Chieu's improved scheme and Lee-Lin-Chang's scheme were proposed so that they will be able to withstand such attacks. In addition, the proposed scheme provides mutual authentication between the user and a remote system and does not require time synchronization or delay-time limitation between the user and the remote system. As a result, in contrast to Wu-Chieu's improved scheme and Lee-Lin-Chang's scheme, the proposed scheme can securely perform key agreement for secure communication.

# Acknowledgements

We would like to thank the anonymous reviewers for their helpful comments in improving our manuscript. This research was supported by the MIC (Ministry of Information and Communication), Korea, under the ITRC (Information Technology Research Center) support program supervised by the IITA (Institute of Information Technology Assessment).

# References

1. Peyret, P., Lisimaque, G., Chua, T.Y.: Smart Cards Provide Very High Security and Flexibility in Subscribers Management. IEEE Transactions on Consumer Electronics. Vol. 36. No. 3. (1990) 744-752
2. Sternglass, D.: The Future Is in the PC Cards. IEEE Spectrum. Vol. 29. No. 6. (1992) 46-50
3. Lamport, L.: Password Authentication with Insecure Communication. Communications of the ACM. Vol. 24. No. 11. (1981) 770-772
4. Hwang, M.S., Li, L.H.: A New Remote User Authentication Scheme Using Smart Cards. IEEE Trans. On Consumer Electronics. Vol. 46. No. 1. (2000) 28-30
5. Sun, H.M.: An Efficient Remote User Authentication Scheme Using Smart Cards. IEEE Trans. on Consumer Electronics. Vol. 46. No. 4. (2000) 414-416
6. Wu, S.T., Chieu, B.C.: A User Friendly Remote Authentication Scheme with Smart Cards. Computers & Security. Vol. 22. No. 6. (2003) 547-550
7. Wu, S.T., Chieu B.C.: A Note on A User Friendly Remote Authentication Scheme with Smart Cards. IEICE Trans. Fund. Vol. E87-A. No. 8. (2004) 2180-2181
8. Yang, C.C., Wang, R.C.: Cryptanalysis of A User Friendly Remote Authentication Scheme with Smart Cards. Computers & Security. Vol. 23. No. 5. (2004) 425-427
9. Lee, C.C., Lin, C.H., Chang, C.C.: An Improved Low Computation Cost User Authentication Scheme for Mobile Communication. Proc. 19th Advanced Information Networking and Applications (IEEE AINA'05). Vol. 2. (2005) 249-252
10. Ding, Y., Horster, P.: Undetectable On-line Password Guessing Attacks. ACM Operating Systems Review. Vol. 29. No. 4. (1995) 77-86

11. Needham, R.M., Schroeder, M.D.: Using Encryption for Authentication in Large Networks of Computers. Communications of the ACM. Vol. 21. No. 12. (1978) 993-999.
12. Menezes, A.J., Oorschot, P.C., Vanstone, S.A.: Handbook of Applied Cryptograph. CRC Press. New York. (1997)
13. Ryu, E.K., Kim, K.W., Yoo, K.Y.: A Promising Key Agreement Protocol. ISAAC 2003. LNCS 2906. (2003) 655-662
14. Diffie, W., Hellman, M.: New Directions in Cryptography. IEEE Trans. Inf. Theory. Vol. IT-22. No. 6. (1976) 644-654

# Two Proxy Signcryption Schemes from Bilinear Pairings

Qin Wang and Zhenfu Cao

Department of Computer Science and Engineering,
Shanghai Jiao Tong University, Shanghai 200030, P.R. China
{wangqin, cao-zf}@cs.sjtu.edu.cn

**Abstract.** Proxy signcryption is a cryptographic primitive which combines the functionalities of a proxy signature scheme and a signcryption scheme. In this paper, based on bilinear pairings, we would like to propose two efficient proxy singcryption schemes. One is certificate based and the other is identity based. Also we analyze the two proposed schemes from efficiency point of view. We show that the certificate based scheme achieves great efficiency in terms of communication cost and computation overhead. And the identity based scheme is much more efficient than the scheme proposed by Li and Chen. What's more, we also argument that the two proposed schemes are secure in the random oracle model without a secure channel.

**Keywords:** proxy signature, signcryption, proxy signcryption, bilinear pairings.

## 1 Introduction

In the areas of computer communications and electronic transactions, one of the important topics is how to send data in a confidential and authenticated way. Usually, the confidentiality of delivered data is provided by encryption algorithms, and the authentication of messages is guaranteed by digital signatures. In 1997, Zheng proposed a primitive that he called *signcryption* [10]. The idea of a signcryption scheme is to combine the functionality of an encryption scheme with that of a signature scheme. It must provide privacy; must be unforgeable; and there must be a method to settle repudiation disputes. This must be done in a more efficient manner than a composition of an encryption scheme with a signature scheme. After that, some research works on signcryption have been done [5–10].

The *proxy signature* primitive and the first efficient solution were introduced by Mambo, Usuda and Okamoto (MUO) [12]. The scheme allows an entity, called the original signer, to delegate another entity, called a proxy signer, to sign messages on its behalf. Proxy signature has found numerous practical applications, particularly in distributed computing where delegation of rights is quite common, such as e-cash systems, global distribution networks, grid computing, mobile agent applications, and mobile communications. A secure proxy signature scheme should satisfy the following five requirements: verifiability, strong

Y.G. Desmedt et al. (Eds.): CANS 2005, LNCS 3810, pp. 161–171, 2005.

unforgeability, strong identifiability, strong undeniability, prevention of misuse [12, 13].

The *proxy signcryption* primitive and the first scheme were proposed by Gamage, Leiwo, and Zheng (GLZ) in 1999 [11]. The scheme combines the functionality of a proxy signature scheme and a signcryption scheme. It allows an entity to delegate its authority of signcryption to a trusted agent. The proxy signcryption scheme is useful for applications that are based on unreliable datagram style network communication model where messages are individually signed and not serially linked via a session key to provide authenticity and integrity. Along with the concept, Gamage, Leiwo, and Zheng also proposed a proxy signcryption scheme [11]. In 2004, Li and Chen proposed an identity based proxy signcryption scheme [17] from pairings, denoted Li-Chen scheme in this paper.

An *identity based cryptosystem* is a novel type of public cryptographic scheme in which the public keys of the users are their identities or strings derived from their identities. For this to work there is a Key Generation Center (KGC) that generates private keys using some master key related to the global parameters for the system. In [18] Shamir proposed an identity-based signature scheme, but for many years identity-based encryption remained an open problem. Until 2001, Boneh and Franklin [2] presented an ID-based encryption scheme based on properties of bilinear pairings on elliptic curves, which appears to be the first fully functioning, efficient and provably secure identity-based encryption scheme. Since then, many cryptographic protocols using pairings were proposed [1-6, 9, 15, 16].

In this paper, we will give two proxy signcryption schemes from bilinear pairings. One scheme is in certificate based public key setting, and the other scheme is in identity based public key setting. The certificate based scheme achieves great efficiency as the Chen-Lee signcryption scheme [5], and completes signcryption and proxy functionality simultaneously. The identity based scheme is much more efficient than Li-Chen scheme[17] in terms of computation overhead. Both of the two proposed schemes need no secure channel. What's more, we argument that they are both secure in the random oracle model.

The rest of this paper is organized as follows: In section 2, we first review some basic concepts of bilinear pairings. Then we propose a certificate based proxy signcryption scheme and analyze its performance and security in section 3. An identity based proxy signcryption scheme and the analysis of its performance and security are presented in section 4. Finally, the conclusion is given in section 5.

## 2     Basic Concepts of Bilinear Pairings

In this section, we will briefly review the basic concept and some properties of bilinear pairing.

Let $(\mathbb{G}, +)$ denote a cyclic additive group generated by $P$, whose order is a large prime $q$, and $(\mathbb{W}, \cdot)$ denote a cyclic multiplicative group of the same order $q$. Let $e : \mathbb{G} \times \mathbb{G} \to \mathbb{W}$ be a pairing which satisfies the following properties:

- Bilinear: $e(aP, bQ) = e(P, Q)^{ab}$.
- Non-degenerate: there exists $P, Q \in \mathbb{G}$, such that $e(P, Q) \neq 1$. This means that if $P$ is a generator of $\mathbb{G}$, then $e(P, P)$ is a generator of $\mathbb{W}$.
- Computable: there is an efficient algorithm to compute $e(P, Q)$ for all $P, Q \in \mathbb{G}$.

The modified Weil paring and the Tate pairing are admissible applications. $\mathbb{G}$ is a cyclic subgroup of the additive group of points of a supersingular elliptic $E(\mathbb{F}_p)$ over a finite field. $\mathbb{W}$ is a cyclic subgroup of the multiplicative group associated to a finite extension of $\mathbb{F}_p$. We can refer to [2] for more details. We consider the following problem in $(\mathbb{G}, \mathbb{W}, e)$.

**BDH Problem:** For $a, b, c \in \mathbb{Z}_q^*$, given $P, aP, bP, cP$, compute $e(P, P)^{abc}$. The advantage of any probabilistic, polynomial-time, 0/1-valued algorithm $\mathcal{A}$ in solving BDH problem in $(\mathbb{G}, \mathbb{W}, e)$ is defined to be:

$$Adv_{\mathcal{A}}^{BDH} = Prob[\mathcal{A}(P, aP, bP, cP, e(P, P)^{abc}) = 1 : a, b, c \in_R \mathbb{Z}_q^*].$$

**BDH Assumption:** For every probabilistic, polynomial-time, 0/1-valued algorithm $\mathcal{A}$, $Adv_{\mathcal{A}}^{BDH}$ is negligible.

# 3   A Certificate Based Proxy Signcryption Scheme

In this section, based on the bilinear pairings, we will propose a new proxy signcryption scheme in certificate based public key setting.

### 3.1   New Proxy Signcryption Scheme CBPSC

The system parameter $\mathbb{G}, \mathbb{W}, P, q, e, E_K(.), D_K(.), H_1, H_2$ are as following: $\mathbb{G}$ is a cyclic additive group generated by $P$, whose order is a large prime $q$. $\mathbb{W}$ is a cyclic multiplicative group of the same order $q$. $e : \mathbb{G} \times \mathbb{G} \to \mathbb{W}$ is a bilinear pairing map. $(E_K(.), D_K(.))$ is a pair of ideal symmetric key encryption /decryption algorithms under the session key $K$. $H_1, H_2$ are two hash functions. $H_1 : \{0, 1\}^{k_1} \to \mathbb{G}^*$, $H_2 : \{0, 1\}^{k_0+k_1+n} \to \mathbb{Z}_q^*$. Here $\mathbb{G}^*$ denotes $\mathbb{G} \setminus \{0\}$, $k_0$ is the number of bits required to represent an element of $\mathbb{G}$, $k_1$ is the number of bits required to represent a warrant, $n$ is the number of bits of a message to be signcrypted. $H_1$ and $H_2$ are viewed as random oracles.

We assume the original sender's key pair is $(X_o, Y_o = X_o P, X_o \in \mathbb{Z}_q)$, the proxy sender's key pair is $(X_p, Y_p = X_p P, X_p \in \mathbb{Z}_q)$, and the receiver's key pair is $(X_r, Y_r = X_r P, X_r \in \mathbb{Z}_q)$. We denote by $X_{pro}$ the proxy private key, $\omega$ the warrant. And concatenation is denoted by $\|$.

The building blocks of the scheme is the short signature proposed by Boneh, Lynn, and Shacham [3], the identity-based signature proposed by Cha and Cheon [4], and the construction method of Bao and Deng [8]. The scheme is described as follows:

**[Proxy Generation]**

1. For delegating his signcryption capability to the proxy sender, the original sender first makes a warrant $\omega$ which includes the restrictions on the class of messages delegated, the original sender and proxy sender's identities and public keys, the period of validity, etc.

2. The original sender computes $S = X_o \cdot H_1(\omega)$, and then sends $(\omega, S)$ to the proxy sender via a public channel.

3. After receiving the proxy certificate $(\omega, S)$, the proxy sender verifies the proxy certificate by checking if $e(P, S) \equiv e(Y_o, H_1(\omega))$.

4. For a valid delegation, the proxy sender computes a proxy private key as: $X_{pro} = S + X_p \cdot H_1(\omega)$.

**[Proxy Signcrypting]**

To signcrypt a plain text $m \in \{0, 1\}^n$ to a receiver on behalf of the original sender, the proxy sender does the following:

1. Randomly choose $t \in \mathbb{Z}_q^*$, and then compute $U = t \cdot H_1(\omega)$, $h = H_2(\omega||m||U)$, $V = (t + h) \cdot X_{pro}$.

2. Compute $k = t \cdot X_{pro}$, and then set $K = e(k, Y_r)$, $C = E_K(\omega||m||V)$.

3. Send $(\omega, U, C)$ to the receiver via a public channel.

**[Proxy Unsigncrypting]**

Upon receiving $(\omega, U, C)$ from the proxy sender, the receiver does the following:

1. Compute $K = e(U, X_r \cdot (Y_o + Y_p))$.

2. Recover $\omega||m||V = D_K(C)$.

3. Compute $h = H_2(\omega||m||U)$

4. Check whether $e(P, V) \equiv e(Y_o + Y_p, U + h \cdot H_1(\omega))$. If it holds, the proxy signcryption is valid.

**[Public Proxy Verification]**

If the receiver wants to prove to a third party, he just needs to release $(\omega, m, U, V)$ which is a proxy signature by the proxy sender on behalf of the original sender. Then any third party can be convinced of the message's origin as follows:

1. Compute $h = H_2(\omega||m||U)$.

2. Check whether $e(P, V) \equiv e(Y_o + Y_p, U + h \cdot H_1(\omega))$. If so, it is indeed the proxy sender's signature on behalf of the original sender.

Note that, the proxy generation algorithm of our scheme is first proposed Zhang *et al.* in [15], and the signcrypting is done in a manner similar to the Chen-Lee scheme from [5].

## 3.2   Correctness

The consistency is easy to verify by the bilinearity of the map:

$$
\begin{aligned}
e(k, Y_r) &= e(t \cdot X_{pro}, X_r \cdot P) \\
&= e(t \cdot (X_o + X_p) H_1(\omega), X_r \cdot P) \\
&= e(t \cdot H_1(\omega), (X_o + X_p) \cdot X_r \cdot P) \\
&= e(U, X_r \cdot (Y_o + Y_p))
\end{aligned}
$$

$$
\begin{aligned}
e(P, V) &= e(P, (t + h) \cdot X_{pro}) \\
&= e(P, (t + h) \cdot (X_o + X_p) \cdot H_1(\omega)) \\
&= e((X_o + X_p) \cdot P, (t + h) \cdot H_1(\omega)) \\
&= e(Y_o + Y_p, t \cdot H_1(\omega) + h \cdot H_1(\omega)) \\
&= e(Y_o + Y_p, U + h \cdot H_1(\omega)
\end{aligned}
$$

## 3.3   Efficiency

Assuming the length of the cipthertext generated from an symmetric encryption algorithm is the same as the length of the plaintext, the length the of ciphertext $(\omega, U, C)$ of our new scheme is only $|k_0 + k_1 + n|$ bits. Our scheme is very efficient in communication cost.

We now discuss the computation cost. We denote by $A$ a point addition in $\mathbb{G}$, by $M$ a scalar multiplication in $\mathbb{G}$, by $H$ a computation of hash function $H_1$, and by $P$ a computation of the pairing. We do not take the computation time for hash function $H_2$ and $(E_K, D_K)$ into account.

Both of the original sender and the proxy sender have to compute $H_1(\omega)$, the proxy generation algorithm requires $1A + 2M + 2H + 2P$. The proxy signcrypting algorithm requires $3M + 1P$. The proxy unsigncrypting algorithm requires $2A + 2M + 1H + 3P$. The public proxy verification algorithm requires $2A + 1M + 1H + 2P$. Because the computation about proxy generation is a one-time cost, compared with the Chen-Lee signcryption scheme proposed by [5], there is no extra cost over it. Moreover, the authors of [5] has compared their scheme with other identity-based signcryption schemes and concluded that their scheme is the most efficient, provably-secure scheme of its type proposed to date. So our proxy signcryption scheme is also of great efficiency.

## 3.4   Security

Because proxy signcryption is an integration of proxy signature and signcryption, we discuss a secure proxy signcryption scheme should satisfy the security requirements to proxy signature and signcryption simultaneously.

[**Security requirements**]

**R1. Verifiability:** From the proxy signcryption text, the recipient can be convinced of the original sender's agreement on the signcrypted message.

**R2. Strong unforgeability:** The original sender and other third parties cannot create a valid proxy signcryption text.

**R3. Strong identifiability:** Anyone can determine the identity of the corresponding proxy sender from the proxy signcryption text.

**R4. Prevention of misuse:** The proxy sender cannot use the proxy private key for other purposes than generating a valid proxy signcryption text.

**R5. Confidentiality:** Except the recipient, any one cannot extract the plaintext from the proxy signcryption text.

**R6. Non-repudiation:** The recipient can efficiently prove to a third party that a message is indeed originated from a specific proxy sender on behalf of an original sender.

Now we analyze our scheme on security.

1. From the proxy unsigncrypting phase, the receiver can be convinced that the proxy sender has the original sender's signature on the warrant $\omega$. The warrant $\omega$ also contains the identity information and the limit of the delegated signcrypting capacity, so the receiver can be convinced of the original sender's agreement on the signcrypted message. Then the scheme satisfies the security requirement R1.

2. Because the proxy sender uses his private key to generate the proxy private key: $X_{pro} = S + X_p \cdot H_1(\omega)$, any one cannot get the proxy private key $X_{pro}$ except the proxy sender himself. In the proxy signcrypting step, we use the Cha-Cheon signature algorithm which is provably secure in the random oracle model [4]. If an attacker forges a valid proxy signcryption text $(\omega, U, C)$ for any message $m$ such that $\omega||m||V = D_K(C)$ where $K = e(U, X_r \cdot (Y_o + Y_p))$, it implies that the attacker has successfully forged a valid Cha-Cheon signature $(U, V)$ for a message $m$, which is in turn contrary to the provable security of the Cha-Cheon signature scheme. So the scheme satisfies the security requirement R2.

3. It contains the warrant $\omega$ in a valid proxy signcryption text, and anyone can determine the identity of the corresponding proxy sender from the warrant $\omega$. So the scheme satisfies the security requirement R3.

4. In our proxy signcryption scheme, using the warrant $\omega$, we have determined the limit of the delegated signcrypting capacity in the warrant, then the proxy sender cannot signcrypt messages that have not been authorized by the original sender. So the scheme satisfies the security requirement R4.

5. Except the receiver, any one else cannot extract the plaintext $m$ from the proxy signcryption text $(\omega, U, C)$. For getting the message, the attacker has to decrypt the ciphertext $C$ directly. To do so, the attacker has to obtain the session key $K$ since $(E_K(\cdot), D_K(\cdot))$ is assumed to be an ideal symmetric key encryption/decrytion algorithm pair. $K = e(k, Y_r)) = e(t \cdot X_{pro}, X_r P) = e(t \cdot (X_o + X_p) \cdot H_1(\omega), X_r P) = e(H_1(\omega), P)^{t \cdot (X_o + X_p) \cdot X_r}$, however, the attacker cannot get the value of $e(H_1(\omega), P)^{t \cdot (X_o + X_p) \cdot X_r}$ from the value of $P, U, Y_o + Y_p, Y_r$, this is the BDH problem, which is widely believed intractable in security community. Furthermore, the proxy signcryption text is $(\omega, U, C)$ and the value $V$ is hidden behind $C$, so the proxy signature on the plaintext is not visible in the proxy

signcryption text. The attacker cannot verify the proxy signature on plaintexts $m_0$ and $m_1$ even the message is chosen from $m_0$ and $m_1$ randomly, which is the requirement of sematic security [14]. Therefore, we conclude that our scheme meets the security requirement R5.

6. A third party can settle repudiation disputes in a similar manner to the public proxy verification algorithm. So the scheme satisfies the security requirement R6.

From above all, we can conclude that

**Corollary 1.** *The proposed certificate based proxy signcryption scheme CBPSC is secure and can work correctly without a secure channel.*

# 4   An Identity Based Proxy Signcryption Scheme

In this section, we propose an identity based proxy signcryption scheme from pairings. Our identity based proxy signcryption scheme is based on Zhang's proxy signature scheme [16].

## 4.1   New Proxy Signcryption Scheme IDBPSC

### [Setup]

The Key Generation Center (KGC) chooses a random number $s \in \mathbb{Z}_q^*$ and sets $P_{pub} = sP$. Then publishes system parameters $\{\mathbb{G}, \mathbb{W}, e, q, P, P_{pub}, H_1, H_2\}$, and keeps $s$ as the *master-key*, which is known only by itself. $H_1 : \{0,1\}^* \to \mathbb{G}^*$ and $H_2 : \{0,1\}^* \to \mathbb{Z}_q^*$ are viewed as random oracles. Other parameters are the same as section 3.1.

### [Extract]

Given an identity $ID$, the KGC computes $Q_{ID} = H_1(ID)$ and the private key $S_{ID} = sQ_{ID}$. Let $(Q_o, S_o)$ be the original sender's key pair, $(Q_p, S_p)$ be the proxy sender's key pair, and $(Q_r, S_r)$ be the receiver's key pair.

### [Proxy Generation]

To delegate the signcrypting capacity to the proxy sender, the original sender uses Hess's identity based signature scheme [1] to make the signed warrant $\omega$. If the following process is finished successfully, the proxy sender gets the proxy key $S_{pro}$.

1. The original sender first makes a warrant $\omega$ which includes the restrictions on the class of messages delegated, the original sender and proxy sender's identities and public keys, the period of validity, etc.

2. The original sender computes $r_\omega = e(P, P)^{k_\omega}$, where $k_\omega \in \mathbb{Z}_q^*$, $V_\omega = H_2(\omega \| r_\omega)$ and $U_\omega = V_\omega S_o + k_\omega P$. Then sends $(\omega, U_\omega, V_\omega)$ to the proxy sender via a public channel.

3. After receiving the proxy certificate $(\omega, U_\omega, V_\omega)$, the proxy sender verifies the validity of the signature on $\omega$: Compute $r_\omega = e(U_\omega, P)e(Q_o, P_{pub})^{-V_\omega}$ and accept the signature if and only if $V_\omega \equiv H_2(\omega \| r_\omega)$.

4. For a valid delegation, the proxy sender computes a proxy private key as: $S_{pro} = V_\omega S_p + U_\omega$.

[**Proxy Signcrypting**]

To signcrypt a plain text $m \in \{0,1\}^n$ to a receiver on behalf of the original sender, the proxy sender does the following:

1. Randomly choose $k \in \mathbb{Z}_q^*$, and then compute $r = e(P,P)^k$, $K = e(S_p, Q_r)^r$, $C = E_K(\omega||m)$, $V = H_2(C||r)$ and $U = V S_{pro} + kP$.
2. Send $(\omega, C, U, V, r_\omega)$ to the receiver via a public channel.

[**Proxy Unsigncrypting**]

Upon receiving $(\omega, C, U, V, r_\omega)$ from the proxy sender, the receiver does the following:

1. Compute $r = e(U,P)(e((Q_o + Q_p), P_{pub})^{H_2(\omega||r_\omega)} \cdot r_\omega)^{-V}$.
2. Check whether $V = H_2(C||r)$. If it holds, the proxy signcryption is valid.
3. Recover $\omega||m = D_K(C)$.
4. Compute $K = e(Q_p, S_r)^r$.

[**Public Proxy Verification**]

Any third party can be convinced of the message's origin as follows:

1. Compute $r = e(U,P)(e((Q_o + Q_p), P_{pub})^{H_2(\omega||r_\omega)} \cdot r_\omega)^{-V}$.
2. Check whether $V \equiv H_2(C||r)$. If so, accept it.

### 4.2    Correctness

The consistency is easy to verify by the bilinearity of the map:

$$
\begin{aligned}
&e(U,P)(e((Q_o + Q_p), P_{pub})^{H_2(\omega||r_\omega)} \cdot r_\omega)^{-V} \\
&= e(U,P)(e(V_\omega \cdot (S_o + S_p), P) \cdot r_\omega)^{-V} \\
&= e(U,P)(e(S_{pro} - k_\omega P, P) \cdot r_\omega)^{-V} \\
&= e(U,P)(e(S_{pro}, P)e(-k_\omega P, P) \cdot r_\omega)^{-V} \\
&= e(U,P)e(S_{pro}, P)^{-V} \\
&= e(V S_{pro} + kP, P)e(S_{pro}, P)^{-V} \\
&= e(P,P)^k \\
&= r
\end{aligned}
$$

### 4.3    Efficiency

Now we compare the efficiency of our IDBPSC with that of Li-Chen scheme proposed in [17] from computation overhead.

We denote by $A$ a point addition in $\mathbb{G}$, by $M$ a scalar multiplication in $\mathbb{G}$, by $E$ an exponentiation in $\mathbb{W}$, and by $P$ a computation of the pairing. We do not take the computation time for hash function $H_2$ and $(E_K, D_K)$ into account.

In the table below we enumerate the various operations necessary for each.

**Table 1.** Comparison of our scheme and the scheme in [17]

| Algorithm | IDBPSC | Li-Chen |
|---|---|---|
| proxy generation | 2A+3M+2E+3P | 1A+2M+1E+3P |
| proxy signcrypting | 1A+2M+2E+2P | 2A+2M+2E+2P |
| proxy unsigncrypting | 1A+3E+3P | 4E+8P |
| public proxy verification | 1A+2E+2P | 2E+4P |

In proxy generation algorithm, our scheme cost a little bit more computation than Li-Chen scheme, but proxy generation algorithm is a one-time cost. In the three algorithms: proxy signcrypting, proxy unsigncrypting, and public proxy verification, our scheme totally requires $5A + 5M + 9E + 10P$, while Li-Chen scheme requires $3A + 10M + 3E + 17P$. We note that the computation of the pairing is most time-consuming. Although there has been many papers discussing the complexity of pairings and how to speed up the pairing computation, the computation of the pairing still remains time-consuming. Our scheme only needs 10 pairing computations, while theirs needs 17 pairing computations. So our scheme is much more efficient than Li-Chen scheme.

In addition, Li-Chen scheme needs a secure channel to send the proxy certificate from the origianl sender to the proxy sender, while ours can be done through public channel.

### 4.4 Security

Now we discuss the security of our new identity based proxy signcryption scheme.

1. It's easy to see the IDBPSC scheme satisfies the security requirements of R1, R3, R4, R6 for the similar reason as the CBPSC scheme.

2. Because the proxy sender uses his private key to generate the proxy private key: $S_{pro} = V_\omega S_p + U_\omega$, any one cannot get the proxy private key $S_{pro}$ except the proxy sender himself. In the proxy signcrypting step, the Hess signature is used which is provably secure in the random oracle model [1]. If an attacker forges a valid proxy signcryption text $(\omega, C, U, V, r_\omega)$ for any message $m$, it implies that the attacker has successfully forged a valid Hess signature $(U, V)$ for a ciphertext $C$, which is in turn contrary to the provable security of the Hess signature scheme. So the scheme satisfies the security requirement R2.

3. Except the receiver, any one else cannot extract the plaintext $m$ from the proxy signcryption text $(\omega, C, U, V, r_\omega)$. For getting the message, the attacker has to decrypt the ciphertext $C$ directly. To do so, the attacker has to obtain the session key $K$ since $(E_K(\cdot), D_K(\cdot))$ is assumed to be an ideal symmetric key encryption/decrytion algorithm pair. $K = e(S_p, Q_r)^r$, however, the attacker cannot get the value of $e(S_p, Q_r)$ from the value of $P, Q_p, Q_r, P_{pub}$, this is the BDH problem which is widely believed intractable in security community. For further details see [2]. Therefore, we conclude that our scheme meets the security requirement R5.

*Remark.* If we compute $V = H_1(m||r)$ instead of $V = H_1(C||r)$, then any adversary can verify the signature on two plaintexts $m_0$ and $m_1$ during the game

IND-IDSC-CCA [6], and find out which one matches to the challenge ciphertext, that is replacing $V = H_1(C||r)$ by $V = H_1(m||r)$ would induce an obstacle to the sematic security.

From above all, we can conclude that

**Corollary 2.** *The proposed identity based proxy signcryption scheme IDBPSC is secure and can work correctly without a secure channel.*

## 5    Conclusion

We proposed two proxy signcryption schemes from bilinear pairings. One was certificate based, and the other was identity based. The scheme CBPSC achieved great efficiency in communication cost and computation overhead. The scheme IDBPSC was much more efficient than Li-Chen scheme in terms of computation overhead. Both of the two proposed schemes were secure in the random oracle model and needed no secure channel.

## Acknowledgment

This work was supported in part by the National Natural Science Foundation of China for Distinguished Young Scholars under Grant No. 60225007, the National Research Fund for the Doctoral Program of Higher Education of China under Grant No. 20020248024, and the Science and Technology Research Project of Shanghai under Grant Nos. 04JC14055 and 04DZ07067.

## References

1. Hess, F.: Efficient Identity Based Signature Schemes Based on Pairings. In: Nyberg, K., Heys, H. (eds.): Selected Areas in Cryptography: 9th Annual International Workshop. Lecture Notes in Computer Science, Vol. 2595. Springer-Verlag, Berlin Heidelberg New York (2003) 310–324
2. Boneh, D., Franklin, M.: Identity-Based Encryption from the Weil Pairing. In: Kilian, J. (ed.): Advances in Cryptology-Crypto. Lecture Notes in Computer Science, Vol. 2139, Springer-Verlag, Berlin Heidelberg New York (2001) 213-229
3. Boneh, D., Lynn, B., Shacham, H.: Short Signatures from the Weil Pairing. In: Boyd,C. (ed.): Advances in Cryptology-Asiacrypt. Lecture Notes in Computer Science, Vol. 2248, Springer-Verlag, Berlin Heidelberg New York (2001) 514-532
4. Cha, J.C., Cheon, J.H.: An Identity-Based Signature from Gap Diffie-Hellman Groups. In: Y.G. Desmedt (ed.): Public Key Cryptography. Lecture Notes in Computer Science, Vol. 2567. Springer-Verlag, Berlin Heidelberg New York (2003) 18–30
5. Chen,L., Lee, J.M.: Improved Identity-Based Signcryption. In: Vaudenay, S. (ed.): Public Key Cryptography. Lecture Notes in Computer Science, Vol. 3386. Springer-Verlag, Berlin Heidelberg New York (2005) 362–379
6. J.M.Lee: Identity based signcryption. 2002. http://eprint.iacr.org/2002/098.
7. Lee, J.M., Mao, W.: Two Birds One Stone: Signcryption using RSA. In: M. Joye (Ed.): Topics in Cryptology-CT-RSA. Lecture Notes in Computer Science, Vol. 2612. Springer-Verlag, Berlin Heidelberg New York (2003) 211–225

8. Bao, F., Deng, R.H.: A Signcryption Scheme with Signature Directly Verifiable by Public Key. In: Imai, H., Zheng, Y. (eds.): Public Key Cryptography. Lecture Notes in Computer Science, Vol. 1498. Springer-Verlag, Berlin Heidelberg New York (1998) 55–59

9. Libert, B., J.Quisquater: A New Identity Based Signcryption Scheme from Pairings, In: IEEE Information Theory Workshop (2003)

10. Zheng,Y.: Digital Signcryption or How to Achieve Cost (Signature and Encryption) ¡¡ Cost(Signature)+Cost(Encryption), In: Kaliski, B.S., Jr. (ed.): Advances in Cryptology-Crypto. Lecture Notes in Computer Science, Vol. 1294. Springer-Verlag, Berlin Heidelberg New York (1997) 165–179

11. Gamage,C., Leiwo, J., Zheng, Y.: An Efficient Scheme for Secure Message Transmission Using Proxy-Signcryption. 22nd Australasian Computer Science Conference. Springer-Verlag, Berlin Heidelberg New York (1999) 420–431

12. Mambo, M., Usuda, K., Okamoto, E.: Proxy Signatures: Delegation of the Power to Sign Messages. IEICE Trans. on Fundamentals, E79-A(9) (1996) 1338–1354

13. Lee,B., Kim, H., Kim, K.: Strong Proxy Signature and its Applications. SCIS-Sypsium on Cryptology and Information Security (2001)

14. Shin, J.B., Lee, K., Shim, K., New DSA-Verifiable Signcryption Schemes. In: Lee, P.J., Lim, C.H. (eds.): Information Security and Cryptology. Lecture Notes in Computer Science, Vol. 2587. Springer-Verlag, Berlin Heidelberg New York (2003) 35–47

15. Zhang, F.G., Safavi-Naini, R., Lin, C.Y., New Proxy Signature, Proxy Blind Signature and Proxy Ring Signature Schemes from Bilinear Pairing. 2003. http://eprint.iacr.org/2003/104

16. Zhang, F., and Kim, K.: Efficient ID-Based Blind Signature and Proxy Signature from Bilinear Pairings. In: R. Safavi-Naini.R, Seberry,J. (eds.): Australasian Conference on Information Security and Privacy. Lecture Notes in Computer Science, Vol. 2727. Springer-Verlag, Berlin Heidelberg New York (2003) 312–323

17. Li, X., Chen, K.: Identity Based Proxy-Signcryption Sheme from Pairings. Proceedings of the 2004 IEEE International Conference on Services Computing. IEEE Comuter Society (2004) 494-497

18. Shamir,A.: Identity-Based Cryptosystems and Signature Schemes. In: Blakley, G.R., David Chaum (eds.), Advances in Cryptology-Crypto. Lecture Notes in Computer Science, Vol. 196. Springer-Verlag, Berlin Heidelberg New York (1984) 47-53

# Constructing Secure Warrant-Based Proxy Signcryption Schemes

Yuan Zhou, Zhenfu Cao, and Rongxing Lu

Department of Computer Science, Shanghai Jiao Tong University,
1954 Huashan Road, Shanghai 200030, P.R. China
zhouyuan@sjtu.edu.cn, {cao-zf, rxlu}@cs.sjtu.edu.cn

**Abstract.** Proxy signcryption, proposed by Gamage et al. [1], is a cryptographic primitive, which combines the functionality of a proxy signature scheme with that of an encryption. But to date, no formal definitions of security have been provided. In this paper, we first propose the syntax of warrant-based proxy signcryption scheme, then formalize notions of security for it. After that, we present a warrant-based proxy signcryption scheme based on integer factorization assumption.

**Keywords:** proxy Signcryption, integer factorization, provable security.

## 1 Introduction

Signcryption is a cryptographic primitive proposed by Zheng [2] to combine a function of a digital signature scheme with that of a encryption scheme. Signcryption not only provides three services (i.e. authenticity and confidentiality and non-repudiation) but also provides them in a single logical step. So it is more efficient than traditional signature-then-encryption. After Zheng' work, some resarch works has been done. Schemes in [3, 4, 5] have all been designed without a precisely specified secure model and corresponding security proof. A formal model of security for signcryption with non-repudiation is proposed in [6]. In [7], Malone-Lee and Mao provide a formal model of security for signcryption and give the corresponding security proofs of an Signcryption scheme using RSA. In their paper, they claim that their scheme offers non-repudiation in a very simple manner. However, their scheme cannot efficiently provides $\mathcal{NR}$ algorithm defined in [6]. The first formal definition signcryption scheme was issued in[8]. The author of paper defines signcryption as a multi-user primitive which simultaneously satisfies chosen ciphertext security for privacy and existential unforgeability for authenticity.

The notion of proxy signature scheme introduced by Mambo et al in 1996 [9]. A proxy signature scheme allows a entity called original signer to delegate his signing capability to another entity, called proxy signer. In a partial delegation with warrant proxy signature scheme, the original signer uses standard signature algorithm to sign a warrant which includes the type of the information delegated, both the parties identities and the period of delegation, etc. The signature of the

Y.G. Desmedt et al. (Eds.): CANS 2005, LNCS 3810, pp. 172–185, 2005.

warrant is called certificate. With the certificate and his private key, the proxy signer generates a proxy private key. After that, the proxy signer can sign any messages according to the warrant. And a third party would verify the validity of the proxy signature. In [10], some formal security notions for warrant based proxy signature schemes are presented. The proxy signature plays an important role in many applications [11–14] and has received great attention since it was proposed.

Recently, e-commerce environments have been paid great attentions. Let us consider an scenario that an president in a company delegates his capability of signing a message to another entity in case of say, temporal absence or lack of time. As a natural idea, a proxy signature scheme can be taken into account. However, if the message involves some commercial secret, a proxy signature scheme cannot satisfy this requirement. In 1999, Gamage et al. [1] extended the proxy signature and introduced a proxy signcryption scheme by combining proxy signature and encryption technology. It allows an entity to delegate its authority of signcryption to a trusted agent. Gamage' scheme is based on discrete logarithm. However, this scheme is not under an secure model, so the corresponding security proof has not been proposed in it. Further, it is desirable to design a proxy signcryption scheme based on other problems, such as integer factorization assumption.

Being inspired with above ideas, in this paper, we extend the syntax of signcryption proposed in [8] and present the syntax of warrant-based proxy signcryption, which combines the function of a warrant-based proxy signature scheme with that of a encryption scheme. Then, we formalize the notion of security for it. To our best knowledge, no similar works have been done. After that, we propose an efficient proxy signcryption scheme, which is based on integer factorization assumption and can be applied to signcrypt some short message. The scheme is based on Rabin signature scheme [15] and the encryption scheme in [16]. Moreover, our scheme's computation is much lower than Gamage'one.

## 2    Warrant-Based Proxy Signcryption Schemes

In [8], the syntax of signcryption schemes and some security notions for such schemes have been presented. In this section, we first review the basic works, then extend them to ones for warrant-based proxy signcryption.

### 2.1    Signcryption Scheme and the Security Notions for It

We recall the components of a signcryption scheme and the notions of security for such schemes [8].

**Definition 2.1 (Signcryption scheme).** Let signcryption $\mathbf{SC}=(\mathcal{G}, \mathcal{K}, \mathcal{SC}, \mathcal{VD}, \mathcal{NR}, \mathcal{V})$ be defined as follows:

- The parameter generation algorithm $\mathcal{G}$ takes as input $1^k$ where $k$ is the security parameter, and outputs some global parameters **params**.

- The key generation algorithm $\mathcal{K}$ takes as input global parameters **params** and outputs key pair (SDK, VEK). SDK is the user's sign/decrypt key, which is kept secret, and VEK the user's verify/encrypt key, which is made public.
- The randomized signcryption algorithm $\mathcal{SC}$ takes as in put the sender's secret key $SDK_s$ and the receiver's public key $VEK_r$ and a message $M$ from the associated message space $\mathcal{M}$, and outputs a signcryption $C$.
- The (usually deterministic) algorithm $\mathcal{VD}$ takes as input the signcryption $C$, the receiver's secret key $SDK_r$ the sender's public key $VEK_s$, and outputs $M \in \mathcal{M} \cup \{\bot\}$, where $\bot$ indicates that the message was not encrypted or signed properly.
- The non-repudiation algorithm $\mathcal{NR}$ takes as input the sender's public key $VEK_s$, the receiver's key pair $(SDK_r, VEK_r)$ and a string $C$, to return either a pair of strings $(M, \sigma)$ or the $\bot$ symbol.
- The (usually deterministic) verification algorithm $\mathcal{V}$ takes input $(VEK_s, M, \sigma)$, and output a bit. We say that $\sigma$ is a valid signature on $M$ relative to $VEK_s$ if $\mathcal{V}(VEK_s, M, \sigma)=1$.

**Remark 2.1.** From the above definition, we know the signcryption $c$ on some message $M$ can be transformed into a signature $\sigma$ on $M$ via the non-repudiation algorithm $\mathcal{NR}$.

In this paper, we only recall the strongest possible notion of insider security for multi-user signcryption [8]. The security for signcryption consists on semantical security against chosen ciphertext attacks(we call this security notion **SC-IND-CCA**) and strong existential unforgeability against chosen message attacks (we call this security notion **SC-UF-CMA**) when attacking some user $U$.

For defining the notion of **SC-IND-CCA**, we consider the following game between a challenger $\mathcal{C}$ and an adversary $\mathcal{A}$.

**Game 1:**

- **Setup.** The challenger $\mathcal{C}$ runs algorithm $\mathcal{G}$ and $\mathcal{K}$ to obtain a key pair $(SDK_U, VEK_U)$. The adversary $\mathcal{A}$ is given $VEK_U$.
- **Phase 1.**
  - Signcryption query $(M, VEK_r)$. The challenger $\mathcal{C}$ responds by running algorithm $\mathcal{SC}$ to signcrypt the message $M$.
  - De-signcryption query $(C, VEK_s)$. The challenger $\mathcal{C}$ responds by running algorithm $\mathcal{VD}$ to de-signcrypt the signcryption $C$.
- **Challenge.** Once the adversary $\mathcal{A}$ decides that Phase 1 is over, it outputs two equal length plaintexts $M_0^*, M_1^* \in \mathcal{M}$ and an arbitrary private key $SDK_s^*$. $\mathcal{C}$ picks a random bit $b \in \{0,1\}$ and computes $C^* = \mathcal{SC}(SDK_s^*, VEK_U, M_b^*)$. $C^*$ is send to $\mathcal{A}$ as a challenge.
- **Phase 2.** The adversary $\mathcal{A}$ performs new queries as in Phase 1.
- **Guess.** Finally, $\mathcal{A}$ output a bit $b'$ and wins if $b' = b$.

Let us define adversary $\mathcal{A}$'s advantage in attacking the scheme **SC** as the following function of the security parameter $k$: $\mathbf{Adv}_{\mathbf{SC},\mathcal{A}}^{\mathbf{IND\text{-}CCA}}(k) = |\Pr[b = b']\text{-}1/2|$.

**Definition 2.2 (SC-IND-CCA).** We say that a signcryption is **SC-IND-CCA** secure if for any probability polynomial time adversary $\mathcal{A}$, the advantage $\mathbf{Adv}_{\mathbf{SC},\mathcal{A}}^{\mathbf{IND\text{-}CCA}}(k)$ is negligible.

For defining the notion of **SC-UF-CMA**, we consider the following game between a challenger $\mathcal{C}$ and a forger $\mathcal{F}$.

**Game 2:**

- **Setup.** The challenger $\mathcal{C}$ runs algorithm $\mathcal{G}$ and $\mathcal{K}$ to obtain a key pair (SDK$_U$, VEK$_U$). The adversary $\mathcal{A}$ is given VEK$_U$.
- **Queries** The forger $\mathcal{F}$ make signcryption queries and de-signcryption queries exactly as in Game 1. Again, these queries can also be produced adaptively.
- **Output.** Finally, $\mathcal{F}$ outputs a signcryption $C$, and a key pair (SDK$_r$, VEK$_r$) and wins the game if (1) the result plaintext of the operation $\mathcal{VD}($SDK$_U$, VEK$_r$, $C$) is a message $M$ such that $C$ is not the output of a signcryption query ($M$, VEK$_r$), (2) the output of the operation $\mathcal{NR}($VEK$_U$, SDK$_r$, VEK$_r$, $C$) is ($M$, $\sigma$) such that the equation $\mathcal{V}($VEK$_U$, $M$, $\sigma)=1$ is hold.

Let us define $\mathbf{Adv}_{\mathbf{SC},\mathcal{F}}^{\mathbf{UF\text{-}CMA}}(k)$ to be the probability that the forger $\mathcal{F}$ wins the Game 2.

**Definition 2.3 (SC-UF-CMA).** We say that a signcryption is **SC-UF-CMA** secure if for any probability polynomial time forger $\mathcal{F}$, the advantage $\mathbf{Adv}_{\mathbf{SC},\mathcal{F}}^{\mathbf{UF\text{-}CMA}}(k)$ is negligible.

## 2.2 Warrant-Based Proxy Signcryption Scheme and the Security Notions for It

We first extend definition 2.1, and give the syntax of warrant-based proxy signcryption schemes. For convenience, we design an environment applied to proxy signcryption schemes. This environment involves three entity: the original sender, the proxy sender and the receiver. The original sender can use an standard signcryption scheme to signcrypt a messagn intended to receiver. However, when he is absent, lack time etc., he can delegate the capacity to another entity, called proxy sender.

**Definition 2.4 (Warrant-based proxy signcryption scheme).** A warrant-based proxy signcryption scheme **WPSC**$=(\mathcal{G}, \mathcal{K}, \mathcal{SC}, \mathcal{VD}, \mathcal{NR}, \mathcal{V}, (\mathcal{D}, \mathcal{P}), \mathcal{PSC}, \mathcal{PVD}, \mathcal{PNR}, \mathcal{PV})$ is defined as follows.

- The parameter generation algorithm $\mathcal{G}$ takes input $1^k$ where $k$ is the security parameter, and outputs some global parameters **params**.
- The key generation algorithm $\mathcal{K}$ takes input global parameters **params** and outputs a original sender' key pair (SDK$_{os}$, VEK$_{os}$), a proxy sender's key pair (SDK$_{ps}$, VEK$_{ps}$) and a receiver's (SDK$_r$, VEK$_r$).

- The algorithms $\mathcal{SC}$, $\mathcal{VD}$, $\mathcal{NR}$ and $\mathcal{V}$ are the same as a standard signcryption scheme ones described in definition 2.1. Here the original sender plays the role of standard sender.
- $(\mathcal{D}, \mathcal{P})$ is a pair of interactive randomized algorithms which form the two-party proxy-delegation protocol. The input to each algorithm includes two public keys $\text{VEK}_{os}$, $\text{VEK}_{ps}$ and the the proxy sender's warrant $M_w$ respectively. $\mathcal{D}$ also takes as input the secret key $\text{SDK}_{os}$ of original sender , and $\mathcal{P}$ also takes as input secret $\text{SDK}_{ps}$ of the proxy sender. As result of the interaction, the output of $\mathcal{P}$ is a proxy signcrypting key $SC_P$, which the proxy sender uses to produce proxy signcryption on behalf of the original sender.
- The proxy signcryption algorithm $\mathcal{PSC}$ takes as input the signcrypting key $SC_P$, public key $\text{VEK}_r$ of the receiver and a message $M \in \{0,1\}^*$ intended to the receiver, outputs the signcryption $C_P$.
- The (usually deterministic) proxy de-signcryption algorithm $\mathcal{PVD}$ takes as input public key $\text{VEK}_{os}$ of the original sender, public key $\text{VEK}_{ps}$ of the proxy sender, secret key $\text{SDK}_r$ of the receiver and a string $C_P$, and returns a string $M \in \mathcal{M}$, or the $\bot$ symbol.
- The proxy non-repudiation algorithm $\mathcal{PNR}$ takes as input the public key $\text{VEK}_{os}$ of the original sender, the public key $\text{VEK}_{ps}$ of the proxy sender, the key pair $(\text{SDK}_r, \text{VEK}_r)$ of the receiver and a string $C_P$, and returns either a pair of strings $(M, \sigma_P)$ or the $\bot$ symbol.
- The (usually deterministic) proxy verification algorithm $\mathcal{PV}$ takes as input $(\text{VEK}_{os}, \text{VEK}_{ps}, M, \sigma_P)$, and output a bit. We say that $\sigma_P$ is a valid proxy signature on $M$ relative to $\text{VEK}_{os}$ and $\text{VEK}_{ps}$ if $\mathcal{PV}(\text{VEK}_{os}, \text{VEK}_{ps}, M, \sigma_P)=1$.

In the course of implementing the two-party proxy-delegation protocol (i.e. implement the interactive randomized algorithms $\mathcal{D}$ and $\mathcal{P}$), some schemes need secure channel (call this case SC), the other ones does not need it (call this case NSC). According to the two cases, we construct two model of warrant-based proxy signcryption schemes.

**Model 2.1 (SC).** Let **WPSC**=$(\mathcal{G}, \mathcal{K}, \mathcal{SC}, \mathcal{VD}, \mathcal{NR}, \mathcal{V}, (\mathcal{D}, \mathcal{P}), \mathcal{PSC}, \mathcal{PVD}, \mathcal{PNR}, \mathcal{PV})$ is a warrant-based proxy signcryption scheme, where **SC**=$\{\mathcal{G}, \mathcal{K}, \mathcal{SC}, \mathcal{VD}, \mathcal{NR}, \mathcal{V}\}$ is a standard signcryption scheme.

- The description of the algorithms $\mathcal{G}$, $\mathcal{K}$, $\mathcal{SC}$, $\mathcal{VD}$, $\mathcal{NR}$ and $\mathcal{V}$ are the same as the corresponding parts in definition 2.4.
- The original sender sends to the designated proxy sender an appropriate warrant $M_w$ in a public channel and a signature $s_w$ for $M_w$ under the secret key $\text{SDK}_{os}$ in a *secure channel*. The warrant $M_w$ includes the public key, identity of the designated proxy sender, etc. When receiving the warrant $M_w$ and its signature $s_w$, by using his key pair $(\text{SDK}_{ps}, \text{VEK}_{ps})$ and $s_w$ the proxy sender generates the proxy signcrypting key $SC_P$.
- When the proxy sender want to generate proxy signcryption $C_P$ on some message $M$, he simply executes ordinary signcrypting operation with the proxy signcrypting key $SC_P$ and the receiver's public key $\text{VEK}_r$.

- When the receiver want to de-signcrypt the signcryption $C_P$, he first computes the proxy de-signcrypting key $VD_P$ using the warrant $M_w$, the original sender's public key $\text{VEK}_{os}$, the proxy sender's public key $\text{VEK}_{ps}$, the receiver's key pair ($\text{SDK}_r$, $\text{VEK}_r$) and some information involved in the proxy signcryption $C_P$, then carries out the de-signcryption by the same checking operation as in the ordinary signcryption scheme.
- When the receiver wants to provide third party with the valid proxy signature on the message $M$, he computes a pair of strings ($M$, $\sigma_P$) using the proxy de-signcrypting key $VD_P$, the key pair ($\text{SDK}_r$, $\text{VEK}_r$) of the receiver and a string $C_P$.
- When the third party verifies the proxy signature, he first computes the proxy public key $PV_P$ using the warrant $M_w$, the original sender's public key $\text{VEK}_{os}$, the proxy sender's public key $\text{VEK}_{ps}$ and some information involved in the proxy signature $\sigma_P$, then carries out the verification by the same checking operation as in the ordinary signature scheme.

**Model 2.2 (NSC).** Let $\textbf{WPSC}=(\mathcal{G}, \mathcal{K}, \mathcal{SC}, \mathcal{VD}, \mathcal{NR}, \mathcal{V}, (\mathcal{D}, \mathcal{P}), \mathcal{PSC}, \mathcal{PVD},$ $\mathcal{PNR}, \mathcal{PV})$ is a warrant-based proxy signcryption scheme, where $\textbf{SC}=\{\mathcal{G}, \mathcal{K},$ $\mathcal{SC}, \mathcal{VD}, \mathcal{NR}, \mathcal{V} \}$ is a standard signcryption scheme.

- The description of the algorithms $\mathcal{G}, \mathcal{K}, \mathcal{SC}, \mathcal{VD}, \mathcal{NR}$ and $\mathcal{V}$ are the same as the corresponding parts in definition 2.4.
- The original signer sends to the designated proxy signer an appropriate warrant $M_w$ together with a signature $s_w$ for $M_w$ under the secret key $\text{SDK}_{os}$ in a *public channel*. The warrant $M_w$ includes the public key, identity of the designated proxy signer, etc.
- When the proxy sender want to generate proxy signcryption $C_P$ on some message $M$, he simply executes ordinary signcrying operation on message $M\|s_w$ with his secret key $\text{SDK}_{ps}$ and the public key $\text{VEK}_r$ of the receiver (In fact, the tuple $\{M_w, s_w, \text{SDK}_{ps}\}$ constitutes the proxy signcrying key $SC_P$ and signcrypting on message $M\|s_w$ with the secret key $\text{SDK}_{ps}$ is equivalent to signcrypting on message $M$ with proxy signcrying key $SC_P$).
- To de-signcrypting $C_P$, the receiver first executes a standard signature verifying operation (i.e. whether $S_w$ is a valid signature of $M_w$), then executes a standard de-signcrypting operation (i.e. whether the result of de-signcryption is $M\|s_w$) for some message $M$.
- When the receiver wants to provide third party with the valid proxy signature on the message $M$, he computes a pair of strings ($M$, $\sigma_P$) using the public key $\text{VEK}_{os}$ of the original sender, the public key $\text{VEK}_{ps}$ of the proxy sender, the key pair ($\text{SDK}_r$, $\text{VEK}_r$) of the receiver and a string $C_P$.
- When the third party verifies the proxy signature, he simply executes two ordinary signature verifying operation. That is, whether $s_w$ is a valid signature of $M_w$ and whether $\sigma_P$ is a valid signature of the message $M\|s_w$.

Similar to the security of proxy-protected signature schemes, the proxy signature also satisfies the following three basic security properties.

**Verifiability:** From a proxy signature generated by the operation of the proxy non-repudiation algorithm $\mathcal{PNR}$, any verifier can be convinced of the original sender's agreement on the signcrypted message.

**Unforgeability:** Only a designated proxy sender can create a valid proxy signcryption for the original sender (even the original sender cannot do it).

**Undeniability:** A proxy sender cannot repudiate a proxy signcryption he created.

**Remark 2.1.** In fact, the property of unforgeability and the property of Undeniability are equivalent.

From the formal angle, the security for proxy signcryption consists on semantical security against chosen ciphertext attacks(we call this security notion **PSC-IND-CCA**) and strong existential unforgeability against chosen message attacks (we call this security notion **PSC-UF-CMA**) when attacking some user $U$.

Before presenting the formal security notions, we first informally describe the adversarial model in the following ways.

When the user plays the role of standard sender, We allow the adversary to corrupt the receivers and learn their secrets.

When the user plays the role of original sender, we have the following cases:

(1) We allow the adversary to corrupt the proxy senders and learn their secrets. It can also add new users and obtain proxy delegation from the original senders. (2) We allow the adversary to corrupt the receivers and learn their secrets.

When the user plays the role of proxy sender, we have the following cases:

(1) We allow the adversary to corrupt the original senders and learn their secrets. (2) We allow the adversary to corrupt the receivers and learn their secrets.

When the user plays the role of receiver, we have the following cases:

(1) We allow the adversary to corrupt the original senders and learn their secrets. (2) We allow the adversary to corrupt the proxy senders and learn their secrets.

Now, we will give the formal security notions for the **SC** model and **NSC** model respectively. First, we consider the **SC** model.

**SC model:** Let $\mathbf{WPSC} = (\mathcal{G}, \mathcal{K}, \mathcal{SC}, \mathcal{VD}, \mathcal{NR}, \mathcal{V}, (\mathcal{D}, \mathcal{P}), \mathcal{PSC}, \mathcal{PVD}, \mathcal{PNR}, \mathcal{PV})$ is a warrant-based proxy signcryption scheme, where $\mathbf{SC} = \{\mathcal{G}, \mathcal{K}, \mathcal{SC}, \mathcal{VD}, \mathcal{NR}, \mathcal{V}\}$ is a standard signcryption scheme. In **WPSC**, the secure channel is used.

For defining the notion of **PSC-IND-CCA**, we consider the following game:

**Game 1:**

- **Setup.** The challenger $\mathcal{C}$ runs algorithm $\mathcal{G}$ and $\mathcal{K}$ to obtain a key pair (SDK$_U$, VEK$_U$) waiting for attack by the adversary $\mathcal{A}$. $\mathcal{A}$ is given VEK$_U$.

- **Phase 1.**
  - Delegation query ($\text{VEK}_{ps}^i$). When the adversary $\mathcal{A}$ runs algorithm $\mathcal{G}$ and $\mathcal{K}$ to obtain a key pair ($\text{SDK}_{ps}^i$, $\text{VEK}_{ps}^i$), and sends $\text{VEK}_{ps}^i$ to the challenger, the challenger $\mathcal{C}$ generates an appropriate warrant $M_w^i$ for $\text{VEK}_{ps}^i$ and a signature $s_w^i$ for $M_w^i$ using the secret key $\text{SDK}_U$, then responds ($M_w^i$, $s_w^i$).
  - Signcryption query ($M_i$, $\text{VEK}_r^i$). The challenger $\mathcal{C}$ responds by running algorithm $\mathcal{SC}$ in model 2.1 to signcrypt the message $M_i$.
  - Proxy signcryption query ($M_i$, $M_w^i$, $s_w^i$, $\text{VEK}_{os}^i$, $\text{VEK}_r$). The challenger $\mathcal{C}$ first computes the signcrypting key $SC_P$ by using $M_w^i$, $s_w^i$ and ($\text{SDK}_U$, $\text{VEK}_U$), then responds by running algorithm $\mathcal{PSC}$ defined in Model 2.1 to proxy-signcrypt the message $M_i$.
  - De-signcryption query ($C_i$, $\text{VEK}_s^i$). The challenger $\mathcal{C}$ responds by running algorithm $\mathcal{VD}$ to de-signcrypt the signcryption $C_i$.
  - Proxy de-signcryption query ($C_P^i$, $M_w^i$, $\text{VEK}_{os}^i$, $\text{VEK}_{ps}^i$). The challenger $\mathcal{C}$ responds by running algorithm $\mathcal{PVD}$ in model 2.1 to proxy-de-signcrypt the proxy signcryption $C_P^i$.
- **Challenge.** Once the adversary $\mathcal{A}$ decides that Phase 1 is over, it does as follows:
  1. Output two equal length plaintexts $M_0^*, M_1^* \in \mathcal{M}$ and an arbitrary private key $\text{SDK}_s$. $\mathcal{C}$ picks a random bit $b \in \{0,1\}$ and computes $C = \mathcal{SC}(\text{SDK}_s, \text{VEK}_U, M_b^*)$. $C$ is send to $\mathcal{A}$ as a challenge.
  2. Or output two equal length plaintexts $M_0^*, M_1^* \in \mathcal{M}$ and an arbitrary private signcrypting key $SC_p$. $\mathcal{C}$ picks a random bit $b_P \in \{0,1\}$ and computes $C_P = \mathcal{PSC}(SC_p, \text{VEK}_U, M_{b_p}^*)$. $C_P$ is send to $\mathcal{A}$ as a challenge.
- **Phase 2.** The adversary $\mathcal{A}$ performs new queries as in Phase 1.
- **Guess.** Finally, $\mathcal{A}$ output a bit $b'$ or $b_P'$, and wins if $b' = b$ or $b_P' = b_P$.

Let us define adversary $\mathcal{A}$'s advantage in attacking the scheme **SC** as the following function of the security parameter $k$: $\mathbf{Adv}_{\mathbf{SC},\mathcal{A}}^{\mathbf{PSC\text{-}IND\text{-}CCA}}(k) = |\Pr[b'{=}b \vee b_P'{=}b_P]{-}1/2|$.

**Definition 2.5 (PSC-IND-CCA).** We say that a signcryption is **PSC-IND-CCA** secure if for any probability polynomial time adversary $\mathcal{A}$, the advantage $\mathbf{Adv}_{\mathbf{SC},\mathcal{A}}^{\mathbf{PSC\text{-}IND\text{-}CCA}}(k)$ is negligible.

For defining the notion of **PSC-UF-CMA** in **SC**, we consider the following game between a challenger $\mathcal{C}$ and a forger $\mathcal{F}$.

**Game 2:**

- **Setup.** The challenger $\mathcal{C}$ runs algorithm $\mathcal{G}$ and $\mathcal{K}$ to obtain a key pair ($\text{SDK}_U$, $\text{VEK}_U$) waiting for attack by the adversary $\mathcal{F}$. $\mathcal{F}$ is given $\text{VEK}_U$.
- **Queries.** The forger $\mathcal{F}_1$ make delegation queries, signcryption queries, proxy signcryption queries, de-signcryption queries and proxy de-signcryption queries exactly as in Game 1.

- **Output.**
  1. $\mathcal{F}$ outputs a proxy signcryption $C_P$, a public key $\text{VEK}_{ps}$ and a key pair $(\text{SDK}_r, \text{VEK}_r)$, and wins in the game, if (1) the output of the operation $\mathcal{PNR}$ is $(M, \sigma_P)$ such that the equation $\mathcal{PV}(\text{VEK}_U, \text{VEK}_{ps}, M, \sigma_P)=1$ is hold, (2) the delegation query $(\text{VEK}_{ps})$ has not been made.
  2. $\mathcal{F}$ outputs a signcryption $C$, and a key pair $(\text{SDK}_r, \text{VEK}_r)$ and wins the game if (1) the result plaintext of the operation $\mathcal{VD}(\text{SDK}_r, \text{VEK}_U, C)$ is a message $M$ such that $C$ is not the output of a signcryption query $(M, \text{VEK}_r)$, (2) the output of the operation $\mathcal{NR}(\text{SDK}_r, \text{VEK}_r, \text{VEK}_U, C)$ is $(M, \sigma)$ such that the equation $\mathcal{V}(\text{VEK}_U, M, \sigma)=1$ is hold.
  3. $\mathcal{F}$ outputs a tuple $(C_P, M_w, s_w, \text{VEK}_{os})$ and a key pair $(\text{SDK}_r, \text{VEK}_r)$, and wins the game if (1) the result plaintext of the operation $\mathcal{PVD}$ is a message $M$ such that $C_P$ is not the output of a proxy signcryption query $(M, M_w, s_w, \text{VEK}_{os}, \text{VEK}_r)$ for $M, M_w, \text{VEK}_{os}, \text{VEK}_r$, (2) the output of the operation $\mathcal{PNR}$ is $(M, \sigma_P)$ such that the equation $\mathcal{PV}(\text{VEK}_{os}, \text{VEK}_U, M, \sigma_P)=1$ is hold.

Let us define $\mathbf{Adv}_{\mathbf{SC},\mathcal{F}}^{\mathbf{PSC\text{-}UF\text{-}CMA}}(k)$ to be the probability that the forger $\mathcal{F}$ wins the Game 2.

**Definition 2.6 (PSC-UF-CMA)** We say that a signcryption is **PSC-UF-CMA** secure if for any probability polynomial time forger $\mathcal{F}$, the advantage $\mathbf{Adv}_{\mathbf{SC},\mathcal{F}}^{\mathbf{PSC\text{-}UF\text{-}CMA}}(k)$ is negligible.

Now we describe the security notion of **NSC** model.

**NSC model:** Let $\mathbf{WPSC}=(\mathcal{G}, \mathcal{K}, \mathcal{SC}, \mathcal{VD}, \mathcal{NR}, \mathcal{V}, (\mathcal{D}, \mathcal{P}), \mathcal{PSC}, \mathcal{PVD}, \mathcal{PNR}, \mathcal{PV})$ is a warrant-based proxy signcryption scheme, where $\mathbf{SC}=\{\mathcal{G}, \mathcal{K}, \mathcal{SC}, \mathcal{VD}, \mathcal{NR}, \mathcal{V}\}$ is a standard signcryption scheme. In **WPSC**, the secure channel is not used.

For defining the notion of **PSC-IND-CCA** in **NSC** model, we consider the following game:

**Game 1:**

- **Setup.** The challenger $\mathcal{C}$ runs algorithm $\mathcal{G}$ and $\mathcal{K}$ to obtain a key pair $(\text{SDK}_U, \text{VEK}_U)$ waiting for attack by the adversary $\mathcal{A}$. $\mathcal{A}$ is given $\text{VEK}_U$.
- **Phase 1.**
  - Delegation query $(\text{VEK}_{ps}^i)$. When the adversary $\mathcal{A}$ runs algorithm $\mathcal{G}$ and $\mathcal{K}$ to obtain a key pair $(\text{SDK}_{ps}^i, \text{VEK}_{ps}^i)$, and sends $\text{VEK}_{ps}^i$ to the challenger, the challenger $\mathcal{C}$ generates an appropriate warrant $M_w^i$ for $\text{VEK}_{ps}^i$ and a signature $s_w^i$ for $M_w^i$ using the secret key $\text{SDK}_U$, then responds $(M_w^i, s_w^i)$.
  - Signcryption query $(M_i, \text{VEK}_r^i)$. The challenger $\mathcal{C}$ responds by running algorithm $\mathcal{SC}$ to signcrypt the message $M_i$.

- Proxy signcryption query $(M_i, M_w^i, s_w^i, \text{VEK}_{os}^i, \text{VEK}_r)$. The challenger $\mathcal{C}$ responds by running the standard signcryption algorithm $\mathcal{SC}$ to signcrypt the message $M_i \| s_w^i$.
- De-signcryption query $(C_i, \text{VEK}_s^i)$. The challenger $\mathcal{C}$ responds by running algorithm $\mathcal{VD}$ to de-signcrypt the signcryption $C_i$.
- Proxy de-signcryption query $(C_P^i, M_w^i, \text{VEK}_{os}^i, \text{VEK}_{ps}^i)$. The challenger responds by running algorithm $\mathcal{PVD}$ in model 2.2 to de-signcrypt the proxy signcryption $C_P^i$.

- **Challenge.** Once the adversary $\mathcal{A}$ decides that Phase 1 is over, it does as follows:
  1. Output two equal length plaintexts $M_0^*, M_1^* \in \mathcal{M}$ and an arbitrary private key $\text{SDK}_s$. $\mathcal{C}$ picks a random bit $b \in \{0,1\}$ and computes $C = \mathcal{SC}(\text{SDK}_s, \text{VEK}_U, M_b^*)$. $C$ is send to $\mathcal{A}$ as a challenge.
  2. Or output two equal length plaintexts $M_0^*, M_1^* \in \mathcal{M}$ and an arbitrary tuple $(\text{SDK}_{ps}, \text{VEK}_{ps}, M_w, s_w)$. $\mathcal{C}$ picks a random bit $b_P \in \{0,1\}$ and computes $C_P$ using algorithm $\mathcal{PSC}$ in model 2.2. $C_P$ is send to $\mathcal{A}$ as a challenge.
- **Phase 2.** The adversary $\mathcal{A}$ performs new queries as in Phase 1.
- **Guess.** Finally, $\mathcal{A}$ output a bit $b'$ or $b_P'$, and wins if $b' = b$ or $b_P' = b_P$.

Let us define adversary $\mathcal{A}$'s advantage in attacking the scheme **SC** as the following function of the security parameter $k$: $\mathbf{Adv}_{\mathbf{NSC},\mathcal{A}}^{\mathbf{PSC\text{-}IND\text{-}CCA}}(k) = |\Pr[b'{=}b \vee b_P'{=}b_P]{-}1/2|$.

**Definition 2.7 (PSC-IND-CCA).** We say that a signcryption is **PSC-IND-CCA** secure if for any probability polynomial time adversary $\mathcal{A}$, the advantage $\mathbf{Adv}_{\mathbf{NSC},\mathcal{A}}^{\mathbf{PSC\text{-}IND\text{-}CCA}}(k)$ is negligible.

For defining the notion of **PSC-UF-CMA** in **NSC** model, we consider the following game between a challenger $\mathcal{C}$ and a forger $\mathcal{F}$.

**Game 2:**

- **Setup.** The challenger $\mathcal{C}$ runs algorithm $\mathcal{G}$ and $\mathcal{K}$ to obtain a key pair $(\text{SDK}_U, \text{VEK}_U)$ waiting for attack by the adversary $\mathcal{F}$. $\mathcal{F}$ is given $\text{VEK}_U$.
- **Queries.** The forger $\mathcal{F}_1$ make delegation queries, signcryption queries, proxy signcryption queries, de-signcryption queries and proxy de-signcryption queries exactly as in Game 1.
- **Output.**
  1. $\mathcal{F}$ outputs a proxy signcryption $C_P$, a public key $\text{VEK}_{ps}$ and a key pair $(\text{SDK}_r, \text{VEK}_r)$, and wins in the game, if (1) the output of the operation $\mathcal{PNR}$ is $(M, \sigma_P)$ such that the equation $\mathcal{PV}(\text{VEK}_U, \text{VEK}_{ps}, M \| s_w, \sigma_P){=}1$ is hold, (2) the delegation query $(\text{VEK}_{ps})$ has not been made.
  2. $\mathcal{F}$ outputs a signcryption $C$, and a key pair $(\text{SDK}_r, \text{VEK}_r)$ and wins the game if (1) the result plaintext of the operation $\mathcal{VD}(\text{SDK}_r, \text{VEK}_U, C)$ is a message $M$ such that $C$ is not the output of a signcryption query $(M,$

VEK$_r$), (2) the output of the operation $\mathcal{NR}(\text{SDK}_r,\text{VEK}_r,\text{VEK}_U,C)$ is $(M, \sigma)$ such that the equation $\mathcal{V}(\text{VEK}_U, M, \sigma)=1$ is hold.

3. $\mathcal{F}$ outputs a tuple $(C_P, M_w, s_w, \text{VEK}_{os})$ and a key pair $(\text{SDK}_r, \text{VEK}_r)$, and wins the game if (1) the result plaintext of the operation $\mathcal{PVD}$ is a message $M$ such that $C_P$ is not the output of a proxy signcryption query $(M, M_w, s_w, \text{VEK}_{os}, \text{VEK}_r)$ for $M, M_w, \text{VEK}_{os}, \text{VEK}_r$, (2) the output of the operation $\mathcal{PNR}$ is $(M, \sigma_P)$ such that the equation $\mathcal{PV}(\text{VEK}_{os}, \text{VEK}_U, M\|s_w, \sigma_P)=1$ is hold.

Let us define $\mathbf{Adv}_{\mathbf{NSC},\mathcal{F}}^{\mathbf{PSC\text{-}UF\text{-}CMA}}(k)$ to be the probability that the forger $\mathcal{F}$ wins the Game 2.

**Definition 2.8 (PSC-UF-CMA).** We say that a signcryption is **PSC-UF-CMA** secure if for any probability polynomial time forger $\mathcal{F}$, the advantage $\mathbf{Adv}_{\mathbf{NSC},\mathcal{F}}^{\mathbf{PSC\text{-}UF\text{-}CMA}}(k)$ is negligible.

# 3   Our Scheme

In this section, we will propose a warrant-based proxy signcryption scheme, whose security is based on integer factorization. Moreover, the scheme is **NSC** model. Rabin signature scheme was proposed in [15]. The improved version of it will be applied in our scheme. For illustrating the scheme compactly, we first review the improved Rabin signature scheme.

## 3.1   Improved Rabin Signature Scheme

Generate an Rabin key pair $\{(N, a), (p, q)\}$ with $N = p \cdot q$, $p \equiv q \equiv 3 \pmod 4$), and $a \in Z_N^*$ satisfying Jacobi symbol $\left(\frac{a}{N}\right) = -1$ where $(N, a)$ is public key and $(p, q)$ is private key. The scheme requires an hash function $H : \mathcal{M} \to Z_N^*$.

**Signature algorithm:** For some message $M \in \mathcal{M}$, First compute $c_1$ and $c_2$ as follows:

$$c_1 = \begin{cases} 0, & \text{if } \left(\frac{H(M)}{N}\right) = 1 \\ 1, & \text{if } \left(\frac{H(M)}{N}\right) = -1 \end{cases}.$$

$$c_2 = \begin{cases} 0, & \text{if } \left(\frac{l}{p}\right) = 1 \\ 1, & \text{if } \left(\frac{l}{p}\right) = -1 \end{cases}.$$

where $l = a^{c_1} \cdot H(M)$.
Then compute $s$ from the following equation:

$$s^2 \equiv (-1)^{c_2} \cdot a^{c_1} H(M) \pmod N.$$

The signature on $M$ is $(s, c_1, c_2)$.

## 3.2   The Proposed Scheme

**Key generation phase:** The original sender generates an Rabin key pair $\{(N_{os}, a_{os}),(p_{os}, q_{os})\}$ with $|p_{os}| = |q_{os}| = k/2$. Here $k$ is an system security parameter. A proxy sender and a receiver likewise generate their Rabin key pair $\{(N_{ps}, a_{ps}),(p_{ps}, q_{ps})\}$ and $\{(N_r, a_r),(p_r, q_r)\}$ respectively. Our scheme requires four hash functions: $H_1 : \{0,1\}^* \to Z_{N_{os}}^*$, $H_2 : Z_{N_r}^* \to \{0,1\}^n$, $H_3 : \{0,1\}^n \times \{0,1\}^* \to Z_{N_{os}}^*$ and $H_4 : \{0,1\}^n \times \{0,1\}^* \times \{0,1\}^* \to Z_{N_{ps}}^*$.

**Signcrypting phase:** To signcrypt a plaintext $M \in \{0,1\}^n$ intended to the receiver , the original sender follows the steps below:

1. Choose a random $r$ satisfying $0 < r < N_r/2$ and $\left(\frac{r}{N_r}\right) = 1$ , and compute $\alpha \equiv r^2 (\mathrm{mod}\, N_r)$.
2. Compute $\beta = H_2(r) \oplus M$.
3. Compute $H_3(M,r)(\mathrm{mod}\, N_{os})$ and then use the improved Rabin signature scheme to compute $(\gamma, c_1, c_2)$ such that $\gamma^2 \equiv (-1)^{c_2} \cdot (a_{os})^{c_1} \cdot H_3(M,r)(\mathrm{mod}\, N_{os})$.

The ciphertext is given by $C = \{\alpha, \beta, \gamma, c_1, c_2\}$.

**De-signcrypting phase:** When receiving a ciphertext $C = \{\alpha, \beta, \gamma, c_1, c_2\}$, the receiver has to run the followinig steps:

1. Compute $r$ from $\alpha$ using the secret key $(p_r, q_r)(\mathrm{mod}\, N_r)$.
2. Compute $M = H_2(r) \oplus \beta$.
3. Compute $h = H_3(M,r)(\mathrm{mod}\, N_{os})$ and then check if $\gamma^2 \equiv (-1)^{c_2} \cdot (a_{os})^{c_1} \cdot h(\mathrm{mod}\, N_{os})$. If this condition does not hold, reject the ciphertext.

The consistency of the scheme is easy to verity.

**Non-repudiation phase:** IF the receiver want to prove to a third party that the proxy sender signed a plaintext $M$, he just forward $(M, \sigma) = \{M, \gamma, r, c_1, c_2\}$.

**Verification:** When the third party receive $(M, \sigma)$, he perform the step 3 in the de-signcrypting phase.

**Delegating phase:** When the original sender delegates his signcryption capability to the proxy sender, they will run the following steps:

1. The original sender first makes a warrant $M_w$, then publishs it.
2. The original sender uses the improved Rabin signature scheme on $M_w$ to generate proxy key $(s_w, c_1^w, c_2^w)$, and send it to the designed proxy sender publicly. Here

$$s_w^2 \equiv (-1)^{c_2^w} \cdot a^{c_1^w} H_1(M_w)(\mathrm{mod}\, N_{os}) \tag{1}$$

3. After receiving the proxy certificate $(M_w, s_w, c_1^w, c_2^w)$, the proxy sender verifies the proxy certificate by checking if the equation (1) holds. If it holds, the proxy key will be accepted.

**Proxy signcrypting phase:** To signcrypt a plaintext $M \in \{0,1\}^n$ intended to the receiver on behalf of the original sender, the proxy sender follows the steps below:

1. Choose a random satisfying $0 < r < N_r/2$ and $\left(\frac{r}{N_r}\right) = 1$, and compute $\alpha \equiv r^2 (\mathrm{mod} N_r)$.
2. Compute $\beta = H_2(r) \oplus M$.
3. Compute $H_4(M, s_w, r)(\mathrm{mod} N_{ps})$ and then use the improved Rabin signature scheme to compute $(\gamma, c_1, c_2)$ such that $\gamma^2 \equiv (-1)^{c_2} \cdot (a_{ps})^{c_1} \cdot H_4(M, s_w, r)$ $(\mathrm{mod} N_{ps})$.

The ciphertext is given by $C_P = \{M_w, s_w, \alpha, \beta, \gamma, c_1^w, c_2^w, c_1, c_2\}$.

**Proxy de-signcrypting phase:** When receiving a ciphertext $C_P = \{M_w, s_w, \alpha, \beta, \gamma, c_1^w, c_2^w, c_1, c_2\}$, the receiver has to run the following steps:

1. Check if $s_w^2 \equiv (-1)^{c_2^w} \cdot a^{c_1^w} H_1(M_w)(\mathrm{mod} N_{os})$. If this condition does not hold, reject the ciphertext.
2. Compute $r$ from $\alpha$ using the secret key $(p_r, q_r)(\mathrm{mod} N_r)$.
3. Compute $M = H_2(r) \oplus \beta$.
4. Compute $h = H_4(M, s_w, r)(\mathrm{mod} N_{ps})$ and then check if $\gamma^2 \equiv (-1)^{c_2} \cdot (a_{ps})^{c_1} \cdot h(\mathrm{mod} N_{ps})$. If this condition does not hold, reject the ciphertext.

The consistency of the scheme is easy to verity.

**Proxy non-repudiation phase:** IF the receiver want to prove to a third party that the proxy sender signed a plaintext $M$, he just forward $(M, p\sigma) = \{M, M_w, s_w, \gamma, r, c_1^w, c_2^w, c_1, c_2\}$.

**Proxy verification:** When the third party receive $(M, \sigma)$, he perform the step 1 and step 4 in the Proxy de-signcrypting phase.

## 4    Security Analysis

In this section, we study the security of the scheme. The following theorems show that the proposed scheme is **PSC-IND-CCA** secure and **PSC-UF-CMA** secure.

**Theorem 4.1.** If integer factorization problem is hard then the proposed scheme is **PSC-IND-CCA** secure in the random oracle model.

The proof of Theorem 4.1 is our full paper [17].

**Theorem 4.2.** If integer factorization problem is hard then the proposed scheme is **PSC-UF-CMA** secure in the random oracle model.

The proof of Theorem 4.2 is in our full paper [17].

# References

1. Gamage C., Leiwo J. and Zheng Y.: An efficient scheme for secure message transmission using proxy-signcryption. In Proceedings of the 22th Australasian Computer Science. Auckland: Springer-Verlag, 1999. 420-431.

2. Zheng, Y.: Digital signcryption or how to archive cost(signature & encryption)$\ll$ cost(signature) + cost(encryption). In Advanes in Cryptology - CRYPTO'97, LNCS 1294, 1997, pp.165-179.

3. Bao, F. and Deng, R.H.: A signcryption scheme with signature directly verifiable by public key. In public key Cryptography'98, LNCS 1431, Berlin: Spinger-Verlag, 1998, pp.26-45.

4. He, W.H. and Wu T.C.: Cryptanalysis and improvement of Petersen-Michels signcryption scheme. IEE Proceedings - Computers and Digital Tchhniques, 146(2), 1999, pp.123-124.

5. Petersen, H. and Michels, M.: Cryptanalysis and improvement of signcryption schemes. IEE Proceedings - Computers and Digital Tchhniques, 146(2), 1999, 123-124 - Computers and Digital Tchhniques, 145(2), 1998 pp.149151.

6. Malonee-Lee, J.: Signcryption with non-repudiation, Technical Report CSTR-02-004, Department of Computer Science, University of Bristol, June 2002.

7. Malonee-Lee, J. and Mao, W.: Two Birds One Stone: Signcryption using RSA. In Topics in Cryptology - CT-RSA 2003, LNCS, 2612, Berlin: Spinger-Verlag, 2003, pp.211-225.

8. An, J.H., Dodis, Y. and Rabin, T.: On the security of joint signature and encrytion. In Advanes in Cryptology - Eurocrypt'02, LNCS 1294, 1997, pp.165-179. LNCS 2332, 2002, pp.83-107.

9. Mambo, M., Usuda, K. and Okamoto, E.: Proxy signatures for delegating signing operation. In Proceedings of the 3rd ACM Conference on Computer and Communications Security (CCS), ACM, 1996, pp.48-57.

10. Boldyreva, A., Palacio, A. and Warinschi, B.: secure proxy signature schemes for delegation of signing rights. http://venona.antioffline.com/2003/096.pdf.

11. Kim, H., Beak, J., Lee, B. and Kim, K.: Secret computation with secrets for mobile agent using one-time proxy signatures. In Cryptography and Information Security 2001, 2001.

12. Lee, B., Kim, H. and Kim, K.: Strong proxy signature and its applications. In Proceedings of SCIS, 2001.

13. Foster, I., Kesselman, C., Tsudik, G. and Tuecke, S.: A security Architecture for Computational Grids. In Fifth ACM Conference on Computers and Communications Security, 1998.

14. Park, H-U. and Lee, L-Y.: A Digital nominative proxy signature scheme for mobile communications. In ICICS 2001, LNCS, 2229, Berlin: Spinger-Verlag, 2001, pp.451-455.

15. Rabin, M. O.: Digitalized signatures. Foundations of Secure Communication, Academic Press, 1978, pp.155-168.

16. Ballare, M. and Rogaway, P.: Random oracle are practical: a paradiam for designing efficient protocols. In First ACM Conference on Computer and Communications Security, ACM, 1993.

17. Zhou, Y. Cao, Z. and Lu, R.: Constructing Secure Warrant-based Proxy Signcryption Schemes. http://tdt.sjtu.edu.cn/YZ/Constructing Secure Warrant-based Proxy Signcryption Schemes.pdf.

# Design and Implementation of an Inline Certified E-mail Service

Stelvio Cimato[1], Clemente Galdi[2], Raffaella Giordano[3], Barbara Masucci[2],
and Gildo Tomasco

[1] Dipartimento di Tecnologie dell'Informazione, Universitá di Milano,
Via Bramante 65, 26013 Crema (CR), Italy
cimato@dti.unimi.it
[2] Dipartimento di Informatica ed Applicazioni, Universitá di Salerno,
Via S. Allende, 84081 Baronissi (SA), Italy
clegal, masucci@dia.unisa.it
[3] Italsime s.p.a.
Via Cinthia 25, Parco S. Paolo, 80126, Napoli (NA), Italy
giordano.r@italsime.it

**Abstract.** Nowadays, e-mail has become one of the most widely used communication medium. Because of its characteristics of inexpensivity and rapidity in the delivery of messages, e-mail is increasingly used in place of ordinary mail. However, the e-mail service exposes users to several risks related to the lack of security during the message exchange. Furthermore, regular mail offers services which are usually not provided by e-mail, and which are of crucial importance for "official" events.

Certified e-mail tries to provide users with additional guarantees on the content and the delivery of the messages, making e-mail equivalent and in some cases more convenient than the ordinary paper-based mail service. In literature, several distributed protocols for certified e-mail have been proposed, relying on an inline trusted third party (TTP) to ensure the fairness of the protocol. In such protocols, the TTP is actively involved in each message exchange. In this paper we provide a novel inline certified e-mail protocol which satisfies all the most important requirements which have been discussed for certified e-mail. Furthermore, we discuss a prototype implementation of our protocol targeted to the Windows platform.

## 1 Introduction

The electronic mail service allows users connected to the Internet to exchange messages containing text or multimedia files. The ease of use of e-mail clients as well as the spreading of the Internet and its associated services has determined a large diffusion of the e-mail service. E-mail is more and more used in place of ordinary mail. However, the use of e-mail in official events poses some problems. Indeed the actual e-mail service is based on the Simple Mail Transfer Protocol (SMTP [2]) which offers no guarantees on the delivery and the authenticity of the messages. Compared to the ordinary mail service, the e-mail is much less

Y.G. Desmedt et al. (Eds.): CANS 2005, LNCS 3810, pp. 186–199, 2005.

reliable: it gives the sender no evidence of having sent a message as well as no return receipt. Furthermore, whenever an e-mail message is received, there is no assurance on the identity of the originator of the message. Even the transmitted message could be eavesdropped over its path from the origin to the destination, and its content could be manipulated or corrupted by a malicious adversary.

Some e-mail clients (e.g., Microsoft Outlook) provide a Read Receipt request facility. Recipients may receive a request for a response to be sent, but they may decline to send the acknowledgement, or could set a switch to forbid confirmations of such a request. Other e-mail clients may simply ignore the request for a receipt. Indeed, such systems give no guarantee that the sender will receive a receipt when the recipient has displayed the message.

IETF RFC 2298 [1] defines a MIME content-type for message disposition notifications (MDNs). An MDN can be used to notify the sender of a message of any of several conditions that may occur after successful delivery, such as display of the message contents, printing of the message, deletion (without display) of the message, or the recipient's refusal to provide MDNs. However MDNs are not enough to satisfy all the properties usually guaranteed by the regular mail service, because they are easily forgeable.

Exploiting the digital nature of the transaction, it is possible to devise methods and techniques that enhance the capabilities of the message transfer protocol, obtaining the same or even additional guarantees with respect to the paper-based counterpart. One example of such guarantees is the following. A registered mail service allows the sender to prove that she sent *a message* at a specific time to a specific destination. Notice that nothing can be said about the *content* of the message sent. In a digital world, the sender may be able to prove that she sent a *message with a specific content* to a destination.

Certified e-mail protocols basically provide the following property: user Bob receives an e-mail message from user Alice if and only if the latter receives a receipt for this communication, i.e., a proof that the message has been delivered to the recipient. The receipt is such that the recipient cannot deny having received the message. Along with this property, many certified e-mail protocols provide other features like confidentiality of the message, proof of integrity, and so forth. Temporal authentication is, in some cases, e.g., patent submissions, a strict requirement. Enhancing e-mail systems with temporal authentication could simplify such kind of applications by reducing them to the simple operation of sending an e-mail. In Section 2 we describe in more detail the most important properties that have been identified in the literature as being crucial for certified e-mail systems.

Recently a lot of research has been dedicated to the problem of designing certified e-mail protocols. Most of the protocols that have been studied involve a trusted third party (TTP for short) which is delegated by the participants to control the behavior of the parties, assist them during the exchange of messages, and resolve any dispute, if necessary. According to the role played by the TTP, protocols have been classified as *inline* or *optimistic*. In inline protocols [10, 28, 17, 23], the TTP is actively involved in each message exchange: both the parties send their messages to the TTP, which checks for their integrity and forwards them to the intended receiver. As pointed out in [3], all commercial system providing a certified e-mail service [15, 22, 30] implement protocols in this class. The main reason of this choice is due to the fact that inline protocols guarantee accountability since the TTP is aware of each message exchange. In optimistic protocols [5, 6], the sender and the receiver first try to exchange the message by themselves, without the intervention of the TTP and rely on the TTP only for the cases where a dispute arises (maybe because one of the parties is trying to cheat). Certified e-mail protocols can be seen as a special case of *fair exchange* protocols. For this general case there exist protocols that do not require any trusted third party. Such solutions use the notion of *gradual exchange* [24, 18], i.e., the information is exchanged one bit at a time, or are *probabilistic* [11, 20], i.e., fairness is achieved with a certain probability. However these protocols usually rely on assumptions on the computational power of the parties and suffer from a high communication overhead. Non repudiation protocols with *transparent* TTP have been proposed in [21]. The term transparent refers to the fact that at the end of a protocol run, it is impossible to decide on the intervention of the TTP during the message exchange, by looking only at the produced evidences.

An interesting survey of non repudiation protocols and of the different roles played by the TTP has been provided by Kremer et al. in [19].

In this paper we propose a new inline protocol for certified e-mail. The protocol requires six messages to be exchanged among the parties and satisfies all the requirements usually taken into account in literature. As far as we know, this is the first inline protocol that meets all these requirements. Furthermore, we describe a prototype implementation targeted to the Microsoft Windows platform, based on the development of a software module compatible with one of the most used e-mail client applications.

The rest of the paper is organized as follows. The next section describes the requirements for a certified e-mail protocol. In Section 3 previous proposals are reviewed and compared to our protocol, which is described and analyzed in Section 4. Finally, some conclusions follow the description of the implementation in Section 5.

## 2    Requirements

Certified e-mail protocols ensure that a participant exchanges a message for a receipt, which the receiver should release at the end of the transaction. Indeed, the aim of such protocols is to provide a method for the secure exchange of messages, which is resistant to possible attempts of cheating by the different participants. Since both the message and the receipt are digital objects, certified e-mail protocols can be seen as instances of fair exchange protocols [6]. Such protocols deal with the fair exchange of objects, i.e., at the end of the exchange, both participants get what they expect or nobody gets any valuable information.

In the following we list the main requirements that a certified e-mail protocol should satisfy.

**Fairness:** In a *fair* certified e-mail protocol, parties should not be able to interrupt or corrupt the protocol obtaining any advantage from the exchanged messages. At the end of the protocol each party should get the desired information or nobody should get any valuable information: the sender should get both sending and delivery receipts, while the receiver should get the e-mail message;

**Sending Receipt:** Since certified email protocols are interactive protocols that may involve human interaction, it could be desirable that the sender obtains an evidence of the fact that he *started* the process of sending a certified email. Notice that this receipt may not contain any information generated by the recipient, e.g., it is produced by a third authority.

**Non-repudiation of origin:** The party which originates the message should not be able to falsely deny having originated it; the receiver should get evidence of the exchange to resolve any dispute;

**Non-repudiation of receipt:** The recipient of the message should not be able to falsely repudiate having received that message; at the end of the protocol the sender should get evidence of the delivery of the message;

**Authenticity:** The participants to the protocol should be guaranteed on their reciprocal identities and on the identities of the other entities involved in the message exchange;

**Integrity:** Parties involved in the exchange of the messages should not be able to alter or corrupt the transmitted messages without being detected;

**Confidentiality:** Only the sender and the receiver should be able to extract the content of the original e-mail message given the exchanged messages;

**Timeliness:** The duration of the protocol should be finite, so that the exchange procedure terminates successfully or any party can decide to abort the exchange within a predefined time bound;

**Temporal Authentication:** The starting time of the exchange should be certified and observable by the participants to the protocols; an arbiter should be able to verify the temporal data attached to messages.

To achieve many of the above properties, many protocols rely on a trusted third party. If the TTP has an active role during the message exchange, such protocols are referred to as *inline protocols*. The drawbacks of such protocols is that the TTP has to be online for the whole duration of the exchange and that the correctness of the protocol is entirely devoted to its behavior: any failure of the TTP could compromise the e-mail exchange. A main advantage of these protocols is that they allow accountability. Indeed, all the commercial systems that provide a certified e-mail service implement a protocol of this kind. On the other hand, optimistic protocols have been introduced by Asokan et al. ([5, 6, 7]), relying on the idea that the TTP takes part in the protocol only in case of failures or to resolve a dispute between the parties. The main drawback of this approach is that this class of protocols does not allow accountability.

# 3  Related Works

Several researchers proposed protocols for certified e-mail using an online third party during the exchange of the message. Bahreman and Tygar [10] proposed an inline protocol requiring six messages to be sent among the parties. In their protocol the sender sends the e-mail message to the TTP, which returns a proof of mailing. Then, the TTP encrypts the message with a session key and sends it to the recipient, who signs the ciphertext and returns the signature to the TTP. Finally, the TTP sends the receipt to the sender and the session key to the recipient. Our protocol is derived from this one. We notice that this protocol presented in [10] does not preserve the confidentiality from the TTP, since the sender sends the e-mail message to the TTP. Furthermore, there is no temporal authentication.

Deng et al. [17] proposed two inline protocols requiring four messages to be sent among the parties. In particular, the second protocol preserves the confidentiality from the TTP, while the first one does not. Coffey and Saidha [16] proposed a non-repudiation protocol which relies on an external time-stamping authority to state the non-repudiation of origin and destination evidence time. Another non-repudiation protocol requiring four messages have been proposed by Zhang and Shi [26]. In such protocol the TTP manages a database containing the session keys used in a protocol run and publishes at the right time, in a publicly accessible database, the keys needed to allow the deciphering of the exchanged messages. One of the main drawback of this technique is that the TTP cannot delete any element from the database as each key should be recovered by a judge in case of a dispute. For this reason the size of the database grows indefinitely.

Schneier and Riordan [23] proposed an inline protocol using a secure database server. Although they claim this server does not need to be trusted, in practice it is a TTP since it should not be able to collude with the sender. In their protocol the sender encrypts the e-mail message with a session key and sends it to the receiver. Then, the receiver asks the sender to publish the session key on a secure database server at a certain time. This message is signed by the receiver and sent to the sender. Afterwards, the sender submits the session key to the server; then, the receiver gets it and decrypts the e-mail.

Several non-repudiation protocols which have been applied to certified e-mail have been proposed by Zhou and Gollman. In [29] the authors present a protocol that requires five messages. The key idea is that the sender and the receiver exchange the signatures on the encrypted message and then interact with the TTP to recover the key and the non repudiation-proofs. In [27] another protocol is proposed where the e-mail message is transmitted from the sender to the receiver through a sequence of trusted third parties. The role of these parties is to deliver the message, collect the receipt signed from the receiver, and route them back to the sender.

Finally, Abadi, Glew, and Pinkas [3] proposed an inline protocol requiring four messages. The protocol does not require any public-key infrastructure. However, the protocol assumes that the TTP has some public keys and that some other authentication mechanism is provided (such as a shared secret) among the participants.

The following table summarizes the properties guaranteed by each of the above mentioned inline protocols. An empty circle means that the property is not satisfied and a bullet means that the property is satisfied. In this paper we propose an inline certified e-mail protocol (last column of the table) satisfying all nine properties.

| Property | [10] | [17] | [16] | [26] | [23] | [29] | [27] | [3] | Ours |
|---|---|---|---|---|---|---|---|---|---|
| Fairness | ● | ● | ● | ● | ● | ● | ● | ● | ● |
| Sending Receipt | ● | ○ | ● | ● | ○ | ○ | ● | ● | ● |
| Non Rep. Origin | ● | ● | ● | ● | ● | ● | ● | ○ | ● |
| Non Rep. Receipt. | ● | ● | ● | ● | ● | ● | ● | ● | ● |
| Authenticity | ● | ● | ● | ● | ● | ● | ● | ○ | ● |
| Integrity | ● | ● | ● | ● | ● | ● | ● | ● | ● |
| Confidentiality | ○ | ○ | ● | ● | ○ | ○ | ○ | ● | ● |
| Timeliness | ● | ○ | ○ | ○ | ○ | ● | ○ | ○ | ● |
| Temp. Auth. | ○ | ○ | ● | ● | ○ | ○ | ○ | ○ | ● |

**Fig. 1.** Summary of properties

## 4   The Protocol

In this section we provide a detailed description of the protocol. Recall that the goal of the protocol is to allow a sender $S$ to send an e-mail message to a receiver $R$, in such a way that the properties discussed in Section 2 are satisfied. Some of these properties derive from the use of cryptographic primitives, others derive directly from the protocol.

### 4.1   Preliminaries

The scenario we consider consists of a number of users who are willing to exchange e-mail messages using a certified e-mail service. The service provides them some additional guarantees on the delivery of the messages and on the security of the communication. To such purpose, the protocol relies on a Trusted Third Party (TTP) actively involved in each message exchange. The TTP is trusted, in the sense that it does not collude neither with the message sender nor with the receiver. Furthermore it is assumed to be reliable. The protocol assumes that each user has a public key, widely available to the other users and whose authenticity can be verified, and a corresponding private key which is kept secret and known only to him. Currently there are a number of techniques that can be used in order to guarantee the above assumption. The most widely used is the existance a public key infrastructure. We just mention certificateless public key encryption schemes introduced in [4] and ID-based encryption schemes [14, 13, 25] as possible alternatives to PKIs. The public key system defines an encryption transformation and an associated decryption transformation which are used to exchange messages between users in such a way that the *confidentiality* of the messages is guaranteed.

## 4.2   Cryptographic Primitives

In the following we describe the cryptographic primitives used in the protocol.

- $Sig_A(m)$: denotes the pair $(m, \sigma)$ where $\sigma$ is the digital signature of the message $m$ using the private key of user $A$ under any secure signature algorithm;
- $h(m)$: indicates the hash of message $m$ using some collision resistant hash function. A collision resistant hash function maps arbitrary length messages to constant size messages such that it is computationally infeasible to find any two distinct messages hashing to the same value.
- $PK_B(m)$: denotes the encryption of message $m$ using the public key of user $B$ under some public-key encryption algorithm.
- $E_k(m)$: denotes the encryption of message $m$ using the key $k$ under some symmetric encryption algorithm.

## 4.3   Description of the Protocol

The protocol we propose is derived from Bahreman and Tygar proposal [10]. In order to ensure time related properties to the exchange of messages, we add a timestamping service, which is performed by the TTP. Whenever the TTP receives a request from the sender $S$, it generates and stores a new transaction associated with the arrival time of the message and the message itself. The transaction is stored for the whole duration of the exchange and can be deleted at the end of the protocol or used as a proof to determine the responsibility of the cheater in case of dispute.

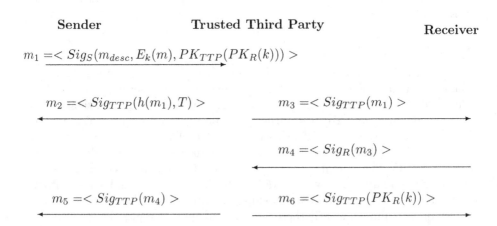

**Fig. 2.** The protocol

Let us describe in more details the protocol, whose sketch is presented in Figure 2. It is composed of six messages and prescribes the interaction of the sender $S$ with the Receiver $R$ through the TTP.

1. When $S$ wants to send an e-mail message $m$ to $R$, he chooses a session key $k$, encrypts the message $m$ using $k$, encrypts $k$ with the public key of $R$ and then with the public key of the TTP. Afterwards, $S$ adds a brief description $m_{desc}$ of the message $m$ and signs the resulting message, obtaining the message $m_1$, which is sent to the TTP.

2. At the reception of the message $m_1$ from $S$, the TTP generates a timestamp $T$ and concatenates it to the hash of $m_1$. Afterwards, it signs the resulting message, obtaining the message $m_2$, which is sent to $S$. The TTP also signs the message $m_1$, obtaining the message $m_3$, which is sent to $R$.

3. At the reception of the message $m_3$ from the TTP , $R$ reads the description of the message and decides whether he wants to get the original e-mail message from $S$. If he does, he signs the message $m_3$, obtaining the message $m_4$, which is sent to the TTP. Otherwise, if $R$ is not interested in the message, he can simply ignore the message and abort the transaction.

4. If the TTP receives the message $m_4$ from $R$ within a time $T < t < T + \delta$, where $\delta$ is a predefined time interval, he verifies that $m_4$ has been obtained by signing the message $m_3$. In such case, he signs the message $m_4$, obtaining the message $m_5$, which is sent to $S$. Finally, the TTP extracts from $m_1$ the encryption of the session key $k$ under the public key of $R$, signs it, and obtains the message $m_6$, which is sent to $R$.

## 4.4   Analysis

In this section we show that our protocol satisfies all the requirements listed in Section 2.

**Fairness.** If both the sender and the receiver behave as expected and messages are delivered on time, at the end of the protocol each party gets the desired information. Indeed, $S$ gets a sending receipt (that is, message $m_2$), even if $R$ is not interested in receiving the original e-mail message and aborts the transaction. After receiving the message $m_3$, containing the encryption of $m$ under the session key $k$, $R$ has to decide whether he is interested in getting the original e-mail. Only if it confirms to be interested in reading the e-mail, by sending the message $m_4$ to the TTP, he gets the message $m_6$, containing the encryption of the session key $k$ under his public key. The protocol ensures that at the same time, the TTP sends the message $m_5$ to $S$. This message constitutes a delivery receipt for $S$, since it contains the signature of the TTP of the message $m_4$, which is the authenticated confirmation that $R$ was interested in receiving the original e-mail message. Notice that, in case the sender maliciously constructs a message $m_1$, e.g., by using $E_k(m)$ and $PK_R(k')$ to compose $m_1$, the receiver will have a proof that the sender cheated during the execution of the protocol.

**Sending receipt.** The sending receipt consists of message $m_2$, which contains the signature of the TTP on the hash of $m_1$. This receipt is sent to $S$ by the TTP before the interaction with $R$, hence it is independent on the reception of the message from $R$.

**Non-repudiation of origin and receipt.** This property is guaranteed since each message sent during the execution of the protocol is signed by its sender.

At the end of the protocol, $R$ gets $m_3$ and $m_6$, which represent the non-repudiation tokens of origin. With these tokens, $R$ can prove that $S$ indeed sent the e-mail. On the other end, $S$ gets $m_5$, which represents the non-repudiation token of receipt. With this token, $S$ can prove that $R$ indeed received the e-mail.

**Authenticity, Integrity, Confidentiality.** The property derive directly from the authenticity and verifiability of the public key. Integrity come from the collision resistance property of the hash function and on the security of the signature scheme. The protocol also preserves the confidentiality of the e-mail message $m$, both from the TTP and from an adversary eavesdropping the messages exchanged. Indeed, the TTP never learns the content of the original e-mail message: it receives the encryption of $m$ under the key $k$, but cannot decrypt it, because $k$ is encrypted with the public key of $R$. The same holds for any adversary eavesdropping the message exchanges.

**Timeliness.** The duration of the exchange is finite. Indeed, let $\tau$ be the maximum transmission time, i.e., the time needed for a message to reach its destination. Furthermore, let $\lambda$ be the maximum computation time. It is clear from inspection that, if the sender starts the protocol at time $T$, the protocol terminates at latest at time $t + 4\tau + 3\lambda$.

**Temporal authentication.** The TTP guarantees the temporal authentication of the exchange, certifying the starting time $T$ of the transaction (such a timestamp is contained in the message $m_2$).

## 5    Implementation

To test the performance and the usability of the proposed protocol, we developed a prototype implementation, targeted to the Windows platform. The implementation relies on the development of applications to manage the messages exchange from both client and server (TTP) side. For the client side, users willing to use the certified e-mail service are requested to install a plug-in, i.e., a piece of software which extends the capability of the usual e-mail client. The plug-in has been designed for Outlook 2000. The extension is conceived in such a way that users are given the option to choose if sending a normal e-mail or using the certified e-mail service.

For the server side, an extension to Exchange Server 2000 has been developed, through the generation of a DLL ActiveX which reacts to the reception of certified e-mail messages and generates the requested messages needed to execute the protocol.

### 5.1    Previous Implementations

In literature several implementations of certified e-mail systems exist. Generally they can be roughly classified as research projects or commercial systems.

TRICERT [8] is an hybrid scheme based on Postal Agents which are distributed servers acting on the behalf of the TTP. The PA must be online, but they are not able to resolve disputes. The PA have been implemented by daemons included in the Apache web servers, while the client applications provide user interfaces through SSL enabled web servers. The trusted party in practice is a human service operator which has to manage the requests logged into the trusted server. Notice that this scheme is neither optimistic nor inline, so it is not possible to compare it with our proposal.

The protocol proposed by Abadi et al [3] has been implemented by combining the usage of a standard e-mail client with a Java-enabled browser. Certified e-mail messages contain both a plaintext part explaining the content of the message and an HTML part containing a link to an applet with appropriate parameters. To read the message, the receiver must double-click on the link to launch the applet and continue the execution of the protocol. While this kind of solution is attractive, since it does not require the users to install any additional software, it has the disadvantage that messages are not easily manageable, since it is necessary to contact the TTP each time one wants to read, print or reply to the received message.

Several companies offer certified e-mail services usually hiding the technical details related to both the protocol and the used application. Usually the parties communicate through a central trusted web server [9, 15]. Another commercial implementation is ZixMail, which has been developed by the ZixIt Company [30]. The service enables the delivery of documents and e-mail messages in a secure way by encrypting and digitally signing the communications. The ZixMail users can choose between two options for message delivery: ZixMail direct method can be used when both the sender and the receiver are provided with a ZixMail client application, which is available also as Lotus Notes or Microsoft Outlook plug-in; ZixMail.net method is used when the receiver does not have a ZixMail client. In the latter case, the receiver can use an SSL enabled browser to retrieve the message.

## 5.2 Exchange Server Extension

To implement the server side of the certified e-mail service, we relied on the event model which is provided with the Web Storage System used by Microsoft Exchange Server 2000.

A Web Storage System is a hierarchical folder system which can store all sorts of documents and data types such as e-mail messages, Web pages, multimedia files, and so on. The Web Storage System provides access to events which fire when certain tasks occur within the Web Storage System, for example whenever an item in the store is saved or deleted.

The event paradigm consists of two main elements: the *event sink*, which is the code that Exchange 2000 executes when an event fires in a specified folder; and a *registration element*, which is a hidden item created in the store at the root of the folder, holding all the information necessary to associate the event with its event sink and its properties.

In our case, a new event sink (`eCertifiedMail.dll`) implemented as DLL ActiveX has been created and registered on the server as a new COM+ component. Each time a new message is received by the TTP the event sink registered with the OnSyncSave event is called before the message is stored into the *Inbox* folder, such that the message can be manipulated according to the protocol specification.

### 5.3  Cmail Plug-In

The plug-in is based on the design of a COM Add-In, which is an ActiveX DLL able to interact with applications coming with the Office 2000 package.

To store the certified e-mail messages in input and output, two new folders have been created in *Inbox* and *Outbox* system folders of Outlook. These folders include other sub-folders which contain the messages generated during the interaction with the TTP. More in detail, in *Outbox*, the *CEMSender* folder contains the subfolder where both sending and return receipts are stored for certified e-mail messages originated from the Sender. The *CEMReceiver* folder contains two subfolders, *Requests* and *Keys*, containing the first and the last messages sent by the TTP and generated during the execution of the protocol whenever an incoming certified e-mail message is received.

The basic cryptographic operations are performed exploiting the cryptographic primitives provided with the Windows operating system, called *CryptoApi*. To this purpose, we used the Visual Basic COM wrappers for the *CryptoAPI* called the *WCCO (Wiley CryptoAPI COM Objects)* [12]. However, to overcome some limitations we developed an extension of the *WCCO* library providing the cryptographic functions needed during the execution of the protocol.

The plug-in is activated whenever the user decides to compose a new message. In this case, a form is displayed on the screen asking the user if she wants to use the usual service or certified e-mail service. If the user chooses to compose a certified e-mail message, a new session key $k_1$ which is 168 bit long is generated and its hash is calculated and stored as a message-id. Since the *CryptoApi* only allows to use public key encryption schemes to encrypt "short" messages, i.e., session keys and hash values, the part of message containing $PK_{TTP}(PK_R(k))$ could not be implemented as stated. We have substituted this part of the message with $(E_{k_2}(PK_R(k_1))||PK_{TTP}(k_2))$, where $k_2$ is another randomly generated session key.

To summarize, the final message is created with an appropriate header, holding in some user-defined fields the message type (in this case new certified e-mail message), the subject, the encrypted message $E_{k_1}(m)$, the other information needed by the TTP to continue the exchange, i.e., $E_{k_2}(PK_R(k_1))||PK_{TTP}(k_2)$ and the signature of the sender of all the above components, i.e.:

$$Sig_S(Header||Subject||E_{k_1}(m)||E_{k_2}(PK_R(k_1))||PK_{TTP}(k_2)).$$

The resulting message is sent to the TTP and a copy is stored in the *CEMSender* folder.

Whenever the TTP receives a certified e-mail request from the Sender, after verifying the integrity and the authenticity of the message, it stores the attachments on the disk, calculates and stores a fresh timestamp for the execution of the protocol, and composes two messages $m_2$ and $m_3$ for the Sender and the Receiver, respectively.

The Sender verifies the integrity and the authenticity of the message sent by the TTP and stores it in the *Receipt* sub-folder of the *Inbox*.

When the Receiver opens the message sent by the TTP a form containing the Sender and the Subject of the e-mail is displayed, and he is asked to refuse or accept the e-mail. In the first case, the message is deleted from the *Inbox*. In the second case, the attachments are saved on the disk, a verification of the message is performed and a copy is stored in the *Request* folder. Then, a new message ($m_4$) is composed and sent to the TTP.

On the reception of the acknowledgment from the Receiver, the TTP verifies it and composes two new messages for the Sender and the Receiver.

The Sender verifies and saves the message $m_5$ in the sub-folder Receipt of the *CEMSender* subfolder.

The Receiver retrieves the session key $k_1$ to decrypt the message and stores the last message holding the key in the Key sub-folder of the *CEMReceiver* of the *Inbox*.

## 6   Conclusions

We have presented a new certified e-mail protocol relying on an online trusted third party. Our protocol enhances the basic e-mail system with *all* the most important features discussed up to now in the literature and reported in Figure 1. In particular the properties of confidentiality and temporal authentication should help to overcome the problems that have prevented the use of e-mail for official communications.

The prototype implementation we provide is composed by an extension for Microsoft Exchange 2000 and by a plug-in developed for the Microsoft Outlook e-mail client. Users can continue to use the regular e-mail service and adopt the certified e-mail facility as an additional service. Since our goal was to demonstrate the applicability of the protocol, currently the prototype simply assumes the public key to be known. It is our intention to enhance the basic prototype so that it can interact with a PKI in order to obtain and verify public keys. Finally we are planning to develop other plug-ins for the most used e-mail clients to confirm the practicality of the approach.

## References

1. RFC 2298. An extensible message format for message disposition notifications, http://www.ietf.org/rfc/rfc2298.txt, March 1998.
2. RFC 2821. Simple mail transfer protocol (smtp), http://www.ietf.org/rfc/rfc2821.txt, April 2001.

3. M. Abadi, N. Glew, B. Horne, and B. Pinkas. Certified email with a light on-line trusted third party: Design and implementation. In *Proceedings of Eleventh International World Wide Web Conference*. ACM Press, New York, US, 2002.

4. S.S. Al-Riyami and K.G. Paterson. Certificateless public key cryptography. In Chi-Sung Laih, editor, *Advances in Cryptology - ASIACRYPT 2003*, volume 2894 of *Lecture Notes in Computer Science*, pages 452–473. Springer, 2003.

5. N. Asokan, M. Schunter, and M. Waidner. Optimistic protocols for fair exchange. In *ACM Conference on Computer and Communications Security*, pages 7–17, 1997.

6. N. Asokan, V. Shoup, and M. Waidner. Asynchronous protocols for optimistic fair exchange. In *Proceedings of the IEEE Symposium on Research in Security and Privacy*, pages 86–99, 1998.

7. N. Asokan, V. Shoup, and M. Waidner. Optimistic fair exchange of digital signatures. In Kaisa Nyberg, editor, *EUROCRYPT 98*, pages 591–606. Springer-Verlag, 1998.

8. G. Ateniese, B. de Medeiros, and M. T. Goodrich. TRICERT: A distributed certified E-mail scheme. In *Proceedings of the Symposium on Network and Distributed Systems Security (NDSS 2001)*, San Diego, CA, February 2001.

9. http://www.authentica.com.

10. A. Bahreman and J. D. Tygar. Certified electronic mail. In Dan Nesset and Robj Shirey, editors, *Proceedings of the Symposium on Network and Distributed Systems Security*, pages 3–19, San Diego, CA, February 1994. Internet Society.

11. M. Ben-Or, O. Goldreich, S. Micali, and R.L. Rivest. A fair protocol for signing contracts. *IEEE Transactions on Information Theory*, 36(1), 1990.

12. R. Bondi. *Cryptography for Visual Basic: a programmer's guide to the Microsoft CryptoAPI*. John Wiley and Sons, Inc., New York, NY, USA, 2000.

13. D. Boneh, X. Boyen, and E. Goh. Hierarchical identity based encryption with constant size ciphertext. In Cramer, editor, *EUROCRYPT 05*, pages 440–456. Springer-Verlag, 2005.

14. D. Boneh and M. K. Franklin. Identity-based encryption from the weil pairing. In Joe Kilian, editor, *Advances in Cryptology - CRYPTO 2001*, volume 2139 of *Lecture Notes in Computer Science*, pages 213–229. Springer, 2001.

15. http://www.certifiedmail.com.

16. T. Coffey and P. Saidha. Non-repudiation with mandatory proof receipt. *ACM Computer Communications Review*, 26, 1996.

17. R. H. Deng, L. Gong, A. A. Lazar, and W. Wang. Practical protocols for certified electronic mail. *Journal of Network and System Management*, 4(3), 1996.

18. S. Even, O. Goldreich, and A. Lempel. A randomized protocol for signing contracts. *Communications of the ACM*, 28(6), 1985.

19. S. Kremer, O. Markowitch, and J. Zhou. An intensive survey of fair non-repudiation protocols. *Computer Communications*, 25(17):1606–1621, 2002.

20. O. Markowitch and Y. Roggerman. Probabilistic non-repudiation without ttp. In *Proceedings of Second Conference on Security in Communication Networks*, 1999.

21. O. Markowithc and S. Kremer. An optimistic non-repudiation protocol with transparent trusted third party. In *Procceding of Information Security Conference (ISC 2001)*, volume 2200 of *Lecture Notes in Computer Science*, pages 363–378. Springer, 2001.

22. http://www.readnotify.com.

23. J. Riordan and B. Schneier. A certified E-mail protocol with no trusted third party. In *Proceedings of the 13th Annual Computer Security Applications Conference*, pages 347–352, 1998.

24. T. Tedrick. Fair exchange of secrets. In *Proceedings of Crypto '84*, volume 196 of *Lecture Notes in Computer Science*, pages 434–438, 1985.

25. B. Waters. Efficient identity-based encryption without random oracles. In Cramer, editor, *EUROCRYPT 05*, pages 114–127. Springer-Verlag, 2005.

26. N. Zhang and Q. Shi. Achieving non-repudiation of receipt. *The Computer Journal*, 39(10):844–853, 1996.

27. J. Zhou and D. Gollmann. Certified electronic mail. In *Proceedings of ESORICS '96*, volume 1146 of *Lecture Notes in Computer Science*, pages 160–171, 1996.

28. J. Zhou and D. Gollmann. A fair non-repudiation protocol. In *Proceedings of the IEEE Symposium on Research in Security and Privacy*, pages 55–61, Oakland, CA, 1996. IEEE Computer Society Press.

29. J. Zhou and D. Gollmann. An efficient non-repudiation protocol. In *PCSFW: Proceedings of The 10th Computer Security Foundations Workshop*. IEEE Computer Society Press, 1997.

30. Zixmail and zixmail.net. http://www.zixmail.com.

# Efficient Identity-Based Protocol for Fair Certified E-mail Delivery

Zhenfeng Zhang[1,2], Jing Xu[1,3], and Dengguo Feng[1,2]

[1] State Key Laboratory of Information Security
[2] Institute of Software, Chinese Academy of Sciences, Beijing 100080, P.R. China
[3] Graduate School of Chinese Academy of Sciences, Beijing 100039, P.R. China
zfzhang@is.iscas.ac.cn

**Abstract.** Certified e-mail delivery has become one of the basic requirement in performing business transactions over the Internet securely. How to construct efficient fair protocols for certified e-mail delivery is of great interest. The notion of identity based cryptosystem has attracted much interest since its introduction by Shamir in 1984, as it eliminates the need of certificates and simplifies the key management. In this paper, we propose a fair protocol for certified e-mail delivery based on identity-based signatures. A semi-trust third party (TTP) is involved in our protocol to ensure fairness, who does not need to store anything except its own private-key. There is no need for an additional registration between users and TTP. The proposed scheme is the first identity-based protocol with such a concise frame and is computation- and communication-efficient.

**Keywords:** Fair exchange, Certified E-mail, Security protocol, Identity-based signature.

## 1 Introduction

Communication by e-mail has become a vital part of everyday business and has replaced most of the conventional ways of communicating. The basic e-mail security services include the provision of privacy (only the intended recipient can read the message) and authentication (the recipient can be assured of the identity of the sender). Cryptographic mechanisms for providing these security services have been applied in Internet mail systems, such as S/MIME [24] and PGP [25]. In addition to sender authentication and message privacy, S/MIME can also provide a signed receipt service. A signed receipt from the recipient (requested by the sender) serves as a non-repudiable proof of receipt for a specific e-mail. However, the return of this receipt relies on the willingness of the recipient to honor the sender's request and provides no protection to the sender if the recipient chooses not to sign and return the acknowledgement after having read the message. In other words, this technique does not truly provide non-repudiation of the receipt security service.

Y.G. Desmedt et al. (Eds.): CANS 2005, LNCS 3810, pp. 200–210, 2005.

Important business correspondence may require certified e-mail delivery service, analogous to that provided by conventional mail service. For a viable certified e-mail service, the following security properties are needed:

- Non-repudiation of origin - the recipient must have a way of proving that a specific e-mail indeed originates from the sender;
- Non-repudiation of receipt - the sender must have a way of proving that the recipient has indeed received a specific e-mail;
- Strong fairness for the exchange - the recipient should obtain a specific e-mail if and only if the sender obtains a receipt for it.

By now, certified e-mail delivery (CEMD) has become one of the central problems in performing business transactions over the Internet securely and can be applied in numerous e-commerce transactions. Briefly speaking, this is the problems of how two mutually distrustful parties can fairly exchange a sender's valuable e-mail for a receiver's digital signature representing a proof of reception. A CEMD protocol [13, 17] shall provide strong fairness to ensure that the recipient receives the e-mail if and only if the sender receives the receipt.

The most practical and efficient approach to the fair exchange problems is to make use of an off-line trusted third party (TTP) to help the participants with the exchange. By this approach, the exchanging parties attempt to exchange their respective items themselves, i.e. without any involvement of the TTP. Should any dispute arise during the exchange process due to a party's misbehavior or a network failure, TTP is invoked to recover the disputed items and restore fairness.

Recently, a new category of off-line TTP-based fair exchange protocols has been proposed based on a cryptographic primitive called *verifiable and recoverable encryption of a signature* (VRES) [1, 2, 3, 4, 8, 10, 11, 14]. The VRES represents a digital signature encrypted in such a way that a receiver of the VRES can verify that it indeed contains the correct signature without obtaining any information about the signature itself (verifiability). The receiver can also verify that a designated TTP can help to recover the original signature from the VRES, in case the original signature sender refuses to do so (recoverability).

In SAC'04, Nenadic et al. [21] proposed a new RSA-CEMD protocol for the two communicating parties to fairly exchange an e-mail message for an RSA-based receipt. The main contribution of their work is a novel RSA-based method for the verifiable and recoverable encrypted signature, which is utilized as a crucial primitive to construct their RSA-CEMD protocol. The proposed protocols has been used as a main cryptographic primitive in the Fair Integrated Data Exchange Services (FIDES) project [22] provided for E-commerce transactions. However, as a building block, their VRES scheme was shown to be insecure recently by [23]: an adversary can easily generate a valid VRES which cannot be recovered by the designated TTP, and hence the proposed certified e-mail delivery protocol can not guarantee the claimed fairness.

As we know, in traditional public key cryptosystems, an entity's public-key is generated from some random information that is unrelated to his identity, and hence needs to be certified to provide users with confidence in the authenticity of the public keys they are using. PKI is an important infrastructure to manage these digital certificates and the trust relationships between entities in a hierarchical manner. Unfortunately, these certificate-based infrastructures turned out to be very heavy to deploy, cumbersome to use and non-transparent for the user.

In order to bypass the trust problems encountered in conventional Public Key Infrastructures, Shamir [18] introduced the concept of ID-based public-key cryptography (ID-PKC) in 1984, where an entity's public key can be a unique binary string identifying its owner non-ambiguously, such as an e-mail address, an IP address combined to a user-name, a social security number, et. al.. The motivation of ID-PKC was to simplify key management and remove the need of public key certificates as much as possible: since a key is the identity of its owner, there is no need to bind them by a digital certificates, and thus end users do not have to enquire for a certificate for their public key. A breakthrough work in the research of ID-PKC shall owe to Boneh and Franklin [7], who proposed the first efficient identity encryption scheme based on the bilinear pairings over elliptic curves. Since then, a great deal of research has been done about the ID-based cryptosystems. Moreover, the identity-based protocols constructed over elliptic curves are more suitable for ad hoc and sensor networks. However, as far as we know, no identity based protocol for certified e-mail delivery has been proposed.

In this paper, we proposed an efficient identity-based fair protocol for certified e-mail delivery, which work with an identity-based signature scheme constructed over elliptic curves. In our protocol, there is no registration between a party and TTP, which makes our protocol much concise and easy to implementation. In fact, TTP generates a trapdoor permutation as the system parameter, and does not need to store anything except the private-key of permutation. The trapdoor kept secret by TTP is only used in the recovery phase to ensure fairness.

The rest of the paper is organized as follows. In section 2, some notations and assumptions that will be used in this paper are given. Then we present our identity-based fair certified e-mail delivery protocol and analysis its security and efficiency in section 3. A conclusion is drawn in section 4.

## 2    Notations and Preliminaries

The following notations will be used in the remaining part of the paper.

- $E_{sk}(m)$ expresses a signature of an item $m$ created with a private key $sk$.
- $h(\cdot)$ is a suitable collision-resistant one-way hash functions.
- $x\|y$ denotes the concatenation of data items $x$ and $y$.

The following assumptions are used in the design of a certified e-mail delivery protocol.

- Alice wishes to send an e-mail message $M$ to party Bob in exchange for Bob's receipt for $M$.
- Alice and Bob have agreed to employ an off-line TTP to help them with the exchange if they cannot reach a fair completion of the exchange themselves.

## 2.1 The Bilinear Pairing

Let $\mathcal{G}_1$ be a cyclic additive group generated by $P$, whose order is a prime $q$, and $\mathcal{G}_2$ be a cyclic multiplicative group of the same order. Let $e : \mathcal{G}_1 \times \mathcal{G}_1 \rightarrow \mathcal{G}_2$ be a pairing which satisfies the following conditions:

1. Bilinearity: For any $P, Q, R \in \mathcal{G}_1$, we have $e(P + Q, R) = e(P, R)e(Q, R)$ and $e(P, Q + R) = e(P, Q)e(P, R)$. In particular, for any $a, b \in \mathbf{Z}_q$,

$$e(aP, bP) = e(P, P)^{ab} = e(P, abP) = e(abP, P).$$

2. Non-degeneracy: There exists $P, Q \in \mathcal{G}_1$, such that $e(P, Q) \neq 1$.
3. Computability: There is an efficient algorithm to compute $e(P, Q)$ for all $P, Q \in \mathcal{G}_1$.

The typical way of obtaining such pairings is by deriving them from the weil-pairing or the tate-pairing on an elliptic curve over a finite field. We refer to [6, 7] for a more comprehensive description on how these groups, pairings and other parameters should be selected for efficiency and security. The interested reader is also referred to [16] for a complete bibliography of cryptographic works based on pairings.

Computation Diffie-Hellman (CDH) Problem: Given $P$, $aP$, $bP \in \mathcal{G}_1$ for randomly chosen $a, b \in_{\mathcal{R}} \mathbf{Z}_q^*$, to compute $abP$.

## 2.2 The Identity-Based Setting

In an identity-based cryptosystem, there is a trusted authority called the private key generator (PKG) who holds a master key and issues private keys for all users in the system domain. The public-key of a user can be derived publicly and directly from his unique identifier information. The following is a brief overview of the identity-based setting. We refer to [7] for a detailed description.

- **Setup.** Given a security parameter $k$, the PKG chooses groups $\mathcal{G}_1$ and $\mathcal{G}_2$ of prime order $q > 2^k$, a generator $P$ of $\mathcal{G}_1$, a bilinear map $e : \mathcal{G}_1 \times \mathcal{G}_1 \rightarrow \mathcal{G}_2$, a randomly chosen master key $s \in \mathbf{Z}_q^*$ and the associated public key $P_{pub} = sP$. It also picks cryptographic hash functions of same domain and range $H_1, H_2 : \{0, 1\}^* \rightarrow \mathcal{G}_1$. The system's public parameters are

$$\texttt{params} = (\mathcal{G}_1, \mathcal{G}_2, e, P, P_{pub}, H_1, H_2).$$

- **Extract.** Suppose the identity of a user is $ID$. Given an identity $ID$, the PKG computes $Q_{ID} = H_1(ID) \in \mathcal{G}_1$ and $d_{ID} = sQ_{ID} \in \mathcal{G}_1$, and then transmits it to the user securely. The private key of the user is $d_{ID}$.

Now we briefly present the identity-based signature scheme proposed by Sakai, Ogishi and Kasahara [19], which has been commonly called SOK-IBS scheme in [5].

- **Sign:** In order to sign a message $M$, the signing algorithm takes as input the signer's private key $d_{ID}$ and its identity $ID$, and performs as following:

    1. Pick $r \in_{\mathcal{R}} \mathbf{Z}_q$, compute $U = rP \in \mathcal{G}_1$ and $H = H_2(ID, M, U) \in \mathcal{G}_1$.
    2. Compute $V = d_{ID} + rH \in \mathcal{G}_1$.

The signature on $M$ is the pair $\sigma = \langle U, V \rangle \in \mathcal{G}_1 \times \mathcal{G}_1$.

- **Ver:** To verify a SOK-IBS signature $\sigma = \langle U, V \rangle \in \mathcal{G}_1 \times \mathcal{G}_1$ on a message $M$ for an identity $ID$, a verifier first takes $Q_{ID} = H_1(ID) \in \mathcal{G}_1$ and $H = H_2(ID, M, U) \in \mathcal{G}_1$, and then accepts the signature if and only if

$$e(P, V) = e(P_{pub}, Q_{ID}) \cdot e(U, H). \qquad (1)$$

In [5, 15], the SOK-IBS signature scheme has been shown to be non-existential forgeable under adaptive chosen message attacks in the random oracle model, assuming the computational Diffie-Hellman problem in $\mathcal{G}_1$ is hard.

## 3   Our ID-CEMD Protocol

Let the system parameter $\mathtt{params} = (\mathcal{G}_1, \mathcal{G}_2, e, P, P_{pub}, H_1, H_2)$ be defined as in the **Setup** algorithm of section 2.2.

**System Setup.** Suppose the identity of user Alice is $ID_A$, and the corresponding private key is $d_A = sQ_A \in \mathcal{G}_1$, which is generated by PKG and is transmitted to Alice via a secure channel, where $Q_A = H_1(ID_A) \in \mathcal{G}_1$. Similarly, assume the identity of Bob is $ID_B$. The private key of Bob is then $d_B = sQ_B \in \mathcal{G}_1$, which is also computed by PKG and transmitted to him via a secure channel, where $Q_B = H_1(ID_B) \in \mathcal{G}_1$.

In our protocol, a designated TTP chooses $x \in \mathbf{Z}_q^*$ at random, generates a public key $PK = xP \in \mathcal{G}_1$ and publishes it as a system parameter, while keeps $SK = x$ secret.

Bob's receipt for a message $M$, denoted as $receipt_B = (U, V)$, is represented by Bob's SOK-IBS signature on $M$.

The ID-CEMD protocol consists of two protocols: the exchange protocol and the receipt recovery protocol.

### 3.1   The Exchange Protocol

In the exchange protocol, Alice and Bob attempt to exchange a message $M$ for its receipt, without any involvement of the TTP. The exchange protocol comprises steps (E1)-(E4), as shown in Table 1.

**Table 1.** The ID-CEMD Protocol

---

(E1): Alice → Bob : $h(M), E_{d_A}(h(M))$
(E2): Bob → Alice : $U, V'$
(E3): Alice → Bob : $M$
(E4): Bob → Alice : $V$

---

**(E1):** Alice first transfers to Bob the hash value $h(M)$ and her digital signature $E_{d_A}(h(M))$ on $M$. This signature is optional. If this option is selected, it will serve as a non-repudiable proof of origin of $M$.

**(E2):** Upon receipt of the two items, Bob verifies Alice's signature $E_{d_A}(h(M))$ with Alice's public key $Q_A = H_1(ID_A)$. If the verification is negative, Bob may either ask Alice to re-send message (E1) or terminate the protocol execution. Otherwise, Bob produces a *verifiable and recoverable encryption* of its receipt for message $M$, denoted as $(U, V')$. To do so, Bob performs as following:

– 1. First choose $r \in \mathbf{Z}_q$ at random and compute $U = rP \in \mathcal{G}_1$, and then let

$$H = H_2(ID_B, h(M), U) \in \mathcal{G}_1.$$

– 2. Compute $V' = d_B + rH + rPK \in \mathcal{G}_1$.

Now $\sigma' = \langle U, V' \rangle \in \mathcal{G}_1 \times \mathcal{G}_1$ is Bob's VRES on $M$ and is delivered to Alice.

**Remark:** Similar to that in [5, 15], the above VRES scheme can also be shown to be non-existential forgeable under adaptive chosen message attacks in the random oracle model, assuming the CDH problem in $\mathcal{G}_1$ is hard.

**(E3):** Upon receipt of this item, Alice performs the following verification to check the correctness of Bob's VRES $(U, V')$. First compute $Q_B = H_1(ID_B) \in \mathcal{G}_1$ and $H = H_2(ID_B, h(M), U) \in \mathcal{G}_1$, and then accept the VRES if

$$e(P, V') = e(P_{pub}, Q_B) \cdot e(U, H + PK), \tag{2}$$

and reject it otherwise. If this verification is negative, Alice may either ask Bob to re-send message (E2) or terminate the protocol execution. Otherwise, Alice transfers the message $M$ to Bob.

**(E4):** Upon receipt of $M$, Bob performs the following verification to ensure the correct message $M$ was received. Confirm that the message $M$ received generates the hash value identical to that received in step (E1), i.e. calculate the fresh hash value $h(M)''$ of the received message $M$ and compare it with the hash value $h(M)$ received from Alice in step (E1).

If the verification is negative, Bob may either ask Alice to re-send message (E3) or terminate the protocol execution. Otherwise, Bob computes $V = V' - rPK$ and transfers it to Alice.

Upon receipt of $V$, Alice uses it to check that

$$e(P, V) = e(P_{pub}, Q_B) \cdot e(U, H). \tag{3}$$

If this verification is positive, the certified e-mail delivery is completed successfully, i.e. Alice has obtained Bob's $receipt_B = (U, V)$ and Bob has obtained Alice's message $M$ together with its proof of origin $E_{d_A}(h(M))$.

## 3.2   The Receipt Recovery Protocol

In case when Alice fails to obtain Bob's correct $receipt_B$ after handing over $M$ to Bob, Alice may request TTP for the receipt recovery by invoking the recovery protocol.

**Table 2.** The Recovery Protocol

> (R1): Alice → TTP : $M, U, V'$
> (R2): TTP → Alice : $V$
> (R3): TTP → Bob : $M$

**(R1):** Alice transfers the items $M$ and $(U, V')$ to TTP, which performs the following verification. Compute $Q_B = H_1(ID) \in \mathcal{G}_1$ and $H = H_2(ID_B, h(M), U) \in \mathcal{G}_1$, and then check

$$e(P, V') = e(P_{pub}, Q_B) \cdot e(U, H + PK). \tag{4}$$

If the verification is negative, TTP rejects Alice's request. Otherwise, TTP uses his knowledge of the trapdoor $x$ to compute

$$V = V' - xU, \tag{5}$$

and returns $V$.

**(R2):** TTP sends $V$ to Alice, who checks that

$$e(P, V) = e(P_{pub}, Q_B) \cdot e(U, H).$$

**(R3):** TTP forwards $M$ to Bob.

Note that, the TTP's public key $PK$ is used for the generation and verification of a VRES, while the private-key $SK$ is sufficient for TTP to extract a SOK-IBS signature from a valid VRES in the recovery protocol. The TTP does not need to maintain an additional state, such as secret-public key pair, for each user via a special registration phase so as to resolve a dispute. What the TTP needs to store is only his own private-key $SK$.

## 3.3   Security and Efficiency Analysis

We shall show that the proposed protocol is secure against various attempts of cheating by either Alice or Bob.

For a malicious Bob, he attempts to cheat by generating a VRES $(U, V')$ on $h(M)$ in (E2), which will pass Alice's verification, but the corresponding $V$ cannot be recovered correctly by the designated TTP in (R2). After getting the message $M$ in (E3), Bob refuses to send $V$ to Alice, or just send a wrong $V$. However, this is always not the case. In fact, for any VRES $(U, V')$ satisfying

$$e(P, V') = e(P_{pub}, Q_B) \cdot e(U, H + PK),$$

and $V = V' - xU$, we have

$$
\begin{aligned}
e(P, V) &= e(P, V')e(P, -xU) \\
&= e(P, V')e(PK, U)^{-1} \\
&= e(P_{pub}, Q_B) \cdot e(U, H).
\end{aligned}
$$

Thus, for the $V$ extracted by TTP, the $(U, V)$ is definitely a valid SOK-IBS signature on $M$, and the signer Bob cannot deny it. Therefore, a malicious Bob cannot gain any advantage over Alice in our ID-CEMD protocol.

Alice may attempt to cheat by refusing to send $M$ or sending an incorrect $M'$ in step (E3). If Bob does not receive $M$ before a timeout or detects the incorrect message $M'$ through the verification in step (E3), Bob will consequently terminate the protocol. Note that it is computationally infeasible for Alice to compute $V$ from $(U, V')$ by himself, without the knowledge of $SK = x$. In fact, since $V' - V = xU = xrP$, to compute $V$ from $(U, V')$ is equivalent to solve the computational Diffie-Hellman problem for the instance of $(P, U = rP, PK = xP)$. This means that Alice will not receive Bob's receipt $receipt_B$, so Alice gains no benefit from this misbehavior.

Alice attempts to cheat by requesting TTP to recover Bob's receipt after step (E2) without sending $M$ to Bob in step (E3). One of the conditions for TTP to accept Alice's request is that Alice must provide message $M$ that can pass the verification in step (R1). If the verification is positive, TTP forwards Alice's message $M$ to Bob while passing $V$ to Alice. Thus, Alice cannot benefit from this misbehavior, as message $M$ will ultimately be delivered to Bob by TTP.

There is another attack we must take into consideration: colluding attack. That is, Alice may attempt to collude with another user, and try to have TTP recover $V$ from $(U, V')$. However, the signer's identity $ID$ is explicitly included in the signature as $H = H_2(ID_B, h(M), U)$, thus the colluding attacks proposed by Bao [4] will not work here.

Finally, we remark that our trust on TTP is minimal: it is only semi-trusted, which means that TTP cannot generate a valid receipt $(U, V)$ without getting the corresponding VRES $(U, V')$. From TTP's point of view, a VRES is actually equivalent to a receipt since he has the trapdoor of the permutation $V = V' - xU$.

Noting the underlying receipt $(U, V)$ is a SOK-IBS signature, which is non-existential forgeable under adaptive chosen-message attacks, a malicious TTP cannot generate a valid receipt $(U, V)$ by himself, without the corresponding VRES $(U, V')$. So, our protocol is also secure against a malicious TTP.

**Efficiency Analysis:** In [21], it is shown that their protocol requires less computation and communication overhead, and places less security and storage requirements on the TTP. It seems appropriate to compare our protocol with [21]. The following analysis shows that our protocol is more efficient and concise.

In Nenadic et al.'s CEMD protocol, it requires an initialization phase for a party and a TTP to agree on a shared secret, which is then used by the TTP for possible receipt recovery. In our protocol, there is no need for such a registration between a user and TTP. This feature will greatly reduce the communication overhead and managing cost. And the time-consuming computations arise from (2) and (3) for verifying a VRES and a signature respectively. The corresponding computational cost is the same to that of a SOK-IBS scheme, which is roughly two pairing operations, as the term $(P_{pub}, Q_B)$ can be pre-computed and stored before the exchange procedure.

In our ID-CEMD protocol, the end-users Alice and Bob need not to have their own certificates. Of course, as all the identity-based cryptosystems, the system parameters and the public key of TTP need to be certified by a certificate. Moreover, the designated TTP can be anyone different from the only PKG of an identity-based system. In fact, if we let PKG be the designated TTP, then we must have full trust in it since each user's private key is escrowed by PKG.

## 4    Conclusions

Certified e-mail delivery over Internet is an important e-commerce application that will proliferate in the coming years. This paper proposed a novel and efficient scheme enabling the *verifiable and recoverable encrypted signature* (VRES) for an identity-based signature scheme. Based upon the identity-based VRES, we presented an efficient identity-based fair protocol for certified e-mail delivery, which provides strong fairness to ensure that the recipient receives the e-mail if and only if the sender receives the receipt, and is more efficient in computation and communication. Moreover, there is no registration between a party and TTP, which makes our protocol much concise and easy to implementation.

## Acknowledgement

The work is supported by National Natural Science Foundation of China under Granted No.60373039, and National Grand Fundamental Research Project of China under Granted No.G1999035802.

# References

1. N. Asokan, V. Shoup and M. Waidner. Optimistic fair exchange of digital signatures. IEEE Journal on Selected Areas in Communications, 18(4): 593-610, 2000.
2. G. Ateniese. Verifiable encryption of digital signatures and applications, ACM Transactions on Information and System Security, 7, 1 (2004), 1-20.
3. G. Ateniese, C. Nita-Rotaru. Stateless-recipient certified E-mail system based on verifiable encryption. Proc. of 2002 RSA Conference-Topics in Cryptology, volume 2271 of Lecture Notes in Computer Science, pages 182-199, Springer-Verlag, 2002.
4. F. Bao, R. Deng and W. Mao. Efficient and practical fair exchange protocols with off-line TTP. Proc. IEEE Symposium on Security and Privacy, pages 77-85, 1998.
5. M. Bellare, C. Namprempre and G. Neven. Security Proofs for Identity-Based Identification and Signature Schemes, Proc. of Advances in Cryptology-Eurocrypt 2004, volume 3027 of Lecture Notes in Computer Science, pages 268-286, Springer-Verlag, 2004.
6. D. Boneh, B. Lynn, H. Shacham. Short signatures from the weil pairing. Proc. of Advances in Cryptology-ASIACRYPT 2001, volume 2248 of Lecture Notes in Computer Science, pages 514-532, Springer-Verlag, 2001.
7. D. Boneh and M. Franklin. Identity-based encryption from the Weil Pairing. Proc. of Advances in Cryptology-Crypto 2001, volume 2139 of Lecture Notes in Computer Science, pages 213-229, Springer-Verlag, 2001.
8. C. Boyd and E. Foo. Off-line fair payment protocols using convertible signatures. Proc. of Advances in Cryptology-ASIACRYPT 1998, volume 1514 of Lecture Notes in Computer Science, pages 271-285, Springer-Verlag, 1998.
9. J. Camenisch and M. Michels. Separability and efficiency for generic group signature schemes. Proc. of Advances in Cryptology-Crypto 1999, volume 1666 of Lecture Notes in Computer Science, pages 106-121, Springer-Verlag, 1999.
10. L. Chen. Efficient Fair Exchange with Verifiable Confirmation of Signatures. Proc. of Advances in Cryptology-ASIACRYPT 1998, volume 1514 of Lecture Notes in Computer Science, pages 286-299, Springer-Verlag, Berlin, Germany, 1998.
11. R. H. Deng, L. Gong, A. A. Lazar, and W. Wang. Practical Protocols for Certified Electronic Mail. J. of Network and System Management, 4(3): 279-297, 1996.
12. S. Even and Y. Yacobi. Relations among public key signature schemes. Technical Report 175, Computer Science Dept., Technion, Israel, 1980.
13. M. Franklin, M. Reiter. Fair exchange with a semi-trusted third party. Proc. ACM Conference on Computer and Communications Security, Zurich, Switzerland, pages 1-5, 1997.
14. J. A. Garay, M. Jakobsson, and P. MacKenzie. Abuse-free optimistic contract signing. Proc. of Advances in Cryptology-CRYPTO 1999, volume 1666 of Lecture Notes in Computer Science, pages 449-466, Springer-Verlag, Berlin, Germany, 1999.
15. B. Libert, J.-J. Quisquater. The Exact Security of an Identity Based Signature and its Applications, IACR Cryptology ePrint Archive, Report 2004/102, 2004.
16. The Pairing-Based Crypto Lounge. Web page maintained by Paulo Barreto: http://planeta.terra.com.br/informatica/paulobarreto/pblounge.html
17. B. Schneier and J. Riordan. A certified E-mail protocol. Proc. of 13th Computer Security Applications Conference, pages 347-352. ACM Press, 1998.
18. A. Shamir, Identity based cryptosystems and signature schemes, Proc. of Advances in Cryptology-Crypto 1984, volume 196 of Lecture Notes in Computer Science, Springer-Verlag, pages 47-53.

19. R. Sakai, K. Ohgishi, M. Kasahara. Cryptosystems based on pairing, In 2000 Sympoium on Cryptography and Information Security, Okinawa, Japan, 2000.
20. I. Ray and I. Ray. An optimistic fair exchange E-commerce protocol with automated dispute resolution, Proc. International Conference on E-Commerce and Web Technologies (EC-Web), volume 1875 of Lecture Notes in Computer Science, pages 84-93, Springer-Verlag, 2000.
21. A. Nenadic, N.Zhang and S.Barton. Fair certified E-mail delivery, Proc. ACM Symposium on Applied Computing (SAC 2004) - Computer Security Track, Nicosia, Cyprus, pages 391-396, 2004.
22. A. Nenadic, N. Zhang, S. Barton. FIDES-A middleware E-commerce security solution, Proc. of 3rd European Conference on Information Warfare and Security (ECIW 2004), London, UK, pages 295-304, 2004.
23. Z. F. Zhang, D. G. Feng, Efficient Fair Certified E-Mail Delivery Based on RSA, Proc. First International workshop on Information Assurance in Distributed Systems, ISPA Workshops 2005, volume 3759 of Lecture Notes in Computer Science, pages 368-377, Springer-Verlag, 2005.
24. S/MIME. *Secure Multipurpose Internet Mail Extensions*. Available at http://www.rsasecurity.com/standards/smime/.
25. The Internet Engineering Task Force (IETF). OpenPGP, *An Open Specification for Pretty Good Privacy*. Available at http://www.ietf.org/html.charters/openpgp-charter.html.

# Similar Keys of Multivariate Quadratic Public Key Cryptosystems

Yuh-Hua Hu[1], Lih-Chung Wang[2], Chun-Yen Chou[3], and Feipei Lai[4]

[1] Department of Computer Science and Information Engineering,
National Taiwan University, Taipei 106, Taiwan
d92015@csie.ntu.edu.tw
[2] Department of Applied Mathematics,
National Donghwa University,
Hualien 974, Taiwan
lcwang@mail.ndhu.edu.tw
[3] Department of Mathematical Education,
National Hualien University of Education,
Hualien 970, Taiwan
choucy@mail.nhlue.edu.tw
[4] Departments of Electrical Engineering & of Computer Science
and Information Engineering,
National Taiwan University, Taipei 106, Taiwan
flai@ntu.edu.tw

**Abstract.** Most multivariate schemes have potentially much higher performance than other public key cryptosystems [15] [4] [1] [2]. Wolf and Preneel [16] show multivariate quadratic public key schemes have many equivalent keys and provide some transformations to identify the keys. In this paper, we propose the idea of similar keys of MQ-based public key cryptosystems(PKCs) and provide a method to reduce the size of private key in MQ-based PKCs to $50\% \sim 70\%$ of its original size. And our method is generic for most MQ-based PKCs except for UOV-like and STS-like schemes. Moreover, our method remains the equivalent security and efficiency with original MQ-based PKCs.

**Keywords:** MQ, multivariate, public key cryptosystem, digital signature, similar key.

## 1 Introduction

Public key cryptography is involving the use of two separate keys, and the use of two keys has profound consequences in the areas of non-repudiation, confidentiality, and authentication. For example, on-line transactions need the digital signature schemes to verify the validness, the e-mail security application like PGP[18] needs the public key cryptosystem to protect the session key, and the heart of the authentication service X.509[18] is public key certificate. Finding a efficient, secure and easy to implement PKC is helpful to the network security

Y.G. Desmedt et al. (Eds.): CANS 2005, LNCS 3810, pp. 211–222, 2005.

application. Most MQ-based PKCs are faster than other PKCs in key genera-
tion/signing or decrypting/verifying or encrypting [15] [4] [1] [2]. Hence, they
may be applied in more occasions. However, the key size of MQ-based PKCs is
their drawback.

Number-theoretical PKCs have relatively small private key size, for example
RSA-1024 bits, ECC-163bits [7] [5]. MQ-based PKCs have a large size of private
key, such as C*[8], HFE[11], QUARTZ[12], SFLASH$^{v3}$[2], TRMS[15], TTS[1]
and UOV[6]. The reason is that most MQ-based PKCs need to store the affine
transformations, consisting of an invertible matrix and constant offset, and the
coefficients of polynomials in $\varphi_2$. The coefficients of the affine transformations
are the major parts of the private key.

Changing the affine transformation is an intuitive way to reduce the size of
private key. Wang et al. [15] used the extension field instead of the ground field
and Hu et al. [4] used the elementary row operations to reduce the size of private
key, and both of them speeded up the signing or decrypting time. Though there
is still no attack to these specific affine transformations, they did not prove that
the specific affine transformation has the same security with arbitrary invertible
matrix.

Wolf and Preneel[16] showed some systematic schemes to analyze the equivalent keys. And they provide the concept and the normal forms to reduce the
private key. In this paper we introduce the idea of similar keys of MQ-based
PKCs, and give a model for most MQ-based PKCs that can reduce the size of
the private key to $50\% \sim 70\%$ of original size except for UOV-like and STS-like
[17] schemes, and we sketch that the new model has the same security as the
original model.

In Section 2, we describe the model of MQ-based public key scheme. In Section 3, we define the similar key of MQ-based PKCs. In Section 4, we give our
model to reduce the keys and the performance. In Section 5, we discuss and
analyze our model. And our conclusion is in Section 6.

## 2    MQ-Based PKCs

For a typical MQ-based PKC, they operate on a base field $\mathbb{K}$. And its public key is
composed of three maps, $\varphi_3 \circ \varphi_2 \circ \varphi_1$, and its private key is the triple $(\varphi_1^{-1}, \varphi_2, \varphi_3^{-1})$.
$\varphi_1$ and $\varphi_3$ are affine transformations in $\mathbb{K}^n$ and $\mathbb{K}^m$ respectively and $\varphi_1^{-1}$ and
$\varphi_3^{-1}$ are their inverse transformations. The $\varphi_2$ is a quadratic transformation and
the structure of $\varphi_2$ in each MQ-based PKC is different (HFE, SFLASH$^{v3}$, C*,
QUARTZ, TTS, TRMS, UOV). We illustrate the idea of similar keys with TRMS.
The following example is revised in the workshop of PKC2005 [13].

### 2.1    Structure of TRMS

There are a variety of schemes of TRMS which are all based on tractable rational
maps. Tractable rational maps on $\mathbb{K}^n$ are invertible affine transformations or,
after a rearrangement of indices if necessary, functions of the following form
$\varphi : \mathbb{K}^n \to \mathbb{K}^n$,

$$
\begin{cases}
y_1 = r_1(x_1) \\
y_2 = r_2(x_2)\dfrac{p_2(x_1)}{q_2(x_1)} + \dfrac{f_2(x_1)}{g_2(x_1)} \\
\quad\vdots \\
y_k = r_k(x_k)\dfrac{p_k(x_1, x_2, \ldots, x_{k-1})}{q_k(x_1, x_2, \ldots, x_{k-1})} + \dfrac{f_k(x_1, x_2, \ldots, x_{k-1})}{g_k(x_1, x_2, \ldots, x_{k-1})} \\
\quad\vdots \\
y_n = r_n(x_n)\dfrac{p_n(x_1, x_2, \ldots, x_{n-1})}{q_n(x_1, x_2, \ldots, x_{n-1})} + \dfrac{f_n(x_1, x_2, \ldots, x_{n-1})}{g_n(x_1, x_2, \ldots, x_{n-1})}
\end{cases}
$$

where for $i = 2, 3, \ldots, n$, $p_i, q_i, f_i, g_i$ are polynomials, and for $i = 1, 2, \ldots, n$, $r_i$ is a permutation polynomial on $\mathbb{K}$. That is, $r_i$ is a polynomial function which is also a bijection from $\mathbb{K}$ onto itself.

Let $\mathbb{K} = GF(2^8)$. We will construct 3 maps $\varphi_1 : \mathbb{K}^{28} \to \mathbb{K}^{28}$, $\varphi_2 : \mathbb{K}^{28} \to \mathbb{K}^{20}$, $\varphi_3 : \mathbb{K}^{20} \to \mathbb{K}^{20}$ where $\varphi_1, \varphi_3$ are invertible affine transformations, $\varphi_2 = \pi \circ \widetilde{\varphi_2} \circ i$ with $\pi$ a projection, $i$ an imbedding, and $\widetilde{\varphi_2}$ identified as a tractable rational map over some extension field over $\mathbb{K}$.

**Public Key.** The public key is the result of the composition map $\varphi_3 \circ \varphi_2 \circ \varphi_1$.

**Private Key.** The private key is the triple $(\varphi_1^{-1}, \varphi_2, \varphi_3^{-1})$.

**Signing.** To sign a message $M$, first we compute its hash $\mathbf{z} = H(M) \in \mathbb{K}^{20}$ by a publicly agreed hash function. Then do $\mathbf{y} = \varphi_3^{-1}(\mathbf{z})$. Then choose 8 nonzero random numbers $r_1, r_2, \ldots, r_8$. Then get $\mathbf{x}$ by identifying it with $(\widetilde{\varphi_2}^{-1} \circ i)(r_1, r_2, \ldots, r_8, \mathbf{y})$ which is computed by a sequence of substitutions. Then get the signature $\mathbf{w} = \varphi_1^{-1}(\mathbf{x})$.

**Verifying.** To verify a signature $\mathbf{w}$, simply check if $V(\mathbf{w}) = (\varphi_3 \circ \varphi_2 \circ \varphi_1)(\mathbf{w}) = (\varphi_3 \circ \pi \circ \widetilde{\varphi_2} \circ i)(\mathbf{x}) = (\varphi_3 \circ \pi)(r_1, r_2, \ldots, r_8, \mathbf{y}) = \varphi_3(\mathbf{y}) = \mathbf{z} = H(M)$.

### 2.2  Details of $\varphi_1$ and $\varphi_3$

Let $\varphi_1, \varphi_3$ be invertible affine maps on $\mathbb{K}^{28}$ and $\mathbb{K}^{20}$ respectively such that $\varphi_1 = T_1 \circ L_1 \circ D_1 \circ U_1$ and $\varphi_3 = T_3 \circ L_3 \circ D_3 \circ U_3$ where

1. $T_1$ is a translation on $\mathbb{K}^{28}$ and $T_3$ is a translation on $\mathbb{K}^{20}$. $T_3$ is used to cancel the constant terms in the public key. Therefore $T_3$ is not chosen but determined.
2. In general, $L_1$ is a $28 \times 28$ lower triangular matrix over $\mathbb{K}$ and $L_3$ is a $20 \times 20$ lower triangular matrix over $\mathbb{K}$ such that both with diagonal entries equal to 1.
3. $D_1$ is a $28 \times 28$ diagonal matrix over $\mathbb{K}$ and $D_3$ is a $20 \times 20$ diagonal matrix over $\mathbb{K}$.
4. In general, $U_1$ is a $28 \times 28$ upper triangular matrix over $\mathbb{K}$ and $U_3$ is a $20 \times 20$ upper triangular matrix over $\mathbb{K}$ such that both with diagonal entries equal to 1.

The scheme in [15] is a special form of $\varphi_1$ and $\varphi_3$.

## 2.3   Details of $\varphi_2$

Let $\mathbb{L}, \mathbb{L}', \mathbb{L}''$ be the finite extension fields of $\mathbb{K}$ such that $\mathbb{K} \subset \mathbb{L}'' \subset \mathbb{L}' \subset \mathbb{L}$ and $[\mathbb{L}'' : \mathbb{K}] = 2$, $[\mathbb{L}' : \mathbb{L}''] = 3$, $[\mathbb{L} : \mathbb{L}'] = 3$. Therefore we can identify an element in $\mathbb{K}^2$ as an element in $\mathbb{L}' = GF(2^{16}) \subset \mathbb{L}' \subset \mathbb{L}$, an element in $\mathbb{K}^6$ as an element in $\mathbb{L}' = GF(2^{48}) \subset \mathbb{L}$, and an element in $\mathbb{K}^{18}$ as an element in $\mathbb{L} = GF(2^{144})$.

Decompose $(x_1, x_2, \ldots, x_{28}) \in \mathbb{K}^{28}$ into five groups: $X_1 = (x_1, x_2, \ldots, x_8)$, $X_2 = (x_9, x_{10}, x_{11}, x_{12}, x_{13}, x_{14})$, $X_3 = (x_{15}, x_{16})$, $X_4 = (x_{17}, x_{18}, x_{19})$ and $X_5 = (x_{20}, x_{21}, \ldots, x_{28})$. Identify $X_1$ with $(0, \ldots, 0, x_1, x_2, \ldots, x_8) \in \mathbb{L}$. Identify $X_2 \in \mathbb{K}^6$ as an element in $\mathbb{L}' \subset \mathbb{L}$. Identify $X_3 \in \mathbb{K}^2$ as an element in $\mathbb{L}'' \subset \mathbb{L}' \subset \mathbb{L}$ and $X_4 \in \mathbb{K}^3$ with $(0, x_{17}, 0, x_{18}, 0, x_{19}) \in \mathbb{L}'' \subset \mathbb{L}$. Identify $X_5 \in \mathbb{K}^9$ with $(0, x_{20}, 0, x_{21}, \ldots, 0, x_{28})$ as an element in $\mathbb{L}$. Hence we have a natural imbedding $i : \mathbb{K}^{28} \hookrightarrow \mathbb{L}^5$ by $i(x_1, x_2, \ldots, x_{28}) = (X_1, X_2, X_3, X_4, X_5)$. Similarly, decompose $(y_9, y_{10}, \ldots, y_{32}) \in \mathbb{K}^{20}$ into four groups: $Y_2 = (y_9, y_{10}, y_{11}, y_{12}, y_{13}, y_{14})$, $Y_3 = (y_{15}, y_{16})$, $Y_4 = (y_{17}, y_{18}, y_{19})$ and $Y_5 = (y_{20}, y_{21}, \ldots, y_{28})$ and identify them as elements in $\mathbb{L}$. For any $r_i \in \mathbb{K}$, $i = 1, 2, \ldots, 8$, identify $R_1 = (r_1, r_2, \ldots, r_8) \in \mathbb{K}^8$ with $(0, \ldots, 0, r_1, r_2, \ldots, r_8) \in \mathbb{L}$. Then we also have

$$i(r_1, r_2, \ldots, r_8, y_9, y_{10}, \ldots, y_{28}) = (R_1, Y_2, Y_3, Y_4, Y_5) \in \mathbb{L}^5.$$

Furthermore, since $\mathbb{K}^{20}$ is a subspace of $\mathbb{L}^5 = \mathbb{K}^{90}$, we have the projection $\pi : \mathbb{L}^5 \to \mathbb{K}^{20}$ such that $(\pi \circ i)(r_1, r_2, \ldots, r_8, y_9, y_{10}, \ldots, y_{28}) = (y_9, y_{10}, \ldots, y_{28})$

Let $\widetilde{\varphi_2} : \mathbb{L}^5 \to \mathbb{L}^5$ be a tractable rational map of the following form.

$$\begin{cases} R_1 = X_1 \\ Y_2 = X_2\, p_2(X_1) + f_2(X_1) \\ Y_3 = r_3(X_3) + f_3(X_1, X_2) \\ Y_4 = X_4\, p_4(X_1, X_2, X_3) + f_4(X_1, X_2, X_3) \\ Y_5 = X_5\, p_5(X_1, X_2, X_3, X_4) + f_5(X_1, X_2, X_3, X_4) \end{cases}$$

such that $\varphi_2 = \pi \circ \widetilde{\varphi_2} \circ i$, and we have the following in $\varphi_2$:

1. $R_1 = X_1$ induces $(r_1, r_2, \ldots, r_8) = (x_1, x_2, \ldots, x_8)$.
2. $Y_2 = X_2\, p_2(X_1) + f_2(X_1)$ induces

$$\begin{pmatrix} y_9 \\ y_{10} \\ \vdots \\ y_{14} \end{pmatrix} = \begin{pmatrix} x_9 \\ x_{10} \\ \vdots \\ x_{14} \end{pmatrix} *_6 \begin{pmatrix} x_1 \\ x_2 \\ \vdots \\ x_6 \end{pmatrix} + \begin{pmatrix} c_1 x_1 x_2 \\ c_2 x_2 x_3 \\ \vdots \\ c_6 x_6 x_7 \end{pmatrix} + \begin{pmatrix} c_7 x_3 \\ c_8 x_4 \\ \vdots \\ c_{12} x_8 \end{pmatrix}$$

where $c_i$'s are constant parameters of user's choice and $\mathbf{u} *_n \mathbf{v}$ denotes first identifying $\mathbf{u}, \mathbf{v} \in \mathbb{K}^n$ in the extension field with degree $n$ then carrying out the multiplication there. For details see Appendix.

3. $Y_3 = r_3(X_3) + f_3(X_1, X_2)$ induces

$$\begin{pmatrix} y_{15} \\ y_{16} \end{pmatrix} = \begin{pmatrix} x_{15} \\ x_{16} \end{pmatrix}^2 + \begin{pmatrix} c_{13}x_1 x_2 + c_{14}x_3 x_4 + \cdots + c_{19}x_{13}x_{14} \\ c_{20}x_{14}x_1 + c_{21}x_2 x_3 + \cdots + c_{26}x_{12}x_{13} \end{pmatrix} + \begin{pmatrix} c_{27}x_1 \\ c_{28}x_2 \end{pmatrix}$$

where $\left(\dfrac{x_{15}}{x_{16}}\right)^2 = \left(\dfrac{x_{15}}{x_{16}}\right) *_2 \left(\dfrac{x_{15}}{x_{16}}\right)$ and $c_i$'s are constant parameters of user's choice.

4. $Y_4 = X_4\, p_4(X_1, X_2, X_3) + f_4(X_1, X_2, X_3)$ induces

$$\begin{pmatrix} y_{17} \\ y_{18} \\ y_{19} \end{pmatrix} = \begin{pmatrix} x_{17} \\ x_{18} \\ x_{19} \end{pmatrix} *_3 \begin{pmatrix} x_8 \\ x_9 + x_{11} + x_{12} \\ x_{13} + x_{15} + x_{16} \end{pmatrix} + \begin{pmatrix} c_{29}x_4 x_{16} \\ c_{30}x_5 x_{10} \\ c_{31}x_{15}x_{16} \end{pmatrix} + \begin{pmatrix} c_{32}x_9 \\ c_{33}x_{10} \\ c_{34}x_{11} \end{pmatrix}$$

where $c_i$'s are constant parameters of user's choice.

5. $Y_5 = X_5\, p_5(X_1, X_2, X_3, X_4) + f_5(X_1, X_2, X_3, X_4)$ induces

$$\begin{pmatrix} y_{20} \\ y_{21} \\ \vdots \\ y_{28} \end{pmatrix} = \left( \begin{pmatrix} x_{19} \\ x_{18} \\ x_{17} \\ x_{10} \\ x_9 \\ x_8 \\ x_1 \\ x_{19} \\ x_{18} \end{pmatrix} \begin{pmatrix} x_{16} \\ x_{15} \\ x_{14} \\ x_7 \\ x_6 \\ x_5 \\ x_{17} \\ x_{16} \\ x_{15} \end{pmatrix} \begin{pmatrix} x_{13} \\ x_{12} \\ x_{11} \\ x_4 \\ x_3 \\ x_2 \\ x_{14} \\ x_{13} \\ x_{12} \end{pmatrix} \right) *_3 \begin{pmatrix} x_{20} \\ x_{21} \\ x_{22} \\ x_{23} \\ x_{24} \\ x_{25} \\ x_{26} \\ x_{27} \\ x_{28} \end{pmatrix} + \begin{pmatrix} c_{35}x_{18}x_{19} \\ c_{36}x_{17}x_{13} \\ c_{37}x_{16}x_{14} \\ c_{38}x_{12}x_{13} \\ c_{39}x_{15}x_{14} \\ c_{40}x_{19}x_{12} \\ c_{41}x_{18}x_{10} \\ c_{42}x_{12}x_6 \\ c_{43}x_{13}x_5 \end{pmatrix} + \begin{pmatrix} c_{44}x_1 \\ c_{45}x_2 \\ \vdots \\ c_{52}x_9 \end{pmatrix}$$

where $c_i$'s are constant parameters of user's choice.

The reason why the formulas in the above assignments represents a permutation polynomial $r_3$ and polynomials $p_2, f_2, f_3, p_4, f_4, p_5, f_5$ is as follows.

1. We identify $X_3 = (x_{15}, x_{16})$ as an element in $\mathbb{L}'' = GF(2^{16})$ which is of characteristic 2. For any finite field of characteristic 2, $X \mapsto X^2$ is an automorphism. Hence let $r_3(X) = X^2$, then $r_3$ is an automorphism on $\mathbb{L}''$, hence a permutation polynomial. And $\left(\dfrac{x_{15}}{x_{16}}\right) \mapsto \left(\dfrac{x_{15}}{x_{16}}\right)^2$ surely represents $r_3$.

2. For polynomials $p_2, f_2, f_3, p_4, f_4, p_5, f_5$, simply notice that on a finite field, any map is a polynomial map. See [14] for details. For example, we show the case of $p_2$ for illustration. Consider a map $\mathcal{P}$ on $\mathbb{L}$ as follows

$$\mathcal{P}(X_1) = \begin{cases} \begin{pmatrix} 0 \\ \vdots \\ 0 \\ 0 \\ 0 \\ x_1 \\ x_2 \\ x_3 \\ x_4 \\ x_5 \\ x_6 \end{pmatrix} & \text{if } X_1 = \begin{pmatrix} 0 \\ \vdots \\ 0 \\ x_1 \\ x_2 \\ x_3 \\ x_4 \\ x_5 \\ x_6 \\ x_7 \\ x_8 \end{pmatrix}, \\[2em] \overrightarrow{0} & \text{otherwise.} \end{cases}$$

Simply let $p_2$ be the polynomial representation for $\mathcal{P}$.

## 2.4   The Key Size of TRMS

As shown above, $\varphi_1 = T_1 \circ L_1 \circ D_1 \circ U_1$, $\varphi_3 = T_3 \circ L_3 \circ D_3 \circ U_3$, and there are 52 parameters $c_1, c_2, \ldots, c_{52}$ for the private key user to choose in $\varphi_2$. Therefore the size for private key is $[28 + (0 + 1 + \cdots + 27) + 28 + (27 + 26 + \cdots + 0)] + [20 + (0 + 1 + \cdots + 19) + 20 + (19 + 18 + \cdots + 0)] + 52 = 1284$ Bytes.

Also, since the public key is 20 general quadratic polynomials in 28 variables without constant terms, its size is $20 \cdot (\dfrac{28 \cdot 29}{2} + 28) = 8680$ bytes. In general, there are two ways to generate the public keys.

# 3   Similar Keys

First, we define the term "Similar Keys" and discuss two transformations of TRMS for similar keys.

**Definition 1.** *Two public keys of MQ-based PKCs are similar if they are identical after a bijective linear transformation by the public key information in polynomial time. Here the polynomial time should be less than the time to attack the original MQ-based PKC.*

We define some terms for discussing later. Let two public keys of TRMS be $V_P = (\varphi_{P3} \circ \varphi_{P2} \circ \varphi_{P1}) = (p_1, p_2, \cdots, p_m)$ and $V_Q = (\varphi_{Q3} \circ \varphi_{Q2} \circ \varphi_{Q1}) = (q_1, q_2, \cdots, q_m)$ ,where $\varphi_{P3}$ and $\varphi_{Q3}$ are invertible affine transformations over $\mathbb{K}^m$, $\varphi_{P1}$ and $\varphi_{Q1}$ are invertible affine transformations over $\mathbb{K}^n$, $\varphi_{P2}$ and $\varphi_{Q2}$ are projections $\mathbb{K}^n \to \mathbb{K}^m$, and $p_1, p_2, \cdots, p_m, q_1, q_2, \cdots, q_m$ are quadratic polynomials in $n$ variables without constant terms.

## 3.1   Invertible Linear Transformation of $\varphi_3$

If $q_1, q_2, \cdots, q_m$ could be expressed as linear combinations of $V_P$. And $p_1, p_2, \cdots, p_m$ could be expressed as linear combinations of $V_Q$. Then $V_P$ and $V_Q$ are similar. More precisely, $V_P = L \circ V_Q$ and $L$ is an invertible linear transformation.

**Lemma 2.** *If $\varphi_{P1} = \varphi_{Q1}$ and $\varphi_{P2} = \varphi_{Q2}$. Then $V_P$ and $V_Q$ are similar keys.*

*Proof.* $V_P = \varphi_{P3} \circ \varphi_{P2} \circ \varphi_{P1}$ and $V_Q = \varphi_{Q3} \circ \varphi_{Q2} \circ \varphi_{Q1}$. Since $\varphi_{P3}$ and $\varphi_{Q3}$ are invertible transformations, there exists $\varphi_{P3}^{-1}$, the inverse of $\varphi_{P3}$, and $\varphi_{Q3}^{-1}$, the inverse of $\varphi_{Q3}$. Hence $\varphi_{P3}^{-1} \circ \varphi_{P3} = \varphi_{Q3}^{-1} \circ \varphi_{Q3} = I_m$.

$$\begin{aligned}
\varphi_{P3} &= \varphi_{P3} \circ I_m \\
&= \varphi_{P3} \circ \varphi_{P3}^{-1} \circ \varphi_{P3} \\
&= \varphi_{P3} \circ \varphi_{Q3}^{-1} \circ \varphi_{Q3} \\
V_P &= \varphi_{P3} \circ \varphi_{P2} \circ \varphi_{P1} \\
&= \varphi_{P3} \circ \varphi_{P3}^{-1} \circ \varphi_{P3} \circ \varphi_{P2} \circ \varphi_{P1} \\
&= \varphi_{P3} \circ \varphi_{Q3}^{-1} \circ \varphi_{Q3} \circ \varphi_{Q2} \circ \varphi_{Q1} \\
&= \varphi_{P3} \circ \varphi_{Q3}^{-1} \circ V_Q
\end{aligned}$$

Then we get the equations $V_P = L \circ V_Q$, where $L = \varphi_{P3} \circ \varphi_{Q3}^{-1}$ is an invertible linear transformation.

Since $p_i$ is a linear combination of $V_Q$, then we get the equation $l_{i,1}q_1 + l_{i,2}q_2 + \cdots + l_{i,m}q_m + p_i = 0$, for $i \in (1, 2, \cdots, m)$ and $l_{i,j}$ is the element of $L$ in $i$-row and $j$-column. It is easy to solve $(l_{i,1}, l_{i,2}, \cdots, l_{i,m})$. We could get L by solving $\frac{n \cdot (n+3)}{2}$ equation in (m+1) variables in time complexity $O(m^2 n^2)$.

### 3.2  Substitution of $\varphi_1$

Let $R$ be a random permutation of $X$, $X = (x_1, x_2, \cdots, x_n)$. If $p_1(X) = q_1(R(X))$, $p_2(X) = q_2(R(X)), \cdots, p_m(X) = q_m(R(X))$. Then $V_P$ and $V_Q$ are similar.

**Lemma 3.** *If $\varphi_{P2} = \varphi_{Q2}$, $\varphi_{P3} = \varphi_{Q3}$ and $\varphi_{P1} = \varphi_{Q1} \circ A$, where $A$ is a permutation matrix. Then $V_P$ and $V_Q$ are similar keys.*

*Proof.* As our definition,

$$V_P = \varphi_{P3} \circ \varphi_{P2} \circ \varphi_{P1} = \varphi_{Q3} \circ \varphi_{Q2} \circ \varphi_{Q1} \circ A = V_Q \circ A.$$

If $A$ could be computed by $V_P$ and $V_Q$, then $V_P$ and $V_Q$ are similar. Let

$$X_{i,v} = (x_1, x_2, \cdots, x_n) \text{ ,where } x_j = v \text{ if } j = i, \text{ and } x_j = 0 \text{ if } j \neq i.$$

For example $X_{1,1} = (1, 0, 0, \cdots, 0), X_{2,3} = (0, 3, 0, \cdots, 0)$. Then we evaluate $V_P(X_{1,1}), V_P(X_{2,1}), \cdots, V_P(X_{n,1})$ and $V_Q(X_{1,1}), V_Q(X_{2,1}), \cdots, V_Q(X_{n,1})$. Since $V_P = V_Q \circ A$ and $A$ is a permutation matrix, we have $V_P(X_{i,1}) = V_Q(A(X_{i,1})) = V_Q(X_{j,1})$, where $j \in (1, 2, \cdots, n)$.

If the values of $V_P(X_{i,1})$ are all different, we could find the mapping of $A(X_{i,1}) = X_{j,1}$ for all $i \in (1, 2, \cdots, n)$.

If $V_P(X_{i,1})$ and $V_P(X_{j,1})$ are equivalent, we evaluate $V_P(X_{i,2}), V_P(X_{j,2})$ and $V_Q(X_{i,2}), V_Q(X_{j,2})$ to find the mapping of $A(X_{i,2}) = X_{k,2}$. If $V_P(X_{i,2})$ and $V_P(X_{j,2})$ are still equivalent, we change $X_{i,2}$ to $X_{i,3}$ and continue to get the permutation matrix $A$.

The probability of $V_P(X_{i,v}) = V_P(X_{j,v})$ is $\frac{1}{|K|^{m-n}} = \frac{1}{256^{(28-20)}} = 2^{-64}$. The probability of $V_P(X_{i,1}) = V_P(X_{j,1})$ and $V_P(X_{i,2}) = V_P(X_{j,2})$ is $2^{-128}$. It is so small that we could ignore this happens. So $A$ could be computed in the time complexity $O(m)$.

## 4  Our Scheme and Performance

We use Lemma 2 to transform the model of TRMS or other MQ-based PKCs. If we fix $\varphi_2$ and $\varphi_1$, we will get the similar key no matter $\varphi_3$ we choose. But we still need $\varphi_3$ to mask the equations of $\varphi_2 \circ \varphi_1$.

### 4.1  Our Scheme

When we generate the key pair of TRMS as Section 2, we add a new affine transformation $\varphi_4$ such that $V_P' = \varphi_{P4} \circ \varphi_{P3} \circ \varphi_{P2} \circ \varphi_{P1} = (p_1', p_2', \cdots, p_m')$ has a

$$p'_i(X) = a_{11}x_1^2 + a_{12}x_1x_2 + \cdots + a_{1i}x_1x_i + \cdots + a_{1n}x_1x_n$$
$$+ \quad a_{22}x_2^2 \quad + \cdots + a_{2i}x_2x_i + \cdots + a_{2n}x_2x_n$$
$$\vdots$$
$$+ \; a_{nn}p_np_n$$
$$+ \; 0x_1 + \quad 0x_2 \quad + \cdots + \quad x_i \quad + \cdots + \quad 0x_n$$

**Fig. 1.** One example of our new model

special form like Fig.1. If the coefficient of $x_i$ in $p'_i$ is zero, we generate $\varphi_1$ again. There are many choices of the above form of $p'_i$. We just give one example to illustrate.

From Lemma 2, any choice of $\varphi_3$ has the unique $\varphi_4$ to form the specific polynomial set. And $\varphi_4 \circ \varphi_3$ is also an affine transformation. The new model is still one of TRMS (or the original MQ-based PKC). Actually we do not have to generate and save $\varphi_3$ and $\varphi_4$, as $\varphi_4 \circ \varphi_3$ is unique. We generate $\varphi_2 \circ \varphi_1$ first, and then use the Gaussian elimination to find the polynomials in Fig.1.

**Public Key.** The public key is the polynomials of $V'_P$, and some terms in public key are always zero so that we do not need to store these values and to compute when encrypting or verifying.

**Private Key.** The private key for the new model of TRMS is only $\varphi_2$ and $\varphi_1^{-1}$.

**Signing and Verifying.** When signing and verifying, we do the same steps of [15], except that when signing, we first read the private key and find $\varphi_4 \circ \varphi_3$. This overhead is the key expansion. This overhead is first introduced in MQ-based PKCs, but it is quite general in symmetric key cryptosystems, like AES, DES. The signing time of the new model equals the original model, and for some zero monomials, the verifying time should be a little faster than the original model.

### 4.2   Performance

**Key Size.** The key size of private key in our model is only $50\% \sim 70\%$ of the one in the original model. We apply our model to other MQ-based PKCs. The result is in Table 1.

**Table 1.** Private key reduction ratio of MQ-based PKCs

| Scheme Name | Original model (Bytes) | Our model (Bytes) | Reduction ratio |
|---|---|---|---|
| TRMS(20,28)[1] | 396 | 276 | 69.7% |
| TRMS(20,28)[2] | 1284 | 864 | 67.3% |
| TTS(20,28) | 1399 | 979 | 70.0% |
| SFLASH$^{v2}$ | 2450 | 1225 | 50.0% |
| SQARTZ | 3914 | 2575 | 65.8% |

[1] computed with the detail in [15]
[2] computed with the detail in Section 2

**Execution Time.** We wrote code to test the execution time of our model and the original model of TRMS in [15]. The result is in Table 2. The environment is that CPU: P4 2.4GHz, RAM: 1024MB, OS: Linux + gcc 3.3, and parameters: gcc -O3 -march=pentium4 -fomit-frame-pointer.

**Table 2.** Execution time of our model and the original model of TRMS

| Operation | Original model | Our model |
|---|---|---|
| Generating Key (ms) | 1.3 | 0.9 |
| Setting Key (ms) | x | 0.1 |
| Signing (ns) | 7 | 7 |
| Verifying (ns) | 20 | 20 |

## 5   Discussion

### 5.1   Remark on Security

As we mentioned in Section 4, the public key of our new scheme is $\varphi_{P4} \circ \varphi_{P3} \circ \varphi_{P2} \circ \varphi_{P1}$ and $\varphi_{P3} \circ \varphi_{P2} \circ \varphi_{P1}$ is the original model. $\varphi_4$ is the unique transformation that is computable by the information of $\varphi_{P3} \circ \varphi_{P2} \circ \varphi_{P1}$. Here we motivate that the security of the new model and the original model are equivalent.

We assume that there is a method $A$ that can make a fake signature of our new model of TRMS (or other MQ-based signature). Hence we can get a fake signature of the original model.

Since $\varphi_4$ can be computed from $\varphi_{P3} \circ \varphi_{P2} \circ \varphi_{P1}$ in time complexity $O(m^2 n^2)$ and $A$ could make a fake signature with $\varphi_{P4} \circ \varphi_{P3} \circ \varphi_{P2} \circ \varphi_{P1}$, for any $H \in \mathbb{K}^m$. Then we get a signature $S$, that satisfies $H = \varphi_{P4} \circ \varphi_{P3} \circ \varphi_{P2} \circ \varphi_{P1}(S)$.

If we want to make a fake signature with $\varphi_{P3} \circ \varphi_{P2} \circ \varphi_{P1}$, we get the hash value $H_{original}$ first. Then we evaluate the $\varphi_4(H_{original})$. Then we apply $A$ to compute $S_{original}$ such that $\varphi_4(H_{original}) = \varphi_{P4} \circ \varphi_{P3} \circ \varphi_{P2} \circ \varphi_{P1}(S_{original})$. And $\varphi_{P4}$ is an invertible affine transformation. Then we get $S_{original}$ is the signature of $H_{original}$.

$$
\begin{aligned}
H_{original} &= \varphi_{P4}^{-1} \circ \varphi_{P4}(H_{original}) \\
&= \varphi_{P4}^{-1} \circ \varphi_{P4} \circ \varphi_{P3} \circ \varphi_{P2} \circ \varphi_{P1}(S_{original}) \\
&= \varphi_{P3} \circ \varphi_{P2} \circ \varphi_{P1}(S_{original}).
\end{aligned}
$$

The other direction is easy to understand as the new model of TRMS is one of the original model. If a method $A'$ can attack the original model, hence $A'$ can attack the new model.

### 5.2   Key Generation

The key generation time is faster than the original model is reasonable. The difference between these models is $\varphi_3$. The original model needs to generate $\varphi_3$ and the inverse of $\varphi_3$. $\varphi_3$ needs a lot of random numbers and the inverse of $\varphi_3$ needs the Gaussian elimination. Though our model needs $\varphi_3$ and $\varphi_4$, $\varphi_4 \circ \varphi_3$

is from the Gaussian elimination of $\varphi_2 \circ \varphi_1$. The Gaussian elimination takes additive and multiplicative operations in the finite field. These operations take less time than the random number generations.

### 5.3    Polynomial Forms

In our experiment, the probability to generate key successfully is $\frac{1000}{1094\sim1108} \approx 0.9$. Some reviewer surprised at this result. As $\varphi_1$, $\varphi_3$, $\varphi_4$ are all invertible, it must be possible to map the linear terms to the identity matrix. The reason is $\varphi_2$ is quadratic. Then the linear terms in public key are not only from the linear terms in $\varphi_2$ and $\varphi_1$ but also the quadratic terms in $\varphi_2$ and the linear terms and constant terms in $\varphi_1$.

Some reviewer suggests to restrict both $\varphi_1$ and $\varphi_3$ to linear transformations and then we always generate key successfully. This is an interesting idea for HFE-like or UOV-like schemes. However, it is not applicable to the current version of TRMS as there are only 11 linear terms in $\varphi_2$.

$$
\begin{bmatrix} p_1(X) \\ p_2(X) \\ \vdots \\ p_m(X) \end{bmatrix} = \begin{bmatrix} a_{111} & \cdots & a_{11n} & a_{122} & \cdots & a_{12n} & \cdots & a_{1nn} & b_{11} & \cdots & b_{1n} \\ a_{211} & \cdots & a_{21n} & a_{222} & \cdots & a_{22n} & \cdots & a_{2nn} & b_{21} & \cdots & b_{2n} \\ \vdots & \vdots & \vdots & \vdots & \vdots & \vdots & \vdots & \vdots & \vdots & \vdots & \vdots \\ a_{m11} & \cdots & a_{m1n} & a_{m22} & \cdots & a_{m2n} & \cdots & a_{mnn} & b_{m1} & \cdots & b_{mn} \end{bmatrix} \begin{bmatrix} x_1^2 \\ \vdots \\ x_1 x_n \\ x_2^2 \\ \vdots \\ x_2 x_n \\ \vdots \\ p_n p_n \\ x_1 \\ \vdots \\ x_n \end{bmatrix}
$$

**Fig. 2.** The matrix form of the public key

The polynomial form in Fig.1 is an example. In order to always generate key successfully, we can change the polynomial form. If $(p_1, p_2, \cdots, p_m)$ is the public key. The public key can be represented in the matrix form like Fig.2. We perform elementary row operations to find the rank of the coefficient matrix and make the first non-zero term in each row to 1. The final coefficient matrix is the new public key. As the polynomial form in Fig.1, the new public key is unique if the original public key is similar. When saving the public key, we first save the index of the first non-zero term in each row and then save the subsequent terms.

## 6    Conclusion

Wolf and Preneel [16] showed multivariate quadratic public key schemes have many equivalent keys. In this paper, we introduce the idea of similar keys of

MQ-based PKCs and utilize the idea for the new model of some MQ-based PKCs. And this new model could reduce the size of private key to 50% ∼ 70%. Moreover, our model remains the equivalent security and has a little advantage of public key in size and verifying time.

We introduce two transformations to find the similar key in affine transformation, and we only apply Lemma 2 to reduce the size of the private key. The methods to compute the number of the similar keys of the MQ-based PKCs are not only these two transformations we provide. We will survey the others in the future. And there may be other methods to reduce the key size with Lemma 3 or new transformations.

In this paper, we concentrate on the two affine transformations for similar keys. There is another way to find the similar keys of a particular MQ-based PKC, like HFE, TTS. That is to utilize the kernel information, $\varphi_2$, to find the similar keys and reduce the private key space.

Finally, our new model is general since most MQ-based PKCs are composed of $(\varphi_1,\varphi_2,\varphi_3)$. There are two kinds of exceptions, STS schemes and UOV-like schemes. STS schemes have a little reduction than others as there are many coefficients in $\varphi_2$. UOV-like schemes are composed of $(\varphi_1,\varphi_2)$. But all still could enjoy the advantage of the size of public key and encrypting time/verifying time.

## Acknowledgements

The authors would like to thank Dr. Christopher Wolf and Dr. Bart Preneel for the fruitful discussions.

## References

1. Jiun-Ming Chen and Bo-Yin Yang, *A More Secure and Efficacious TTS Scheme*, ICISC 2003, LNCS v. 2971, pp. 320-338, full version at http://eprint.iacr.org/2003/160.
2. N. Courtois, L. Goubin, and J. Patarin, *SFLASH$^{v3}$, a Fast Asymmetric Signature Scheme*, eprint 2003/211, available at http://eprint.iacr.org/2003/211.
3. M. Garey and D. Johnson, *Computers and Intractability, A Guide to the Theory of NP-completeness*, 1979, p. 251.
4. Yuh-Hua Hu, Lih-Chung Wang, Jiun-Ming Chen, Feipei Lai, and Chun-Yen Chou, *An implementation of public key cryptosystem TTM with linear time complexity for decryption*, Proceedings. IEEE International Symposium on Information Theory 2003, pp. 17.
5. Neal Koblitz, *Elliptic curve cryptosystems*, Mathematics of Computation 48 (1987), pp.203-209.
6. A. Kipnis, J. Patarin, and L. Goubin, *Unbalanced Oil and Vinegar Sigature Schemes*, CRYPTO 1999, LNCS v. 1592, pp. 206-222.
7. V.S. Miller, *Use of elliptic curves in cryptography*, CRYPTO 1985, LNCS v. 218, pp. 417-426.
8. Tsutomu Matsumoto and Hideki Imai, *Public Quadratic Polynomial-Tuples for Efficient Signature-Verification and Message-Encryption*, EUROCRYPT 1988, LNCS v. 330, pp. 419-453.

9. *New European Schemes for Signatures, Integrity, and Encryption*, project homepage at http://www.cryptonessie.org.
10. *Performance of Optimized Implementations of the NESSIE primitives, version 2.0* http://www.cryptonessie.org.
11. J. Patarin, *Hidden Fields Equations (HFE) and Isomorphisms of Polynomials (IP) Two New Families of Asymmetric Algorithms*, EUROCRYPT 1996, LNCS v. 1070, pp. 33-48.
12. J. Patarin, N. Courtois, and L. Goubin, *QUARTZ, 128-Bit Long Digital Signatures*, CT-RSA 2001, LNCS v. 2020, pp. 282-297. Updated version available at http://www.cryptonessie.org.
13. http://www.am.ndhu.edu.tw/ lcwang/lcwang.htm.
14. Lih-Chung Wang and Fei-Hwang Chang, *Tractable Rational Map Cryptosystem*, eprint 2004/046, available at http://eprint.iacr.org/2004/046.
15. Lih-Chung Wang, Yuh-Hua Hu, Bo-Yin Yang, Feipei Lai, Chun-Yen Chou and Bo-Yin Yang, *Tractable Rational Map Signature*, PKC 2005, LNCS v. 3386 pp. 244-257.
16. Christopher Wolf and Bart Preneel, *Large Superfluous Keys in Multivariate Quadratic Asymmetric Systems*, PKC 2005, LNCS v. 3386 pp. 275-287.
17. Christopher Wolf and Bart Preneel, *Taxonomy of Public Key Schemes based on the problem of Multivariate Quadratic equations*, eprint 2005/077, available at http://eprint.iacr.org/2005/077.
18. William Stallings, *CRYPTOGRAPHY AND NEWWORK SECURITY Principles and Practice*, Second Edition, pp. 356.
19. Bo-Yin Yang, Jiun-Ming Chen, and Yen-Hung Chen, *TTS: High-Speed Signatures on a Low-End Smart Card*, CHES 2004, LNCS v. 3156, pp. 371-385.

# A Note on Signed Binary Window Algorithm for Elliptic Curve Cryptosystems

Fanyu Kong and Daxing Li

Institute of Network Security, Shandong University, Shanda Nanlu Road,
Jinan 250100, Shandong, R.P. China
phd_kong@yahoo.com, lidaxing@vip.sina.com

**Abstract.** The window algorithms for various signed binary representations have been used to speed up point multiplication on elliptic curves. While there's been extensive research on the non-adjacent form, little attention has been devoted to non-sparse optimal signed binary representations. In the paper, we prove some properties of non-sparse optimal signed binary representations and present a precise analysis of the non-sparse signed window algorithm. The main contributions are described as follows. Firstly, we attain the lower bound $k+1/3$ of the expected length of non-sparse optimal signed binary representations of $k$-bit positive integers. Secondly, we propose a new non-sparse signed window partitioning algorithm. Finally, we analyze Koyama-Tsuruoka's non-sparse signed window algorithm and the proposed algorithm and compare them with other methods. The upper bound $\frac{5}{6} \cdot 2^{w-1} - 1 + \frac{(-1)^w}{3}$ of the number of precomputed windows of the non-sparse signed window algorithms is attained.

**Keywords:** elliptic curve cryptosystems, point multiplication, signed window algorithm, signed-digit number representations.

## 1 Introduction

Elliptic Curve Cryptosystems, as introduced by Koblitz [1] and Miller [2], are based on the intractability of the discrete logarithm problem on elliptic curves. The fundamental operation on elliptic curves is point multiplication, which is an analogous operation as exponentiations on multiplicative groups. Hence, the binary algorithm, the $m$-ary algorithm and the sliding window algorithm [3–7] for exponentiations can be applied to point multiplication on elliptic curves.

Fortunately, a significant property of elliptic curve cryptosystems is that the inverse of a point can be computed essentially for free. Therefore, signed binary representations of an integer $n$, as introduced by Booth [8] and Reitwiesner [9], can be used to speed up point multiplication. In 1990, Morain and Olivos [10] firstly suggested to apply the non-adjacent form (NAF) to construct the addition-subtraction chain for point multiplication, which can save 11.11% operations compared to the binary algorithm. Furthermore, at Crypto'1992, Koyama and Tsuruoka [11] proposed a signed binary window algorithm for a non-sparse

Y.G. Desmedt et al. (Eds.): CANS 2005, LNCS 3810, pp. 223–235, 2005.

optimal signed binary representation (called the KT recoding), which requires fewer operations by using the sliding window method.

In [11], the KT recoding was considered better than the NAF with respect to window technique since that the former has a larger average zero-run length. However, it was noted in [12, 13] that in comparing various signed binary window algorithms, it is important to take into account the number of the precomputations. By far, in the previous literature [11-13, 21] the number of precomputed windows of Koyama-Tsuruoka's signed window algorithm [11] is counted by $2^{w-1} - 1$. It is still a problem what is the precise number of precomputed windows of the non-sparse signed window algorithm.

Note that an efficient sliding window technique, known as the width-$w$ nonadjacent form ($w$-NAF), was independently introduced by Miyaji, Ono and Cohen [14] and Solinas [15]. Some properties of the $w$-NAF have be extensively discussed in [16, 17, 18]. Recently, much attention has been devoted to left-to-right $w$-NAF recodings. Joye and Yen [19] first developed a left-to-right NAF recoding algorithm. Some left-to-right recodings with the same weight as the $w$-NAF ($w > 2$), are respectively proposed by Avanzi [20], by Okeya et al. [21], and by Muir and Stinson [22]. Furthermore, Möller [23, 24] introduced the fractional window method, which can provide more flexibility in order to make best use of the memory that is available.

In this paper, we propose some properties of non-sparse optimal signed binary representations and make a precise analysis of the non-sparse signed binary window algorithm. Firstly, we prove the lower bound $k+1/3$ of the expected length of non-sparse optimal signed binary representations. Secondly, we propose a new non-sparse signed window partitioning algorithm, which is slightly better than Koyama-Tsuruoka's algorithm practically for the window width $w = 4, 5, 6, 7$. Finally, we analyze the two non-sparse signed window algorithms, i.e. Koyama-Tsuruoka's algorithm and the proposed algorithm, and prove the upper bound $\frac{5}{6} \cdot 2^{w-1} - 1 + \frac{(-1)^w}{3}$ of the number of precomputed windows. Furthermore, we give a comparison of various algorithms based on signed binary representations including the $w$-NAF and the fractional window method.

The rest of this paper is organized as follows. Section 2 reviews signed binary representations. Section 3 proves some properties of non-sparse optimal signed binary representations of positive integers. Section 4 proposes a new non-sparse signed window algorithm. Section 5 analyzes Koyama-Tsuruoka's algorithm and the proposed algorithm and compare them with other algorithms, such as the $w$-NAF and so on. Finally, Section 6 concludes the paper.

## 2     Background

### 2.1     Notation

If an integer $n = \sum_{i=0}^{k-1} n_i 2^i$ with $n_i \in \{0, 1\}$, we call $(n_{k-1}, \ldots, n_1, n_0)_2$ the binary representation of $n$. In a signed-digit number system, if $n = \sum_{i=0}^{k} n_i' 2^i$ with $n_i' \in \{\bar{1}, 0, 1\}$, we call $(n_k', \ldots, n_1', n_0')_2$ a signed binary representation of $n$. Moreover, let $\bar{1}$ denote $-1$ for convenience.

## 2.2 Signed Binary Representations

A signed binary representation $(n'_{k-1}, \ldots, n'_1, n'_0)_2$ is called an optimal signed binary representation of $n$, if its hamming weight (the number of non-zero digits) is minimal among all the signed binary representations. One of the most important optimal signed binary representations is the non-adjacent form (NAF). Some properties of signed binary representations have be presented in the literature [8, 9, 25-31]. We now give some required definitions and results.

**Definition 1.** *[9] A signed binary representation $(n'_{k-1}, \ldots, n'_1, n'_0)_2$ with no two adjacent digits being both non-zero is variously called the canonical, sparse or non-adjacent form (NAF), which satisfies $n'_i \cdot n'_{i+1} = 0$ for all $0 \leq i \leq k-1$.*

*Property 1.* [9, 25, 26, 27] The NAF has the following properties:

(1) Every integer $n$ has a unique NAF.

(2) The NAF is an optimal signed-digit binary representation.

(3) For any integers $n$, the length of the NAF of $n$ is at most one digit larger than that of the binary representation of $n$.

**Lemma 1.** *[29, 32] The probability that in an NAF the digit immediately to the left of a 0 is another 0 is 1/2 and that it is 1 or −1 is in each case 1/4.*

Let $T_k$ denote the number of integers requiring at most $k$ bits in the NAF representations. Let $T'_k$ denote the number of integers requiring exactly $k$ bits in the NAF representations. Let $T''_k$ denote the number of positive integers requiring exactly $k$ bits in the NAF representations.

**Theorem 1.** *[27, 29]*

$$T_k = (2^{k+2} + (-1)^{k+1})/3, \quad T'_k = (2^{k+1} + (-1)^{k+1} \cdot 2)/3, \quad T''_k = (2^k + (-1)^{k+1})/3$$

Various optimal signed binary representations can be obtained. Optimal signed binary representations other than the NAF are called non-sparse optimal signed binary representations. For example, the binary representation of the integer $n = 413$ is $(110011101)_2$. The NAF representation is $(10\bar{1}0100\bar{1}01)_2$ and a non-sparse optimal signed-digit representation is $(110100\bar{1}\bar{1})_2$.

## 3 Properties of Non-sparse Optimal Signed Binary Representations

While there's been extensive research on the properties of the NAF, little attention has been devoted to non-sparse optimal signed binary representations. Now we propose two theorems on the lengths of non-sparse optimal signed binary representations, which can be applied to the analysis of the non-sparse signed window algorithm.

Note that the NAF representation can be converted into a non-sparse optimal signed-digit representation by replacing '$10\bar{1}$' and '$\bar{1}01$' with '$011$' and '$0\bar{1}\bar{1}$'.

Hence, we can derive the expected length of non-sparse optimal signed binary representations by counting the corresponding NAF representations. According to the property of the NAF, the length of the corresponding NAF of a $k$-bit positive integer is $k$ or $k+1$ bits. In fact, the NAF representations of the exactly $k$-bit positive integers consist of three cases:

(1) the $k$-bit NAF representations.

(2) the $(k+1)$-bit NAF representations, which have the leading digits '$10\bar{1}0$'.

(3) the $(k+1)$-bit NAF representations, which have the leading digits other than '$10\bar{1}0$'.

**Lemma 2.** *If the leading digits of $(k+1)$-bit NAF representations of an integer $n$ are '$10\bar{1}0$', the length of the binary representation of $n$ is $k$ bits.*

*Proof.* According to the property of the NAF, the NAF representation of an integer $n$ is unique and the $(k+1)$-bit NAF representation has a corresponding $k$-bit or $(k+1)$-bit binary representation. Since that the leading digits of the $(k+1)$-bit NAF representation of $n$ are '$10\bar{1}0$', we have

$$n = 2^k + (-1) \times 2^{k-2} + \sum_{i=0}^{k-4} n_i' 2^i, \qquad n_i' \in \{\bar{1}, 0, 1\}$$

Since $2^{k-2} > \sum_{i=0}^{k-4} n_i' 2^i$, we can obtain $n < 2^k$. Hence the integer $n$ must be a $k$-bit binary integer. □

**Theorem 2.** *For the exactly $k$-bit positive integers:*

*(1) the number of the $k$-bit NAF representations is $C_k = 2^{k-1}/3 + 1/2 + (-1)^{k+1}/6$.*

*(2) the number of the $(k+1)$-bit NAF representations, which have the leading digits '$10\bar{1}0$', is $C_k' = (2^{k-1} + (-1)^k)/3$.*

*(3) the number of the $(k+1)$-bit NAF representations, which have the leading digits other than '$10\bar{1}0$', is $C_k'' = 2^{k-1}/3 - 1/2 + (-1)^{k+1}/6$.*

*Proof.* First consider the second case. When the leading digits of the $(k+1)$-bit NAF representations are '$10\bar{1}0$', the remaining bit string can be any of the $(k-3)$-bit NAF representations. By Theorem 1, the number of the $(k-3)$-bit NAF representations is $T_{k-3} = (2^{k-1} + (-1)^k)/3$. Hence, we obtain $C_k' = (2^{k-1} + (-1)^k)/3$.

Let $C_k$ denote the number of the $k$-bit NAF representations of the exactly $k$-bit positive integers and $C_k''$ denote the number of the $(k+1)$-bit NAF representations of the exactly $k$-bit positive integers, which have the leading digits other than '$10\bar{1}0$'. Hence we have

$$\begin{cases} C_k + C_k' + C_k'' = 2^{k-1} \\ C_k + C_{k-1}' + C_{k-1}'' = T_k'' \end{cases} \tag{1}$$

By solving the above equation (1), we obtain $C_k = 2^{k-1}/3 + 1/2 + (-1)^{k+1}/6$ and $C_k'' = 2^{k-1}/3 - 1/2 + (-1)^{k+1}/6$. □

**Theorem 3.** *For the exactly k-bit positive integers, the lower bound of the expected length of the non-sparse optimal signed binary representations is $k + 1/3$ and the upper bound is $k + 2/3$.*

*Proof.* Note that a non-sparse optimal signed binary representation can be obtained by replacing '$10\bar{1}$' and '$\bar{1}01$' with '011' and '$0\bar{1}\bar{1}$' from the NAF representation. Moreover, only the conversion from '$10\bar{1}0$' to '0110' of the most significant digits of the $(k + 1)$-bit NAF representations can reduce the length by 1. Hence the expected length of the shortest non-sparse optimal signed binary representation is $k + C_k''/2^{k-1}$, which is approximately $k+1/3$.

Similarly, the expected length of the longest non-sparse optimal signed binary representation of the exactly $k$-bit positive integers is approximately $k+2/3$, which is equal to the expected length of the NAF representation.     □

## 4   New Non-sparse Signed Window Partitioning Algorithm

Koyama and Tsuruoka [11] proposed a signed window algorithm based on the KT recoding, which is a non-sparse optimal signed binary representation. The KT recoding allows a few adjacent non-zeros, which can reduce the number of the non-zero windows. Before the analysis of the non-sparse signed window algorithm, we propose a new signed window partitioning algorithm, which can obtain non-sparse signed windows by scanning the NAF representation. The basic idea is converting the most significant digits '$10\bar{1}$' or '$\bar{1}01$' of a window into '011' or '$0\bar{1}\bar{1}$', which increases the window length by 1. The proposed method is described as Algorithm 1.

Note that for $w=3$, the proposed Algorithm 1, Koyama-Tsuruoka's signed window algorithm [11] and the window algorithm for the NAF [29, 32] have the same expected zero-run length 1.5 and are indeed equivalent. For $w \geq 4$, we obtain the following Theorem 4.

**Theorem 4.** *For a k-bit NAF representation and the window width $w \geq 4$, the expected number of non-zero windows of Algorithm 1 is*

$$\frac{k}{w + \frac{4}{3} + \frac{(-1)^w}{3 \cdot 2^{w-1}} - (\frac{1}{2})^{w-3} + (2 + (-1)^w) \cdot (\frac{1}{2})^{\frac{w}{2} - \frac{3}{4} \cdot (1 - (-1)^w)}}.$$

*Proof.* The window partitioning process in Algorithm 1 can be modeled as a Markov chain, whose states are the different possible windows. In [32], Semay analyzed the the sliding window algorithm for the NAF representation. Since Algorithm 1 outputs the non-sparse signed windows by scanning the NAF, we adopt a similar analysis as that in [32]. Let $i$ be the number of the non-zero digits of a width-$w$ window for the NAF representation. Let $\star$ denote a non-zero digit 1 or $\bar{1}$. For $w \geq 4$, the different windows (states) are:

---

**Algorithm 1.** New signed window partitioning algorithm

---

Input: the NAF $n = \sum_{i=0}^{k} n_i 2^i$, $n_i \in \{\bar{1}, 0, 1\}$, $0 \leq i \leq k$, the window width $w \geq 3$.
Output: the windows $W_1, W_2, \ldots, W_r$.

1.    $j := 1$;
2.    $i := k$;
3.    while $i \geq 0$ do
4.        if $n_i = 0$ then
5.            $W_j := 0$;
6.            $j := j + 1$;
7.            $i := i - 1$;
8.        else if $(n_i, \ldots, n_{i-w+1}) = (1, 0, \bar{1}, \ldots)$ or $(\bar{1}, 0, 1, \ldots)$ then
          /* For $i - w + 1 < 0$, take $(n_i, \ldots, n_0)$. Similarly, so do Step 9 and 13. */
9.            $W_j := (0, 1, 1, n_{i-3}, \ldots, n_{i-w})$ or $(0, \bar{1}, \bar{1}, n_{i-3}, \ldots, n_{i-w})$;
10.           $j := j + 1$;
11.           $i := i - w - 1$;
12.       else
13.           $W_j = (n_i, \ldots, n_{i-w+1})$;
14.           $j := j + 1$;
15.           $i := i - w$;
16.       end if.
17.   end while.

---

$i = 0$        $S_1 = 0$
$i = 1$        $S_2 = \star 0 \ldots 0$                                    (length $w$)
$i = 2$        $S_3 = \star 0 \ldots 0 \star$                              (length $w$)
               $S_4' = 1010 \ldots 0$ or $\bar{1}0\bar{1}0 \ldots 0$        (length $w$)
               $S_4'' = 10\bar{1}0 \ldots 0$ or $\bar{1}010 \ldots 0$       (length $w+1$)
               $S_4''' = 10\bar{1}0 \ldots 0 \star$ or $\bar{1}010 \ldots 0 \star$  (length $w+1$)
               $S_4'''' = \star 0 \ldots 0 \star 0 \ldots 0$               (length $w$)

$\ldots$

$3 \leq i \leq \lfloor \frac{w+1}{2} \rfloor$  $S_{2i-1}' = 1010(0| \star 0)^* \star$ or $\bar{1}0\bar{1}0(0| \star 0)^* \star$  (length $w$)
               $S_{2i-1}'' = 10\bar{1}0(0| \star 0)^* \star 0$ or $\bar{1}010(0| \star 0)^* \star 0$ (length $w+1$)
               $S_{2i-1}''' = \star 00(0| \star 0)^* \star$                 (length $w$)
               (When $w = 2i - 1$, $S_w'''$ is not included.)

               $S_{2i}' = 1010(0| \star 0)^*$ or $\bar{1}0\bar{1}0(0| \star 0)^*$   (length $w$)
               $S_{2i}'' = 10\bar{1}0(0| \star 0)^* 0$ or $\bar{1}010(0| \star 0)^* 0$  (length $w+1$)
               $S_{2i}''' = 10\bar{1}0(0| \star 0)^* \star$ or $\bar{1}010(0| \star 0)^* \star$  (length $w+1$)
               $S_{2i}'''' = \star 00(0| \star 0)^*$                        (length $w$)
               (When $w = 2i$, $S_w''''$ is not included.)

Note that the states $S_{2i-1}', S_{2i-1}''$ and $S_{2i-1}'''$ correspond to the state $S_{2i-1}$ in [32] and the states $S_{2i}', S_{2i}'', S_{2i}'''$ and $S_{2i}''''$ correspond to the state $S_{2i}$ in [32]. By a similar analysis as that in [32], we can calculate the stationary distribution of the Markov chain, which is $(\pi_1, \pi_2, \pi_3, \ldots, \pi_w', \pi_w'', \pi_w'')$ for $w$ odd and

$(\pi_1, \pi_2, \pi_3, \ldots, \pi'_w, \pi''_w, \pi'''_w)$ for $w$ even. Let $f(w) = \frac{3}{7 \cdot 2^{w-1} + (-1)^w}$, then the probabilities are obtained as follows.

$$\pi_1 = f(w) \cdot (2^{w+1} + (-1)^w)/3, \qquad\qquad \pi_2 = \pi_3 = f(w) \cdot 2.$$

For $i \geq 2$:

$$\pi'_{2i} = f(w) \cdot 2^{i-1}, \qquad\qquad \pi'_{2i+1} = f(w) \cdot 2^{i-1},$$
$$\pi''_{2i} = f(w) \cdot 2^{i-2}, \qquad\qquad \pi''_{2i+1} = f(w) \cdot 2^{i-1},$$
$$\pi'''_{2i} = f(w) \cdot 2^{i-2}, \qquad\qquad \pi'''_{2i+1} = f(w) \cdot \left[ \binom{w-i-2}{i-1} - 1 \right] \cdot 2^i,$$
$$\pi''''_{2i} = f(w) \cdot \left[ \binom{w-i-1}{i-1} - 1 \right] \cdot 2^i.$$

The expected number of the non-zero windows is :
— For $w$ odd:

$$k \cdot \frac{1 - \pi_1}{1 \cdot \pi_1 + w \cdot (1 - \pi_1) + \sum_{i=2}^{\frac{w-1}{2}} [f(w) \cdot 2^i]}$$
$$= \frac{k}{w + \frac{4}{3} + \frac{(-1)^w}{3 \cdot 2^{w-1}} - (\frac{1}{2})^{w-3} + (\frac{1}{2})^{\frac{w-3}{2}}} \tag{2}$$

— For $w$ even:

$$k \cdot \frac{1 - \pi_1}{1 \cdot \pi_1 + w \cdot (1 - \pi_1) + \sum_{i=2}^{\frac{w-2}{2}} [f(w) \cdot 2^i] + f(w) \cdot 2^{\frac{w}{2}-1}}$$
$$= \frac{k}{w + \frac{4}{3} + \frac{(-1)^w}{3 \cdot 2^{w-1}} - (\frac{1}{2})^{w-3} + 3 \cdot (\frac{1}{2})^{\frac{w}{2}}} \tag{3}$$

Thus, by (2) and (3) we have the result

$$\frac{k}{w + \frac{4}{3} + \frac{(-1)^w}{3 \cdot 2^{w-1}} - (\frac{1}{2})^{w-3} + (2 + (-1)^w) \cdot (\frac{1}{2})^{\frac{w}{2} - \frac{3}{4} \cdot (1 - (-1)^w)}}. \tag{4}$$

$\square$

According to Theorem 4, we obtain the average zero-run length of Algorithm 1 in Table 1.

**Table 1.** The Average Zero-run Length of Algorithm 1

| width  | w=3 | w=4   | w=5    | w=6     | w=7      | w=8       |
|--------|-----|-------|--------|---------|----------|-----------|
| length | 1.5 | 1.625 | 1.5625 | 1.59375 | 1.515625 | 1.4921875 |

It is shown that the proposed algorithm is slightly better than Koyama-Tsuruoka's signed window algorithm [11] for $w = 4, 5, 6$ and $7$, which cases are particularly attractive for elliptic curve cryptosystems.

# 5   Analysis and Comparisons

## 5.1   Analysis of Non-sparse Signed Window Algorithms

Now we analyze Koyama-Tsuruoka's signed window algorithm and the proposed Algorithm 1, which have the same upper bound of the number of precomputed windows. There are two problems on the analysis of Koyama-Tsuruoka's signed window algorithm in the literature [11–13]:

(1) In [11], the average length of the KT recoding is counted by $k + 1/4$. However, according to Theorem 3 in Section 3, the lower bound of the average length of the shortest non-sparse optimal signed binary representations is $k+1/3$. Therefore, the previous result is incorrect and we revise it.

(2) In [11–13], the number of precomputed windows for non-sparse signed window algorithm is counted by $2^{w-1} - 1$. However, we note that some window values can't appear in non-sparse optimal signed binary representations and needn't be precomputed. Hence there must be a upper bound smaller than $2^{w-1} - 1$ and the previous analysis is inaccurate.

Now we consider the second problem. The sliding algorithm for computing point multiplication $n \cdot P$ on elliptic curves is described as Algorithm 2. The overall number of operations includes the number of the precomputations, the number of the non-zero windows and the number of point doublings. Moreover, since the inverse of a point on elliptic curves is easily computed, only odd positive windows need be precomputed.

The overall number of operations of Koyama-Tsuruoka's signed window algorithm is $(k + 1.75 - w) + \frac{k+1/4}{w+1.5} + (2^{w-1} - 1)$ in [11, 13], where $k = \lfloor \log n \rfloor + 1$. Now we count the precise number of precomputed windows.

---

**Algorithm 2.** The sliding window algorithm for point multiplication $Q = n \cdot P$

---

Input: $n = \sum_{i=0}^{k} n_i' 2^i$, $n_i \in \{\bar{1}, 0, 1\}$, $0 \leq i \leq k$, a point $P$, the window width $w$.
Output: $Q = n \cdot P$.

1.    Partition and precompute the left-to-right windows $W_1, W_2, \ldots, W_r$ .
2.    $Q := W_1 P$;
3.    for $i = 2$ to $r$ do
3.1        $Q := 2^{L(W_i)} Q$;
3.2        $Q := Q + W_i \cdot P$;
4.    end for.
5.    Output $Q$.

---

**Theorem 5.** *For the window width* $w \geq 2$, *the sliding window algorithm for non-sparse optimal signed binary representations has:*

*(1) The upper bound of the number of precomputed windows is* $\frac{5}{6} \cdot 2^{w-1} - 1 + \frac{(-1)^w}{3}$.

*(2) The maximum precomputed window is* $\frac{5}{6} \cdot 2^w - \frac{1}{3}$ *for* $w$ *even, whose representation is* $11(01)^{w/2-1}$ *and* $\frac{5}{6} \cdot 2^w - \frac{5}{3}$ *for* $w \geq 5$ *and odd, whose representation*

*is* $11(01)^{(w-1)/2-2}001$. *For* $w = 3$, *the maximum precomputed window is* 5, *whose representation is* 101.

*Proof.* Note that only odd positive windows of at most $w$ bits need be precomputed. The number of precomputed windows of non-sparse optimal signed representations includes the number of precomputed windows of the NAF representation and the number of the $(k+1)$-bit NAF representations, which have the leading bits '$10\bar{1}0$'.

According to [29, 32], the number of precomputed windows of the NAF representation is $\frac{1}{3} \cdot 2^w - 1 - \frac{(-1)^w}{3}$.

By Theorem 2, for the exactly $k$-bit positive integers, the number of the $(k + 1)$-bit NAF representations, which have the leading bits '$10\bar{1}0$', is $C_k' = (2^{k-1} + (-1)^k)/3$. Hence, we can obtain the number of the odd positive integers, which have the leading bits '$10\bar{1}0$' in their $(k + 1)$-bit NAF representations, is $\frac{1}{6} \cdot 2^{w-1} + \frac{(-1)^w}{6} + \frac{(-1)^w}{2}$.

Therefore, the number of precomputed windows of the sliding window algorithm for non-sparse optimal signed binary representations has is $\frac{5}{6} \cdot 2^{w-1} - 1 + \frac{(-1)^w}{3}$. The results on the maximum precomputed window follows. $\square$

*Remark 1.* Note that modified-NAF has been analyzed in [27]. In fact, the modified-NAF can be converted into non-sparse optimal signed binary representations by replacing some '$10\bar{1}$' or '$\bar{1}01$' with '$011$' or '$0\bar{1}\bar{1}$' and vice versa.

Let $m$ is an odd positive integer such that $1 \le m \le 2^{w-1} - 3$ for the fractional $w$-NAF method by Möller [23,24]. We present the maximum precomputed window for various representations in Table 2. Taking $w = 5$ as an example, the maximum precomputed window for non-sparse optimal signed binary representations is 25, whose representation is $(11001)_2$. The representation $(11011)_2$, $(11101)_2$ and $(11111)_2$ of the odd positive integers 27, 29 and 31 can't appear in non-sparse optimal signed binary representations.

**Table 2.** The Maximum Precomputed Window

| Representation | $w=2$ | $w=3$ | $w=4$ | $w=5$ | $w=6$ |
|---|---|---|---|---|---|
| Binary | $3=(11)_2$ | $7=(111)_2$ | $15=(1111)_2$ | $31=(11111)_2$ | $63=(111111)_2$ |
| NAF | $1=(1)_2$ | $5=(101)_2$ | $9=(1001)_2$ | $21=(10101)_2$ | $41=(101001)_2$ |
| Non-sparse | $3=(11)_2$ | $5=(101)_2$ | $13=(1101)_2$ | $25=(11001)_2$ | $53=(110101)_2$ |
| $w$-NAF | $1=(1)_2$ | $3=(11)_2$ | $7=(111)_2$ | $15=(1111)_2$ | $31=(11111)_2$ |
| Factional $w$-NAF | $1=(1)_2$ | $4+m$ | $8+m$ | $16+m$ | $32+m$ |

**Theorem 6.**
*(1) The expected number of operations of Koyama-Tsuruoka's non-sparse signed window algorithm is:*

$$(k - w + \frac{11}{6}) + \frac{k + 1/3}{w + 3/2} + \frac{5}{6} \cdot 2^{w-1} - 1 + \frac{(-1)^w}{3}.$$

(2) Let $s = \frac{4}{3} + \frac{(-1)^w}{3 \cdot 2^{w-1}} - (\frac{1}{2})^{w-3} + (2 + (-1)^w) \cdot (\frac{1}{2})^{\frac{w}{2} - \frac{3}{4} \cdot (1 - (-1)^w)}$. The expected number of operations of Algorithm 1 is:

$$(k + \frac{1}{3} - w + s) + \frac{k + 1/3}{w + s} + \frac{5}{6} \cdot 2^{w-1} - 1 + \frac{(-1)^w}{3}$$

*Proof.* By Theorem 5, the number of precomputed windows is $\frac{5}{6} \cdot 2^{w-1} - 1 + \frac{(-1)^w}{3}$. By Theorem 3, the lower bound of the average length of non-sparse optimal signed-digit representations is $k + 1/3$. Due to the equation in the literature [12, 13, 28, 29], this result can be obtained.    □

### 5.2   Comparisons with Other Algorithms

Let $L$ denote the length of the signed or unsigned binary representation of $n$. Let $s$ and $t$ denote the average zero-run length and the number of precomputed windows. The number of the non-zero windows can be determined by $\frac{L}{w+s}$. Note that $t$ precomputed windows $\{3P, 5P, 7P, \ldots, (2t+1)P\}$ can be obtained via the addition chain $P, 2P, 3P, 5P, 7P, \ldots, (2t+1)P$. Hence, the number of operations of the sliding window algorithm is counted by as follows [11-14, 28, 29]:

$$L - w + s + (\frac{L}{w+s} - 1) + (t + 1)$$

The expected zero-run length of the binary representation is 1. The expected zero-run length of the NAF representation is $\frac{4}{3} + \frac{(-1)^{w+1}}{3 \cdot 2^{w-2}}$ [12, 13, 28, 29, 32]. The expected zero-run length of the KT recoding [11] is $3/2$. Note that the $w$-NAF should be seen as a width-$(w-1)$ window algorithm with the zero-run length 2.

Let $m$ be an odd positive integer such that $1 \le m \le 2^{w-1} - 3$. The fractional $w$-NAF method has the signed fractional windows $\{\pm 1, \pm 3, \ldots, \pm(2^{w-1} + m)\}$ and the number of precomputed windows is $2^{w-2} - 1 + (m + 1)/2$ for $w \ge 3$. The average density of the fractional $w$-NAF method is $\frac{1}{w + \frac{m+1}{2^{w-1}} + 1}$.

Therefore, we give a comparison of the non-zero density and the number of precomputed windows of various representations in Table 3. Note that $m$ is an odd positive integer such that $1 \le m \le 2^{w-1} - 3$. It is shown that when $w \le 5$, there is a difference not more than 2 between the NAF and non-sparse signed-digit representations.

For a signed window algorithm, there is an optimal window width $w$ for $k$-bit integers, which minimizes the number of operations. When $k$ varies from 160 to 600, the optimal window width $w$ varies from 3 to 6. For example, for $k=233$, the binary method (double-and-addition) and the NAF method (double-and-addition/subtraction) require 347.5 and 309.5 operations, respectively. For $k=233$ and $w=4$, a comparison of various sliding window algorithms is given in Table 4.

It is shown in Table 4 that there is a small difference among the various signed window algorithms for $k = 233$. The $w$-NAF combined the fractional window method can achieve the best performance by choosing a proper $m$.

**Table 3.** The Non-zero Density and Number of Precomputed Windows

| Representation | $w=2$ | $w=3$ | $w=4$ | $w=5$ | $w=6$ |
|---|---|---|---|---|---|
| Binary | 0.333(1) | 0.250(3) | 0.200(7) | 0.167(15) | 0.143(31) |
| NAF | 0.333(0) | 0.222(2) | 0.190(4) | 0.157(10) | 0.137(20) |
| KT recoding | 0.286(1) | 0.222(2) | 0.182(6) | 0.154(12) | 0.133(26) |
| Algorithm 1 | 0.333(0) | 0.222(2) | 0.178(6) | 0.152(12) | 0.132(26) |
| $w$-NAF | 0.333(0) | 0.250(1) | 0.200(3) | 0.167(7) | 0.143(15) |
| Fractional $w$-NAF | 0 | $1+(m+1)/2$ | $3+(m+1)/2$ | $7+(m+1)/2$ | $15+(m+1)/2$ |

**Table 4.** Comparison of Various Algorithms ($k = 233, w = 4$)

| Algorithm | Precomputed | Number of Operations |
|---|---|---|
| Binary+Window | 7 | 283.6 |
| NAF+Window | 4 | 278.5 |
| KT's window | 6 | 279.2 |
| Algorithm 1 | 6 | 278.4 |
| 5-NAF | 7 | 277.4 |
| Fractional 4-NAF ($m = 5$) | 6 | 278.36 |
| Fractional 5-NAF ($m = 1$) | 8 | 277.5 |

# 6  Conclusion

We present a precise analysis of Koyama-Tsuruoka's signed window algorithm and the new proposed non-sparse signed window algorithm. We also give comparisons of various algorithms and it is shown that the $w$-NAF combined the fractional window method is more efficient than the others. Furthermore, the properties of non-sparse signed binary representations can be applied to analyze the performance of various algorithms based on non-sparse signed binary representations.

**Acknowledgments.** The authors are very grateful to the anonymous referees for their valuable comments, corrections and suggestions, and for drawing the authors' attention to related work on the $w$-NAF and the fractional window method. The authors would also like to thank Ming Li for his interesting discussions on this paper.

# References

1. N. Koblitz, "Elliptic curve cryptosystems," Mathematics of Computation, vol. 48, pp. 203-209, 1987.
2. V. S. Miller, "Use of elliptic curve in cryptography," Advances in Cryptology - CRYPTO'85, LNCS 218, Springer-Verlag , pp. 417-426, 1986.
3. D. E. Knuth, The Art of Computer Programming, vol. 2: Seminumerical Algorithms, Addison-Wesley, 3rd edition, 1998.

4. H. Cohen, A Course in Computational Algebraic Number Theory, vol. 138 of Graduate Texts in Mathematics, Springer-Verlag, 1993.

5. C. K. Koc, "Analysis of sliding window techniques for exponentiation," Computers and Mathematics with Applications, 30(10), pp.17-24, 1995.

6. O. Rizzo, "On the complexity of the $2^k$-ary and of the sliding window algorithms for fast exponentiation," Rivista di Matematica dell'Università dell'Università di Parma. 7(3). 2004.

7. D. M. Gordon, "A Survey of Fast Exponentiation Methods," Journal of Algorithms, vol. 27 , pp. 129-146,1998.

8. A. D. Booth, "A Signed Binary Multiplication Technique," Q. J. Mech. Appl. Math., vol. 4, no. 2, pp. 236-240, 1951.

9. G. W. Reitwiesner, "Binary arithmetic," Advances in Computers, vol. 1, pp. 231-308, 1960.

10. F. Morain and J. Olivos, "Speeding up the computations on an elliptic curve using addition-subtraction chains," Theoretical Informatics and Applications, vol. 24, pp. 531-543, 1990.

11. K. Koyama and T. Tsuruoka, "Speeding up elliptic curve cryptosystems using a signed binary window method," Advances in Cryptology - CRYPTO'92, LNCS 740, Springer-Verlag , pp. 345-357, 1992.

12. N. Kunihiro and H. Yamamoto, "Window and extended window methods for addition-subtraction chain," IEICE Trans. on Fundamentals, vol.E81-A, no.1, pp. 72-81, Jan. 1998.

13. E. De Win, S. Mister, B. Preneel and M. Wiener, "On the Performance of Signature Schemes based on Elliptic Curves," Proc. of ANTS'98, Springer-Verlag, LNCS 1423, pp. 252-266, 1998.

14. A. Miyaji, T. Ono and H. Cohen, "Efficient elliptic curve exponentiation," In Proceedings ICICS'97, LNCS 1334, pp. 282-290, Springer-Verlag, 1997.

15. J. A. Solinas, "An improved algorithm for arithmetic on a family of elliptic curves," In Proceedings of CRYPTO '97, LNCS 1294, pp. 357-371, Springer-Verlag, 1997.

16. J. A. Solinas, "Efficient arithmetic on Koblitz curves," Designs, Codes and Cryptography, vol. 19 , pp. 195-249, 2000.

17. H. Cohen, "Analysis of the sliding window powering algorithm," J. of Cryptology, vol. 18, no.1, pp.63-76, 2005.

18. J. A. Muir and D. R. Stinson, "Minimality and Other Properties of the Width-$w$ Nonadjacent Form," to appear in Mathematics of Computation. Available at: http://www.ccsl.carleton.ca/~jamuir/papers/wNAF-revised-3.pdf.

19. M. Joye, and S. M. Yen, "Optimal left-to-right binary signed-digit recoding," IEEE Trans. on Comp. 49 (7), pp. 740-748, 2000.

20. R. M. Avanzi, "A Note on the Signed Sliding Window Integer Recoding and a Left-to-Right Analogue," In: H. Handschuh and A. Hasan (Eds.): SAC 2004, LNCS 3357, pp. 130-143, Springer-Verlag, 2005.

21. Katsuyuki Okeya, Katja Schmidt-Samoa, Christian Spahn, Tsuyoshi Takagi, "Signed Binary Representations Revisited," CRYPTO 2004, LNCS 3152, pp. 123-139, Springer-Verlag, 2004.

22. J. A. Muir, and D. R. Stinson, "New Minimal Weight Representations for Left-to-Right Window Methods," CT-RSA 2005 ,Lecture Notes in Computer Science 3376, pp. 366-383, Springer-Verlag, 2005.

23. B. Möller, "Improved Techniques for Fast Exponentiation," Information Security and Cryptology - ICISC 2002, Lecture Notes in Computer Science 2587, pp. 298-312, Springer-Verlag, 2002.

24. B. Möller, "Fractional Windows Revisited: Improved Signed-Digit Representations for Efficient Exponentiation," Information Security and Cryptology - ICISC 2004, Lecture Notes in Computer Science 3506 , pp. 137-153, Springer-Verlag, 2005.

25. S. Arno and F. S. Wheeler, "Signed digit representations of minimal hamming weight," IEEE Transactions on Computers, vol. 42, no. 8, pp. 1007-1010, 1993.

26. O. Egecioglu and C. K. Koc, "Exponentiation using canonical recoding," Theoretical Computer Science, 129(2), pp. 407-417, 1994.

27. W. Bosma, "Signed Bits and Fast Exponentiation," J. Théor. Nombres Bordeaux, 13(1), pp. 27-41, 2001.

28. R. M. Avanzi, "On multi-exponentiation in cryptography," Technical Report 2002/154, Cryptology ePrint Archive(2002), Available at:
http://eprint.iacr.org/2002/154.

29. R. M. Avanzi, "On the complexity of certain multi-exponentiation techniques in cryptography," J. of Cryptology, Online First, 2005.

30. Clemens Heuberger and Peter Grabner, "On the number of optimal base 2 representations of integers," Preprint available at:
http://www.opt.math.tu-graz.ac.at/~cheub/publications.

31. B. Phillips and N. Burgess, "Minimal Weight Digit Set Conversions," IEEE Transactions on Computers, vol.53, no.6, pp. 666-677, 2004.

32. Olivier Semay, "Efficiency analysis of window methods using Markov chains," Diplomarbeit, Sommer 2004. Available at: http://www.cdc.informatik.tu-darmstadt.de/reports/reports/KP/Olivier_ Semay.diplom.ps.

# Constructions of Almost Resilient Functions

Pin-Hui Ke[1,2,3], Tai-Lin Liu[1,4], and Qiao-Yan Wen[1]

[1] School of Science,
Beijing University of Posts and Telecommunications,
Beijing,100876, P.R. China
keph@eyou.com, tlinliu@sina.com, wqy@bupt.edu.cn
[2] State Key Laboratory of Information Security, Chinese Academy of Sciences,
Beijing 100039, P.R. China
[3] School of Mathematics and Computer Science,Fujian Normal University,
Fujian 350007, P.R. China
[4] School of Literature and Science , Shandong Finance Institute,
Shandong 250014, China

**Abstract.** The relation between almost resilient function and its component functions is investigated in this paper. We prove that if each nonzero linear combination of $f_1, f_2, \cdots, f_m$ is an $\varepsilon$-almost$(n, 1, k)$-resilient function, then $F = (f_1, f_2, \cdots, f_m)$ is a $\frac{2^m-1}{2^m-1}\varepsilon$-almost$(n, m, k)$-resilient function. In the case $\varepsilon$ equals 0, the theorem gives another proof of Linear Combination Lemma for resilient functions. As applications of this theorem, we introduce a method to construct a balanced $\frac{9}{2}\varepsilon$-almost $(3n, 2, 2k+1)$-resilient function from a balanced $\varepsilon$-almost $(n, 1, k)$-resilient function and present a method of improving the degree of the constructed functions with a small trade-off in the nonlinearity and resiliency. At the end of this paper, the relation between balanced almost CI function and its component functions are also concluded.

## 1 Introduction

An $\varepsilon$-almost$(n, m, k)$-resilient function is an $n$-input $m$-output function $f$ with the property that the deviation of output's distribution from uniform distribution is not great than $\varepsilon$ when $k$ arbitrary inputs are fixed and the remaining $n - k$ inputs run through all the $2^{n-k}$ input tuples. The concept of almost resilient functions was introduced by K.Kurosawa et al.[1] and is the generalization of the concept of resilient function. It was showed to have parameters superior to resilient functions. The notations of independent sample space was introduced by Naor and Naor [2], which has been proved to have many cryptographic applications, such as multiple authentication codes[3], almost security cryptographic boolean functions[4] and so on. In [1], the relations between the almost resilient functions and the large sets of almost independent sample spaces were established. So if some efficient methods to construct almost resilient functions are found, more large sets of almost independent sample spaces are also obtained. However up to the present, the only construction method is by using almost independent sample space. So we wish to investigate the relations between the

Y.G. Desmedt et al. (Eds.): CANS 2005, LNCS 3810, pp. 236–246, 2005.

almost resilient functions and its component functions and look for some other construction methods.

Linear Combination Lemma , which is also called XOR-*lemma* in binary case, establishs a bridge which links the vector resilient function and its component functions and plays an important role in the characterization and construction of vector resilient functions[5]. It is also expressed in terms of independence of random variables in [6]. However, the proof method cannot be directly adapted to the almost case. So in this paper we firstly present a useful lemma , which will be used to look insight into the relation between a vector function and its component function. If $F$ is an $\varepsilon$-almost$(n, m, k)$-resilient function , it is easy to prove that each nonzero linear combination of $f_1, f_2, \cdots, f_m$ is a $2^{m-1}\varepsilon$-almost$(n, 1, k)$-resilient function. Furthermore it is naturally for us to consider the opposite direction which has never been discussed before. We prove that if each nonzero linear combination of $f_1, f_2, \cdots, f_m$ is $\varepsilon$-almost$(n, 1, k)$-resilient function then $F$ is a $\frac{2^m-1}{2^m-1}\varepsilon$-almost$(n, m, k)$-resilient function. The proof of the theorem depends on some technical observations. Especially in the case $\varepsilon$ equals 0, the theorem gives another proof of Linear Combination Lemma. Then we present a method to construct a balanced $\frac{9}{2}\varepsilon$-almost$(3n, 2, 2k + 1)$-resilient function from a balanced $\varepsilon$-almost$(n, 1, k)$-resilient function. As pointed out in [7], one important task of construction of vector resilient functions is to construct $(n, m, k)$-resilient functions with degree $d > m$ and high nonlinearity. By above theorem, we will describe a method of improving the degree of the constructed functions with a small trade-off in the nonlinearity and resiliency. Almost correlation immune (for simplicity, CI) functions is the generalization of CI functions, which was introduced by K.Kurosawa[1] and the case of single output also independently introduced by Yi-Xian Yang [8]. At the end of this paper, the relation between balanced almost CI function and its component functions are also concluded.

## 2  Preliminaries

The vector spaces of $n$-tuples of elements from GF(2) is denoted by $F_2^n$. Let $F$ be a function from $F_2^n$ to $F_2^m$.

**Definition 1.** *The function $F$ is called an $(n, m, k)$-resilient function if*

$$Pr[F(x_1, \cdots, x_n) = (y_1, \cdots, y_m)|x_{i_1}x_{i_2} \cdots x_{i_k} = \alpha] = 2^{-m}$$

*for any $k$ positions $i_1 < i_2 < \cdots < i_k$, for any $k$-bit string $\alpha \in F_2^k$, and for any $(y_1, \cdots, y_m) \in F_2^m$, where the values $x_j (j \notin \{i_1, i_2, \cdots, i_k\})$ are chosen independently at random.*

Following proposition is well-known and useful in understanding the relationship between a resilient functions and its component functions. It has appeared in many references (see, for example, [5]).

**Proposition 1.** *Let $F = (f_1, \cdots, f_m)$ be a function from $F_2^n$ to $F_2^m$, where $n$ and $m$ are integers with $n \geq m \geq 1$, and each $f_i$ is a function on $F_2^n$. Then*

$F$ is an $(n, m, k)$-resilient function if and only if every nonzero combination of $f_1, \cdots, f_m$

$$f(x) = \bigoplus_{i=1}^{m} c_i f_i(x)$$

is a $(n, 1, k)$-resilient function, where $c = (c_1, \cdots, c_n) \in F_2^n$.

K.Kurosawa et al. introduced a notation of $\varepsilon$-almost$(n, m, k)$-resilient function[1].

**Definition 2.** *The function $F$ is called a $\varepsilon$-almost$(n, m, k)$-resilient function if*

$$|Pr[F(x_1, \cdots, x_n) = (y_1, \cdots, y_m)|x_{i_1} x_{i_2} \cdots x_{i_k} = \alpha] - 2^{-m}| \leq \varepsilon$$

*for any $k$ positions $i_1 < i_2 < \cdots < i_k$, for any $k$-bit string $\alpha \in F_2^k$, and for any $(y_1, \cdots, y_m) \in F_2^m$, where the values $x_j (j \notin \{i_1, i_2, \cdots, i_k\})$ are chosen independently at random.*

An almost $k$-wise independent sample spaces is a probability space on $n$-bit tuples such that any $k$-bits are almost independent. A large set of $(\varepsilon, k)$-independent sample spaces, denoted by $LS(\varepsilon, k, n, t)$ , is a set of $2^{m-t}(\varepsilon, k)$-independent sample spaces, each of size $2^t$, such that their union contains all $2^n$ binary vectors of length $n$. For details about $k$-wise independent sample spaces and $LS(\varepsilon, k, n, t)$, we refer to [1, 2].

The relation between $LS(\varepsilon, k, n, t)$ and almost resilient function is revealed in [1].

**Proposition 2.** *If there exists an $LS(\varepsilon, k, n, t)$, then there exists a $\delta$-almost $(n, n - t, k)$-resilient function, where $\delta = \frac{\varepsilon}{2^{n-t-k}}$.*

A $(n, m)$-function $F$ is called balanced if

$$Pr[F(x_1, \cdots, x_n) = (y_1, \cdots, y_m)] = 2^{-m}$$

for all $(y_1, \cdots, y_m) \in F_2^m$.

**Proposition 3.** *If there exists a balanced $\varepsilon$-almost $(n, m, k)$-resilient function, then there exists a $LS(\delta, k, n, n - m)$, where $\delta = \frac{\varepsilon}{2^{k-m}}$.*

Using Weil-Carlitz-Uchiyama bound, K.Kurosawa et al.[1] present a construction of $t$-systematic $(\varepsilon, k)$-independent sample spaces and then extended to large set of almost independent sample spaces. So by proposition 2, some almost resilient functions are obtained.

Let $F(X) = (f_1, f_2, \cdots, f_m)$ be an $(n, m)$-function, the *nonlinearity* of $F$ is defined to be $nl(F) = min\{nl(l \circ f) : l$ is a non-constant $m$-variable linear function$\}$, where $nl(f)$ is the least hamming distance between boolean function $f$ and all affine functions. And the *degree* of $F$ defined to be the minimum of the degree of $l \circ f$, where $l$ ranges over all non-constant $m$-variable linear function.

# 3   A Useful Lemma

In this section, we will present a useful lemma. Firstly, an example for $n = 3$ will be given. Then we will prove the general case.

Let $h$ be a function from $F_2^n$ to $F_2^m$ or $F_2$. Denote

$$L(h(X) = Y) = \{(x_1, x_2, \cdots, x_n) : h(x_1, x_2, \cdots, x_n) = Y\}. \tag{1}$$

Let $X_i, 1 \leq i \leq 3$ be three independent random variables on $F_2$. By above notation, we have

$$L(X_1 \oplus X_2 \oplus X_3 = 0) = \{(000), (110), (011), (101)\}$$
$$L(X_1 \oplus X_2 \oplus X_3 = 1) = \{(001), (100), (010), (111)\}$$
$$L(X_1 \oplus X_2 = 0) = \{(000), (001), (110), (111)\}$$
$$L(X_1 \oplus X_2 = 1) = \{(100), (101), (010), (011)\}$$
$$L(X_1 \oplus X_3 = 0) = \{(000), (010), (101), (111)\}$$
$$L(X_1 \oplus X_3 = 1) = \{(100), (110), (001)(, 011)\}$$
$$L(X_2 \oplus X_3 = 0) = \{(000), (100), (011), (111)\}$$
$$L(X_2 \oplus X_3 = 1) = \{(001), (101), (010), (110)\}$$
$$L(X_1 = 0) = \{(000), (001), (010), (011)\}$$
$$L(X_1 = 1) = \{(100), (101), (110), (111)\}$$
$$L(X_2 = 0) = \{(000), (001), (100), (101)$$
$$L(X_2 = 1) = \{(010), (011), (110), (111)\}$$
$$L(X_3 = 0) = \{(000), (010), (100), (110)\}$$
$$L(X_3 = 1) = \{(001), (011), (101), (111)\}.$$

There are $2^3 - 1 = 7$ nonzero linear combination of $X_1, X_2, X_3$ totally. We divide them into two parts with 4 and 3 elements , denote as $A_1$ and $A_2$ respectively. Without loss of generality, we assume $A_1 = \{X_1 \oplus X_2 \oplus X_3, X_1 \oplus X_2, X_2 \oplus X_3, X_3\}$ and $A_2 = \{X_1 \oplus X_3, X_1, X_2\}$. Given an element $(y_1, y_2, y_3) \in F_2^3$ and a nonzero linear combination of $X_1, X_2, X_3$, it determine a set $L(\oplus_{i=1}^3 c_i X_i = \oplus_{i=1}^3 c_i y_i)$, $c_i \in F_2$. We call the set *determined* by $(y_1, y_2, y_3)$. Take $(y_1, y_2, y_3) = (001)$, for each element in $A_i$, we can write out the determined sets. They are
$$L(X_1 \oplus X_2 \oplus X_3 = 1), L(X_1 \oplus X_2 = 0), L(X_2 \oplus X_3 = 1), L(X_3 = 1) \text{ and}$$
$$L(X_1 \oplus X_3 = 1), L(X_1 = 0), L(X_2 = 0).$$

Furthermore, we call the set $L(\oplus_{i=1}^3 c_i X_i = \oplus_{i=1}^3 c_i y_i \oplus 1)$ the *determined complement set* induced by $(y_1, y_2, y_3)$. The collections of the sets determined by $(001)$ in $A_1$ are

$$\{L(X_1 \oplus X_2 \oplus X_3 = 1), L(X_1 \oplus X_2 = 0), L(X_2 \oplus X_3 = 1), L(X_3 = 1)\} =$$

$$\{(001), (100), (010), (111), (000), (001), (110), (111), (001), (101), (010), (110),$$
$$(001), (011), (101), (111)\}.$$

We can rearrange above collection as

$$\{\underline{(001), (001), (001), (001)}, \underline{(100), (101), (110), (111)}, \underline{(010), (011), (110), (111)},$$
$$\underline{(000), (010), (101), (111)}\}.$$

And the collections of the determined complement set induced by (001) in $A_2$ are

$$\{L(X_1 = 1), L(X_2 = 1), L(X_1 \oplus X_3 = 0)\} =$$

$$\{(100), (101), (110), (111), (010), (011), (110), (111), (000), (010), (101), (111)\}.$$

Note that we allow an element to appear repeatedly in above collections. It is interesting to see that except the element (001) which is used to determined these sets the two collections are equal, i.e. except (001) each element in the collection and its multiplicity are identical. It is also true for an an arbitrary element of $F_2^3$ chosen as determine element and arbitrary partition of nonzero linear combination of $X_1, X_2, X_3$ provided that $|A_1| = 4$ and $|A_2| = 3$.

Above assertion is also true in the general case. Let $X_i, 1 \leq i \leq m$, be $m$ independent random variables on $F_2$. The number of nonzero combination of $X_1, X_2, \cdots, X_m$ is $C_m^1 + C_m^2 + \cdots + C_m^m = 2^m - 1$. We divide it into two parts, each contains $2^{m-1}$ and $2^{m-1} - 1$ elements respectively. Denote them as $A_1$ and $A_2$. For each nonzero $m$-bit string $(c_1, c_2, \cdots, c_m) \in F_2^m$ and $a \in F_2$, by (1) it is easy to check that

$$|L(\oplus_{i=1}^m c_i X_i = a)| = 2^{m-1}, L(\oplus_{i=1}^m c_i X_i = 0) \cup L(\oplus_{i=1}^m c_i X_i = 1) = F_2^m. \quad (2)$$

**Lemma 1.** *Let notations defined as above. For an arbitrary $m$-bit string $Y = (y_1, y_2, \cdots, y_m) \in F_2^m$, then the collection of sets in $A_1$ determined by $Y$ equals to the collection of determined complement sets in $A_2$ induced by $Y$ added $2^{m-1}Y$. Note again that we call the two collections are equal if and only if the elements and its multiplicity in the two collections are identical.*

Proof. It is easy to verified that the number of the elements in the two collections are both $2^{2m-2}$. In order to prove the Lemma, we only need to verify that each element in one collection appears in another collection with the same multiplicity.

Firstly by the definitions of two collections , it is clearly that the determine element $Y$ appears with the same multiplicity. For any $m$-bit string $Y' = (y_1', y_2', \cdots, y_m') \neq Y$, assume that $Y'$ is in the collection of sets in $A_1$ determined by $Y$ and its multiplicity is $r, 1 \leq r \leq 2^{m-1}$. Then there exist exactly $r$ linear combination $\oplus_{j=1}^m c_{i_j} X_j$ in $A_1$, with $c_{i_j} \in F_2$ and $1 \leq i \leq r$, such that $\oplus_{j=1}^m c_{i_j} y_j = \oplus_{j=1}^m c_{i_j} y_j'$. On the other hand, by $Y' \neq Y$, $\oplus_{i=1}^m c_i(y_i - y_i') = 0$ have $2^{m-1} - 1$ nonzero solutions $(c_1, c_2, \cdots, c_m) \in F_2^m$. Hence there are $2^{m-1} - r - 1$ linear combination of $X_i, 1 \leq i \leq m$, in $A_2$ such that $\oplus_{j=1}^m c_{i_j}' y_j = \oplus_{j=1}^m c_{i_j}' y_j'$. From (2), for the residual $r$ linear combination $\oplus_{j=1}^m c_{i_j}' y_j$ in $A_2$, we have $\oplus_{j=1}^m c_{i_j} y_j = \oplus_{j=1}^m c_{i_j} y_j' + 1$. By the above definition, they are just the determined complement sets in $A_2$. So $Y'$ just belong to $r$ determined complement sets in $A_2$, i.e. $Y'$ is in the determined complement sets in $A_2$ and its multiplicity is also $r$. With the arbitrariness of $Y'$, we complete the proof.

# 4   Construction of Almost Resilient Functions

## 4.1   Relation Between Almost Resilient Function and Its Component Functions

In this section, we consider the relation between almost resilient function and its component functions .

**Theorem 1.** *Let $F = (f_1, \cdots, f_m)$ be a function from $F_2^n$ to $F_2^m$, where $n$ and $m$ are integers with $n \geq m \geq 1$, and each $f_i$ is a function on $F_2^n$. If $F$ is an $\varepsilon$-almost$(n, m, k)$-resilient function, then each nonzero combination of $f_1, \cdots, f_m$*

$$f(x) = \bigoplus_{i=1}^{m} c_i f_i(x)$$

*is a $2^{m-1}\varepsilon$-almost $(n, 1, k)$-resilient function, where $x = (x_1, \cdots, x_n) \in F_2^n$.*

Proof. From the definition of almost resilient function, it is easy to prove.

**Theorem 2.** *Let $F = (f_1, \cdots, f_m)$ be a function from $F_2^n$ to $F_2^m$, where $n$ and $m$ are integers with $n \geq m \geq 1$, and each $f_i$ is a function on $F_2^n$. If each nonzero combination of $f_1, \cdots, f_m$*

$$f(x) = \bigoplus_{i=1}^{m} c_i f_i(x)$$

*is an $\varepsilon$-almost $(n, 1, k)$-resilient function, then $F$ is an $\frac{2^{m}-1}{2^{m-1}}\varepsilon$-almost$(n, m, k)$-resilient function , where $x = (x_1, \cdots, x_n) \in F_2^n$.*

Proof. For any $k$ positions $i_1 < i_2 < \cdots < i_k$, any $k$-bit string $\alpha \in F_2^k$, and any $Y = (y_1, \cdots, y_m) \in F_2^m$, by (1), we have

$$Pr[F(x_1, \cdots, x_n) = (y_1, \cdots, y_m) | x_{i_1} x_{i_2} \cdots x_{i_k} = \alpha]$$

$$= \frac{|L(F(X) = Y | x_{i_1} x_{i_2} \cdots x_{i_k} = \alpha)|}{2^{n-k}}. \tag{3}$$

Let $f_i = X_i$ in Lemma 1, and divide all the nonzero linear combination of $f_i, 1 \leq i \leq m$ into two part $A_1$ and $A_2$ with $|A_1| = 2^{m-1}$ and $|A_2| = 2^{m-1} - 1$. Assume

$$A_1 = \{\oplus_{j=1}^{m} c_{i_j} f_j, 1 \leq i \leq 2^{m-1}\} \overset{\triangle}{=} \{h_i, 1 \leq i \leq 2^{m-1}\} \text{ and}$$

$$A_2 = \{\oplus_{j=1}^{m} c_{i_j}' f_j, 1 \leq i \leq 2^{m-1} - 1\} \overset{\triangle}{=} \{h_i', 1 \leq i \leq 2^{m-1} - 1\}.$$

And the collection of determined sets in $A_1$ and the collection of determined complement sets in $A_2$ induced by $Y$ are denoted as $DS_{A_1}(Y)$ and $DCS_{A_2}(Y)$ respectively.

By the condition of the theorem, we have

$$2^{m-1}(-2^{n-k}\varepsilon + 2^{n-k-1}) \leq \sum_{h_i \in A_1} |L(h_i(X) = \oplus_{j=1}^m c_{i_j} y_j | x_{i_1} x_{i_2} \cdots x_{i_k} = \alpha)|$$

$$\leq 2^{m-1}(2^{n-k}\varepsilon + 2^{n-k-1}). \tag{4}$$

By Lemma 1,

$$\sum_{h_i \in A_1} |L(h_i(X) = \oplus_{j=1}^m c_{i_j} y_j | x_{i_1} x_{i_2} \cdots x_{i_k} = \alpha)|$$

$$= \sum |\{(x_1, x_2, \cdots, x_n) : F(X) = Y', Y' \in DS_{A_1}(Y) \text{ and } x_{i_1} x_{i_2} \cdots x_{i_k} = \alpha\}|$$
$$= 2^{m-1}|\{(x_1, x_2, \cdots, x_n) : F(X) = Y \text{ and } x_{i_1} x_{i_2} \cdots x_{i_k} = \alpha)\}|$$
$$+ \sum |\{(x_1, x_2, \cdots, x_n) : F(X) = Y', Y' \in DCS_{A_2}(Y) \text{and } x_{i_1} x_{i_2} \cdots x_{i_k} = \alpha\}|$$
$$= 2^{m-1}|L(F(X) = Y | x_{i_1} x_{i_2} \cdots x_{i_k} = \alpha)|$$
$$+ \sum_{h_i' \in A_2} |L(h_i'(X) = \oplus_{j=1}^m c_{i_j}' y_j \oplus 1 | x_{i_1} x_{i_2} \cdots x_{i_k} = \alpha)|. \tag{5}$$

By the condition of the theorem again, we have

$$(2^{m-1} - 1)(-2^{n-k}\varepsilon + 2^{n-k-1}) \leq \sum_{h_i' \in A_2} |L(h_i(X) = \oplus_{j=1}^m c_{i_j}' y_j \oplus 1$$

$$|x_{i_1} x_{i_2} \cdots x_{i_k} = \alpha)| \leq (2^{m-1} - 1)(2^{n-k}\varepsilon + 2^{n-k-1}). \tag{6}$$

From (4)-(6), we have

$$-(2^m - 1)2^{n-k}\varepsilon + 2^{n-k-1} \leq 2^{m-1}|L(F(X) = Y | x_{i_1} x_{i_2} \cdots x_{i_k} = \alpha)|$$

$$\leq (2^m - 1)2^{n-k}\varepsilon + 2^{n-k-1}.$$

Hence, by (3) we have

$$|Pr[F(x_1, \cdots, x_n) = (y_1, \cdots, y_m) | x_{i_1} x_{i_2} \cdots x_{i_k} = \alpha] - 2^{-m}| \leq \frac{2^m - 1}{2^{m-1}}\varepsilon.$$

Thus the proof is completed.

**Remark.** In the case $\varepsilon = 0$, Theorem 2 gives another proof of Linear Combination Lemma and Proposition 1.

## 4.2     A Construction Based on a Balanced Almost $(n, 1, k)$-Resilient Function

If a balanced $\varepsilon$-almost $(n, 1, k)$-resilient function is given , we show in this section that it is possible to construct a balanced $\frac{9}{2}\varepsilon$-almost $(3n, 2, 2k + 1)$-resilient function.

**Lemma 2.** *If $F$ be an $\varepsilon$-almost $(n, m, k)$-resilient function, then $F$ is also an $\varepsilon$-almost $(n, m, r)$-resilient function, for any $r \leq k$.*

Proof. From the Definition 2, it is easy to prove.

**Theorem 3.** *Let $f$ be a balanced $\varepsilon$-almost $(n, 1, k)$-resilient function, then $g(X, Y, Z) = (f(X) \oplus f(Y), f(Y) \oplus f(Z))$ is a balanced $\frac{9}{2}\varepsilon$-almost $(3n, 2, 2k+1)$-resilient function.*

Proof. Let $h(X, Y) = f(X) \oplus f(Y)$. It is well known that $wt(h) = 2^n wt(f(X)) + 2^n wt(f(Y)) - 2wt(f(X))wt(f(Y))$, where $wt(h) = |L(h(X) = 1)|$. For $wt(f(X)) = 2^{n-1}, wt(f(Y)) = 2^{n-1}$, we have $wt(h) = 2^{2n-1}$. For any fixed $2k+1$ positions $x_{i_1} = a_1, \cdots, x_{i_r} = a_r, y_{i_1} = b_1, \cdots, y_{i_{2k+1-r}} = b_{2k+1-r}$ , we can assume $r \leq k$, otherwise we have $2k+1-r \leq k$ and consider $f(Y)$ instead. By Lemma 1 , we have

$$\frac{1}{2^n}|wt(f(X)) - 2^r wt(f(X)|x_{i_1} = a_1, \cdots, x_{i_r} = a_r)| \leq \varepsilon.$$

So

$$|Pr(h(X, Y) = 1) - Pr(h(X, Y) = 1|x_{i_1} = a_1, \cdots, x_{i_r} = a_r,$$
$$y_{i_1} = b_1, \cdots, y_{i_{2k+1-r}} = b_{2k+1-r})|$$

$$= \frac{1}{2^{2n}}|wt(h(X, Y)) - 2^{2k+1}wt(h(X, Y)|x_{i_1} = a_1, \cdots, x_{i_r} = a_r, y_{i_1} = b_1, \cdots,$$
$$y_{i_{2k+1-r}} = b_{2k+1-r})|$$

$$= \frac{1}{2^{2n}}|2^{2n-1} - 2^{2k+1}(2^{n-(2k+1-r)}wt(f(X)|x_{i_1} = a_1, \cdots, x_{i_r} = a_r) + 2^{n-r}wt($$
$$f(Y)|y_{i_1} = b_1, \cdots, y_{i_{2k+1-r}} = b_{2k+1-r}) - 2wt(f(X)|x_{i_1} = a_1, \cdots, x_{i_r} = a_r)$$
$$wt(f(Y)|y_{i_1} = b_1, \cdots, y_{i_{2k+1-r}} = b_{2k+1-r}))|$$

$$\leq \frac{1}{2^n}|2^{n-1} - 2^r wt(f(X)|x_{i_1} = a_1, \cdots, x_{i_r} = a_r)| + \frac{1}{2^{2n}}2^{2k+2-r}wt(f(Y)|$$
$$y_{i_1} = b_1, \cdots, y_{i_{2k+1-r}} = b_{2k+1-r})|2^{n-1} - 2^r wt(f(X)|x_{i_1} = a_1, \cdots, x_{i_r} = a_r)|$$
$$\leq \varepsilon + 2\varepsilon = 3\varepsilon.$$

The case $f(Y) \oplus f(Z)$ and $f(X) \oplus f(Z)$ can be similarly proved. And each of them is balanced, so $g$ is also balanced. By Theorem 2, the proof is complete.

## 4.3   An Improved Construction

In this section, we will describe a method of improving the degree of the constructed functions with a small trade-off in the nonlinearity and resiliency.

It was pointed out in [7] that the current state of art in resilient functions functions can be classified into two approaches:

1. Construction of $(n, m, k)$-resilient function with high nonlinearity.
2. Construction of $(n, m, t)$-resilient function with degree $d > m$ and high nonlinearity.

The first problem has abundant results [7, 9, 5]. But the second problem has been less studied. Next we will describe a method of improving the degree of the constructed functions with a small trade-off in the nonlinearity and resiliency.

**Theorem 4.** *Let $F = (f_1, \cdots, f_m)$ be a $(n, m, k)$-resilient function with high nonlinearity and the degree of each $f_i < n - 1$. Then it is possible to construct of an $\varepsilon$-almost$(n, m, k)$-resilient function with degree $n - 1$ and nonlinearity is not less than $nl(F) - (m + 1)$, where $\varepsilon = \frac{2^m - 1}{2^m - 1} \frac{m+1}{2^{n-k}}$.*

Proof. For $1 \leq i \leq m$, define $g_i(x_1, x_2, \cdots, x_n) = f_i(x_1, x_2, \cdots, x_n) \oplus x_1 x_2 \cdots x_{i-1} x_{i+1} \cdots x_n$, and $G(X) = (g_1, g_2, \cdots, g_m)$. By construction, the degree of each $g_i$ is $n - 1$. And the degree $n - 1$ terms in each $g_i$'s are different. Hence any nonzero linear combination of $g_i$ has degree $n - 1$. So the degree of $G(X)$ is $n - 1$.

For any nonzero linear combination of $g_i$,

$$g(X) = \oplus_{i=1}^{m} c_i g_i = \oplus_{i=1}^{m} c_i f_i \bigoplus \oplus_i x_1 x_2 \cdots x_{i-1} x_{i+1} \cdots x_n,$$

$$c_i \in F_2, 1 \leq i \leq m. \tag{7}$$

By Proposition 1, for any $k$ positions $i_1 < i_2 < \cdots < i_k$, any $k$-bit string $\alpha \in F_2^k$ and any $a \in F_2$,

$$|L(\oplus_{i=1}^{m} c_i f_i = a | x_{i_1} x_{i_2} \cdots x_{i_k} = \alpha)| = 2^{n-k-1}.$$

The term $\oplus_i x_1 x_2 \cdots x_{i-1} x_{i+1} \cdots x_n$ change at most $m + 1$ output of $\oplus_{i=1}^{m} c_i f_i$. Hence

$$2^{n-k-1} - (m + 1) \leq |L(\oplus_{i=1}^{m} c_i g_i = a | x_{i_1} x_{i_2} \cdots x_{i_k} = \alpha)| \leq 2^{n-k-1} + (m + 1).$$

From (3), we have

$$|Pr[\oplus_{i=1}^{m} c_i g_i = a | x_{i_1} x_{i_2} \cdots x_{i_k} = \alpha] - 2^{-1}| \leq \frac{m + 1}{2^{n-k}}.$$

Hence, $\oplus_{i=1}^{m} c_i g_i$ is an $\frac{m+1}{2^{n-k}}$-almost $(n, 1, k)$-resilient function. By Theorem 2, $G(X)$ is an $\frac{2^m - 1}{2^m - 1} \frac{m+1}{2^{n-k}}$-almost $(n, m, k)$-resilient function.

Similarly, with (7) and the fact that the term $\oplus_i x_1 x_2 \cdots x_{i-1} x_{i+1} \cdots x_n$ change at most $m+1$ output of $\oplus_{i=1}^{m} c_i f_i$, $nl(\oplus_{i=1}^{m} c_i g_i) \geq nl(\oplus_{i=1}^{m} c_i f_i) - (m+1)$. By the definition of nonlinearity, the nonlinearity of $G$ is at least $nl(F) - (m+1)$. The proof is thus complete.

In the case $n \gg k + 1$, $\varepsilon = \frac{2^m - 1}{2^m - 1} \frac{m+1}{2^{n-k}}$ is little and could be ignored in practical.

## 5    The Relation Between Almost Resilient Function and Almost CI Function

Similar to the resilient function, correlation immune function can also be generalized. K.Kurosawa et al.[1] called it the almost correlation immune function. In fact, in earlier Yi-Xian Yan[8] has generalized the single output case and presented some results.

**Definition 3.** *The function $F$ is called an $\varepsilon$-almost $(n, m, k)$-correlation immune function if*

$$|Pr[F(x_1, \cdots, x_n) = (y_1, \cdots, y_m)|x_{i_1} x_{i_2} \cdots_{i_k} = \alpha] -$$

$$Pr[F(x_1, \cdots, x_n) = (y_1, \cdots, y_m)]| \leq \varepsilon$$

*for any $k$ positions $i_1 < i_2 < \cdots < i_k$, for any $k$-bit string $\alpha \in F_2^k$, and for any $(y_1, \cdots, y_m) \in F_2^m$, where the values $x_j (j \notin \{i_1, i_2, \cdots, i_k\})$ are chosen independently at random.*

The relation between almost CI function and nonuniform $LS(\varepsilon, k, n, t)$ is given in [1]. It is well-known that an $(n, m, k)$-resilient function is equivalent to an balanced $(n, m, k)$-CI function.

By the Definition 2 and 3, it is easy to see that if $F$ is balanced, then $F$ is an $\varepsilon$-almost $(n, m, k)$-CI function if and only if $F$ is an $\varepsilon$-almost $(n, m, k)$ resilient function.

**Theorem 5.** *Assume $F = (f_1, \cdots, f_m)$ is a balanced function, then if $F$ is an $\varepsilon$-almost $(n, m, k)$-CI function, every nonzero combination of $f_1, \cdots, f_m$*

$$f(x) = \bigoplus_{i=1}^{m} c_i f_i(x)$$

*is a balanced $2^{m-1}\varepsilon$-almost $(n, 1, k)$-CI function. If every nonzero combination of $f_1, \cdots, f_m$*

$$f(x) = \bigoplus_{i=1}^{m} c_i f_i(x)$$

*is a balanced $\varepsilon$-almost $(n, 1, k)$-CI function, $F$ is a $\frac{2^m-1}{2^{m-1}}\varepsilon$-almost $(n, m, k)$-CI function , where $x = (x_1, \cdots, x_n) \in F_2^n$.*

Proof. The conclusion follows from Theorem 2 and above discussion directly.

# 6 Conclusion

In this paper, we have study the relation between an almost resilient function and its component functions. We prove that if each nonzero linear combination of $f_1, f_2, \cdots, f_m$ is $\varepsilon$-almost$(n, 1, k)$-resilient function, then $F$ is a $\frac{2^m-1}{2^{m-1}}\varepsilon$-almost$(n, m, k)$-resilient function. In the case $\varepsilon$ equals 0, the theorem gives another proof of Linear Combination Lemma. As application of this theorem, we show it is possible to construct a balanced $\frac{9}{2}\varepsilon$-almost $(3n, 2, 2k+1)$-resilient function from a balanced $\varepsilon$-almost $(n, 1, k)$-resilient function and present a method of improving the degree of the constructed functions with a small trade-off in the nonlinearity and resiliency. At the end of this paper, we conclude the relations between the almost CI function and its component functions.

From this paper we see that the Theorem 2 is the basis of many constructions. So it remain for us to improve Theorem 2 i.e. if each nonzero linear combination of $f_1, f_2, \cdots, f_m$ is $\varepsilon$-almost$(n, 1, k)$-resilient function, is it possible to prove that $F$ is a $\varepsilon'$-almost$(n, m, k)$-resilient function such that $\varepsilon' < \frac{2^m-1}{2^m-1}\varepsilon$? Because allow small deviation from the uniform distribution, the almost resilient function have better parameters. we believe that the almost resilient functions have wider application than resilient function . And as a further work, we wish to find more construction methods and cryptographic applications of almost resilient function.

## Acknowledgement

The authors wish to thank the referees for their comments and suggestions that helped to improved the correspondence. This work was supported by the National Natural Science Foundation of China(No.60373059), the National Research Foundation for the Doctoral Program of Higher Education of China(No. 20040013007) and the Research Foundation of the State Key Laboratory of Information Security.

## References

1. K.Kurosawa,T.Johansson,D.Stinson. Almost k-wise independent sample spaces and their applications. *J.Cryptology*, vol.14, no.4, pp.231-253,2001.
2. J.Naor,M.Naor. Small bias probality spaces:efficient constructions and applications. In *SIAM Journal on Computing* 22, pp.838-856, 1993.
3. M.N.Wegman,J.L.Carter. New hash functions and their use in authentication and set equality. *Journal of Computer and System Sciences* 22, pp.265-279, 1981.
4. K.Kurosawa,R.Matsumoto. Almost security of cryptographic boolean functions,*IEEE Tran. on Info. theory*, IT-50 No.11, pp.2752-2761, November 2004.
5. Xian-Mo Zhang, Yu-Liang Zheng. Cryptographically resilient functions. *IEEE Tran. on Info. theory*, IT-43. No.5, pp.1740-1747. September 1997.
6. Guo-Zhen Xiao,J.Massy. A special characterization of correlation immune combining functions,*IEEE Tran. on Info. theory*, IT-34, pp.569-571, May 1988.
7. K.C.Gupta,P.Sarkar. Improved construction of nonlinear resilient S-Boxes. *IEEE Tran. on Info. theory*,IT-51,No.1, pp.339-348, January, 2005.
8. Yi-Xian Yan, Xu-Duan Lin. Coding Theory and Cryptography. People Post and Telecomunication Publisher,1992.(in chinese).
9. T.Johansson,E.Pasalic. A construction of resilient functions with high nonlinearity. *IEEE Tran. on Info. theory*,IT-49, No.2 , pp.494-501, Feburary 2003.

# A Novel Method to Maintain Privacy in Mobile Agent Applications

Kun Peng, Ed Dawson, Juanma Gonzalez Nieto, Eiji Okamoto,
and Javier López

Information Security Institute,
Queensland University of Technology
{k.peng, juanma, e.dawson}@qut.edu.au
http://www.isrc.qut.edu.au/people/pengk

**Abstract.** Two methods to implement privacy in network communication, anonymity and DCSC (data confidentiality and secure computation) are analysed and compared in regard to privacy in mobile agent applications. It is illustrated that privacy through DCSC is more suitable in mobile agent applications. To support this conclusion, privacy is concretely implemented in a bidding mobile agent scheme in this paper. Success of this example demonstrates that privacy can be practically achieved in mobile agent applications through DCSC without compromising the advantage of mobile agent.

**Keywords:** Mobile agent, privacy, DCSC, secure computation.

## 1 Introduction

Mobile agents [9, 8, 19, 20] are autonomous software entities that relay code, data and state through multiple nodes. Usually, an originator generates the mobile agent and sends it out to collect data, which is then used by the originator for a special purpose. The advantage of mobile agent is that it is a real-time service, so can visit dynamically chosen nodes to collect data instantly. For example, with the help of a bidding mobile agent, a buyer (seller) can instantly get the bids from a dynamic set of bidders. Then he can immediately choose one bid as the winning bid. Compared to the traditional e-auction schemes [12, 15, 17], a bidding-mobile-agent-based auction is more instant, flexible and convenient.

Usually, compared to traditional network applications like traditional e-auction and e-voting [14, 2, 10, 11], a mobile agent application has the following properties.

- Dynamic: the nodes in the communication network are usually temporally connected terminals fitted with a relay function.
- Instant: network service must be available instantly without preparation or delay.
- Flexible: various nodes and communication patterns may be involved.

Y.G. Desmedt et al. (Eds.): CANS 2005, LNCS 3810, pp. 247–260, 2005.

With these properties, mobile agent has its advantage in circumstances where dynamic and instant network services are needed. Without these properties, mobile agent has no advantage over the traditional network applications.

As the nodes usually may want to conceal their personal privacy in mobile agent applications, in certain cases no node may permit his identity to be linked to his data. More precisely, a node's privacy is the unlinkability between his identity and his data. A definition of privacy in a mobile agent application is as follows.

**Definition 1.** *A mobile agent application is private if no node's data can be linked to its identity.*

For example, a bidding mobile agent application is private if except for the winner no bidder can be linked to its bid. The only known private mobile agent schemes are [19, 20], two bidding agents. In [19, 20], privacy is implemented through anonymity of the nodes, a method which is inefficient and inconsistent with the properties and advantages of mobile agent application. So designing practical privacy mechanism in mobile agent application is a challenging task. The design must take into account the important fact that as a real-time network application mobile agent has its advantages, which should not be sacrificed in the implementation of privacy.

In this paper, a new privacy mechanism is proposed in mobile agent scheme. The new mechanism, called DCSC, employs data confidentiality and secure computation to achieve privacy in network communication. Basing privacy on data confidentiality and secure computation is not a new idea. For example, it is widely applied to traditional network applications like electronic auction [12, 15] and e-voting [10, 11]. Although this privacy mechanism has not been applied to mobile agent schemes, it has some advantages in regard to mobile agent over the privacy mechanism based on anonymity. The DCSC privacy mechanism is more efficient and does not conflict with the advantages of mobile agent applications. So it is more suitable to mobile agent than the privacy mechanism based on anonymity. DCSC is applied to a new bidding mobile agent scheme with the same circumstance as [19, 20]. The new bidding mobile agent scheme illustrates that privacy can be practically achieved in mobile agent applications without compromising its advantages.

The remainder of this paper is organised as follows. In Section 2, privacy in network communication is analysed and two privacy mechanisms are compared. It is shown that DCSC privacy has its advantages in some applications. In Section 3, it is illustrated that DCSC privacy is more suitable for privacy in mobile agent and often the only feasible solution for private mobile agent application. In Section 4, secure computation techniques are introduced to support DCSC. Especially, an efficient secure computation technique to be used later in the paper, ciphertext comparison, is recalled. In Section 5, a concrete application of DCSC privacy in mobile agent, private bidding mobile agent, is designed on the base of ciphertext comparison. In Section 7, the paper is concluded.

## 2    Privacy in Network Communication

A communication network is composed of a few nodes and used to transmit messages through the nodes. There are many security requirements on network communication. This paper focuses on one of them, privacy, a property widely desired in network applications.

**Definition 2.** *Network communication is private if no node in the network can be linked to his data transmitted in the network.*

This unlinkability in network communication is frequently required. For example, on-line buyers using e-cash [5], on-line bidders in e-auction [12, 15, 17] and on-line voters in e-voting [10, 11] do not want to be linked to the items they buy, their bids and their votes respectively.

There are two methods to implement privacy in a communication network: anonymity and DCSC (data confidentiality and secure computation). Anonymity of a node requires that the identity of the node or its other identification information like IP address or geographic location is concealed. Anonymity ensures that no node is identified, not to mention to be linked to any data. Under DCSC, all the data are always confidential (encrypted) even when being processed such that no identification can be linked to any data in plaintext.

The idea of the anonymity mechanism is simple: if a party is anonymous, his behaviour cannot be linked to his identity. To implement anonymity of a party, a pseudonym for him and untraceability of his data are usually necessary. The party can use the pseudonym to label his data such that his identity does not appear in the network communication. The data in the network communication must be untraceable such that any data cannot be linked to its owner by tracing it back to its origin (e.g. address of its owner). Another role of the pseudonym is that recoverable pseudonym can be designed such that anonymity can be revoked by recovering the corresponding identity from a pseudonym. The only known practical method to implement untraceability is mix network [1, 7]. A mix network is an additional communication network interleaving with the existing communication network, whose role is to relay and shuffle the data transmitted between any two nodes in the existing communication such that data transmission in the existing communication network becomes untraceable. Although the idea of the anonymity mechanism is simple and direct, it has the following drawbacks.

-   Anonymity is difficult to achieve in special applications with certain communication patterns. For example, implementation of privacy is difficult between neighbouring nodes when relay communication pattern is employed. Mobile agent is such an example. When a mobile agent visits a node, the node excutes the agent to determine the next node to relay the agent to. So each node definitely knows the identity of the next node.
-   Pseudonym is usually implemented through special signature schemes like blind signature, group signature or ring signature. Especially, when authentication is required, complex and inefficient group signature [4] or ring signature must be employed. Compared to normal signature schemes, these

signature schemes require costly set-up, complex maintenance, inefficient generation and verification and intensive network communication.

- Mix network needs additional network communication interleaving with the existing network communication, which may affect or even conflict with the existing network communication. For example, when the existing network communication is temporal, instant and dynamic, it is inconsistent with mix network, which is not always temporally or instantly available and requires setting up beforehand and verification afterwards. Moreover, mix network is inefficient (especially when its correctness is required to be publicly verifiable) and needs intensive network communication.

DCSC is composed of two key cryptographic techniques: data confidentiality through encryption and secure computation of the encrypted data without revealing them. Under DCSC, data in the communication network are encrypted (with a semantically secure encryption algorithm[1]) and never decrypted. After the encrypted data is transmitted and collected and the network communication finishes, the encrypted data may be processed and used for a certain purpose. When the data is processed, a secure computation technique [18, 15, 16] is employed to compute a required function of the data without decrypting them. Although all the encrypted data is traceable and labelled with its owner's identity, they are kept confidential for ever. So no party can be linked to any known data (in plaintext). Note that the secure computation takes place after the network communication finishes and out of the communication network, so is independent of the network.

Data confidentiality can be easily and efficiently implemented as any semantically secure encryption algorithm can be employed. Complexity and cost of secure computation depends on which function of the data is computed. Usually, a general secure computation solution to compute any function is less efficient, while secure computation solution to certain functions are more efficient. With the progress in secure computation techniques, more and more functions can be efficiently computed with encrypted inputs. Another advantage of DCSC is that data confidentiality is achieved. As in some applications, it is desired to conceal the statistic information of the data, data confidentiality is needed even if anonymity has been implemented to prevent the link between the data and their owners.

Both privacy mechanisms are widely employed in cryptographic applications. Anonymity-based privacy is more popular in e-cash [5], while DCSC privacy is employed in most private e-auction schemes [12, 15] (the only known anonymity-based private e-auction is [17].). In e-voting, both anonymity-based privacy [14, 2] and DCSC privacy [10, 11] are common. When choosing which privacy mechanism to use, the following factors should be considered.

---

[1] An encryption algorithm is semantically-secure if given a ciphertext $c$ and two messages $m_1$ and $m_2$, such that $c = E(m_i)$ where $i = 1$ or 2, there is no polynomial algorithm to find out $i$.

- Semantically secure encryption is much simpler and more efficient than group signature or ring signature, which require costly operation both before and during the network communication.
- Mix network is inefficient and needs an additional interleaving network service, which may affect or even compromise the existing network.
- Secure computation is independent of the communication network, so brings no side effect to communication.
- Appropriate and efficient secure computation technique is necessary for success of DCSC.

So, if secure computation of the function of the data is relatively efficient, or the pseudonym technique or mix network is inconsistent with the existing communication, or data confidentiality is desired, DCSC instead of the anonymity-based privacy mechanism should be applied.

## 3   Privacy in Mobile Agent Applications

Privacy is important in mobile agent like in other network applications. As stated before, the advantage of mobile agent over traditional network applications is that it is a temporal, dynamic, instant and flexible real-time service. Unlike traditional network services, a mobile agent application does not involve preparation or setting-up work, long-lasting network connection or communication delay. A mobile agent can instantly travel through temporal network connection and implement a certain application without any interference or delay. Without this advantage, mobile agent is useless. For example, if real-time service is not required, traditional e-auction and e-voting scheme are more mature, stable and reliable than bidding agent and voting agent.

In the known private mobile agent applications [19, 20], privacy is implemented through anonymity of the nodes. However, in the privacy implementation in [19, 20] only pseudonym is covered while untraceability, a more essential primitive, is not mentioned. So these privacy implementations are incomplete and unreliable. Careful study shows that implementing privacy in mobile agent application through anonymity is unsuitable and in most cases infeasible. Besides the efficiency concern caused by group (ring) signature and mix network, the following drawbacks demonstrate that anonymity-based privacy is inconsistent with mobile agent.

- Group signature and ring signature require every participant to register at a certain time before the network communication starts, which is contradictory to the requirement of instant service in mobile agent applications.
- An additional mix network is involved in the communication. If the mix network is not ready between any two neighbouring nodes, communication fails. Note that a mix network is not often available locally at any temporal time and dynamic location (in many cases, it is impossible to set up a mix network instantly at a certain given location.). On the other hand, mobile agent employs the relay communication pattern and requires instantly

available local relay communication service. Even if a local mix network is instantly available, the relay communication pattern still reveals information about address or location between neighbouring nodes. Moreover, shuffling in a mix network is essentially a batch operation instead of a instant service. So the dynamic and instant behaviour of the mobile agent application must depend on mix network, a service not dynamically or instantly available. This is a serious inconsistency.

– Generation of group signature and ring signature is less efficient than normal encryption or signature generation. Additionally, group signature and ring signature produce longer messages. So the nodes with limited computation capability and wireless communication with limited bandwidth cannot afford this additional computation and communication.

On the other hand, DCSC is suitable for privacy in mobile agent. Data confidentiality is efficient to implement using encryption. Data confidentiality does not increase communication burden. Although secure computation brings additional computation and communication, it does not delay the communication. With progress of secure computation technology [16], efficient secure computation is possible in many mobile agent applications. The most important fact is that DCSC does not compromise the advantages of mobile agent. As a result, DCSC is a better solution to privacy than anonymity in mobile agent applications.

## 4    Secure Computation

Secure computation techniques are essential for DCSC privacy, so are introduced in this section. Secure computation [18, 15, 16, 13] is also called multiparty computation or secure evaluation in some literature. Its role is to compute a function with encrypted inputs. The private key is shared by multiple parties such that no input can be decrypted under a threshold trust assumption. The function is evaluated by the multiple parties such that the function result is obtained while no input is revealed. It is demonstrated in [13] that any Boolean function with a circuit of linear size can be efficienctly evaluated without revealing the inputs, while a function with a $k$ bit output can be deduced to $k$ Boolean functions. Current secure computation techniques [15, 13] can provide solution to a wide range of functions. So DCSC can be generally implemented in mobile agent schemes in many application. Function-oriented special evaluation techniques can be employed to improve efficiency. For example, addition through secure computation is very efficient with the help of an additive homomorphic encryption algorithm[2]. In another example, e-auction, both general secure computation techniques [15, 13] and more efficient specially-purposed secure computation techniques [12] have been proposed to process the encrypted bids without decrypting them in recent private auction schemes.

---

[2] An encryption with encryption function $E()$ is additive homomorphic if $E(m_1)E(m_2) = E(m_1 + m_2)$.

The millionaire problem is the most intensively studied function in secure computation. When Yao [18] first proposed secure computation, he studied the millionaire problem as an example. In the millionaire problem, two ciphertexts are compared without being decrypted to determine which encrypts a larger message. So solution to the millionaire problem is called ciphertext comparison. The millionaire problem is important as many complex computations can be deduced to it. In this paper, ciphertext comparison is employed to achieve privacy in a bidding mobile agent scheme. In the recent years, progress has been made in finding an efficient solution to the millionaire problem. The most efficient verifiable ciphertext comparison technique so far is proposed in [16], which is efficient enough for practical applications.

In [16], two $L$-bit messages $m_1$ and $m_2$ are bitwise encrypted and then compared as follows.

1. The two messages $m_1$ and $m_2$ are represented bit by bit as $(m_{1,1}, m_{1,2}, \ldots, m_{1,L})$ and $(m_{2,1}, m_{2,2}, \ldots, m_{2,L})$.
2. The two messages are bitwise encrypted $c_1 = (c_{1,1}, c_{1,2}, \ldots, c_{1,L}) = (E(m_{1,1}), E(m_{1,2}), \ldots, E(m_{1,L}))$ and $c_2 = (c_{2,1}, c_{2,2}, \ldots, c_{2,L}) = (E(m_{2,1}), E(m_{2,2}), \ldots, E(m_{2,L}))$ where $E()$ is a additive homomorphic encryption algorithm. The private key is shared by multiple participants such that any decryption is possible only when the number of cooperating participants is over a threshold.
3. $c_1$ and $c_2$ are sent to the participants, who are required to test whether

$$(D(c_{1,1}) = 1 \land D(c_{2,1}) = 0) \lor$$
$$(D(c_{1,1}) = D(c_{2,1}) \land D(c_{1,2}) = 1 \land D(c_{2,2}) = 0) \lor \ldots \lor \qquad (1)$$
$$(D(c_{1,1}) = D(c_{2,1}) \land D(c_{1,2}) = D(c_{2,2}) \land \ldots \land D(c_{1,L-1}) = D(c_{2,L-1})$$
$$\land D(c_{1,L}) = 1 \land D(c_{2,L}) = 0)$$

without decrypting any bit encryption. $m_1 > m_2$ if and only if logic test (1) returns TRUE.
4. The participants exploits homomorphism of the encryption algorithm and use two cryptographic primitives, batch verification and zero test, to test

$$D(c_{1,1}/(E(1)c_{2,1})) = 0 \lor D(c_{1,1}/c_{2,1})^{t_1}(c_{1,2}/(E(1)c_{2,2}))^{t_2} = 0 \lor$$
$$\ldots \lor D(\textstyle\prod_{i=1}^{L-1}(c_{1,i}/c_{2,i})^{t_i})(c_{1,L}/(E(1)c_{2,L}))^{t_L}) = 0 \qquad (2)$$

where $t_1, t_2, \ldots, t_L$ are randomly chosen. Logic test (2) is equivalent to logic test (1). If and only if logic test (2) returns TRUE, the participants declare $m_1 > m_2$. Details of batch verification and zero test are described in [16].

It is proved in [16] that the ciphertext comparison technique is correct and sound: $m_1 > m_2$ if and only if the zero test in (2) returns $true$. It is also illustrated in [16] that the ciphertext comparison technique is private: if the colluding participants are not over the sharing threshold of the private key, no information about $m_1$ or $m_2$ is revealed except which one is larger. In this paper, the ciphertext comparison technique above is denoted as $CC(c_1, c_2)$.

# 5   Implementation of DCSC Privacy in Bidding Mobile Agent Scheme

In this section, DCSC privacy mechanism is implemented in a typical mobile agent application: bidding mobile agent. A bidding agent is generated and sent out by an originator to sell or buy an item. It migrates to multiple bidding nodes to collect their price quotes, and is free to choose its next move dynamically based on the data it acquired from its journey. The agent finally returns to the originator with the bids of all the bidders. Then the originator chooses a winning offer (bid). As the bidding nodes usually want to conceal their personal privacy, no node permits his identity to be linked to his bid. So privacy is necessary in the application of bidding mobile agent. The existing bidding mobile agent schemes with privacy are [19] and [20]. As stated before, these two schemes employ anonymity mechanism to implement privacy, which is incomplete, unreliable and inefficient.

A new bidding mobile agent scheme is designed, which employs DCSC to implement privacy. In the new scheme, there are an originator, some potential bidders and a third party. It is assumed that originator and the third party do not collude. The originator sends out a mobile agent to visit the nodes to collect bids. The mobile agent finally returns to the originator with encrypted bids from all the bidders. The function for the originator to compute is to find out the highest or lowest bid from all the encrypted bids without decrypting them. Namely, he has to find out the ciphertexts encrypting the largest or smallest message from multiple ciphertexts by executing secure computation with the third party. His task is similar to the auctioneer's task in e-auction schemes [15, 12]. However, the secure computation techniques in these traditional auction schemes cannot be employed in mobile agent schemes. The general secure computation techniques in the existing auction schemes [15] are too inefficient. The specially-purposed

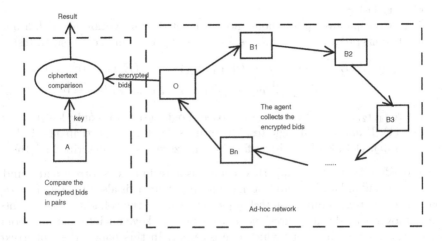

**Fig. 1.** DCSC private bidding mobile agent

secure computation techniques in the existing auction schemes [12] require each bidder to make a choice for every biddable price in his bid. This bid format causes high computational cost for bid encryption and heavy burden for communication. Fortunately, the function for the originator to compute in a bidding mobile agent application can be implemented through repeated ciphertext comparisons. If the encrypted bids are compared pair by pair, the highest or lowest bid can be found. The ciphertext-comparison-based secure computation is implemented between the originator and the third party (e.g. a hardware like smart-card), who do not collude with each other. More precisely, the third party shares the private key with the originator and cooperates with the originator to perform the ciphertext comparison on the encrypted bids pair by pair. As the ciphertext comparison technique in [16] is publicly verifiable, the third party does not need to be trusted in regard to correctness of computation. Nothing is revealed to the originator except the comparison result as the ciphertext comparison technique in [16] is private if the third party does not collude with the originator.

The new private bidding mobile agent scheme is described in Figure 1 where $A$ is the third party, $O$ is the originator and $B_i$ is the $i^{th}$ bidder. To suit the ciphertext comparison technique in [16], the bids are bitwise encrypted. The symbols to be used in this section are as follows.

- $p$ and $q$ are large primes such that $p = 2q + 1$.
- $G$ is the cyclic subgroup in of $Z_p$ with order $q$ and $g$ is a generator of $G$.
- $L$ is the bit length of a bid.

The new bidding mobile agent scheme is as follows.

1. Publishing public key
   An additive homomorphic encryption scheme is chosen. The third party chooses private key $x_1$ from $Z_q$ and publishes his public key $y_1 = g^{x_1}$. The originator chooses his private key $x_2$ from $Z_q$ and publishes his public key $y_2 = g^{x_2}$.
2. Starting a mobile agent
   The originator generates a mobile agent, which will visit the potential bidders and collect their bids. The public key for data encryption, $y_1 y_2$, is published in the agent, while the corresponding private key is shared by the originator and the third party.
3. Visiting the potential bidders
   When the mobile agent arrives at a potential bidder, the bidder encrypts, signs and submits his bid to the agent. The $i^{th}$ bidder $B_i$ chooses a bid $b_i$ with bitwise representation $(b_{i,1}, b_{i,2}, \ldots, b_{i,L})$. He then encrypts his bid into $c_i = (c_{i,1}, c_{i,2}, \ldots, c_{i,L})$ where $c_{i,k} = (a_{i,k}, \ b_{i,k}) = (g^{r_{i,k}}, \ g^{b_{i,k}}(y_1 y_2)^{r_{i,k}})$ for $k = 1, 2, \ldots, L$. Note this encryption is a variant of ElGamal encryption. Its difference from a standard ElGamal encryption is:
   - the public key is $y_1 y_2$, so the corresponding private key is $x_1 + x_2$, which is shared by the third party and the originator;
   - decryption of ciphertext $(a, b)$ is $\log_g(b/a^{x_1+x_2})$

This modified ElGamal encryption is bitwise and additively homomorphic, so consistent with the ciphertext comparison technique in [16], which will be employed later to compare the encrypted bids. Although decryption of this modified ElGamal encryption algorithm requires computation of discrete logarithm, the computation of discrete logarithm is easy as the message is a bit.

4. Determining winning bid and winner

When the mobile agent returns to the originator, it brings $n$ encrypted bids $c_1, c_2, \ldots, c_n$. The originator compares them in pairs to find the winning bid using the ciphertext comparison technique described in Section 4. For example, after $n - 1$ comparisons, the highest or lowest bid can be found. Note that all the bids are additively homomorphically encrypted bit by bit, so is consistent with the ciphertext comparison technique. Comparison of two encrypted bids $c_i$ and $c_j$ is as follows.

(a) The originator randomly chooses $R_{i,k}$ and $R_{j,k}$ for $k = 1, 2, \ldots, L$ from $Z_q$. He then calculates $c'_i = (c'_{i,1}, c'_{i,2}, \ldots, c'_{i,L})$ and $c'_j = (c'_{j,1}, c'_{j,2}, \ldots, c'_{j,L})$ where

$$c'_{i,k} = (a'_{i,k}, b'_{i,k}) = (g^{R_{i,k}} a_{\pi(i),k}, (y_1 y_2)^{R_{i,k}} b_{\pi(i),k})$$
$$c'_{j,k} = (a'_{j,k}, b'_{j,k}) = (g^{R_{j,k}} a_{\pi(j),k}, (y_1 y_2)^{R_{j,k}} b_{\pi(j),k})$$

and $\pi()$ is a permutation of $\{i, j\}$. Finally, he sends $c'_i$ and $c'_j$ to the third party. Namely the originator re-encrypts and shuffles $c_i$ and $c_j$ and sends them to the third party. The oroginator demonstrates that $D(c'_i)$ and $D(c'_j)$ is a permutation of $D(c_i)$ and $D(c_j)$ without revealing the permutation by proving

$$(\log_g a'_{i,1}/a_{i,1} = \log_{y_1 y_2} b'_{i,1}/b_{i,1} \wedge \log_g a'_{i,2}/a_{i,2} = \log_{y_1 y_2} b'_{i,2}/b_{i,2} \wedge \ldots$$
$$\wedge \log_g a'_{i,L}/a_{i,L} = \log_{y_1 y_2} b'_{i,L}/b_{i,L} \wedge \log_g a'_{j,1}/a_{j,1} = \log_{y_1 y_2} b'_{j,1}/b_{j,1} \wedge$$
$$\log_g a'_{j,2}/a_{j,2} = \log_{y_1 y_2} b'_{j,2}/b_{j,2} \wedge \ldots \wedge \log_g a'_{j,L}/a_{j,L} = \log_{y_1 y_2} b'_{j,L}/b_{j,L})$$
$$\vee (\log_g a'_{i,1}/a_{j,1} = \log_{y_1 y_2} b'_{i,1}/b_{j,1} \wedge \log_g a'_{i,2}/a_{j,2} = \log_{y_1 y_2} b'_{i,2}/b_{j,2} \wedge \ldots$$
$$\wedge \log_g a'_{i,L}/a_{j,L} = \log_{y_1 y_2} b'_{i,L}/b_{j,L} \wedge \log_g a'_{j,1}/a_{i,1} = \log_{y_1 y_2} b'_{j,1}/b_{i,1} \wedge$$
$$\log_g a'_{j,2}/a_{i,2} = \log_{y_1 y_2} b'_{j,2}/b_{i,2} \wedge \ldots \wedge \log_g a'_{j,L}/a_{i,L} = \log_{y_1 y_2} b'_{j,L}/b_{i,L})$$

This proof can be simplified using batch verification technique [3] into proof of

$$\log_g(\prod_{k=1}^{L}(a'_{i,k}/a_{i,k})^{t_k} \prod_{k=1}^{L}(a'_{j,k}/a_{j,k})^{t'_k}) =$$
$$\log_{y_1 y_2}(\prod_{k=1}^{L}(b'_{i,1}/b_{i,1})^{t_k} \prod_{k=1}^{L}(b'_{j,1}/b_{j,1})^{t'_k}) \qquad (3)$$
$$\vee \log_g(\prod_{k=1}^{L}(a'_{i,k}/a_{j,k})^{t_k} \prod_{k=1}^{L}(a'_{j,k}/a_{i,k})^{t'_k}) =$$
$$\log_{y_1 y_2}(\prod_{k=1}^{L}(b'_{i,1}/b_{j,1})^{t_k} \prod_{k=1}^{L}(b'_{j,1}/b_{i,1})^{t'_k})$$

where $t_k$ and $t'_k$ are short integers randomly chosen by the originator. Proof (3) can be implemented using ZK proof of equality of logarithm [5] and ZK proof of partial knowledge [6]. The proof can be publicly verified by anyone.

(b) The third party re-encrypts and shuffles $c_i'$ and $c_j'$. He randomly chooses $S_{i,k}$ and $S_{j,k}$ for $k = 1, 2, \ldots, L$ from $Z_q$. He then calculates $c_i'' = (c_{i,1}'', c_{i,2}'', \ldots, c_{i,L}'')$ and $c_j'' = (c_{j,1}'', c_{j,2}'', \ldots, c_{j,L}'')$ where

$$c_{i,k}'' = (a_{i,k}'', \ b_{i,k}'') = (g^{S_{i,k}} a_{\pi'(i),k}', \ (y_1 y_2)^{S_{i,k}} b_{\pi'(i),k}')$$
$$c_{j,k}'' = (a_{j,k}'', \ b_{j,k}'') = (g^{S_{j,k}} a_{\pi'(j),k}', \ (y_1 y_2)^{S_{j,k}} b_{\pi'(j),k}')$$

and $\pi'()$ is a permutation of $\{i, j\}$. The third party demonstrates that $D(c_i'')$ and $D(c_j'')$ is a permutation of $D(c_i')$ and $D(c_j')$ without revealing the permutation by proving

$$(\log_g a_{i,1}''/a_{i,1}' = \log_{y_1 y_2} b_{i,1}''/b_{i,1}' \ \wedge \ \log_g a_{i,2}''/a_{i,2}' = \log_{y_1 y_2} b_{i,2}''/b_{i,2}' \ \wedge \ldots$$
$$\wedge \ \log_g a_{i,L}''/a_{i,L}' = \log_{y_1 y_2} b_{i,L}''/b_{i,L}' \ \wedge \ \log_g a_{j,1}''/a_{j,1}' = \log_{y_1 y_2} b_{j,1}''/b_{j,1}' \ \wedge$$
$$\log_g a_{j,2}''/a_{j,2}' = \log_{y_1 y_2} b_{j,2}''/b_{j,2}' \ \wedge \ \ldots \wedge \ \log_g a_{j,L}''/a_{j,L}' = \log_{y_1 y_2} b_{j,L}''/b_{j,L}')$$
$$\vee \ (\log_g a_{i,1}''/a_{j,1}' = \log_{y_1 y_2} b_{i,1}''/b_{j,1}' \ \wedge \ \log_g a_{i,2}''/a_{j,2}' = \log_{y_1 y_2} b_{i,2}''/b_{j,2}' \ \wedge \ldots$$
$$\wedge \ \log_g a_{i,L}''/a_{j,L}' = \log_{y_1 y_2} b_{i,L}''/b_{j,L}' \ \wedge \ \log_g a_{j,1}''/a_{i,1}' = \log_{y_1 y_2} b_{j,1}''/b_{i,1}' \ \wedge$$
$$\log_g a_{j,2}''/a_{i,2}' = \log_{y_1 y_2} b_{j,2}''/b_{i,2}' \ \wedge \ \ldots \wedge \ \log_g a_{j,L}''/a_{i,L}' = \log_{y_1 y_2} b_{j,L}''/b_{i,L}')$$

This proof can be simplified using batch verification technique [3] into proof of

$$\log_g(\prod \nolimits_{k=1}^{L}(a_{i,k}''/a_{i,k}')^{t_k} \prod \nolimits_{k=1}^{L}(a_{j,k}''/a_{j,k}')^{t_k'}) =$$
$$\log_{y_1 y_2}(\prod \nolimits_{k=1}^{L}(b_{i,1}''/b_{i,1}')^{t_k} \prod \nolimits_{k=1}^{L}(b_{j,1}''/b_{j,1}')^{t_k'}) \qquad (4)$$
$$\vee \ \log_g(\prod \nolimits_{k=1}^{L}(a_{i,k}''/a_{j,k}')^{t_k} \prod \nolimits_{k=1}^{L}(a_{j,k}''/a_{i,k}')^{t_k'}) =$$
$$\log_{y_1 y_2}(\prod \nolimits_{k=1}^{L}(b_{i,1}''/b_{j,1}')^{t_k} \prod \nolimits_{k=1}^{L}(b_{j,1}''/b_{i,1}')^{t_k'})$$

where $t_k$ and $t_k'$ are short integers randomly chosen by the originator. Proof (4) can be implemented using ZK proof of equality of logarithm [5] and ZK proof of partial knowledge [6]. The proof can be publicly verified by anyone.

(c) The originator verifies the third party's proof, then performs $CC(c_i'', c_j'')$ with him.

The winning bid can be found by repeated comparisons of the encrypted bids in pair. For example, in a first bid auction, the ciphertext containing a larger bid in $c_i''$ and $c_j''$ is compared in the next comparison with a ciphertext which has not been compared. After $n-1$ such comparisons, the highest bid is found as the winning bid. After the winning bid is found, the originator and the third party cooperate to decrypt it. The winner can claim his winning by revealing his bid and encryption details. If no bidder claims to be the winner, the originator and the third party cooperate recover the shuffling of the winning bid to trace it back to its submitted format. As each submitted bid is signed by the bidder, the winner cannot deny he submitted the winning bid.

## 6  Analysis

The winning bid is determined through ciphertext comparison. Before each encrypted bid is compared, it is re-encrypted and shuffled by both the originator and the third party. As the re-encryption and shuffling have been publicly verified to be correct, no bid is tampered with before the comparison. As the ciphertext comparison technique in [16] is correct and sound, the comparison of the encrypted bids finds the winning bid.

As the private key is shared between the originator and the third party, no losing bid is decrypted if they do not collude. As the modified encryption algorithm in this paper is semantically secure, no information about the losing bids is revealed before they are compared if the originator and the third party do not collude. The ciphertext comparison technique in [16] is private, so no information about the bids is revealed in each comparison of ciphertext pair except which ciphertext in the pair contains a larger message. As each pair of bids are shuffled by the originator and the third party before they are compared, each comparison does not reveal which bid is larger although it can find the ciphertext containing the larger bid. So no information about the losing bids is revealed in the comparison if the originator and the third party do not collude. Therefore, the new mobile agent scheme achieves data confidentiality and privacy. Note that shuffling of each compared bids is very important for the sake of privacy. Wihtout the shuffling, ranking of all the bids is publicly known, which compromises privacy.

The new private bidding mobile agent is compared against the existing private bidding mobile agents [19, 20] in Table 1. Efficiency advantage of the new private

**Table 1.** Comparison

| Schemes | Data confi--dentiality | Anonymity | Privacy | Advantegs of mobile agent | Implemen--tation |
|---|---|---|---|---|---|
| [19, 20] | No | Incomplete | Incomplete | Inconsistent | Mix network not implemented |
| New scheme | Yes | No | Complete | Consistent | Completely implemented |

**Table 2.** Efficiency advantage

| [20] | | | The new scheme | | |
|---|---|---|---|---|---|
| computation | | communication | computation | | communication |
| recoverable anonymity and encryption | anonymous channel | | encryption | ciphertext comparison | |
| $2n^2 + 4n$ | not mentioned but inefficient | $n^2(n+1)$ | $2nL$ | $(13L+2)(n-1)$ | $n(n-1)L$ |

mobile agent is demonstrated in Table 2 where first bid auction is run. [19] is not included in Table 2 as [20] is an optimisation of [19]. In Table 2, full-length exponentiations are counted in terms of computation, while full-length integers are counted in terms of communication. In Table 2, $n$ is the number of servers and $L$ is the bit-length of the bids. Usually, $L$ is a small integer, while $n$ is much larger. Comparisons in the two tables show that the new private bidding mobile agent scheme is more efficient and provides better service than the existing private bidding mobile agent schemes.

# 7    Conclusion

Possible methods to implement privacy in network communication are analysed and compared. As a result, DCSC, a privacy mechanism never employed in mobile agent schemes before, is demonstrated to be the appropriate mechanism to implement privacy in mobile agent schemes. DCSC privacy in bidding mobile agent scheme is designed and analysed to demonstrate the advantages of DCSC privacy in mobile agent schemes.

# References

1. Masayuki Abe and Fumitaka Hoshino. Remarks on mix-network based on permutation networks. In *Public Key Cryptography 2001*, volume 1992 of *Lecture Notes in Computer Science*, pages 317–324, Berlin, 2001. Springer-Verlag.
2. Masayuki Abe and Hideki Imai. Flaws in some robust optimistic mix-nets. In *Advances in Cryptology—ACISP 03*, pages 39–50, 2003.
3. Riza Aditya, Kun Peng, Colin Boyd, and Ed Dawson. Batch verification for equality of discrete logarithms and threshold decryptions. In *Second conference of Applied Cryptography and Network Security, ACNS 04*, volume 3089 of *Lecture Notes in Computer Science*, pages 494–508, Berlin, 2004. Springer-Verlag.
4. Giuseppe Ateniese, Jan Camenisch, Marc Joye, and Gene Tsudik. A practical and provably secure coalition-resistant group signature scheme. In *ACISP 2003*, volume 1880 of *Lecture Notes in Computer Science*, pages 255–270, Berlin, 2000. Springer-Verlag.
5. D. Chaum and T. P. Pedersen. Wallet databases with observers. In *CRYPTO '92*, volume 740 of *Lecture Notes in Computer Science*, pages 89–105, Berlin, 1992. Springer-Verlag.
6. R. Cramer, I. B. Damgård, and B. Schoenmakers. Proofs of partial knowledge and simplified design of witness hiding protocols. In *CRYPTO '94*, volume 839 of *Lecture Notes in Computer Science*, pages 174–187, Berlin, 1994. Springer-Verlag.
7. Jens Groth. A verifiable secret shuffle of homomorphic encryptions. In *Public Key Cryptography 2003*, volume 2567 of *Lecture Notes in Computer Science*, pages 145–160, Berlin, 2003. Springer-Verlag.
8. G. Karjoth. Secure mobile agent-based merchant brokering in distributed marketplaces. In D. Kotz and F. Mattern, editors, *Proceedings of the 2nd International Symposium on Agent Systems and Applications and 4th International Symposium on Mobile Agents*, volume 1882 of *Lecture Notes In Computer Science*, pages 44 – 56. Springer-Verlag, London, UK, 2000.

9.  G. Karjoth, N. Asokan, and C. Gülcü. Protecting the computation results of free-roaming agents. In K. Rothermel and F. Hohl, editors, *Proceedings of the 2nd International Workshop on Mobile Agents (MA '98)*, volume 1477 of *Lecture Notes in Computer Science*, pages 195–207. Springer-Verlag, Berlin Heidelberg, 1998.

10. Jonathan Katz, Steven Myers, and Rafail Ostrovsky. Cryptographic counters and applications to electronic voting. In *Advances in Cryptology—EUROCRYPT 01*, volume 2045 of *Lecture Notes in Computer Science*, pages 78–92, Berlin, 2001. Springer-Verlag.

11. Aggelos Kiayias and Moti Yung. Self-tallying elections and perfect ballot secrecy. In *Public Key Cryptography, 5th International Workshop—PKC 02*, volume 2274 of *Lecture Notes in Computer Science*, pages 141–158, Berlin, 2002. Springer-Verlag.

12. Hiroaki Kikuchi. (m+1)st-price auction. In *The Fifth International Conference on Financial Cryptography 2001*, volume 2339 of *Lecture Notes in Computer Science*, pages 291–298, Berlin, 2001. Springer-Verlag.

13. Eyal Kushilevitz, Rafail Ostrovsky, and Adi Rosn. Characterizing linear size circuits in terms of pricacy. *Journal of Computer System Science 58(1)*, pages 129–136, 1999.

14. Byoungcheon Lee and Kwangjo Kim. Receipt-free electronic voting scheme with a tamper-resistant randomizer. In *Information Security and Cryptology, ICISC 2002*, volume 2587 of *Lecture Notes in Computer Science*, pages 389–406, Berlin, 2002. Springer-Verlag.

15. Moni Naor, Benny Pinkas, and Reuben Sumner. Privacy perserving auctions and mechanism design. In *ACM Conference on Electronic Commerce 1999*, pages 129–139, 1999.

16. Kun Peng, Colin Boyd, Ed Dawson, and Byoungcheon Lee. An efficient and verifiable solution to the millionaire problem. In *Pre-Proceedings of ICISC 2004*, volume 3506 of *Lecture Notes in Computer Science*, pages 315–330, Berlin, 2004. Springer-Verlag.

17. Kun Peng, Colin Boyd, Ed Dawson, and Kapali Viswanathan. Efficient implementation of relative bid privacy in sealed-bid auction. In *The 4th International Workshop on Information Security Applications, WISA2003*, volume 2908 of *Lecture Notes in Computer Science*, pages 244–256, Berlin, 2003. Springer-Verlag.

18. Andrew Chi-Chih Yao. Protocols for secure computations (extended abstract). In *IEEE Symposium on Foundations of Computer Science 1982, FOCS 1982*, pages 160–164, 1992.

19. M. Yao, M. Henricksen, E. Foo, and E. P. Dawson. A mobile agent system providing offer privacy. In *proceedings of 9th Australasian Conference on Information Security and Privacy (ACISP 2004)*, pages 301–312, Berlin, 2004. Springer-Verlag. Lecture Notes in Computer Science 3108.

20. M. Yao, M. Henricksen, E. Foo, and E. P. Dawson. Offer privacy in mobile agents using conditionally anonymous digital signatures. In *proceedings of First International Conference on Trust and Privacy in Digital Business (Trustbus 2004)*, pages 132–141, Berlin, 2004. Springer-Verlag. Lecture Notes in Computer Science 3184.

# Non-expanding Transaction Specific Pseudonymization for IP Traffic Monitoring

Lasse Øverlier[1,2], Tønnes Brekne[3], and André Årnes[3]

[1] Norwegian Defence Research Establishment, P.B. 25, 2027 Kjeller, Norway
lasse.overlier@ffi.no, http://www.ffi.no/
[2] Gjøvik University College, P.B. 191, 2802 Gjøvik, Norway
lasse@hig.no, http://www.hig.no/
[3] Centre for Quantifiable Quality of Service in Communication Systems,
Norwegian University of Science and Technology,
O.S. Bragstads plass 2E, N-7491 Trondheim, Norway
{tonnes, andrearn}@q2s.ntnu.no, http://www.q2s.ntnu.no/

**Abstract.** This paper presents a scheme for transaction pseudonymization of IP address data in a distributed passive monitoring infrastructure. The approach provides high resistance against traffic analysis and injection attacks, and it provides a technique for gradual release of data through a key management scheme. The scheme is non-expanding, and it should be suitable for hardware implementations for high-bandwidth monitoring systems.

## 1 Introduction

This paper presents a scheme for transaction pseudonymization[1] of IP addresses in traffic data collected from distributed passive network monitoring sensors on high-capacity network links. This work continues our earlier work in evaluating candidate solutions for anonymization of passive monitoring data in the context of the LOBSTER[2] and SCAMPI [3] projects. The motivation for this research is that pseudonymization of network monitoring data becomes challenging when it must simultaneously satisfy the conflicting requirements of privacy and traffic analysis applications. Also, the huge amount of real-time data handled at high-capacity backbone network connections imposes strict resource constraints.

We begin by introducing some terminology, along with the context and motivation for this work. After listing some pivotal assumptions, we give a brief overview of injection attacks, which our work is designed to protect against. Some related work is mentioned, before we proceed with a description of the

---

[1] We employ this term in the sense of "one-time pseudonyms" as mentioned in [1]. We have previously used the term *instance specific pseudonymization* in our papers.

[2] LOBSTER is a pilot European Infrastructure for large-scale monitoring of broadband Internet infrastructure, see http://www.ist-lobster.org/

[3] SCAMPI is a EU project for creating a scalable and programmable monitoring platform for the Internet, see http://www.ist-scampi.org/

Y.G. Desmedt et al. (Eds.): CANS 2005, LNCS 3810, pp. 261–273, 2005.
© Springer-Verlag Berlin Heidelberg 2005

scheme and its associated key management scheme. The paper ends with a description of the scheme's capabilities, and an analysis of some of its security properties. Finally, we present the conclusions of this work.

We have previously shown that an active adversary could efficiently attack prefix-preserving pseudonymization of IP addresses gathered using passive network monitors[2]. We have also demonstrated how *any* static pseudonymization scheme fails in the face of injection attacks, where an adversary sends forged IP packets with arbitrary source and destination IP addresses in such a way that they are recognizable in their pseudonymized forms [3].

The term *static pseudonymization*, refers to a scheme where each plaintext value has a unique and unchanging pseudonym. *Transaction pseudonymization* refers to a scheme where each pseudonym for a plaintext value is unlinkable[4] to any other pseudonym of the same plaintext value. In this way, there is no recognizable relationship between different pseudonyms of the same plaintext value.

The scheme presented in this paper is transaction specific, providing protection against injection attacks, while supporting efficient matching of pseudonyms for an authorized user through the use of partial disclosure of address information. The scheme is non-expanding and requires no more storage space than the original plaintext address. It is intended to provide a flexible solution for pseudonymization in high-capacity networks, supporting different applications and user groups with various requirements and trust levels.

### 1.1   Context and Threat Model

In the following, we base our context and threat model assumptions on [2, 3]. A reiteration is given here for the benefit of the reader. We consider only the pseudonymization of IP-addresses, although our methods are applicable to other data types as well. The IP addresses are assumed to be $n$ bits in length.

The context is that of passive sensors monitoring an IP network, and anonymizing captured traffic data. The sensors are programmable network monitoring cards[5] capable of operating on high-capacity links ($\leq$ 10Gbit/s). The IP addresses are anonymized at the sensor node, and a sensor identifier is appended to the data. The data rates involved impose strict performance requirements on all processing tasks. As the network monitoring system is distributed, the pseudonymization scheme has to be consistent across the sensors in order to support distributed analysis applications.

We wish to prevent adversaries from reidentifying IP addresses under the following assumptions:

**Assumption 1.** *The adversary may send forged network traffic with arbitrary source and destination IP addresses.*

**Assumption 2.** *The adversary is capable of ensuring that injected packets are captured by at least one passive sensor.*

---

[4] Unlinkability means that "two or more items within a system are no more and no less related than they are related concerning a-priori knowledge" [1].

[5] Examples of such cards are SCAMPI cards and Endace DAG cards.

**Assumption 3.** *The adversary may access all anonymized data from a set of sensors, such that their monitoring data contains the injected packets.*

In other words, the adversary is capable of performing injection attacks, a special case of the cryptographic *chosen plaintext attack*. An attacker can send an IP packet with arbitrary source and destination IP addresses. By forging the packet header so that it is recognizable in its anonymized form, the attacker will be able to find an exact match between an original and an anonymized IP address. This is a general problem with pseudonymization schemes, as shown in [2, 3].

## 1.2 Protecting Network Monitoring Data Against Injection Attacks

In [3], we suggested the use of non-static pseudonyms for IP addresses as a possible countermeasure against the attacks that have been discovered. Such a solution should ideally satisfy the following criteria:

- Each pseudonymization of the original data should be a transaction pseudonym, so that there is no recognizable relationship between different pseudonyms of the same original data;
- the data should be efficiently searchable for an authorized user with the appropriate credentials; and
- only the the minimum information about the plaintext data required by an authorized application should be revealed.

If these criteria can be met by a pseudonymization scheme, the scheme should provide both resistance against traffic analysis, as well as support for authorized analysis applications. This concept of pseudonymization is similar to multi-show anonymity. The multi-show capability [4] bases itself on proving the existence of a constant credential, and that the credential satisfies certain criteria. In our case, we generate a number of different unique pseudonyms for the original value in order to prevent injection attacks and the most obvious cryptographic attacks.

An example where partial disclosure of information might be needed, but plaintext data is not needed, is in performance measurements for the network backbone. In such a case, only some topology information is needed, and this does not require the use of plaintext IP addresses. One important operation is matching packets in order to carry out performance measurements in the network. Also the ability to efficiently match addresses is necessary for analysis where request/response packets are paired. Thus a primary criterion deciding the usefulness of any transaction pseudonymization is how efficiently address matching can be done without compromising the pseudonyms. Alternately, the question is to what degree one must reveal information in order to allow efficient matching.

We can imagine the following two variations of non-static pseudonymization schemes for IP traffic data:

- *transaction specific*, where each occurrence of a datum $d$ has a unique pseudonym; and
- *session specific*, where occurrences of a datum $d$ have pseudonyms unique to a session.

We have decided to concentrate on transaction specific pseudonymization, and believe this to be the best one. Sessions have no general upper bound on the number of packets required for them to run to completion. Also, depending on the type of session in question, and the design quality, the semantics of whether or not a session is active or terminated at any given point in time can be ambiguous. Thus there appear to be some fundamental problems associated with doing session specific pseudonymization.

The basic property we want to achieve is unlinkability between different pseudonyms—even if they are instances of the same IP address. The schemes discussed are generally applicable to the anonymization of both individual IP-addresses, pairs of IP-addresses, as well as other types of data. The cryptographic approaches are generally reversible, but they can be made irreversible through the use of one-way functions[6].

## 1.3   Related Work

Much of the early work in anonymization was related to solving the problem of traffic analysis. Two solutions to this problem was published by Chaum in 1981 [6] and 1988 [7], called mix networks and dc networks respectively. Similarly, there has been an ongoing effort to improve traffic analysis methodologies in order to compromise such networks. Raymond [8] has provided an overview of current traffic analysis research, and another overview, with a proposal for terminology for the field of anonymity, was published by Pfitzmann and Koehntopp [1].

The issue of using pseudonymous network monitoring traces is discussed in [9, 10], and later work in this area has focused on prefix-preserving pseudonymization [11, 12]. An efficient implementation of prefix-preserving pseudonymization for network processors was proposed in [13]. However, we demonstrated in [2, 3] that all static pseudonymization schemes, and prefix-preserving pseudonymization schemes in particular, are vulnerable to injection attacks.

In [14] Pang and Paxton address the problem of anonymization of logged traffic data at a higher level of abstraction. They suggested a scheme and implemented a tool for transforming higher level content to an anonymized state using transformation scripts. However, this requires that every protocol be parsed and scrubbed, and the many possible covert channels in known protocols can be used to achieve injection attacks even against anonymized protocols.

Related work in solving the pseudonymization problem has been suggested using revocable privacy [15] and zero-knowledge proofs [16]. Camenish and Lysyanskaya [4] presented a protocol for revocable anonymity for users within different organizations, but it depends on the use of asymmetric cryptography and an unproven cryptographic primitive. The multi-show capability [4] bases itself on proving the existence of a constant credential, and that the credential satisfies certain criteria. Some work on multi-show anonymous credentials in the context of constructing anonymous networks has been done in [17], and systems for anonymous multi-show credentials have also been presented in [4].

---

[6] See definition 9.9, page 327 in [5].

# 2   A Stream Cipher-Based Pseudonymization Scheme

This section shows how stream ciphers can be employed to construct a non-expanding transaction specific pseudonymization scheme. The fact that it is non-expanding means that it does *not* increase storage complexity, and in turn storage costs.

The essence of the scheme is to partition each IP address into $l$ bitstring segments of length $w_1, w_2 \ldots, w_l$, respectively. The pseudonymization proceeds by running a stream cipher for each of the $l$ segments. The stream cipher for each segment $j$ runs in counter mode [5], operates on the segments of length $w_j$, and increments the "counter" for each crypto block. We refer to this counter as the initialization vector (IV).

First we describe the stream cipher mode used in this paper. Based on this, we present a *bitwise pseudonymization scheme* which is a specific instance of a more general *segmented pseudonymization scheme* working on segments (i.e. bitstrings). Using the bitwise scheme we describe how to construct a more general scheme.

## 2.1   Stream Ciphers

Stream ciphers (see [5, 18]) are algorithms that encrypt plaintext a number of bits at a time. For the purpose of this paper we are using all bits from the output, 1 bit at a time. A stream cipher can be either synchronous or self-synchronous, depending on whether the key stream is independent of the message stream or not. In a synchronous stream cipher, the key stream is independent of the message stream, so that the encrypting and decrypting parties have to be synchronized with respect to the key stream generation.

A *counter mode* stream cipher is a type of synchronous stream cipher that uses a simple next-state function (usually a counter) and a nonlinear output transformation dependent on a key to produce its output (see [19]). An advantage of this mode is that it provides random access to plaintext data. However, self-synchronization with the ciphertext stream is not possible—it is not possible to start the decryption based on availability of a sufficient amount of ciphertext. Random access to data is only possible given the right initialization vectors and decryption keys. Another advantage with synchronized block ciphers is that there is no inherent error propagation. Accordingly, error correction is not considered in this paper, although it may be required for some applications.

## 2.2   Bitwise Non-expanding Pseudonymization

We start our discussion with a method for individual bitwise pseudonymization of IP addresses. A generalization of this scheme is outlined in Sect. 2.3. We encrypt each bit in a block of data with an individual key stream applied to that specific bit position in every concurrent block of data.

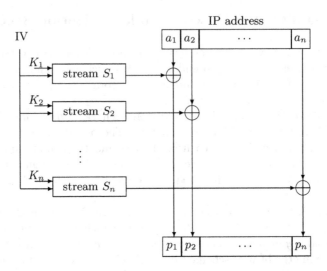

**Fig. 1.** Example of bitwise pseudonymization using a counter mode stream cipher

The collected traffic data can be considered an ordered list of rows. Each row contains the data collected from one packet. Before applying the pseudonymization itself, this list is split into a series of sublists in order to facilitate the key management scheme presented in Sect. 3.

In the bitwise scheme, applied to a sublist, we have an IP address of $n$ bits, $a_1 a_2 \cdots a_n$, that is to be pseudonymized. Figure 1 shows how this scheme works on individual bits in the IP addresses. We have $n$ individual stream ciphers in counter mode, $S_1, S_2, \ldots, S_n$, individually keyed with keys $K_1, K_2, \ldots, K_n$, using the same initialization vector IV and supplying a stream of $b$ bits per round. This bitstream is used to encrypt one bit column in $b$ consecutive IP addresses. In other words, for every bit from stream $S_j$, one bit from the IP address $a_j$ is pseudonymized into $p_j$. IV is incremented synchronously for all streams after $b$ IP addresses have been pseudonymized. In this way, individual bit columns in the pseudonymized IP addresses can be revealed to users in a non-expanding manner.

When the rows of encrypted data are written to log files there will be no information linking two log entries with the same plaintext. The scheme also allows partial release of individual bits. For example, we release the first 24 bits in an IP address to allow a view of class C subnet activity without revealing information about the 256 individual addresses within that subnet. This also hides information about the traffic distribution to between individual hosts on within the subnet.

### 2.3   General Non-expanding Pseudonymization

We extend this bitwise model to a more general scheme introducing $l$ segments of bitstrings, $w_1, w_2, \ldots, w_l$ covering all $n$ bits of the IP address, $\Sigma_{i=1}^{l} w_i = n$,

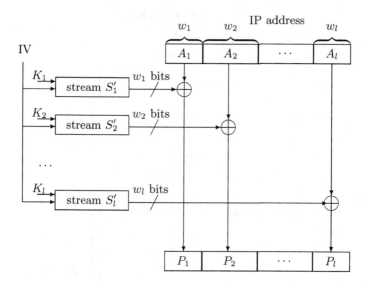

**Fig. 2.** General non-expanding stream pseudonymization

as shown in Fig. 2. The reason for grouping the bit columns is that users most often do not need access to individual bits.

For each segment $j$ we have a generalized stream cipher, $S'_j$, that in essence consists of $w_j$ bitwise stream ciphers as in Sect. 2.2. However, these stream ciphers are individually keyed from a strong pseudorandom sequence based on one key, $K_j$.

The bitwise stream ciphers are used even in the general scheme, as it is easier to implement, while preserving the flexibility of grouping the bits as needed. We still have the same number of encryptions due to the constant amount of data to be encrypted, and we observe that this must be the minimal number of encryptions needed in order to have partial release of the individual groups.

## 3 Key Scheme

The key scheme has been designed with the following criteria in mind:

1. key generation must be easy, given some master key, so that it is not necessary to store and administer large numbers of keys;
2. access to individual address pseudonyms should be as close to random access as possible; and
3. release of key material to enable disclosure should result in an access capability which is limited in both time and space.

The captured traffic data can be viewed as a long list of rows, each row containing packet header data for one packet. This list is split into a series of sublists as shown in Fig. 3. Each IP address is split into a series of segments.

IP address lists

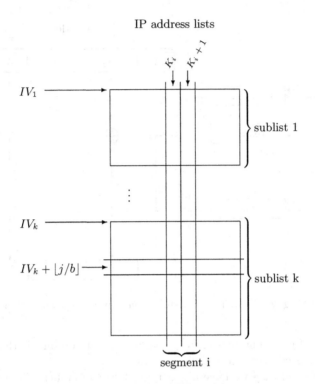

**Fig. 3.** Segments, sublists, IVs and key usage

Fix the three stream ciphers below.

1. One cipher encrypts each column of bits in the IP addresses as a bit stream, and is referred to as the *column cipher*. This cipher is thus used for the pseudonymization itself, which is done sublist by sublist.
2. One cipher is used to generate the initialization vectors for each sublist, and is referred to as the *sublist IV generator*.
3. One cipher is used to generate the keys for the column cipher, and is referred to as the *segment key generator*.

**Assumption 4.** *The stream ciphers employed are semantically secure.*

To enforce limited access in time and space, each sublist is assigned a unique initialization vector, and each segment in the IP addresses is assigned a unique key.

The column cipher operates in counter mode, and encrypts segments. The key for this cipher is determined by which segment (i.e. the $i^{\text{th}}$ segment) out of the $l$ possible segments is being encrypted. For reasons of efficiency, however, $w_i$ stream ciphers are used in parallel for segment $i$. In order to avoid use of the same key for all $w_i$ stream ciphers, the key for the stream cipher encrypting the $h^{\text{th}}$ bit in segment $i$ uses key $K_i + h - 1$.

The initialization vector for the cipher is determined by the initialization vector for the sublist in which it is currently operating, and the number of rows from the top. If it is $j$ rows from the top, then the effective initialization vector is $IV+g(j)$, where $g(j)$ is some function of $j$ such that $g(j) \leq j$. $g$ is necessary, as a stream cipher in counter mode generally produces a number $b$ of bits. Instead of using only one bit, we would like to use as many as possible before incrementing the initialization vector. Typically $g(j) = \lfloor j/b \rfloor$.

The $l$ keys for each of the $l$ segments are fixed for the entire list. The segment key generator is used to generate keys for each bit column. Thus these keys number at most $n$, which is the number of bits in an IP address, and can easily be stored and managed.

The sublist IV generator is used to generate a key stream. This key stream is split into a series of bitstrings of equal length. The length is selected so that these bitstrings can be used as initialization vectors for the column cipher. this way, the initialization vectors for individual sublists can be generated quickly and securely. One such initialization vector is stored for each sublist. If this should be too much, the complexity of regenerating the relevant initialization vector on demand should be surmountable.

Random access to specific segments of individual addresses is then possible by knowing: the segment key, the initialization vector of the block, the function $g$ (which is fixed for a list and public), and the row number of the packet data in question.

## 4    Properties of the Scheme

In this section, we describe important functional aspects of the scheme and its use.

### 4.1    Transaction Specificity

We now show that we have produced a transaction specific pseudonymization scheme. Assume that the initialization vectors have length $v$. Each IP address instance has been given a unique pseudonym, in spite of the fact that each pseudonym has a length equal to the original address. To see how this is possible, note that decrypting a pseudonym depends on knowledge of a number of keys, and *in addition* the exact position in the list of the specific pseudonym instance. Strictly speaking, the pseudonym is thus the pair $(i, p)$, where $i$ is the row number, and $p$ is the encrypted address. Since, however, $i$ is implicitly given, it is not necessary to store, and so the scheme ends up as non-expanding. As a result, it is important that the pseudonymized list be stored with captured packet information in the order in which it was pseudonymized. Thus the scheme is transaction specific, but only probabilistically so.

### 4.2    Random Access to Pseudonyms

Access to the pseudonyms themselves is as close to random access as efficient use of the stream ciphers will allow. Rows are effectively accessed in groups of

$b$ consecutive rows at a time, and the specific group of rows can be accessed directly without any other processing than that required to generate decryption keys (in the case where segments may contain more than one bit), and generate the appropriate IV. Both these generation tasks are exercises in table lookups and a small number of addition operations, bounded by $n$ for the keys, and by a constant for the IV. Thus an access form very close to true random access is efficient, and possible, given that sublists are not reordered, or that their ordering is explicitly marked.

### 4.3   Limiting Access with Initialization Vectors and Segment Keys

With respect to limiting access, first note that each sublist has its own IV. Since each such IV is generated by a secure stream cipher, there is no exploitable statistical correlation between the sublist IVs. Thus knowledge of one IV does not allow an adversary to deduce IVs for previous or subsequent sublists. Similarly, knowledge of one segment key does not allow deduction of the other segment keys, provided they are randomly chosen. Because decryption of one or more address bits requires knowledge of *both* IV and at least one segment key, knowledge of a segment key alone does not enable decryption of bits in that same segment in other sublists than the ones for which an adversary has IVs.

### 4.4   Combination of Schemes: Anonymity and Protection

The scheme as presented so far provides access to a number of bits of address information in *plaintext* to authorized users. Partial disclosures of plaintext data may however be unacceptable in some situations. In such cases, the data could be pseudonymized with a static pseudonymization scheme, such as cryptographic prefix-preserving pseudonymization[7], *before* it is protected with transaction specific pseudonymization. In this way trusted users are given access to parts of the prefix-preserving pseudonym. These users are obviously able to perform injection attacks, but the effect of such attacks are reduced through the practice of partial disclosure.

The combined scheme suggested above provides partial disclosure of data in a flexible manner, while still protecting private data. Disclosure is performed in two steps:

1. disclosure of encryption keys and relevant IVs for the transaction specific pseudonymization function discloses partial information about the static pseudonym; and
2. disclosure of encryption keys for the cryptographic prefix-preserving discloses information about the plaintext address.

This combination scheme provides full support for *pseudonymity revocation*.

---

[7] An anonymization scheme is prefix-preserving if, for any two original IP addresses sharing a $k$-bit prefix, their anonymized versions will also share a $k$-bit prefix. The tools TCPdpriv, wide-tcpdpriv, and Crypto-PAn are examples of prefix-preserving schemes, as discussed in [11, 12].

# 5 Security Aspects of the Scheme

In this section we analyze the security of our transaction specific pseudonymization scheme, concentrating on the collision properties of the components. We demonstrate that the criteria stated in section 1.2 can be systematically determined and met. The security of the scheme presented in this paper depends on the security of the ciphers used to:

1. generate the individual column keys (segment key generator);
2. encrypt the segments themselves (column cipher); and
3. generate the initialization vectors for the sublists (sublist IV generator).

Assumption 4 implies that any two bits the stream ciphers output are statistically independent, and that it is not possible to infer any simple functional relation between any two bits in the stream without knowledge of both key and initialization vector. Furthermore, the sublist IV and segment key generators should be ciphers with key length no less than that employed for the column cipher.

## 5.1 Security of the Segment Key Generator

Since IP addresses are split into $l$ segments, the segment key generator generates a set $\kappa = \{K_1, \ldots, K_l\}$ of $L$-bit keys. One or more of these keys may be released to a party granted access to the corresponding IP address segments in one or more sublists. There are $\prod_{i=1}^{l} 2^L = 2^{lL}$ possible ways of selecting $\kappa$.

A possible weakness arises if a key is selected more than once. $w_i - 1$ additional keys are generated from $K_i$ as a series of successive increments from $K_i$. Thus the effective set of keys is $K_1, \ldots, K_1 + w_1 - 1, \ldots, K_l, \ldots, K_l + w_l - 1$. There are $2^L - \sum_{j=1}^{i} (w_j + w_{i+1} - 1)$ ways of selecting key number $i + 1$ so that no key is used twice. Thus the probability of no collision is:

$$p_0 = \prod_{i=1}^{l} \frac{2^L - \sum_{j=1}^{i-1} (w_j + w_i - 1)}{2^L}. \tag{1}$$

## 5.2 Column Cipher Security

In this subsection ignore key generation aspects and assume that the key for the individual column is genuinely random and unknown to attackers. Given such keys, the cipher and its use within this scheme is semantically secure by assumption.

## 5.3 Security of the Sublist IV Generator

Assuming that counter mode encryption is secure, it is conceivable that a collision can occur. Initialization vectors are generated at random for each sublist. If sublists have length $s$, and two sublists have initialization vectors $I_i$ and $I_j$, $i \neq j$, such that $|I_i - I_j| < s/b$, there is a possibility that the same address has been encrypted with the same effective IV twice.

The column cipher produces $b$ bits per round of encryption. Assume that $s$ is a multiple of $b$. When $m$ sublists of length $s$ have associated IVs generated for them, the number of possible effective IVs is $ms/b$ in all. This is selected from in all $2^L$ IVs, where $L$ is the key length of the sublist IV generator. There are $\prod_{i=1}^{m} 2^L$ possible IVs. Assume that $i - 1$ IVs have been selected so that their respective sublists have no overlap of effective IVs. Selecting the $i^{\text{th}}$ IV with no resulting overlap can be done in $2^L - i\left(\frac{2s}{b} - 1\right)$ ways. Thus the probability of selecting IVs so that there is no IV collision anywhere is:

$$p_0 = \prod_{i=0}^{m-1} \frac{\left(2^L - \left(\frac{2s}{b} - 1\right) i\right)}{2^L} = \prod_{i=0}^{m-1} \left(1 - 2^{-L}\left(\frac{2s}{b} - 1\right) i\right). \tag{2}$$

Ignoring products with factors of the form $2^{-Li}$, where $i > 1$, one conservative approximation is:

$$p_0 \approx 1 - 2^{-L} \sum_{i=0}^{m-1} \left(\frac{2s}{b} - 1\right) i = 1 - 2^{-L}\left(\frac{2s}{b} - 1\right) \frac{m}{2}(m - 1). \tag{3}$$

Thus the approximate probability of at least one collision occurring is

$$p_c = 1 - p_0 \approx \frac{2^{-L-1}}{b}\left(2m^2 s - 2ms - m^2 b + mb\right). \tag{4}$$

Fix $p_c$ at a desired level, then:

$$L \approx -\log_2 b - \log_2 p_c + \log_2 m + \log_2\left(2ms - 2s - mb + b\right) - 1. \tag{5}$$

## 6    Conclusion

We have presented a scheme for non-expanding transaction specific pseudonymization. This scheme provides protection against injection attacks and still allows individual release of bit columns in the addresses. We have also proposed a key management scheme and a combination scheme that provides practical trust management for the application of the scheme.

We have analyzed selected aspects of the scheme and shown that it allows efficient, nearly random access of pseudonymized data with a surmountable overhead. It is easily amenable to parallelization in a way which should allow efficient hardware implementation. This is important for the scheme's application potential in large scale traffic data collection.

## Acknowledgements

This work was funded by The Centre for Quantifiable Quality of Service in Communication Systems, Gjøvik University College, and the Norwegian Defence Research Establishment. The Centre for Quantifiable Quality of Service in Communication Systems, is a Centre of Excellence appointed by The Research Council of Norway, and is funded by the Research Council, NTNU and UNINETT.

# References

1. Pfitzmann, A., Koehntopp, M.: Anonymity, unobservability, and pseudonymity – a proposal for terminology. In: Workshop on Design Issues in Anonymity and Unobservability. (2000)
2. Brekne, T., Årnes, A., Øslebø, A.: Anonymization of ip traffic monitoring data: Attacks on two prefix-preserving anonymization schemes and some proposed remedies. In: Proceedings of Privacy Enhancing Technologies workshop (PET 2005). (2005)
3. Brekne, T., Årnes, A.: Circumventing ip-address pseudonymization in $o(n^2)$ time. In: Proceedings of IASTED Communication and Computer Networks (CCN 2005). (2005)
4. Camenisch, J., Lysyanskaya, A.: An efficient system for non-transferable anonymous credentials with optional anonymity revocation. In Pfitzmann, B., ed.: Advances in Cryptology - EUROCRYPT 2001: Second Symposium, PADO 2001, Springer-Verlag, LNCS 2045 (2003)
5. Menezes, A.J., van Oorschot, P., Vanstone, S.: Handbook of Applied Cryptography. CRC Press (1996)
6. Chaum, D.: Untraceable electronic mail, return addresses, and digital pseudonyms. Communications of the ACM **4** (1981)
7. Chaum, D.: The dining cryptographers problem: Unconditional sender and recipient untraceability. Journal of Cryptology **1** (1988) 65–75
8. Raymond, J.F.: Traffic analysis: Protocols, attacks, design issues, and open problems. In: Workshop on Design Issues in Anonymity and Unobservability, Springer-Verlag, LNCS 2009 (2000)
9. Biskup, J., Flegel, U.: On pseudonymization of audit data for intrusion detection. In: Workshop on Design Issues in Anonymity and Unobservability, Springer-Verlag, LNCS 2009 (2000)
10. Sobirey, M., Fischer-Hübner, S., Rannenberg, K.: Pseudonymous audit for privacy enhanced intrusion detection. In: SEC. (1997) 151–163
11. Xu, J., Fan, J., Ammar, M., Moon, S.B.: On the design and performance of prefix-preserving ip traffic trace anonymization. In: Proceedings of the ACM SIGCOMM Internet Measurement Workshop 2001. (2001)
12. Xu, J., Fan, J., Ammar, M., Moon, S.B.: Prefix-preserving ip address anonymization: Measurement-based security evaluation and a new cryptography-based scheme. ICNP 2002 (2002)
13. Ramaswamy, R., Weng, N., Wolf, T.: An IXA-basednetwork measurement node. In: Proc. of Intel IXA University Summit. (2004)
14. Pang, R., Paxson, V.: A high-level programming environment for packet trace anonymization and transformation. In: SIGCOMM '03: Proceedings of the 2003 conference on Applications, technologies, architectures, and protocols for computer communications, New York, NY, USA, ACM Press (2003) 339–351
15. Stadler, M.: Cryptographic Protocols for Revocable Privacy. PhD thesis (1996)
16. Lysyanskaya, A., Rivest, R.L., Sahai, A., Wolf, S.: Pseudonym systems. In Heys, H., Adams, C., eds.: Selected Areas in Cryptography: 6th Annual International Workshop, SAC'99, Springer-Verlag, LNCS 1758 (1999)
17. Persiano, G., Visconti, I.: An efficient and usable multi-show non-transferable anonymous credential system. In: Financial Cryptography: 8th International Conference, Springer-Verlag, LNCS 3110 (2004) 196–211
18. Schneier, B.: Applied Cryptography. John Wiley & Sons, Inc. (1996)
19. Diffie, W., Hellman, M.E.: Privacy and authentication: An introduction to cryptography. In: Proceedings of the IEEE. Volume 67. (1979) 297–427

# Revaluation of Error Correcting Coding in Watermarking Channel[*]

Limin Gu[1,3], Yanmei Fang[1,2], and Jiwu Huang[1,2]

[1] School of Information Science and Technology, Sun Yat-Sen University,
Guangzhou 510275, P.R. China
{issfym, isshjw}@zsu.edu.cn
[2] The Guangdong Key Laboratory of Information Security Technology
[3] Beijing Research and Development Center,
China Construction Bank, Beijing

**Abstract.** Robustness is one of the most important issues in digital watermarking. By modeling digital watermarking as digital communications, several researchers proposed using error correcting coding (ECC) to improve watermark robustness. However, the following important facts are neglected. i) The robust watermark channel suffers from a very high bit error ratio (BER), which may exceed the capability of ECC; ii) Due to the imperceptibility requirement, the redundancy introduced by ECC will lead to a decrease of the watermark magnitude. Could the usage of ECC effectively improve the robustness of watermark? This paper addresses this problem from the perspectives of both theoretical analysis and experiments. Our investigation shows that ECC cannot effectively improve the robustness of watermarking against a vast majority of various attacks except for cropping and jitter attacks. Hence, ECC should not be considered as a universal method applied to enhance the watermark robustness.

## 1 Introduction

Imperceptibility and robustness are two basic requirements of watermarking in many applications. Hence, one of the important goals of watermarking is to improve robustness while keeping the watermark imperceptive. This presents a great challenge.

To improve the robustness of watermarking, much effort has been made. Due to similarities between digital watermarking and digital communications, some papers in the literature viewed watermarking as a digital communication problem [1,2] and hence applied the theories and methods of digital communications to watermarking. It was reported that some watermarking algorithms applied ECC to lower BER of watermarks and thus improve robustness. For example, BCH code, convolutional code [3], RS code [4], and Turbo code [5] have been adopted.

---

[*] Support by NSFC (60325208, 60133020), NSF of Guangdong (04205407).

Y.G. Desmedt et al. (Eds.): CANS 2005, LNCS 3810, pp. 274–287, 2005.

The above idea seems straightforward since ECC is effectively used in noisy channel in digital communications. It should be, however, noted that there are some differences between watermarking and digital communication. That is, watermark, as a very weak signal, is embedded in a media under the constraint of imperceptivity, and often suffers from extremely noisy attack. In fact, this difference has been overlooked in literature. When applying ECC to enhance robustness of watermarking, the following problems will arise. i) Is ECC effective in the improvement of watermark robustness? And to what extent could ECC improve the robustness? ii) Which error correcting code performs best for watermarking? iii) How to choose the coding ratio in using ECC?

Some efforts to address above issues have been reported. Huang et al. [6] compared the performance of repetition coding and BCH coding, hard-decision decoding and soft-decision decoding. Zinger et al. [7] investigated the performance of BCH coding, repetition coding, and their concatenations over watermarking channel modeled as binary symmetric channel (BSC). They claimed that if the channel error rate is high, it makes sense to adopt repetition coding to embed few watermark bits; if the channel error rate is not high, it is better to apply hybrid coding; if the payload is quite large and the channel error rate is lower than 10%, BCH coding with subtraction is the best choice. Baudry et al. [8] addressed ECC strategies in watermarking. They analyzed the performance of BCH coding, repetition coding, and their concatenations. A new algorithm for BCH soft decoding is proposed. Balado et al. [9] pointed out that Turbo coding schemes has lower error rate than hybrid coding for the same amount of hidden information.

However, the following important facts are neglected in the above efforts, when applying ECC to watermarking. i) The robust watermark channel suffers from a very high BER, sometimes, which may exceed the capability of ECC; ii) Due to the imperceptibility requirement, the redundancy introduced by ECC will lead to a decrease of the hidden watermark magnitude. Naturally, a problem arises: Could the usage of ECC effectively improve the robustness of watermarking?

In this paper, we address this problem from the perspectives of both theoretical analysis and experimental investigation. Based on the analysis of the relationship between embedded watermark strength and ECC coding length, the paper discusses the ECC coding length and the robustness of watermarking. By comparing the robustness performance by applying BCH coding and not using ECC, we claim that for common signal processing including compression and noise corruption, ECC cannot improve the robustness of watermarking. ECC is beneficial only in those attacks where the bit error rate in watermark detection does not depend on the watermarking strength.

The paper is organized as follows. Section 2 describes a general communication model for watermarking channel. In Section 3, we analyze the watermarking channels with different error correcting ability. Experimental results supporting the analysis are given in Section 4. Finally, conclusions are drawn in Section 5.

## 2    Watermarking Scheme and Coding Gain of ECC

The watermarking procedure can be viewed as a digital communication problem [2]. In this section, we present the watermarking scheme and the block codes at a high-BER traditional communication channel.

### 2.1    Watermarking Scheme

In watermark embedding, LSB-based model [10] is frequently used. In this paper, we use a similar method. Let matrix $A$, $A = \{a_{ij}\} \in I^{M \times N}$, $i = 1, 2, \ldots, M$, $j = 1, 2, \ldots, N$, denote the original image and matrix $B$, $B = \{b_{ij}\} \in I^{M \times N}$, the transform domain matrix of $A$. Vector $Y$, $Y = \{Y_k\} \in I^k, k = 1, 2, \ldots, K$, is a subset of $B$, specifically the vector $Y$ consists of low-frequency or mid-frequency coefficients in the matrix $B$. The watermark embedding is fulfilled when the watermark $W$, $W = \{w_k\}$, $k = 1, 2, \ldots, K$, is embedded in the vector $Y$. The following formula is used for watermark embedding [11]:

$$\begin{cases} y'_k = y_k - (y_k \mod S) + \frac{3}{4}S & \text{if } w_k = 1 \\ y'_k = y_k - (y_k \mod S) + \frac{1}{4}S & \text{if } w_k = 0 \end{cases} \tag{1}$$

where parameter $S$ controls the watermark embedding strength and should be as large as possible under the constraint of imperceptivity. In what follows, we call $S$ the embedding strength. The operator $mod$ calculates the modulo of $y_k$ with respect to $S$. If $y_k < 0$, its absolute value is used in Eq.1.

In the watermark extraction, the maximum likelihood method is first employed to retrieve each hidden bit, and then the extracted bits were decoded to obtain an estimated version, $W'$, of the original watermark $W$. The watermark error rate can be obtained by comparing $W'$ with $W$. Generally, when the embedded bits are demodulated to produce a binary codeword, the watermarking channel can be modeled as a BSC channel [12]. In this paper, hard-decision decoding is exploited, and hence, the watermarking channel is modeled as BSC channel.

### 2.2    Coding Gain at High BER

As well known, during the performance analysis of traditional communication systems, the curves, between the SNR (Signal-to-Noise Ratio)$(E_b/N_0)$ and the BER $(p_e)$ are more significant. Given a BER, the coding gain of ECC in a specific system is defined as the reduction of decibels corresponding to the one without ECC. Hence, coding gain is not only dependent on the type of ECC, and also the SNR.

When introducing ECC into a practical system, just as depicted by works [12-14], there is a low limitation ($10^{-2}$ or so) of SNR for communication channel. If actual SNR is lower than the bound, ECC cannot improve the quality of communication. That is, ECC is efficient only when the errors are below the correction capacity of ECC, which is seldom the case with high BER systems. Fig.1 illustrates a comparison of BERs between the uncoded case and the case of

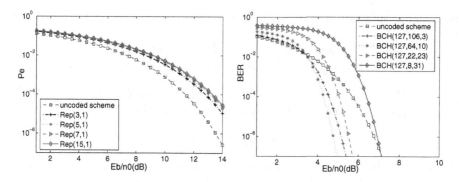

**Fig. 1.** The relationship of $E_b/N_0$ and $p_e$: (a) in the uncoded case and repetition coding case; (b) in the uncoded case and BCH coding case

BCH or repetition codes with hard-decision. The conclusion can be drawn from the figure that the coding gain of BCH (127, 64, 10) is 2.15dB for $10^{-5}$ of the BER, and 1.35dB for $10^{-3}$. When the SNR is extremely low, the coding gain presents a negative value. That is, the performance degrades after introducing the ECC. For repetition codes, the coding gain always presents a negative value.

In many attacks, the watermark may undergo a high BERs above 0.2 or 0.3, e.g. in case of very noisy channels. In these situations, the majority of extracted hidden bits present a number of errors exceeding the correction capacity of ECC. We need to understand the behavior of ECC in watermarking system in order to select them deliberatively.

## 3   Analyses of ECC in Watermark Channel

### 3.1   Watermark Coding Length vs. Embedding Strength

Due to the constraint of imperceptibility, watermark embedding strength and coding length, if ECC is applied, are conflicting with each other. Given a PSNR (peak signal-to-noise ratio), there is a trade-off between these two factors. According to [15], for the unitary transform domain embedding algorithms using the following popular additive embedding equation

$$y'_k = y_k + S \cdot w_k, \quad k = 1, 2, \ldots, K, \tag{2}$$

we can derive the following inequality for the lower bound of PSNR, $T_{PSNR}$.

$$T_{PSNR} \leq 20 \log_{10} \frac{N \cdot b_m}{\sqrt{\sum_k (S \cdot w_k)^2}} \tag{3}$$

where the size of image is $N \times N$ and the maximum grayscale level in the image is $b_m$, $S$ is the embedding strength. $w_k$ is the watermark signal. Therefore, it is clear that, given a lower bound of PSNR, $T_{PSNR}$, there exists a upper bound of embedding strength $S$ to ensure watermark imperceptibility. For the data embedding using Eq.1, the change of transform coefficient due to the embedding is:

$$
\begin{cases}
\Delta y_k = y_k \mod S - \frac{3}{4}S, & \text{if } w_k = 1 \\
\Delta y_k = y_k \mod S - \frac{1}{4}S, & \text{if } w_k = 0
\end{cases} \tag{4}
$$

Let $X$, $Y$ and $Z$ be random variables, and defined as $X \in \{\frac{1}{4}, \frac{3}{4}\}$, $Y \in [0, 1)$ and $Z \in \{\Delta y_k\}$, $k = 1, 2, \ldots, K$, then Eq.4 can be rewritten as

$$
Z = (Y - X) \cdot S \tag{5}
$$

$X$ and $Y$ can be considered as independent. Then, with Eq.1, Eq.3 is expressed as

$$
\begin{aligned}
T_{PSNR} &\leq 20 \log_{10} \frac{N \cdot b_m}{\sqrt{K \cdot E(Z^2)}} \\
&= 20 \log_{10} \frac{N \cdot b_m}{\sqrt{K \cdot S^2 \cdot [E(X^2) + E(Y^2) - 2E(X)E(Y)]}}
\end{aligned} \tag{6}
$$

where $K$ and $S$ denote the length and strength of the watermark signal, respectively, $E(\cdot)$ indicates the expectation operation.

If keeping the original image, hidden watermark signal, the type of channel code, and embedding model unchanged, for different length of hidden bits $K$ and embedding strength $S$, we have

$$
\sqrt{K_1} \cdot S_1 = \sqrt{K_2} \cdot S_2 \tag{7}
$$

where $K_1$, $S_1$, $K_2$, and $S_2$ denote the length of hidden bits and embedding strength in two different schemes, respectively.

From the viewpoint of digital communications theory, for a repetition code, an increase of repetition times $R$ leads to a decrease of error rate. However, in digital watermarking, the increase of $R$ will result in a longer coding length. Under the constraint of imperceptibility, say, maintaining the same PSNR of watermarked image, we have to lower the embedding strength as Eq.7. In Fig.2, $S$-$R$ curves were obtained with Lena image, and data were embedded in the mid-frequency coefficients of $8 \times 8$ block DCT with a 64-bit watermark.

Similar results have been obtained for BCH codes as shown in Table 1, where PSNR=50.72dB, also with Lena image, a 64-bit watermark signal is embedded in the mid-frequency coefficients of $8 \times 8$ block DCT. Table 1 illustrates the impact of different BCH coding length on embedding strength for a given PSNR. When encoding the 64-bit watermark, BCH code (31, 6) has a longer coding length, and hence brings embedding strength down dramatically.

It is clear that when watermark error bits occur during extraction, on the one hand, ECC can correct some error bits by introducing redundancy. On the other hand, the redundancy leads to a decrease of embedding strength and thus an increase of error rate. It is known that large embedding strength can decrease error bits in watermark detection. Therefore, there is a trade-off between the coding length and the embedding strength.

## 3.2  Lowering BER by Increasing Embedding Strength

The BER varies with different codes and channel properties. Here, we discuss the problem under the assumption of BSC channel corrupted by additive white Gaussian noise (AWGN). The detected watermark signal can be modeled as follows:

$$r = q + \tau, \text{ and } v = r \bmod S \tag{8}$$

where $q$ is a random variable, representing embedded watermark signal, i.e. $q \in \{S/4, 3S/4\}$. $\tau$ is the AWGN component, $\tau \in N(0, \sigma^2)$. $S$ is the embedding strength. $r$ is the received signal, and $v$ is a decision variable. Then, the watermark bit is derived, by comparing $v$ with $S/2$.

When binary "0" is transmitted, the received signal is $r = q_0 + \tau = S/4 + \tau$. Similarly, when binary "1" is transmitted, the received signal is $r = q_0 + \tau = 3S/4 + \tau$. Hence, the two conditional probability density function (pdf) of $r$ are

$$p(r|q_0) = \frac{1}{\sqrt{2\pi}\sigma} \exp\{-\frac{(r - S/4)^2}{2\sigma^2}\} \tag{9}$$

$$p(r|q_1) = \frac{1}{\sqrt{2\pi}\sigma} \exp\{-\frac{(r - 3S/4)^2}{2\sigma^2}\} \tag{10}$$

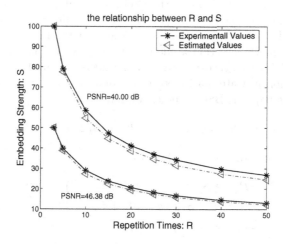

**Fig. 2.** The relationship between repetition times $R$ and embedding strength $S$. The mid-frequency coefficients of $8 \times 8$ DCT are used for embedding with Lena image.

**Table 1.** BCH coding length $K$ vs. embedding strength $S$ (64 bits in watermark)

| BCH Codes | Coding Length K | Estimated Strength $S$ | Experimental Strength $S$ |
|-----------|-----------------|------------------------|---------------------------|
| BCH (31, 6) | 341 | 21.8 | 21.8 |
| BCH(63, 18) | 252 | 25.4 | 25.8 |
| BCH (63, 30) | 189 | 29.3 | 30.2 |
| BCH(127, 64) | 127 | 35.7 | 34.4 |

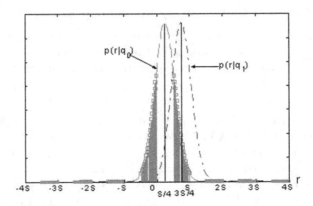

**Fig. 3.** Gaussian pdf of random variable $r$, and the false negative regions of case $q = S/4$

It is the modulo $S$ in Eq.8 that makes error probability of watermarking different from that of common communications. Owing to the property of modulo $S$, the interval of is mapped onto interval of $(-\infty, +\infty)$. The received signal $r$ can be expressed as $r = kS + v$, where $k \in Z$. In fact, whenever $r$ is in the intervals of $[(k + 1/2)S, (k + 1)S)$, the decision variable $v$ will be greater than $S/2$, and consequently the decision is made in favor of $q = 3S/4$. If $q = S/4$ was transmitted and the decision variable $v$ was greater than or equal to $S/2$, false decision in watermark detection would occur (as shown in Fig.3 by the shadowed parts). If $q = 3S/4$ was transmitted and the decision variable $v$ was less than $S/2$, false decision in watermark detection would also occur. Since the channel discussed in this paper is BSC channel, we have

$$P(v \geq S/2 \mid q = S/4) = P(v < S/2 \mid q = 3S/4) \tag{11}$$

So, the channel bit error rate is as follows.

$$\begin{aligned}
P_b &= P(v \geq S/2 \mid q = S/4)P(q = S/4) \\
&\quad + P(v < S/2 \mid q = 3S/4)P(q = 3S/4) \\
&= P(v \geq S/2 \mid q = S/4) \\
&= \frac{1}{\sqrt{2\pi}\sigma} \sum_{k=-\infty}^{\infty} \left[ \int_{(k+1/2)S}^{(k+1)S} \exp\{-\frac{r - 3S/4^2}{2\sigma^2}\} \right] \\
&= 2\sum_{k=0}^{\infty} \left[ Q(\frac{(4k + 1)S}{4\sigma}) - Q(\frac{(4k + 3)S}{4\sigma}) \right]
\end{aligned} \tag{12}$$

Obviously, the distribution of error regions here are different from that of general binary signals in AWGN, due to modulo $S$ operation in Eq.8. Note that at three times standard deviation from the mean value, Gaussian pdf has dropped to close to zero. Hence, the series turn to be finite many items, and the above equation can be written as

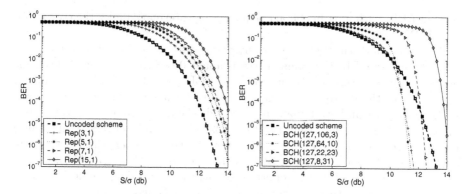

**Fig. 4.** Performance of repetition codes and BCH codes

**Table 2.** Bit error probability expressions [8, 14]

| Code Scheme | Symbol Bit Error |
|---|---|
| Repetition$(r, 1)$ | $P_{rep} = \sum\limits_{i=r/2+1}^{n} \binom{n}{i} P_b^i (1 - P_b)^{r-i}$ |
| BCH$(n, k, t)$ | $P_{BCH} = \frac{1}{n} \sum\limits_{i=t+1}^{n} i \binom{n}{i} P_b^i (1 - P_b)^{n-i}$ |

$$P_b = 2 \sum_{k=0}^{M} [Q(\frac{(4k + 1)S}{4\sigma}) - Q(\frac{(4k + 3)S}{4\sigma})] \tag{13}$$

where $M$ is a finite integer number.

Owing to the power constraint in watermarking, the energy per symbol $E_c$ after using ECC with code ratio $k/n$ satisfies the following equation [14]:

$$\frac{E_c}{N_0} = (\frac{k}{n}) \frac{E_b}{N_0} \tag{14}$$

where $N_0$ is the variance of AWGN. $E_b$ is the energy per bit before applying ECC. We use the following equation to calculate the channel BER for ECC at coding ratio $k/n$.

$$P_b = 2 \sum_{k=0}^{M} [Q(\frac{(4k + 1)S}{4\sigma} \sqrt{\frac{k}{n}}) - Q(\frac{(4k + 3)S}{4\sigma} \sqrt{\frac{k}{n}})] \tag{15}$$

Since the channel BER, $P_b$, is available, we can investigate the final BER of ECC after decoding. Table 2 shows the expressions used in this paper to calculate the BER of various repetition and BCH codes, using the channel BER derived in Eq.13.

Thus, it is feasible to compare the performance of schemes using ECC with that of uncoded scheme. Fig.4 illustrates the performance of several codes in term of BER, with a 64-bit binary sequence as watermark under the corruption of AWGN noise.

The watermark channels are usually very noisy (BER from 0.1 to 0.5) [16]. In this range of BER, the value of $S/\sigma$ is about $0 \sim 8$dB. The uncoded scheme obviously outperforms repetition code and BCH code. Only when the value of $S/\sigma$ is bigger than 10dB, which is uncommon in watermarking channels, some BCH codes perform better than the uncoded scheme. Since our watermark is a 64-bit sequence, schemes using BCH (127,22,23) and BCH (127,8,31) introduce too much redundancy and thus have lower embedding strengths. So they are outperformed by the schemes of BCH (127,64,10) and BCH (127,106,3). Curves in Fig. 4 show that it is more important to increase embedding strength in order to improve the robustness of watermarking against Gaussian noise.

However, the noise introduced by some testing functions in the StirMark 3.1, e.g. cropping and jitter attacks, cannot be modeled as AWGN. So, the corresponding performance needs to be further investigated.

## 4   Experimental Works

To answer the questions listed in Section 1, we conducted extensive experiments to investigate the relationship between coding scheme and robustness of watermarking.

It is known that different coding schemes with similar coding length have similar embedding strength. Hence, the more powerful correcting ability a coding scheme has, the better robustness of watermarking the scheme achieves. For different coding schemes with different coding lengths and correcting abilities, our investigation of watermarking robustness takes this factor into account.

To address the relationship between the coding types and watermarking robustness (in terms of BER), we compare the following four coding schemes.

- Scheme without using ECC (uncoded scheme). In this case, the length of information bits is the shortest in the four schemes. Hence, we can use the highest embedding strength. This scheme is used to investigate to what extent an increase of embedding strength could improve the robustness of watermark.
- BCH coding. Considering the contending relationship between correcting capability and redundancy introduced by using ECC, we choose BCH (63,36) in case of 32-bit informative watermark, while BCH (127,64) is employed in case of 64-bit and 128-bit informative watermarks. Here, no interleaving is employed.
- Convolutional coding. Similarly, with regard to the trade-off between correcting ability and coding length, we use convolutional code with coding ratio 1/2, maximum free distance 10, constraint length 8.
- Repetition coding. To have similar length of information bits with BCH and convolutional coding schemes, we choose repetition code (3,1). In detection, we use hard-decision to extract each hidden bit, and then determine the watermark bit to be "1" or "0" by means of majority decision. We compare

the extracted watermark with the original watermark, thus obtaining the error rate in detection.

In experiments, the watermark bits are embedded in the mid-frequency coefficients of $8 \times 8$ block DCT for DCT-based scheme and the mid-frequency as well as the low-frequency coefficients for DWT-based scheme. The informative watermarks are composed of 32, 64, and 128 bits.

In the investigation, we test the above four schemes with the same amount of watermark bits. By adjusting the embedding strength $S$, the watermarked images with the four schemes have approximately the same PSNR. That is, we decrease the embedding strength $S$ for a long to-be-embedded bit sequence, and increase the embedding strength for a short to-be-embedded bit sequence. The requirement of invisibility is maintained. Then, we can expect to compare the robustness performance of watermark with the four schemes.

The experiments were carried out on the images with different texture complexity, including Lena, Pepper, Boats, and Baboon. Due to the limitation to the pages, we only report in this paper the results on Lena and Baboon. The similar results can be obtained on Pepper and Boats.

Fig.5 shows the performance comparison between different coding schemes in term of BER for different JPEG compression quality levels, as a 64-bit watermark was embedded in the mid-frequency DCT coefficients of $8 \times 8$ blocks. Note that for JPEG compression, there is little difference between the performance of BCH coding and convolutional coding with similar coding length, while repetition coding scheme is outperformed by both BCH and convolutional coding schemes. Note that, the uncoded scheme has the lowest error rate for all different JPEG compression quality levels. The experiments with a 64-bit watermark, embedded in the low-frequency DCT coefficients of $8 \times 8$ blocks also achieve similar results. Furthermore, experiments with a 32-bit watermark or a 128-bit watermark, embedded in the low- and mid-frequency DCT coefficients of 88 blocks and DWT, demonstrates similar trend too. This indicates that ECC cannot improve the robustness of watermarking against JPEG compression.

Fig.6 shows the robustness of watermark with different coding schemes under Gaussian noise attack (measured by PSNR of the attacked watermarked image versus the original watermarked image), as a 64-bit watermark signal embedded in the mid-frequency DCT coefficients of $8 \times 8$ blocks. Obviously, all the schemes have high BERs when strong noise is added. However, we can see that the uncoded scheme has the lowest error rate than other schemes for the most of time, meaning that ECC cannot improve the robustness of watermarking against additive Gaussian noise attack. Schemes with different size of watermark, embedded in both low- and mid-frequency of DWT and mid-frequency of $8 \times 8$ DCT, exhibited the same trend too.

Note that, experimental results are shown for three different PSNR value, i.e. 44.2dB, 42.0dB, 38.1dB, in both Fig.5 and Fig.6. It is felt that the experimental works are sufficient to support the observations made above.

Table 3 lists the robustness performance of the uncoded and BCH coding schemes when StirMark 3.1 testing functions were applied, as a 64-bit water-

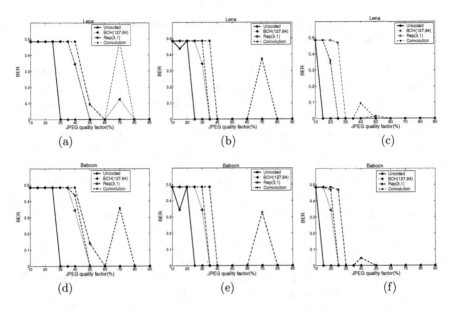

**Fig. 5.** Robustness achieved by different codes vs. JPEG quality levels as watermark embedded in the mid-frequency of $8 \times 8$ DCT. PSNR of watermarked images are: (a), (d) 44.2 dB; (b), (e) 42.0 dB; (c), (f) 38.1 dB.

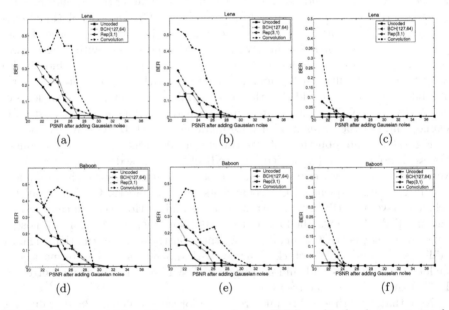

**Fig. 6.** Robustness achieved by different codes vs. JPEG quality levels as watermark embedded in the mid-frequency of $8 \times 8$ DCT. PSNR of watermarked images are: (a), (d) 44.2 dB; (b), (e) 42.0 dB; (c), (f) 38.1 dB.

**Table 3.** Performance of two different coding schemes on *Lena* and *Baboon* as watermark was embedded in the mid-frequency coefficients of 8 × 8 blocks

| StirMark functions | Lena(38dB) | | Baboon(38dB) | | Lena(44dB) | | Baboon(44dB) | |
|---|---|---|---|---|---|---|---|---|
| | Uncoded | BCH | Uncoded | BCH | Uncoded | BCH | Uncoded | BCH |
| 1_row_5_col_removed | 0.219 | 0.141 | 0.234 | 0.125 | 0.219 | 0.141 | 0.250 | 0.156 |
| 5_row_1_col_removed | 0.141 | 0.266 | 0.141 | 0.234 | 0.125 | 0.297 | 0.141 | 0.313 |
| 5_row_17_col_removed | 0.250 | 0.234 | 0.219 | 0.313 | 0.219 | 0.266 | 0.234 | 0.266 |
| 4x4_median_filter | 0.469 | 0.484 | 0.469 | 0.484 | 0.484 | 0.484 | 0.484 | 0.484 |
| 3x3_median_filter | 0.453 | 0.484 | 0.344 | 0.406 | 0.438 | 0.484 | 0.438 | 0.438 |
| 2x2_median_filter | 0.484 | 0.484 | 0.438 | 0.484 | 0.469 | 0.484 | 0.469 | 0.484 |
| Gaussian_filtering_3_3 | 0.484 | 0.484 | 0.484 | 0.484 | 0.484 | 0.484 | 0.484 | 0.375 |
| linear_1.010_0.013_0.009_1.011 | 0.438 | 0.484 | 0.469 | 0.484 | 0.453 | 0.484 | 0.453 | 0.484 |
| linear_1.007_0.010_0.010_1.012 | 0.453 | 0.484 | 0.453 | 0.484 | 0.453 | 0.484 | 0.469 | 0.484 |
| linear_1.013_0.008_0.011_1.008 | 0.453 | 0.484 | 0.422 | 0.484 | 0.469 | 0.484 | 0.453 | 0.484 |
| ratio_x_1.00_y_1.20 | 0.141 | 0.141 | 0.109 | 0.156 | 0.125 | 0.125 | 0.109 | 0.141 |
| ratio_x_1.00_y_1.10 | 0.016 | 0 | 0.047 | 0.094 | 0 | 0 | 0.016 | 0 |
| ratio_x_0.90_y_1.00 | 0.094 | 0.188 | 0.125 | 0.141 | 0.047 | 0.266 | 0.047 | 0.234 |
| ratio_x_0.80_y_1.00 | 0.016 | 0.125 | 0.063 | 0.141 | 0.047 | 0.141 | 0.047 | 0.125 |
| rotation_-0.50 | 0.375 | 0.484 | 0.375 | 0.375 | 0.375 | 0.484 | 0.375 | 0.484 |
| rotation_0.50 | 0.391 | 0.484 | 0.375 | 0.484 | 0.391 | 0.484 | 0.375 | 0.484 |
| rotation_scale_-0.25 | 0.328 | 0.359 | 0.313 | 0.297 | 0.359 | 0.328 | 0.359 | 0.281 |
| rotation_scale_0.25 | 0.359 | 0.359 | 0.375 | 0.344 | 0.359 | 0.344 | 0.359 | 0.328 |
| scale_0.90 | 0.406 | 0.484 | 0.438 | 0.484 | 0.438 | 0.484 | 0.438 | 0.484 |
| scale_1.10 | 0.266 | 0.375 | 0.297 | 0.344 | 0.141 | 0.438 | 0.234 | 0.391 |
| scale_1.50 | 0 | 0 | 0 | 0 | 0 | 0 | 0 | 0 |
| scale_2.00 | 0 | 0 | 0 | 0 | 0 | 0 | 0 | 0 |
| sharpening_3_3 | 0.297 | 0.375 | 0.453 | 0.391 | 0.484 | 0.469 | 0.578 | 0.375 |
| Shearing_x_1.00_y_0.00 | 0.297 | 0.281 | 0.234 | 0.328 | 0.297 | 0.328 | 0.266 | 0.313 |
| Shearing_x_1.00_y_1.00 | 0.422 | 0.422 | 0.406 | 0.406 | 0.406 | 0.422 | 0.406 | 0.406 |
| Shearing_x_5.00_y_0.00 | 0.422 | 0.453 | 0.391 | 0.453 | 0.406 | 0.484 | 0.422 | 0.484 |
| Shearing_x_5.00_y_5.00 | 0.469 | 0.484 | 0.469 | 0.484 | 0.469 | 0.484 | 0.469 | 0.484 |
| JPEG_50 | 0 | 0 | 0 | 0 | 0 | 0 | 0 | 0 |
| JPEG_40 | 0 | 0.344 | 0 | 0.344 | 0 | 0 | 0 | 0 |
| JPEG_35 | 0 | 0.484 | 0 | 0.484 | 0 | 0 | 0 | 0 |
| JPEG_30 | 0 | 0.484 | 0 | 0.484 | 0 | 0 | 0 | 0 |
| JPEG_25 | 0.484 | 0.484 | 0.484 | 0.484 | 0 | 0 | 0 | 0 |
| JPEG_20 | 0.484 | 0.484 | 0.484 | 0.484 | 0 | 0.344 | 0 | 0.344 |
| JPEG_15 | 0.484 | 0.484 | 0.484 | 0.484 | 0 | 0.484 | 0 | 0.484 |
| FMLR | 0.266 | 0.484 | 0.016 | 0.297 | 0.031 | 0.156 | 0 | 0 |

mark was embedded into the mid-frequency DCT coefficients of 8 × 8 blocks. It is observed that, the uncoded scheme performs better than BCH scheme for the most of testing functions in StirMark 3.1, except for cropping and jitter attacks. For jitter attacks, the uncoded scheme outperforms BCH scheme in some cases while being outperformed in other cases. Note that all the cropping testing functions in StirMark 3.1 are not listed in Table 3. For cropping, situation is different because enhanced embedding strength does not play a role. Instead, ECC can resist these two types of attacks to a certain extent. Furthermore, since DCT and DWT cannot preserve geometrical invariant property, all schemes have high error rates under geometrical attacks. Even so, we can see that BER corresponding to the uncoded scheme is lower, compared with the BCH scheme.

Under the constraint of imperceptibility, embedding strength and length of embedded bits are conflicting with each other. ECC can correct some error bits in watermark extraction by means of introducing redundancy. At the same time, however, redundancy introduced by using ECC will lower the embedding strength, hence increasing BER in decoding. Although having no error correcting capability possessed by ECC, the uncoded scheme does lower error rate by means of increasing watermark strength. The above experiments show that it is more important to increase embedding strength in the improvement of watermark robustness against most of attacks except cropping and jitter attack.

It is noted that error bits caused by some attacks, e.g. cropping in image/audio watermarking, or losing frame in video, are independent of embedding strength. In such cases, the higher embedding strength in the uncoded scheme does not make sense, whereas ECC can improve the robustness of watermarking. This observation has been supported by our experiments. In the case of burst errors, it has been reported [17] that better performance can be achieved by combining ECC and interleaving coding.

## 5    Conclusions

In this paper, we have addressed an interesting issue, i.e. whether applying ECC can always lead to the robustness enhancement of watermark signal. The main contributions and conclusions are listed below.

- Having emphasized the differences between watermarking channel and common communication channel. First, robust watermarking channel may be a very noisy channel with a high BER exceeding the capability of ECC. On the other hand, the imperceptibility of original media signal is a peculiar constraint in digital watermarking, which does not exist in common communication systems.
- Having analyzed the contending relationship between watermark embedding strength and total amount of embedded bits (length of embedded sequence) both theoretically and experimentally, from the perspective of the imperceptibility constraint.
- Having analyzed and revaluated, both theoretically and experimentally, the BER of watermarking noisy channel with different error correcting ability, from a different view of low energy to noise ratios. It is shown that using ECC in a very noisy watermarking channel can not effectively improve the robustness of watermarking.
- Having conducted extensive experiments. In experiments, both StirMark 3.1 testing functions and additive Gaussian noise are tested. Data are embedded in the mid-frequency $8 \times 8$ DCT coefficients, and the mid-frequency DWT coefficients as well as the low-frequency DWT coefficients. The informative watermarks composed of 32bits, 64bits, and 128bits are all tested. The performance of four coding schemes, i.e. uncoded scheme, BCH scheme, Repetition scheme and convolutional codes scheme, are compared.
- Having pointed out that it is more important to increase embedding strength in the improvement of watermark robustness against most of attacks except for cropping and jitter attack. The experimental results support our analysis and conclusions.

Hence, using ECC to achieve robust watermarking is not straightforward. It may be used for some specific purposes in watermarking, and it should not be considered as a universal measure that can be employed to enhance robustness of watermarking.

# References

1. I.J. Cox, M.L. Miller, A.L. McKellips: Watermarking as Communications with Side Information, Proc. of the IEEE, 1999, 87(7): 1127-1141.
2. J. Huang and Y. Q. Shi: Reliable Information Bit Hiding, IEEE Trans. on Circuits and Systems for Video Technology, 2002, 12(10): 916-920.
3. F.Prez-Gonzlez, J. R. Hernndez, B. Felix: Approaching the Capacity Limit in Image Watermarking: A Perspective on Coding Techniques for Data Hiding Applications, Signal Processing, 2001, 81(6): 1215-1238.
4. C. F. Wu, W. S. Hsieh: Image Refining Technique Using Watermarking, IEEE Trans. on Consumer Electronics, 2000, 46(1): 1-5.
5. S. Pereira, S. Voloshynovskiy, T. Pun: Effective Channel Coding for DCT Watermarking, Proc. IEEE Int. Conf. on Image Processing, 2000, vol. 3, pp. 671-673.
6. J. Huang, G. F. Elmasry, Y. Q. Shi: Power Constrained Multiple Signaling in Digital Image Watermarking, Proc. of IEEE Int. Workshop on Multimedia Signal Processing, 1998, pp. 388-393.
7. S. Zinger, Z. Jin, H. Maitre, B. Sankur: Optimization of Watermarking Performance Using Error Correcting Codes and Repetition, Proc. of Comm. and Multimedia Security, 2001, 229-240.
8. S. Baudry, J.F. Delaigle, B. Sankur, B. Macq, H. Maitre: Analyses of Error Correction Strategies for Typical Communication Channels in Watermarking, Signal Processing, 2001, 81(6): 1239-1250.
9. F. Balado, F. Perez-Gonzalez, S. Scalise: Turbo Coding for Sample-level Watermarking in the DCT Domain, Proc. of IEEE Int. Conf. on Image Processing, 2001, vol. 3, pp. 1003-1006.
10. R.G van Schyndel, A.Z Tirkel, C.F. Osborne: A Digital Watermark, Proc. of IEEE Int. Conf. on Image Processing, 1994, vol. 2, pp.86 -90.
11. M. J. Tsai, K. Y. Yu, and Y. Z. Chen: Joint Wavelet and Spatial Transformation for Digital Watermarking, IEEE Trans. on Consumer Electronics, 2000, 46(1): 241-245.
12. X. M. Wang, G. Z. Xiao: Principles and Applications of Error Correcting Coding, Xidian University Press, Xian, China, 2001.
13. V. Jovanovic, S. Budisin: On the Coding Gain of Linear Binary Block Codes, IEEE Trans. on Communications., Vol. COM-32, May 1984.
14. Z. G. Cao, Y. S. Qian: Modern Communication Theory, Tsinghua University Press, Beijing, China, 1992.
15. R.Z. Liu, T.N. Tan: A General Watermarking Framework for Optimal Energy Estimation, Chinese J. Computers, 2001, 24(3):242-246
16. C. Desset, B. Macq, L. Vandendorpe: Block Error-Correcting Codes for Systems with a Very High BER: Theoretical Analysis and Application to the Protection of Watermarks, Signal Processing: Image Communication, 2002, 17(5): 409-421.
17. F. Elmasry, Y. Q. Shi,: 2-D Interleaving for Enhancing the Robustness of Watermarking Signals Embedded in Still Images, Proc. of IEEE Int. Conf. on Multimedia & Expo, New York, July 2000.

# On the Performance and Analysis of DNS Security Extensions*

Reza Curtmola, Aniello Del Sorbo, and Giuseppe Ateniese

Information Security Institute and Department of Computer Science,
Johns Hopkins University, Baltimore, MD 21218, USA
{crix, anidel, ateniese}@cs.jhu.edu

**Abstract.** The Domain Name System (DNS) is an essential component of the critical infrastructure of the Internet. The role of DNS is vital, as it is involved in virtually every Internet transaction. It is sometimes remarked that DNS works well as it is now and any changes to it may disrupt its functionality and add complexity. However, due to its importance, an insecure DNS is unacceptable for current and future networks. The astonishing simplicity of mounting an attack against the DNS and the damaging potential of such an attack should convince practitioners and system administrators to employ a secure version of DNS. However, security comes with a cost. In this paper, we examine the performance of two proposals for secure DNS and we discuss the advantages and disadvantages of both. In particular, we analyze the impact that security measures have on the performance of DNS. While it is clear that adding security will lower DNS performance, our results show that the impact of security can be mitigated by deploying different security extensions at different levels in the DNS tree.

We also describe the first implementation of the SK-DNSSEC [1] protocol. The code is freely downloadable and released under an open-source license.

## 1   Introduction

The Domain Name System (DNS) is one of the world's largest distributed databases, whose main function is to translate human readable *domain names* to their corresponding IP *addresses*. Its tree-like structure allows a hierarchical distribution of domain names that facilitates fast name resolution and sub-division of the management load for domain administrators. The role of DNS is vital as it is involved in virtually every Internet transaction. Considering the importance of DNS, it is surprising that a secure version of it is not currently deployed. Vulnerabilities in the DNS system were noticed as early as 1990, in the seminal paper by Bellovin [2]. Several known threats to the DNS system are summarized in [3], some of which include packet interception, packet ID guessing, query prediction and cache poisoning. Because the DNS packets are not cryptographically

---

* The full version of the paper is available on the authors' website.

Y.G. Desmedt et al. (Eds.): CANS 2005, LNCS 3810, pp. 288–303, 2005.

signed, it is possible for a malicious party to inject, intercept or modify these packets with the intent of disrupting the DNS service [2, 3, 4, 5].

To have a secure DNS, two security requirements have to be met at a minimum: *Data origin authentication* and *data integrity*. The main proposal to secure the existing DNS is based mostly on public-key cryptography (PK-DNSSEC [6]), has received a lot of attention and exists as an IETF standard. A different solution (SK-DNSSEC [1]) makes use almost exclusively of symmetric-key cryptography.

This work presents the first implementation of the SK-DNSSEC protocol, which allows us to compare its performance with plain-DNS and PK-DNSSEC. We evaluated the performance tradeoff induced by the security overhead and identified the advantages and disadvantages of both security extensions. With regard to the computational cost, we show that PK-DNSSEC outperforms SK-DNSSEC for authoritative and referral name servers, while SK-DNSSEC performs better for recursive name servers. We argue that a hybrid approach with PK-DNSSEC deployed for top-level domains, where the information is static, and SK-DNSSEC for low-level domains, where the information is more dynamic, would leverage the benefits of both worlds.

Our experiments also show that PK-DNSSEC generates considerably more network traffic and has higher query latency than plain-DNS or SK-DNSSEC. Furthermore, SK-DNSSEC exhibits several other advantages over PK-DNSSEC, some of which are: it has simpler key management, it is less intrusive for zone files and it uses less memory for caching. All these aspects make SK-DNSSEC a valid alternative to PK-DNSSEC, especially if DNS security is needed in dynamic environments.

The rest of this paper is structured as follows. We review background and related work in Sect. 2. We present some details of the SK-DNSSEC implementation in Sect. 3. In Sect. 4 we empirically evaluate the performance of plain-DNS, SK-DNSSEC and PK-DNSSEC and conduct a comparative analysis of these three models. In Sect. 5 we discuss several aspects that can have a significant impact on the functionality of a secure DNS. Section 6 concludes the paper.

## 2    Background and Related Work

A *zone* is a part of the domain name space and the name server that manages a zone is called *authoritative* for that zone. The basic data unit in a zone is called a *Resource Record (RR)*. Clients that query name servers are called *resolvers*. The process by which resolvers retrieve data on a domain name is called *resolution*, and it usually involves a series of queries to servers along the path from the root node to the target name. A *recursive (caching)* name server, upon receiving a query, will resolve the query, cache it and return the answer. A *referral* name server does not return a final answer, but rather does a referral, meaning it redirects the query to the next name server in the DNS tree on the path to the server authoritative for the queried name.

***The Public Key DNS Security Extensions.*** PK-DNSSEC uses three new Resource Records ($RR$) in order to provide end-to-end authenticity and data integrity: KEY (to encode the public key associated with a zone), SIG (to encode digital signatures over an $RR$ set) and NXT (to indicate what does not exist in a zone). DNS servers need to sign the $RR$ sets in zones for which they are authoritative, and answer queries by returning the corresponding SIG RRs along with the queried resource record set. An authenticated NXT RR is returned to indicate that a queried $RR$ does not exist in the zone. On the other hand, a DNS resolver has to verify signed answers by validating the SIG RRs that cover each $RR$ set. The resolver can be configured to trust a set of public keys. If the answer is from a zone whose public key is trusted, the resolver can perform the verification without taking additional steps. Otherwise, the resolver needs to establish a chain of trust starting from one of the trusted public keys (usually of the root name server) down to the public key of that zone. During this process, the resolver may need to make additional queries for public keys of intermediate name servers.

***The SK-DNSSEC protocol.*** PK-DNSSEC is based on public-key cryptography and places a considerable computational burden on resolvers as they have to verify the authenticated DNS answers. Moreover, the answers containing signed $RR$ sets generate considerably more network traffic than plain DNS. In an effort to minimize such undesired effects, SK-DNSSEC [1] proposes a different approach, mostly based on symmetric key algorithms. SK-DNSSEC introduces the notion of DNS symmetric certificates which provide integrity and authenticity by combining encryption techniques with MAC functions (specifically HMAC [7, 8]). A DNS symmetric certificate is similar to a public-key certificate in the sense that it binds the owner's identity to a key. To obtain a secure answer, a DNS resolver establishes a chain of authentication from a trusted DNS server to the authoritative name server using symmetric certificates. Initially, the resolver needs to acquire a long-term root certificate from a root server. This is the only step in which public-key cryptography is used, and it is done only once in order to bootstrap the chain of trust. Root certificates are never queried again until they expire, usually when the public key of the root server changes. Each node in the DNS hierarchy shares a symmetric key with its parent, called *master key*. Master keys are used to generate symmetric certificates which allow safe transport of secret keys from the parent to the child in the DNS tree. A resolver needs to acquire a DNS symmetric certificate for each DNS server encountered while the chain of trust is being built from the root server to the authoritative name server. These certificates can be cached and contain the secrets shared by the resolver with the DNS servers queried during the resolving process. Thus, a DNS server does not need to store any of the information shared with the resolvers.

The strategy deployed in SK-DNSSEC is similar to the one introduced by Davis and Swick [9] and Kerberos [10, 11]. In particular, DNS symmetric certificates can be viewed as *tickets* used by the ticket-granting server in Kerberos to provide clients with access capabilities to certain resources. We refer the reader to [1] and to the full version of this paper for a more detailed description of SK-DNSSEC and its operation.

## 3    Implementation

One of the major contributions of this work is the first implementation of the SK-DNSSEC protocol since it was originally proposed [1]. BIND is the most widely deployed implementation of DNS protocols and its source code is freely available. We selected version 9 of BIND as the base for the SK-DNSSEC implementation. This version provides the most complete implementation of the PK-DNSSEC extensions.

The current version of the SK-DNSSEC implementation uses AES in CBC mode as the symmetric cipher, HMAC with MD5 [1] as the MAC function, and RSA with PKCS1 padding as the public-key cipher. The implementation can be easily extended to accommodate additional algorithms. However, certain algorithms may not be appropriate. For example, Blowfish is a symmetric cipher with a high speed encryption rate, but in our experiments it did not perform as expected. The reason is that Blowfish has a low key agility as opposed to other standard algorithms [14]. Switching frequently between different keys, as required by SK-DNSSEC, can significantly influence the throughput. Thus, we recommend the use of symmetric ciphers with high key agility, like AES.

Due to space constraints, we give a more detailed description of the SK-DNSSEC implementation in the full version of the paper.

## 4    Performance

Our primary goal is to perform a comparative analysis between plain-DNS, SK-DNSSEC and PK-DNSSEC, in order to evaluate the performance tradeoff induced by the security overhead.

In this paper, we consider the public-key DNS security extensions (PK-DNSSEC) defined in RFC2535 [6]. There are several work-in-progress IETF drafts [15, 16] that will eventually supersede RFC2535, but the results presented in this paper will still be valid since we are mainly concerned with performance evaluation. The most important change in these drafts is the addition of a *Delegation Signer* (DS) record delegating trust from a parental key to a child's zone key. This simplifies key management, but does not reduce the computational cost for a resolver and will not affect the overall performance.

### 4.1    Setup

For our experimental analysis, we have setup the DNS tree depicted in Fig. 1. Each of the domains corresponding to the nodes in the tree is hosted on a separate machine. The machines are part of a single Ethernet LAN segment. They reside on the same subnet, connected by a Trendnet TEG-S240TX Gigabit switch, with no intermediate routers in between. All machines have the same hardware configuration, namely single Athlon XP 2.2 GHz processor, 1

---

[1] Even if MD5 is not collision resistant ([12, 13]), HMAC-MD5 still provides adequate security in the context of this application.

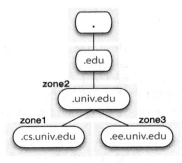

**Fig. 1.** The test DNS tree

GB SDRAM memory, running Red Hat Linux 8.0 (kernel 2.4.20) and BIND 9.2.1 compiled with OpenSSL 0.9.7d.

Each node in the DNS test tree is responsible for exactly one zone. The zones for `.` and `.edu` contain only one host as well as basic delegating records. The real zones used for testing are `.cs.univ.edu`, `.univ.edu` and `.ee.univ.edu` (zones 1, 2 and 3 respectively). Contents of these zones are elaborated on later, as they are adapted to the different types of tests performed. In the case of PK-DNSSEC, the zones were signed using 1024-bit RSA keys (with public exponent $e = 2^{16} + 1$, the default in OpenSSL), while for SK-DNSSEC we used AES 128-bit symmetric keys. All the machines used in the DNS tree have EDNS0 enabled [17], so UDP packets are not limited to 512 bytes.

To compensate for the small number of name servers in the test DNS tree, the TTL (time to live) values for zones were chosen smaller than values of realistic TTLs. This implies that the records expire faster. A small TTL forces name servers to query for records more frequently, thus effectively simulating a high workload which is closer to a real-world scenario. Experiments were performed with TTL values between 1 and 60 seconds. We argue that using small TTLs does not bias the results in favor of any of the considered models. We also argue that the results give an approximation of the behavior when larger TTLs are used. The experiments were conducted on a smaller scale and our goal was to give a preliminary performance evaluation.

### 4.2   Experiments

We group the performance tests in three categories: query throughput, network traffic and query latency. We believe that for network traffic performance evaluation, it is more important to simulate a realistic DNS traffic pattern than it is for the query throughput performance tests. Querying for different types of RRs has less impact on the query processing rate of a name server than on the size of DNS responses. Thus, for the network traffic tests, we chose to model the traffic pattern and zone contents after a real DNS trace. However, we did not follow the same principles for the query throughput evaluation because we wanted to minimize the influence of network overhead caused by larger DNS messages.

## 4.3   Query Throughput

The query throughput of a DNS server is defined as how many queries per second the DNS server is capable of handling. Each of the zones 1, 2 and 3 contains 10,000 hosts and consists of one SOA resource record (RR), one NS RR and 10,000 A RRs (with distinct IP addresses chosen from different class B address pools). Since we are only going to query for A RRs, the zones do not have other types of resource records[2]. The workload for the name servers was generated using *queryperf*, a DNS query performance testing tool bundled within the BIND9 distribution [18]. A query throughput performance test is considered a stress test that measures the raw query throughput of a DNS server. *Queryperf* can have a specified amount of outstanding queries, and we used the default setting of 20. To avoid additional load on the machines hosting the zones, *queryperf* was executed on a separate machine, outside the DNS test tree, but still inside the same Ethernet segment. In accordance with the SK-DNSSEC protocol, we also modified *queryperf* to include symmetric certificates. In the case of PK-DNSSEC, *queryperf* was executed with the flag -D enabled to ensure that DNS-SEC records are requested. Furthermore, we verified that in all answers the authentic data bit (AD) was set, indicating that all authentications had been successful.

To maintain consistency in the comparative tests, each category of tests was run with the same batch of queries for all the three configurations of the DNS tree: plain-DNS, SK-DNSSEC and PK-DNSSEC. The tests in different categories were executed independently from each other, by restarting all the name servers between executions. For each category of tests, the results were averaged over a set of ten measurements. The experimental results are described in the next sections and analyzed in Sect. 4.3.

**Performance of a Recursive (Caching) DNS Server.** When a caching name server answers a query from the cache, it requires much less CPU time and fewer packets of network traffic than when it answers a query for which the server needs to perform a recursive lookup by querying authoritative servers. Therefore, just like in [19], we characterize the throughput of a caching server by two numbers: (1) the throughput when the answers are not in the cache, and (2) the throughput when answers are already in the cache. The actual throughput with a mixed production load will be somewhere between these two numbers, closer to one or the other depending on the cache hit rate.

Our basic query batch consists of 10,000 queries, matching all the A RRs in *zone3* (.ee.univ.edu). Using *queryperf*, the queries were directed to the name server authoritative for *zone1* (.cs.univ.edu), which played the role of a caching resolver. This means that a query for host1.ee.univ.edu will require two queries to the authoritative servers: one to the univ.edu server returning a referral and one to the ee.univ.edu server returning the answer. We designed this test in order to simulate the behavior of typical web surfing clients: a typical

---

[2] This simplifies the measurement process and minimizes the influence of network overhead caused by *RRs* of larger size.

**Table 1.** Caching server performance for entirely uncached and entirely cached answers

| Configuration | uncached (qps) | cached (qps) |
|---|---|---|
| plain-DNS | 2550 | 17800 |
| SK-DNSSEC | 1860 | 17793 |
| PK-DNSSEC | 1313 | 17779 |

**Table 2.** Authoritative and referral server performance (in queries per second)

| Configuration | authoritative (qps) | referral (qps) |
|---|---|---|
| plain-DNS | 18070 | 17200 |
| SK-DNSSEC | 8633 | 5206 |
| PK-DNSSEC | 11440 | 13535 |

lookup for the uncached web server address `www.domain.com` requires a query to the `com` server and one to the `domain.com` server.

Table 1 shows the results when the answers are entirely uncached and entirely cached. These results were obtained using the basic query batch and are independent of the zone TTL. In addition to the basic query batch, we performed tests with query batches of $n$ thousand queries, with $n \in \{20, 30, 40, 50, 90, 100\}$, obtained by repeatedly concatenating the basic query batch of 10,000 queries. Using these batches we simulated a mixed production load, where some of the queries will be answered from the cache, depending on the zone TTL. Results are shown in Fig. 2.

**Performance of an Authoritative and Referral DNS Server.** To test the performance of an authoritative name server, the query batch was constructed by choosing hosts from *zone1* and then directed to the name server authoritative for *zone1*. In the case of a referral server, the queries were for hosts from *zone1* and were directed to the name server authoritative for *zone2*. This name server had recursion turned off and made referrals by answering with the data it had about the name server authoritative for *zone1* (the answer consists of NS RRs, called *delegation points*, and A RRs, called *glue addresses* [6]). For the SK-DNSSEC tests, a modified version of *queryperf* was used, in order to ensure that symmetric certificates are validated, new ones are created in case of referrals, and answers are authenticated for authoritative answers, as required by the SK-DNSSEC protocol. Table 2 shows the results. Note the results are independent from the zone TTL, as they are not influenced by caching.

**Performance of a Root DNS Server.** In the case of SK-DNSSEC, the root name server receives requests for root certificates and this is the only step in which public-key cryptography is used. To determine the rate at which a name server can handle root certificate requests, we directed the query batch to the root name server in the test DNS tree. Once more, the modified version of *queryperf* was used, to include root certificate requests. The root name server

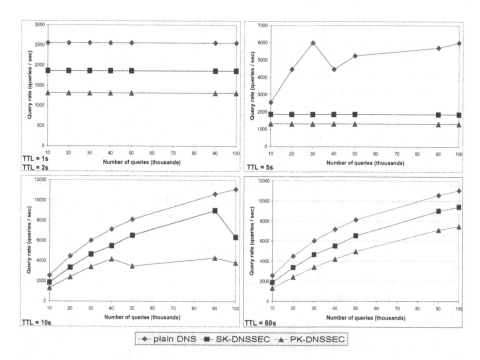

**Fig. 2.** Query throughput performance for a caching server, for various zone TTLs, averaged over ten measurements (note that each graph has a different scale)

was able to handle approximately 305 root certificate requests per second[3]. We believe this is acceptable since root certificates are requested only once (when resolvers become operative for the first time) and their validity can be set arbitrarily long[4]. It is important to stress that root certificate requests are distinct from root DNS queries: A root server may receive millions of DNS queries but may have to handle only a small number of root certificate requests. An alternative is to deploy PK-DNSSEC at the top level of the DNS tree and SK-DNSSEC below. This would distribute the load among several servers. Another possibility is to deploy standard mechanisms to prevent DoS attacks at the root, such as client puzzles [20, 21, 22].

**Query Throughput Performance Analysis.** All the query throughput percentage values described in this section are expressed relative to the plain-DNS

---

[3] Incidentally, notice that this is approximately the same number of queries a PK-DNSSEC-enabled server would be able to handle if signatures would have to be computed on the fly and it is the main reason why we argue that PK-DNSSEC is not suitable for dynamic environments.

[4] More specifically, a root certificate can be valid, for example, for 6 months or 1 year or more given that the public keys of root servers are chosen to last for a long period of time. In principle, a root certificate is valid as long as the public key of the root server is not changed.

results. The most significant burden for PK-DNSSEC is on recursive name servers that act as caching resolvers. Observe in Table 1, for uncached queries, that SK-DNSSEC causes a smaller decrease of the query throughput than PK-DNSSEC does: while SK-DNSSEC stays at 73%, PK-DNSSEC gets as low as 51%. If the queried name server is not authoritative for a queried domain and if a query is not cached, then a portion of the DNS tree is traversed during the resolving process. Thus, testing for the performance of a recursive server is a good indicator for the performance of the whole DNS tree, since it also involves referrals and authoritative answers in addition to purely recursive answers. Since PK-DNSSEC performs better at answers that are purely referral or authoritative, the difference in performance for a recursive server can only be attributed to the additional burden placed on resolvers by PK-DNSSEC. Indeed, for PK-DNSSEC, caching resolvers have to verify the signed answers, which involves a public-key verification; for SK-DNSSEC, caching resolvers only have to send an already pre-computed symmetric certificate, thus no cryptographic operations are necessary.

In Fig. 2, for the zone TTL of 1 and 2 seconds, caching was not effective for any of the tested configurations. Indeed, it took plain-DNS 3.9 seconds to finish querying for all the 10,000 hosts in the query batch, while it took 5.3 seconds for SK-DNSSEC and 7.6 seconds for PK-DNSSEC. For zone TTL of 5 seconds, we start to see the effects of caching for plain-DNS, while for SK-DNSSEC and PK-DNSSEC caching is visible only starting with zone TTL of 10 seconds. Observe that in some cases, when the number of queries increases, the query rate drops; take for example the case of TTL=5s, plain-DNS, from 30000 to 40000 queries. The explanation is that resolving 30000 queries falls just inside the 5 seconds interval, the zone TTL, and the additional 10,000 queries are treated as uncached queries, thus lowering the average query rate.

On the other hand, Table 2 shows that PK-DNSSEC performs better than SK-DNSSEC for an authoritative name server (63% compared to 47%) and for a referral name server (78% compared to 30%). The increased performance for authoritative answers was expected, since PK-DNSSEC needs no additional computations, while for SK-DNSSEC a symmetric certificate needs to be verified and a MAC needs to be computed. Similarly, for referral answers, PK-DNSSEC only serves the pre-signed data, while SK-DNSSEC needs to verify a symmetric certificate, create a new one, and also encrypt and authenticate a new pair of symmetric keys. Also, we suspect that the difference in performance between authoritative and referral answers for PK-DNSSEC is caused by the additional $RR$s present in authoritative answers.

It is worth mentioning that, according to our measurements, the cryptographic operations in the SK-DNSSEC implementation accounted for only a small percentage of the total cost added by SK-DNSSEC (28% for the referral name server test and 26% for the authoritative name server test). The overhead seems to be mostly caused by the rest of the code (data structures handling, DNS message re-parsing etc), that can potentially be optimized in future releases, thus further improving the performance of SK-DNSSEC.

## 4.4   Network Traffic

**Testbed Setup.** To obtain a realistic query type and query outcome distribution for our query batch, we have monitored the DNS network traffic at the main DNS server of our institution. The data was recorded for 8 consecutive days, 8 hours daily, between 8AM-4PM. In this interval more than four million queries were observed, with the query type and query outcome distributions as shown in Table 3 and Table 4, respectively. The query type distribution in Table 3 is consistent with the numbers observed for a root server [23] and for the MIT LCS and AI labs [24][5].

**Table 3.** Observed query type distribution

| Query Type | A | PTR | AAAA | MX | A6 | SOA | SRV | NS | other |
|---|---|---|---|---|---|---|---|---|---|
| Percentage(%) | 60.452 | 16.605 | 15.164 | 7.311 | 0.211 | 0.111 | 0.093 | 0.042 | <0.010 |

**Table 4.** Observed query outcome distribution: *'success'* represents successful queries the name server handled that did not result in referrals or errors; *'referral'* are the queries that resulted in referrals; *'nxrrset'* are the queries that resulted in error responses because the queried domain existed, but the queried resource record did not exist for that domain; *'nxdomain'* are queries that resulted in error responses because the queried domain did not exist; *'failure'* are the queries that resulted in errors other than those covered by *'nxrrset'* and *'nxdomain'*

| Query Type | Percentage(%) | | | | | |
|---|---|---|---|---|---|---|
| | success | referral | nxrrset | nxdomain | failure | total |
| A | 55.26 | <0.01 | <0.01 | 4.97 | 0.21 | 60.45 |
| PTR | 15.35 | <0.01 | <0.01 | 1.02 | 0.23 | 16.60 |
| MX | 5.97 | <0.01 | 1.11 | 0.08 | 0.15 | 7.31 |
| AAAA | 0.61 | <0.01 | 11.48 | 1.55 | 1.52 | 15.16 |
| Total | 77.19 | 0.01 | 12.59 | 7.62 | 2.11 | 99.52 |

The query type distribution is relevant when evaluating the network traffic because queries of different types can result in differently sized answers. Also, the query outcome distribution plays an important role if we consider, for example, the cost of processing queries for non-existent hostnames in the case of PK-DNSSEC: validation for signed negative answers is usually more expensive than for signed positive answers. Thus, we considered both query type distribution and query outcome.

While trying to maintain the same query type distribution as in Table 3 for the query batch, a few changes were made that should have a negligible impact

---

[5] The only exception is the large number of AAAA queries in our trace, which we suspect occurred because of a bug in version 8.12.9 of `sendmail`: IPv6 DNS lookups are attempted before IPv4 lookups, even if IPv6 is not enabled in the kernel of the operating system.

on the performance results: Instead of queries for PTR records, we used queries for A records. This should not make a difference since an answer to a query for a reverse address mapping (PTR) record has about the same size of an answer to a query for a regular address (A) record. Also, since all the other types of resource records, besides A, PTR, AAAA and MX account for less than 0.5% of the total number of queries, we argue they have a negligible impact and we do not include them in our query batch.

In addition, resemblance to a real-world scenario was considered for the contents of the zones in the DNS tree. The test zones consist of one SOA resource record (RR), two NS RRs and one A RR for each of the 10,000 hosts in the zone. It is a common practice to have at least two NS RRs per zone and two MX RR per domain for redundancy reasons. With only three test zones in our DNS tree, having only two MX RRs per zone causes an overwhelming majority of queries for MX RRs to be answered from the cache. To avoid this and simulate what happens in the real DNS with a much larger name space, we assigned two MX RRs to 1000 of the hosts in each zone. This setting is satisfactory given the amount of MX records (over 7%) in the query batches.

**Network Traffic Performance Tests.** Using the same DNS test tree, a batch of 10,000 queries was directed to the name server responsible for *zone1*. The queried domains were chosen from *zone3*, while the query type distribution followed the description in Sect. 4.4 and Table 3. The percentage of queries that resulted in error (*nxrrset* + *nxdomain* + *failure*) is considerable (over 22%), and we included queries with such outcome in the query batch[6], according to the data in Table 4. The queries were run from a machine outside the test DNS tree, but still inside the same Ethernet segment.

*Queryperf* was used to generate the workload, with the default setting of 20 outstanding queries, for intervals of $i$ seconds, with $i \in \{10, 20, 60, 300\}$. For some configurations of the name servers in the DNS tree, it was possible to run the query batch multiple times during an interval. The results were gathered using *tcpdump* from yet another machine outside the DNS tree, but inside the same Ethernet segment. Tests were run with the zones in the DNS tree having a TTL of $t$ seconds, with $t \in \{1, 10, 25, 60\}$. Results are aggregated in Fig. 3 and summarized in Table 5.

With $t = 1$ and $i = 10$ (Fig. 3(a)), SK-DNSSEC averages to 733 KB/sec, relatively close to the average of 652 KB/sec for plain-DNS. In contrast, PK-DNSSEC imposes a much higher bandwidth with an average of 1724 KB/s. Moreover, during the test interval, the SK-DNSSEC resolver was able to complete 80% of the number of queries resolved by plain-DNS, as opposed to only 57% in the case of PK-DNSSEC. Thus, for SK-DNSSEC, not only was the amount of traffic generated much smaller than for PK-DNSSEC, but also the number of resolved queries was considerably larger.

---

[6] To generate a *failure* outcome for a query, we create a lame delegation of a domain, and ask a query for a host in that domain. For outcomes such as *nxrrset* and *nxdomain*, we query for a non-existent RR set or hostname.

**Table 5.** Network traffic statistics

| Configuration | TTL (sec) | Traffic Avg (KB/sec) | Queries resolved | Configuration | TTL (sec) | Traffic Avg (KB/sec) | Queries resolved |
|---|---|---|---|---|---|---|---|
| plain-DNS | 1s | 652 | 20283 | plain-DNS | 25s | 639 | 243964 |
| SK-DNSSEC | 1s | 733 | 16283 | SK-DNSSEC | 25s | 669 | 233482 |
| PK-DNSSEC | 1s | 1724 | 11761 | PK-DNSSEC | 25s | 1844 | 231766 |
| plain-DNS | 10s | 726 | 79845 | plain-DNS | 60s | 384 | 738013 |
| SK-DNSSEC | 10s | 768 | 69198 | SK-DNSSEC | 60s | 391 | 699924 |
| PK-DNSSEC | 10s | 1730 | 34330 | PK-DNSSEC | 60s | 1024 | 694919 |

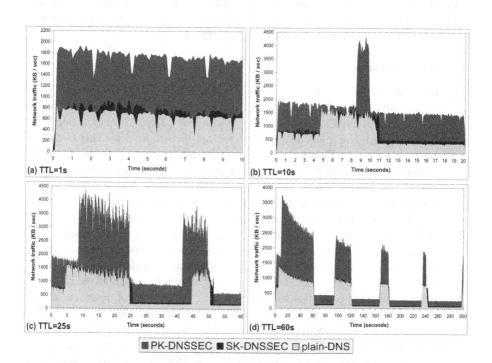

**Fig. 3.** Network traffic evolution over time (note that each graph has a different scale)

With $t = 10$ and $i = 20$ (Fig. 3(b)), we observe an interesting behavior. After the batch of 10,000 queries is exhausted between seconds 5 and 6 for plain-DNS and SK-DNSSEC, *queryperf* runs the query batch multiple times during the specified interval, and since the TTL of the zones is now 10s, after this moment all the queries in the batch are already cached. That explains the sudden increase in network traffic and in number of queries resolved: The resolver is able to answer from the cache a higher number of queries, thus generating more traffic (mostly between the resolver and the client that issued the queries). After the 10 second mark, we observe a gradual decrease in the amount of network traffic, as the TTL of the cached records expires. The same caching behavior is seen for

PK-DNSSEC, but for a shorter interval, since it took more time to resolve the first 10,000 queries.

With $t = 25$, $i = 60$ (Fig. 3(c)) and $t = 60s$, $i = 300$ (Fig. 3(d)), the caching behavior becomes more obvious; also, as the TTL increases, the number of resolved queries converges to the same value for the three models.

The full version of the paper also contains experiments showing the amount of traffic as a function of the number of queries. In all cases we can see that PK-DNSSEC generates a considerably larger amount of network traffic than plain-DNS (between 164%-188% more traffic), while SK-DNSSEC stays relatively close to plain-DNS (between 1%-12% more traffic). This considerable difference is caused by the large message size in the PK-DNSSEC model. Among other issues, the increased size of DNS responses confirms that PK-DNSSEC-aware servers can act as denial-of-service amplifiers, as hypothesized in [3].

### 4.5   Query Latency

The query latency of a caching DNS server is the time it takes to answer any single DNS query. It can be a real issue for DNS, since it is the aspect of server performance that is most visible to the individual end user. Another experiment was run to evaluate the query latency. The name servers used for this test were configured as shown in Figure 1, but were physically located so that realistic network delays were involved: the name server authoritative for *zone1* was part of a network (located in Italy), while the rest of the name servers were part of a different network (located in the USA). In the test, queries for hosts in *zone3* were directed to the name server authoritative for *zone1*, which played the role of a resolver. The answers for these queries were not previously cached and the following results (expressed in milliseconds) are averaged over a set of 100 queries: plain-DNS - 505.76, SK-DNSSEC - 509.70 and PK-DNSSEC - 1360.82.

The latency for SK-DNSSEC is slightly higher than for plain-DNS, since additional cryptographic operations are involved in the process of query resolving. On the other hand, SK-DNSSEC has a lower query latency than PK-DNSSEC, mainly because in PK-DNSSEC the resolver has to contact the name servers in the DNS tree twice: once to get the actual signed answer and once to get the key material required to validate the answer. SK-DNSSEC, just like plain-DNS, only contacts the intermediate servers once. Basically, if the answer is not already cached, then the round trip time between name servers involved in the resolving process has a higher influence over the query latency in PK-DNSSEC than in SK-DNSSEC. Note that the query latency will not significantly depend on the speed of the machines running the name servers, because it is dominated by external network delays rather than by processing time [19].

## 5   Remarks

We saw that the computational cost of adding security to DNS is different depending on the type of name server. If a hybrid approach is considered, with PK-DNSSEC deployed for the top-level domains, where the information is static, then SK-DNSSEC would be suitable for the low-level DNS tree, which is characterized by a more dynamic environment. Such a hybrid approach has several positive aspects. Our experiments showed that the computational cost of PK-DNSSEC is high for caching resolvers, while SK-DNSSEC places most of the computational cost on non-recursive servers above the zone that is being searched. Thus, PK-DNSSEC pushes the computational cost towards the bottom of the DNS tree, while SK-DNSSEC pushes it upwards. A hybrid approach would eliminate these shortcomings: with PK-DNSSEC on top, referrals are efficient (which is important for servers that handle high-volume traffic), while SK-DNSSEC on the bottom reduces the computational burden for caching resolvers (since resolvers are usually at the bottom of the hierarchy).

We also noticed that the cryptographic core of the signing routine in SK-DNSSEC is responsible only for a fraction of the total cost incurred in generating symmetric certificates and that its performance can be further improved by employing faster cryptographic primitives. For instance, one could substitute HMAC with UMAC which appears to be one order of magnitude faster [25].

While experimenting with the three versions of DNS, we have analyzed some aspects and considered techniques we plan to include in a future release of the code. In particular, one issue we are addressing is the fact that pre-computation in SK-DNSSEC is not possible since authentication is always achieved via freshly generated secret keys. This offers a high level of security against replay attacks but it requires secret keys to be stored on-line so that they are readily available to the DNS server. This does not apply to PK-DNSSEC since signatures are pre-computed over entire $RR$ sets and re-used until they expire. However, key management in PK-DNSSEC is a big issue, particularly in the case of *dynamic updates* [26], and it appears that the only way to effectively address it is to have certain keys online. We plan to devise techniques to mitigate this online-key issue with a combination of intrusion detection and proactive security mechanisms [27].

Finally, we are addressing the fact that SK-DNSSEC employs public-key cryptography whenever a root symmetric certificate is needed either because a new resolver is being set up or because an existing root certificate has expired. In both cases, we argued that a root server can handle the load caused by legitimate requests but an SK-DNSSEC-enabled root server is potentially susceptible to a denial of service attack. In a future release of the code we are planning to incorporate the following strategy which may mitigate the issue above: The root private key is kept off-line and root certificate requests are only collected and later elaborated offline at certain time intervals. The delay between the request and the response from the root server could be fixed and predetermined. In this way, a resolver with an expiring certificate will have a time window before the expiration date in which it is allowed to request the new certificate. This should be enough to limit service disruptions. Alternatively, we are also looking at mechanisms based on client puzzles [20, 21, 22] but tailored to the specific needs of DNS.

# 6  Conclusions and Future Work

We have presented a functional implementation of the SK-DNSSEC protocol and we performed a comparative analysis between plain-DNS, SK-DNSSEC and PK-DNSSEC in order to evaluate the performance tradeoff induced by the security overhead.

We saw that a hybrid approach, with PK-DNSSEC deployed for top-level domains and SK-DNSSEC for the low-level DNS tree, can leverage the benefits of both security extensions. PK-DNSSEC significantly increases the size of DNS response packets, generating considerably more network traffic and higher network latency than plain-DNS or SK-DNSSEC. In general, SK-DNSSEC appears to be a valid alternative to PK-DNSSEC since it improves on several other important aspects. For instance, it simplifies key management, it is less intrusive than PK-DNSSEC, given that zone files do not have to be changed, and no NXT RRs are needed. In addition, since response packets in SK-DNSSEC are smaller, less memory for caching is required.

**Availability.** The implementation of the SK-DNSSEC-enabled BIND9 name server is available at http://skdnssec.isi.jhu.edu.

**Acknowledgments.** We are grateful to Fabian Monrose for his insightful comments that notably improved this paper. We thank Daniel Massey, Adam Stubblefield, Breno de Medeiros, Kevin Fu and Emil Sit for their feedbacks on the paper. Many thanks to Steve Rifkin for helping to collect DNS traffic data. We are also grateful to Scott Rose for his suggestions on setting up the performance testbed. We thank the anonymous reviewers for their helpful comments. This work was supported by an NSF grant.

# References

1. G. Ateniese and S. Mangard, "A new approach to DNS security (DNSSEC)," in *8th ACM Conference on Computer and Communications Security*, pp. 86–95, ACM Press, 2001.
2. S. M. Bellovin, "Using the Domain Name System for system break-ins," in *Proceedings of the Fifth USENIX UNIX Security Symposium*, pp. 199–208, June 1995.
3. D. Atkins and R. Austein, *Threat Analysis Of The Domain Name System*. IETF - Network Working Group, August 2004. RFC3833.
4. P. Vixie, "DNS and BIND security issues," in *Proceedings of the Fifth USENIX UNIX Security Symposium*, pp. 209–216, June 1995.
5. T. de Raadt, N. Provos, T. Miller, and A. Briggs, "Bind vulnerabilities and solutions," April 1997. http://niels.xtdnet.nl/papers/secnet-bind.txt.
6. D. Eastlake, *Domain Name System Security Extensions*, March 1999. RFC2535.
7. M. Bellare, R. Canetti, and H. Krawczyk, "Keying hash functions for message authentication," in *Crypto '96 Proceedings*, vol. 1109 of *LNCS*, Springer-Verlag, 1996.
8. H. Krawczyk, M. Bellare, and R. Canetti, *HMAC: Keyed-Hashing for Message Authentication*. IETF - Network Working Group, February 1997. RFC2104.

9. D. Davis and R. Swick, "Network security via private-key certificates," in *Proceedings of the Third USENIX UNIX Security Symposium*, pp. 239–242, September 1992. Also in ACM Operating Systems Review, v. 24, n. 4 (Oct. 1990).

10. B. C. Neuman and T. Ts'o, "Kerberos: An authentication system for computer networks," in *IEEE Communications*, vol. 32(9), pp. 33–38, IEEE, September 1994.

11. J. Kohl and C. Neuman, *The Kerberos Network Authentication System (V5)*. IETF - Network Working Group, September 1993. RFC1510.

12. X. Wang and H. Yu, "How to break MD5 and other hash functions," in *EuroCrypt 2005*, vol. 3494 of *Lecture Notes in Computer Science*, pp. 19–35, Springer-Verlag, 2005.

13. A. Lenstra and B. de Weger, "On the possibility of constructing meaningful hash collisions for public keys," in *ACISP 2005*, vol. 3574 of *LNCS*, pp. 267–279, Springer-Verlag, 2005.

14. D. Whiting, B. Schneier, and S. Bellovin, "AES key agility issues in high-speed IPsec implementations."

15. R. Arends, M. Larson, R. Austein, D. Massey, and S. Rose, "Protocol modifications for the DNS security extensions," Internet draft 09, IETF - DNS Extensions, October 2004.

16. R. Arends, M. Larson, R. Austein, D. Massey, and S. Rose, "Resource records for the DNS security extensions," Internet Draft 11, IETF - DNS Extensions, October 2004.

17. P. Vixie, *Extension Mechanisms for DNS (EDNS0)*, August 1999. RFC2671.

18. "BIND." http://www.isc.org/sw/bind.

19. NOMINUM, "How to Measure the Performance of a Caching DNS Server," 2002. http://www.nominum.com/content/documents/CNS_WP.pdf.

20. D. Dean and A. Stubblefield, "Using client puzzles to protect TLS," in *Proceedings of the Tenth USENIX Security Symposium*, August 2001.

21. A. Juels and J. Brainard, "Client puzzles: A cryptographic defense against connection depletion attacks," in *Proceedings of NDSS '99* (S. Kent, ed.), pp. 151–165, 1999.

22. B. Waters, A. Juels, J. A. Halderman, and E. W. Felten, "New client puzzle outsourcing techniques for DoS resistance," in *11th ACM CCS 2004*, ACM, 2004.

23. D. Wessels and M. Fomenkov, "Wow, that's a lot of packets," in *PAM2003*, April 2003.

24. J. Jung, E. Sit, H. Balakrishnan, and R. Morris, "DNS performance and the effectiveness of caching," in *ACM SIGCOM Internet Measurement Workshop '01*, November 2001.

25. J. Black, S. Halevi, H. Krawczyk, T. Krovetz, and P. Rogaway, "UMAC: Fast and secure message authentication," in *Advances in Cryptology - Crypto '99 Proceedings*, vol. 1666 of *LNCS*, pp. 216–233, Springer-Verlag, 1999.

26. P. Vixie, S. Thomson, Y. Rekhter, and J. Bound, *Dynamic Updates in the Domain Name System (DNS UPDATE)*. IETF - Network Working Group, April 1997. RFC2136.

27. R. Ostrovsky and M. Yung, "How to withstand mobile virus attacks," in *10th ACM Symposium on Principles of Distributed Computing*, pp. 51–59, ACM Press, 1991.

# On Securing RTP-Based Streaming Content
# with Firewalls*

Liang Lu, Rei Safavi-Naini, Jeffrey Horton, and Willy Susilo

Centre for Communication Security Research,
School of Information Technology and Computer Science,
University of Wollongong, Australia
{1197, rei, jeffh, wsusilo}@uow.edu.au

**Abstract.** Delivery of real-time streaming content is an increasingly important Internet application. Applications involved in processing streaming content may have exploitable vulnerabilities, as many other applications have been discovered to have, and using a firewall to filter out malicious traffic may provide some benefit. However, as these applications largely rely on traffic carried by RTP/UDP, firewalls that are unaware of the behaviour of RTP data streams have difficulties in filtering out malicious traffic injected into a stream by an attacker. In this paper, we observe a vulnerability in the current RTP protocol which allows an attacker to inject malicious traffic into a data stream, and present a scheme that allows a stateful firewall that keeps state from RTP packets to detect such malicious traffic. Our technique uses non-static fields such as RTP sequence numbers to improve the inspection scheme by modelling streaming traffic and detecting malicious streams based on deviation for this model. We show effectiveness of our approach by giving the results of our experiments.

**Keywords:** Network security, firewall, streaming content.

## 1  Introduction

Recent years have seen increasing applications of streaming content online, such as live video or audio broadcast, IP telephony and teleconferencing. This growth is driven by technology advancement such as PC performance, residential broadband access and virtual-reality technologies and is expected to continue. Like other networking applications, applications involved in processing streaming content may have exploitable vulnerabilities. It is highly desirable to have a firewall that can filter out malicious traffic in streaming content.

However, streaming applications have different behavior to conventional networking applications. Unlike conventional networking applications which are mostly based on TCP, streaming applications based on open protocols (e.g. [16],

---

* This work is partially supported by Cooperative Research Center - Smart Internet Technology (CRC-SIT), Australia.

Y.G. Desmedt et al. (Eds.): CANS 2005, LNCS 3810, pp. 304–319, 2005.

[3], [21]) largely rely on RTP [17] for data delivery. RTP typically uses UDP as the underlying transport protocol. Although TCP may also be used, it is mainly used for tunneling through firewalls at the cost of timely delivery of stream data when there is packet loss. Because conventional firewalls have difficulties in detecting malicious UDP injection due to its connectionless nature, they cannot effectively filter out malicious traffic injected in streaming content.

In this paper, we first discuss the difficulties that various types of conventional firewalls have when filtering UDP-based streaming applications. Then we give an overview of the protocol stack of streaming applications, from where we can obtain more reliable information that distinguishes legal traffic from injected traffic. This information is not utilized effectively in current systems and results in vulnerabilities which an attacker can exploit to "hijack" a streaming session. That is, an innocent stream is replaced by a malicious one without the receiver detecting this replacement. We provide a novel and effective inspection scheme that can be used in stateful firewalls to filter out malicious traffic injected into streaming content, and hence prevent the injection. Finally, experimental results are given to show the effectiveness of our scheme.

The rest of this paper is organized as follows. Section 2 provides a brief introduction to streaming content and firewalls, and explains the reasons why conventional firewall techniques have difficulties in handling streaming content. Section 3 explains the vulnerability that allows an attacker to inject malicious traffic into streaming content. Section 4 presents a formal modelling of streaming content behavior, based on which our filtering scheme is then introduced. Section 5 gives experimental results showing the effectiveness of our scheme. Section 6 summarizes related work, and section 7 concludes the paper.

## 2   Preliminaries

### 2.1   Streaming Content Overview

Prior to the development of effective content streaming techniques, users needed to fully download media files to local storage devices before they could begin playing them. This could take from seconds to hours depending on the file size.

With streaming technology, users can start playing media files immediately or after a short buffering time. A chunk of media file content is packetized into a large number of small portions, which stream like little drops of water through network pipes to local devices. Streaming technology also enables users to select a particular section of a media file such as the second half of a soccer game, or communicate with other peers in realtime. Major applications of streaming content include IP telephony, live video/audio broadcast and stock monitoring. The main disadvantage of streaming technology from a user perspective is that received content cannot be archived or redistributed easily.

Streaming application protocols such as *Real Time Steaming Protocol (RTSP)* [16], *Session Initiation Protocol (SIP)* [21], and *H.323* [3] are defined at the application layer. Typically, these protocols use TCP to reliably deliver session control messages such as setup, manipulate, and tear down commands. The data stream containing the streaming content itself is typically delivered using a UDP based protocol, because timeliness is typically more important to data delivery than reliability and waiting for retransmission of a lost frame would have worse impact on viewers' impression than omitting the frame.

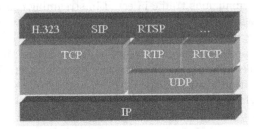

**Fig. 1.** Typical Protocol Stack of Streaming Applications

UDP does not provide sequence reconstruction, so packets arriving out of order cannot be reconstructed to their original sequence. To solve this problem, IETF developed the *Real Time Protocol (RTP)* [17], which was also published by ITU-T as *H.225.0*. Same as UDP and TCP, RTP is also defined at the transport layer. It provides protocol elements necessary for the delivery of streaming content such as:

- Sequence number: a 16-bit number that increments by one for each RTP data packet sent for the receiver to detect packet loss or to restore packet sequence.
- Timestamp: a 32-bit number reflecting the sampling instant of the first octet in the RTP data packet.
- Payload type: a 7-bit number indicating RTP payload format and its interpretation by the application.

RTP is typically run on top of UDP which provides the end-to-end delivery for RTP data packets. *RTP Control Protocol (RTCP)* [17] can be optionally used to provide feedback on the quality of the data distribution.

Putting all the above protocols together, we show the typical protocol stack and data packet format of streaming applications in Figure 1.

## 2.2   Firewall Overview

A firewall is a security system consisting of a combination of hardware and/or software that limits the exposure of a protected network to attacks from outside. It protects a network against malicious attacks and penetration by filtering out unwanted network traffic coming into the secured portion of the network. The filtering decision is made according to a predefined rule set. There are 3 major types of firewalls today, which are packet filtering firewalls, application gateways [9] and stateful firewalls [7].

Packet filtering firewall is the most basic, fundamental type of firewall. Access control is governed strictly by a statically predefined rule set mainly consisting of IP addresses and port numbers. Hence, it is unsuitable for inspection of streaming content, which sends/receives data via dynamically negotiated ports.

Application gateways are firewalls that provide filtering functions at the application layer in addition to access control at the network and transport layer. It has numerous advantages over packet filtering firewalls, such as user authentication, application logging, and content filtering. However, in order to filter application headers and payloads in addition to IP and TCP headers, application gateways need to spend time copying packets from system kernel space to user space. Hence, they are "are not generally well suited to high-bandwidth or real-time applications [19]".

Similar to packet filtering firewalls, stateful firewalls also enforce access control at the network and transport layer. They are more effective than packet filtering firewalls in that they enforce the notion of "stateful connection", i.e. incoming packets are passed through only if they belong to an established session. Compared with the above 2 types of firewalls, stateful firewalls have the following advantages in inspecting streaming content:

- They are able to open dynamic ports for packets that belong to an established session.
- Working at the transport and network layer, they are suitable for high-bandwidth and real-time applications.

## 3   Injection of Malicious Traffic

TCP traffic contains more stateful information about an established connection than UDP traffic does. This includes TCP flags and sequence and acknowledgment numbers. Stateful firewalls thus can handle TCP traffic effectively. On the other hand, inspection of UDP traffic is usually based merely on IP addresses, port numbers, and a virtual timer [7]. These fields do not change over time in an established session and are easy to forge. Consequently, injection into a continuous UDP traffic sequence is straightforward if the IP addresses and port numbers are known by an attacker. Therefore, although possessing some advantages in scanning streaming content, stateful firewalls cannot prevent injection of packets when streaming applications use UDP for data delivery.

Although sequence numbers that change over time are also provided at the transport layer of RTP-based streaming applications, their behavior is very different to TCP sequence numbers. Most notably, sequence numbers in an RTP session may form a loose sequence with missed sequence numbers. Sequence numbers can be missed if a packet is dropped because UDP does not provide for retransmission of dropped packets. Packets with duplicate sequence numbers are not expected to be received before sequence numbers wrap around for the same reason.

Therefore, RTP sequence numbers cannot be used in the same way in which TCP sequence numbers are employed in stateful firewalls. Schulzrinne *et al.*

[17] proposed a sequence number validation scheme, where a sequence number is considered valid only if it is no more than $MAX\_DROPOUT$ ahead of the max sequence number ever received nor more than $MAX\_MISORDER$ behind, where $MAX\_DROPOUT$ and $MAX\_MISORDER$ are constants determined by an administrator. Additionally, a stream is considered restarted if two consecutive packets with neighboring sequence numbers, both considered invalid, are received. This scheme utilizes RTP sequence numbers to a certain extent, but leaves a number of exploitable vulnerabilities unsolved:

- Packet Injection: Legal packets and injected packets are placed into a "fairly-competing" situation. A packet is considered legal as long as it hits the acceptable range of sequence numbers. Currently, the RFC for RTP defines a 16-bit sequence number, resulting in a good chance of randomly hitting this range. Moreover, this acceptable range may be "pushed" forward by an injected packet, resulting in successive legal packets being rejected for falling behind the acceptable range. Consequently, an attacker may take over the entire session if he can completely "push" the acceptable range off the legal stream. To increase the chance of a successful injection, an attacker can inject a sequence of packets whose sequence numbers increase by more than 1, or at a faster rate than a legal sequence.
- Session Restart: The validation scheme considers that a session is restarted if two consecutive packets with neighboring sequence numbers, both considered invalid, are received. An attacker may exploit this scheme to take over a session by injecting packets at a faster rate than a legal stream. As long as two consecutive injected packets arrive in the gap between two legal packets, the streaming session will be restarted, and consequently the next legal packet may be rejected for falling out of the acceptable range set by the injected packets.
- Use of Magic Numbers: Use of $MAX\_DROPOUT$ and $MAX\_MISORDER$ is a trade-off between fault-tolerance and effectiveness of sequence validation. Administrators may have difficulties in selecting appropriate values of such numbers as their effectiveness is connection dependent. For instance, by assuming a maximum misordering time of 2 seconds at 50 packets/second and a maximum dropout of 1 minute, H. Schulzrinne el al [17] set $MAX\_DROPOUT$ and $MAX\_MISORDER$ to 3000 and 100 respectively. That being said, any injected packet with a random sequence number has about 4.7% (3100/65535) success rate. We can see that although setting a maximum dropout of 1 minute allows a certain degree of fault-tolerance, it also increases the success rate of random packet injection to a non-trivial level.

## 4    Streaming Content Modelling and the Inspection Scheme

Our inspection scheme is based on modelling the arrival process of streaming content. Packet arrival process in the past was often assumed to be Poisson process because such process has attractive theoretical properties [26]. However, some recent research has pointed out failures of Poisson Process in modelling packet arrival process of both wide-area and local-area network traffic [23], [11], [15], [22], [27]. Hence, we have not assumed arrival process of RTP-based streaming traffic to be Poisson process. Our inspection scheme uses the *Central Limit Theorem* [12], which does not require that the population follow a particular statistical distribution.

## 4.1   Arrival Process Modelling of Streaming Content

A streaming session essentially delivers a large number of packets of media content from a server to a receiver. Packets arrive sequentially at the receiver with non-overlapping time intervals. Let $P$ denote the set of all packets in a particular streaming sequence, and $p_i$ denote the $i$th packet that arrives in sequence, then $P$ can be represented by an ordered set of sequential packets $\{p_0, p_1, \ldots, p_n\}$, where $p_{i+1}$ arrives after $p_i$. Each packet $p_i$ essentially consists of a 4-tuple: $\{seq, time, ordered, rate\}$, meanings of which are explain in the following.

*p.seq* and *p.time* denote the sequence number and arrival time (wall clock time) of a packet $p$. $p$ is accepted if *p.seq* falls in the acceptable range at *p.time*.

Packets may arrive out of order. We represent whether a packet $p$ arrives out of order with *p.ordered*, which is formally defined as follows,

$$p.ordered = \begin{cases} false, & \text{if } p.seq < MAX\_SEQ \\ true, & \text{if } p.seq > MAX\_SEQ \\ null, & \text{if } p.seq = MAX\_SEQ \end{cases}$$

where $MAX\_SEQ$ denotes the maximum valid sequence number previously received. In practice, sequence numbers can wrap around. Hence, when comparing *p.seq* and $MAX\_SEQ$, we may need to add 65535 to the one that is wrapped around. Unless otherwise stated, we will refer to *p.seq* as $p.seq + k * 65535$ in the following discussion, where $k$ denotes the number of times that a sequence has wrapped around.

*p.rate* denotes a packet $p$'s arrival rate which is defined as the ratio between sequence number increment and arrival time difference from the last ordered packet. Formally, assume we have a sequence of packets $P = \{p_0, p_1, \ldots, p_n\}$, then $\forall p_i \in P$ where $i > 0$, we define the arrival rate of a packet $p_i$ as follows,

$$p_i.rate = \begin{cases} \frac{p_i.seq - p_j.seq}{p_i.time - p_j.time}, & \text{where } p_j.seq = MAX\_SEQ \ (p_i.ordered = true) \\ \\ \frac{p_i.seq - p_j.seq}{p_i.time - p_j.time}, & \forall k, 0 \le k \le i-1,\ 0 < p_i.seq - p_j.seq < p_i.seq - p_k.seq, \\ & \text{i.e., } p_j.seq \text{ is nearest to } p_i.seq \text{ in any sequence numbers} \\ & \text{less than } p_i.seq \\ & (p_i.ordered = false) \\ \\ null, & (p_i.ordered = null) \end{cases}$$

Confining packet arrival rate to a reasonable range is essential to filtering out injected malicious traffic from a legal stream. This prohibits an attacker from increasing his chance of success by sending a stream whose sequence numbers increase faster than those of the legal stream, as we discussed in section 3.

Due to characteristics of streaming content, the following restrictions apply to $P$:

- $\forall i, j$, if $i \neq j$, then $p_i.seq \neq p_j.seq$
- $\forall i, j$, if $i > j$, then $p_i.time > p_j.time$
- $\forall i$, if $p_i.ordered = true$, then $\forall j$ where $0 \leq j < i$, $p_j.seq < p_i.seq$
- $\forall i$, if $p_i.ordered = false$, then $\exists j$ where $0 \leq j < i$, $p_j.seq > p_i.seq$
- $\forall i$, $p_i.rate > 0$

## 4.2    Application of the Central Limit Theorem

Before the detailed discussion on our inspection scheme, we provide a review of the relevant statistical background.

Assume we have a sample $S = \{s_1, s_2, \ldots, s_n\}$ gathered from a population $P$, regardless of what statistical distribution $P$ follows. Let $\bar{S}$ and $\bar{P}$ denote the average of $S$ and $P$ respectively, and $\sigma_P$ denote the standard deviation of $P$. The *Central Limit Theorem* tells us that distribution of

$$\frac{\bar{S} - \bar{P}}{\sigma_P / \sqrt{n}} \tag{1}$$

is increasingly well approximated by the normal distribution $N(0, 1)$ as the sample size, $n$, gets larger. Since we have the statistical table for this normal distribution, we can figure out the probability that $\frac{\bar{S}-\bar{P}}{\sigma_P/\sqrt{n}}$ lies in a particular interval $(a, b)$ using the equation

$$\lim_{n \to \infty} [a \leq \frac{\bar{S} - \bar{P}}{\sigma_P / \sqrt{n}} \leq b] = \alpha \tag{2}$$

where $\alpha = \int_a^b \frac{1}{\sqrt{2\pi}} e^{-\frac{u^2}{2}} du$. This means that, with the specified probability $\alpha$, we believe that

$$a \leq \frac{\bar{S} - \bar{P}}{\sigma_P / \sqrt{n}} \leq b \tag{3}$$

which can be transformed to

$$\bar{S} - b * \frac{\sigma_P}{\sqrt{n}} \leq \bar{P} \leq \bar{S} - a * \frac{\sigma_P}{\sqrt{n}} \tag{4}$$

This enables us to estimate the range of $\bar{P}$ based on the value of $\bar{S}$ with a certain confidence level $\alpha$. The meaning of $\alpha$ can be explained intuitively as follows: if, for example, we set $\alpha = 0.95 = 95\%$, then the possibility that any $\bar{S}'$ lies in the estimated interval of $\bar{P}$ is 95% on average.

### 4.3    Inspection Scheme

Typically, packetized streaming content arrives at a relatively constant rate. Change or fluctuation of arrival rate usually takes place gradually over a non-trivial period of time. Even though there exists on-demand media encoding techniques such as *Variable Bitrate (VBR)*, they are more applicable to the application layer than the transport layer. Moreover, there exist smoothing techniques which can smooth and reduce imposed burstiness [24].

For this reason, we can assume that, in a particular streaming session, arrival rates of successive packets follow the same distribution as preceding packets. An empirical justification of this assumption was provided by media traffic captured using *mmdump* [18]. By the *Central Limit Theorem*, we can estimate the interval in which arrival rates of successive packets will lie based on arrival rates of preceding packets. Assuming that we have a sample of legal packets $P = \{p_0, p_1, \ldots, p_n\}$ collected at the beginning of a streaming session, we are then able to estimate the acceptable range of arrival rate for packets in this stream using equation (4), where $a$ and $b$ are specified by equation (2) given a certain confidence level $\alpha$. Successive packets are accepted if their arrival rates lie in the corresponding estimated interval, or otherwise dropped.

The algorithm that enforces our inspection scheme is presented in algorithm 1. Because of the fact that arrival rate may change gradually over time, we estimate the acceptable interval of arrival rate for packet $p_{n+1}$ from the arrival rates of the most recent $n$ packets preceding $p_{n+1}$.

Validating RTP-based streaming packets on the basis of their arrival rates has the following advantages over the validation scheme based on sequence numbers [17]:

- It is more difficult to forge a packet's arrival rate than its sequence number. Unlike real fields such as IP addresses, port numbers and sequence numbers, packet arrival rates are dynamically computed using non-static sequence numbers and packet arrival times. To successfully inject a packet, an attacker must be able to choose a suitable sequence number and launch the injection at the right time for the selected sequence number. More subtly, even though an attacker may be able to launch an injection at a precisely specified time, he still has difficulties in foreseeing the arrival time which is governed by the *Round Trip Time (RTT)* between the receiver and himself.
- Administrators are relieved from selecting magic numbers such as *MAX_DROPOUT* and *MAX_MISORDER*. This is a difficult task as the effectiveness of *MAX_DROPOUT* and *MAX_MISORDER* is connection-dependent. For example, smaller *MAX_DROPOUT* and *MAX_MISORDER* would be expected in a stable connection. In our scheme, we just need to select the confidence level, the value of which determines the effectiveness of the inspection scheme. This is achieved by the underlying statistical model.
- Packet arrival rate is a relatively stable measurement. Packets arriving after a network disruption period, regardless of how long it is, are expected

---

**Algorithm 1.** Validate($p_0 - p_n$, $p_{n+1}$)

---

/* The function infers the validity of a packet $p_{n+1}$ based on $n$
   preceding packets $p_0 - p_n$ that have been assumed or verified as
   valid.                                                              */
/* $p_{n+1}$: the packet to be validated.                             */
/* $p_0,\ldots,p_n$: $n+1$ packets that precede $p_{n+1}$ and have been assumed or
   verified as valid                                                  */
/* $r_1,\ldots,r_{n+1}$: arrival rates of packet $p_1,\ldots,p_{n+1}$  */

**begin**

/* the confidence level associated with the estimation            */
**const** $CONFIDENCE\_LEVEL$;

/* set up sample parameters                                       */
**for** $l = 1$ **to** $n+1$ **do**
    $r_l = p_l.rate$

set $\bar{r} = \frac{\sum_{l=1}^{n} r_l}{n}$

set $\sigma_r = \sqrt{\frac{\sum_{l=1}^{n}(r_l - \bar{r})^2}{n-1}}$

set $r_{max} = \bar{r} + CONFIDENCE\_LEVEL * \frac{\sigma_r}{\sqrt{n}}$

set $r_{max} = \bar{r} - CONFIDENCE\_LEVEL * \frac{\sigma_r}{\sqrt{n}}$

/* set up parameters of the validated packet                      */
set $\bar{r}' = \frac{\sum_{l=1}^{n} r_l}{n+1}$

**if** $r_{min} \leq \bar{r}'$ and $\bar{r}' \leq r_{max}$ **then**
|    accept $p_{n+1}$ ;
**else**
    drop $p_{n+1}$ ;

**end**

---

to present arrival rates similar to previously received packets so that they
will be accepted. Hence, fault-tolerance ability is increased without trading
off effectiveness, as opposed to the use of $MAX\_DROPOUT$ and
$MAX\_MISORDER$ which represents a trade-off between fault-tolerance
and effectiveness.

## 5   Experiments and Results

### 5.1   Experimental Setup

To send and receive RTP-based streaming content, we employed the *Java Media
Framework (JMF)* [25] which enables audio, video and other time-based media
to be added to applications built on Java technology.

For packet injection, we employed *Nemesis* [1] which is a command-line network packet crafting and injection utility. We modified its source code and enabled it to craft RTP packets with some configurable RTP parameters as follows,

- Sequence Hop (-h): Sequence hop between a pair of crafted RTP packets. For example, we can send a sequence of crafted packets with sequence number $\{1, 2, 3, ...\}$, or $\{100, 200, 300, ...\}$, where h = 1 or h = 100 respectively.
- Injection Interval (-i): The interval between which two RTP packets are crafted and injected, measured in milliseconds.
- Packet Count (-c): Number of crafted packets to be injected.

Setup of our experiments is depicted in Figure 2, where arrival rates of crafted RTP packets vary in the following 3 categories,

- Fast: Sending crafted RTP packets without specifying an injection interval, which means no substantial interval between crafting and sending two packets. Arrival rate of an injected sequence is around hundreds of thousands of packets per second.
- Medium: Sending crafted RTP packets with a substantial interval as specified by the "-i" parameter. We are then able to inject a sequence of packets with an arrival rate similar to the legal stream, typically around 30-60 packets per second, i.e. i ≈ 16-33.
- Slow: Sending only one crafted RTP packet each time when *Nemesis* is invoked. Number of injected packets in this case is governed by a for-loop script which repeatedly creates a new process to invoke *Nemesis*. The "-c" parameter (packet count) is implicitly set to be 1, and need not be specified. Typically, arrival rate is around 5 packets per second, as process creation and invocation takes quite a bit time.

## 5.2   Result on Packet Injection

We send a clip of music using *JMF* and inject a clip of human conversation by *Nemesis*, representing legal and injected sequence respectively.

When we use fast injection with sequence hop (the "-h" parameter) 1, we are always able to hijack the legal session and replace its content with the selected conversation. This is caused by the restarting mechanism as we analyzed in section 3. As we can see from Figure 2, any two consecutive crafted packets that arrive between a pair of legal packets can take over the streaming session and "push away" the acceptable range of sequence numbers so that packets belonging to the legal stream are not accepted.

When we use slow or medium injection with a large sequence hop (e.g. 500), we can inject some noise being voice fragment into a legal stream, as sequence numbers of the injected stream travel faster and can "catch up" the acceptable range. However, we have not been able to hijack an entire session. Although an injected packet that accidentally falls in the acceptable range of sequence numbers can push it away, any two consecutive legal packets that arrive between a pair of injected packets can take over the streaming session and "pull back" the acceptable range of sequence numbers so that packets belonging to the injected stream are dropped. On the contrary, two injected packets that arrive consecutively at the receiver cannot "pull back" the acceptable range since their sequence numbers are not consecutive.

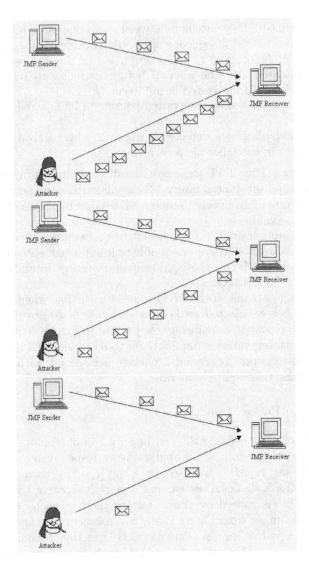

**Fig. 2.** Experimental Setup

## 5.3   Effectiveness of the Inspection Scheme

With a statistical approach, it is always possible that legal packets are dropped or injected packets are accepted. We refer to these cases as false-positive and false-negative respectively. A low false-positive rate guarantees system usability, while a low false-negative rate assures legitimacy of received streaming content. To measure effectiveness of our inspection scheme by false-positive and false-negative rates, we performed an offline analysis on RTP-based streaming content from various sources, including web radio stations (lexp web radio[1] and webtalk radio[2]), Microsoft *MSN* live conversation, and *JMF*-generated streaming content.

**Result on Passing Through Legal Streaming Content.** We first performed an experiment on normal streaming content, i.e. streaming content that is delivered without injection. We have included experiments during which the network cable was disconnected for 10 to 61 seconds to simulate network disruption. Similarly, we have included silent periods in *MSN* conversations to simulate bustiness in VoIP.

The experimental result is summarized in Table 1. It can be seen from the false-positive rate that a very small proportion of the legal packets are marked as being injected. This is a slight disadvantage of our scheme.

**Table 1.** Experimental result under confidence level $\alpha = 0.98$

|  | lexp radio | webtalk radio | JMF | MSN |
|---|---|---|---|---|
| bit rate | 128kbps | 28kbps | not specified | not specified |
| number of packets | 47135 | 36471 | 54023 | 55738 |
| number of bytes | 64.9M | 28.9M | 11.9M | 42.8M |
| duration | 4021.1s | 6819.2s | 1832.6s | 1474.6s |
| false-positive | 0.004% | 0.0% | 0.06% | 0.2% |
| false-negative | N/A | N/A | N/A | N/A |

Figure 3 demonstrates variation of packet arrival rates in the above experiments, as well as that of the estimated acceptable range. It illustrates that a very small portion of legal packets are dropped because of dramatic fluctuations in their arrival rates. Apart from that, arrival rates of most packets belonging to a particular stream do not fluctuate greatly.

**Result on Filtering Out Injected Streaming Content.** Our experimental environment is separated from the outside world by a firewall not under our control that prohibits incoming UDP traffic, so that we have not had the opportunity to test the inspection scheme with injection against streaming content received from a commercial streaming server on Internet, such as the lexp or webtalk server. Instead, we performed experiments on filtering out injected packets with streaming content generated by *JMF* which is open source and free to use.

We performed experiments for all 3 categories of packet injection methods as discussed in section 5.1. The result is summarized in Table 2. It can be seen from the false-negative rate that all injected packets are successfully marked as illegal. On the other hand, a very small number of legal packets are also marked as illegal as shown by the false-positive rate.

---

[1] www.lexp.org
[2] http://www.webtalkradio.com/

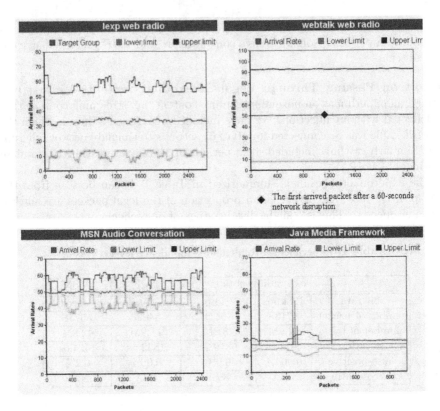

**Fig. 3.** Variation of Packet Arrival Rates: Legal Traffic

**Table 2.** Experimental result under confidence level $\alpha = 0.98$

|  | fast injection (-c=$10^4$, -h=1) | fast injection (-c=$10^4$, -h=$10^2$) | slow injection (-c=$10^3$, -h=500) | medium injection (-c=$10^4$, -h=$10^2$) |
|---|---|---|---|---|
| number of packets | 22761 | 24746 | 28085 | 29986 |
| number of bytes | 17.0M | 18.7M | 20.9M | 22.9M |
| duration | 329.2s | 405.7s | 461.1s | 738.0s |
| false-positive | 0.067% | 0.17% | 0.033% | 0.012% |
| false-negative | 0.0% | 0.0% | 0.0% | 0.0% |

Figure 4 demonstrates variation of packet arrival rates of legal and injected packets. We can see that the arrival rates of injected packets significantly deviate from those of legal packets.

The experiment shows a remarkable result against packet injection and hijacking. It is because that sequence numbers of injected packets have to travel substantially faster than those of legal packets in order to "catch up" a legal stream. On the other hand, some legal packets are also filtered out because they accidentally present an arrival rate substantially distinct from other packets. However, this is acceptable for streaming content due to its redundant nature.

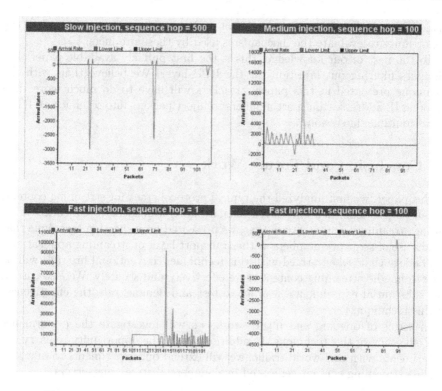

**Fig. 4.** Variation of Packet Arrival Rates: Legal and Injected Traffic

# 6   Related Work

People in the research and industry communities have given strong attention to streaming content delivery. Mostly, they focus on monitoring and tailoring multimedia traffic. A number of RTP capture and monitoring tools are publicly available in the research community. Among these are *rtpdump* [13] and *rtpmon* [14]. *rtpdump* parses on a specified address and port pair for RTP and RTCP packets, and generates report to output files. *rtpmon* monitors RTP session by viewing packet loss rate and jitter information presented in RTCP feedback packets.

Fung *et al.* [10], [20] proposed a transport-level proxy to secure multimedia streams. An extended SOCKS UDP binding model with appropriate socket calls is proposed to provide complete support for UDP-based, multimedia streaming applications. However, they mainly analyzed streaming applications at the application and UDP layer, without considering the in-between RTP layer. As a result, packet injection and session hijacking are only prevented at the UDP layer, i.e. based on IP addresses and port numbers.

In industry, although several commercial firewalls that support streaming content [6], [2], [4], [5], [8] are available, their internal details have not been made public and their source code is not available. Hence, we have not had the opportunity to evaluate the mechanisms used by these products.

To the best of our knowledge, this is the first publicly available paper that discusses filtering out injections at the RTP layer. We believe that, with the technique presented in this paper, attackers will have to do much more than spoofing IP addresses and port numbers to inject packets into or hijack an RTP-based multimedia session.

## 7    Conclusion and Future Work

In this paper, we first analyzed the typical protocol stack for streaming content, and discussed deficiencies in conventional firewalls which lead to difficulties in securing streaming content. After that, we presented an inspection technique that makes use of sequence numbers at the transport layer of streaming applications. We believe that, when armed with this technique, conventional firewalls will be able to handle streaming content more effectively and securely. We also carried out substantial experiments in order to test and demonstrate the effectiveness of this technique.

In terms of ongoing and future work, we will investigate the performance and efficiency of this technique. In addition, given the opportunity to carry out experiments with real-world traffic, we will extend our experiments to injection against streaming content generated by commercial streaming servers.

## References

1. http://nemesis.sourceforge.net/.
2. Packeteer. http://www.packeteer.com.
3. Recommendation H.323: Visual Telephone Systems and Equipment for Local Area Networks Which Provide a Nonguaranteed Quality of Service. ITU-T, 1996.
4. Connecting the World's Voice, 2003. Available at
   http://www.packetcomm.org/Documents/Netrake_Comptel0205.ppt.
5. NetScreen Concepts & Examples ScreenOS Reference Guide, Volume II: Fundermentals. Technical report, Juniper Networks, 2004.
6. SnowShore Media Firewall. Technical report, Brooktrout Technology, 2004.
7. Stateful Inspection Technology. Technical report, CheckPoint Software Technologies Ltd, 2004.
8. Cisco IOS Firewall. Technical report, Cisco Systems, 2005. Available at
   http://www.cisco.com/application/pdf/en/us/guest/products/ps1018/c1244
   /cdccont_0900aecd8029d0a6.pdf.
9. W. R. Cheswick and S. M. Bellovin. *Firewalls and Internet Security, Repelling the Wily Hacker*. Addison-Wesley, 1994.
10. K. P. Fung. SOCKS5-based Firewall Support for UDP-based Applications. Master's thesis, The Hong Kong Polytechnic Univ., Dept. of Computing, Hong Kong, PRC, http://www2.comp.polyu.edu.hk/~csrchang/MSc/Billy.pdf, 1999.
11. R. Gusella. A Measurement Study of Diskless Workstation Traffic on an Ethernet. *IEEE Transactions on Communications*, 38(9):1557–1568, 1990.

12. R. A. Johnson and D. W. Wichern. *Applied Multivariate Statistical Analysis*. Upper Saddle river, New Jersey: Prentice Hall, 1998.
13. H. Schulzrinne. rtpdump. http://www.cs.columbia.edu/~hgs/rtp/rtpdump.html.
14. D. Bacher, A. Swan, and L. A. Rowe. rtpmon: A Third-Party RTCP Monitor. http://bmrc.berkeley.edu/people/drbacher/projects/mm96-demo/index.html.
15. H. Fowler and W. Leland. Local Area Network Traffic Characteristics, with Implications for Broadband Network Congestion Management. *IEEE JSAC*, 9(7):1139–1149, 1991.
16. H. Schulzrinne, A. Rao, and R. Lanphier. Real Time Streaming Protocol (RTSP). RFC 2336, Apr 1998.
17. H. Schulzrinne, S. Casner, R. Frederick, and V. Jacobson. RTP: A Transport Protocol for Real-Time Applications. RFC 3550, Jul 2003.
18. J. Merwe, R. Cceres, Y. Chu and C. Sreenan. mmdump: a tool for monitoring internet multimedia traffic. *ACM SIGCOMM Computer Communication Review*, 30:48–59, 2000.
19. J. Wack, K. Cutler, and J. Pole. Guidelines on Firewalls and Firewall Policy. Technical report, National Institute of Standards and Technology, 2002.
20. K. P. Fung and Rocky K. C. Chang. Secure media streaming & secure adaptation for non-scalable video. *ICIP*, 3:1763 – 1766, 2004.
21. M. Handley, H. Schulzrinne, E. Schooler, and J. Rosenberg. SIP: Session Initiation Protocol. RFC 2543, Mar 1999.
22. P. Danzig, S. Jamin, R. Caceres, D. Mitzel, and D.Estrin. An Empirical Workload Model for Driving Widearea TCP/IP Network Simulations. *Internetworking: Research and Experience*, 3(1):1–26, 1992.
23. R. Jain and S. Routhier. Packet Trains - Measurements and a New Model for Computer Network Traffic. *IEEE JSAC*, 4(6):986–995, 1986.
24. R. Zimmermann, K. Fu, C. Shahabi, and M. Jahangiri. A Multi-Threshold Online Smoothing Technique for Variable Rate Multimedia Streams. submitted for journal publication.
25. Sun Microsystems Inc. Java Media Framework, 1994-2005.
26. V. Frost and B. Melamed. Traffic Modeling for Telecommunications Networks. *IEEE Communications Magazine*, 32(3):70–80, 1994.
27. V. Paxson and S. Floyd. Wide-Area Traffic: The Failure of Poisson Modeling. *IEEE/ACM Transactions on Networking (TON)*, 3(3):226 – 244, 1995.

# Safeguard Information Infrastructure Against DDoS Attacks: Experiments and Modeling

Yang Xiang and Wanlei Zhou

School of Information Technology, Deakin University,
221 Burwood Highway, Vic 3125, Australia
yxi@deakin.edu.au, wanlei@deakin.edu.au

**Abstract.** Nowadays Distributed Denial of Service (DDoS) attacks have made one of the most serious threats to the information infrastructure. In this paper we firstly present a new filtering approach, Mark-Aided Distributed Filtering (MADF), which is to find the network anomalies by using a back-propagation neural network, deploy the defense system at distributed routers, identify and filtering the attack packets before they can reach the victim; and secondly propose an analytical model for the interactions between DDoS attack party and defense party, which allows us to have a deep insight of the interactions between the attack and defense parties. According to the experimental results, we find that MADF can detect and filter DDoS attack packets with high sensitivity and accuracy, thus provide high legitimate traffic throughput and low attack traffic throughput. Through the comparison between experiments and numerical results, we also demonstrate the validity of the analytical model that can precisely estimate the effectiveness of a DDoS defense system before it encounters different attacks.

## 1 Introduction

Distributed denial-of-service attacks (DDoS) currently bring a tremendous threat to the information infrastructure. In a DDoS attack, multiple malicious hosts (zombies) that are recruited by the attacker launch a coordinate attack against one host or network victim, which cause denial of service to legitimate users. To defend against DDoS attacks, much of the current research focus on filtering [1], traceback [2], and congestion control [3]. Many demonstrate the effectiveness of the countermeasures under some preset conditions and assumptions. Among the traceback schemes, packet marking overwrites some fields in the IP header, which are called marks, to record the information needed to reconstruct the sources. It includes two main streams: Probabilistic Packet Marking (PPM) [4] and Deterministic Packet Marking (DPM) [5]. In particular, an improved DPM scheme, Flexible Deterministic Packet Marking (FDPM) [6], requires a small number of IP packets to find out more sources than other schemes, and has a built-in overload prevention mechanism to intelligently mark packets when system is overloaded in high-speed networks. The work in this paper is based on FDPM. Firstly, we present Mark-Aided Distributed Filtering (MADF) and

Y.G. Desmedt et al. (Eds.): CANS 2005, LNCS 3810, pp. 320–333, 2005.

its experiments. This system is to find the network anomalies by using a back-propagation neural network, deploy the defense system at distributed routers, identify and filtering the attack packets before they can reach the victim. Then secondly we propose an analytical model for the interactions between DDoS attack party and defense party, which allows us to have a deep insight of the interactions between the attack and defense parties.

## 2    Experiments on DDoS Defense by MADF

### 2.1    Background

Flexible Deterministic Packet Marking (FDPM) [6] deploys its encoding modules are deployed at the edge routers that are close to the attack source end. When packets enter the network, they are marked by the encoding modules. The real source IP addresses of the entry points and hash of the address (we call these bits digest bits) are stored in the marking fields. The mark will not be changed when the packet traverses through the network. The address digest bits make sure the group of packets comes from the same entry point, they also provide a picture of the aggregation feature of packets; and segment number is used to reconstruct the real source in it original order. When the packets reach the victim end, the source IP addresses of entry points can be reconstructed. More details of the marks can be found in related references.

If the attacker sends attack packets through the same entry point, there will be a special pattern of marked packets with the same destination IP address and address digest bits. Therefore, in a global view, there will be a pattern with several groups of packets with corresponding address digest bits, and the same destination IP address. The pattern reflexes clearly the character of DDoS traffic that come from multiple sources and aggregate at one destination. This information is especially beneficial to find out attack traffic and remove them from legitimate traffic. In our work, the pattern is recognized by neural network.

### 2.2    System Design

As it is shown in figure 1, Mark-Aided Distributed Filtering (MADF) can be deployed at any point between the source end (one hop behind FDPM encoding module) and the victim end. The system includes two parts, the Offline Training System (OTS) and Online Filtering Systems (OFSs). The reason for this design is that most of the computation time is spent on the training of neural network. Once the network is trained, the filtering system can perform filtering at almost real time because the test phase of a neural network is very fast. The OTS is a lightweight neural network [7] with back-propagation algorithm [8]. This offline system collects traffic features and trains the neural network without influencing the normal operation of the network. In order to save the computation time of training, we propose a serialized neural network approach, which is that the trained neural networks can be serialized and be shared for different OFSs. In

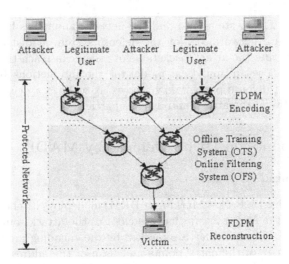

**Fig. 1.** System architecture of MADF and FDPM

our experiments, a serialized file is from 100kb to 330kb, which is convenient to be exchanged periodically to other OFSs.

There are 3 layers in this neural network, which consists of input layer, hidden layer and output layer. The number of the units (neurons) in the input layer is dictated by the dimensionality of the input vectors (features of traffic). There is one unit in the output layer, representing a value between 0 and 1 (legitimate and attack traffic, respectively). The number of hidden units governs the expressive power of the net. In terms of minimum Bayes error [9] the features of input with good discriminatory power can be chosen. However, because in practice it is difficult to know the class probability densities, selecting features by Bayes error is much less effective in non-linear classifiers than linear classifiers. In [10] a Support Vector Machine (SVM) approach is used to rank the features. In this paper we use some extracted network traffic features with high ranks in the previous reference and some features by experience, as the input of the neural network for training and test (as shown in table 1), and let the output as the likelihood of attack packets. We apply time window to collect the information of network traffic. Besides the common packet features, the mark (address digest bits) that the FDPM writes into the IP header, is also concerned. Let

$$x_{mark} = \frac{Number\_of\_Packets}{Number\_of\_digests} \tag{1}$$

This feature means the concentration of the packets that have same digest bits. In practice, we adjust the scale of this special feature, to make the neural network adjust weights from it more than other features during training, because if the neural network prefers this feature over the others, it will be more sensitive to DDoS attacks, according to our experiments. Let

$$x'_{mark} = \beta x_{mark} \tag{2}$$

where $x'_{mark}$ and $x_{mark}$ are the adjusted mark feature and the original mark feature respectively, and is the scaling ratio. In our experiments, the optimized value for the scaling ratio is 10.

**Table 1.** Features used in neural network

| Feature | Description | Protocol |
|---------|-------------|----------|
| SrcIP | Number of source IP address | Any |
| DestIP | Number of destination IP address | Any |
| SrcPort | Number of source port | Any |
| DestPort | Number of destination port | Any |
| Length | Total length of packets | Any |
| Chksum | Number of wrong checksum | Any |
| SYN | Number of SYN flag | TCP |
| FIN | Number of FIN flag | TCP |
| ACK | Number of ACK flag | TCP |
| Mark | Concentration of the packets with same digest bits | Any |

The Online Filtering System (OFS) use the trained neural network to find attack traffic according. Just as the OTS, it can be deployed at any point in the protected network. When the attack is confirmed, those packets with specific marks as the attack packets are filtered out. We test the incoming packets by the trained neural network. If the output indicates anomalies, we further investigate the composition of marked packets. If the number of packets that have the same address digest bits exceeds a threshold $N_{drop}$ (this value is decided by experience), this flow of packets will be filtered. This two-step design can not only protect legitimate traffic but also punish entirely the attack traffic. First, because the anomaly detection is performed by a nonlinear neural network classifier with the assistance of concentration of the packets of same digest bits, the legitimate traffic will be less likely decided as an anomaly than by other coarse granite classifiers such as statistical models. Second, once the attack traffic flow is identified, this flow can be totally filtered by differentiating the identity address digest bits that FDPM marks.

# 3 Performance of MADF

## 3.1 Data Sets

Currently there is very few data that can describe the whole profile of a DDoS attack. Therefore, we use the data generated by SSFNet [11] simulator and the embedded DDoS tools [12] in project Distributed Denial of Service Simulators at Deakin University. We also implement FDPM by SSFNet, so the data generated have FDPM marks for the evaluation of the MADF. In the above project, two

DDoS tools, TFN2K and Trinoo, are adopted and integrated into SSFNet to create virtual DDoS networks to simulate the attacks. In order to simulate the DDoS attack as real as possible, we also use the real Internet topology from Cooperative Association for Internet Data Analysis (CAIDA)'s Skitter project [13]. The data set used is generated from server aroot ipv4.20040120 on 09/Jan/2004. To simplify the problem, we connect all routers by 100M network interfaces. We randomly choose the 1000 attack hosts and let the rest be legitimate clients, and let the Skitter server be the victim. Constant rate attack of 300KBps is applied to all attack hosts. According to the hop distribution (number of routers between the victim and its clients), most of the clients locate in the distance between 10 hops and 25 hops. Therefore, we deploy the FDPM encoding module at routers 10 hops from the victim, and the Mark-Aided Distributed Filtering systems at routers from 1 to 9 hops from the victim.

### 3.2  Metrics of Performance

The ultimate goals of MADF are to find out the attack traffic as accurately as possible, and to filter out the attack traffic as much as possible and at the mean time let as much legitimate traffic pass through as possible (but not to detect anomalies). Therefore, the main performance criteria are average value of legitimate traffic passed rate (LTPR) and attack traffic passed rate (ATPR) of distributed filtering systems. Let

$$LTPR = \frac{Number\_of\_legitimate\_packets\_passed}{Number\_of\_total\_legitimate\_packets} \tag{3}$$

$$ATPR = \frac{Number\_of\_attack\_packets\_passed}{Number\_of\_total\_attack\_packets} \tag{4}$$

Another criterion to measure the performance is the LTPR/ATPR ratio LAR, as it is shown in formula (5). A perfect DDoS defense system can achieve this value of $+\infty$ because the denominator ATPR will reach 0. On the other hand, a worst case of defense system has this value of 0 because the numerator LTPR will reache 0. Therefore, a high LAR indicates a strong defense system.

$$LAR = \frac{LTPR}{ATPR} \tag{5}$$

Besides the above criteria, we also introduce a network flooding ratio NFR as in formula (6) because the above criteria can only denote how good the filtering function is, but can not denote the overall defense result of a distributed defense. As we discussed before, like other distributed defense systems, MADF can be deployed at any point between the source end (one hop behind FDPM encoding module) and the victim end. A criterion is needed to measure how effective is that the defense system can prevent the overall network flooding caused by DDoS attacks. Unfortunately, most research that has been done so far did not pay much attention to this important criterion. A low NFR represents a strong distributed defense to protect the whole network. Let

$$NFR = \frac{\sum\limits_{i=1}^{n} Number\_of\_attack\_packets\_passed\_in\_router\,(i)}{\sum\limits_{i=1}^{n} Number\_of\_total\_packets\_passed\_in\_router\,(i)} \quad (6)$$

Where $n$ is the total number of routers in the whole network.

### 3.3 Performance Evaluation

The MADF system is deployed at different distances from the victim and conduct experiments based on both TFN2K and Trinoo DDoS simulator tools. Random algorithms in SSFNet are used to generate legitimate traffic. After the neural network is trained, the DDoS tools are initiated to start the attack with different attack rates. Then the traffic on the deployment points is monitored. The following figures show the average values of LTPR and ATPR at routers that locate at different hops from the victim. From the figures we can see our scheme can filter out most of the attack traffic and let most of the legitimate traffic pass through. This also proofs MADF can be deployed at any place in the protect network without sacrificing much performance.

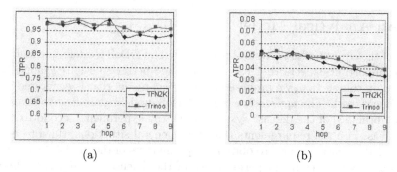

(a)                                        (b)

**Fig. 2.** Average LTPR and ATPR at different distances

Figure 3(a) shows the LTPR/ATPR ratio LAR at different routers from the victim. The value is from 18.32 to 27.71, which means a strong and precise filtering. Our system is better than many other current defense systems in terms of LAR. For example, the best LAR of Pi [14] is about 7 and the intelligent packet filtering [15] is about 18, which both are lower than MADF. Moreover, from this figure we can see the LAR becomes higher when the system is deployed more close to the attack sources $LAR_{hop9} > LAR_{hop1}$. This gives the justification to support argument of the source end deployment instead of the traditional victim end deployment. Figure 3(b) shows the network flooding ratio NFR curves of both TNF2K and Trinoo attacks at 300KBps attack rate. When the defense system is deployed close to the victim end, most of the network is still saturated by the attack packets (0.2741 for TFN2K and 0.2845 for Trinoo at hop 1). However, when it is deployed close to the source end, this value gradually decreases to a

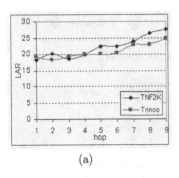
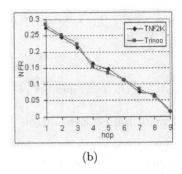

(a)                                          (b)

**Fig. 3.** LAR and NFR at different distances

very low level (0.0154 for TFN2K and 0.0162 for Trinoo at hop 9). Therefore, this figure shows the NFR decreases when the system is deployed more close to the attack sources. This is another justification to support argument of the source end deployment instead of the traditional victim end deployment. Moreover, it proves if MADF is properly deployed it can not only protect the single victim but also prevent overall network congestion.

## 4    An Analytical Model

Most of the current effort has not been invested on DDoS modeling, which is one of the important aspects that can help provide better solutions against DDoS attacks. In this section, we propose an analytical model that is generated by the experiment work. The approaches of this DDoS modeling are first to investigate the performance of the defense system MADF by experiment, second to build a model based on the requirements that meet general situations, third to use one attack and defense scenario to obtain the parameters of the model, fourth to use the built model to estimate performance of the defense system under different scenarios, and finally compare the numerical performance with the experimental one and show the validity of the model.

### 4.1    Definitions and Assumptions

*Definition 1* strength functions. In a DDoS attack and defense scenario, there are two parties. One is the attack party $X$ and the other is the defense party $Y$. Let $x(t)$ and $y(t)$ respectively denote the strength functions of the DDoS attack party $X$ and defense party $Y$ at time $t$. The strength function here means the function of the factors that can cause the part to win or lose. For example, for the attack party $X$ the factors can be the number of the hosts that participate in the attack, the rate of the hosts send attack packets, etc. For the defense party $Y$ the factors can be technologies used in defense, the deployment points of the defense systems, the skills of the technicians operating the defense systems, etc. In order to simplify the problem, we instantiate the strength of defense as the LTPR/ATPR ratio LAR.

*Definition 2* termination of the combat. The termination of the combat is defined as a stable condition after a period of time of interaction, either the attack traffic tends to a successful flood (attacker wins) or the defense system filters out most of the attack traffic (defender wins).

*Assumption 1* both $x(t)$ and $y(t)$ are continuous differentiable functions of time and are nonnegative. This idealization allows us to model the strength functions by differential equations. The minimum value of $x(t)$ and $y(t)$ is zero because any negative value has no physical meaning in practice.

*Assumption 2* the casualty rate for the attack party $X$ is proportional to the strength of the defense party $Y$, and vice versa. This assumption is reasonable because in the actual cases if there are more powerful defense systems deployed then it would be less possibility for the attack party to win (but the security and the strength of defense systems do not necessarily follow a linear proportional relationship [16]). On the contrary, if the attack part puts more resources such as attacking hosts then the defense party will more likely to lose. We model this assumption as these following two equations.

$$\frac{dx}{dt} = -ay, a > 0 \qquad (7)$$

$$\frac{dy}{dt} = -bx, b > 0 \qquad (8)$$

Where $a$ is the rate that a defense party can mitigate the attack strength and $b$ is the rate an attack party can deteriorate the defense strength. These two parameters are defined as attrition rates.

At the initial status $t=0$, we have

$$x(0) = x_0, y(0) = y_0, t = 0 \qquad (9)$$

From the chain rule we have

$$\frac{dy}{dx} = -\frac{-bx}{-ay} \qquad (10)$$

Separating the variables in equation (10) yields

$$-aydy = -bxdx \qquad (11)$$

Integrating the above equation by using the condition in equation (9) we have

$$a\left(y^2 - y_0^2\right) = b\left(x^2 - x_0^2\right) \qquad (12)$$

Then the equation follows the Lanchester square law [17]. Let

$$C = ay_0^2 - bx_0^2 \qquad (13)$$

Then we have

$$ay^2 - bx^2 = C \qquad (14)$$

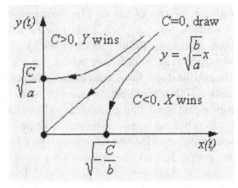

**Fig. 4.** Trajectories of the basic model

Typical trajectories in the phase plane represented by equation (14) are shown in figure 4. The trajectories for $C \neq 0$ are hyperbolas, and when $C = 0$ the trajectory is the straight line $y = \sqrt{ba}x$. When $C < 0$ the trajectory intersects the $x$-axis at $x = \sqrt{-Cb}$ then the attack party $X$ wins because the defense party $Y$ has been decreased to zero. On the other hand, if $C > 0$ the defense party wins with a final strength level of $y = \sqrt{Ca}$.

### 4.2    Analysis of the Model

Under the assumptions in the previous section, the condition that satisfy the win of defense party is $C > 0$. Then from equation (13) we have

$$\left(\frac{y_0}{x_0}\right)^2 > \frac{b}{a} \tag{15}$$

From the inequality we can see if the attack strength $X$ remains at the same initial level $x_0$ for constant $a$ and $b$, a doubling of the initial defense strength $Y$ results in a fourfold advantage for the defense party. This means the attack party $X$ must increase its rate $b$ that it can deteriorate the defense strength (for example its attack technology) by a factor of 4 to render a successful attack

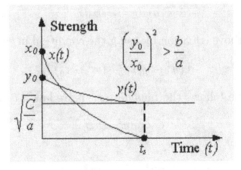

**Fig. 5.** The conditions when the defense party wins

if the initial attack strength $x_0$ is kept at the same level. Although it does not exactly inform how much strength will be enough for a security system to defend against a DDoS attack, it indicates that a more secure system requires attackers expend even much more on a successful attack.

Figure 5 shows the typical strength curves for $x(t)$ and $y(t)$ and the condition when the defense party wins. At time $t_s$ the defense party wins with the strength level at $\sqrt{Ca}$ while the attack strength level at zero. The initial value of the defense strength $y_0$ is not necessarily greater than the initial attack strength $x_0$ to ensure a successful defense. However, if the relationship between these two parties meets the requirement in inequality (15) the defense party can win. Solve the differential equation system in equation (7) and (8) by initial condition in equation (9) we have

$$y(t) = y_0 cos\left(\sqrt{abt}\right) - x_0\sqrt{\frac{a}{b}}sin\left(\sqrt{abt}\right) \tag{16}$$

$$x(t) = x_0 cos\left(\sqrt{abt}\right) - y_0\sqrt{\frac{a}{b}}sin\left(\sqrt{abt}\right) \tag{17}$$

Equation (16) can also be written as

$$\frac{y(t)}{y_0} = cos\left(\sqrt{abt}\right) - \left(\frac{x_0}{y_0}\right)\sqrt{\frac{a}{b}}sin\left(\sqrt{abt}\right) \tag{18}$$

Where $y(t)/y_0$ means the normalized defense strength level, which depends on two parameters, $\sqrt{a/b}$ and $\sqrt{abt}$. The parameter $\sqrt{a/b}$ shows the relative effectiveness of the attack and defense parties. The parameter $\sqrt{ab}$ represents the intensity of the DDoS attack and defense scenario, which determines how quickly the scenario ends (defense party successes or attack party successes).

## 5   Validity of the Model

In this section we show the validity of the model by comparing the numerical performance with the experimental one. As we introduced in the previous section, the parameters $a$ and $b$ are obtained by the experiments then used to estimate the numerical performance.

In the model we instantiate the parameter $a$ in equation (7) as the marking rate and solve the parameter $b$ in equation (8) according to the experimental data. Because the above performance is the metric when the defense system approaches a stable status, the time factor in the model become not correlative with our results, and the actual correlation can be adjusted by the parameter $a$ and $b$. The model is fitted with the experimental data of the attack rate 100KBps and the $b$ can be evaluated as 8.780430744. We solve the model with parameter $a$ and $b$ and let the attack rate as 200KBps and 300KBps. Then the fitted LAR curves by numerical method of our model are obtained as figure 6.

From figure 6(a) we can see when the attack rate is 200KBps the numerical curve from the model can fit very well will the experimental curve. This proves

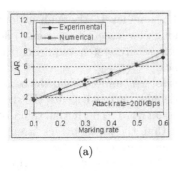
(a)

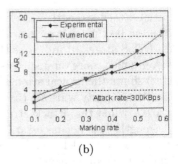
(b)

**Fig. 6.** Experimental and numerical curves of LAR

our analytical model can precisely estimate the effectiveness of the DDoS defense system under different scenarios. It is beneficial to know in advance the effectiveness of a defense system without experiencing many different real attacks. Moreover, this estimation can give a guide that how secure is the system and how much reinforcement is needed. Figure 6(b) shows when the attack rate is 300KBps the numerical curve can also fit well with the experimental curve, although more errors occur in this situation than the one of 200KBps attack rate. Actually we can expand this model with the non-constant parameters $a$ and $b$ to have a more flexible model (the expanded model results in better fit). However, to setup these sub-models is beyond the scope of this paper.

## 6   Related Work

DDoS attacks usually cause network anomalies, such as increase of traffic volumes and source IP addresses, change of other network features such as packet length, flow duration, percentage composition by protocol and application, etc., and relationships between those network features.

Statistical method [18] is a straight forward method to detect anomalies. However, it requires a strong assumption that the network traffic variables obey a Normal Distribution. Another popular method to detect change point problem is nonparametric Cumulative Sum (CUSUM) method [19]. It is stateless, lightweight, and sensitive to persistent sudden changes caused by DDoS attacks instead of Internet flash crowd. This method has been used to detect many DDoS anomalies such as SYN flood [20]. However, this method can only consider one network feature, and can only deal with the change point problem. If the network anomaly is not an intensive flood, this method may not discover the attack timely. Rather than analyzing the change of features, multivariate correlation analysis [21] that is proposed to detect subtle DDoS attacks considers the correlations among the features. The normal network traffic patterns are different from the abnormal patterns in terms of correlation. Loss of self-similarity [22] is also a representation of relationships between features. However, it is no theoretical proof to decide which features are valid for the correlation models and how important each feature is. Additionally, those methods can only represent the changes of correlation, but not the causality between those changes and attacks.

Ingress filtering [1] is proposed to be deployed on the external interface of a network and drops all spoofed incoming packets. It requires a global deployment and also a knowledge base of legitimate IP addresses that can be very large. Park [23] proposed a router-based Distributed Packet Filtering (DPF). Another filtering mechanism is proposed as Hop-Count Filtering (HCF) [24] to drop spoofed IP packets by detecting the number of hops a packet takes to reach its destination. However, it could be infeasible to cover the whole network by such defense systems in current Internet environment, although in a theoretically perfect situation, it can filter spoofed IP packets. Some filtering approaches [25] depend on the network congestion, which means only intensive congestion can trigger the filtering mechanisms. Actually, most network congestion control such as RED [3] and RED-related schemes [26] can probabilistically limit the throughput of the flows that share unfair bandwidth. However, it could be ineffective to detect and filter low attack rate DDoS traffic.

On DDoS modeling, a random flow network model was proposed by [27] to evaluate the effectiveness of a DDoS countermeasure framework. Their simulation reveals the general relationship among several metrics derived from the model. They also suggest to build a more complete and effective DDoS countermeasure framework using complementary solutions to achieve DDoS attack detection, prevention, and tolerance at same time. DDOS-DATA project [28] is to analyze Distributed Denial of Service (DDOS) attacks and mitigation technologies to develop an understanding of how well mitigation technologies perform and how they can be combined to limit the potential attack space. They discuss analysis results for the Proof of Work, Rate Limiting, and Active Monitor mitigation technologies considered both individually and when deployed in combinations. From a higher level, an improved McCumber model for information assurance was proposed by [29] to evaluate security from aspects of security services, information states and security countermeasures. However, all the previous work is in short of the capability to describe the interaction between DDoS attack party and defense party, and lacks practical applications.

# 7   Conclusions

In this paper, we present the experiments of Mark-Aided Distributed Filtering (MADF) system and an analytical model that is generated by the experiments. The experimental results show that our approach is sensitive and accurate in finding DDoS attacks. It can filter out most of attack traffic, and let most of legitimate traffic pass through. As currently many information infrastructures are deluged by DDoS floods, our approach can effectively protect the information infrastructure from the attacks. The analytical model can not only estimate the effectiveness of a DDoS defense system before it encounters different attacks but also be used to model some other network security problems such as virus and spam defense.

# References

1. Ferguson, P., Senie, D.: Rfc 2267 - network ingress filtering: Defeating denial of service attacks which employ ip source address spoofing. Technical report, Network Working Group (1998)
2. Aljifri, H.: Ip traceback: A new denial-of-service deterrent? IEEE Security & Privacy **1** (2003) 24–31
3. Floyd, S., Jacobson, V.: Random early detection gateways for congestion avoidance. IEEE/ACM Transactions on Networking **1** (1993) 397–413
4. Savage, S., Wetherall, D., Karlin, A., Anderson, T.: Network support for ip traceback. ACM/IEEE Transactions on Networking **9** (2001) 226–237
5. Belenky, A., Ansari, N.: Ip traceback with deterministic packet marking. IEEE Communications Letters **7** (2003) 162–164
6. Xiang, Y., Zhou, W., Rough, J.: Trace ip packets by flexible deterministic packet marking (fdpm). In: IEEE International Workshop on IP Operations & Management (IPOM 2004). (2004)
7. Mller, B., Reinhardt, J., Strickland, M.: Neural Networks : An Introduction. 2 edn. Springer-Verlag, New York (1995)
8. Haykin, S.: Neural Networks: A Comprehensive Foundation. 2 edn. Prentice Hall (1998)
9. Bernardo, J.M., Smith, A.F.M.: Bayesian Theory. John Wiley and Sons, England (1994)
10. Mukkamala, S., Sung, A.H.: Detecting denial of service attacks using support vector machines. In: The IEEE International Conference on Fuzzy Systems. (2003) 1231–1236
11. SSFNet: Scalable simulation framework. (`http://www.ssfnet.org`)
12. Chen, R.C., Shi, W.and Zhou, W.: Simulation of distributed denial of service attacks. Technical report, School of Information Technology, Deakin University, Australia (2004)
13. Skitter: Skitter project, cooperative association for internet data analysis (caida). (`http://www.caida.org/tools/measurement/skitter/`)
14. Yaar, A., Perrig, A., Song, D.: Pi: A path identification mechanism to defend against ddos attacks. In: 2003 IEEE Symposium on Security and Privacy. (2003) 93–107
15. Sung, M., Xu, J.: Ip traceback-based intelligent packet filtering: A novel technique for defending against internet ddos attacks. IEEE Transactions on Parallel and Distributed Systems **14** (2003) 861–872
16. Gordon, L.A., Loeb, M.P.: The economics of information security investment. ACM Transactions on Information and System Security **5** (2002) 438–457
17. Lanchester, F.W.: Mathematics in warfare. The World of Mathematics **4** (1956) 2138–2157
18. Gil, T.M., Poletto, M.: Multops: a data-structure for bandwidth attack detection. In: 10th Usenix Security Symposium. (2001) 23–38
19. Pollak, M.: Optimal detection of a change in distribution. Ann. Statist **13** (1986) 206–227
20. Wang, H., Zhang, D., Shin, K.G.: Change-point monitoring for the detection of dos attacks. IEEE Transactions on Dependable and Secure Computing **1** (2004) 193–208
21. Jin, S., Yeung, D.S.: A covariance analysis model for ddos attack detection. In: IEEE International Conference on Communications (ICC 2004). Volume 4. (2004) 1882–1886

22. Allen, W.H., Marin, G.A.: The loss technique for detecting new denial of service attacks. In: IEEE SoutheastCon 2004. (2004) 302–309
23. Park, K., Lee, H.: On the effectiveness of route-based packet filtering for distributed dos attack prevention in power-law internet. In: ACM SIGCOMM 2001. (2001) 15–26
24. Jin, C., Wang, H., Shin, K.G.: Hop-count filtering: An effective defense against spoofed ddos traffic. In: 10th ACM Conference on Computer and Communication Security (CCS 2003). (2003) 30–41
25. Hu, Y.H., Choi, H., Choi, H.A.: Packet filtering for congestion control under dos attacks. In: 2nd IEEE International Information Assurance Workshop (IWIA 2004). (2004) 3–18
26. Mahajan, R., Bellovin, S.M., Floyd, S.: Controlling high bandwidth aggregates in the network. Computer Communications Review **32** (2002) 62–73
27. Kong, J., Mirza, M., Shu, J., Yoedhana, C., Gerla, M., Lu, S.: Random flow network modeling and simulations for ddos attack mitigation. In: IEEE International Conference on Communications (ICC 2003). Volume 1. (2003) 487–491
28. Blackert, W.J., Gregg, D.M., Castner, A.K., Kyle, E.M., Hom, R.L., Jokerst, R.M.: Analyzing interaction between distributed denial of service attacks and mitigation technologies. In: DARPA Information Survivability Conference and Exposition (DISCEX 03). (2003)
29. Maconachy, W.V., Schou, C.D., Ragsdale, D., Welch, D.: A model for information assurance: An integrated approach. In: The 2001 IEEE Workshop on Information Assurance and Security. (2001)

# Distributed Credential Chain Discovery in Trust-Management with Parameterized Roles

Xian Zhu, Shaobin Wang, Fan Hong, and Junguo Liao

College of Computer, Huazhong University of Science & Technology,
Wuhan 430074,China

**Abstract.** Trust-management subjects face the problem of discovering credential chain. In this paper, the distributed credential chain discovery algorithms in trust-management with parameterized roles are proposed. The algorithms extend the $RT_0$'s and are goal-oriented also. Based on the concept of parameterized roles in $RT_1$, they search the credential graph via the constant matching and variable solving mechanisms. The algorithms can perform chain discovery in most trust-management systems and can support the protection of access control policies during automated trust negotiation. Soundness and completeness of the algorithms are given.

## 1  Introduction

It is a hotspot how to solve the access control problem effectively in decentralized collaborative environments. In these systems, resources and the subjects requesting them belongs to different security domains controlled by different authorities. So traditional access control mechanisms cannot be used in these environments. In [1], Blaze et al introduced the trust-management (TM) systems to deal with the problem. Then, some famous TM systems, such as KeyNote [2], SPKI/SDSI [3,4] and RT [5,6,7] were proposed. Delegation is a core concept in these systems, which is the ability of an entity A to give another entity B the authority to act on A's behalf. To make the access control decisions, a credential chain from the source of authority to the requester must be discovered. We call this the credential chain discovery problem. With the tenet of TM systems—decentralized control, the credentials are typical issued and stored in a distributed manner. So the problem evolved to the distributed credential chain discovery problem.

Now there are some algorithms to solve the problem [8,9,10]. But most of them assume the credentials are stored with its issuer, which will make some bottleneck. In [6], Li Ninghui et al present some goal-oriented algorithms. The credentials can be stored with its issuer or subject. The query can be answered by doing backward, forward or bi-direction searching, which makes the searching efficiency improved greatly. However, $RT_0$ is a basic language in RT family. $RT_1$ is the most important extension to $RT_0$, which extends $RT_0$ to allow parameterized roles. In RBAC96 [11], a role name is an atomic string. But parameterized role name is constructed by applying a role identifier to a tuple of data terms (the parameter). The parameterized roles can be used as follows [5,12,13]:

Y.G. Desmedt et al. (Eds.): CANS 2005, LNCS 3810, pp. 334–348, 2005.

. With the same role identifier plus some different parameters, it can be used to aggregate some roles with few differences between them. The numbers of roles will be decreased greatly, thus simplifying the management of roles.

. It can represent relationships between entities, thus supporting more fine-grained access control. For example, we can use Alpha.managerOf(employee) to name the manager of an employee.

. It can represent attributes that have fields. For example, a diploma typically contains school, degree, year, *etc.*

. It can also represent access permissions that take parameters identifying resources and access modes.

The credential in KeyNote and SPKI/SDSI can be expressed in $RT_1$ with the parameterized roles [5,7,14], so the algorithms are more general when it's based on $RT_1$. In addition, automatic trust negotiation (ATN) based on $RT_0$ has the problem of supporting the protection of access control policies [15,16]. However, if we design ATN based on $RT_1$, the problem may be solved. For example, when Alice requests a service in a server, the server responds with the target: IBM.employee$\xleftarrow{?}$Alice. It will reveal that the server have a business relationship with IBM, which may be a secret. Based on $RT_1$, the target can be transformed to CoalitionA.employee(?company)$\xleftarrow{?}$Alice.

To make the algorithms in $RT_0$ more applicable, we must extend it to be based on $RT_1$ and to support parameterized roles. Although there are some distributed credential chain discovery algorithms supported parameterized roles proposed, but they are imperfectness[1]. In this paper, we give some algorithms based on $RT_1$. They extend the $RT_0$'s and are goal-oriented also. The credential chain can be discovered by searching from the issuer side, subject side or both when the credentials are stored distributed. We first proposed the centralized algorithms. And the distributed algorithms are designed by incorporating the type systems of $RT_0$ with them. The algorithms are based on a graphical representation of $RT_1$ credentials. They construct the credential graph via the constant matching and variable solving mechanisms to find the path connecting the source of authority and the requester. We present the time and space complexity. And the soundness and completeness theorems with respect to the $RT_1$'s logic program semantics are proved.

The rest of this paper is organized as follows. Section 2 introduces $RT_1$'s syntax and semantics. In section 3, the new algorithms based on $RT_1$ are proposed. Soundness and completeness of the algorithms are given in section 4. Some related work is discussed in section 5. We conclude the paper in section 6.

## 2   $RT_1$'s Syntax and Semantics

RT is a newly proposed trust management system with many advanced features. RT combines the strengths of RBAC and TM systems. An entity in RT is a uniquely identified individual or process. Entities are also called principals in the

---

[1]   It will be discussed in section 5.

literature. They can issue credentials and make requests. In some environments, an entity could also be, say, a secret key or a user account. Entities in RT correspond to users in RBAC. A role name is an identifier, say, a string. A role takes the form of an entity followed by a role name, separated by a dot. Roles in RT can represent both roles and permissions from RBAC. By credential, an entity can define members of the role in its namespace. RT introduces a family of language including $RT_0$, $RT_1$, $RT^T$ and $RT^D$. $RT_0$ is the most basic language and $RT_1$ is the most important extension to $RT_0$.

As $RT_0$'s syntax is similar to $RT_1$'s except that the role name in $RT_0$ can not have parameters, we describe the $RT_1$'s syntax directly. The parameter is either a constant or a variable, and the variable takes the form of a question mark "?" followed by an alpha-numeric string. There are four kinds of credentials. The semantics is defined by presenting a translation from credentials to Datalog rules. $RT_1$ introduces a special binary predicate isMember, which takes an entity and a role as arguments. Credentials are defined and translated as follows:

. Type-1: $A.r(h_1,...,h_n) \leftarrow D$. It means that A defines D to be a member of A's $(h_1,...,h_n)$ role. It is translated to isMember(D,A.R). For convenience, we use R to denote $r(h_1,...,h_n)$ sometimes.

. Type-2: $A.r(h_1,...,h_n) \leftarrow B.r_1(s_1,...,s_m)$. It means that A defines its R role to include all members of B's $R_1$ role. It is translated to isMember(?z,A.R)$\leftarrow$isMem- ber(?z,B.$R_1$).

. Type-3: $A.r(h_1,...,h_n) \leftarrow A.r_1(t_1,..,t_l).r_2(s_1,...,s_m)$. It means that A defines its R role to include all members of B's $R_2$ role, where B is a member of A's $R_1$ role. It is translated to isMember(?z,A.R)$\leftarrow$isMember(?x,A.$R_1$), isMember(?z,?x.$R_2$). In addition, the parameter in the role name $R_1$ can be a special keyword "this". Each appearance of "this" is translated to the variable ?z. We call $A.r_1(t_1,..,t_l).r_2$ $(s_1,...,s_m)$ a linked role.

. Type-4: $A.R \leftarrow B_1.R_1 \cap B_2.R_2 \cap ... \cap B_k.R_k$. It means that if an entity is a member of $B_1.R_1$, $B_2.R_2$,..., and $B_k.R_k$, then it is also a member of A.R. It is translated to isMember(?z,A.R)$\leftarrow$isMember(?z,$B_1.R_1$),...,isMember(?z,$B_k.R_k$). We call $B_1.R_1 \cap B_2.R_2 \cap ... \cap B_k.R_k$ an intersection.

A role expression is an entity, a role, a linked role, or an intersection. All credentials take the form, $A.R \leftarrow e$, where e is a role expression. We say this credential defines the role A.R.

$RT_1$ credentials are well-formed, which means all variable should appear in the body. In the latter three types credentials, a variable ?x may optionally have one or more constraints following its name. Each constraint is translated to a logical atom pv(?x). For convenient, we omit pv(?x) in the translation formulas.

Rules resulting form the above translation can be translated into Datalog by translating isMember(?z,A.$r(h_1,...,h_n)$) into m(A,r,$h_1,...,h_n$,?z). Given a set of $RT_1$ credentials C, let Trans(C) be the Datalog program resulting from the translation. The implications of C, defined as the set of membership relationships implied by C, is determined by the minimal model of Trans(C). $RT_1$ has been proved to be tractable.

# 3 Credential Chain Discovery

The algorithms proposed in this paper are extensions to $RT_0$'s [6]. In this section, we first discuss the centralized algorithms. Then extend them to the distributed algorithms via the type system proposed in $RT_0$[6].

As the parameter can be a constant or a variable, the algorithms should answer the following kinds of queriers:

. CoalitionA.employee(IBM)$\xleftarrow{?}$Alice. The parameter is a constant. It needs to answer whether Alice can get the role.

. CoalitionA.employee(?company)$\xleftarrow{?}$Alice. The parameter is a variable. It needs to answer whether Alice can get the role with the parameter. At the same time, it should also answer what roles Alice can get. That is to say, the algorithms should give the solution of the variable ?company.

## 3.1 The Backward Search Algorithm

The backward search algorithm determines the member of a give role expression $e_0$. It proceeds from node $e_0$ and constructs the subgraph related to the query. It maintains a queue of nodes to be processed, which initially contains only a node for $e_0$. Nodes are processed one by one until the queue is empty and the algorithm is terminated. We call "variable=constant" a *variable solution*. For example, "y=a". Multiple variable solutions can be connected to construct a variable solution. For example, "y=a,x=b". We use $\cup$ to denote connection operator. For example, "y=a"$\cup$"x=b"="y=a,x=b". The node's solution is constructed by "variable solution, entity name". We call the entity name in the solution an *entity solution*. A node can have multiple solutions. We call constraint in $RT_1$ the *variable constraint*. For example, $x_{¿}5$ and $y_{¡}10$. The edge in the graph has weight, which is used to store the variable solution and variable constraint. The node is identified by a role expression and it stores its solutions. Figure 1 illustrates a node $B.r_2(?x,a)$.

The variable solution on the edge is used to store the corresponding variable's solution when the edge being added. The variable constraint on the edge is used to store the corresponding variable's constraint. Only the solution satisfied the constraint could be propagated through the edge.

The algorithm is described as follows.

1) For a role expression without parameters, the algorithm processes it as same as $RT_0$'s.

| $B.r_2(?x, a)$ |
| --- |
| x = c, Alice; <br> x = d, Bob |

**Fig. 1.** An example of the node's structure used in backward algorithm

2) To process a role node $A.r(h_1,..,h_n)$, the algorithm finds all credentials taking the form, $A.r(h_1',...,h_n') \leftarrow e$. For each credential, it creates two symbols $A.r(h_1',...,h_n')$ and e. Then it processes as follows:

For each symbol $h_i$ in $\{h_1,...,h_n\}$,

if $h_i$ is a constant, then,

if $h_i'$ is a constant and $h_i' \neq h_i$, then it goes to the next credential. (Because it cannot build a valid chain in that case.)

if $h_i'$ is a variable, then,

if $h_i$ can not satisfy the constraint on $h_i$, then it goes to the next credential.

let $h_i'=h_i$, and it replaces every occurrence of $h_i'$ in e with $h_i$.

if $h_i$ is a variable, then,

if $h_i'$ is a constant, then it creates a variable solution "$h_i=h_i'$" and adds it to variable solution VS.

if $h_i'$ is a variable, then let $h_i'=h_i$, and it replaces every occurrence of $h_i'$ in e with $h_i$. (In fact, it is a rename processing of variable, to make the variable in the path of the credential graph has a consistent name. Some name conflict may occur in the processing. So we must implement it with some temporary name mechanisms. For example, we can let $h_i'=@+h$temporarily and remove the prefix @ at last.)

It creates two nodes for $A.r(h_1',...,h_n')$ and e, and adds the edge $A.r(h_1',...,h_n')$ $\leftarrow e$. If $h_i'$ is a variable and there is a constraint on it, it adds the constraint to the edge. If $A.r(h_1,..,h_n)$ is different from $A.r(h_1',...,h_n')$ (it must have created a variable solution.), it adds the edge $A.r(h_1,..,h_n) \leftarrow A.r(h_1',...,h_n')$, and adds VS to the edge.

3) To process a linked role node $A.r_1(h_1,..,h_n).r_2(s_1,...,s_m)$, the algorithm creates a node for $A.r_1(h_1,..,h_n)$, and creates a linking monitor to observe the node. When the monitor observes the node has received a new solution S, it gets the entity solution B from the solution, and creates a symbol $B.r_2(s_1',...,s_m')$. If there are some variables coexisting in $(h_1,..,h_n)$ and $(s_1,...,s_m)$, it replaces these variables in $(s_1',...,s_m')$ with the corresponding variable solution; otherwise, let $s_i'=s_i$. Then it creates a node for $B.r_2(s_1',...,s_m')$ and adds the edge $A.r_1(h_1,..,h_n).r_2(s_1,...,s_m) \leftarrow B.r_2(s_1',...,s_m')$. At the same time, it gets the variable solution from S and adds it to the edge. (Here, it might have multiple edges between two nodes and each edge has different variable solution on it.)

To process the "this" parameter in the linked role, the algorithm translates it into a constraint on the edge $A.r_1(h_1,..,h_n).r_2(s_1,...,s_m) \leftarrow B.r_2(s_1',...,s_m')$. When the node $A.r_1(h_1,..,h_n)$ has received a new solution, it adds the variable solution of "this" to the edge as a constraint, which means only when the entity solution in a solution equals to the variable solution of "this", the solution can be propagated through the edge.

4) To process an intersection node $e=B_1.R_1 \cap B_2.R_2 \cap ... \cap B_k.R_k$ the algorithm creates a intersection monitor for e and k nodes, one for each $B_i.R_i$. When it observes that $B_i.R_i$ has received a new solution, it checks whether the entity solution D in the solution is also included in all the other k-1 node's solutions. If it does, it checks whether the variable coexisting in the k nodes has the same

solution. If it does also, it adds the edge e←D, and adds the solution to the edge. (Here, it might have multiple edges between two nodes and each edge has different variable solution on it.)

As for the algorithm, there are some other details should be presented as follows.

Node's creation: it is similar to $RT_0$'s. Each time it tries to create a node, it first checks whether it already exists. If not, it creates a new node and adds it into the queue. Otherwise, it does not create it.

Solution's propagation: when a node is notified to add a solution, it first checks whether the solution exists in the node. If not, it adds the solution. Just before it adds the solution, for each variable in the solution, it checks whether the variable exists in the node's name; if not, it removes the variable solution from the solution. Then it propagates the solution to all its children. Only when a solution satisfied the constraint on an edge, it could be propagated through the edge. And when a solution propagated through an edge, the algorithm connects the solution with the variable solution on the edge to create the solution for its children. (If no solution exists, then this step is omitted.) When a node $e_1$ is first added as a child of $e_2$ (as the result of adding $e_1 \leftarrow e_2$), all existing solutions on $e_2$ are propagated to $e_1$ through the edge.

**Example 1.** There are the following credentials:

Alpha.payRaise←Alpha.evaluatorOf(this).goodPerformanceAlpha.evaluator-Of(Bob)←Alice
Alpha.evaluatorOf(Charle)←Alice
Alice.goodPerformance←Bob
Alice.goodPerformance←Darl.

Figure 2 shows the result of doing backward search from Alpha.payRaise. The edge is labeled with variable constraint and variable solution, and the constraint is marked with underline. The first line of each node gives the node number in order of creation. The solution in the second part of a node, the constraint and the variable solution on the edge are labeled by the number of the node that was being processed when they were added. The edge labeled with 1 is a linking monitor. "4 this=Bob" and "4 this=charle" are constraints as well as variable solutions. "2 this=Bob" and "2 this=Charle" are variable solutions only. As only the solution "Bob" of node 6 can satisfy the constraint on the edge 1←6, so node 1 is notified to add the solution "this=Bob,Bob". When the solution is propagated to node 0 further, "this=Bob" is removed because "this" does not exist in the node 0's name. At last, the algorithm adds the solution "Bob" to node 0.

There are many details in the algorithm. However, we can only give a relative simple example due to the space limitations. But the main characters are revealed by the example. In the similar way as $RT_0$'s, we can prove the following theorem.

**Theorem 1.** Given a set C of $RT_1$ credentials, assuming that each credential in C has at most v variables and that each role name has at most p arguments. Let N be the number of credentials in C. Then the worst-case time complexity of the backward search algorithm is $O((pN)^{3p}N^3+(pN)^{p+v}N^2)$, and the space complexity is $O(\max((pN)^{3p}N^2,(pN)^{p+v}N^2))$.

The proofs for this and other theorems are omitted due to space limitation. They can be found in the full version of this paper [18].

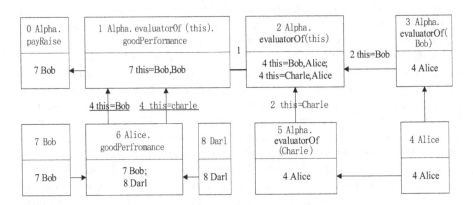

**Fig. 2.** An example of proof graph constructed by doing backward search

From the theorems, we can find that the role name should not include so many arguments. Otherwise, the search efficiency will decrease sharply. When p=0 and v=0, the time and space complexity is the same as $RT_0$'s.

## 3.2   The Forward Search Algorithm

An intuitive design of the forward search algorithm is that it searches at the same credential graph as the backward search algorithm, which makes it be similar to the backward algorithm. We do not take this approach but propose a more concise algorithm.

There are no variable and constraint in the graph of the algorithm. It can do this lies in the fact that the credentials in RT are well-formed. As the algorithm searches from an entity with no parameters, it will create a role node with no variable via a type-1 credential. And as each variable in the head of a credential must also appear in the body, so each variable in the role expression is instantiated as the algorithm proceeding. And the constraints are evaluated as the variables are instantiated, so it does not add the constraints to the graph. Then the data structure of node and edge is the same as $RT_0$'s.

As there is a special parameter "this", a node e stores both the entities (entity solution) that are members of e and roles (role solution) that e is a member of. As the variable solution is included implicitly in the node's name, so variable solution needn't be included in the node's solution. It only needs to add the node's name to the solution. Entity solution is propagated to a node's children and role solution is propagated to a node's parents.

In addition, similar to $RT_0$'s, there are full solution and partial solution mechanisms. Each full solution on e is a role that e is a member of. Each partial

solution is used to deal with the intersection and has the form
$(B_1.R_1 \cap B_2.R_2 \cap ... \cap B_k.R_k, B_i.R_i)$, where $1 \leq i \leq k$.

We introduces a special predicate $InstanceOf(e_1, e_2)$, where both $e_1$ and $e_2$ are role expressions with parameters. It is interpreted as follows:

$InstanceOf(e_1, e_2) = True$ iff:

1) All the entities and role identities are the same between $e_1$ and $e_2$.

2) For each constant in $e_1$'s role parameters, if the corresponding role parameter in $e_2$ is also a constant, then they must be equal.

For each variable in $e_1$'s role parameters, the corresponding role parameter in $e_2$ must also be a variable.

3) For homonymous variables in $e_1$'s role parameters, the corresponding role parameters in $e_2$ must also be homonymous variables.

For the homonymous variables in $e_2$'s role parameters, the corresponding role parameter in $e_1$ must also be homonymous variables or same constants.

For example, $InstanceOf(A.r_1(a,b), A.r_1(a,?x) = True$, $InstanceOf(A.r_1(a,b), A.r_1(b,?x)) = false$, $InstanceOf(A.r_2(?x,b,c), A.r_2(?x,?y,c)) = ture$, and $InstanceOf(A.r_1(a,b).r_3(a,c), A.r_1(?x,?y).r_3(?x,?z)) = True$.

The algorithm is described as follows.

1) For a role expression without parameters, except the processing given above, the algorithm processes it as same as $RT_0$'s.

2) For a role expression $e$ with parameters, it involves the following three steps.

2.1) If $e$ is a role node $B.r_2(s_1,...,s_m)$, add itself as a solution to itself, then add entity node $B$ and a linking monitor observing $B$. When $B$ gets a full solution $A.r_1(h_1,..,h_n)$, the monitor creates the node $A.r_1(h_1,..,h_n).r_2(s_1,...,s_m)$ and adds edge

$B. r_2(s_1,...,s_m) \rightarrow A.r_1(h_1,..,h_n).r_2(s_1,...,s_m)$.

2.2) Find all credentials of the form $A.r(h_1,...,h_n) \leftarrow e_1$, where $InstanceOf(e,e_1) = True$. For each such credential, create a symbol $A.r(h_1,...,h_n)$. Then process as follows:

If there is a "this" parameter included in $e_1$, then add a "this" monitor observing $e$. When $e$ gets an entity solution $D$ and for the "this" parameter in $e_1$, the corresponding constant in $e$ is $D$, then go on processing.

If there are constraints in the credential, and the constants in $e$ do not satisfy the constraints, then go to the next credential.

For each variable $h_i$ (each variable in the head of a credential must also appear in the body.), replace it with the corresponding constant in $e$. Then create the node $A.r(h_1,...,h_n)$ and add edge $A.r(h_1,...,h_n) \leftarrow e$.

2.3) If $e$ is a role node $B.r(s_1,...,s_m)$ ($f_i$ in intersection of $RT_1$ can only be a role.), find all credentials of the form $A.r(h_1,...,h_n) \leftarrow B_1.R_1 \cap B_2.R_2 \cap ... \cap B_k.R_k$ such that there exists a $B_i.R_i$, where $InstanceOf(B.r(s_1,...,s_m), B_i.R_i) = True$. For each credential, if there are constraints in the credential and the constants in

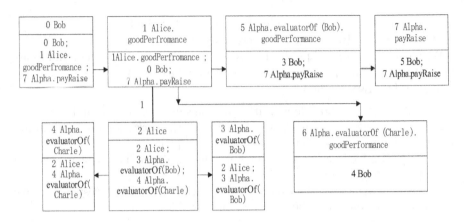

**Fig. 3.** An example of proof graph constructed by doing forward search

e satisfy the constraints, then add $(B_1.R_1 \cap B_2.R_2 \cap ... \cap B_k.R_k, B.r(s_1,...,s_m))$ as a partial solution on e.

As for the algorithm, there are some other details should be presented as follows.

. Node's creation: it is the same as backward algorithm.

. Solution's propagation: when a node is notified to add a solution, it first checks whether the solution exists in the node. If not, it adds the solution. Then it propagates the entity solution (or role solution) to all its children (or parents). When a node $e_2$ is first added as a parent of $e_1$ (as the result of adding $e_1 \leftarrow e_2$), all existing entity solutions on $e_2$ are propagated to $e_1$ through the edge, and all existing role solution on $e_1$ are propagated to $e_2$ through the edge.

. The processing of partial solution: when an entity node D gets the partial solution, it checks whether it has all other k-1 pieces. If it does, it checks whether all homonymous variables in $B_1.R_1 \cap B_2.R_2 \cap ... \cap B_k.R_k$ have the same solutions. If it does also, it replaces all the variables in $B_1.R_1 \cap B_2.R_2 \cap ... \cap B_k.R_k$ with corresponding constants in the partial solution. Then it creates the node $B_1.R_1 \cap B_2.R_2 \cap ... \cap B_k.R_k$ and adds edge $D \rightarrow B_1.R_1 \cap B_2.R_2 \cap ... \cap B_k.R_k$.

With the same credentials as exmaple 1, figure 3 shows the result of doing forward search from Bob. The edge labeled with 1 is a linking monitor. There are "this" monitors on the node 5 and 6, which are omitted to keep the graph concise.

**Theorem 2.** Under the same assumptions as in theorem 1, the time complexity for the forward search algorithm is $O((pN)^{3p}N^3 + (pN)^{p+v}N^3)$, and the space complexity is $O(\max((pN)^{3p}N^2, (pN)^{p+v}N^2))$.

## 3.3   Bi-direction Search Algorithm

The bi-direction search algorithm is designed by combining forward and backward algorithms. When answering the query $A.r(s_1,...,s_m) \leftarrow B$, if each $s_i$ is a constant, the the algorithm stops when $A.r(s_1,...,s_m)$ gets the solution B. However, if there are variables, it will not stop because it should get all the variable's solutions. When the two graphs constructed respectively by the backward and forward algorithms are being connected, the entity solutions of the nodes created by forward algorithm are propagated to the nodes created by backward algorithm; as the nodes create by backward algorithm have no role solutions, there are no role solutions to propagate to nodes created by forward algorithm. The required credential chains (if exists) will not lost in this way. Finally, although the role solution of B may not include $A.r$ $(s_1,...,s_m)$, but $A.r(s_1,...,s_m)$ must have get the entity solution B. So we can always get the right answer although there are no role solutions in nodes created by backward algorithm.

### 3.4   Distributed Credential Discovery Algorithms

As the algorithms are goal-oriented, it can be used when credential storage is distributed. In $RT_0$, when the credential type system is defined, the centralized algorithms can be extended to distributed discovery algorithms. With the type system which specifies the storage type of the credential, the credential can be stored by its subject or issuer. The completeness of the distributed algorithms is guaranteed by the type system [6]. The type system in $RT_0$ is closely related to the role name. In $RT_1$, although the role name is extended to include parameters, it has no effect on the type system. For example, a role StateU.diploma is issuer-trace-none and subject-trace-all in $RT_0$, which means the subject, who gets the diploma of StateU, stores the credential. In $RT_1$, we add parameters to the role and upgrade it to Statu.diploma(?degree,?year). It's natural that the credential is still stored by the people who get the diploma. To add the parameters to roles can increase the expressive power of TM system, but the store mechanism is the same. So the distributed algorithms are designed by incorporating the type systems of $RT_0$ directly with the centralized algorithms discussed above.

## 4   Soundness and Completeness of the Algorithms

The algorithms proposed in this paper construct the proof graph related to the query, which is a subgraph of the credential graph. In this section, we prove that the credential graph is consists with the credential's semantics, that is to say, its soundness and completeness theorems. With these two theorems, it's easy to prove the soundness and completeness theorems of the algorithms in ways similar to $RT_0$'s.

In a weighted directed graph, if the weight on the edge is defined as variable constraint and variable solution, and the variable solution of the same variable does not appear twice on a path, then we call the connection of all variable solution on the path *variable solution on the path*. It is easy to prove that the variable solution of the same variable will not appear twice on all paths in the credential graph defined by definition 2 given below.

**Definition 1.** (Reachable path) In the weighted directed graph described above, if there exists a path $D \xrightarrow{*} A.R$, and for each edge $e_i \xrightarrow{CS} e_j (i \neq j)$ on the path, if all variable solutions on the path $D \xrightarrow{*} e_i$ satisfy the constraint $CS$, then we call $D \xrightarrow{*} A.R$ a reachable path. If there are "this" constraints in CS, D must be the solution of "this".

**Definition 2.** (Credential graph) For a set of credentials C, the corresponding credential graph is given by $Gc=(Nc,Ec)$, where Nc and Ec are the least set of nodes and edges that satisfy the following closure properties:

**Property 1:** If $A.R \leftarrow e \in C$, then $e \rightarrow A.R \in Ec$ and $\{e,A.R\} \subseteq Nc$; if $A.R \in Nc$, then $A \in Nc$; if $A.R_1.R_2 \in Nc$, then $A.R_1 \in Nc$; if $B_1.R_1 \cap B_2.R_2 \cap ... \cap B_k.R_k \in Nc$ then $\{B_1.R_1,...,B_k.R_k\} \subseteq Nc$.

**Property 2:** If $A.r(h_1,...,h_n) \in Nc$, $A.r(h_1',...,h_n') \leftarrow e \in C$, and the following conditions hold:

1) If both $h_i$ and $h_i'$ are constants, then $h_i = h_i'$;
2) If $h_i$ is a constant, $h_i'$ is a variable, and there is a constraint on $h_i'$, then $h_i$ must satisfy the constraint. then $\{A.r(h_1",...,h_n"),e'\} \subseteq Nc$ and $e' \xrightarrow{CS} A.r(h_1",...,h_n") \in Ec$, where CS is the constraint on the edge; if there is a variable solution VS, then $A.r(h_1",...,h_n") \xrightarrow{VS} A.r(h_1,...,h_n) \in Ec$, where:
  . if $h_i$ is a constant, then $h_i" = h_i$;
  . if $h_i$ is a variable and $h_i'$ is a constant, then $h_i" = h_i'$ and it creates a variable solution $h_i = h_i'$;
  . if both $h_i$ and $h_i'$ are variables, then $h_i" = h_i$.
  . if there are variables in $(h_1",...,h_n")$, then CS is the corresponding variable's constraint in the credential $A.r(h_1',...,h_n') \leftarrow e$;
  . e' is created by e with each variable $h_i'$ in e being replaced with the corresponding $h_i"$.

**Property 3:** If $A.r_1(h_1,..,h_n).r_2(s_1,...,s_m) \in Nc$ and there is a reachable path $B \xrightarrow{*} A.r_1(h_1,..,h_n)$, where VS is the variable solution on the path, then $B.r_2(s_1',..., s_m') \in Nc$, where:
if there are homonymous variables between $(s_1,...,s_m)$ and $(h_1,...,h_n)$, for example $s_i = h_j$, then let $s_i' =$ the solution of $h_j$. Otherwise, let $s_i' = s_i$.

And $B.r_2(s_1',...,s_m') \xrightarrow{VS} A.r_1(h_1,..,h_n).r_2(s_1,...,s_m) \in Ec$. If there exists a "this" parameter in $(h_1,..,h_n)$, then it adds the solution of "this" on the edge as a constraint.

**Property 4:** If $D, B_1.R_1 \cap B_2.R_2 \cap ... \cap B_k.R_k \in Nc$, and for each $j \in [1,...,k]$, there is a reachable path $D \xrightarrow{*} B_j.R_j$, where $VS_j$ is the variable solution on each path; in addition, if there are homonymous variables between $VS_1,...,VS_k$ and the solution of these variables are same, then $D \xrightarrow{VS} B_1.R_1 \cap B_2.R_2 \cap ... \cap B_k.R_k \in Ec$, where $VS = VS_1 \cup ... \cup VS_k$.

The edges and nodes discussed in property 5 and 6 do not include any variables.

**Property 5:** If $e \in Nc$, $A.r(h_1,..,h_n) \leftarrow e_1 \in C$, where $IstanceOf(e,e_1)=True$, and the following conditions hold:

1) If there exists a "this" parameter in $e_1$, assuming the corresponding constant in e is D, then there must be a reachable path $D \xrightarrow{*} e$;

2) If there exists a constraint in credential $A.r(h_1,..,h_n) \leftarrow e_1$, then the constants in e must satisfy the constraint.

then $A.r(h_1',...,h_n') \in Nc$, where:

if $h_i$ is a variable, then $h_i'$ is created by $h_i$ in $e_1$ being replaced with the corresponding constant in e;

otherwise, let $h_i'=h_i$.

And $e \rightarrow A.r(h_1',...,h_n') \in Ec$.

**Property 6:** If $B.r_2(s_1,...,s_m) \in Nc$, and there is a reachable path $B \xrightarrow{*} A.r_1(h_1, ..,h_n)$, then $B.r_2(s_1,...,s_m) \rightarrow A.r_1(h_1,..,h_n)$. $r_2(s_1,...,s_m) \in Ec$ and $A.r_1(h_1,..,h_n)$. $r_2(s_1,...,s_m) \in Nc$

**Property 7:** If $DB_1.R_1 \cap B_2.R_2 \cap ... \cap B_k.R_k \in Nc$, and for each $j \in [1,...,k]$, there is a reachable path $D \xrightarrow{*} B_j.R_j'$ ($R_j'$ does not include variable), where Instance $Of(B_j.R_j',B_j.R_j)=true$ and for each homonymous variable in $B_j.R_j$, the corresponding constant in $B_j.R_j'$ is the same, then $B_1.R_1' \cap B_2.R_2' \cap ... \cap B_k.R_k' \in Nc$ and $D \rightarrow B_1.R_1' \cap B_2.R_2' \cap ... \cap B_k.R_k' \in Ec$.

With definition 2, we can inductively construct a sequence of set $\{(Nc^i, Ec^i)\}_i \in_N$ whose limit is $Gc=(Nc,Ec)$. Ec is constructed as follows:

$$Ec^0 = \{e \rightarrow A.R | A.R \leftarrow e \in C\};$$

$Ec^{i+1}$ is constructed from $Ec^i$ by adding one or two edges according to either closure property from 1 to 7. Given a set C of $RT_1$ credentials, assuming that each role expresssion in C has at most p parameters. Let N be the number of credentials in C. As each parameter in the roles can be instantiated only to the (at most $O(pN)$) constants that appear in the head of credentials, it's easy to prove that at some finite stage, no more edges and nodes will be added, and the sequence converges to Gc.

Given a symbol $(h_1,..,h_n)$ and a variable solution VS, and the following conditions hold:

if $h_i$ is a variable, then there is a solution of $h_i$ in VS.

then the symbol $(h_1',...,h_n')$ can be created as follows:

. if $h_i$ is a constant, then let $h_i'=h_i$;

. otherwise, $h_i'$ is created by $h_i$ being replaced with the corresponding solution in VS.

We call this process *replacing $(h_1,..,h_n)$ with VS*. As there are no variables in type-1 credentials, and all credentials are well-form credentials, each variable solution of $(h_1,..,h_n)$ must be included in the variable solution VS on the path $D \xrightarrow{*} A.r(h_1,..,h_n)$. Obviously, replacing is transitive. For example, if $(h_1',...,h_n')$ is created by replacing $(h_1,..,h_n)$ with VS1 and $(h_1'',...,h_n'')$ is created by replacing $(h_1',...,h_n')$ with VS2, then $(h_1'',...,h_n'')$ can be created by replacing $(h_1,..,h_n)$ with VS1∪VS2.

**Theorem 3.** (Soundness) Let LC be the set of rules translated from C. If there is a reachable path $D \xrightarrow{*} A.r(h_1,..,h_n)$ in Gc, and VS is the variable solution on the path, then LC implies $m(A,r,h_1',...,h_n',D)$, where $(h_1',...,h_n')$ is created by replacing $(h_1,..,h_n)$ with VS.

**Lemma1.** (Completeness lemma) If $m(A,r,h_i^*,...,h_n^*,D)$ holds, add $A.r(h_1,...,h_n)$ to credential graph and InstanceOf$(A.r(h_i^*,...,h_n^*),A.r(h_1,...,h_n))=$ true, then there exists a reachable path $D \xrightarrow{*,VS} A.r(h_1,...,h_n)$ in the graph constructed by property 1,2,3 and 4, where $(h_i^*,...,h_n^*)$ can be created by replacing $(h_1,...,h_n)$ with VS.

**Theorem 4.** (Completeness) If $m(A,r,h_i^*,...,h_n^*,D)$ holds, then there exists a reachable path $D \xrightarrow{*,VS} A.r(h_1,...,h_n)$ in the graph constructed by property (1,2,3,4) and (1,5,6,7) respectively, where $(h_i^*,...,h_n^*)$ can be created by replacing $(h_1,...,h_n)$ with VS.

Since the backward algorithm is based on property (1,2,3,4) and forward algorithm is based on property (1,5,6,7), the completeness theorem needs to be presented in this two cases respectively.

## 5   Discussions and Related Work

In the RT family, $RT_2$ adds to $RT_1$ the notion of o-sets, which are used to group logical related objects such as resources, access modes, etc; $RT^T$ introduces the notion of manifold roles to support threshold and separation–of–duty (SoD) policies; $RT^D$ has the notion of delegation of role activations, which can be used to express user-to-session and process-to-process delegation of capacity and to support the least privilege policy. As these characters are the unique mechanisms introduced by RT framework, we do not discuss the credential discovery algorithms supporting all these characters in this paper. However, it is easy to design the algorithms to support all these characters with the approaches discussed in this paper.

OASIS [12] and Cassandra [17] are also TM systems supporting parameterized roles. Oasis is a role-based access control architecture for achieving secure interoperation of services in an open, distributed environment. It relies on a distributed event infrastructure to trace the status of role activation. Revocation is triggered whenever a role membership condition ceases to hold. Oasis does not deal with automatic credential discovery. Cassandra is a TM system based on Datalog with constraints. The predicate in the rules can attach a location, which make it support distributed credential discovery and storage. However, the issuer must know and specify the location of the predicate's verifier when he or she issues a credential. This implicitly assumes that issuer stores all credentials, because the knowledge about the location of the credential's subject is difficult to get and the location is different with different subject. It will make some bottleneck and every query is answered by doing backward searching when issuer stores all credentials. This is impractical for many applications [6]. And it is difficult for the subject to specify the access control policy on credential. Then it cannot support ATN effectively.

SD$^3$ [8], REFEREE [9] and TPL [10] are other TM systems addressing distributed credential discovery. SD$^3$ is an extension of Datalog. It stands for Secure Dynamically Distributed Datalog. It is a high-level policy language without any special predicate related to access control. The predicate is similar to Cassandra that it can attach a location. REFEREE is an early TM system, which defines a language to code the trust policy. The policy writer can write policies that cause certificates to be retrieved. Both these two TM systems are not role based, then they have no the virtue of role-based access control. And they assume that issuer stores all credentials. TPL assigns roles to the users based on the credential submitting by user and it supports automatic credential retrieval. When the verifier finds some credentials missing, it can crawl the network and retrieve credentials from remote credential repositories. TPL declares itself a credential format independent system. It is compatible with most existing credential format but requires some mandatory components, such as issuerCertRepository and subjectCertRepository. X.509 certificate is the example discussed in TPL. However, the X.509 certificate chains are signature chains, which are more simple than the name chains in some TM systems, such as SPKI and RT. TPL does not give the credential discovery algorithm in detail.

## 6 Conclusions

In this paper, the distributed credential chain discovery algorithms in trust-management with parameterized roles are proposed. The algorithms extend the $RT_0$'s and are goal-oriented also. Based on the concept of parameterized roles in $RT_1$, they search the credential graph via the constant matching and variable solving mechanisms. The algorithms can perform chain discovery in most trust-management systems and can support the protection of access control policies during automated trust negotiation. Soundness and completeness of the algorithms are given. The algorithms have polynomial time and space complexity. It is easy to design the algorithms to support all characters in RT framework with the approaches discussed in this paper. The practical ATN technologies proposed up-to-date are based on $RT_0$, but they are imperfectness. It's our future work to develop ATN based on this paper.

## References

1. M. Blaze, J. Feigenbaum and J. Lacy. Decentralized trust management. *In Proceedings of the 17$^{th}$ Symposium of Security and Privacy*, pages 164-173. IEEE CS Press, 1996.
2. M. Blaze, J. Feigenbaum, J. Ioannidis and A. Keromytis. The KeyNote trust-management version 2. IETF RFC 2704, September 1999.

3. D. Clarke, J.E. Elien, C. Ellison, M. Fredette, A. Morcos and R.L. Rivest. Certificate chain discovery in SPKI/SDSI. *Journal of Computer Security*, 9(4):285-322, 2001.

4. C. Ellison, B. Frantz, B. Lampson, R. Rivest, B. Thomas and T. Ylonen. SPKI certificate theory. IETF RFC 2693, September 1999.

5. N. Li, J.C. Mitchel and W.H. Winsborough. Design of a role-based trust-management framework. In *Proceedings of he 2002 IEEE Symposium on Security and Privacy*, pages 114-130. IEEE Computer Society Press, May 2002.

6. N. Li, W.H. Winsborough, and J.C. Mitchell. Distributed credential chain discovery in trust management. *Journal of Computer Security*, 11(1): 35-86, Feb. 2003.

7. N. Li and J.C. Mitchell. Datalog with constraints: A foundation for trust-management languages. In *Proceedings of the Fifth International Symposium on Practical Aspects of Declarative Languages (PADL 2003)*, pages 58-73. Springer, January 2003.

8. T. Jim. SD3: a trust management system with certificate evaluation. *In Proceedings of the 2001 IEEE Symposium on Security and Privacy*, pages 106-115. IEEE Computer Society Press, May 2001.

9. Y. Huachu, J. Feigenbaum, B. LaMacchia, P. Resnick and M Strauss. REFEREE: Trust management for web applications. *The World Wide Web Journal*, 2(3): 127-139, 1997.

10. A. Herzberg, Y. mass, J. Michaeli, D. Naor and Y. Ravid. Access contorl meets public key infrastructure, or: Assigning roles to strangers. *In IEEE Symposium on Security and Privacy*, May 2000.

11. R.S. Sandhu, E.J. Coyne, H.L. Feinstein and C.E. Youman. Role-based access control models. *IEEE Computer*, 29(2): 38-47, February 1996.

12. W. Yao, K. Moody and J. Bacon. A model of OASIS role-based access control and its support of active security. *ACM Transactions on Information and System Security*, 5(4), 2002.

13. Luigi Giuri and Pietro Iglio. Role templates for content-based access control. In Proceedings of the Second ACM Workshop on Role-Based Access Control (RBAC'97) pages 153-159 Novemeber 1997

14. N. Li, W.H. Winsborough, and J.C. Mitchell. Beyond proof-of-compliance: safety and availability analysis in trust management. *In Proceedings of the 2003 IEEE Symposium on Security and Privacy*, pages 123-139. IEEE Computer Society Press, May 2003.

15. Wiliam H. Winsborough and N. Li. Towards practical automated trust negotiation. In *Proceedings of the 3rd IEEE International Workshop on Policies for Distributed Systems and Networks* (POLICY 02), pages 92-103, 2002.

16. K. Seamons, M. Winslett and T. Yu. Limiting the disclosure of access control policies during automated trust negotiation. In Network and Distributed System Security Symposum(NDSS 01), 2001.

17. M.Y. Becker and P. Sewell. Cassandra: Distributed access control policies with tunable expressiveness. In *Proceedings of the Fifth IEEE International Workshop on Policies for Distributed Systems and Networks (POLICY'04)*, pages 159-168. IEEE Computer Society Press, June 2004.Appendix: Springer-Author Discount

18. X. Zhu, S. Wang, F. Hong, and J. Liao. Distributed credential chain discovery in trust-management with parameterized roles. 2005. ftp://211.69.196.141/pub.

# Author Index

# Lecture Notes in Computer Science

For information about Vols. 1–3719

please contact your bookseller or Springer